THE MORAL SCIENCE

PSYCHOLOGY AS THE SCIENCE OF CONFLICT RESOLUTION

NORMATIVE PUBLICATIONS: VOLUME SEVEN

DR. ALBERT LEVIS, M.D. & MAXWELL LEVIS, PH.D.

Other ALBERT and MAX LEVIS PUBLICATIONS

Contribution of the Formal Theory, Volume 1, 1977
Conflict Analysis, the Formal Theory of Behavior
A Theory and its Experimental Validation, (Normative Publications), 1988, Volume 2
Conflict Analysis Training, a Program of Emotional Education (Normative Publications), 1988, Volume 3
Science Stealing the Fire of the Gods and Healing the World, 2011, Volume 4
Creativity and Power Management, 2016, Volumes 5 and 6

THE WILBURTON INN in Manchester, VT, home of the Museum of the Creative Process and the Institute of Conflict Analysis.

FOR MORE INFORMATION
Contact Albert Levis, MD, Max Levis, PhD,
MuseumOfTheCreativeProcess.com, ArtToScience.org
CreativityAndPowerManagement.org under construction
WilburtonInn.com
POBox 203, Manchester, VT, 05254, Tel 802 362 2500

Albert Levis, MD
Museum of the Creative Process
http://www.museumofthecreativeprocess.com
http://www.wilburtoninn.com
802-379-6350

DEDICATION AND ACKNOWLEDGEMENTS BY ALBERT LEVIS

I dedicate this book to my four children, who have worked over the years as a close-knit family team adopting complementary roles in the project inspired by my mission of identifying a unifying moral paradigm protecting the world from the catastrophes that shaped my childhood and that still upset our contemporary lives. These kids have been my companions in the journey in the search for wisdom. They have been the new heroes encountering the secret power of the Wizard as the riddle that needs to be solved for the healing of the person and the world.

Tajlei, the first born, has assumed the role of her mother as the innkeeper of the Wilburton Inn. She is like the scarecrow becoming the mayor of the Emerald City. Quiet and modest, beautiful and inspired, she has been enjoying the difficult task of innkeeping by working with kindness, diligently, organizing events including like her mother, Georgette, writing murder mysteries.

Melissa has been the emotional power house of the family. She is full of energy and love, enjoying and celebrating life. Her exuberance is manifested in her love for her dog, Jetson, symbolizing her role as Dorothy on the journey to the Wizard. She shows her love for animals with dog lover's weekends at the Wilburton Inn, and by being a wonderful hostess for all guests celebrating their visits, collecting images and statements preserved in her prolific video collection on YouTube and Facebook. She has worked closely with myself forever, as recorded in her journal as a child, as manifested in her high school composing the Odyssey, a fun-filled musical, and Eureka, a dramatic musical about myself as Prometheus, her thesis at Brown; in recent years she has been writing and singing songs about the concepts of the Formal Theory so people can sing and dance learning about science.

Oliver has been the non-cowardly lion of the family story. He, with his hard working wife, Bonny, have had the courage to have a big family, four children, and a house full of woofers, farmers in training, together transforming our family home into a farm, bakery, solar power-driven homestead and lumberyard, offering lively music festivals for the community while espousing liberal political causes.

Finally Max, the youngest sibling, is the family's spiritual leader, combining traditional rituals with contemporary personalized moral significance. He is our Tin Man promoting science with an armor of spirituality. He graduated Harvard Divinity and continued with a career as a psychologist PhD from Boston University. His PhD thesis was developing the online delivery of my Formal Theory's self-assessment and pursuing its development and delivery as a training program at the Wilburton Inn. This has lead to the publication of the museum book, two volumes of case studies, and his collaboration in the prepartion of this volume.

I thank Mark Puryear, who has helped me over the years presenting my ideas to the public as guest art exhibits of the Gorski Retrospective, by organizing a Ted X event on the creative process, and by helping me to develop at Champlain College the Moral Monopoly educational game, reconciling religions into the Moral Science. I thank Kevin Metcalfe for helping me over the years with typesetting volumes, such as the well-illustrated museum exhibits book, Science Stealing the Fire of the Gods, and currently the Moral Science Primer. He will be helping me in managing the new project, a learning center, identified as the Creative Process Runway. I thank Gisela Gamper for being my companion for the last four years, both of us recovering from the trauma of losing a beloved spouse and dealing with the reality of running out of time by thoroughly enjoying the bonus years of our lives.

I want to thank my students and my patients for sharing their stories in this publication illustrating the concepts of the science and how tapping creativity is the highway to self-discovery and healing. In particular I would like to thank Gladys Furphy for sharing her poetry, which she introduced as the subtle way of overcoming the difficulty in revealing her emotions. It is the patients' creativity throughout this volume that helps to better understand oneself but also to understand psychology as a science. My role as a therapist has been to educate people on the thesis of the unconscious as a syndrome of emotions modified by the alternative relational modalities and then to demonstrate this process utilizing creativity for self-discovery and healing.

FORMAL THEORY'S PREMISE INTRODUCING SCIENCE IN BEHAVIOR

Formal Theory's premise is that the creative process, reflecting the unconscious, is a conflict resolution, moral order, energy transformation mechanism abiding by two phenomena of science. The thesis is founded on considering emotions as energetic quantities that are organized by the unconscious as units of conflict resolution through an attitude transformation mechanism. The unconscious reduces psychic tension increasing social adjustment by changing a person's attitude following two natural science phenomena: the first is the laws of the Simple Harmonic Motion, the process capturing energy, and the second is the laws of the equilibrial scale, the mechanism transforming this energy as one's attitude along three formal operations.

Conflict energy is generated upon a normative deviation and conflict resolution occurs upon the restoration of the rest state, as a normative correction. It takes three oscillations to retore the rest state. The pendulum is guided by three formal operations: reciprocity transforming passivity to activity, negation transforming antagonism to cooperation, and correlation transforming alienation to mutual respect.

The two scientific phenomena represent the unconscious' two components: A syndrome, a six emotions chain reaction: stress/response, anxiety/defense, and reversal/compromise. The psyche as a pendulum deviation captures this energy; the three formal operations transform it leading to resolutions along four alternative r elational alternatives, the relational modalities. The three oscillations are an emotional dialectic, a six-role state syndrome, graphically portrayed as a sine curve leading to the four alternative ways of resolving graphically portrayed as vectors in a set of concentric circles and ellipses.

Thus the unconscious is defined as a physiological, homeostatic, energy transformation mechanism, with psychological and sociological functions directed by an innate software. Motivation is experienced as the psychological need to reduce psychic tension by resolving conflicts as generated by multiple physiological needs/appetites. Morality thus is a psychological physiological need/motivation for conflict resolution. Religions evolved as normative systems improving the sociological effectiveness of conflict resolutions.

This volume presents evidence validating this premise utilizing three type of creativity studies: first, art exhibits illustrating the conflict resolution process, second, utilizing the Conflict Analysis Battery, a self-assessment to study how individuals resolve conflict, and third, Moral Monopoly, a game of cultural stories, identifying how religions discovered the alternative ways of resolving conflicts improving the family institution. The scientific unconscious radically changes psychology into the exact Moral Science.

The Moral Science redefines the unconscious

Evidence provided in the volume confirms that the creative process, reflecting the unconscious, is a scientific energy transforming conflict resolution process that is graphically portrayable, measurable, qualifiable, and quantifiable, clarifying the unconscious as the unit entity of the social sciences.

The science introduces wellness diagnostic categories

The new unconscious revamps the current illness -based diagnostic categories. It identifies the two components of the unconscious: the six part syndromal structure of the process and the relational modalities, based on the formal distinctions about power and attitude. According to power we recognize submissiveness and dominance and according to attitude, we recognize the alternatives of cooperation versus antagonism. According to the two formal operations we identify four relational modalities. The new diagnoses represent a wellness personality typology. According to the third principle, correlation, we identify the distinction between alienation versus mutual respect corresponding to the difference between illness and wellness.

The science introduces a new assessment

The unconscious is measurable. A new self-assessment, the Conflict Analysis Battery combines projective tests with an inventory. A dozen creativity exercises as a set of projective metaphor-creation exercises reconstruct the set of six role-states, a chain reaction, a rollercoaster, the syndrome of interconnected emotions. The personality inventory has five scales. Four scales identify one's relational modality or spectrum of modalities; the fifth scale assesses psychic tension. The use of the Conflict Analysis Battery self-assessment leads to self-discovery. The battery helps the test taker to become conscious of the unconscious as a syndrome and a relational modality. Completing the battery leads to catharsis, self-awareness, and into identifying by oneself the relational power and attitude management changes.

Knowledge of the unconscious as a scientific conflict resolution phenomenon, a syndrome and a set of modalities, and the ease of determining them through the self-assessment leads to insights and guidance for changes. The assessment is didactic, diagnostic and therapeutic.

Science introduces wellness psychoeducation as the alternative to psychotherapy

The combination of the clarity of concepts on the nature of the unconscious and of wellness diagnoses, and the availability of the assessment technology, modify psychotherapy into psychoeducation, a standardized emotional education. Psychoeducation changes the focus of therapy from symptoms and psychodynamic object relations to the subject evolving self-awareness, identifying one's relationally determined diagnosis and related pathologies. Instead of identifying the problem as a DSM illness diagnosis, and seeking to control symptoms with CBT, or a therapist's insights and guidance for changes, the test taker by oneself may become aware of one's relational modality as the source of conflicts and can reverse pathologies. Such education may and should be delivered preventively by educators to the general public.

The science restructures therapists' and patients' roles

The factors of understanding pathology as generated by relational modalities, wellness diagnoses, rather than by symptom-based behaviors, phobias, eating disorders, etc. and that insights and changes are generated through the self-assessment, identified by the test taker, reduces the traditional patients' dependence on therapists. It changes the role of the therapist from a diagnostician, interpreter, to that of an educator and a role model. The role of a patient is changed to the role of a student. The new therapist/educator explains the nature of the unconscious, of the relational modalities and of the related pathologies and encourages completing changes in terms of power management. Psychoeducation also changes the role of the educator from one providing information on neuroscience to providing meaningful moral integration of the organization of emotions based on motivation inspired by resolving conflicts. Psychoeducation also changes the role of clergy from preaching a single moral paradigm to educating the public that religions have identified and deified the alternative relational modalities; it is important that clergy learn to integrate religions as moral monopolies into the Moral Science.

Leaders and religions manage power according to their relational modality preferences. Science provides us with criteria to judge moral leadership as inspired by the leaders' relational choices. The world has suffered tremendous conflicts evoked by leaders and religions monopolistic relational modalities. The Moral Science provides the criteria, the principles of reduction of conflict as moderation, cooperation and mutual respect. These parameters are readily evaluated. They may be used to judge the moral competence of ideologies and of political leaders. The public should be able to use science to protect itself from conflict generating leadership.

OVERVIEW OF THE MORAL SCIENCE

The unconscious is a scientific entity, the atomistic unit of the social sciences

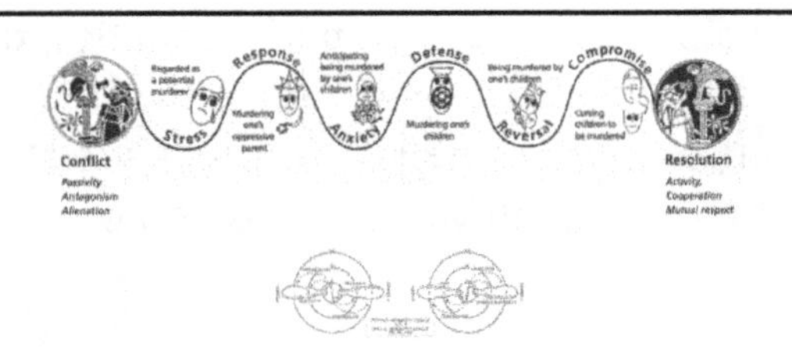

The unconscious is an energy transformation homeostatic morality determined mechanism.

SOCIAL SYNDROMES

Subordinancy		Dominance	
Cooperative	Antagonistic	Cooperative	Antagonistic
RA RO	RO RA	RA ARR	ARR RA
Passive Dependent	Passive Aggressive	Active Dependent	Active Aggressive

Diagnoses are a wellness personality typology

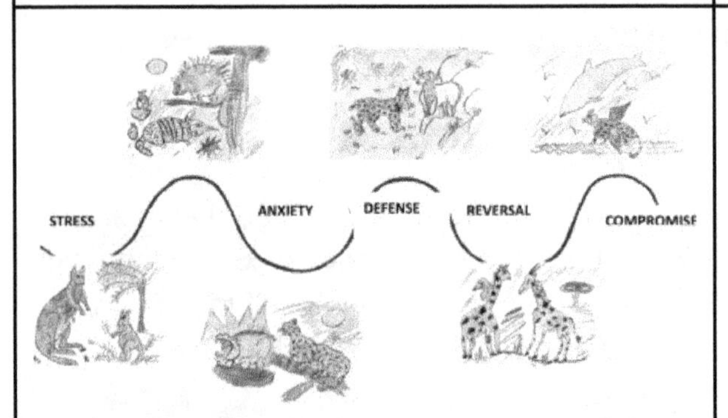

Assessment is becoming conscious of the unconscious as syndromes and modalities.

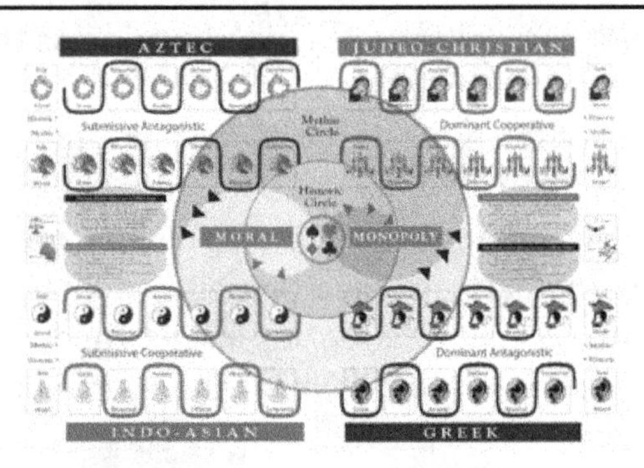

Science demystifies religions by identifying the conflict r esolution process defined by Gods. Religions identified the syndrome as in Genesis, and the relational modalities as spelled by the respective commandments.

The unconscious integrates the disciplines of psychology into the Moral Science

Motivation is driven by the need to reduce psychic tension and improve social adjustment.	Personality typology consists of syndromes and four relational modalities, wellness and pathologies typology.
The Conflict Analysis Battery is a self-assessment that is didactic, diagnostic and therapeutic.	Religions are normative institutions that identified and deified sequentially the four relational modalities. They evolved in abstraction and fairness, but have remained moral monopolies. They may be integrated into the Moral Science.

The Moral Science integrates psychology, religions, and modifies education and politics

The Moral Science integrates art and science, psychology and morality, physiology and sociology, religions among themselves.	We understand art as symbolic systems organized as syndromes and relational modalities leading to the alternative types of conflict resolution.
Psychoeducation may be delivered to everybody leading to self-awareness and to developing skills of power and attitude management.	Religions are measurable normative institutions that have evolved improving the family institution. The public has the criteria to evaluate leadership's type of power management and the right to protect itself from unjust norms.

FOREWORD

This volume consists of four books, an extensive introduction and a conclusion. The introduction examines the challenges for a scientific theory of behavior. The four books present the scientific study of the unconscious integrating the four disciplines of psychology, (epistemology, diagnosis and therapy, assessment, and morality), into the Moral Science. The conclusion examines the relevance of the Moral Science in rethinking psychology and religions.

The information on the science and its application is structured by examining two educational art exhibits presented on the four walls of the square Sanctuary of Wisdom: the exterior exhibit introduces the scientific analysis of four metaphors of the story of the Wizard of Oz: the yellow brick road, pertaining to the analysis of the unconscious as a scientific conflict resolution phenomenon, the four characters representing wellness diagnoses as the alternative ways of resolving conflict, killing the witch, as using creativity for self-discovery, and encountering Oz, as examining the nature of religions as discoveries of the alternative ways to conflict resolution. The interior exhibit of the corresponding walls features murals presenting personal and cultural samples of creativity, illustrating the scientific analysis of metaphors as introduced by the Oz exhibit. The panels and murals, thus introduce the scientific study of the creative process as the integrative unit periodic phenomenon of the social science disciplines.

The 'Moral Science Primer' conveys a significant contribution in the field of the social sciences. It places them on a scientific foundation, leading to their integration with the sciences. This volume presents the concept on the unconscious resolving conflict and evidence validating the premise, thus demonstrating that psychology is the natural science of morality or conflict resolution.

The book introduces the creative process unconscious as the definitive scientific moral paradigm, the origin of all moral thought as the atomistic unit of behavior as an energy transformation phenomenon. The case studies with their visual manifestation with art and the art exhibits of the Museum of the Creative Process deliver solid evidence revamping the social sciences. This book's contribution is groundbreaking.

The volume consists of a synthesis of published information. It is a compilation of excerpts from my several publications. I must give tribute to the early writings studying the creative process as a scientific phenomenon inspired by the study of the Greek cosmogony departing from the 'Argives' a play examining the family dynamics leading to the Trojan war and the Homeric epics,1970. The volume borrows from the Contributions article, 1975, introducing the graphic portrayal of psychological concepts. It borrows from the textbook Conflict Analysis, the Formal Theory of Behavior and the Conflict Analysis Training workbook, 1987, introducing the use of creativity for self-discovery. It borrows the artwork of the panels and the murals of the Sanctuary of Wisdom, from the museum book, 2011.

I must attribute gratitude to Henry Gorski, as his retrospective is used to document predictability of the conflict resolution process illustrating the science of the creative process. Our partnership began in 1972. I have borrowed case studies from two volumes on Creativity and Power Management, 2016. I also extracted the study of religions integrated with the Moral Monopoly game of cards. The new volume presents how the Formal Theory evolved and was validated with art exhibits and the self-assessment to become the Moral Science.

The Moral Science Primer examines the personal thought process, but also that of religions, as paradigms of conflict resolution. We study the history of religions as a continuum of discoveries of science, new ways of resolving conflicts, improving the family institution by establishing covenants, rules about power and attitude management. Science underlies psychological behavior as well as religious doctrines. The theory's practical impact is the introduction of science into psychology and religions, allowing individuals and cultures to identify wellness and pathology. These institutions have relational preferences, which have sociological psychological consequences in both reducing but also in increasing conflict. Science alerts the public to demystify psychology and morality, to diagnose and manage the influence of people and religions through critical analysis of their paradigms.

The bottom line of this theoretical perspective is in our ability to recognize objectively the nature of the unconscious in terms of syndromes and relational modalities. This concept allows us to enter a new era of transparency in individual behavior, philosophies, religions and ideologies. Science identifies the criteria in assessing behavior both in the conduct of individuals and that of moral paradigms. Morality should not be based on distorting individual and cultural perceptions of reality. The role of psychology is to further the meaningful interpretation of behavior and direct the public to manage power and attitude toward the reduction of personal and societal conflicts, thus finding peace, love, and harmony. Science sets the new standards in examining psychology as the Moral Science.

Science in behavior entails making conceptual changes in psychology such as introducing wellness diagnoses replacing the DSM diagnostic categories, evolving better assessment technologies, finally psychology understanding the inner need for morality and religions.

Science entails refocusing education teaching students about psychology identifying their own relational modalities and understanding the importance of morality as optimal power and attitude management. School children should learn about religions to resolve family conflicts with alternative approaches.

The public should be aware of the psychological makeup of political leaders creating and generating conflicts in their leadership approaches. The public should be able to differentiate the influence of leaders like Trump, Putin and Jihadist leaders, versus Christ, Buddha and Moses in managing power.

Religions are accountable to the Moral Science. They should be humbled in their self-righteousness presenting themselves as the total truth. They need to understand their evolution and their limitations as partial truths and that they are subject to relational pathologies. Moral norms should not be determined by one modality. Norms impacting population control need to address global resources and sustainability.

It is very important to recognize the history of civilization and detecting growth in conflict resolution, in recognizing moral order underlying all creativity, be that movies, plays, the study of history, fairy tales and literary works. All creativity reveals the personal and societal quest for conflict resolution.

TABLE OF CONTENTS

INTRODUCTION...17

CHAPTER ONE: INTRODUCTION TO THE FORMAL THEORY
The Moral Science: a conceptual revamping of psychology
The Primer: Four books about psychology's four disciplines
The formal thesis is that the creative process is an energetic transformation phenomenon

A methodological paradigm shift
What is science?
Psychology's multiple aspects seeking integration
Formal Theory's premise of the creative process as an energetic and attitude transformation mechanism
Conflict as energy generation, resolutions as energy transformation

CHAPTER TWO: HISTORY OF THE FORMAL THEORY...25
The Formal Theoretical Publications

CHAPTER THREE: THE VALIDATION OF THE FORMAL THEORY...28
The Assessment Tool
2. About the art exhibits of the Museum of the Creative Process
3. Moral Monopoly
4. The Sanctuary exhibits: 12 Wizard of Oz Panels and 12 Metaphoria Murals

CHAPTER FOUR: INTEGRATING THE FOUR DISCIPLINES OF PSYCHOLOGY INTO THE MORAL SCIENCE............35
The four walls of the Sanctuary as the four disciplines of psychology

CHAPTER FIVE: THE CONFLICT RESOLUTION UNCONSCIOUS
A SCIENTIFIC AND MORAL ORDER MECHANISM...40
The Conflict Resolution Process as scientific and morality bound entity
The exhibits as illustrations and as validations
The educational value of the Sanctuary exhibits

BOOK ONE: EPISTEMOLOGY...44
IDENTIFYING THE STRUCTURE OF THE CREATIVE PROCESS THROUGH
THE SCIENTIFIC INTERPRETATION OF METAPHORS

INTRODUCTION
Wall # 1. Epistemology: the scientific structure and the moral function of the unconscious

CHAPTER ONE: PANELS ABOUT THE YELLOW BRICK ROAD..46
Panel 1: The analysis of the plot of stories as a sequence of six interrelated role-states:
stress, response, anxiety, defense, reversal, and compromise
Panel 2: Myths and religions, art and drama, psychology, as humankind's quests for meaning
Panel 3: Finally, the quests for meaning, find in the unit the science-based paradigm of moral order
The scientific laws underlying moral order were derived by equating the unit, a social science periodic phenomenon, with the Simple Harmonic Motion, a periodic phenomenon from the natural sciences and the formal operations restoring balance to the trays of a scale

CHAPTER TWO: MURALS #1, 3, 2; ABOUT SYNDROMES AND MODALITIES....................................49
Mural 1, Three creation stories as the six-role syndrome

Mural 3: The physics of metaphysics and of relational modalities
Mural 3b: The three Abrahamic religions are formally interrelated alternative ways of resolving conflict
Mural 2: The flag of the united metaphors of the world shows that the conflict resolution process is a measurable and graphically portrayable conflict resolution natural science phenomenon

CHAPTER THREE: PARADIGM SHIFT FROM THE PROPOSITIONAL TO THE RELATIONAL METHOD....................58
Methodology: Shift from the propositional to the relational method
Exemplifying the differences between propositional versus relational method in the history of science

CHAPTER FOUR: FORMAL THEORY'S ANALYSIS OF THE CREATIVE PROCESS AS A SCIENTIFIC PHENOMENON REFLECTING THE UNCONSCIOUS..61
The first observation: periodicity of a pattern
The second observation: the cross-cultural differences in resolving conflicts
The scientific analysis of the creative process
The difference between the thought process and the Simple Harmonic Motion's perpetual motion
Motivation as the psychological need to resolve conflicts
The unconscious as a mechanism that transforms energy and creates moral order
The graphic representation of the unconscious
The epistemology of the unconscious: The physics and logic of mental operations
The formal operations model, the relational and moral variables of the unconscious equilibrium of scales
Differences between Piaget's and the Formal Theory's epistemology
Equivalences in emotional and behavioral transactions
Differences between mind and machines

CHAPTER FIVE: THE UNCONSCIOUS AS THE INTEGRATIVE PARADIGM...75
The formal thesis clarifies the scientific origin of psychological and of moral order
The unconscious is a homeostatic physiological phenomenon
Relational diagnoses and their syndromal unfolding as the six-role process
The unconscious is measurable with the Conflict Analysis Battery
The unconscious determines the cultural normative constraints
Morality is an essential and integral aspect of psychology
The formal integration of the disciplines
Criteria qualifying psychology as a natural science
Applying the theory to the interpretation of metaphors

CHAPTER SIX: PSYCHOLOGY'S FOUR DISCIPLINES..80
Epistemology: The unconscious defined with scientific constructs
Wellness diagnoses: Syndromes and relational modalities
The Conflict Analysis Battery, a didactic, diagnostic, and therapeutic self-assessment
Morality: Religions determined by the unconscious Conflict Resolution Process

CHAPTER SEVEN: INTEGRATION OF FREUD'S CONCEPTUAL MODELS..87
Conceptual parallels between the theories of Freud, Jung, and Levis
Table: The Moral Science integrating Freud's theoretical models
Table: The science integrates therapeutic interventions

BOOK TWO: DIAGNOSIS AND THERAPEUTIC ASSESSMENT.................................90
CHAPTER ONE: ON DIAGNOSTIC CATEGORIES
Identifying diagnoses as the alternative types of conflict resolution as a wellness personality typology

and using the Conflict Analysis Battery as a didactic, diagnostic and therapeutic intervention
Table: DSM 5's psychiatric illness diagnoses versus Relational Modalities wellness personality types
Murals case studies recognize the differences between dominance and submissiveness relational modalities

CHAPTER TWO: PANELS ABOUT THE FOUR HEROES OF THE OZ STORY..94
The four Wizard of Oz heroes as metaphors of the syndromal relational modalities as wellness diagnoses, a personality typology
Panel 4: The unit of conflict resolution, the unconscious, as a syndrome, a sequence of six formally interrelated role states, as a dialectic of interrelated emotions
Panel 5: The four relational modalities as the alternative specific responses to stress
The modalities correspond to different distortions of reality
The formal range of relational modalities constitutes the spectrum of wellness personality typology
Panel 6: Complete Conflict Resolution as a paramount objective
Therapy and Psychoeducation as the Deliberate Pursuit of Conflict Resolution

CHAPTER THREE: FORMAL THEORY'S WELLNESS DIAGNOSES AS SYNDROMES OF FOUR RELATIONAL MODALITIES VERSUS DIAGNOSTIC STATISTICAL MANUAL #5'S MENTAL ILLNESS DIAGNOSES........................99
The syndromal mechanism is modified by the four relational modalities
The four relational modalities
The unfolding of the syndromal process
The significance of the syndromal diagnosis
About the shortcomings of the DSM
Graphic portrayal
Table: The graphic representation of relational modalities, Psycho-assessment and psychotherapy
The sanctification of conflict resolutions
Relational Modalities as Normative Alternatives
Wellness diagnoses as syndromal relational modalities
Table Relational modalities key features
Consequences of the DSM diagnostic categories, the medicalization of wellness
The medical versus relational formulation of diagnoses
Measuring personality, the assessment of the relational modalities and syndromes
The CAB self-assessment is didactic, diagnostic and therapeutic.
Table DSM 5, illness diagnostic categories versus the four relational modalities as wellness personality types
Psychology of Relational Modalities

CHAPTER FOUR: MEASURING THE UNCONSCIOUS..109
The Conflict Analysis Battery (CAB)
The battery's two instruments

Table: Creativity tasks arranged to reconstruct the six-role process

Interpretation of the assessment along the Formal Analysis Profile,
the scientific analysis of the conflict resolution process
Test Delivery and the computer generated report
Three functions of the testing

Discussion of assessment literature
Formal versus descriptive distinctions
Table of equivalence between formal and propositional distinctions
Table: Differences of traditional assessments and the Conflict Analysis Battery
Contrasting features of traditional assessments to those of the Conflict Analysis Battery
Overview of the battery's innovations

CHAPTER FIVE: EVALUATION OF THE SELF-ASSESSMENT...132
Two professors' analysis of the Conflict Analysis Batter
1. Professor Shawky F. Karas,Ed.D. - Experimental testing of the Personality Inventory
2. Professor Donald Mosher - Investigation of the Projective Testing

BRIEF BATTERY ONLINE DELIVERY
Four case studies as diagnostic evaluation with the brief battery
1. Submissive cooperative: the peacock and the dog
2. Submissive antagonistic: two dogs
3. Moderate dominant antagonistic: dog fish
4. Dominant cooperative: lion fish

SAMPLE COMPLETE BATTERY ONLINE DELIVERY
An assessment report with the complete online delivered battery
COMPUTER GENERATED REPORT
VALIDATION STUDIES OF THE ONLINE COMPLETE BATTERY
Query results confirming the effectiveness of the online delivery of the battery as an emotional education program that is didactic, diagnostic and therapeutic

Summary of statistics on the group of 47 test takers regarding the assessment experience as educational, diagnostic and therapeutic

VALIDATION STUDIES OF THE WORKBOOK DELIVERY OF THE COMPLETE BATTERY
Comments by students completing the assessment
Patients' comments

THE TRAINING PROGRAM
DISCUSSION OF THE ASSESSMENT EXPERIENCE
EMOTIONAL EDUCATION

CHAPTER SIX : MURAL #10, THE EVERYDAY PSYCHOPATHOLOGY OF THE DOMINANCE AND SUBORDINANCE RELATIONAL MODALITIES 168
Intern #1 Melissa: The dominance scenario
Intern #2 Chris: Badger vs. Rabbit, the subordinancy scenario

CHAPTER SEVEN: CONFLICT ANALYSIS BATTERY CASE STUDIES ILLUSTRATING THE INTERPRETATION OF METAPHORS AS SYNDROMES AND RELATIONAL MODALITIES...196
Psychiatric Versus Relational Diagnoses
<u>About the submissiveness relational modality. Review of the seven Case Studies</u>
Case Study 1: The Caribou Falling Behind the Herd and the Predatory Wolf
Case Study 2: Trying to Survive as a Dog
Case Study 3: The Anteater and the Lion
Case Study 4: The Horse That Wanted to Jump a Fence, also identified as The Wise Oak
Case Study 5: The Wolf and the Bird with the Broken Wing, case reviewed in therapy outcome chapter
Case Study 6: The Vulture and the Snake, case reviewed on the therapy outcome chapter
Case Study 7: The Foot Fetish Youth
Characteristics Of Submissive Persons' Artwork, Animal Metaphors and the Transparent Mask Sequence
Submissiveness Case Study: Evaluation of a Judge, "The Sacrificial Lamb", alternatively, "The Caribou that Falls Behind the Herd"

The Dominance Relational Modality, Review of the seven Case Studies
Introduction And Definition Of the Dominance Relational Modalities
Identifying Characteristics Of Dominant Persons' Artwork
Clinically Diagnosed Patients
Case Study #1: Holocaust Survivor Lion Versus Lion: A Therapeutic Evaluation
Case Study #2: The Ant And The Flea: A Four Workbooks Case Study
Case Study #3: The Elephant And The Butterfly
Case Study #4: The Dragon And The Unicorn
Case Study #5: The Turkey And The Mountain Lion
Case Study #6: The Cheshire Cat And The Pit-bull
Case Study #7: The Bull and the Cow, The Study Of A Couple, A Dominant Husband and The Submissive Wife
Dominant Case Study Four: The Dragon And The Unicorn

CHAPTER EIGHT: RECORDING THE COURSE OF THERAPY OUTCOME UTILIZING THE CONFLICT ANALYSIS BATTERY..244
Formal Theory's conceptual distinctions and Conflict Analysis Battery's technology
The deck of cards as the template of the unconscious, an orderly system of transformations
Relational diagnoses pertain to wellness and pathology
Advantages of the Conflict Analysis Battery
Sample of the formal analysis method by observing two images illustrating the process of change and capturing it conceptually and graphically
Adopting the dialectic organization of the deck of playing cards as a model of organizing therapeutic changes
Moral Monopoly introduces cultural stories exemplifying the relational modalities
Psychotherapy outcome research
The Gorski Retrospective as an example of the spontaneous evolution in resolving conflicts

Dominance case studies
Segmet, the mighty black cat
Four phases in the healing process
Dominant patient number two: Kathy, the spider that weaves a web connecting the people in her life

Submissiveness case studies
Alicia, how the scared troll became the moon
Conflict Analysis Battery, Book one: the metaphor profile upon the evaluation phase of therapy
Table: Conflict Analysis Battery, Book two: The metaphor profile reflecting many changes in the equivalent tests
Gladys, How Pijagu: The pig that eats too much, the jaguar who desires control and the seagull who wants freedom became a Dolphin, who enjoys companionship or How a "we" becomes an "I"
Personal Essay: An Autobiography Illustrated by Metaphors and Poetry
Patient's Analysis of the Relapse
My Anger, My Moat, My Quiet

Table: Two dominant clinically diagnosed patients with interpersonal conflicts
Table: Two submissive clinically diagnosed case studies: with inner conflicts, eating disorder and self-mutilation
Detecting therapy changes
Training facility and programs
The methodological significance of the Formal Theory
The therapeutic relationship
Concluding Comments

BOOK THREE: THE ASSESSMENT..302
THE CONFLICT ANALYSIS BATTERY'S SCIENTIFIC STRUCTURE AND EMOTIONAL FUNCTION

CHAPTER ONE: PANELS ABOUT KILLING THE WITCH
Introduction: Overview of the third wall panels and murals
Panel 7: The function of the Conflict Analysis Battery self-assessment
Panel 8: The unit as the superhighway to wisdom
Panel 9: The unit integrates knowledge, self-knowledge, and clarity of values

CHAPTER TWO: THE SCIENTIFIC INTERPRETATION OF THE SELF-ASSESSMENT METAPHORS........................311
Introduction: Murals # 4, 7, 8, and 9 illustrate the battery's metaphors and their interpretation
SUB-CHAPTER ONE: Mural 4: My Metaphors, Myself: 1983
SUB-CHAPTER TWO: Mural 7 validates the foundation for the interpretation of CAB's metaphors in that emotions and the respective images are formally interrelated by the three formal operations
SUB-CHAPTER THREE: Mural 8 validates the foundation for the interpretation of CAB's metaphors in that emotions and the respective images have the natural science dimensions of three pendulum oscillations
SUB-CHAPTER FOUR: Mural 9: the metaphor process is a cost-effective methodology for self-discovery and self-healing

BOOK FOUR..346
MORALITY, THE MEANINGFUL INTEGRATION OF KNOWLEDGE

CHAPTER ONE: ON MORALITY AS A SCIENTIFIC PHENOMENON

CHAPTER TWO: PANELS ABOUT THE WIZARD OF OZ...348
Three panels establish the moral function of the creative process: panels #10, 11, and 12
Panel 10: Piety as respect of the universal moral order
Panel 11: Reconciling psychology and religion
Panel 12: The Gorski retrospective as a validation of the creative process, predictably resolving conflict

CHAPTER THREE: MURALS 4, 5, AND 6 OF THE FOURTH WALL ARE ABOUT UNDERSTANDING RELIGIONS AS MEASURABLE CONFLICT RESOLUTIONS SPONTANEOUSLY EVOLVED TOWARD THE MORAL SCIENCE...........353
Mural 5: Our cultural metaphors as a continuum of evolving moral order
Mural 6: From art to science in the search for a better paradigm

CHAPTER FOUR: THE CONFLICT RESOLUTION PROCESS AS THE ATOMISTIC UNIT OF BEHAVIOR..................361
Phenomenology versus formal reductionism as the epistemology of the unconscious
Method: The conflict resolution process as the atomistic unit of behavior
Findings: The six comparative tables attest to the advantages of reductionism
Discussion: The moral significance of the science based unconscious process

CHAPTER FIVE: MORAL MONOPOLY, AN EDUCATIONAL GAME
COMPLETING THE PROGRESSION OF RELIGIONS INTO THE MORAL SCIENCE..396
SUB-CHAPTER ONE: MORALITY GENERATED BY FORMAL THEORY'S UNCONSCIOUS
Religions as complementary discoveries of science
Formal Theory's methodology: the thought process as syndromes and relational modalities
The unconscious as a scientific conflict resolution process, the new moral paradigm
The formal analysis of diagnostic categories as four relational modalities
The evolution of religions as discoveries of the formal operations: mastery, cooperation, and mutual respect
Biblical metaphors as discoveries of science

SUB-CHAPTER TWO: FORMAL ANALYSIS OF THE DECK OF CARDS
Formal analysis of the signs of the card game
Formal Analysis of the structure of the deck of cards
The game board as the map of the unconscious
The natural science dimensions of the game board
The game board portrays syndromes and relational modalities
The card game presents the self-improving, self-adjusting unconscious

SUB-CHAPTER THREE: THE RULES OF THE GAME
The game retraces the history of religions on the scientifically constructed template of the unconscious. It thus integrates the humanities and the sciences
Examining the cultural stories questioning the premise of the Formal Theory
Conclusions from playing the game
The formal analysis of religions
The process of conflict resolution organizes personal and cultural symbolic systems

SUB-CHAPTER FOUR: FORMAL ANALYSIS OF MORAL MONOPOLY'S CULTURAL STORIES
Eight stories as psychological and sociological measurable phenomena
The numbered cards correspond to the six syndromal episodes of cultural stories
Description of the face cards of the cultural suits
The face cards reflecting the relational modalities
Formal transformation from the mythic to the historical story
The first set as mythic role model cards
The second set as historic role model cards
The four cultures are connected dialectically as discoveries of relational operations
Evolution of religions by establishing relational continuity
Sample exchanges between partners in each culture identifying the key family conflict
The cultural stories inscribed on the game board as a continuum of discoveries of science
In depth study of cultures: The Matriarchal Culture
Greece dealt with matriarchy by discovering the principle of reciprocity, turning passivity to activity, men domesticating the fight and flight, Sphinx-like, identity of women
India discovery cooperation as the mode of resolving conflicts
Judaism discovered the operation of mutual respect between father and son
The definition of the inequities in the Abrahamic Family, as a sculpture by Judith Brown

SUB-CHAPTER FIVE: PREPARATION TO PLAY THE GAME BY LEARNING ABOUT THE PREVALENCE OF A RELATIONAL PATTERN IN THE GREEK CULTURE

SUB-CHAPTER SIX: THE GAME SPIRITUALIZES PSYCHOLOGY AND DEMYSTIFIES MORALITY
Establishing continuity among the cultures
The traditional card game insignia corresponding to the evolution of relational effectiveness
The evolution of cultural conflict resolutions
The scientific morality makes religions accountable to science
The challenges for the players: evolving scientific moral consensus
Confirming the scientific and moral unconscious
The Moral Science, the scientific and moral psychology
A methodological Paradigm Shift: the end of idolatry
Insights based on the discovery: normative relativity
The moral of the game: The experiential validation of Formal Theory's claims

SUB-CHAPTER SEVEN: THE BENEFITS OF THE EDUCATIONAL GAME
Healing the world by demonstrating that morality is an exact science putting an end to cross-cultural conflicts.
Why is the scientific and moral unconscious a significant discovery?
Values and norms
The players learn about psychology as the Science of Conflict Resolution
The relevance of the formal interpretation of metaphors is in the integration of psychology and religions into the Moral Science
The players evolve moral consensus
The players reach a consensus on the scientific nature of morality, as the moral psychology
The game entails insights and changes
Religions demystified and humanized
Religions misunderstand the nature of morality
Clarifying the concepts of the Moral Science
Overcoming traditions, refuting dated paradigms
End of idolatry as the shift of paradigms from the content to the process of stories
Normative relativity
The game as the experiential validation of Formal Theory's claims
Why is the scientific and moral unconscious a significant discovery?
Religions' progression in redefining the divine is completed by identifying the unconscious as the scientific conflict resolution process
Reviewing the benefits of the educational game

CONCLUSION..445
INTEGRATING PSYCHOLOGY AND MORALITY INTO THE MORAL SCIENCE

CHAPTER ONE: THE SCIENTIFIC AND MORAL NATURE OF THE UNCONSCIOUS AS THE UNIT ORDER OF PSYCHOLOGY

CHAPTER TWO: MORALITY DEFINED THROUGH NORMATIVE CRITERIA....................446
The Moral Science retraces the evolution of normative systems

CHAPTER THREE: RELIGIONS ARE MEASURABLE NATURAL SCIENCE MORAL ORDER PHENOMENA.............449
The Moral Science addresses religions normative choices as originating in the relational modality of their creators
Applying formal analysis to the conflict between Trump and Islam
Formal Theory's conceptual relevance

CHAPTER FOUR: THE SCIENTIFIC MORAL PARADIGM....................................452
Moral Science's role as the moral authority
Science challenges our sanctified paradigms
The world needs the scientific moral paradigm
Political and psychological self-awareness needed

CHAPTER FIVE: EMOTIONAL EDUCATION FOR ALL.......................................457
Emotional Education as the application of the science
Mission Statement as the implementation of wisdom
Accountability of all humanities to the Moral Science
Mission statement: Healing the person, healing the world

BIBLIOGRAPHY...465

INTRODUCTION TO THE MORAL SCIENCE PRIMER

The Moral Science, the conceptual revamping of psychology

'If there is one thing that theoretical and historical psychologists and other scholars of the field do consensually agree on, it is that there is no consensus about what psychology is or means. ... how could we possibly develop a language for designing real world assessments and interventions for mental health? In other words, a fragmented chaotic pluralism in psychotherapy is an inevitable and natural consequence of a broken, fragmented pluralistic psychology'. Gregg Henriques

'What is this new perspectivistic slice, this new epistemic community of Albert Levis and The Formal Theory of Behavior? What is this new lever this modern Archimedes offers us to lift the world to newer heights? It is nothing less than a new way of ordering and conceptualizing human behavior that bridges the here-and-now with man's long behavioral history, and it does so with both the possibility of predictive accuracy and the opportunity for variability and change. It also bridges the conceptual gaps which have existed between cognitive and emotive schools of thought, between psychoanalysis and learning theory, between the work of Jean Piaget and that of the neo-Freudians-- and, finally, between the worlds of psychology and sociology. The Formal Theory achieves this by reconciling the methodology of the "hard sciences," such as physics, logic and mathematics with that of the "soft sciences," the disciplines of human behavior.' (CFTB 1) William Grey

CHAPTER ONE: INTRODUCTION TO THE FORMAL THEORY

The formal thesis is that the creative process reflects the unconscious, as a natural science conflict resolution phenomenon

Formal Theory's key concept is based on observing the creative process, the plot of stories, reflecting the unconscious, as a scientific conflict resolution phenomenon. The process begins with a conflict, unpleasant emotions, and ends with resolutions, 'happily ever after', as social adjustment. The Formal Theory posits that emotions are energy, and that the unconscious is a homeostatic energy transformation mechanism automatically reducing unpleasant psychic tension by enhancing social adjustment through changing a person's attitude.

The unconscious energetic process is analyzed as consisting of two components: a syndrome of six emotions and a set of four alternative types of conflict resolution. These two components abide by two phenomena of science allowing the introduction of scientific constructs and formulas into psychology. The unit order unconscious becomes a scientific, measurable, graphically portrayable entity that clarifies diagnoses, assessment and morality. This unconscious is the unit of the social sciences. It is the master key to knowledge. Science changes psychology from the agnostic, and non-rational study of behavior to the natural Science of Conflict Resolution, the Moral Science. The scientific understanding of psychology and religions can heal the person and can heal the world by spiritualizing psychology and by demystifying religions.

The 'Moral Science Primer' launches the conceptual revamping of psychology into a rigorous science introducing the scientific study of the unconscious revamping psychology into an exact natural and moral science. The volume examines the disciplines of psychology beginning with rethinking concepts, then examining new diagnostic categories as alternative types of conflict resolution, and utilizing creativity for self-discovery and therapeutic growth. It also addresses understanding religions evolving as complementary discoveries of the types of conflict resolution evolving in abstraction and fairness.

The book was conceived as four volumes, each introducing one of the four disciplines of psychology as a natural and moral or conflict resolution science. I designed the jackets and identified the files. But viewing the reality of introducing the theory in a concise manner, I decided starting with one rather than four publications, one lengthy volume, by reducing the files of the four original volumes into one.

The concept of four volumes may be noticed as each segment of this volume is identified as a book. The four books correspond to the four disciplines. Each begins with a book-jacket of the original publication project. I like the 'Flag of the United Metaphors' as the design for the jacket of this volume. It presents the two aspects of the American flag: the stars and the stripes unifying moral paradigms in a meaningful and measurable context to each other in the context of the two aspects of the conflict resolution process: the syndromal and the relational modality configuration of the new unconscious.

The four books apply the theory to the formal analysis of the disciplines as implementation and as validation of the Formal Theory's thesis. Epistemology introduces science in the study of the creative process unconscious. Diagnosis and Therapeutic Assessment introduces the process leading to four types of conflict resolution as wellness diagnostic categories. Assessment technology examines the scientific structure and the moral function of the self-assessment. On morality we study religions as discoveries of the alternative ways of resolving conflict integrated into the Moral Science.

The evidence on the scientific and moral /conflict resolution nature of the unconscious is introduced through the analysis of two art exhibits of the Sanctuary of 'the Wizard and of Wisdom'. It contains two art exhibits. The first analyzes the metaphors of the story of the Wizard of Oz by introducing phenomena of science in the analysis of the creative process. The exhibit's twelve panels introduce the formal analysis of the story's familiar metaphors founded on scientific principles applied to the constructs of to the four disciplines. The Metaphoria Murals exhibit applies the principles of science in the formal analysis of cultural and personal stories illustrating and validating the formal premise, the conflict-resolving nature of the thought process. The evidence provided by the two exhibits both explains and validates the Formal Theory.

The new volume is number 7 of a series of Formal Theory books, six of which have been already published under the imprint of Normative Publications as archives of the research on the Formal Theory. This volume familiarizes the public with the scientific analysis of the creative process, the scientific interpretation of metaphors. It introduces the four disciplines of the Moral Science with the analysis of the creative process as the atomistic unit, a scientific conflict resolution entity, as the integrative paradigm of the social sciences. The four books address application of the theory to the rethinking of the four disciplines of psychology as the Moral Science.

BOOK ONE is on Epistemology as The Scientific Interpretation of Metaphors, examines critically the conceptualization of the disciplines of psychology. It presents Formal Theory's analysis of the creative process as a conflict resolution or moral order mechanism reflecting the unconscious as an energetic and formal transformation process manifested as a syndrome of six-emotions and as four alternative types of conflict resolution that abide by the laws of two scientific phenomena. The unconscious is analyzed as three pendulum oscillations manifested as a syndrome of six interrelated role states, as an emotional dialectic, guided by the three formal equilibrial operations. Conflict is defined as passivity, antagonism, and alienation; it is resolved transformed to a state formally defined as mastery, cooperation, and mutual respect. According to the formal distinctions the process leads to four alternative ways of resolving conflict, the relational modalities.

The unconscious ushers in the scientific conceptualization of the humanities. The process revamps psychology's concepts. The new unconscious changes the diagnostic categories into the four types of conflict resolution. It changes the assessment of the unconscious as a therapeutic and educational intervention, and changes our understanding of the nature of religions. Foremost is the point of the scientific analysis of the unconscious resolving conflicts as the origin of all moral thinking. The creative process, as a scientific moral order phenomenon, as an energy and attitude transformation homeostatic mechanism, unifies science, psychology and morality in the pursuit of conflict resolution as the principle motivational force.

BOOK TWO introduces the 'Wellness Diagnoses, and Therapy'. We identify in the unit process two entities: a six-role state syndrome and the spectrum of four relational modalities as the four alternative ways of resolving conflicts. The formal relational equilibrial operations: reciprocity, negation and correlation are attitude-directed energetic transformations. They modify attitudes as relational operations leading to four types of conflict resolutions. Resolutions differ: according to power, we distinguish dominance versus subordinancy, and according to attitude, we distinguish cooperation versus antagonism. We recognize these as wellness diagnostic categories, the relational modalities as four syndromal categories, a personality typology as the scientific, qualifiable and quantifiable, graphically portrayable, conflict resolution alternatives. These distinctions as four wellness diagnoses, the range of syndromal alternative types of conflict resolution, replace medical diagnoses by understanding a personality typology as wellness categories. They also account for pathology upon intensification of psychic and societal tension.

The Conflict Analysis Battery is a user-friendly self-assessment available as a workbook and also online. It helps a person to become conscious of the unconscious. The battery combines two types of tests: a personality inventory and a set of metaphor creation projective tasks. The two instruments identify the two components of the unconscious: the relational modality with the personality inventory and the emotional dialectic, the six-role syndrome, with the set of metaphors. The battery guides the test taker to identify one's personality type, a relational modality, and to generate metaphors, to subject them to formal analysis, thus to identify one's syndrome as the six-part emotional path of conflict resolution. The key to therapy hinges on diagnosing one's relational modality and its manifestation as a syndrome founded on the distinctions of power and attitude. The assessment generates insights by recognizing one's syndromal and relational modality.

The manual driven self-assessment, the Conflict Analysis Battery, is a concise program of psychoeducation and psychotherapy. The battery assists the person both in becoming aware of her unconscious way of resolving conflicts, and also how to deliberately modify one's power and attitude to optimize conflict resolution. The self-assessment is educational, diagnostic, and therapeutic; it changes psychotherapy into psychoeducation. Relational self-awareness through the testing changes the role of the therapist into that of an educator. Case studies show the diagnostic and therapeutic effectiveness of the interpretation of metaphors. They also illustrate the universality of the unconscious process as scientific and measurable validating the theory. Four case studies illustrate the evolution of patients' emotional progress in long-term therapy as attitude transformation correcting relational pathology.

BOOK THREE, Assessment, 'From Trauma to Healing', examines the measurement of the unconscious reviewing case studies using the Conflict Analysis Battery; we introduce the formal and energetic aspects of the symbolic language of metaphors and learn about symbolism having physical, energetic, and formal dimensions. Case studies present the importance of traumas in determining the organization of thoughts and emotions as symbolic systems leading spontaneously to conflict resolution as healing.

BOOK FOUR, on Morality as 'The Meaningful Integration of Knowledge' focuses on the study of the process as the integrative paradigm. Moral Monopoly is an educational game studying the interpretation of cultural stories reflecting the evolution of religions as a continuum of complementary discoveries of science that may be integrated into the Moral Science. The game uses the structure of the deck of cards as a template of the unconscious conflict resolution process. The structure of all suits represents the conflict resolution process. The four suits identify the four modalities; finally the four signs, spade, club, diamond and heart are formally interrelated as the dialectic evolution of modalities improving the effectiveness in resolving domestic relations conflicts. The game retraces the history of religions following the signs of the card game as symbols of a progression along the four modalities unified into the Moral Science. The game also educates on the periodicity of evolutions in resolving conflict as a reality that explains developmental dynamics, and emotional growth manifested observing the creative process in therapy as well as in spontaneous creativity. Moral Monopoly analyzes cultural stories identifying how religions resolve conflicts, and how they evolved improving the family system. The Moral Science reconciles them and helps them to complete their mission for peace on earth.

A methodological paradigm shift

The Formal Theory is validated by identifying the scientific conflict resolution structure in samples of creativity like the art exhibits of the Museum of the Creative Process and by completing the Conflict Analysis Battery, identifying the syndromal structure, and the relational modality of the personal creative process. Contemporary psychology and religions are theories without a scientific foundation. Though the humanities pertain to the same entity, human behavior, religion and psychology are unable to find a common denominator reconciling them with each other and with the sciences. Each domain struggles with vague conceptualizations and a variety of conceptual paradigms. The world today is in crisis because the humanities, religion and psychology, lack scientific grounding.

Contemporary psychology has dissociated itself from psychodynamic thinking. Psychology is a medical specialty, pertinent to illness rather than wellness; clinicians identify symptoms without psychodynamic causation; they seek answers in the brain. People have no idea about their personality types and how these affect one's emotions as variations in choices of power and attitude. Current theorists have difficulty in conceptualizing the unconscious, morality, and religions. They have not continued paying attention to psychodynamic issues inherent in psychology as initiated by Freud and Jung. Religions promote different values and norms, which they attribute to gods rather than science. They are normative institutions, arbitrary moral paradigms, moral monopolies, based on dogma, regulating conduct, incompatible with each other, accountable to their own theistic authorities but not to reason.

The Moral Science represents a paradigm shift revamping psychology into an exact science:

1. The Moral Science identifies the unconscious as a psychodynamic conflict resolution scientific mechanism, the integrative core paradigm, contradicting contemporary psychiatry's medicalization and agnosticism.

2. The Moral Science recognizes wellness diagnostic categories as syndromes of six emotions leading to four relational modalities as the alternative types of conflict resolution and examining pathology on purely relational terms contradicting DSM5, diagnoses of emotional problems as illness conditions identifying them as clusters of symptoms.

3. The MS introduces the Conflict Analysis Battery, a self-assessment, which identifies with an inventory the person's relational modality and with creativity tasks the syndromal six-role sequence of the conflict resolving emotions; the inventory is diagnostic of wellness and illness and the creativity tests are therapeutic. The new assessment contradicts current assessments that are non-theoretical, identifying unrelated traits, statistical factors that are meaningless to the test taker as acronyms of arbitrary sets of four or five letters, either inventories or projectives without coincidence in the interpretations of the two types of assessment.

4. The MS understands morality and spirituality as the innate need for conflict resolution having evolved to religions as normative institutions. It recognizes religions as psychological theories that with metaphors have captured both the conflict resolution process syndrome, as in Genesis, and the range of modalities as paths to resolutions, optimized by moral injunctions as in the Ten Commandments. Religions have attributed to the divine the characteristics of the unconscious conflict resolution mechanism. The Moral Science reclaims the characteristics of the divine as those of the unconscious and examines religions as complementary discoveries of science that are now merged into the Moral Science. It contradicts contemporary psychology's agnosticism the dismissal of morality as a non-scientific domain, and contradicts religions defining morality along theistic models, their sanctifying norms, frozen in time, in determining people's contemporary lives. It defends them as institutions of conflict resolution but explains their failure in promising peace on earth but instead evoking personal and cross-cultural conflicts.

The Moral Science introduces the unconscious as the conflict resolving entity, the origin of all moral thought and integrates psychology and morality. It reduces personal and cross-cultural conflicts. It is able to help education to deliver its three objectives: the integration of the humanities and the sciences, self-knowledge, and clarity on moral values. The world needs the scientific unit of the social sciences, a universal moral order.

After fifty years of ongoing research and publications, the Formal Theory has been validated into the exact science of psychology, redefining the current notions on the unconscious, diagnoses, assessment and morality as having the process as the common denominator, and thus integrates them into a rigorous science. The new science clarifies the unconscious as a homeostatic, physiological energy and attitude transforming conflict-resolving mechanism; it identifies wellness diagnoses as the alternative types of conflict resolution also accounting for pathology. It introduces a theory-based self-assessment instrument that is diagnostic and therapeutic and finally it clarifies religions as determined by the unconscious as alternative types of conflict resolution, integrated into the Moral Science.

The Moral Science evolves psychology into a science, by identifying the appropriate object of study and the correct method for its analysis, the unconscious studying the creative process as a conflict resolution mechanism transforming energy, as the atomistic unit of the social sciences. It understands creativity with concepts from physics and logic demystifying religions and psychology. The science thus addresses education's aspiration for integrating the humanities and the sciences, self-knowledge and clarity of values.

The Moral Science contradicts the scholars seeking science in behavior who have resorted to two types of reasoning: dualism, separating rational, or empirical from spiritual thinking. Jung endorsed dualism as two types of reasoning. He introduced the concept of alchemy, the unconscious reasoning as based on innate cultural archetypes. The Frankfurt formalists examined linguistic structure to find morality but failed. Haidt researches the popularity of moral values as the means of defining morality.

The theory is validated by interpreting the personal and cultural metaphors generating meaningfulness. The evidence integrates art and science, introduces clarity in the realms of behavior and religions; it heals the person and can heal the world. Hence the Moral Science revolutionizes the field of psychology, by extension of all the humanities, through the study of the creative process as a scientific conflict resolution or moral order phenomenon. Identifying the unit order of the social sciences as a natural science entity, the Moral Science, begins a new era in the conceptualization of behavior, launching the scientific study of psychology and morality.

What is science?

Science is confused with the use of methodological principles in conducting research. Science hinges on abstract thinking, correct choice of object of study and proper methodology. A scientific phenomenon is characterized as attaining periodicity, predictability, measurability, reduction of complexity to the simplest elements, energy, principles of systemic order, parts that are interrelated with each other with formulas: such as

Energy= Force x Displacement, velocity is distance divided by time, etc.

Scientific hypotheses are readily validated. Sciences identify a unit order, as the universal periodic phenomenon, the measuring rod within every field of inquiry. Objects of study are well defined, i.e. in geometry it is the meter or the yardstick, in chemistry, it is the elements, reduced to the structure of the atom, and accounting for their combinations in molecules, chemical interactions, etc. In physics science reduces everything to energy examining conservation in its many forms including breaking down matter into energy, Einstein's formula. In the biological realm: science recognizes photosynthesis as a homeostatic physiological mechanism.

Psychology's multiple aspects seeking integration

The challenge to evolve psychology into a natural science hinges in identifying a universal common denominator for all aspects of psychology. The core concept has to encompass psychological, spiritual or moral order, and biological phenomena. It must account for all the items listed below:

The unconscious: It must understand the unconscious in terms of emotions and behaviors, their psychodynamic interrelation as patterns, define personality differences, clarify diagnostic categories, differentiate wellness from illness, and identify the types of pathology. The unconscious must be measurable, qualifiable and quantifiable, graphically portrayable. The unconscious must be therapeutically manageable.

Symbolic systems: Science must understand art, ideas, the nature of the symbolic systems, make sense of the creative process
Sociology: The unit order must understand the continuity between the individual and the community, family role relations, authority subordinate relations, the structure of social and political systems.
Biology: The concept must clarify homeostatic mechanisms in sustaining levels of emotional stability, psychic tension, understanding emotions of pleasure and pain, anxiety and peace of mind, it must account for the EEG, the chemistry of synapses and explain the pharmacology of psychological phenomena. The theory must explain diagnoses and the role of neuroscience.

Thus the science of behavior must reconcile psychology, morality with biology and physics.
Science: Everything about behavior has to be reduced to science's elemental substance: energy; the energetic reduction must abide by formulas, parts or variables must be interrelated, such as emotions and behaviors, ideas in a story, phenomena should be measurable and graphically portrayable.

Morality. The paradigm must address the issue of the universality of religions; it must understand dogma, spirituality and explain their diversity and their evolution; it must clarify moral values, religions, normative and political institutions as natural science phenomena.

Religions are psychological theories delivered metaphorically defining types of conflict resolution. Metaphors or parables are intuitive paradigms of order but have been perceived by the faithful as the ultimate truths. They are liable to misinterpretation. Hence they are divisive and responsible for generating cross-cultural conflicts. The Formal Theory identifies the creative process as its object of study. It examines metaphors, be those of religions and cultural stories, all samples of creativity. It identifies alternative types of conflict resolution. It examines continuity between stories as resolutions evolving as complementary discoveries of science. The formal analysis understands metaphors as scientific phenomena. Hence it increases insights into religions and clarifies them as pioneers of psychology as a science.

Formal Theory's premise of the creative process as an energetic and attitude transformation mechanism
Formal Theory reconciles psychology, biology, sociology, morality also religions among themselves by studying the creative process as a natural science phenomenon. It is identified as an energetic phenomenon resolving conflicts abiding by the laws of science. The creative process represents the unconscious as a scientific moral order mechanism, thus behavior becoming a scientific field of conflict resolution.

The means of examining behavior as a science is by identifying the nature of the creative process, reflecting the unconscious, as an energetic and attitude transformation. The process transforms conflict, as labile energy into resolution, as energy of higher organization. We refer to that as increasing negative entropy. The creative process transforms energy as a sequence of emotions and attitudes. This sequence, a syndrome of six emotions, leading to four types of resolution becomes the unit entity of behavior. The six emotions and the modalities are measurable. The unconscious then becomes the yardstick for the scientific analysis and measurement of individual and cultural behavior.

Conflict as energy generation, resolutions as energy transformation
The Formal Theory described the creative process, reflecting the unconscious, as a periodic phenomenon having the homeostatic function of transforming conflict energy incurred upon a normative deviation, to resolutions as normative conciliation, corresponding to both improved attitude and increased social adjustment. Conflict energy is upgraded as negative entropy, and as attitude change as moral growth. Psychic energy

generated upon the experience of a conflict, upon a person's normative deviation, is transformed to negative entropy, catharsis, upon the conflict's resolution as the individual undoes normative deviation with normative compliance, or social adjustment. Simply said: The mind transforms energy from a conflict to a resolution, from unstable psychic tension to a stable format, negative entropy, resolution as normative consensus.

Formal analysis as the scientific interpretation of metaphors

The unconscious is defined abstractly as having an energetic structure and a moral or conflict resolution function. The conflict resolution unconscious mental process is conceptualized as formal transformations of emotional energy manifested as attitude changes. The process starts from a conflict and leads to resolution as a formal reconciliation, converting diversity and pluralism into meaningful totalities, paradigms of moral order. Moral order then is not generated by an external authority or by revelation. It is generated by the personal unconscious conflict resolution unifying process. Religions are reconciled by attributing them to the homeostatic intuitive unconscious reasoning process as the universal human need for reducing psychic and societal conflicts.

Religions' metaphors evolved in abstraction of the underlying order

An example of this mechanism is in the evolution of religions from concreteness to abstraction, from polytheism to monotheism, introducing universality and aspiring for the integration of morality and science. Religions pursue peace. The world Shalom means peace or conflict resolution. Love and peace are the poetic attributes of conflict resolution. The object for the study of conflict resolution is the analysis of the creative process. The secret of peace is in the formal and energetic analysis of stories as associations corresponding to emotions as energies integrated and transformed in the course of the thought process encompassed in samples of creativity such as completed stories.

Peace is in the universality of the plot of stories as a dialectic leading to conflict resolution, which we know as the state of 'living happily ever after'. All religions are psychological theories about conflict resolution introducing equivalent metaphors for the unconscious process. They are discoveries of the process, relying on metaphorical language. An example of formal analysis of religions as metaphors is presented with the examination of Judaism. It advanced metaphors and developed an ethical system that is very close to Moral Science's educational delivery. Below we apply the formal analytical principles in reviewing Judaism's key principles of faith.

The biblical use of metaphors integrating psychology with morality and science

The Formal Theory examines metaphors as scientific conflict resolving phenomena. God is a metaphors of creation as an emotional dialectic. Judaism's metaphors provided the divine as a unifying moral order. Worshiping the One God is equivalent to recognizing the scientific understanding of the unconscious conflict resolution imperative. God is not a person, but a set of formulas manifested in the creative process as the software of the mind. Formal Theory's deficit: Science lacks the emotional power of the divine emotive superpower.

God is one. Adonai Ehad. Ehad means one; oneness, monas, monotheism. It corresponds to the unit order of psychology recognizing causality, but founded on a theistic rather than scientific reductionism. The notion implies that all thoughts have a moral purpose, the universality of conflict resolution. The Formal Theory interprets God, moral causality, as the unit of the unconscious conflict resolution founded on scientific principles, morality is bound to an energetic transformative mechanism that reduces emotional discomfort.

We interpret Genesis, the creation of the universe in six days, as a periodic conflict resolution phenomenon, corresponding to the dialectic of six emotions as three pendulum oscillations, an energetic transformation. We then account for Sabbath the day of rest, as the metaphor of conflict resolution as an event that is celebrated as the relief from conflict, as its resolution. Other religions discovered the conflict resolution process in their creation stories as an emotional dialectic of six parts: The Greek version was the cosmogony as a periodic dramatic process repeated five times leading to the religion of the gods of Olympus. Asian cultures captured it as the Yin Yang equilibrial process as a six-part entity and as six chakras along the spine, the seventh on top of one's head.

We may interpret the Ten Commandments as the moral injunctions required in resolving conflicts. They identify the principles of optimal conflict resolution, the equilibrial principles of the scale. The religion identified them as the guiding principles in resolving conflicts. The moral injunctions coincide with of the formal principles of mastery with moderation, cooperation and mutual respect.

Judaism imparts notions of conflict resolution with its ritual celebrations in cycles of holly days as multiples of 7, enforcing periodicity and insights. The religion gives permission to seek explanations and meaning discussing weekly segments of the Bible. It is allowed to wrestle with tradition pursuing rationality and justice. It empowers youth through joining the community upon puberty. Yom Kippur reviews yearly life's path to seeking relief of guilt through the ritual of atonement, intensified by the exercise of self-control, abstaining from eating, correcting behavior by improving one's attitude. Judaism also identified biological issues factored in as homeostatic regulations like diet following kosher rules, washing hands, rituals of circumcision, and regulations of conduct in consideration of women's menstrual cycle.

The Passover celebration is a well dramatized model conflict resolution experience as a program of emotional education: Exodus exemplifies a people's destiny in pursuing conflict resolution by seeking freedom, a moral process supervised by God. It unfolds as a three act drama beginning with being slaves seeking freedom, 'let my people go'. The response is exodus, as negotiating with the pharaoh authority with a progression of plagues, exiting early with unleavened bread. This is followed by the anxiety of being persecuted; the defense is didactic on conflict resolution as learning about attitudes recognizing four personality types with the simplicity of an assessment, that is a question: What is special about this night? The Four kids of the Haggadah illustrate awareness of the range of relational modalities, based on attitudes.

The responses to the four children differ as the appropriate therapeutic interventions. The parents correct attitudes. Reversal is optimal. The relief of surviving corresponds to enjoying a great meal with symbolic reminders of the heroic past. The meal is completed with a compromise: expressing gratitude for the happy outcome with songs about the experience. Haggadah is a song explaining escalation of conflicts, resolved through divine intervention. Dayenu is a song expressing gratitude. 'What is one?' is a song enumerating the principles of faith providing a scientific summation of the metaphorical wisdom.

Religions favor, like people, alternative types of conflict resolution
As such they represent moral monopolies, normative institutions promoting alternative types of conflict resolution as the total truth; though they are valuable psychological theories they have sanctified diverse norms improving family relations by deifying and mystifying the alternative conflict resolution principles; thus they are divisive. They are partial truths misleading the public as total truths.

The formal analysis of the Judaic dogma validates religions as scientific discoveries presented metaphorically. The problem is that metaphors can be misinterpreted and norms may be challenged. The Formal Theory interpreting metaphors with scientific constructs introduces objectivity and universality in understanding morality, thus completing the mission of religions for peace on earth. The Formal Theory interprets the religions as measurable metaphors and integrates them as complementary discoveries of science. Science fulfills the mission of religions by understanding morality as a science. Science evolves moral consensus by recognizing the process as an homeostatic energetic transformation regulated by the guiding formal operations as universal principles of conflict resolution, as moral values, governing the unconscious creative process.

CHAPTER TWO: HISTORY OF THE FORMAL THEORY

The Formal Theoretical Publications

How did I come to this theoretical perspective? I was born in 1937 in Athens, Greece, a Jewish child in a Christian world, and experienced the second World War, the holocaust, and the communist uprising, leading to the death of good people, including my loving father, grandfather and the great Jewish community of Salonica, a community, which had survived the Inquisition in Spain, and which was exterminated by Hitler. I witnessed Athens being bombarded and saw Europe in ruins. The Formal Theory is the wisdom I developed to understand what happened to the world, all these people, who perished as victims of religions and ideologies. My life has been a journey in the search for meaning and healing.

I tried to understand destructiveness searching history, science and art and found an explanation in the nature of the creative process as a periodic phenomenon that led to alternative resolutions competing with each other. I tested the creative process in therapy with patients, and in delivering wellness emotional education. A person could use creativity for self-discovery, to become conscious of the unconscious, without needing professional help. I developed the Conflict Analysis Battery, sampling creativity for self-discovery, and the Moral Monopoly game, using cultural stories to understand how religions evolved as a continuum of discoveries of conflict resolutions, improving the family institution. Science could help religions to complete their mission.

To share my findings I acquired the Wilburton Inn, incorporated it as Art to Science, Inc. and installed there the art exhibits of the Museum of the Creative Process to inform the public of the scientific nature of the creative process unconscious and the technologies that can readily educate patients and well people.

My confidence in the discovery motivated my ongoing effort to share the news about behavior becoming the Moral Science. It analyzed creativity as both a scientific and a moral order entity. It represented a conceptual and technological development that changes the way we look at art, that unites psychology, religions and science by clarifying the nature of the unconscious, of diagnoses, assessment and morality. The Moral Science impacts education, therapy, politics and religious beliefs. The process as the scientific moral paradigm represents the unifying path to personal wellness and peace in the world. It interprets metaphors with the use of science. Morality becomes the motivational force of the energy transforming unconscious. The analysis of the process introduces science into psychology.

The new paradigm unites the diversity of religions as partial and complementary discoveries of science. It introduces the unconscious as an innate energy transformation mechanism, as the origin of all psychological and moral thinking. The unconscious automatically transforms conflict to resolution. It conducts psychosynthesis, which is like photosynthesis. Spirituality begins in needing to reduce personal discomfort, finding inner peace.

The scientific insights have many theoretical implications and many practical applications. Two new technologies offer easy access to the wisdom of abstract thinking. The Moral Science challenges our understanding of psychology and can free the world from cross-cultural moral differences. The unconscious becomes measurable and graphically portrayable; diagnoses are reduced to the four relational modalities, the alternative ways of resolving conflict, clarifying personality types; the many religions of the world are integrated into the Moral Science healing the world by reinforcing the universality of the values of mastery, cooperation and mutual respect. Understanding psychology and religions as scientific phenomena improves education. The science can understand relational pathology in terms of attitude and power management.

The Formal Theory was inspired by a play I composed, 'The Argives', completed in 1967, a Greek style tragedy, examining king Agamemnon's family conflicts. He was the leader of the Trojan War, who was murdered by his wife, Clytemnestra upon coming home victorious. She was murdered by her son Orestes and daughter Electra. This playwriting exercise ushered me to the study of the Greek Cosmogony, where I detected the emotional dynamics of a pattern repeated five times across generations. The cruel pattern in the Greek creation stories ended with the establishment of a great religion. I explained the periodicity leading to a religion as representing the scientific concept of conflict resolution.

The observation of a scientific phenomenon: The creative process was identified as a scientific phenomenon in the study of the Greek cosmogony as a pattern repeated across five generations leading from extreme family conflicts, infanticides, patricides, etc. to resolution as the creation of the religion of the Olympic Gods. The Formal Theory departed from the analysis of the cosmogony by identifying the universal structure of stories as consisting of a six-role process leading to four alternative relational modalities. The pattern, a mental process was analyzed as both energetic and relational or formal abiding by two phenomena of science. We identified two phenomena of science accounting for this development: an energy transformative process present in every story and a set of three equilibrial formal operations restoring balance. Two scientific phenomena were introduced with their constructs and formulas into the analysis of the thought process.

In 1976 I published an article, which spelled the formal / scientific analysis of the cosmogony pattern reflecting the unconscious as a scientific conflict resolution phenomenon. I republished the article as a booklet on 'The Contributions of the Formal Theory' introducing the formal analysis of the cosmogony pattern as a periodic phenomenon representing the software of the mind. The theory ushered in the integration of psychology, morality and science presenting psychological phenomena interpreted as scientific conflict resolution ones. The unconscious was described as a syndrome illustrated as a sine curve of six-role states, three pendulum oscillations, guided by a set of three formal operations, leading to four relational modalities portrayable graphically as concentric circles with vectors. The vectors identified the distinction-making formal operations restoring balance in equilibrial scales: reciprocity, negation, and correlation. The booklet identified the unconscious capturing energy and transforming it into moral growth.

Eleven years later, in 1987, I published simultaneousness the textbook of the Formal Theory and a workbook. Volume 1, was the textbook*:* Conflict Analysis the Formal Theory of Behavior, a theory and its experimental validation, 1987. The textbook expanded in ten chapters the ten contributions of the first volume. Volume 3 was Conflict Analysis Training, a Concise Program of Emotional Education. The workbook included the self-assessment, the Conflict Analysis Battery, and the processing of its information. Currently the testing is available online, in several formats: brief educational evaluation, and a lengthy therapeutic delivery.

The Formal Theory revamped psychology's epistemology, its concepts of the unconscious, diagnoses, assessment, and morality. Formal Theory's concepts were graphically portrayable and measurable with the assessment. I introduced the assessment into my psychiatric practice. It was well received by the community. It was used for the evaluation of New Haven, CT's police cadets, the screening of seminarians, and the training of school teachers.

At a lecture to the medical community in New Haven, in 1972, I used canvases by Henry Gorski to illustrate the formal theoretical concepts. I collected his work illustrating the science of the creative process. In 2011, I published: 'Volume 4: Science Stealing the Fire of the Gods and Healing the World', a well-illustrated volume presenting the Gorski Retrospective and five other art exhibits of the Museum of the Creative Process. The volume used art as evidence of science illustrating and validating the concepts of the Formal Theory. In 2016, collaborating with my son Maxwell, we digitized the assessment for its online delivery and interpretation. The online delivery of the battery facilitated its evaluation as useful for diagnostic, therapeutic and educational deliveries. We published two volumes of case studies: 'Creativity and Power Management' a Program of Emotional Education, demonstrating the clinical and educational effectiveness of the testing as a therapeutic modality. The two volumes present case studies utilizing the self-assessment as a therapeutic modality; one volume presents the clinical delivery of the program and the other its educational delivery. The second volume includes information about the educational game of Moral Monopoly presenting the formal integration of religions as discoveries of science. The game presents religions as evolving by identifying the alternative modalities of conflict resolution improving the family institution restructuring family role relations and redefining the divine. The six published volumes are available for inspection.

BOOKS BY ALBERT AND MAXWELL LEVIS

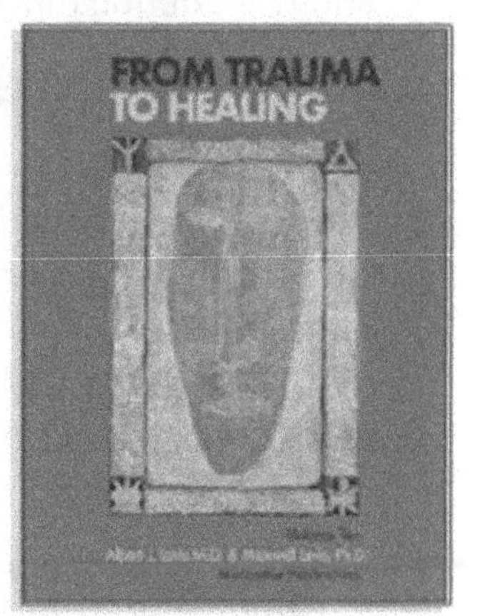

INTEGRATING PSYCHOLOGY WITH MORALITY INTO THE MORAL SCIENCE 2016 - 2021

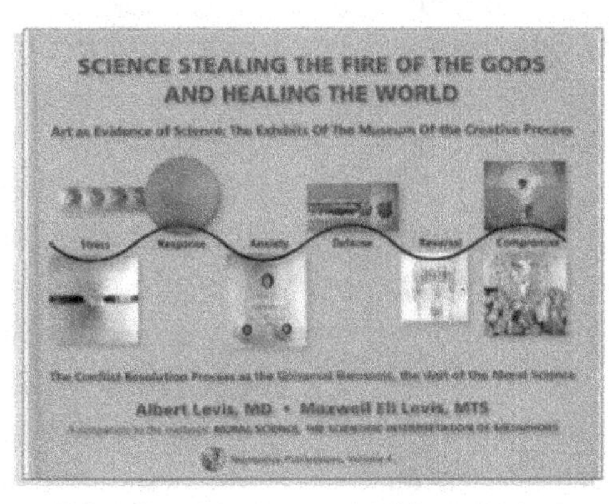

VALIDATING THE FORMAL THEORY WITH ART EXHIBITS AND CASE STUDIES 2000 - 2016

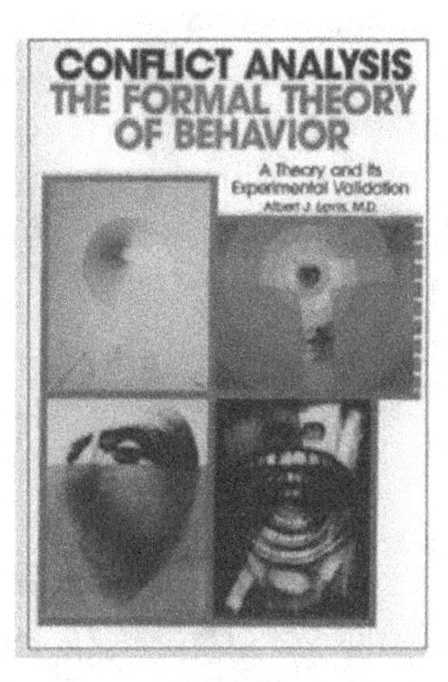

THE FORMAL THEORY STUDYING THE CREATIVE PROCESS
AS A SCIENTIFIC CONFLICT RESOLUTION PHENOMENON 1970 -1987

INTRODUCING PSYCHOLOGY AS THE MORAL SCIENCE

CHAPTER THREE: THE VALIDATION OF THE FORMAL THEORY

Formal Theory's validations have been accomplished by testing the theory's practical applications utilizing the analysis of the creative process in three different domains:

- Presenting case studies utilizing the self-assessment and demonstrating its didactic, diagnostic and therapeutic functions.
- Examining art exhibits at the Museum of the Creative Process. The exhibits illustrate and validate the theoretical thesis. They include the Gorski Retrospective, the Sculptural Trail in the History of Love retracing the evolution of religions, the Sanctuary of the Wizard and of Wisdom illustrating how the creative process integrates the disciplines of psychology into the Moral Science and the Silver Fence exhibit displaying the process as the yardstick elucidating the relational dimensions of symbolic systems.
- Playing Moral Monopoly, an educational card-game, demonstrating the formal analysis of cultural stories, integrating religions identifying the modalities improving the family as discoveries of the Moral Science, and integrating them into a continuum completing their mission for peace in the world.

The two technologies, the Conflict Analysis Battery and Moral Monopoly, the game of cultural stories, validate the premise of the scientific nature of the creative process as the unifying paradigm integrating the humanities, psychology and religions, with the rigorous sciences. Integrating the concepts of psychology and morality improves education. Emotional and moral education can use the two technologies: the battery and the study of religions as a game, as a concise program of emotional education for the general public. The educational program is an effective intervention healing the person and potentially healing the world.

We need awareness of the unconscious and of the modalities and its applications as significant for mental health, and for the reconciliation of cultures, through popularizing emotional education as a universal program of emotional education. Education's objectives may finally become attainable. The Formal Theory by understanding the creative process as a scientific moral order phenomenon integrates the humanities and the sciences; by utilizing the self-assessment students can achieve self-knowledge and by understanding religions as alternative ways of resolving conflicts believers can understand moral values as the principles of science. The public needs this education, reducing the divisiveness of religions by understanding morality as a science, by improving gender relations, family roles, organizational collaboration, reduction of the pathology of relational modalities.

To validate the Formal Theory we examine samples of creativity to identify that the mind transforms energy from conflict to resolution in six steps and following the four modalities. Do our samples of the creative process, abide by the laws of the Simple Harmonic Motion, SHM, and the formal operations restoring balance to the trays of a symbolic role-system?

Validations of the premise show art as evidence of science in that the associations of a circumscribed symbolic system, a story; emotions are connected as a sequence of six-role states bound by three formal operations leading from a conflict to its resolution. Validations of the theory confirm the process as the atomistic unit of the social sciences.

Accordingly we examine stories as liable for interpretation as scientific conflict resolution phenomena by identifying the six-role state energetic process, and by analyzing them as relational modalities that is as phenomena resolving conflicts abiding by the three formal operations.

1. The Assessment Tool

Formal Theory's measurable unconscious led to an assessment, the Conflict Analysis Battery (CAB: Levis, 1988b), which has been used to validate the formal theoretical premise. The CAB combines a diagnostic personality inventory, the Relational Modality Evaluation Scale (RMES), with a set of therapeutic projective tasks.

The self-assessment departs from traditional atheoretical psycho-assessments. It is didactic by beginning the experience with an informational essay about the unconscious and the relational modality diagnoses. It is diagnostic informing the test taker about her relational modality, and it is therapeutic as the prompts guide the test-taker to generate samples of creativity, the Metaphor Creation Tasks, which become meaningful by revealing one's pattern of conflict resolution. The metaphors reconstruct the syndromal sequence of six-role states providing emotional release, generating insights, and clarifying changes to improve one's adjustment. The online delivered assessment is concluded with an informative report, a useful document for the test taker, and for related professionals.

We identify the assessment experience as Creativity and Power Management, a concise program of emotional education as it combines education with insights and guidance for changes. The well-structured self-assessment is a manual-driven emotional education, which can be delivered for patients as psychotherapy and for students as a concise program of emotional education. It is available online and as a workbook. It delivers self-discovery without requiring professional services, but this learning process may enhance traditional therapy. As a psychoeducation, it fulfills the three elusive objectives of education: The integration of art and science, self-knowledge, and clarity of moral values as the three principles of conflict resolution: moderation, cooperation, and mutual respect provides the evaluation of the self-assessment as an emotional experience with responses to twenty statements. (Book two, contain files derived from the self-assessment delivered to cohorts of online test takers. Responses examining separately the experience in achieving its three objectives: didactic, diagnostic, and therapeutic).

Volumes 5 and 6 of the Normative Publications: *Creativity and Power Management, A Concise Program of Emotional Education,* present case studies utilizing the CAB (Levis, A. & Levis. M, 2016a; 2016b). The studies present evidence of the program's effectiveness. The first volume presents clinical case studies illustrating its dramatic effectiveness in diagnosis and therapeutic outcomes. The second volume of case studies reports on the delivery of the battery as a training program in educational settings and finally, through its online delivery without any professional services. The studies demonstrate the measurability of the variables of the unconscious both as relational modalities and also as six-role states syndromal sequences (Levis, A. & Levis, M., 2016a; 2016b).

Mural 4. My Metaphors, Myself is an example of utilizing the self-assessment for personal growth and for the validation of the Formal Theory.

2. About the art exhibits of the Museum of the Creative Process

Upon my 50th birthday having completed the Formal Theory volume and the associated workbook, a concise program of emotional education, I acquired the Wilburton Inn as the future forum for a theoretical innovation. I incorporated the inn as the Art of Science, Inc. On the grounds of the inn I installed the exhibits of the Museum of the Creative Process with the function to introduce the scientific method in the analysis of the creative process reflecting the orderly unconscious. The exhibits validate the Formal Theory illustrating the creative process as a scientific conflict resolution phenomenon reflecting the unconscious. The creative process is analyzed as reflecting the unconscious as a scientific conflict resolution phenomenon abiding by two energy-transforming phenomena: the pendulum and the scale. They present art as evidence of the new science.

In the quest for evolving awareness of the theory, we established a learning center, the Museum of the Creative Process, at a country inn as the location of several 'art as evidence of science' exhibits. Five major art exhibits introduce the new way of looking at art, shifting the focus in art appreciation from the aesthetic value of art to its relevance in observing science, as the universality of conflict resolution, underlying all creativity. The art exhibits focus on the illustration and validation of the concepts through the formal analysis of the art, as illustrated in Volume 4 of the Normative Publications: *Science Stealing the Fire of the Gods and Healing the World (A. Levis & M. Levis, 2011).*

My vision has been the development of a training center, the facility serving as the forum for understanding psychology as the Science of Conflict Resolution, the Moral Science, reconciling art and science, psychology and religions. The science completes the mission of religions for peace in the world by eliminating the arbitrariness of medicalization of psychology releasing humanity from the need for dogma, as beliefs in divine revelation.

The conclusion from visiting this museum is that psychology is the natural science of morality and that creativity, be that as cultural or personal stories, becomes a measurable, graphically portrayable natural science phenomenon. The exhibits validate the creative process as an energetic transformation following the two scientific phenomena upgrading energy as the moral function of the unconscious. They show the creative process as consisting of two segments corresponding to the two scientific phenomena, the pendulum oscillation capturing energy and the scale's equilibrial principles transforming it into the alternative types of conflict resolution. The scientific phenomena being measurable and graphically portrayable introduce the human unconscious as a purely orderly phenomenon. We recognize in them the universality of the six-role process and the four modalities of resolving conflicts as confirming the theoretical premise.

The science reconciles diversity of stories, be they conveyed as canvases, metaphors, and religions or psychological theories as the solutions of the two scientific phenomena. The two phenomena of science present the key to the interpretation of stories, of metaphors, by identifying the orderly process, thus reducing the complexity of stories, myths, to formulas yielding predictability and measurability. The analysis of the creative process in all exhibits demonstrates the function of the unconscious as capturing energy of conflicts and transforming it to resolutions as social adjustment, as types of moral order.

The exhibits are imagery understanding the unconscious as upgrading energy by changing one's attitude. Einstein pointed out that matter is energy released as the breakdown of the atom. We point out that emotions upgrade energy as the opposite of Einstein's releasing energy by splitting the atom. We thus proceed from philosophies, religions and psychological theories' vague conceptualizations of reality, to science by identifying the unconscious as an energetic phenomenon that is measurable, graphically portrayable, predictably upgrading energy.

The museum exhibits introduce the thought process as an energetic transformation following the two scientific phenomena: one capturing energy as conflicts, another converting this energy to moral paradigms improving the person's attitude and her social adjustment. The exhibits are validations of the science integrating psychology and religions spirituality, mythology, poetry, into the Moral Science. They validate the premise of the Formal Theory identifying emotions as energetic phenomena that proceed automatically transforming conflict to resolution, the origin of all moral thought. Viewing the art as a scientific psychological phenomenon leads to energetic cleansing or catharsis as the unit integrating the disciplines of psychology into the Moral Science. This represents a major conceptual breakthrough. The scientific process illustrates how emotions are energy with a distinct human functionality, catharsis as creating order.

The collection of art began in 1972 upon utilizing Henry Gorski's canvases to illustrate formal distinctions pictorially. The Gorski retrospective shows creativity resolving conflicts as a spontaneous healing process and one that leads to moral discoveries. The Gorski Retrospective shows the progression of the canvases of the artist reflecting the spontaneous healing function of the creative process leading to moral discoveries concluding the artist's lifetime conflictual experiences. The Gorski Retrospective demonstrates this entity resolving the artist's conflicts as a series of six canvases corresponding to six emotions predictably leading to the four types of resolution.

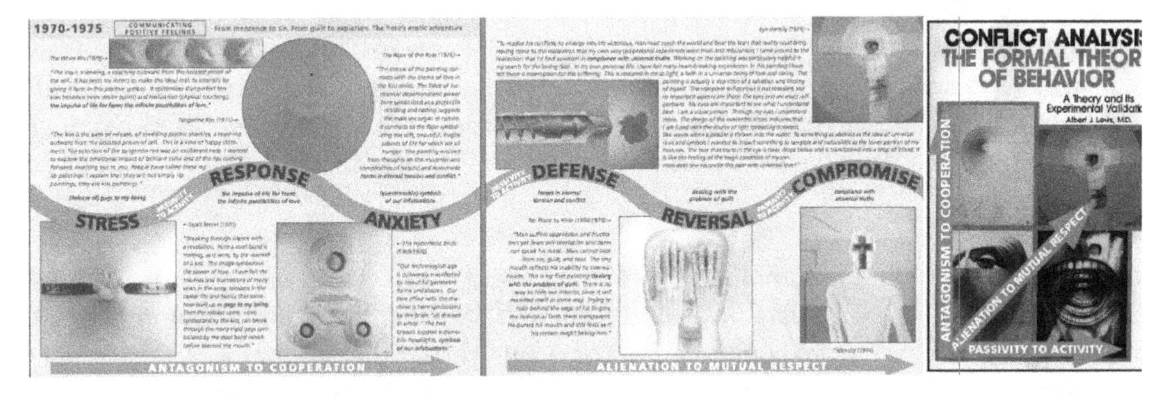

The Gorski Retrospective illustrating the conflict resolution process leading to the theme of moral ending, crucifixion, illustrating conflict resolution as a moral discovery. The science makes the canvases of the artist meaningful as resolving conflicts along the underlying scientific operations of the unconscious reflected in the six-role process and the three formal operations.

The Gorski exhibit was followed by the 'Sculptural Trail in the History of Love' consisting of 30 major installations retracing the evolution of religions as discoveries of the science of conflict resolution, improving the family institution and redefining the divine more abstractly.

The Abrahamic Family, by Judith Brown, one of the stations in 'The Sculptural Trail in the History of Love', is one of the six exhibits of the Museum of the Creative Process. The sculpture illustrates the inequity between the genders: three patriarchs, sitting on thrones, towering over four matriarchs, and two concubines, the Horus birds with beaks to peck on the wives. The sculpture includes the altar for the sacrifice of Isaac as Abraham's method to test the loyalty of his son and of his wives to the notion of a loving divine.

The Silver Fence is a sculpture illustrating the unconscious as the scientific way of conceptualizing behavior Upon my 84th birthday I celebrated completing the project as the Museum of the Creative Process with a pavilion clarifying the scientific nature of the creative process and a new exhibit, the Silver Fence as the sculpture of the unconscious as a scientific phenomenon transforming energy along the two phenomena of science symbolized graphically. The pendulum motion as waves, and the scale as four spirals representing the four relational modalities. The unit of waves and spirals presents the unconscious as the measuring rod of all emotional systems.

The message of the museum exhibits is summed up with the Silver Fence sculpture of the unconscious. The 140 feet long Silver Fence consists of repeated waves and spirals, clarifying the scientific and moral nature of the creative process by identifying its two components. The waves reflect the emotional energetic dialectic as pendulum oscillations. The four spirals identify the four formal alternative types of conflict resolution. The fence exhibit of waves and spirals, syndromes and relational modalities, is applied to illustrate the formal alternatives present in a variety of symbolic systems. It presents the unconscious as a scientific energy-transforming conflict resolving mechanism as the new way of looking at art as fulfilling a rational emotional need, conflict resolution, as a scientific phenomenon structuring the thought process consisting of two components. The waves represent the six-role emotional dialectic and the four spirals illustrate the four alternative ways of resolving conflict. The unit sculpture describes the emotional energetic transformation. The waves present three pendulum oscillations; the four spirals illustrate the alternative directions of the four ways of resolving conflict following the equilibrial principles of the scale. The process is the measuring rod of emotional systems.

Thus the waves represent the three pendulum oscillations as six emotions: Stress, Response, Anxiety, Defense, Reversal and Compromise. The spirals have graphic dimensions; on the right we have power, dominance, and on the left powerlessness as submissiveness; antagonism is graphically presented as counterclockwise spirals and co-operation as clockwise ones. The four spirals represent the conflict resolutions alternatives guided by two formal attitude-changing operations as the relational modalities, wellness diagnoses. The Silver Fence, the sculpture of the unconscious, has physical dimensions measuring the four alternative ways of resolving conflict.

The initial part of the fence acknowledges this order in the formal symbolism of the game of cards: the spade, club, diamond and heart represent the four types of conflict resolution in the symbolic language of the cards. The spade and the heart are in formal relation to each other as reciprocal, passivity versus activity, and as the opposite alternatives: black versus red signs as the antagonistic versus the cooperative relating. The four spirals identify the relational modalities.

In the second half of the silver fence the formal distinctions confer the relational characteristics of the process as the modalities in a number of symbolic systems. The relational dimensions clarify the differences between the four personality types of the heroes of the story of the Wizard of Oz, the children of the Haggadah, the four cultures dealing with temptation, the three prophets of the Abrahamic religions responding to the riddle of the sphinx. They mark the difference between the presidents of the United States: Trump and Biden as dominant versus submissive and as antagonistic versus cooperative and as alienating versus respectful of others. Finally my own response to the riddle is presented by my offering a branch of olive tree to the Sphinx highlighting the condition for conflict resolution between the genders as mutual respect.

The third segment of the fence presents complete resolution as a couple getting married. In the middle of two images of happy lovers we see the family and friends celebrating. At the tail end of the fence, we see symbolically fireworks as the combined DNA of the couple transforming genetically embedded energy to the children of the couple.

This fence's energetic unconscious illustrating the six-role process as a chain reaction syndrome of emotions and the four resolutions is the key to all art exhibits at the Museum of the Creative Process. Thus the exhibits validate the Formal Theory into the Moral Science.

The integration of art and science, of the social and rigorous sciences, begins at the Moral Science Project located in the village by identifying the correspondence of emotions, the conflict resolution process with the two phenomena of science. Three exhibits on the grounds of the gallery focus on using the creative process to connect psychology, religions, and science.

The Park exhibit illustrates how using the Conflict Analysis Battery generates personal creativity leading to insights on the personal pattern of resolving conflicts. Emotions, the conflict resolution process, are presented as the Sin to Catharsis installations. In parallel science clarifies the process presenting it in terms of two energetic equilibrial phenomena, a pendulum and a scale. The significance of this equation is that psychology inherits science's constructs, formulas and graphic portrayal. The unconscious is reduced to a scientific phenomenon, three pendulum oscillations, manifested as sequences of six emotions, a syndrome, and as four types of conflict resolutions.

3. Moral Monopoly

Formal Theory has further been validated through the formal analysis of cultural stories playing Moral Monopoly, an educational card game based on the organization of the deck of cards as the metaphor of the conflict resolution unconscious. The game establishes equivalences between the suits, the relational modalities, and four groups of religions. The game-board is divided into four quadrants along the dichotomies of power and powerlessness horizontally, and cooperation and antagonism as opposite vectorial directions inserted in a central concentric system (Figure 4). The four suits overlap with the four modalities. The suits of the deck as the relational modality diagnoses are illustrated with cultural stories illustrating the relational modalities with two cultural stories, one from mythology, the other from historical times. Each story consists of a face card and six cards as the six-role states of a conflict resolution sequence, each card featuring an image and a statement. The signs of the deck symbolize the upgrading of order from one suit or modality to another as improvements in the mode of resolving conflict departing from the spade, a black upside-down heart, pocked by a needle, the sequence completed with the red upright heart, symbol of perfecting resolutions into love relations. The players learn about the stories and the respective religions as having measurable dimensions. They recognize how religions are in formal relation to each other and integrate them as a continuum of resolutions. They also examine the Abrahamic family's unfinished business in the sense of the inequity of gender relations (Figure 11). The board incorporates religions as a complement of discoveries of science reflecting their evolution, improving the family institution toward optimal resolution of family relations (Levis 2016a; 2016b). The experience educates on the features of the formal analysis of stories as resolving conflicts along the four alternative modalities, as syndromes of six role states and along the effectiveness differential of the alternative modalities.

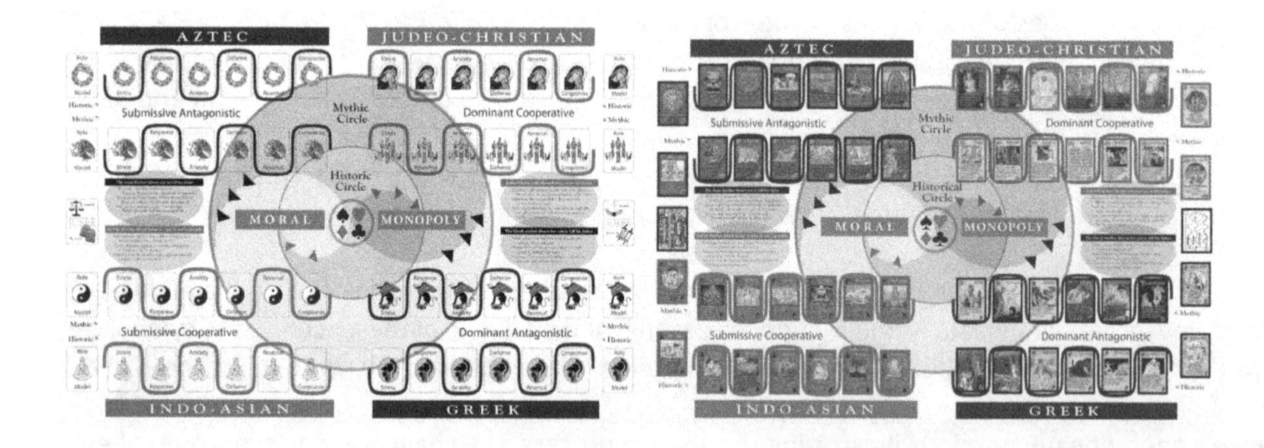

The game-board of the Moral Monopoly game of cards and the board featuring the storytelling cards of eight religions illustrating the attributes of the creative process as measurable
The game board illustrates the organization of the deck of cards as reflecting the unconscious resolving conflicts along the four relational modalities, the six-role process, and as a progression of improvements in the alternative types of conflict resolution. The assumptions of the Formal Theory are examined by the players, who question each story as a measurable conflict resolution reflecting the measurable attributes of the unconscious. The players thus learn about the Moral Science and that religions evolved as complementary discoveries of science. They also examine the conditions for improving the unfinished business of the Abrahamic family.

4. The Sanctuary exhibits: 12 Wizard of Oz Panels and 12 Metaphoria Murals.
Two art exhibits validate the formal hypothesis on the universality of the conflict resolving unconscious as the integrative unit order of the social sciences disciplines: Epistemology, diagnosis, assessment and morality as integrated into the Moral Science.

CHAPTER FOUR: THE SANCTUARY EXHIBITS INTRODUCE THE INTEGRATION OF THE DISCIPLINES OF PSYCHOLOGY INTO THE MORAL SCIENCE

In the two exhibits of the Sanctuary, we recognize the two levels of reduction of symbolic systems: Oz metaphors are reduced to formulas and then the formulas are tested by being applied to the phenomena of psychology. The two physical entities are demonstrated as applicable in the elucidation of complex systems as having a scientific structure and a moral function. We conclude then that the conflict resolving mechanism is an energetic six-role process, a syndrome, and that syndromes lead to four relational modalities. This is the definition of the unconscious as a scientific phenomenon and the beginning of clear rational rethinking of the realms of psychology and morality.

The Wizard of Oz panels exhibit illustrates the analysis of the story's four metaphors corresponding to the four disciplines of psychology. Each section of the volume begins with the analysis of one of the metaphors of the Wizard of Oz. The four metaphors reconcile the disciplines of psychology epistemology, diagnosis, assessment and morality.

The murals exhibit shows the plot of cultural and personal stories as the six-role process clarifying the unconscious as a scientific phenomenon, identifying four wellness diagnoses as the alternative ways of resolving conflict. The murals present the syndrome of six emotions, the emotional dialectic resolving conflicts.

The process as a scientific and moral order phenomenon is demonstrated as the core phenomenon in each discipline of psychology. The Oz panels and the murals present the conflict resolution process along the four disciplines: epistemology, personality diagnoses and therapy as the predicted evolution in attitude and power in all samples of creativity reflecting the universality of the process. Formal analysis establishes continuity between the four disciplines integrating them into the Moral Science. Thus, the art exhibits of the Sanctuary demonstrate the scientific analysis of the creative process applied in the interpretation of metaphors, leading to the reduction of complexity.

The volume has four sections corresponding to the four disciplines of the new psychological theory explaining the formalization of the key concepts of psychology: the unconscious as a conflict resolution phenomenon, the alternative diagnoses as a wellness personality typology accounting for pathologies and their correction using the new assessment as a diagnostic and therapeutic instrument, finally the study of religions as complementary discoveries of the Science of Conflict Resolution.

We introduce the four sections examining separately each discipline of psychology using the two art exhibits of the Sanctuary of Wisdom as metaphorical studies of the creative process.

Each section as a discipline, is introduced by using an Oz metaphor and followed by its validation with murals displayed on the interior walls of the Sanctuary. The exterior walls of the Sanctuary present the four familiar metaphors of the Wizard of Oz story reducing their complexity to the simplicity of the disciplines of science. The scientific insights from the Oz panels are applied to understanding the complexities of 12 murals of the interior walls of the Sanctuary examining cultural and personal stories as demonstrating the presence of the two scientific phenomena.

- *The Yellow Brick Road* allows us to focus on the epistemology, the science of the process as the totality, the scientific unit order of the conflict resolution process.
- *Dealing with the four companions* we identify the personality typology as the alternative ways of resolving conflicts and becoming aware of relational modalities and their syndromal unfolding as therapy by learning how to manage power and attitude.
- *Killing the Witch* allows us to consider using creativity as a measurable transformative entity for self-discovery and also self-help.
- *Dealing with the Wizard* allows us to examine the scientific nature of morality, and of religions as psychological theories promoting the optimizations of conflict resolution.

The four disciplines are integrated into the Moral Science. While the metaphors of the Wizard story identify the disciplines as scientific studies of the unit order, the murals of the interior aspect of the Sanctuary exemplify the study of each discipline with case studies. They exemplify the formal analysis of cultural and personal creativity leading to the validation of the Formal Theory's premise: each case study is analyzed successfully as a six-role state process leading to one of the four modalities.

Thus the Oz metaphors advance the science, the interpretation of art as reducible to two orderly scientific phenomena: the principles of energy transformation along the SHM guided by the three formal operations restoring balance to the equilibrial scale. The Oz exhibit illustrates aspects of the creative process and the corresponding murals illustrate and validate this premise showing the predicted scientific structure and moral function in the thought process in the case studies exhibits. Science connects the Oz metaphors and the stories, as measurable syndromes and identifiable types of conflict resolution.

The four disciplines as books in the volume are summed up in a single image below, the overview of the Sanctuary exhibits, as four rows of representative images.

Each row pertains to a discipline. The four walls as four disciplines are thus summed up by the overview images jackets of the four books. Each row features the topic of the discipline illustrated by a book jacket accompanied by one image form the Oz exhibit and one from the interior case study murals. The metaphors of the Wizard story clarify the science. The murals apply the science in examining case studies. The four books of the volume examine then in detail the three panels and the three murals of each of the four disciplines represented in the four rows of this image. Four chapters introduce the creative process analyzing the two Sanctuary exhibits integrating the four disciplines of psychology into the Science of Conflict Resolution

The four books define the disciplines of psychology with pertinent metaphors
The conclusion of the study is that the unconscious is a natural science conflict resolving homeostatic phenomenon reducing psychic tension by leading to the individual's power and attitude change experienced as social adjustment. The Formal Theory innovates psychology into a science by examining art and finding science, examining science and finding morality reflecting the unconscious as a natural science entity transforming conflict energy to resolution following the innate attitude-changing formal operations. The new knowledge allows us to apply scientific constructs and formulas to all psychological phenomena and there to recognize the personal pattern of conflict resolution. This orderly energetic unconscious is the unit order of the social sciences. It integrates psychology and morality based on science thus ending the need for dualism. We now may

understand psychology and religions as natural science energetic phenomena with abstract concepts, which we can portray graphically as having natural science dimensions.

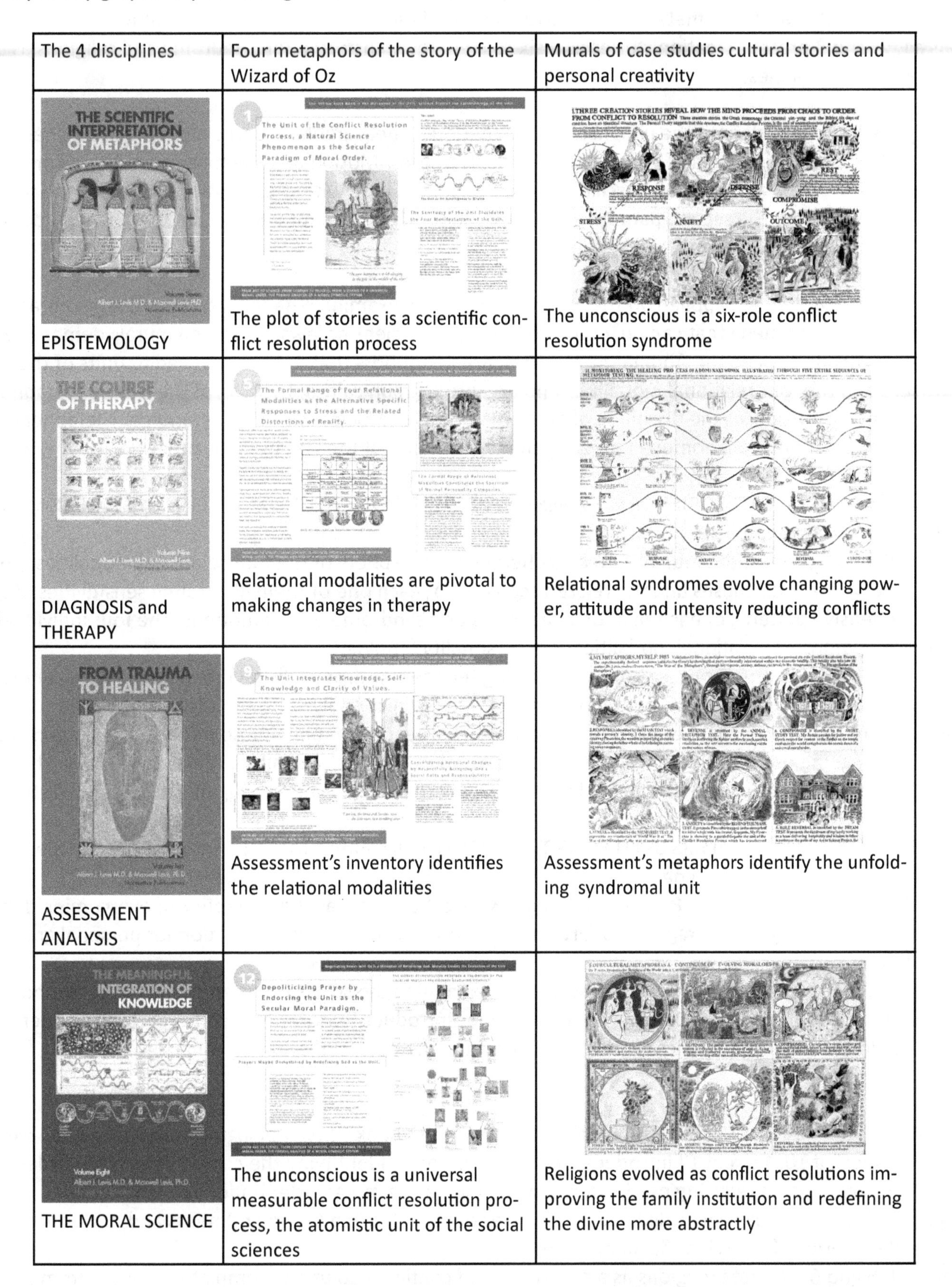

The 4 disciplines	Four metaphors of the story of the Wizard of Oz	Murals of case studies cultural stories and personal creativity
EPISTEMOLOGY	The plot of stories is a scientific conflict resolution process	The unconscious is a six-role conflict resolution syndrome
DIAGNOSIS and THERAPY	Relational modalities are pivotal to making changes in therapy	Relational syndromes evolve changing power, attitude and intensity reducing conflicts
ASSESSMENT ANALYSIS	Assessment's inventory identifies the relational modalities	Assessment's metaphors identify the unfolding syndromal unit
THE MORAL SCIENCE	The unconscious is a universal measurable conflict resolution process, the atomistic unit of the social sciences	Religions evolved as conflict resolutions improving the family institution and redefining the divine more abstractly

Four books analyzing the two Sanctuary exhibits integrate the disciplines of psychology into the Science of Conflict Resolution, the Moral Science

WALL # 1. EPISTEMOLOGY: THE SCIENTIFIC STRUCTURE OF THE PROCESS
Title:_The Scientific Interpretation of Metaphors.
Panels #1, 2, and 3 analyze the metaphor of the Yellow Brick Road as a scientific phenomenon.
Murals #1, 2, and 3 present creation stories as a six-role energy transformation syndrome and religions as sanctified relational modalities.

Analyzing the brick road defines the unconscious as a periodic, measurable, moral order upgrading phenomenon, following two phenomena of science: the Simple Harmonic Motion and the formal operations of the scale. Thus the process, as the mental oscillation, may be understood with the abstract constructs and formulas of physics and logic. The second panel presents the unit bridging the humanities and the sciences identifying in detail constructs, formulas and diagrams.

The laws of science then are applied on the interior murals. We examine creation stories and religions as relational energetic phenomena that can be interpreted along the scientific laws. The three murals demonstrate that the creation stories and the Abrahamic religions, are metaphors that may be reduced to units of the six-role process and the four relational modalities and organized graphically in the Flag of the United metaphors. Thus the first wall introduces the discipline of epistemology as the 'Scientific Interpretation of Metaphors' utilizing the two scientific phenomena reflecting the organization of the unconscious process.

WALL # 2. DIAGNOSTIC CATEGORIES OF WELLNESS AS POWER AND ATTITUDE MANAGEMENT ALTERNATIVES,
Title: Diagnoses and Therapy
Panels #4, 5, and 6 present the four Wizard of Oz heroes as metaphors of the four relational modalities, prototypes of four wellness diagnoses and the related scenarios of each one of them illustrating sensitivities, distortions and defensive patterns of each relational diagnosis as a syndrome of six emotions. The four individuals differ in their syndromal relational modalities as a personality typology.
Murals #10, 11, and 12 present case studies illustrating the four syndromes as relational modality diagnoses confirming the scientific analysis of metaphors utilizing the Conflict Analysis Battery. Two case studies use the assessment to monitor changes occurring during therapy leading to ongoing self-discovery and personal growth. The ongoing use of the testing generate a record of the progress a patient makes in therapy. The use of the battery is shown to generate actionable insights leading to changes and healing of the personal distress.

WALL # 3. THE CONFLICT ANALYSIS BATTERY AS THE SCIENTIFIC INTERPRETATION OF METAPHORS: Title of the third book: From Trauma to Healing.
The third wall's three panels # 7, 8, and 9 are about 'Killing the Witch' as the metaphor of overcoming dependency needs and having the courage to go forth on one's own, by utilizing introspection for personal growth and self-awareness.
Murals # 7, 8, and 9, correspond to three case studies examining the scientific organization of the symbolic language of the Conflict Analysis Battery. The case studies introduce features of the interpretation of personal metaphors along formal and physics distinctions illustrating the nature of symbolic language departing from art but leading to science.

WALL # 4. THE MORAL FUNCTION OF THE PROCESS, Title of fourth book: The Meaningful Integration of Knowledge.
The three panels: # 10, 11, and 12 introduce the Oz metaphor by identifying the conflict resolution order as an energetic transformation reducing psychic tension and increasing moral order underlying Biblical principles as metaphors of scientific relevance: Yigdal, the principles of faith, the Ten Commandments and prayer are interpreted as discoveries of the scientific moral order.
Murals # 4, 5 and 6 integrate religions as a progression of conflict resolutions completed as a syndrome composed of the alternative ways of resolving conflict, improving the family institution.

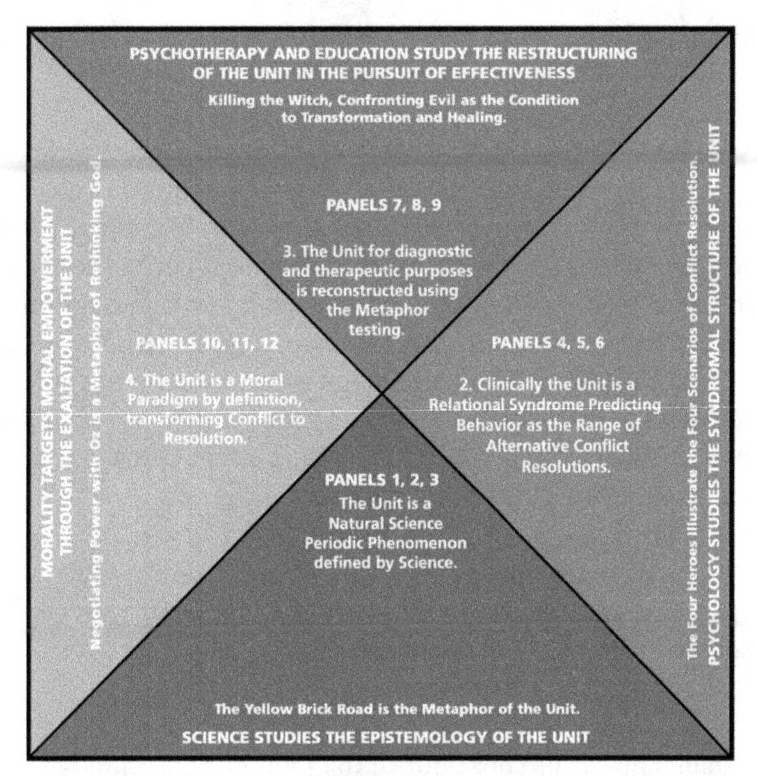

The external exhibit of the Sanctuary consists of twelve conceptual Wizard of Oz panels

The internal exhibit consists of twelve hand painted murals.

CHAPTER FIVE: THE CONFLICT RESOLUTION UNCONSCIOUS AS A SCIENTIFIC AND MORAL ORDER MECHANISM

The conclusion of the study is that the unconscious is a natural science conflict resolving homeostatic phenomenon reducing psychic tension by leading to the individual's power and attitude change experienced as social adjustment. The Formal Theory innovates psychology into a science by examining art and finding science, examining science and finding morality reflecting the unconscious as a natural science entity transforming conflict energy to resolution following the innate attitude-changing formal operations. The new knowledge allows us to apply scientific constructs and formulas to all psychological phenomena and there to recognize the personal pattern of conflict resolution. This orderly energetic unconscious is the unit order of the social sciences. It integrates psychology and morality based on science thus ending the need for dualism. We, now, may understand psychology and religions as natural science energetic phenomena with abstract concepts, which we can portray graphically as having natural science dimensions.

The analysis of the metaphors of the two exhibits reconciles art and science, psychology, and morality as founded on scientific principles. The conclusion: morality as conflict resolution is generated by the unconscious, and religions represent the sanctification of the alternative ways of resolving conflicts improving the family institution and the abstract redefinition of the divine.

The formal analysis of the exhibits makes us conscious of the merger of psychology, morality, and science and how we can apply the science to the technology of metaphors for self-discovery and healing. Through self-analysis of one's metaphors, the individual may benefit from insights about one's way of resolving conflicts to learn how to further one's adjustment by introducing the effectiveness of complete understanding of the conflict resolution process.

The critical assumption of Conflict Analysis-The Formal Theory of Behavior is that the creative process is a natural science conflict resolution mechanism. The implication of this assumption is that it represents the unconscious as a predictable, qualifiable, quantifiable, and graphically portrayable mechanism representing the atomistic unit of the social sciences. This hypothesis of art as science is validated by examining the structure and function of samples of creativity. The validation of the assumption confirms the unconscious as a conflict resolution mechanism and as the origin of moral thought and of all thought as morality bound.

This conclusion cancels the need for an evolutionist/biological and of the neuroscientific explanations of psychology and of the deterministic apocalyptic approach of religion-based moral paradigms. The formal assumption introduces the unconscious as an innate/homeostatic physiological formal and natural science phenomenon of conflict resolution that reduces conflicts in the person and in one's social system. This assumption explains morality as conflict resolution, as a science, as religions, as art, as the alternative conflict resolution modalities, and cultures as the alternative normative institutions. The religions have evolved as a progression of discoveries of the Conflict Resolution Science motivated by the psychological and sociological need to reduce conflict in the person and in the family institution.

The final level of interpretation is defining the scientific moral paradigm as a spiritual inspirational scientific entity. We cannot worship scientific formulas but we can be inspired by good stories and meaningful art. We can enjoy creativity, also become creators, creating art, discovering the universal moral order in all art, including our own thinking and that of religions.

The Conflict Resolution Process as scientific and morality bound

Science rediscovers morality as measurable solutions of the formulas for different values of the variables. The fundamental assumption of the Conflict Resolution Process as the scientific moral paradigm is introduced in the central tile of the upper tier of Mural #3. It features the formal definition of the conflict resolution process inscribed in the sacred tablets of Moses in the place of the Ten Commandments. The image shows that the three Conflict Resolution Principles: Reciprocity as Passivity transformed to Activity, Negation as Antagonism transformed to Cooperation, and Correlation transforming Alienation to Affiliation or Mutual Respect, coincide with the Ten Commandments. The Commandments identified descriptively the principles of moderation, cooperation and mutual respect as dictated by God to Moses. In reality, the three principles are formal operations of the formula of the equilibrial scale. Identity as conflict is equal to the product of Reciprocity times Negation times Correlation as the conflict's resolution. Religions, besides the Bible, discovered the alternative conflict resolutions intuitively and attributed them to the evolving divine.

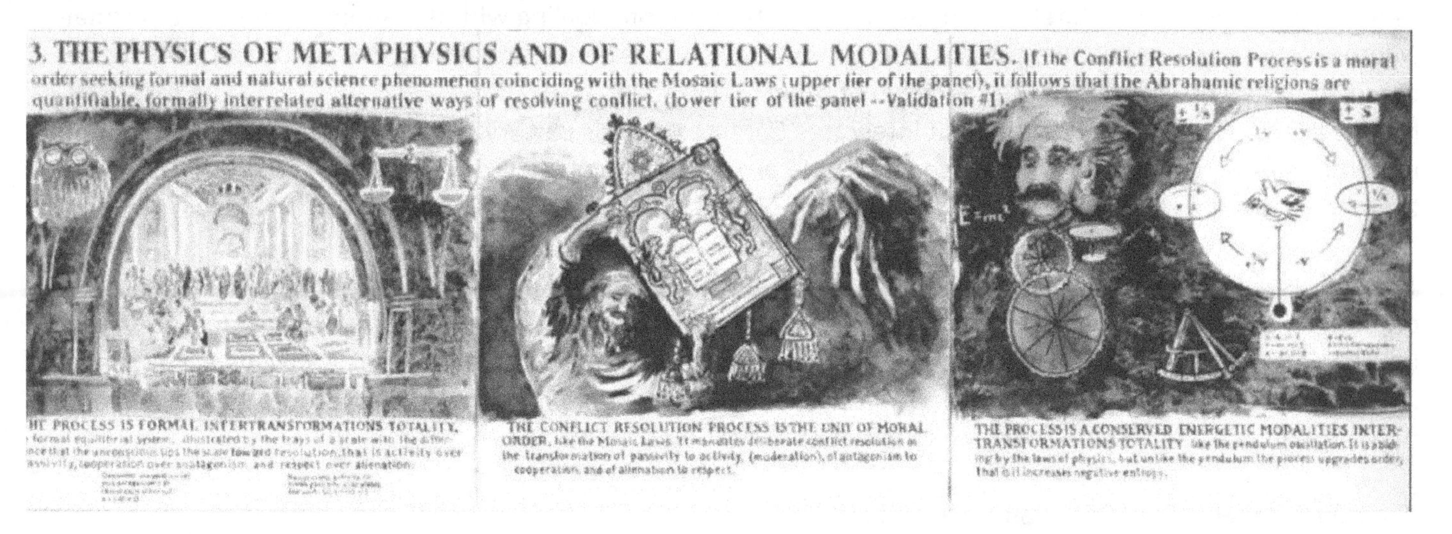

Mural 3B, the laws of moral order

While the moral nature of the process as formal injunctions is inscribed in the middle tile, the other two tiles of the top tier clarify the formulas of the conflict resolution process as forms on the left and as energy on the right: On the left, conflict resolution is equated with the formulas of logic describing opposites and reciprocals. These forms are encompassed in the equilibrial scale's equation about three principles restoring the scale's balance after tipping it with a weight or stressor. The mental mechanism differs from the reversible equilibrial system of the trays of a scale. The mind's equilibrium automatically predictably shifts the process toward restoring balance: the formal transformations pursue reduction of psychic tension, unpleasantness, relating socially with mastery, cooperation and mutual respect.

On the right of the Mosaic tablets, the tile examines the process as energetic. It equates it with Physics' Simple Harmonic Motion, an energetic transformation phenomenon. There is a difference between the mental oscillation of the Conflict Resolution Process and the mechanical Simple Harmonic Motion in that the mental process raises the order of the ideational system; it increases the negative entropy, in three oscillations. Upon its transformation the motion of the mental oscillation stops, whereas in nature the Simple Harmonic Motion continues the oscillation till it dissipates the energy by increasing disorder or entropy in the mechanical oscillation system. While the mind conserves energy upgrading order, machines downgrade energy, transforming order to heat as chaos. We identify this mental energy transforming operation as psychosynthesis parallel to plants' photosynthesis.

The exhibits as illustrations and as validations

The formal analysis of The Wizard of Oz story confirms the universality of the six-role process and resolutions leading to four alternative types of relational modalities. The Sanctuary murals validate this thesis by rediscovering the six-role state process and the four modalities consistently upgrading order as the manifestation of conflict resolutions in each mural. The creative process is seen as a formal and as an energetic periodic entity that helps to interpret metaphors integrating the disparate data of the respective symbolic systems of the 12 murals confirming the process as the unit of the social sciences:

Mural #1 illustrates the conflict resolution process integrating the lifetime events of the Greek cosmogony gods leading to the conflict resolution as the creation of the Olympian religion.
Mural #2, the Flag of the United Metaphors, illustrates how the unit sequence integrates all moral paradigms, including the ideologies of Communism and Capitalism.
Mural #3, illustrates how the unit integrates the three Abrahamic religions as formally interrelated relational modalities.
Mural #5 illustrates how the unit integrates the major world religions as formally interrelated to each other into the abstract order-increasing harmonic process.
Mural #6 presents four cultural ways of dealing with temptation, dealing with the apple metaphor, as formally interrelated and quantifiable conflict resolutions, the four relational modalities. It is reflecting religions as complementary discoveries of the spectrum of relational modalities.
Murals #4, #7-12 illustrate how the unit integrates Conflict Analysis Battery's test-elicited personal metaphors integrated into reconstructing the personal six-role process leading to self-discovery and effective actionable therapeutic insights.

The murals and the panels of the Sanctuary present evidence that the mind progresses along the conflict resolution process integrating fragments of an ideational system along the formal operations characterizing the unconscious process, decreasing conflict, increasing social adjustment, moral order as social justice in relationships. Thus, this study provides evidence that the mental process is a mechanism that promotes the upgrading of energy, increasing negative entropy as moral or social adjustment.

The educational value of the Sanctuary exhibits

The exhibits provide the basis for a scientific and moral psychology, the Moral Science. The exposure to the exhibits represents an emotional education entailing understanding psychology as a science, learning about oneself, and enjoying clarity on moral values as the principles of conflict resolution. The individual motivated to pursue her own favorite relational alternatives may be unconsciously generating particular syndromally determined conflicts within her/his own mind. Health and happiness are attainable through the deliberate pursuit of the principles of conflict resolution as moderation, cooperation, and mutual respect.

The Formal Theory's methodological perspective reconciles the scientific analysis of behavior, with moral order, by postulating that the human unconscious is a natural science phenomenon, a mechanism abiding by the formulas of the rigorous sciences, logic, mathematics, and physics that targets the objective of moral order by automatically resolving conflicts. The formal theoretical unconscious is a mental phenomenon that resolves conflicts upgrading meaning, experienced as spirituality.

The murals and panels study validates the formal thesis of the redefined unconscious by systematically interpreting metaphors by identifying the two components of the unconscious illustrated in Mural #3. The premise postulates that the Conflict Resolution Process is both a moral entity reconciling the Abrahamic religions and a perfect totality of formal and energetic inter-transformations abiding by the laws of logic as those of the scale and of the laws of physics of the pendulum oscillation.

The two exhibits present a series of validations establishing the uniform manifestations of the process, integrating fragments into totalities both at the levels of the individual unconscious and at that of societal organization of values such as those of religions. They illustrate and demonstrate the manifestation of this process by confirming its presence in several order-upgrading phenomena as how the unconscious dictates the evolution of personal and societal attitudes consistently in the direction of conflict resolution. The exhibits show the logic underlying the thought process as the gradual transformation of any one choice role-state to its reciprocal, to its opposite, and its correlative. This formal evolution integrates fragments into the continua of the abstract totality. Each sample of creativity shows how fragments of individual imagery, as well as sociological reality, evolve through a dynamic interplay along the identical formal process, decreasing conflict and increasing psychological and sociological order. Pathology is also identified in terms of the process leading to escalation of conflicts along the alternative modalities. The criteria of pathology are intensity of relational modalities, lack in resolution, leading to the rise of psychic tension.

The first six murals show how the universal reductionist methodology of this process serves the creation of cultural moral orders, while the balance of the murals illustrate the process leading to personal alternative paths to meaning, pathological states and their correction through therapy and education. The conclusion is that a rigorous methodology leads to the integration of personal and cultural order into the formal, totally abstract, conceptualization of psychology, sociology, wellness and pathology.

The Oz panels on the exterior walls of the Sanctuary apply the formal analysis to the four metaphors of one story illustrating the integrative quality of the unit of the scientific moral order. The murals present the manifestation of formal relational order connecting parts into totalities of conflict resolution: Nine murals integrate six fragments, corresponding to each one of the six-role states, into the six-role syndromal sequence (Murals #1, 4, 5, 7-12).

In each of the Conflict Resolution Process murals, the six fragments are in a relation of the opposite, reciprocal and correlative to each other. The conflict as tension between opposites, a duality, is identified in the stress state. The conflict or inception phase or state is resolved or reduced by the end state, the compromise or resolution state. The beginning of conflict, the stress state, is in formal relation to the conflict resolution state, compromise, as passivity is transformed to activity, antagonism to cooperation, and alienation to mutual respect.

Murals two and six address that each conflict resolution process may be quantified, qualified, and graphically portrayed. The circle is the social system normative totality. The ellipses present the personal self-other dialectic as a pendulum ball within the normative or social gravitation field. Three revolutions around the circle constitute the unit syndromal unfolding of the process. Vectors portray the natural science constructs as role states in relation to each other as defined by the laws of science.

This study then corroborates the central assumption of Conflict Analysis - The Formal Theory of Behavior that the Conflict Resolution Process unconscious is a formal and energetic natural science mechanism and, as such, that it is the atomistic unit of behavioral phenomena.

The validations show:
First, that the elements of symbolic systems are formally interrelated to each other as advanced in the definition of the process and that this six-role states pattern transforms conflict to resolution, thus creating order in the respective system. (For more information on the concepts and their diagrammatic presentation, the reader should review the textbook, Conflict Analysis -The Formal Theory of Behavior, sections of Methodology.)
Second, the validations confirm the hypothesis of the Formal Theory that the Unit phenomenon of behavior consists methodologically of a series of energetic transformations bound together within a moral end-product, increased negative entropy as catharsis occurring upon the conflict resolution experience. The sequence of murals shows how the unit is a natural science moral order phenomenon, and therefore, we may reduce behavior and morality to the constructs of physics and logic.

Accordingly, the sequence of images first, represents transformations automatically pursuing balance like the purely formal system of the scale in which formal transformations are connected by a formula. Second, they also represent a periodic natural science phenomenon like the pendulum oscillation, the Simple Harmonic Motion. The images constitute inter-transformable modalities of energy whose sum-total is conserved, but which, unlike other natural science phenomena, proceed deterministically, one-directionally toward upgrading order (labile psychic discomfort or tension is transformed to stable social adjustment as negative entropy).

THE SCIENTIFIC INTERPRETATION OF METAPHORS

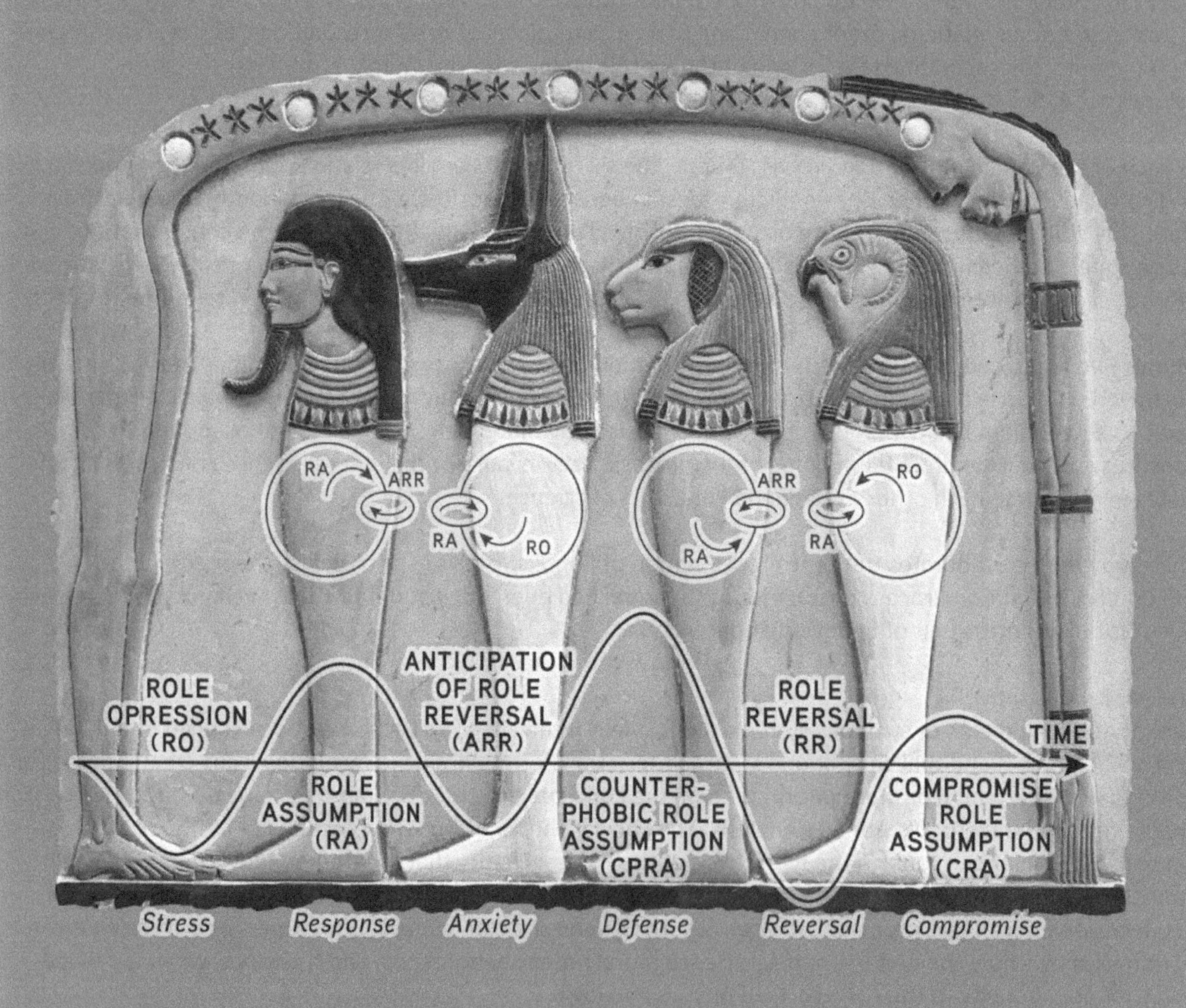

Volume Seven

Albert J. Levis M.D. & Maxwell Levis PhD

Normative Publications

BOOK ONE: EPISTEMOLOGY
IDENTIFYING THE STRUCTURE OF THE CREATIVE PROCESS THROUGH THE SCIENTIFIC INTERPRETATION OF METAPHORS

EPISTEMOLOGY

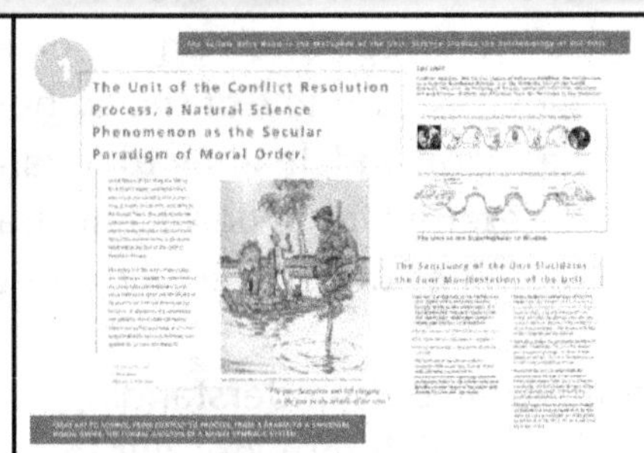

The plot of stories is a scientific conflict resolution process

The unconscious is a six-role conflict resolution syndrome

INTRODUCTION

Wall # 1. Epistemology: the scientific structure and the moral function of the unconscious

The jacket of this book exemplifies the analysis of the creative process, of a story, as a syndrome of six formally interrelated role states and as four relational modalities. The image presents the Goddess Nut and four anthropomorphic characters depicting the Egyptian creation story interpreted by the Formal Theory as a syndrome, the six-part emotional sequence of a conflict resolution, encompassing its heroes, each identified as a relational modality. The metaphor of the creation story is interpreted as leading to a conflict resolution. While moral order as conflict resolution is implicit usually in stories, in this story it is explicit as introducing a religion-associated moral message.

This image shows how the Formal Theory superimposes art, science and morality interpreting metaphors as measurable scientific and moral processes. The image sums up the position advanced on the nature of the unconscious as a scientific conflict resolution mechanism consisting of an energetic six-part dialectic propelled by three formal operations, leading to four alternative types of conflict resolution.

The formal analysis clarifies the unconscious as a natural science conflict resolution phenomenon with measurable and graphically portrayable dimensions. The unconscious becomes the unit of meaning and the measuring rod of emotional reality. It consists of a six-role state syndromal entity and four types of resolutions, the range of wellness diagnoses, a personality typology; it entails the use of creativity for self-discovery, and it clarifies morality as a scientific innate homeostatic conflict resolution mechanism, the origin of all moral thought.

The first book is about the discipline of Epistemology. The book focuses in the formal and energetic analysis of the creative process representing the unconscious as the atomistic unit of the social sciences; it makes the creative process, the plot of stories, the core object of scientific psychology. It allows us to analyze behavioral phenomena as measurable and graphically portrayable variations of the unit conflict resolution process.

The study of the unconscious departs by examining the *Yellow Brick Road* as the metaphor of the process having a beginning, middle and end states that is analyzed as abiding by the laws of two equilibrial phenomena, whose function is an energetic attitude-modifying transformation. The corresponding murals of the first wall present creation stories and religions effectively analyzed by the two phenomena attesting to the validation of the scientific premise on the nature of the creative process.

Panel 1: The analysis of the plot of stories as a Sequence of Six Interrelated Role-States: Stress, Response, Anxiety, Defense, Reversal, and Compromise.
Panel 2: Myths and Religions, Art and Drama, Psychology, Religion as Humankind's Quests for Meaning, for the Hidden Moral Order.
Panel 3: Finally, the Quests for Meaning, find in the Unit the Science-based Paradigm of Moral Order.

CHAPTER ONE: PANELS ABOUT THE YELLOW BRICK ROAD

The scientific laws underlying moral order were derived by equating the unit, a social science periodic phenomenon, with the Simple Harmonic Motion, a periodic phenomenon from the natural sciences and the three formal operations restoring balance to the trays of a scale. The three panels on the exterior wall, present the analysis of the Yellow Brick Road as the metaphor of the plot, the journey, of the Oz heroes; it unites Dorothy's adventures into a totality with a beginning, a middle, and a moral end, leading to a transformation. According to the Formal Theory, this path of surprises and adventures exemplifies a perfect abstract and predictable system of emotions dictated by the unconscious, defining the Unit of the Conflict Resolution Process.

The secrets and the magic of psychology and religion are revealed by understanding this measurable and predictable unconscious mechanism, which governs our lives and determines our fortunes. In uncovering this process as the unconscious across four disciplines of psychology studying samples of creativity, the metaphors of the Oz story, the Formal Theory demystifies psychology and morality into a scientific phenomenon making life less scary and more manageable for Dorothy and humankind.

We interpret the Yellow Brick Road, as a journey of personal transformations, equivalent to the Greek Cosmogony's lifetime cycle of emotional experiences of each generation of the Greek gods. We regard both the Yellow Road and the Greek cosmogony, Mural #1, as metaphors of the creative process. We recognize the process as a scientific conflict resolution phenomenon representing the unconscious as the scientific paradigm of moral order.

Panel 1: The Unit of the Conflict Resolution Process, a natural science phenomenon

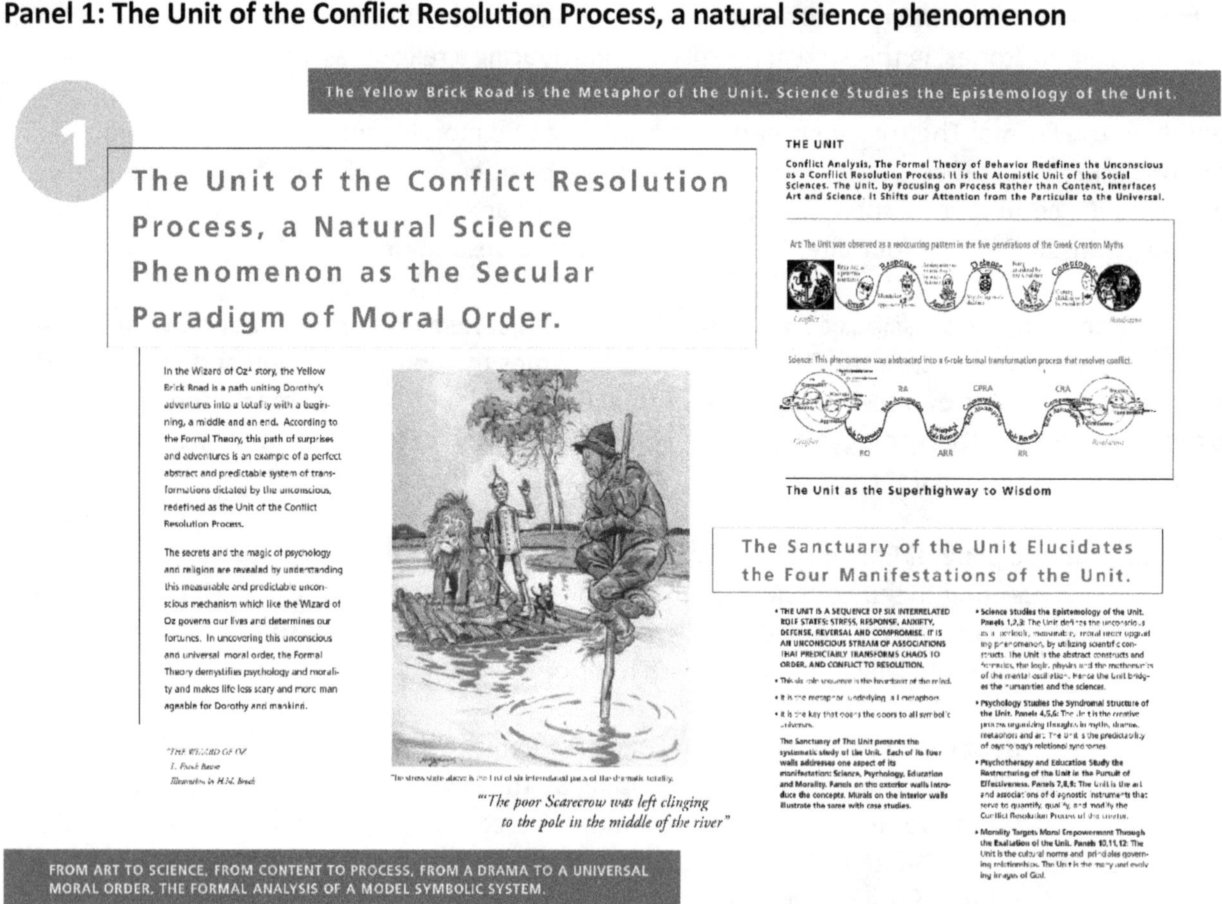

The analysis of the plot of stories is a Sequence of Six Interrelated Role-States: Stress, Response, Anxiety, Defense, Reversal, and Compromise. The Yellow road is the unconscious string of emotions manifested as a stream of associations that predictably transform energy from chaos to order and from conflict to resolution.

- This six-role sequence is the heartbeat of the mind.
- It is the syndrome of formally interrelated emotions underlying all creativity, all metaphors.
- It is the master key that opens the doors to all symbolic universes.

Panel 2: Myths and Religions, Art and Science, Psychology and Morality as Humankind's Quests for Meaning, the Hidden Moral Order .

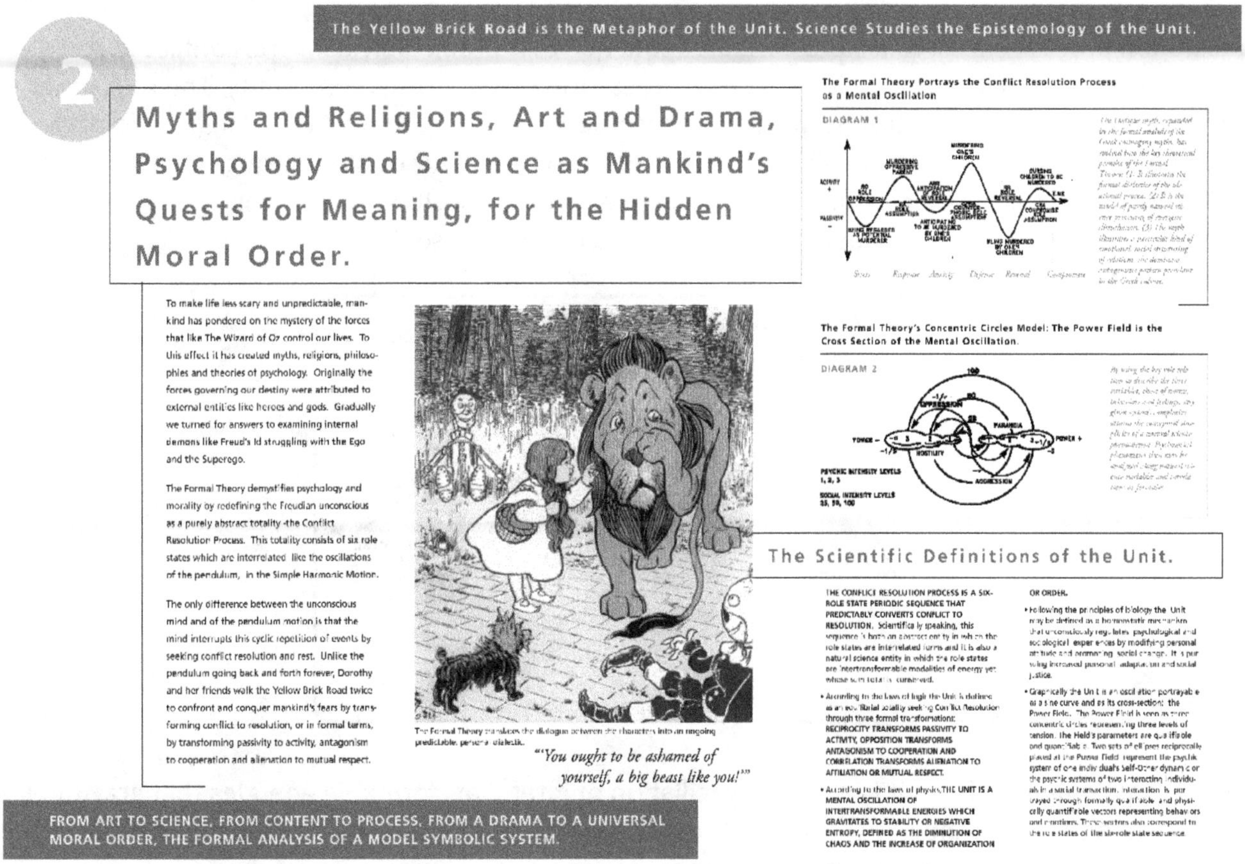

The Yellow Brick Road is the Metaphor of the Unit. Science Studies the Epistemology of the Unit.

2

Myths and Religions, Art and Drama, Psychology and Science as Mankind's Quests for Meaning, for the Hidden Moral Order.

To make life less scary and unpredictable, mankind has pondered on the mystery of the forces that like The Wizard of Oz control our lives. To this effect it has created myths, religions, philosophies and theories of psychology. Originally the forces governing our destiny were attributed to external entities like heroes and gods. Gradually we turned for answers to examining internal demons like Freud's Id struggling with the Ego and the Superego.

The Formal Theory demystifies psychology and morality by redefining the Freudian unconscious as a purely abstract totality -the Conflict Resolution Process. This totality consists of six role states which are interrelated like the oscillations of the pendulum, in the Simple Harmonic Motion.

The only difference between the unconscious mind and of the pendulum motion is that the mind interrupts this cyclic repetition of events by seeking conflict resolution and rest. Unlike the pendulum going back and forth forever, Dorothy and her friends walk the Yellow Brick Road twice to confront and conquer mankind's fears by transforming conflict to resolution, or in formal terms, by transforming passivity to activity, antagonism to cooperation and alienation to mutual respect.

"You ought to be ashamed of yourself, a big beast like you!"

The Formal Theory Portrays the Conflict Resolution Process as a Mental Oscillation

DIAGRAM 1

The Formal Theory's Concentric Circles Model: The Power Field is the Cross Section of the Mental Oscillation.

DIAGRAM 2

PSYCHIC INTENSITY LEVELS 1, 2, 3

SOCIAL INTENSITY LEVELS 25, 50, 100

The Scientific Definitions of the Unit.

THE CONFLICT RESOLUTION PROCESS IS A SIX-ROLE STATE PERIODIC SEQUENCE THAT PREDICTABLY CONVERTS CONFLICT TO RESOLUTION. Scientifically speaking, this sequence is both an abstract entity in which the role states are interrelated forms and it is also a natural science entity in which the role states are intertransformable modalities of energy yet whose sum total is conserved.

- According to the laws of logic the Unit is defined as an equilibrial totality seeking Conflict Resolution through three formal transformations: RECIPROCITY TRANSFORMS PASSIVITY TO ACTIVITY, OPPOSITION TRANSFORMS ANTAGONISM TO COOPERATION AND CORRELATION TRANSFORMS ALIENATION TO AFFILIATION OR MUTUAL RESPECT.
- According to the laws of physics, THE UNIT IS A MENTAL OSCILLATION OF INTERTRANSFORMABLE ENERGIES WHICH GRAVITATES TO STABILITY OR NEGATIVE ENTROPY, DEFINED AS THE DIMINUTION OF CHAOS AND THE INCREASE OF ORGANIZATION OR ORDER.
- Following the principles of biology the Unit may be defined as a homeostatic mechanism that unconsciously regulates psychological and sociological experiences by modifying personal attitude and promoting social change. It is pursuing [illegible] personal adaptation and social justice.
- Graphically the Unit is an oscillation portrayable as a sine curve and as its cross-section: the Power Field. The Power Field is seen as three concentric circles representing three levels of tension. The Field's parameters are qualifiable and quantifiable. Two sets of ellipses reciprocally placed at the Power Field represent the psychic system of one individual's Self-Other dynamic or the psychic systems of two interacting individuals in a social transaction. Interaction is portrayed through formally qualifiable and physically quantifiable vectors representing behaviors and emotions. These vectors also correspond to the role states of the six-role state sequence.

FROM ART TO SCIENCE, FROM CONTENT TO PROCESS, FROM A DRAMA TO A UNIVERSAL MORAL ORDER, THE FORMAL ANALYSIS OF A MODEL SYMBOLIC SYSTEM.

To make life less scary and less unpredictable, humanity has pondered the mystery of the forces that, like The Wizard of Oz, control our lives. To this effect, it has created myths, religions, philosophies, and theories of psychology. Originally the forces governing our destiny were attributed to external entities like heroes and gods. Gradually we turned for answers to examining internal demons like Freud's Id struggling with the Ego and the Superego. The Formal Theory demystifies psychology and morality by redefining the Freudian unconscious as a purely abstract totality, the Conflict Resolution Process. This totality consists of six-role states which are interrelated, like the oscillations of the pendulum, in the Simple Harmonic Motion, guided by three attitude modifying formal operations. These are the equilibrial formal operations of the trays of the scale.

The only difference between the unconscious mind and of the pendulum motion is that the mind interrupts this cyclic repetition of events by seeking conflict resolution and rest. Unlike the pendulum going back and forth forever, Dorothy and her friends walk the Yellow Brick Road twice to confront and conquer humanity's fears by transforming conflicts to resolutions, or in formal terms, by transforming passivity to activity, antagonism to cooperation, and alienation to mutual respect. The transformation reflects the moral nature of the unconscious, which corrects the individual's relational tendencies as alternative types of conflict resolutions.

The Formal Theory Portrays the Conflict Resolution Process as a Mental Oscillation
The formal analysis of the Greek cosmogony myths has evolved into the key theoretical premise of the Formal Theory: (1) It illustrates the formal dialectics of the ideational process. (2) It is the model of purely natural science processing of energetic disturbances. (3) The Greek myth illustrates a particular kind of emotional, social structuring of relations, the dominant antagonistic pattern prevalent in this culture.

The Formal Theory's Concentric Circles Model as The Power Field is the Cross-Section of the Mental Oscillation
By using the key role relation to describe the three variables, those of norms, behaviors, and feelings, any given

system's complexity attains the conceptual simplicity of a natural science phenomenon. Psychosocial phenomena then may be analyzed along with natural science variables and correlations or formulas.

The conflict resolution process is a six-role state periodic sequence that predictably converts conflict to resolution. Scientifically speaking, this sequence is both an abstract formal and an energetic entity. The role states are interrelated energetic quantities, whose sum-total is conserved. According to the laws of logic, and of the equilibrial scale, the unit is defined as an equilibrial totality seeking Conflict Resolution through three formal transformations: reciprocity transforming states of passivity to activity, opposition transforms antagonism to cooperation, and correlation transforms alienation to affiliation or mutual respect.

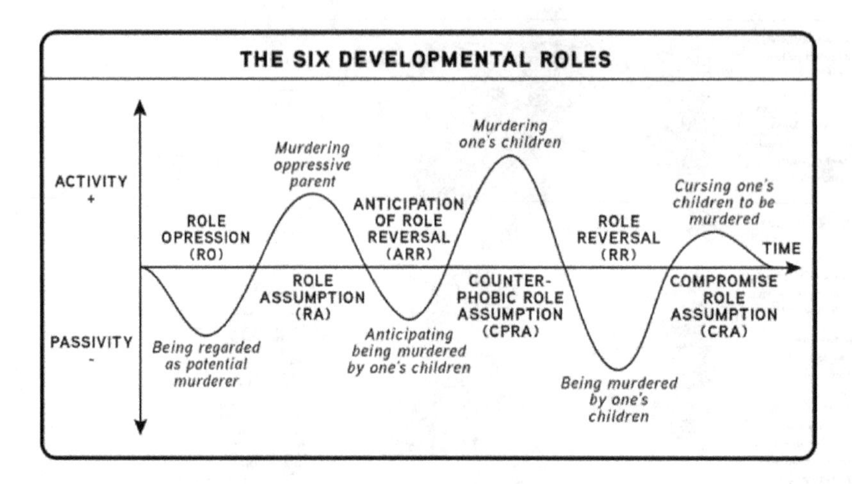

According to the laws of physics, the unit is a mental oscillation of inter-transformable energies that gravitates to stability or negative entropy, defined as the diminution of chaos as psychic tension, and the increase of organization or social order. Graphically, the unit is an oscillation portrayable as a sine curve of the six-role process. Its cross-section is the normative or power field presented as three concentric circles corresponding to three levels of tension. Two sets of ellipses reciprocally placed at the Power Field represent the psychic system of one individual's Self-Other dynamic or alternatively the psychic systems of two interacting individuals in a social transaction. Interaction is portrayed through formally qualifiable and physically quantifiable vectors representing behaviors and emotions. These vectors also correspond to the role states of the six-role state sequence.

Following the principles of biology, the unit may be defined as a homeostatic mechanism that unconsciously regulates psychological and sociological experiences by modifying personal attitude and power promoting social adjustment. The unconscious process pursues increased personal adaptation and social justice.

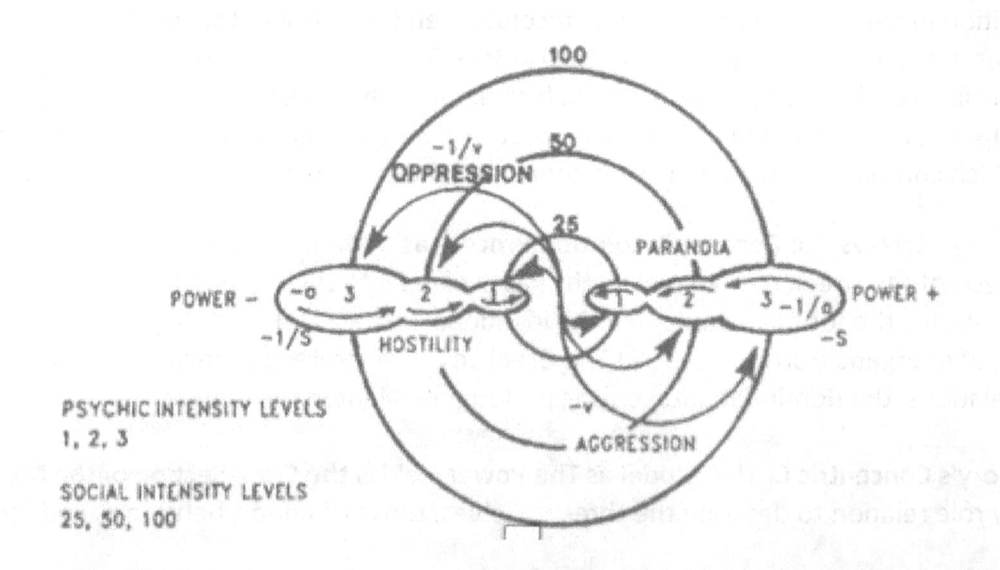

Panel 3: Finally, the Quests for Meaning, find in the Unit the Science-based Paradigm of Moral Order.

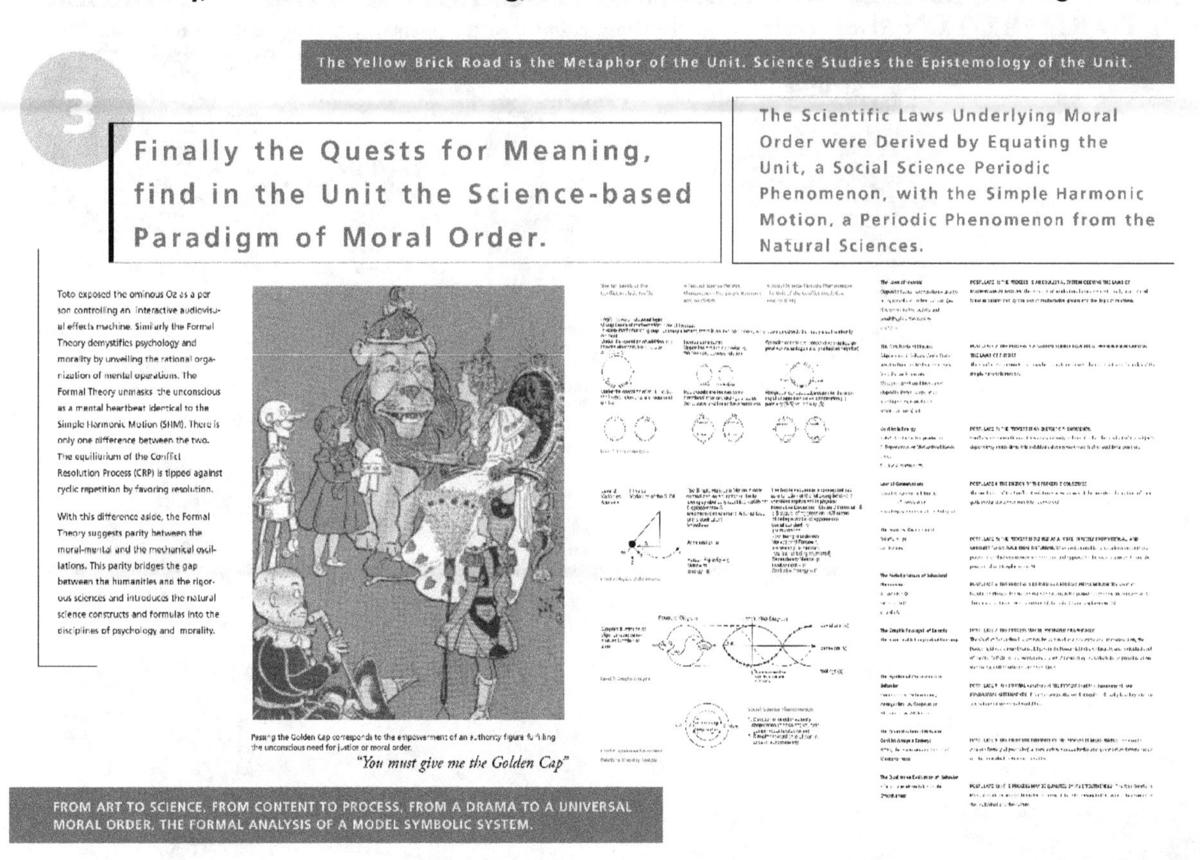

The scientific laws underlying moral order were derived by equating the unit, a social science periodic phenomenon, with the Simple Harmonic Motion (SHM), a periodic phenomenon from the natural sciences and the formal operations restoring balance to the trays of a scale.

Toto exposed the ominous Oz as a person controlling an interactive audiovisual effects machine. Similarly, the Formal Theory demystifies psychology and morality by unveiling the rational organization of mental operations. The Formal Theory unmasks the unconscious as a mental heartbeat identical to the SHM. There is only one difference between the two. The equilibrium of the Conflict Resolution Process (CRP) is tipped against cyclic repetition by favoring energetic upgrading work, as power and attitude changes, as conflict resolutions, the unconscious seeking to reduce psychic discomfort, conflict energy, with a set of formal operations. With this difference aside, the Formal Theory suggests parity between the moral-mental and the mechanical oscillations. This parity bridges the gap between the humanities and the rigorous sciences and introduces the natural science constructs and formulas into the disciplines of psychology and morality.

CHAPTER TWO: MURALS #1, 3, AND 2
SYNDROMES AND MODALITIES

Mural #1: Three Creation Stories Reveal How the Mind Proceeds from Chaos to Order, From Conflict to Resolution. It describes the Conflict Resolution Process as a Perfect Totality, The Unit of Moral Order.
The first mural focuses on the formal analysis of the Greek creation stories as a sequence of interrelated events completing the six-role transformation from conflict to resolution. The Greek creation drama provides clear imagery of the cyclic process summed up in six transformations of one key behavior: murder. This periodic phenomenon allows us to introduce scientific conceptualization into the study of behavior as the orderly, formal, and moral sequencing of thoughts present in all samples of creativity.

The mural presents the Conflict Resolution Process as a composite of three creation stories: The Oriental Yin Yang, the Greek Cosmogony, and the Biblical Genesis. The elements of the three stories are intertwined to reinforce awareness of the universality of the dialectic six-role process, accomplishing the transformation of chaos to order. The dialectic of the Oriental Yin and Yang, the primordial parental antithesis of earth/sky, up/down/male/female, coincides with the six-role process dialectic of the Greek cosmogony generation of Kronos interacting with his father Uranus with his children, the Olympians. Finally, this six-role dialectic coincides with the Biblical Genesis' six days of creation, followed by the day of rest. It alludes to Genesis resolving conflict as a six-part continuum leading to the Sabbath, the day of rest. The Conflict Resolution Process is then affirmed as the universal unconscious underlying Hindu Pantheism, Greek Cosmogony's Dodekatheon, and biblical Monotheism.

2.RESPONSE:	4.DEFENSE:	6.COMPROMISE:
Mother Earth armed Kronos, her youngest son, with a flint sickle. Kronos castrated his father. Father Sky's severed phallus falling on the water was transformed into the beautiful Aphrodite.	Upon their birth, out of fear of being killed by them, Kronos devoured the Olympian children.	Dying Kronos cursed Zeus to be killed in turn by his child. Zeus, scared of this predicament, swallowed his wife Metis as soon as she became pregnant. A few months later, Hephaestus, the smith, opened his skull, and Zeus' daughter Athena emerged. His screams and curses shook the universe.

1.STRESS: Following their union, Father Sky threw his children into Tartarus (Hell), to the dismay of his wife, Mother Earth.	3.ANXIETY: Dying Father Sky cursed Kronos to be killed in his turn by his children, the Olympians. Kronos panicked at the sight of his children.	5.ROLE REVERSAL: Mother Rhea hid her youngest, Zeus, from his father. Zeus grew up, freed his brothers, Hades and Poseidon, and the three killed their father. Hades, hidden in his helmet of darkness, disarmed Kronos, Poseidon with his trident pinned him down, and Zeus finished him off with a lightning bolt.

7. REST: Athena was born dressed like a warrior to protect herself from men and the curse of being killed by her children. Yet Athena was raped by Hephaestus and had a son, Erichthonius, whom she promptly got rid of by putting him in foster placement. Having come of age, to appease his mother, Erichthonius built her a temple on the Acropolis. Athena reassured, gave Athens her olive tree and her owl.

Structurally the three creation stories are reduced to their common denominator, the six-role Conflict Resolution Process. The six roles are given two sets of names. One designates the roles in a role transformation system. The other one emphasizes the continuum's phenomenological development as a sequence of cause-effect relations. The first set of designations describes the events as Role Oppression, RO, Role Assumption, RA, Anticipated Role Reversal, ARR, Counterphobic Role Assumption, CPRA, Role Reversal, RR and Compromise Role Assumption, CRA. The second set of designations describes the same events as stress, response, anxiety, defense, reversal, and compromise. This process is portrayed as a sine curve whose six modulations correspond to the events in a person's lifetime as six formally interrelated role states. This sequence also corresponds to The Aristotelian "perfect universe," describing the structure of Greek Tragedies.

The six-role sequence is predictably evolving passivity to activity, antagonism to cooperation, and alienation to mutual respect. The lower left side of Mural 2 illustrates how the Conflict Resolution Process is repeated in successive generations and leads gradually to improved conflict resolution and the foundation of faith. The graphics of Mural 2 illustrate the same sine wave repeated for each of the four generations of the Greek Cosmogony. The difference for each repetition is the diminution of the distance or alienation between gods and mortals. As each individual God evolves through the life cycle, we detect an ongoing rapprochement between gods and humans occurring in each of the four generations: Uranus (generation n-1), Kronos (n), Zeus (n +1), and Athena (n + 2). Erichthonius, the mortal is the fifth generation (n+3); his lifetime curve is not represented. The Conflict Resolution of each generation brings the gods closer to the Earth. The gods represent this transition with Uranus identified with the sky, Kronos, with the stars, Zeus with Olympus, and finally Athena with her temple, the Parthenon on the Athenian hill of Acropolis. Finally, her son Erichthonius, the 'man born from the Earth,' is identified as a citizen, the King of Athens.

We can look at the role states of any one of the sine curves as representing the formally correlated events in a person's lifecycle as the abstract Conflict Resolution Process.
We address Kronos as generation n, the first of the six role states, stress or role oppression (RO) describes the interaction of Kronos -his being a child threatened to be killed by his father Uranus (generation n-l).
The second role, the response or role assumption (RA), describes Kronos as assuming the reciprocal role: murdering his father, Uranus. His Role of Oppression or Stress leads to the reciprocal Role Assumption or Response.
His Anticipated Role Reversal or anxiety, reinforced by his father's cursing him to die in his turn, corresponds to the anticipation that he would be killed by his children.
His Counter Phobic Role Assumption or Defense pertains to Kronos swallowing his children to avert the dreaded predicament.
His Role Reversal or Outcome state corresponds to the fulfillment of this prophecy: Kronos is killed by his children, headed by Zeus (generation n +1).
His Compromise Role Assumption, the Compromise, corresponds to Kronos cursing Zeus, to receive the same

treatment by his children (generation n +2) as Uranus, his father before him, and now himself, and then Zeus after him. Indeed, the mural #1 image illustrates Athena emerging from Zeus's head.

The conflict resolution process is characterized by a series of three methodologically important formal transformations:

First, t*he reciprocal transformation* of passivity turned into activity as Kronos evolves from the states of passivity: stress, anxiety, and reversal to those of activity: response, defense, and compromise.

A second formal transformation called *opposition/negation gradually transforms antagonism to cooperation* as the child is being banished to lesser oppressions entailed in the reduction of punishments. The site of the exiled child is shifted from the very alien place called Tartarus, which is "as far below the earth as the sky is above it" to the proximity of being banished only to one's father's stomach and emerging from his head.

The third transformation is called *correlation*. According to this principle, correlation generalizes on what has happened to all sets of cosmogony individuals. Those who violate will be violated. This predicament reminds Zeus that suffering is also his predicament. *Correlation is the generalization transforming alienation to the respect for a unifying abstract principle of order.* The global dynamic process of the six-role states entails then a methodology of formal transformations binding the sequence of role states into a three-phase formal transformation process evolving in the span of the lifetime. Roles in a lifetime are bound by the six-role process syntax and by the formal operations grammar.

The transmission of the cyclic phenomenon across several generations is a methodological advantage of the Greek Cosmogony as a paradigm of the Conflict Resolution Process. This periodic intergenerational pattern emphasizes two features: *First,* the predictability of the six-role, three-cycle of activity-passivity states entity; three roles of the lifetime sequence connect the person as a child to the parental generation, and three role states connect the person as an adult, a parent, to the filial generation. *Second,* the Cosmogony illustrates the ongoing progressive upgrading of order, the fact of the qualitative upgrading the moral evolution of the conflict resolution in each successive generation.

The intergenerational sequence starts with serious conflicts-oppression, antagonism, and alienation- between genders and generations and ends several generations later with the reconciliation of a child and a parent. Erichthonius, son of Athena, Zeus' daughter, reconciled himself with his mother and founded the Athenian civilization. Ultimately conflict resolution transforms the conflict as oppression, antagonism, and alienation to resolution as mastery, activity with moderation of power, cooperation in relationships, and affiliation, that is, mutual respect between genders and generations.

Similarly, to the Greek Cosmogony, the Biblical Story defines God as the God of three generations in a family saga. God is referred to as the God of Abraham, Isaac, and Jacob. The Hebrew god is redefined more clearly as the respect of the totality of the moral discoveries completed through the journey of the Jews from Mesopotamia through Egypt to the Promised Land reviewed in the annual cycle of the study of the Torah, the Bible. This education combines learning of history with the awareness of a people's emotional growth or maturation. A people's story is abstracted to a set of rules and regulations. God is oneness. He represents the concept of universal order leading from a conflict to its resolution. While Genesis corresponds to the six-role process, the Ten Commandments essentially coincide with the three formal operations connecting the six-role process to its moral resolution. (See Mural #3).

Mural #3: The Physics of Metaphysics and of Relational Modalities
Mural #3B, upper level of the mural, Two scientific phenomena determining moral order
Mural 3#A, lower level of the mural, The Abrahamic religions as complementary relational modal

2. The process is a sequence of formal transformations. It is an equilibrial system illustrated by the balance of a scale. The unconscious tips the scale toward resolution, transforming passivity to activity, antagonism to cooperation, and alienation to mutual respect. Opposites: cooperation + antagonism cancel each other out. Reciprocals: Activity x passivity yields the unit.	4. The Conflict Resolution Process is the unit of moral order. It mandates deliberate conflict resolution as the transformation of passivity to activity, antagonism to cooperation, and alienation to mutual respect. The universal laws of morality coincide with the Ten Commandments.	6. The process is a sequence of energetic transformations, like those of the pendulum oscillation. The process abides by the laws of physics, but unlike the pendulum, the process upgrades order; it increases negative entropy.
1. Christianity illustrates the subordinacy syndrome. Jesus, the son of an unwed mother, espoused cooperation, non-violence, asexuality, and self-sacrifice: this represents the relational choices of the submissive-cooperative syndrome.	3. Judaism illustrates the assertiveness syndrome. Jacob, the favored son of a powerful mother, is assertive. He extracts blessings from his father and 'wrestles with God.' Becoming empowered as Israel. He is respectful of his discriminated brother Hesau and a fair judge for his wives and sons. The Passover Seder's querying sons illustrate the four relational modalities; those of the wise, wicked, simple, and quiet alternatives. The Judaic values of the wise child reinforce the desirability of assertiveness and respect, qualities of cooperative dominance.	5. Islam illustrates the dominance syndrome. Mohammed espoused dominance, the relational choice attributed to Ishmael. Ishmael was the first-born son of Abraham and Hagar. Hagar and Ishmael were banished to the desert. Feeling unjustly deprived, Ishmael could feel justified in dominating peers and rivals. This relational choice is experienced as controls, and anxiety, the characteristics of dominant-antagonism.

The upper tier of the mural presents the Conflict Resolution Process as a natural science phenomenon of moral order. The three formal operations driving the process coincide with the Mosaic Laws. The upper row middle tile highlights Moses holding the tablets of the Ten Commandments. In them are inscribed the three principal formal operations transforming conflict to resolution. On the left and right, we see the Commandments have scientific essence; they are formulas of logic and physics.

Below we see the three Abrahamic religions as alternative conflict resolutions corresponding to alternative relational modalities. The text provides sociological explanations of the respective religions, representing psychologically and sociologically determined alternative relational modality responses to stress.

The unit redefines the unconscious abstractly as an order-upgrading-mechanism-processing-ideas along with three morally-directed formal operations. It is transforming passivity to activity, antagonism to cooperation, and alienation to mutual respect. It follows that the Abrahamic religions are alternative ways of resolving conflict.

The upper tier of this mural presents the hypothesis that the Conflict Resolution Unit Process is a Formal and Natural Science Entity. Mural #1 highlights the discovery of the 6-role process, as this was observed in three creation stories. Mural #2 highlights the usefulness of this unit process in integrating the moral paradigms of the world. The unit's periodicity and modifiability introduce predictability and measurability, that is, scientific order, in the social and the moral sciences.

Formal logic on the left side is represented by the classical scene of Greek philosophy in the Agora, also by an owl, the bird of wisdom whose eyes depict vectors in balance.
Physics on the right tile is illustrated by a portrait of Einstein, a mechanical configuration, a clock, and its oscillating pendulum on the right. The animals of the respective sciences, the wise owl and the dumb but predictable cuckoo bird, accompanied by formulas, provide a counterpoint to the traditional lions framing the tablets of Moses. These images clearly suggest the equation of the unconscious process with our paradigm of moral order and the orderly two well-known phenomena of the rigorous sciences.

These equations constitute the key hypothesis of the Formal Theory. The unconscious is a periodic Simple Harmonic Motion entity, the mental heartbeat. The unconscious also follows the principles of the equilibrial scale's three basic operations, restoring the rest state, the transformation of passivity to activity, (a reciprocal formal transformation), of antagonism to cooperation, (an opposite- operation), and of alienation to affiliation, (a correlative operation).

The necessary assumption to bridge moralities and science is postulated in these images advancing Formal Theory's major hypothesis that the process is the scientific unit of moral order suggesting the equivalence between the 10 Commandments as the paradigm of moral order abiding by the rigorous laws of logic, mathematics, and physics. Thus, it is advanced that the unit process is both a moral and an orderly phenomenon abiding by the laws of formal logic and by the laws of the Simple Harmonic Motion.

This postulation, therefore, binds together both scientific and moral orders in the unit of the Conflict Resolution Process, making the process as meaningful as the moral paradigm of the Mosaic Commandments and as predictable and measurable as the laws of logic and physics.

Mural #3B: The Three Abrahamic Religions are Formally Interrelated Alternative Syndromal Ways of Resolving Conflict

The three religions differ along psychology's three formal operations following variations of the formal injunctions: Christianity follows submissiveness, Judaism assertiveness as cooperative dominance, and Islam follows dominant antagonism by commanding obedience. Science clarifies that moral values are defined as moderation, cooperation, and mutual respect.

Though the same principles govern Psychology and Morality leading to conflict resolution, there are normative differences determined by cultures and individuals. The alternative directions of resolving conflict are identified as syndromal relational modalities. Each relational modality may be illustrated as a set of graphically portrayable sine curves and as vectors, respectively, within both social concentric circles and psychic ellipses.

Thus, conflict resolution may vary along the relational parameters of dominance versus subordinacy, cooperation versus antagonism, and its intensity varying along the states of alienation versus mutual respect. Because of the unconscious unit abiding by the formulas of logic and physics, it is expected that both the individual and cultural moral orders may be seen to pursue alternative ways of resolving conflict. We identify the relational modalities as the basic set of the 6-role process or syndrome, leading to the formal relational alternatives of cooperative versus antagonistic and subordinacy versus dominance variations. This relational typology manifests both in the individual clinical and in the sociological or cultural realms. Both therapy and morality steer the unconscious process of conflict resolution to deliberately and consciously complete effective conflict resolution. Indeed, the four syndromal conflict resolutions or relational modalities differ in their degree of effectiveness of conflict resolution. Personal and cultural moral tendencies evolve in the course of the individual life span, that is, ontogenetically, and in the course of cultural growth or phylogenetic evolution. Relational Ontogenesis and Phylogenesis lead toward more complete or effective conflict resolution: less polarization, more moderation, less antagonism, more cooperation, less alienation, and more mutual respect.

Validation studies, therefore, address detecting the occurrence of these alternative relational syndromes in individual behavior and cultural thinking. Other studies address the evolution of conflict resolution along one's lifetime from ineffective ways of resolving conflict to more effective ones. Finally, cross-cultural studies may address the evolution of moral paradigms toward effectively greater interpersonal conflict resolution.

We can measure both personal and cultural relational systems in terms of their respective formal and physical characteristics of their symbolic systems. Religious doctrines and norms regulate the structuring of the conflict resolution process. The lower tier of Mural #3 consists in diagnosing religions differing as relational modalities. The Abrahamic Religions are diagnosed as alternative relational modalities, as the range of alternative restructurings of the father-son covenant.

The mental-moral systems are diagnosed or measured by their formal attributes (activity vs. passivity, cooperation vs. antagonism, affiliation vs. alienation) and by their constellation of natural science variables, e.g., energetic quantity as entailed in choice of relational intensity at the level of the pursuit of power as manifested through one's behaviors and emotions. These features characterize both personal and societal structuring of relationships and determine the conflict resolutions as a series of predictable syndromes, as sequences of interrelated events or experiences. These syndromes constitute diagnostic personal and cultural categories.

The formal organization of moral orders allows us to examine the relational characteristics of religions as syndromal entities. The mural highlights the three Abrahamic religions as reflecting alternative relational modalities and related power distribution in the family system. This power distribution is determined both by innate personality typology but also by the personal formative childhood experiences of the respective Abrahamic prophet.

Accordingly, the human unconscious and the Ten Commandments emphasize the moral imperatives of moderation, cooperation, and respect. Yet, the language of the respective prophets, Moses, Jesus, and Mohammed, provided different implementations of the general principles of conflict resolution. The three religions reflect three alternative formally related syndromal choices. The Judaic is the dominant cooperative; the Christian is the submissive cooperative; the Islamic is the dominant antagonistic. This shift of analysis to diagnose religions as relational patterns reconciles the range of possible moral solutions as formally related alternatives. Moses laid down the principles of a moral constitution, but his fellow prophets modified this constitution. The Formal Theory rediscovers the interrelatedness of the three moral paradigms as relational modalities and exposes the universal conflict resolution above the partial truths of the separate moral paradigms. Therefore, it is possible to conceive a conceptual reconciliation of the Abrahamic religions by considering the family's unresolved gender relations.

Mural #2: The Flag of the United Metaphors of the World shows that the Conflict Resolution Process is the common denominator of all moral paradigms and that these, religions and ideologies, are measurable and graphically portrayable moral order natural science phenomena.

Mural # 2 presents this unit as the universal structure underlying all ideologies, those based on religions as well as those based on economic principles. The Flag of the United Metaphors illustrates the formal and natural scientific graphic representation of the world cultures as formally integrated conflict resolution processes representing alternative relational modalities.

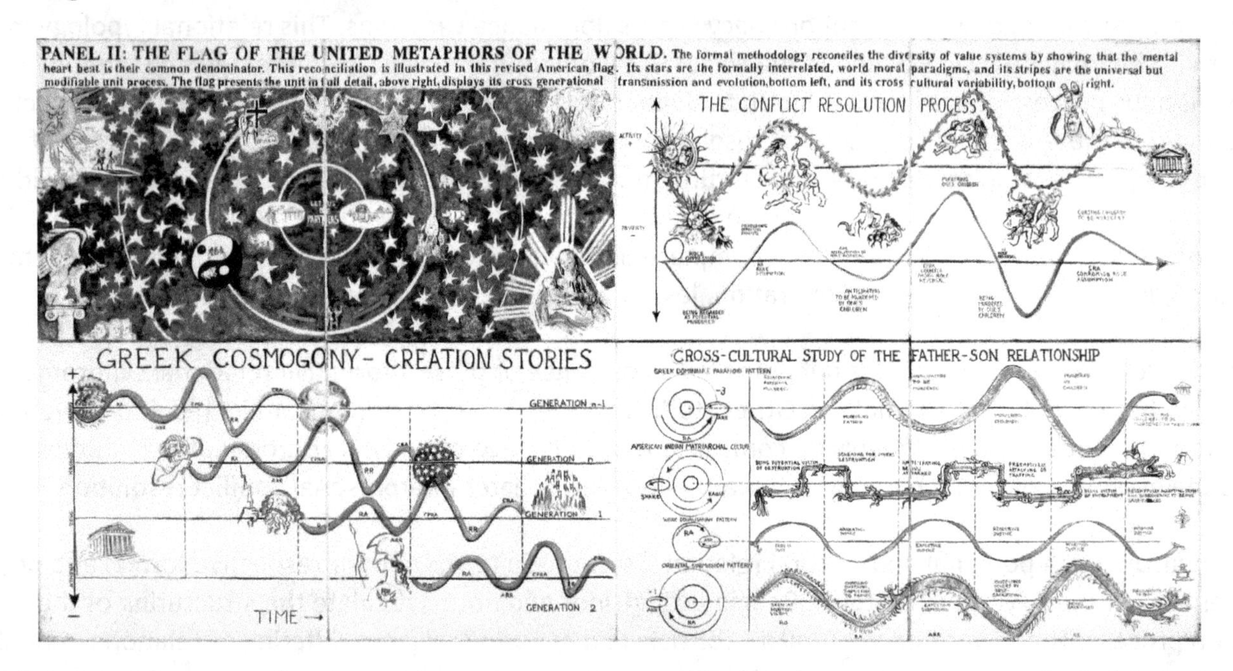

The stripes of the Flag present the Conflict Resolution Process

Integrating Art and Science	*Greek Cosmogony*	*Cross Cultural Study*
The flag presents the unit in full detail as the evolution from art to science.	The flag displays the unit in its cross-generational transmission and evolution.	The flag shows the unit's cross-cultural variability.

The formal methodology reconciles the diversity of value systems by showing that the mental heartbeat and the moral compass, syndromal structure and relational modality function --the unit--is their common denominator. This reconciliation is illustrated in this revised American flag uniting all religions and ideologies through the scientific interpretation of moral paradigms. It is based on the universality of the principles of Conflict Resolution governing unconscious thinking. This flag celebrates the discovery that the unit process integrates the diversity of hitherto alienated belief systems into a new universal moral order. This conceptual integration is used as the paradigm of integration in all disciplines of psychology. It allows us to integrate theoretical perspectives, assessment instruments, therapeutic modalities, and to examine art work and cultural systems in terms of the unit conflict resolution process. Thus all phenomena of behavior become measurable and graphically portrayable. This then is an essay about the integration of knowledge on the foundation that the unconscious creative process, a scientific conflict resolution phenomenon, is the integrative paradigm.

The stripes of the flag are the universal, but modifiable, syndromal unit process. The striped section of the flag represents the Universal Harmonic, the unit of the social sciences, and reflects the graphic representation of the six-role process. The flag's stripes consist of variations of the Conflict Resolution Process, the common denominator, the atomistic unit of all moral metaphors, religions, and ideologies. There are three sets of stripes.

One set recapitulates the Unit Process from art to science as presented in the first mural. A second set focuses on the cross-generational transmission of the pattern, as observed in the four consecutive generations of the Greek Cosmogony Myths. A third set addresses the cross-cultural variability of the Unit Process as it is used to depict four principal relational alternatives. Thus, the flag's stripes illustrate the unit, the unit's cross-generational transmission, and its variability and transformation.

The stripes interlock cross-generationally along with the six role states and transmit the particular process across generations. The interlocking of the four generations of the Greek Cosmogony conveys the evolving qualities of the transmitted pattern. This variability eases the recognition of four pronounced variations corresponding to the four major cultures; the Greek snake, the Mexican Indian feathered serpent, the Judaic scroll, and the Oriental dragon. These four cultural paradigms serve another function. They illustrate four relational modalities or diagnostic categories of everyday psychopathology.

The Stars of the Flag identifying the relational modality dimensions of religions and ideologies
The stars section presents the unit's cross-section as the power field integrating the cultural metaphors of the world, religions, and ideologies along their relational or attitudinal dimensions.

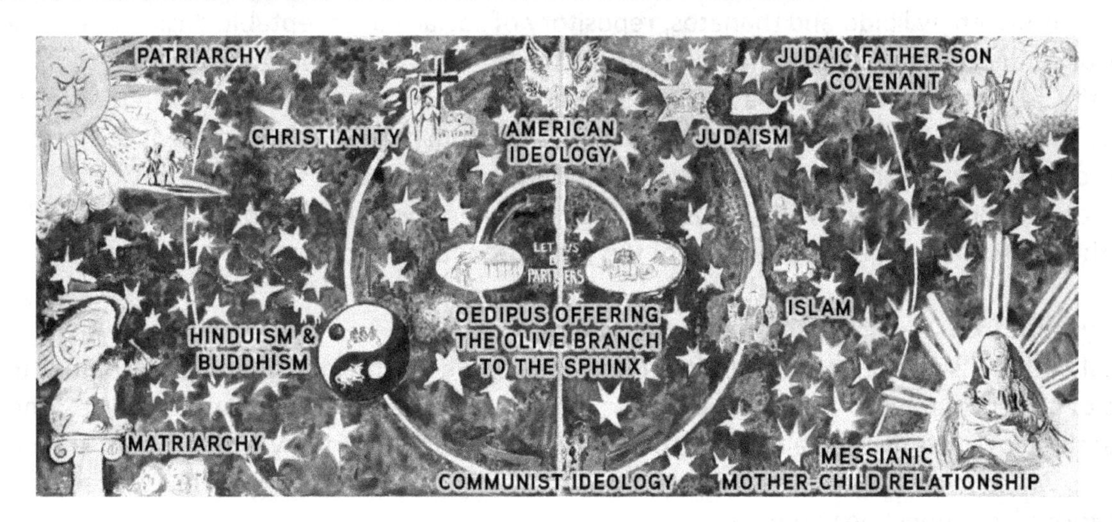

The stars of this flag are the many formally interrelated, world moral paradigms. They represent the cultural and ideological stories in their formal dimensions and interrelations. Unlike the disconnected stars of a usual flag, these stars are put on a map of formal distinctions. They are then interrelated to each other placed on suitable orbital positions. That implies that the constellations of the symbols of religions and cultures, the metaphors of the world: the Cross, the Star of David, the Islamic Crescent and Star, the Oriental Yin-Yang, the bear brandishing the communist hammer and sickle, and the capitalist eagle, the world's religions and economic philosophies are in specific relation to each other around the normative power field.

The Power Field has a specific structure. It consists of a system of concentric circles, a magnetic field with a power axis from left to right and with implicit connotations about cooperative clockwise and antagonistic counter-clockwise directions. Accordingly, the power field positioning reflects the formal properties of each cultural symbol as a measurable metaphor.
The placement of paradigms along this power field qualifies and quantifies the paradigms as alternative power choices entailing the respective syndromal emotional correlates. Thus, the cultural metaphors are given an accurate social/emotional formal qualitative and quantitative dimension on the power field in the context of each other's power dimensions, i.e., the Judaic is an entity qualified as cooperative dominance (or assertiveness), Christianity is characterized as the cooperative subordinacy choice, Islam is characterized by dominant antagonistic variation, (the Jihad as Holy war morality).
The four corners of the star section of the flag are occupied by four pronounced relational alternatives. The matriarchy and patriarchy on the left side indicate the antagonistic and polarized nature of the primitive

religions. The images indicate the parents frightening their children. The images of the religions on the right corners represent the cooperative Abrahamic religions. The parents are accepting and caring of their children.

The concept of the Flag of the United Metaphors highlights the sociological implications of the discovery of the orderly unconscious Conflict Resolution Process. A flag that unites moral orders is a flag of the conceptually united metaphors of the world, a truly international and cross-cultural flag. This flag integrates the conflicted and contradictory metaphors of diverse faiths as formally interrelated and quantitatively identified alternative ways of resolving conflict. It confirms that the metaphors of the world may be united by the fact that they all constitute quantifiable modulations of the universal Conflict Resolution Process and that they all fit together as complementary solutions. The impact of this message is significant. All ideologies are instantly reduced to partial truths, but they are also elevated to equivalent testimonials of the universal nature of the moral order seeking human unconscious.

CHAPTER THREE:
PARADIGM SHIFT FROM THE PROPOSITIONAL TO THE RELATIONAL METHOD

Freud defined the unconscious using several conceptual models (Freud, 1955). Initially as the Oedipal complex, viewed it as driven by libido and thanatos, repository of socially unacceptable desires. He established it as a process of conflict between three mental agencies the id, ego, and superego. He also described it as an energetic entity, also one manifested in a pattern of interpersonal relations reoccurring in therapy identified as transference. The Formal Theory introduced a paradigm shift from relying on the content of stories, the propositional method, axiomatic thinking, to identify what is universal in all stories, the plot of stories, as the formal interrelation of parts in a totality having the function of resolving conflicts. This observation introduced into psychology the relational method in the place of the propositional method.

Methodology: shift from the propositional to the relational method

The relational method is a shift from the arbitrariness of axiomatic formulations and philosophies to identifying the features of closed systems, in which we examine variables as interrelated by formulas. The conflict resolution process: the plot of stories pertains to the circumscribed totality of a story with a beginning middle and a moral end. It is within such a totality in which energy is conserved but transformed that we can observe internal order as formulas connecting variables.

Psychoanalysis' theoretical models rely on propositional logic (Sabelli, 1984). Propositional statements depend on the truth or falsity of their assumptions (Royce, Crouch, 2004). On the other hand, Formal Theory introduces the relational method, which studies circumscribed realms, such as a story as a perfect symbolic universe of emotions, as an energetic totality characterized by formally interrelated variables (Gensler, 2017). The formal relational analysis of the thought process identifies relations between parts within the totality of testable formula-bound variables. Thus, the relational method shifts our awareness from focusing on the content of stories as arbitrary truisms to recognizing the formal organization of emotions in an emotional continuum, like in a story, as interrelated parts, emotions, also as energetic transformations of one quantity, abiding by laws of science, here the physics of the pendulum oscillation and the formal operations of an equilibrial system predictably leading to a conflict resolution.

Exemplifying the differences between propositional versus relational method in the history of science

The Biblical story of Genesis and Freud's Oedipus Complex represent, methodologically, the axiomatic arbitrary non-relational analysis of moral and psychological phenomena. The great debate regarding Genesis focused on the correctness or falsity of the content of the creation story. Creationists supported it, evolutionists refuted it, yet both erred methodologically by focusing on the veracity or falsity of the content of Genesis as a story. The Formal Theory's relational interpretive approach views Genesis as a metaphor for the scientific nature of the creative process; Genesis in Greek means creation or creativity. The six days of creation leading to the Sabbath identifies metaphorically the unconscious' six-role states interrelated in the totality of a creation as a conflict resolution totality. The six days is a metaphor symbolizing the six roles of the emotional dialectic of the unconscious leading to the upgrading of order; six days are a metaphor of the transformative six emotions of the unit process. The day of rest is symbolic of the state of resolution.

Similarly, the assumption that the Oedipus Complex as a universal genetically determined order exemplifies the incorrectness of propositional thinking. The relational method provides a means of examining the Oedipus Complex as an episode in the context of the totality of the *Oedipus Rex* play as a dramatic system of six interrelated episodes or emotions leading to a resolution. The play begins with a conflict, the hubris of patricide and incest, and ends with its punishment. The Formal Theory examines the formal structure of the play as three acts, corresponding to six emotions, reflecting the conflict resolution unconscious. The dramatic conclusion shows the upgrading of order in the cathartic moral outcome of the play. The audience experiences the tragedy as an emotional six-role state rollercoaster departing from the hubris of a transgression, as an energetic load, and ending with the energetic transformation symbolized in the punishment of the hero/transgressor, thus confirming a societal norm reducing antagonism, affirming mastery and mutual respect between fathers and sons, instead of antagonism and alienation of transgressive relating. The drama resolves conflicts upgrading order/energy, accomplishing a normative improvement conveyed by its resolution.

The moral or conflict resolution significance of the play reflects the unconscious correcting the antagonistic gender relations structure reported in the matriarchal family of the Greek Cosmogony in which mothers, in alliances with their sons, murdered fathers. The formal theoretical view is that the drama corrects the norm of antagonistic matriarchy to the less antagonistic patriarchal family. Matriarchy interfered in the father-son relationship by supporting antagonism between fathers and sons. The *Oedipus Rex* play corrects this antagonistic relation between domestic partners identified in the Greek Cosmogony's power struggles as the alliance of a mother and sons against the father. The play changes this antagonistic, alienating alliance to the cooperative and mutually respectful relations between family members experienced upon the corrective completion of the play. This pattern of conflict resolution occurs in many Greek tragedies. They have had the function of transforming matriarchy's powerful antagonistic women, like Helen of Troy and her sister Clytemnestra, who killed her husband Agamemnon upon his homecoming from the Trojan War, to domesticated loyal cooperative, self-restrained partners, like Odysseus' wife Penelope, the heroine of the new moral order.

The axiomatic or propositional explanations advanced by Freud's Oedipus complex represent narrow, concrete truisms that have limited metaphorical significance and no scientific foundation. On the contrary, the relational method interprets the play as an abstract order following the formulas of science and logic. The unconscious conflict resolution then is viewed by the Formal Theory as a physiological, psychological, and sociological homeostatic natural science periodic phenomenon.

Simply said, the relational method allows us to analyze the unconscious as a conflict resolution process, an energetic transformation. It determines the unconscious as a mental function that seeks automatically the social adjustment of the individual by reducing psychological and sociological tensions. The unconscious then as a Conflict Resolution Process is the origin of all moral thinking, where morality is defined as conflict resolution through normative compliance or alternatively as normative change. The mind aspires for morality as normative compliance or deliberate normative restructuring to reduce the painful experience of psychic and social tensions. Thus, the Formal Theory connects meaningfully parts into totalities and advances the relational method to the abstractions of scientific formulas on the nature of the unconscious.

Methodological changes

The Formal Theory introduces this key methodological change in the evaluation of unconscious dynamics, shifting from the propositional to the relational method. This foundational change shifts the study of the unconscious from Freud's and Jung's multiple theoretical propositions to the formal and energetic analysis of the circumscribed creative process. In the place of the multiple models advanced by psychoanalytic theorists the Formal Theory focuses on one key assumption on the scientific nature of the creative process as resolving conflicts through the thought process analyzed as a circumscribed homeostatic energetic and formal transformation.

Specifically, Formal Theory defines the unconscious as having an orderly physical, energetic structure serving an adjustive normative moral or conflict resolution function identified as the upgrading of order that is increasing negative entropy, transforming labile psychic energy to stable social adjustment. This study introduces Formal Theory's thesis that the creative process reflects the unconscious automatically transforming energy, psychic tension, developed upon an individual's normative deviation, to sociological adjustment resolving conflicts as normative conciliation founded on the scientific analysis of the creative process. The creative process is defined as a conflict resolving homeostatic mechanism following the laws of two scientific phenomena, the Simple Harmonic Motion and Felix Klein's equilibrial principles.

While Freud defined libido as a sexually founded drive and Jung identified it as psychic energy stemming from the personal and collective unconscious, the Formal Theory identifies the unconscious as a purely physical energy transforming engine. Energy generated upon the personal experience of a normative deviation as though the psyche were a pendulum ball shifted away from its position of rest is transformed to moral order. The unconscious is conceived of as abiding by the laws of the physics of the Simple Harmonic Motion thus conceptualized with the constructs, formulas, and graphic portrayal of a physical energetic phenomenon. It is steered by formal operations determined by another phenomenon of science thus abiding by the laws of logic.

While Freud seeks repressed libidinally motivated phenomena and Jung explores archetypes in the process of individuation, the Formal Theory simply identifies emotions as energetic quantities requiring processing as an energetic transformation along the six-role state continuum departing from a distressing conflict and completed with spontaneous, spiritually meaningful social adjustment. The resolutions vary; they lead to four alternative types of conflict resolution. The unconscious transforms energy as an emotional dialectic consisting of six-role states, emotions, as three pendulum oscillations, a six emotions psychodynamic sequence driven by the three formal operations of the formula of equilibrial principles, to resolve conflicts as four alternative relational modalities.

The modalities establish a wellness psychodynamic personality typology. The Formal Theory unconscious is motivated by the need to transform unpleasant psychic tension to social comfort, establishing continuity between physiological, psychological, sociological, and scientific phenomena. Thus the Formal Theory (Levis, 1988a) replaces the many theoretical models by providing a coherent, scientifically rigorous conceptualization of the unconscious as a homeostatic physiological function reducing psychic tension, conflict, and increasing social adjustment.

This chapter reviews in detail the scientific, structure of the unconscious, following laws of logic and physics, as the core concept of psychology, and its relevance to psychological diagnosis, assessment, and the recognition of morality, rethinking psychology as the Moral Science, (Levis, 1988b).

This definition of the unconscious has broad relevance for psychology, assessment, pathology and therapy also in understanding religions. As such it is an entity that introduces morality as a natural science motivational force as the primary concept in all social sciences. The unconscious readily identified using creativity for self-discovery modifies education, therapy, and morality. It addresses thus the three key objectives of education: the integration of art and science, self-knowledge and clarity of moral values.

CHAPTER FOUR:
FORMAL THEORY'S ANALYSIS OF THE CREATIVE PROCESS AS A SCIENTIFIC PHENOMENON REFLECTING THE UNCONSCIOUS

The first observation: periodicity of a pattern

Research on the Formal Theory departed from the observation of a pattern that was repeated five times in the Greek Cosmogony that ended with the creation of a religion: the Greek culture's Olympic Gods. The orderly nature of the pattern was identified as consisting of six-role states by examining the interlocking of five successive generations perpetuating the transmission of the pattern and also its modification. The formal theoretical hypothesis was that the pattern, representing the unconscious, consisted of six interrelated role states, three connecting an individual with the parental and three with the filial generation (Figure 2). This observation led to identify the six-role states, the structure of the plot of stories, as a natural science phenomenon equated with three pendulum oscillations regarding the process as an energetic transformation.

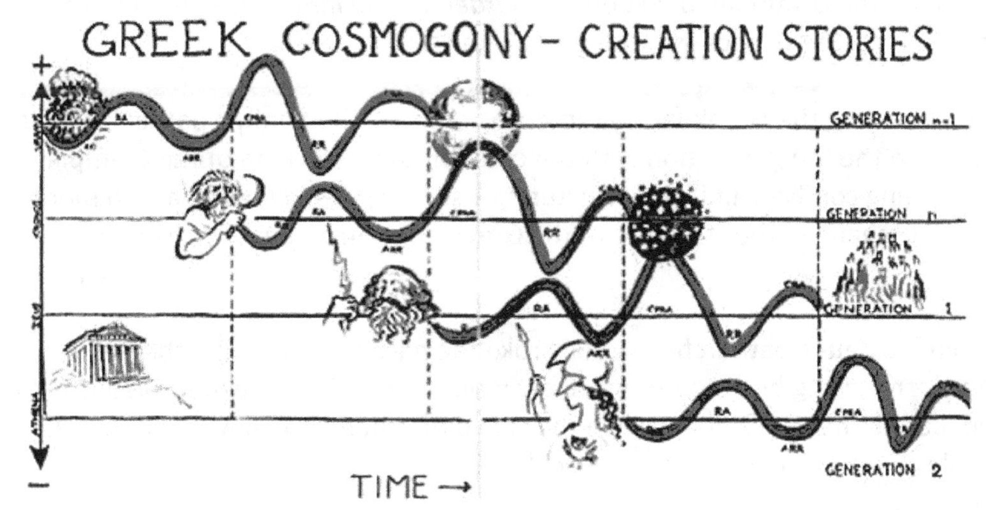

Observation #1, Mural #2 of the Sanctuary of the Wizard, Museum of the Creative Process illustrates the unfolding process in the Greek Cosmogony as a sine curve reoccurring across four generations of patricidal infanticidal behaviors. The insight on the nature of the unconscious originated in the observation of this periodic phenomenon. Periodicity was accounted for by the cross-generational transmission of the six-role state harmonic that resolved conflicts upgrading energy in terms of leading to a set of normative changes identified by the religion of the twelve Olympic Gods (Levis, 2011).

The Greek Creation Story identifies the pattern repeated in five generations of the Greek cosmogony analyzed as the unit of the conflict resolution process.

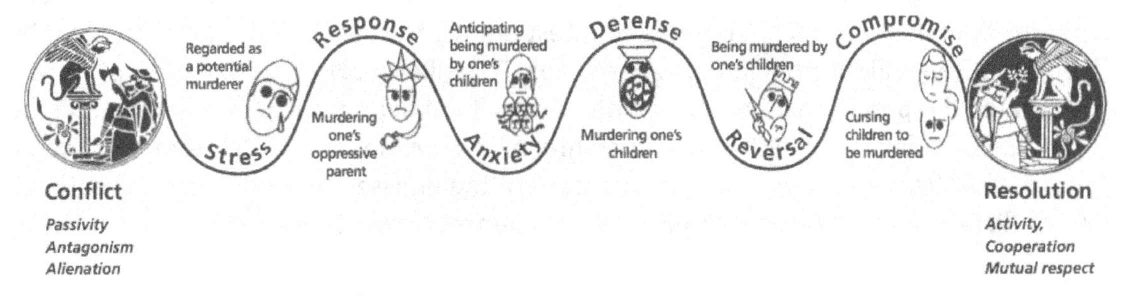

The unconscious is defined as a conflict resolution process integrating emotions and behaviors into syndromes of six interrelated role states predictably leading to social adjustment following three conflict resolution scientific principles as the innate motivational forces. These principles operating unconsciously steer the person to social adjustment as conflict reducing normative conciliation. The unconscious process may be graphically portrayed as a six-part harmonic oscillation. Its cross section as a system of concentric circles allows portraying the place of the person in its deviation from the normative center, the point of moral gravity. The diagrams illustrate the physical structure of the conflict resolution process as a natural science measurable oscillatory phenomenon.

The creative process reflects the unconscious as a conflict resolution phenomenon integrating six emotions and behaviors into the syndrome of interrelated role states predictably leading to a social adjustment, here the invention of the religion of the Olympic gods. The mural presents the six images of the Cosmogony cycle illustrating the six-role process as a syndromal entity illustrating the continuity of one action, murdering:

Stress, Role Oppression, corresponds to a son oppressed as murderous,
Response, Role Assumption, as the son murdering his father,
Anxiety, Anticipations of Role Reversal, anticipating being murdered by one's children,
Defense, Counterphobic Role Assumption, as murdering one's children counterphobically,
Reversal or Outcome, Role Reversal, as being murdered by one's children and
Compromise, Compromise Role Assumption, as cursing one's children to be murdered in their turn (Levis, 1988, and 2011).
The formal interpretation was that the creation stories illustrated the upgrading of order as a series of conflict resolutions. The resolutions represented the continuity of action, as *murder*, a verb integrating the six role states in each of the five generations of the Greek gods into the six-role pattern.

The five-generation pattern evolved resolving the Greek family's intense conflicts. The family's patricidal, infanticidal Oedipal conflicts were resolved in the 5th generation with the creation of the religion of the Olympian gods. Morality was generated by resolving conflicts and by restructuring a social system creating a new moral order. The conflict resolution effectively changed the structure of the Greek family from matriarchy to patriarchy.

Medusa's matriarchy was transformed to Zeus's patriarchy as Zeus broke the pattern of antagonistic domestic relations by eating up his wife, Metis, and giving birth to Athena a few months later. The dreaded Medusa, the primitive matriarch was beheaded, but her head was featured in the shield of Athena, the new goddess, illustrating the transformation of the role of women in the patriarchal culture.

The epics of Homer address the gender conflicts towards consolidating this new family institution. Helen, a run-away wife, was worth an epic war, the Iliad. Odysseus subduing sirens and matriarchs by himself, humanity's Odyssey led to Penelope, the loyal wife, consolidating the covenant of the vows as the condition for a happier family. Orestes and Electra, killing their mother put an end to matriarchy. Odysseus homecoming to the loyal spouse represented the inception of patriarchy. The new moral covenant established new roles for gender relations. Vows taking was the new norm based on mutual respect between men and women. The transition was not easy. Greek tragedies bear the names of many unhappy and angry women.

Tragedies as conflict resolution games, were the healing method of the dominant antagonistic Greek culture. The theater of Epidaurus built next to Argos, Mycenae, is a testimony of Greece's quest for emotional balance pursuing healing by dramatizing painful conflictual experiences. Tragedies inspired the analysis of the dramatic process. Aristotle examined the process as three acts with continuity of action: the process beginning from a hubris and ending with justice, deke, and catharsis as a painful moral development. The Roman scholars identified moral revelations with the Deus ex Machina, the descent of the emissary of gods on the theatrical stage. Dealing with family conflicts inspired dramaturgy, philosophy, science, democracy and the rules of Olympic games.

The second observation: the cross-cultural differences in resolving conflicts
In the Greek family the father son relation was antagonistic, while in the Judaic the father son covenant was the cooperative alternative. In matriarchy men as fathers were victims and in patriarchy they were masters. Antagonism and cooperation, were related as opposite; passivity and activity were related as reciprocal to each other. Reciprocal and opposite were formal relations. These operations integrated the religions as formally related alternative conflict resolutions.

This observation inspired me to learn about formal operations and to identify the Kleinian formula of Identity as equal to the product of three other formal operations. I introduced the formal relations to the-six role process and there I developed the new insights on the nature of the unconscious as both an energetic and a formal transformational process. The unconscious used the formal operations resolving one's conflicts by changing automatically one's attitude from a state of passivity, antagonism and alienation to a state of mastery, cooperation and mutual respect.

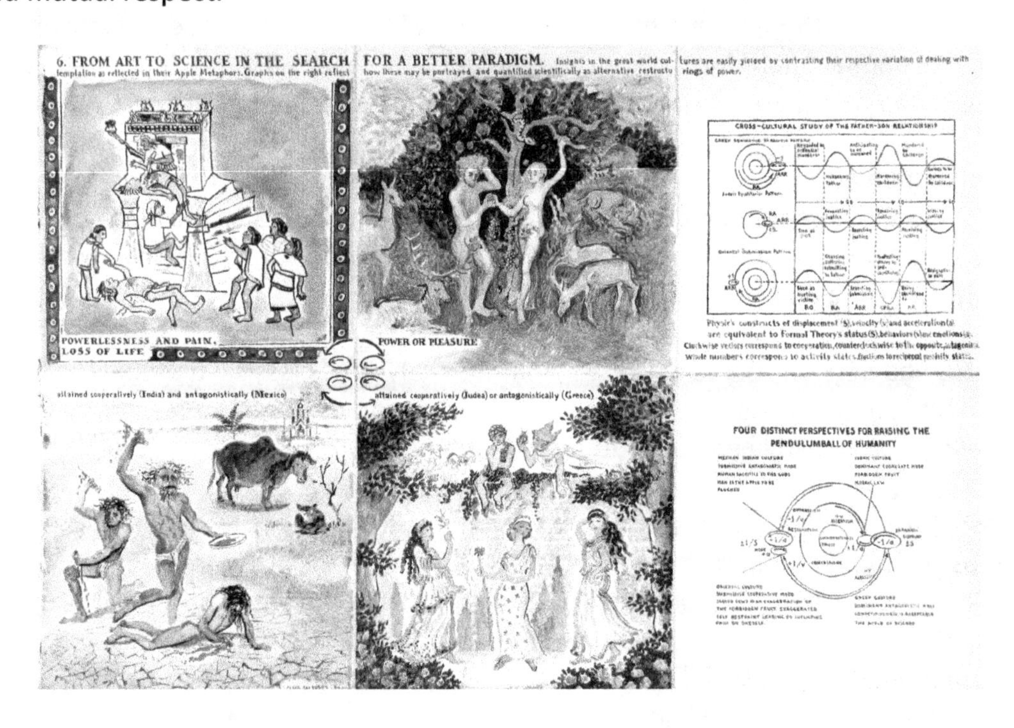

Observation #2, Mural #6 of the Sanctuary of the Wizard, Museum of the Creative Process.
Mural #6 illustrates four cultural alternative ways of dealing with temptation identifying the range of power and attitude choices and their graphic representations. The four cultures represent the spectrum of four formal alternative ways in resolving conflicts along the dichotomies of power and powerlessness and cooperative versus antagonistic attitude. The Aztec eagle versus snake myth and the Greek Cosmogony Oedipal dynamics represent antagonistic relating, while the Indian ascetic and the Judaic monotheistic stories represent cooperative relating. Both the Greek and the Judaic cultures strived for dominance, while the Indian and Aztec cultures represent the pursuit of the reciprocal alternative: subordinacy. The cultures were configured as formally interrelated and as graphically portrayable with vectorial differences within the 'normative field of concentric circumferences' (Levis, 2011).

I contrasted the Greek creation story with three other creation stories as providing formal alternative resolutions of conflict as coveting the apple symbol of power, contrasting their respective metaphors in dealing with temptation. I analyzed the differences and detected formal continuity between them. They resolved conflicts differently from each other, but the resolutions were formally interrelated. The Greek antagonistic father-son relationship was viewed as the opposite of the Judaic religion's cooperative respectful father-son-covenant relationship. The Judaic apple was forbidden versus the Greek apple was coveted. It was inscribed to the fairest. Similarly the Indian apple corresponded to the sacred cow and people chose asceticism, while the Aztec culture regarded the heart of the sacrificial person as the apple of the gods.

The four cultures differed along two formal distinctions, opposite alternatives attitudes of cooperation versus antagonism, and reciprocal distinctions as choices of activity/power versus passivity/powerlessness. India, people sacrificing themselves, cooperative attitude, versus being victims of sacrifice in the Aztec tradition relating antagonistically. The Aztec and Indian cultures accept powerlessness, while the Greek and Judaic cultures aspire for power, the apple.

While this periodic process was accounted for as an energetic transformation, departing from chaos and leading to order or negative entropy, these cultural differences were explained as four alternative ways of resolving conflict, reflecting two equilibrial dichotomies in relating along the reciprocal and opposite alternatives. These formal alternatives were accounted for by the formal operations of the trays of a scale (Flavel, 2015). It was concluded that the unconscious transforms energy of conflict into relief of tension upon the reconciliation of opposites and reciprocals in the moral or social adjustment conclusion of the six-role process. The Formal Theory explained the unconscious thought process both as a natural science periodic energetic phenomenon and one following formal relational operations to conflict resolution. This formulation defined the unconscious as a conflict resolution process with physical and formal natural science dimensions.

The six roles: stress, response, anxiety, defense, reversal, and compromise, were the syntax of the verb murdering corresponding to three pendulum oscillations. The relational changes as the dialectic of the passive and active, antagonistic to cooperative forms etc. were the grammar of the verb murdering corresponding to three formal operations restoring balance to the trays of a scale.

This dramatic process had been observed by Aristotle in the analysis of classical tragedies as having a continuity of action, a beginning, middle, and a transformative or moral end corresponding to catharsis, identified as entelechy. We redefine it as negative entropy (Butcher & Gassner, 1951). (Halliwell, 1998).

The graphic representation of the unconscious

The process as an oscillation is graphically portrayable as a sine curve. Its cross-section is presented as a set of three concentric circles quantifying the normative field in terms of power, as diametrically opposed positions, and vectors portray relational opposite choices along the opposite forms of cooperation and antagonism. This unconscious is the unit entity of the social sciences. It is the origin of all psychological and moral behavior. As it is measurable, the premise may be tested and validated.

The unconscious as a periodic phenomenon

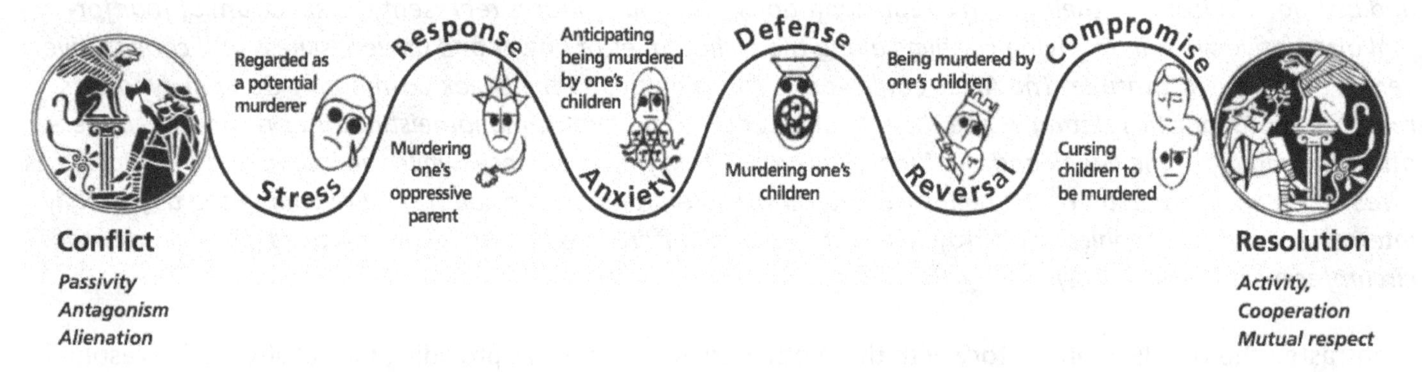

The Formal Theory identifies the creative process, the plot of stories as an innate homeostatic, energy transformative, and attitude modifying process, as a natural science moral order physiological phenomenon. The energetic transformation follows the laws of the Simple Harmonic Motion. It completes the transformation of energy in the span of three pendulum oscillations guided by the three equilibrial operations of the Kleinian formula of operations restoring balance to the trays of a scale.

Periodicity was accounted for by the cross-generational transmission of the six-role state harmonic attributed to three pendulum oscillations graphically portrayed as a six-part harmonic. The function of this physiological process is the reduction of psychic and social tension coinciding with the individual's normative adjustment (Levis, 2011). Analysis of the antagonistic father-son relationship portrayed as incremental polarization in the normative field. The cross-section of the harmonic is presented as a system of concentric circles portraying the sociological normative positions of interrelated behaviors. The individuals in conflict are positioned as ellipses on the circumference in reciprocal deviations. Intensity is presented as the distance from the normative center, the point

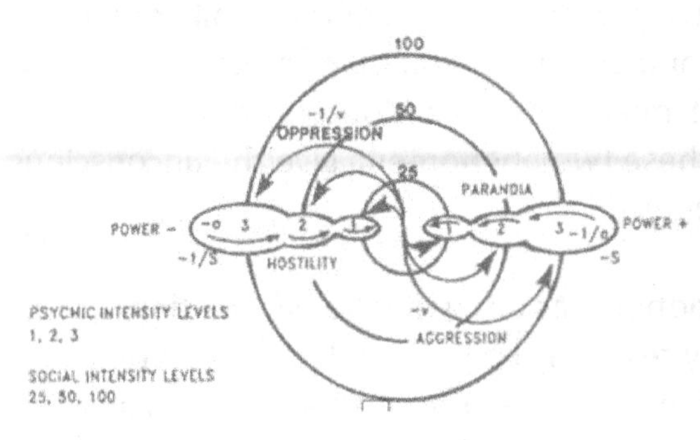

of moral gravity. The personal tension presented as vectors within the ellipses identify emotions as forces of acceleration in reciprocal relation to deviations. The two diagrams: the lengthy six-role process and personal psychic systems in energetic balance, illustrate the physical structure of the unconscious conflict resolution process as a natural science measurable oscillatory phenomenon.

The scientific analysis of the creative process

I identified the structure of the story reflecting the unconscious as a scientific phenomenon abiding by the laws of two phenomena of science first, by examining periodicity in the repetition of a pattern in the five generations of the Greek cosmogony and second, by contrasting the resolutions of the alternative creation stories. I analyzed the periodicity of the pattern of the Greek cosmogony as corresponding to an energetic cyclic six-role process transmitted from generation to generation and there I detected the dynamics of the pendulum oscillation, the Simple Harmonic Motion. I identified the alternative conflict resolutions as interrelated by formal operations, such as the equilibrial operations restoring balance in the trays of a scale.

Periodicity of a pattern in five generations of the Greek cosmogony was analyzed as the unit of the conflict resolution process reflecting the unconscious as consisting of both a syndrome of six-role states transforming energy and as alternative resolutions, as the four relational modalities, each corresponding to a cultural moral system and a human personality type.

The six role states are illustrated as episodes in the lifecycle of Kronos, Greek for Time. They presented as six events, six-role states, predictably leading to a conflict resolution as the religion of the Olympians. Kronos' lifecycle is completed with the temple of goddess Athena, the temple of the Virgin, Parthenon. The resolution corresponds to restructuring the family role relations from cruel matriarchy to sanctified even handed patriarchy.

The cultural differences in resolving conflicts were presented metaphorically as dealing with temptation in the symbolism of the apple. The apple is the person's heart in the Aztec culture of life sacrifice; in Greece it is the apple of discord, men and women competing for power, a reward. In India it is the sacred cow with men seeking self-sacrifice; in Judea the apple is the forbidden fruit. I theorized that religions evolved as normative institutions that identified the alternative ways of resolving conflict improving the family institution. I created a game of cards Moral Monopoly. The suits of the deck as cultures evolved resolving conflict. The four suits corresponded to the four modalities. The four signs were formally interrelated, spade to heart, and reflected the spontaneous progression of improvements in resolving conflicts in the family institution. The suits evolve from matriarchy, to patriarchy, through asceticism to monotheism and the messianic religions.

Thus, I identified the unconscious as a homeostatic phenomenon transforming psychic conflict to social adjustment as motivation, seeking pleasure as a social and as an energetic experience, and as a phenomenon abiding by the laws of two scientific phenomena.

The difference between the thought process and the Simple Harmonic Motion's, SHM, perpetual motion

The mind achieves an energetic transformation upgrading order into pleasurable moral growth in three pendulum oscillations guided by the three formal attitude modifying operations. Like photosynthesis in plants transforming sunlight into sugar, flowers and fruit, three formal operations of the human unconscious transform conflict energy automatically to conflict resolutions, art capturing moral growth as wisdom.

The simplicity and user friendliness of the formal energetic premise is in that it generates meaningfulness.

Science establishes respect for the religions by observing the creative process in terms of the familiar plot and moral of stories. The science is readily demonstrated in the formal and energetic analysis of metaphors, following the dynamics of the two scientific phenomena: the laws of the Simple Harmonic Motion and of the equilibrial scale. The practical advantage of introducing science is in that these two phenomena give the unconscious their constructs, formulas and their respective graphic representations.

The theory explained the plot of stories as a cyclic pattern of six emotions, as energetic transformations, with the function of reducing psychic tension, experienced as conflict, by resolving conflicts in the context of a desirable attitudinal sociological adjustment. The theory examined the creative process as a natural science energetic transformation, with measurable dimensions and a homeostatic physiological and sociological moral function: conflict resolution. The unconscious was thus conceived as an energy and attitude-transformation mechanism proceeding to conflict resolution defined as attaining a moral end. The unconscious process transforms unpleasant psychic energy, restoring the emotional rest state, by transforming the energetic disturbance of one's emotional balance through attitude changes leading to the individual's relief from stress through social adjustment and emotional expiation or catharsis.

This adjustive psychic mechanism unfolds as a six-role state dialectic in the mind of the actor: stress, response, anxiety, defense, reversal and compromise. One of the states is anxiety as anticipations of role reversal. The person's anticipations are ascribed to powerful external authorities; in cultures these evolve into divine figures, monitoring one's conduct as deviations from acceptable norms, reminding the person to conform. Compromise behaviors follow. They consist in making concessions. In religions these evoke the need to offer sacrifices to expiate from one's sense of deviation. The process has pertinence to psychological and sociological reality.

Motivation as the psychological need to resolve conflicts

Formal Theory's unifying abstraction is that the mechanical process conducting conflict resolution transforms energy through an innate attitude-modifying process. This process transforms psychic energy, distress, to social adjustment experienced as pleasant emotional growth and as moral or social adjustment. Thus the Formal Theory conceived the creative process as an energetic transformation process motivated by the pleasure of reducing psychic tension and improving social adjustment. The transformation was completed in three pendulum oscillations as six emotions, guided by three formal operations automatically transforming one's attitude, restoring peace of mind, the rest state, peace in the person's emotional system.

The dialectic of six emotions as an energetic quantity, was complying to the laws of the pendulum oscillation. The six emotions are forms of one energetic quantity modified by three formal operations reflecting the individual's relational disposition within the social or normative system. Emotions, states of passivity, as energies are transformed to actions as states of mastery, and actions are transformed to emotions, back and forth.

The unconscious, the core psychological entity, is defined as a natural science entity, an energetic transformation following the laws of the pendulum oscillation and the laws of the equilibrial scale. The first is an energetic process, the plot of stories, as a six-role state emotional oscillation, clinically identifiable as a syndrome, an emotional rollercoaster; the second component is the conflict resolutions determined by the combination of the three formal operations of the Kleinian formula. The formal operations identify four types of resolutions, the relational modalities, alternative wellness diagnoses.

The Unconscious Abiding by Two Scientific Phenomena as a Mechanism that Transforms Energy into Attitude Change, that is, Moral Order

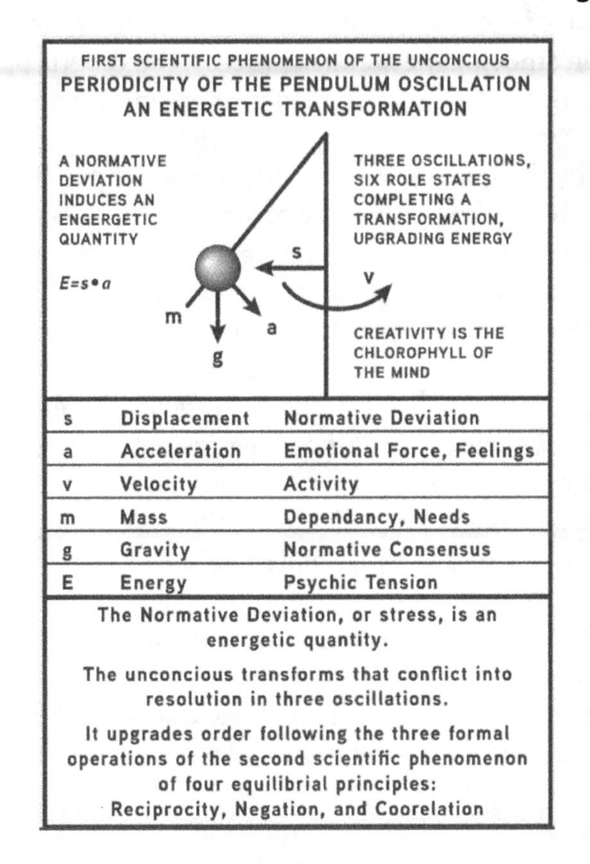

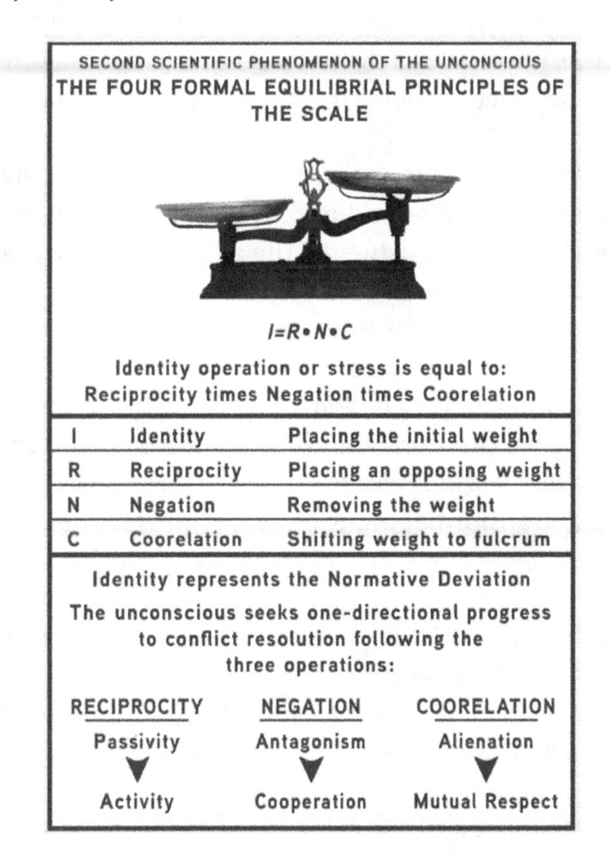

The unconscious, the core psychological entity, is defined as a natural science entity, an energetic transformation following the laws of the pendulum oscillation and the laws of the equilibrial scale.

The oscillations are guided by the set of three formal equilibrial operations. We know them as Felix Klein's set theory as operations applied by Piajet to the balance of the trays of a scale. The mind uses them as innate attitude-changing formal operations restoring balance to the emotional system by transforming a person's attitude within the social system.

The oscillations are emotional energetic states affected by motivation defined by three formal equilibrial operations as in Felix Klein's equilibrial formula:

$$I=RxNxC$$

Identity, or conflict, is equal to the product of three formal operations restoring the balance of a system: Reciprocity, R, transforms passivity to activity, Negation ,N, transforms antagonism to cooperation, and Correlation, C, transforms alienation to mutual respect.

Piajet illustrated the formal operations with the three operations restoring the balances of the trays of a scale.

The equilibrial operations transform energy from psychic conflict as passivity, antagonism and alienation to resolution, social adjustment, as mastery, cooperation and mutual respect.

This energetic process is a conflict resolution mechanism, that addresses both one's emotional state and her disposition toward others. The unconscious is a natural science, biologically supported moral or social order phenomenon. The structure and function of the creative process was identified as a scientific conflict resolution or a moral order mechanism defining the unconscious as the atomistic unit of the social sciences. It was identified as a natural science moral mechanism that is measurable and that can be graphically portrayed.

The process abiding by the laws of the SHM and the equilibrial scale then becomes a natural science phenomenon, and one of psychological and moral order as it resolves personal and societal conflicts. The Formal Theory thus resolves the conceptual problem of the integration of the humanities and the sciences by providing psychology's unconscious the natural science foundation in studying the creative process, the orderly plot of stories as a conflict resolving mechanism with the characteristics of a natural science energetic phenomenon.

A conflict, whatsoever, is energy processed automatically by the unconscious mechanism leading to the reduction of psychic discomfort or tension through attitude change, the person conforming to the social norms, achieving a sense of adjustment. The structure of the creative process is a six-role state energy transformation process. The transformation occurs spontaneously as conflict energy is experienced as unpleasant. The energetic correction unfolds as three pendulum oscillations following three formal attitude-modifying operations.

The two natural science phenomena, the SHM and the equilibrial principles of the scale, guide the emotional/energetic unconscious process. They are the software of the unconscious. This conflict resolution mechanism defines the unconscious as a natural science energetic periodic phenomenon with a certain function, energy and attitude transformation. The creative process unconscious as a unit conflict resolution mechanism, a periodic entity, becomes the object for the scientific study of both psychology and morality.

The unconscious completes the energetic transformation in three pendulum oscillations, amounting to six formally interrelated emotions: stress and response, anxiety and defense, reversal, and compromise. This series of role states is guided by three formal attitude modifying formal operations transforming conflict defined as a state of passivity, antagonism, and alienation to the state of resolution defined as mastery, cooperation, and mutual respect.

Conflict resolution, attitude correction, leading to social adjustment is defined emotionally as the moral unconscious. Understanding the energetic and formal nature of the unconscious makes psychology into the Science of Conflict Resolution or in brief the Moral Science. Thus, conflict resolution, an energetic and moral order transformation becomes the atomistic unit, the scientific moral paradigm.

The unconscious then is seen as a unit entity that has a physical, energetic structure and a formal conflict resolution, or relational emotional transformative function. The six-role process is the mental heartbeat, and the formal relational resolution is the unconscious' moral compass. These two components are identified by the two instruments of the Conflict Analysis Battery, its inventory identifies the modality and its dozen metaphor creation tasks identify the syndrome. The assessment validates the theoretical premise by identifying a test taker's relational modality and its manifestation as a syndrome of six emotions leading to a conflict resolution, as being meaningful and helpful by the person, who can attest of becoming conscious of the unconscious.

The pleasure principle motivational force

The six-role process entity is the syndromal organization of emotions as a conflict resolution mechanism, where conflicts are experienced upon an individual's normative deviation generating psychic tension in the individual's mind. Motivation is the need for relief of tension experienced as pleasure upon the transformation of conflict energy to order coinciding with the return of the pendulum to its rest state, experienced as a normative conciliation. Thus, the unconscious process is a homeostatic mechanism reducing psychic and social tension through normative conciliation or alternatively through normative change

The Epistemology of the Unconscious: The Physics and Logic of Mental Operations

The unconscious mind has the function of transforming conflict energy to moral growth, as personal and social change. This inner-need for resolution as transformation of energy guides behaviors, defining motivation as the pursuit of conflict resolution following the formal and moral principles of mastery, cooperation, and mutual respect. The unconscious then corrects personal deviations modifying one's attitude seeking social adjustment or inner justice.

The plot of stories reflects this scientific and moral unconscious as the unit of the social sciences as the formal organization of parts/emotions/role-states in the conflict resolving structure of one's stories. Formal analysis applied to the totality of a story identifies the unconscious as the processing of emotions pursuing compromises.

Formal Theory applies physics and logic to the realm of emotions and societal norms as a moral, social, and personal transformative entity. The physical structure and the moral function of the dramatic totality define the unconscious as the atomistic unit of the social sciences, the engine upgrading emotional order. The study of the dramatic plot of stories bridges psychology with morality and science. The unconscious is the origin of all moral thought. For humans, the unconscious is like the chlorophyll in the realm of plants; it binds energy into moral growth.

The Formal Theory builds on the physics and logic of two equilibrial phenomena: the formulas of energetic transformations of the pendulum oscillation and the formal operations correcting imbalance in the trays of a scale (Klein, 1945). According to the Formal Theory, the unconscious process consists of six-role emotional and energetic states connected by three formal operations transforming conflict as a state of passivity to one of activity, of antagonism to one of cooperation, and one of alienation to one of mutual respect.

Pendulum Oscillation: The creative process was examined as having the structure of the Simple Harmonic Motion (Figure 6) interpreting the six-role pattern as representing three pendulum oscillations with the energetic quantity conserved but modified. The interlocked generations perpetuated the pattern but allowed resolutions as relational transformations in every generation. Resolutions were experienced as conservation of energy leading to negative entropy, a state of stable energy, referred to as the rest position or the end state upon a story's moral conclusion as normative adjustment.

Figure 6. The Pendulum Oscillation.

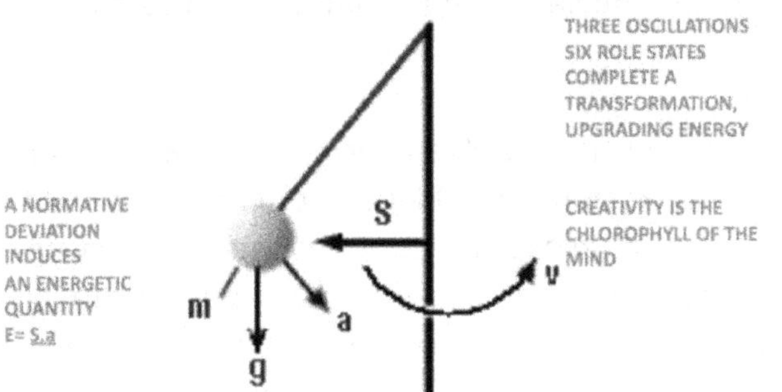

The transformation of a conflict to a resolution is an emotional and energetic process that has the characteristics of the Simple Harmonic Motion, the pendulum oscillation. The unconscious experiences conflict as a deviation from a norm in a parallel fashion as a pendulum upon its displacement in the field of gravity.

There are three variables, or constructs in the physics of the pendulum oscillation, that help to understand the physical nature of the experience of conflict as an energetic and directional phenomenon: norms, emotions, and behaviors as interrelated. These are the concepts of the normative field: Displacement, S, corresponds to the normative deviation within the structure of a social system, Acceleration, F, corresponding to emotions and Velocity, V, corresponding to behaviors. These variables are in formal relation to each other specified by the trigonometric formulas of:

S, normative distance = R sin w,
F, acceleration or emotions, motivation = negative R sin w
and V, behaviors = R cosine w
Where R corresponds to a 'role' behavior.

Resolution occurs as the energy E is transformed into work performed mentally or socially as an attitude and a normative change. The equilibrial dynamics of the unconscious restore the state of rest, through an energetic upgrading, in three pendulum oscillations.

The mind experiences a force of acceleration F, opposite to the displacement, S.
F is emotions, proportional, and opposite to the normative displacement. K is a constant, assumed to vary with individual responsiveness.

$$F = -KS$$

Within Formal Theory, conflict as a normative deviation S of a given mass, dependency needs, is experienced as an energetic quantity equal to the product of displacement S times the dependency needs F:

$$E = S \times F.$$ (F for the Force of acceleration opposite to the deviation S).

This energy E corresponds to the psychic tension experienced upon any normative deviation. This is the driving force energizing the Conflict Resolution Process into a pendulum oscillation. It represents the motivational need to transform this energy through the resolution process. The unconscious transforms this energy from chaos, or unstable energy, to sociological and emotional order, a stable energetic state. Order is identified as the normative conciliation or conformity, the individual experiencing mutual respect with the norms of the social system. This reconciliation reduces the psychic tension experienced by the individual and defines moral order as a new psycho-social logical agreement as the definition of 'conflict resolution.' The variables of this unconscious are determined by the six-role state energetic structure of the oscillation and by its formally determined relational parameters.

The unconscious as a conflict resolving process is about emotions conceived of as energetic quantities generated through induction. The emotions are like electricity generated in a spool opposing changes experienced through its rotation in a magnetic field. The unconscious generates psychic tension as it resists change upon an individual's shift within the societal magnetic/normative field. A person being oppressed generates hostility, while one transgressing experiences guilt; both emotions oppose the respective social shifts. Cooperative conduct generates positive emotions. Assertiveness generates considerateness; concessions generate hope for rewards. Conflict then may be defined as the energy generated by the deviation of the self within the normative field, defined by the formulas listed above.

Each of the six-role states, as emotions, are energetically charged; they are inter-transformable types of energy; passivity is experienced as a state of dynamic energy and activity as the state of kinetic energy. Stabilizing or upgrading the energy propels the individual unconsciously to resolution as societal conformity, respect of universal norms/rules, experienced as relief of tension coinciding with emotional growth. This is the moral end of stories and the beginning of religious philosophies. Religions are psychological phenomena respected as normative institutions that have evolved as intuitive discoveries of the principles of conflict resolution.

Conflict resolution is a process defined as an energetic transformation coinciding with emotional 'work.' The energy generated upon a normative deviation: the individual deviating within the gravitational or magnetic field of one's culture, is transformed to order, negative entropy, entelechy, meaning, creations, and resolution through attitudinal change as normative compliance. Resolution coincides with arresting the mental oscillation by completing the six-step three formal operations unit entity. Upon conflict resolution, the motion stops as its energy is conveyed into the performance of moral or abstract thinking work. The work consists of the individual's change of attitude (embracing the cultural order) or alternatively in the individual negotiating a social or normative change, as the condition for the completion of a resolution.

The Equilibrium of Scales' Formal Operations Model, the Relational and Moral Variables of the Unconscious
The unconscious, as a phenomenon of physics, abides by the law of the conservation of energy and, as a phenomenon of formal organization, abides by the laws of mathematics and the logic of the equilibrial trays of a scale (Klein, 1945). Thus, the unconscious was examined following the three formal operations of the equilibrial scale as determining the alternative moral directions identified as the four alternative ways of resolving

conflicts. The model of formal operations governing the equilibrial trays of a scale has been studied by Piaget as pertaining to the conservation of intellectual constructs (Piaget, 2015). We use the formal operations method to explain conservation of emotional states instead of unemotional/cognitive or intellectual constructs.

THE SECOND SCIENTIFIC PHENOMENON OF THE UNCONSCIOUS:
The three formal equilibrial principles of the scale

I=RxNxC

Identity operation or stress is equal to the product of: Reciprocity times Negation times Correlation

Equilibrium of the trays of the scale.
The unconscious as a phenomenon of energy abides by the law of the conservation of energy, and as one of formal operations, it abides by the laws of mathematics and logic of the equilibrial trays of a scale
(Felix Klein, 1945).

Differences between Piaget's Epistemology and that of the Formal Theory

Piaget considered the mental formal operations as reversible, while Formal Theory considers the emotional process as one-directional, as it seeks conflict resolution. Conservation of Freud's cathexis as the physical energy of emotions is the key to the continuity of the process from the beginning to the moral end, the resolution of a conflict. The process is about the transformations of the conserved emotional energy, in relational balance following the formal operations of the trays of a scale as an equilibrial system. Resolution is simply and universally manifested in the formal structure of the symbolic universe described by the principal law of the set theory illustrated with the equilibrial trays of the scale. The psyche abides by these laws. Morality as resolution is simply and universally manifested in the formal restructuring of the symbolic universe described by the laws of the equilibrial scale. Relational changes may be observed in the organization of associations in every sample of creativity. The following formula explains the alternative pathways of restoring emotional balance:

I=RNC

Accordingly, change or stress as the Identity (I) operation is in equilibrial balance with the product of three other formal operations: Reciprocity (R), Negation (N), and Correlation (C).
An identity operation as a weight placed on a tray may be offset or balanced out by the three different operations: reciprocity transforming passivity to activity, as adding an equal weight on the other tray, opposition or Negation, transforming antagonism to cooperation, as removing the weight, and third by Correlation, transforming alienation to mutual respect, as a shift of the weight on the fulcrum. The moral responses of the mind may seek balance along all or one of the three formal operations.

Equivalents in Emotional and Behavioral Transactions

1. Reacting by reciprocating transforming passivity to activity, the morality of an eye for an eye, as balancing the scale by placing a weight on the other tray.
2. Alternatively, reacting to antagonism with cooperation as in asceticism and the Christian ethic of responding as equivalent to removing the weight on the loaded tray.
3. Responding to alienation with mutual respect as in understanding is exemplified by the father-son covenant: it corresponds to grasping connections, correlating facts and factors into formulas of science or philosophies; this type of relating is equivalent to shifting the cursor on the fulcrum.

The mental responses to a stressor seek balance along all or one of the three formal operations. The conflict resolution process then unfolds spontaneously from a conflict defined as passivity, antagonism, and alienation to resolution as mastery, cooperation, and mutual respect. At the point of conflict resolution, the trays of the mental scale are in an equilibrial balance, experienced by the person as the restoration of the state of rest.

The formal alternatives clarify personality types as responding to stressors along the alternative relational modalities. The personality types correspond to the range of alternative formal operations determining resolutions. The religions of the world evolved as discoveries of science by identifying the alternative equilibrial principles and the respective relational modalities. Formal analysis integrates the religions of the world as the range of relational modalities into the Moral Science.

Differences between mind and machines

The consequence of identifying the structure of the mental process with the two mechanical models allows us to introduce their constructs and formulas into the study of behavior. Physics and logic become the conceptual language or epistemology of the social sciences. Although the mind abides by the natural laws of these two equilibrial machines, the pendulum, and the scale, it differs from them in several ways.

1. The pendulum differs from the mind in the sense that the mind converts the energy of the oscillation into useful work, the development of connections, whereas the pendulum oscillates until its energy is dissipated. The emotional dialectic of a six-part conflict resolution process achieves its goal, conflict resolution, in six exchanges, and then it stops oscillating. Resolution is completed upon the third cycle, as the mind transforms the energy of conflict to order and goes to the state of rest. So, the mental equilibrial oscillation differs from mechanical Simple Harmonic Motion in that it transforms energy as modifying attitudes; it completes the work of resolving a conflict, increasing moral order, and it thus upgrades the energy of the system, I.e., the relational pattern communicated in the circumscribed length of a story.

2. The mental scale differs from mechanical equilibrial scales as it spontaneously seeks the restoration of the mental equilibrium. The formal mental process is homeostatic. It automatically restores balance as its function; this differs from the mechanical scale where the equilibrium is reversible. The mind proceeds one directionally, reducing stressful tension and restoring the mental equilibrium. The equilibrial trays of the mental scale self-correct by transforming the role states energy along three formal operations from passivity to activity, its reciprocal, from antagonism to cooperation, its opposite, and from alienation to mutual respect, its correlative. These principles are reinforced by psychic comfort, which varies modified by one's personality type, but also by societal norms, which have identified these principles through their normative institutions (Levis, 2016).

The conceptual equivalences between scientific constructs and formulas and psychological variables introduced above are summarized in the table below as the Ten Levels of the Formal Analysis Profile as the Scientific Laws Underlying Moral Order. The implication of the introduction of scientific unconscious entails radical innovation rethinking psychology's concepts and respective disciplines.

Postulate 1: The Process Is an Equilibrial System Obeying the Laws of Mathematical Groups.
The elements of an ideational universe are formally interrelated ideas as determined by the laws of mathematical groups and the logic of relations.
The Laws of Inverse:
Opposite States:
cooperation + antagonism, cancel each other out: $a+(-a) = 0$
Reciprocal States:
activity and passivity, yield the totality: $a \times 1/a = I$
Formal operations are also conceptualized as the set of equilibrial principles, formal operations restoring

balance to a scale following the formula of Invers equal to the product of reciprocity, negation and correlation:
I=RxNxC
The formal operations are innate attitude modifying forces leading the emotional transformation of passivity, antagonism and alienation to activity, cooperation and mutual respect.

Postulate 2: The Process Is A Natural Science Equilibrial Phenomenon Obeying the Laws of the Physics of the Simple Harmonic Motion. The Conflict Resolution Process may be conceptualized with the constructs and formulas of the Simple Harmonic Motion.
The Constructs of Physics:
Displacement: S = Power, Social Status.
Acceleration: a = Motivational Force
Velocity: v = Behaviors,
Mass: m = Emotional Investment

Postulate 3: The Process Is an Energetic Phenomenon
Conflicts are energetic quantities whose intensity is determined as the product of the subject's dependency needs times this individual's displacement from his/her equilibrial position.
Level 3: Energetic Analysis, Conflict is Energy
E = FxS
Conflict is the product of : F = Dependency or Motivational Needs times S = Social status shift = normative displacement

Postulate 4: The Energy of The Process Is Conserved
The oscillation of the Conflict Resolution Process consists of the inter-transformation of energetic modalities whose sum total is conserved.
Level 4: Transformation of Energies abides by the Law of Conservation of energy.
Etotal = E dynamic + E kinetic + E momentum
Etotal = Epsychic + E social + E Biological

Postulate 5: Emotions are a Force Directly Proportional And Opposite To An Equilibrial Disturbance as the Normative Deviation
The motivational force (acceleration: a) that a person in conflict experiences is proportional and opposite to the social status shift from the position of rest (displacement: S).
Level 5: Conflict Analysis: The Force is proportional and opposite to the social status shift, the Displacement Relationship: a = -1/2 KxS

Postulate 6: The Process Is Defined As A Periodic Phenomenon
The Conflict Resolution Process, the six-role dialectic pattern, is the periodic trigonometric function of its three covariant constructs: emotions (a), behavior (v), and displacement (S).
Level 6: Syndromal Analysis The Periodic Nature of Behavioral Phenomena
a = -ac sin H
v = vc cos H
s = a sin H

Postulate 7: The Process May Be Portrayed Graphically
The Conflict Resolution Process may be portrayed as a sine curve and its cross-section, the Power Field as a circumference. Ellipses in the Circle Power Field illustrate one individual's set of mental Self-Other representations or a set of interacting individuals in a reciprocal relationship to each other orbiting the Power Circle.
Level 7: Graphic Analysis The Graphic Portrayal of Behavior The Structural & Longitudinal Drawings

Postulate 8: The Formal Variations Of The Process Lead To A Taxonomy Of Four Syndromal Alternatives: From this perspective, we distinguish clinically four key alternative relational syndromal modalities.
Level 8: Diagnostic Analysis Relational Modality and The Syndromal Organization of Behavior
Dominance vs. Subordinacy • Antagonism vs. Cooperation • Alienation vs. Affiliation

Postulate 9: The Energetic Intensity Of The Process Is Measurable: The Conflict Analysis Battery of psychological tests leads to the qualitative and quantitative determination of the individual behavioral variables.
Level 9: The Quantification of Behavior through the Conflict Analysis Battery:
RMES, the inventory, identify a person's relational modality and the set of Metaphor tests reconstruct the syndrome of six roles.

Postulate 10: The Process May Be Qualified By Its Effectiveness: The four Relational Modalities differ among themselves in terms of the interpersonal effectiveness they confer to the individual and the culture.
Level 10: The Qualitative Evaluation of Behavior
Efficiency =n=E useful/ E total= Effectiveness

The Scientific Laws Underlying Moral Order were Derived by Equating the Unit, a Social Science Periodic Phenomenon, with the Simple Harmonic Motion and the Equilibrial System of a Scale

Level 1: Formal Analysis

POSTULATE 1: THE PROCESS IS AN EQUILIBRIAL SYSTEM OBEYING THE LAWS OF MATHEMATICAL GROUPS. The elements of an ideational universe are formally interrelated ideas as determined by the laws of mathematical groups and the logic of relations.

The Laws of Inverse:
Opposite States:
cooperation + antagonism,
cancel each other out:
$a+(-a) = 0$

Reciprocal States:
activity and passivity,
yield the totality:
$a \times 1/a = I$

The Ten Levels of the Conflict Analysis Profile

Logic: Laws of relational logic
Group theory of mathematics: Law of Inverse:
In every mathematical group, for every element, there is an inverse element, which, combined with the first, yields the identity element

Under the operation of addition, the inverse elements are opposite
$a + (-a) = 0$

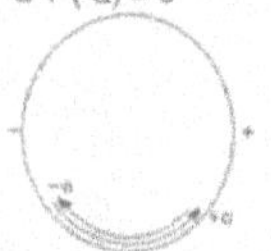

Under the operation of multiplication the inverse elements are reciprocal
$a \cdot 1/a = 1$

A Natural Science Periodic Phenomenon: The Simple Harmonic Motion (SHM)

Inverse constructs:
Opposites are the clockwise vs. the counterclockwise rotation

Reciprocals are the two same directional rotations distinguished as the passive and the active alternatives

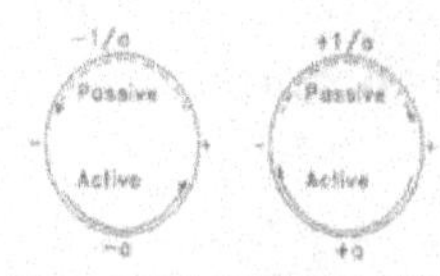

A Social Science Periodic Phenomenon: The Unit of the Conflict Resolution Process (CRP)

Opposite constructs: cooperative (marked as positive) vs. antagonistic (marked as negative)

Reciprocal constructs:Direction for the scoring of antagonism (-) vs. cooperation (+) passivity (1/S) vs. activity (S)

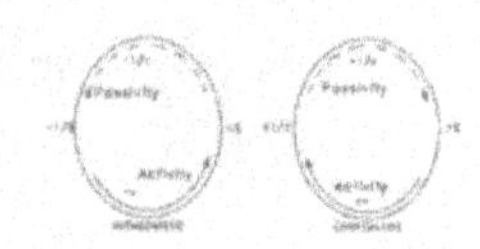

Level 2: Physics of the Process

POSTULATE 2: THE PROCESS IS A NATURAL SCIENCE EQUILIBRIAL PHENOMENON OBEYING THE LAWS OF PHYSICS. The Conflict Resolution Process may be conceptualized with the constructs and formulas of the Simple Harmonic Motion.

The Constructs of Physics:
Displacement: S = Power,Social Status.
Acceleration: a = Motivational Force
Velocity: v = Behaviors,
Mass: m = Emotional Investment
Opposite States: cooperation + antagonism, cancel each other out: $a+(-a) = 0$

Level 2 Variables Analysis

Physics Variables of the SHM

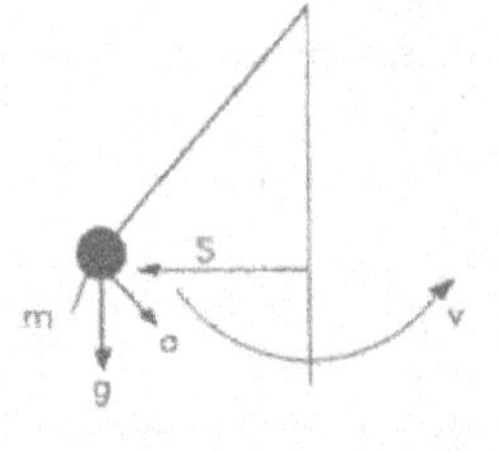

The Simple Harmonic Motion is conceptualized as a function of the following symbolically identified variables:
Displacement= S
Maximum displacement=A (amplitude of the oscillation)
Velocity=v

Acceleration=a

Force= F gravity = g
Mass= m
Energy= E

The 6-role sequence is conceptualized as a function of the following behavioral variables equivalent to physics:
Normative Deviation= Status Differential= S
(-S status of aggression; -1/S status of being a victim of aggression)
Social conduct =v
(-v murdering
-1/v being murdered)
Motivational Force= a
(-a wishing to murder;
-1/a fear of being murdered)
Dependency Needs=g
Involvement = m
Conflict = Energy = E

POSTULATE 4: THE ENERGY OF THE PROCESS IS CONSERVED
The oscillation of the Conflict Resolution Process consists of the intertransformation of energetic modalities whose sum total is conserved.

Level 4: Transformation of Energies Analysis
Law of Conservation:
Etotal = E dynamic + E kinetic + E momentum
Etotal = Epsychic + E social + E Biological

POSTULATE 5: THE PROCESS IS DEFINED AS A FORCE DIRECTLY PROPORTIONAL AND OPPOSITE TO AN EQUILIBRIAL DISTURBANCE
The motivational force (acceleration: a) that a person in conflict experiences is proportional and opposite to the social status shift from the position of rest (displacement: S).

Level 5: Conflict Analysis
The Force vs. Displacement
Relationship: $a = -1/2\ KxS$

POSTULATE 6: THE PROCESS IS DEFINED AS A PERIODIC PHENOMENON
The Conflict Resolution Process, the six-role dialectic pattern, is the periodic trigonometric function of its three covariant constructs : emotions (a), behavior (v) and displacement (S).

Level 6: Syndromal Analysis
The Periodic Nature of Behavioral Phenomena
$a = -ac \sin H$ • $v = vc \cos H$ • $s = a \sin H$

POSTULATE 7: THE PROCESS MAY BE PORTRAYED GRAPHICALLY
The Conflict Resolution Process may be portrayed as a sine curve and its cross-section, the Power Field as a circumference. Ellipses in the Power Field Circle illustrate one individual's set of mental Self-Other representations or a set of interacting individuals in reciprocal relationship to each other orbiting the Power Circle.

Level 7: Graphic Analysis
The Graphic Portrayal of Behavior
The Structural & Longitudinal Drawings

Structural Diagram
Longitudinal Diagram

Graphic illustration of trigonometric variables as function of time:

deviations (S)
behaviors (v)
feelings (a)
TIME
For cross-section see the structural diagram.

POSTULATE 8: THE FORMAL VARIATIONS OF THE PROCESS LEAD TO A TAXONOMY OF FOUR SYNDROMAL ALTERNATIVES: From this perspective we distinguish clinically four key alternative relational syndromal modalities.

Social Science Phenomenon

1. Direction of circular velocity cooperation (clockwise) vs. antagonism (counterclockwise)
2. Direction toward pole of dominance or subordinancy.

Level 8: Diagnostic Analysis
Relational Modality Analysis

The Syndromal Organization of Behavior
Dominance vs. Subordinancy
Antagonism vs. Cooperation
Alienation vs. Affiliation

POSTULATE 9: THE ENERGETIC INTENSITY OF THE PROCESS IS MEASURABLE: The Conflict Analysis Battery of psychological tests leads to the qualitative and quantitative determination of the individual behavioral variables.

Level 9: The Quantification of Behavior
Conflict Analysis Battery:
RMES, the Inventory and the set of Metaphor tests

POSTULATE 10 : THE PROCESS MAY BE QUALIFIED BY ITS EFFECTIVENESS: The four Relational Modalities differ among themselves in terms of the interpersonal effectiveness they confer to the individual and the culture.

Level 10: The Qualitative Evaluation of Behavior
Efficiency =n=E useful/ E total= Effectiveness

CHAPTER FIVE: THE UNCONSCIOUS AS THE INTEGRATIVE PARADIGM

The unconscious is a homeostatic physiological phenomenon

The premise of the Formal Theory is that the unconscious transforms conflict energy into moral growth. The conceptual innovation of the Formal Theory consists in examining emotions as energy and the function of the unconscious as the transformation of conflict energy to entelechy, meaning, moral order, social adjustment through spontaneous attitude change.

• The formal thesis clarifies the scientific origin of psychological and of moral order. The unconscious becomes a periodic phenomenon steering the person to adapt to and alternatively to change the norms of the societal environment.

• It automatically reduces psychic tension, similar to the autonomous regulations of blood pressure and sugar levels. This function manifests in dreaming, and with deliberate thinking as in completing any sample of creativity.

• The unconscious manifests at the psychological level as relational diagnoses and their psychodynamic syndromal unfolding as the six-role process.

• Emotions are interdependent and inseparable as the six-role states syndrome. The unconscious introduces syndromes constituting a personality typology of wellness relational modality diagnoses, which represent four psycho-dynamically organized formally interrelated alternative ways of resolving conflicts. They are accountable for wellness and for psychopathology entailing psychotherapeutic interventions.

• The unconscious is measurable with the Conflict Analysis Battery, a didactic, diagnostic, and therapeutic self-assessment.

• The assessment makes the test taker conscious of the unconscious and guides one to the deliberate management of power and attitude, in reducing psychopathology and dysfunctional adjustments.

• The unconscious manifests at the sociological interactional level as culturally determined normative constraints regulating individual behavior. Religions represent normative institutions inspiring conflict resolution (Levis, A & Levis, M., 2016b).

Morality is an essential and integral aspect of psychology and physiology

The Moral Science departs from the contemporary psychology's agnostic trend and from the theistic attribution of morality. It explains morality as an essential and integral aspect of psychology and physiology. Morality reflects the innate physiological need for conflict resolution as the reduction of psychic tension; it originates in the psyche as a motivational force, more prevalent and powerful than sexuality. It drives our thinking when we are alert and when we are asleep. It propels our creativity across all art forms to celebrate conflict resolutions as the universal quest for justice. The Formal Theory examines the creative process as an emotional six-part dialectic leading to four alternative types of conflict resolutions. The unconscious is identified as an energy processing homeostatic function.

The fundamental law of the natural sciences is the conservation of energy. The key to introducing science into psychology is in identifying ideational actions and emotions as energy, which entails processing emotions and behaviors as energetic transformations abiding by the laws of nature. The mind has eluded scientific analysis because it has defied being reduced to the physics of energy. Cartesian Dualism addressed this difficulty suggesting an alternative to rational thinking suitable for comprehending spiritual matters. Freud introduced primary and secondary thinking processes. Jung endorsed dualism by distinguishing rational from empirical reasoning. He introduced the concept of mental alchemy and innate cultural archetypes.

The Formal Theory suggests the key to making behavior into a science is in the fact that the mind transforms conflict energy to an upgraded form of energy, moral growth, entelechy, catharsis, meaning as the change of attitudes. The Formal Theory explains how the mind practices psychosynthesis, parallel to plants' photosynthesis. It transforms conflict energy to meaning, as moral growth through three innate attitude changing formal operations. Aristotle identified the outcome of Greek tragedies as cathartic leading to entelechy implying transformation of attitude as an energetic upgrading.

Examining psychological phenomena as energetic allows their study as natural scientific ones. We no longer need dualism and alchemy, mysticism and revelation to comprehend morality or spirituality. Entelechy, as inner meaning in Greek, is about energy transformed to moral growth, emotional and social restructuring through an innate process of attitude change.

The new psychology focuses on the energetic structure and formal operations of the unconscious as a conflict resolution attitude modifying mechanism. The mind is the automatic processor of emotional/conflict energy leading to its transformation through an attitude-modifying set of formal operations. These operations transform conflict defined as a state of passivity, antagonism and alienation to resolution as a state of mastery, cooperation and mutual respect. Science rediscovers the Ten Commandments as the innate transformative function of the unconscious. Science understands morality and provides for the public's need for a moral paradigm offering a rational alternative to dogma, yet respecting religions as forerunners of the science.

Religions evolved concepts improving the family institution by introducing intuitively metaphorical descriptions of the creative process resolving conflicts: Genesis identified the six-role process leading to the day of rest, and the Ten Commandments identified the principles of conflict resolution describing injunctions promoting mastery with moderation, cooperation and mutual respect. Morality is attributed to God, as the unifier of art and science.

The Moral Science begins a new era in the conceptualization of behavior launching the scientific study of psychology and morality bound together into a unifying science. It is a surprise that we finally have an answer to the quest of integrating art and science, psychology and morality. The Formal Theory innovates by examining art and finding science. It analyzes the creative process, reflecting the unconscious, as a natural science energetic entity allowing us to apply scientific constructs and formulas to psychological phenomena, as resolving conflict, recognizing conflict resolution as moral thinking; the Formal Theory integrates psychology and morality based on rigorous phenomena ending the need for dualism.

The Formal Theory points out that the creative process, the plot of stories, represents conflict resolution, that is moral order, as an energetic transformation process. It recognizes emotions as energetic quantities abiding by the laws of two phenomena of science: the Simple Harmonic Motion, SHM, and the formal operations restoring balance to the equilibrial scale. The Formal Theory's premise is that the unconscious manifested in the creative process transforms unpleasant psychic energy by upgrading its order, seeking social adjustment, conflict resolution or morality. This unconscious is defined as an innate homeostatic mechanism transforming energy following three attitude-modifying formal operations.

The creative process unconscious has a scientific structure with a moral function. This innate process is the origin of all moral thought. It is defined as a syndromal dialectic of six emotions that leads to four alternative paths of conflict resolutions, the set of relational modalities.

Religions evolved by discovering the process, as in Genesis meaning creation, and in the Greek cosmogony as a six-part continuum, they also identified the alternative types of resolving the conflicts of the family restructuring role relations and redefining the divine attributing to it the characteristics of the unconscious. Divines evolved as the alternative role models of conflict resolution. The modalities were attributed to many gods in the religion of the Olympians and to one god in Judaism. The Formal Theory introduces the analysis of the creative process as reflecting the unconscious linking science and physiology, psychology and religions, and religions among themselves.

The hypothesis is that the mind resolves conflicts through an attitude-modifying process that transforms psychic energy, distress, to social adjustment as personal moral growth. The process helps the person unconsciously to change his/her power play and attitude and to become reconciled with the social system, the normative reality. The concept also allows to challenge societal norms. Conflict energy is transformed to social adjustment as moral growth. Like photosynthesis in the plant world, the mind transforms emotional conflict energy as psychosynthesis. It transforms conflicts into creating poetry, art, stories and mystifying them as religions inspiring communal synergy in creating civilizations.

Integration of the disciplines

The study integrates the disciplines of psychology into the brand new Moral Science by demonstrating the scientific structure and the moral function of the creative process unconscious representing the common denominator of the disciplines of psychology. The volume presents evidence validating the Formal Theory. The evidence is based in examining the creative process as following formulas of science.

The volume brings about theory and clinical evidence, case studies, for each of the four disciplines. Metaphors are analyzed as science, as measurable types of conflict resolution. All metaphors become measurable graphically portrayable phenomena of science.

Science, while respecting religions also points out that they are partial discoveries of science and as partial truths incomplete in their wisdom and hence unable to complete their mission for peace on earth. They are moral monopolies, normative institutions, promoting alternative types of conflict resolution; in that sense they are valuable psychological theories that have sanctified norms improving family relations by deifying and mystifying the alternative conflict resolution principles. The great news is that that the Moral Science can integrate them as measurable natural science phenomena and fulfill their mission by establishing scientific consensus on moral values as the universal principles of conflict resolution governing the unconscious and manifested in the creative process.

Criteria qualifying psychology as a natural science

The Formal Theory has introduced science in behavior by examining the creative process as an energetic transformation phenomenon reflecting the unconscious need to reduce psychic tension and increase social adjustment. It is Aristotle, who first described the formal structure of symbolic systems in his treatise on dramatic plays -The Poetics. He observed how tragedies are characterized by the following: Dramas have the characteristics of Perfect Universes (Teleion Holon). They consist of three parts: a beginning, a middle, and an end. The parts are interrelated and are in proper proportion to each other. They consist of a system of role transformations, starting from a hybris, an arrogant action, culminating through an adventure, peripetia, to the turn of fortune- the role reversal, ending with a moral resolution, deke, justice, experienced by the audience as catharsis. Catharsis coincides with a state of conflict resolution, attitude change, an emotional transformation upon the end of the drama. While Aristotle studied the moral order governing ideas in dramatic plays in abstract terms, he did not have access to the scientific analysis of energetic and equilibrial phenomena.

The creative process, as the unconscious, transforms energy to negative entropy or moral order. It is then the engine of moral growth. Human psychosynthesis is equivalent to photosynthesis, theism is equivalent to heliotropism, the unconscious is the chlorophyll of humans. The unconscious seeks morality, conflict resolution, like plants seek light. The metaphors help to understand the universality of conflict resolution as a biological homeostatic moral mechanism following principles of nature. Through conflict resolution equated with morality, and religions identified as conflict resolutions, rigorous science becomes the foundation of all humanities.

Applying the theory to the interpretation of metaphors

The Formal Theory thus, interprets psychological and moral reality as founded on science. It understands the unconscious through a simple paradigm shift from multiple stories to what is universal in all stories, their plot. Theories and religions capturing reality with stories, as metaphors are approximate views of reality, but all stories, theories and religions, have a common denominator, their plot, which is now measurable as a six-part, syndromal, energetic mechanism guided by three formal operations. The metaphors, partial truths, may now be interpreted as structured by the universal process, energy transformation, and relational modalities; stories become measurable natural science conflict resolution phenomena.

The formal theoretical claim is validated by examining samples of creativity as metaphors of the process and there identifying the scientific aspects of the process as a six-role state syndrome and as one of four relational modalities. The current concepts of psychology: the unconscious, diagnoses, and the concepts of religions, are metaphors, mere approximations of reality perpetuating uncertainty, ambiguity, divisiveness and ineffectiveness in delivering services. Metaphors are the beginning of science, but not the end. Metaphors inspire but compete with the truth. They lead to the frontiers of the world's wisdom, but do not cross them.

Metaphors reduce the complexity of reality by identifying equivalences with familiar, meaningful symbolisms. Examples of metaphors are religions, dreams, art, animal stories, and fairy tales, metaphorically presenting the meaningful manifestation of an underlying pattern as a particular conflict and its resolution. We can fathom the order underlying the stories and their solutions by interpreting stories as the manifestation of the conflict resolution scientific process. The content of metaphors as multiple theories may now be interpreted as measurable conflict resolution entities analyzing them as natural science phenomena.

The Formal Theory's interpretation of metaphors identifies the unconscious as consisting of energy transformation, a conflict resolution syndrome propelled by three attitude-modifying innate formal equilibrial operations seeking to restore a disturbed emotional rest state. The conflict resolution analysis of metaphors examines them as samples of the creative process analyzing them with the constructs and formulas of the pendulum, the Simple Harmonic Motion, and those of the scale, as principles of balance. Thus, the creative process, physiology, psychology, morality, religions, may be measured by the constructs and the formulas of the physics of the pendulum as energetic transformations, and the scale's equilibrial principles as formal moral order relational entities. The unit process in accurate and scientific terms is a measuring rod, equivalent to the unit in arithmetic, the cell in biology, and the orbit in stars.

This finding, capturing science and morality as a unit order, transforms agnostic and medicalized psychology as well as dogma based religions into the natural Science of Conflict Resolution. This integration represents a dramatic development. Psychology becomes a science founded on conflict resolution or morality. At the same time, this science clarifies wellness and illness, psycho-assessment, psychodynamics and psychotherapy. It demystifies religions as psychological measurable phenomena promoting conflict resolution. The science clarifies how to deliberately modify behavior as a power and attitude management emotional balance reducing psychopathology.

The formal thesis clarifies the scientific origin of psychological and of moral order

The Formal Theory's interpretation of metaphors identifies the unconscious as consisting of energy transformation, a conflict resolution syndrome and four relational modalities transforming energy propelled by three attitude-modifying innate formal equilibrial operations. This transformation of energy accounts for the creation of moral order. Conflict resolution is moral order, scientific laws improve interpersonal relations. The Formal Theory clarifies that psychological and moral reality are founded on science.

The Formal Theory understands the unconscious through a simple paradigm shift from our multiple stories to what is universal in all stories, their plot. Stories, theories and religions, are metaphors; they have content, partial views on matters, but as stories they all have a plot, this is the core process. The metaphors as the content of theories are intuitive truths; the process of stories be those theories, and religions, the plot of stories, is the yardstick measuring the stories as quantifiable alternative types of conflict resolution.

This finding, capturing science and morality as a unit order transforms dogma-based beliefs and agnostic and medicalized psychology into the natural Science of Conflict Resolution. This finding represents a dramatic development. Science accounts for psychology but also for spirituality. At the same time, this science clarifies wellness and illness, psycho-assessment, psychodynamics and psychotherapy. It also demystifies religions as psychological measurable phenomena and clarifies how to deliberately modify behavior as a power and attitude management emotional equilibrium reducing psychopathology.

CHAPTER SIX: PSYCHOLOGY'S FOUR DISCIPLINES

1. Epistemology: The unconscious defined with scientific constructs

We contrast psychological theories as differences in their definition of the unconscious. The Formal Theory redefines the unconscious. It departed from the Freudian irrational and immoral conflict-creating Oedipal strivings to define it as a scientific conflict resolution process, a homeostatic biological function reducing psychic tension and improving the person's social adjustment. Psychology and sociology are conceptually integrated with scientific constructs and formulas. The Formal Theory introduces science in the study of the unconscious as both a natural science energetic entity and one of conflict resolution or moral order. It understands the unconscious as the origin of moral thinking. It recognizes the unconscious as graphically portrayable and as readily measurable.

The Formal Theory departed with a paradigm shift by examining what is universal in all stories and there detecting their plot as a conflict resolution mechanism. The Formal Theory introduced the study of the creative process as a scientific energy transforming mechanism, as a well-organized symbolic universe that resolves conflict abiding by two phenomena of science: The Simple Harmonic Motion and the formal operations of the equilibrial scale.

The unconscious was defined as a homeostatic physiological mechanism automatically processing energy of conflicts as a normative deviations into resolutions as normative adjustments, a periodic energetic oscillation phenomenon of six emotions, as a syndrome guided by three attitude-changing formal operations. The formal operations led to resolutions as a set of alternative relational modalities. Unconsciously operating homeostasis preserves the individual's state of rest by reducing energy experienced as unpleasant psychic conflict by transforming it through catharsis to normative conciliation.

The first scientific phenomenon captures energy and the second phenomenon transforms it. The first, the SHM, captures energy upon a normative deviation as the shift of a pendulum ball, a deviation. This energy is transformed in three oscillations as six emotions, formally interrelated symbolic ideas along the three equilibrial attitude-changing operations of the second phenomenon: reciprocity, negation and correlation, restoring balance in the trays of a scale by transforming attitudes from passivity to activity, antagonism to cooperation, and alienation to mutual respect.

The unconscious is a homeostatic physiological psychological sociological entity

The observation of periodicity in the Greek creation story was accounted for as a conceptual continuum connecting psychology and sociology leading to a religion. The analysis of the periodic pattern led to the identification of the two scientific phenomena: the Simple Harmonic Motion accounting for the energetic transformation in the pattern, and the equilibrial scale both restoring the balance, the mental rest state, transforming energy from dynamic to kinetic, from emotions to action, then to moral growth through catharsis.

The clinical manifestation of the unconscious: a syndrome and four alternative ways of resolving conflict
The creative process unconscious was identified as an emotional dialectic, an energetic transformation process, that resolves conflicts leading to four alternative types of resolution, the relational modalities. The new unconscious was a homeostatic entity representing the software of the mind as an automatism triggered by normative deviations generating conflict and as the inner physiological, scientific, sociological, psychological response seeking to reduce psychic discomfort through attitudinal relational changes, seeking social or normative adjustment as resolutions.

The unconscious was defined as transforming energy from chaos to order. It differed from the pendulum machine in that the process completes in three oscillations, six emotional role states, the transformation of energy to moral order, entelechy and catharsis. In the span of three oscillations, the conflict resolution process following the scale's three formal operations transformed psychic distress energy to social adjustment order turning discomfort of passivity to its reciprocal, mastery, of antagonism to its opposite, cooperation, and of alienation to the correlative state of mutual respect.

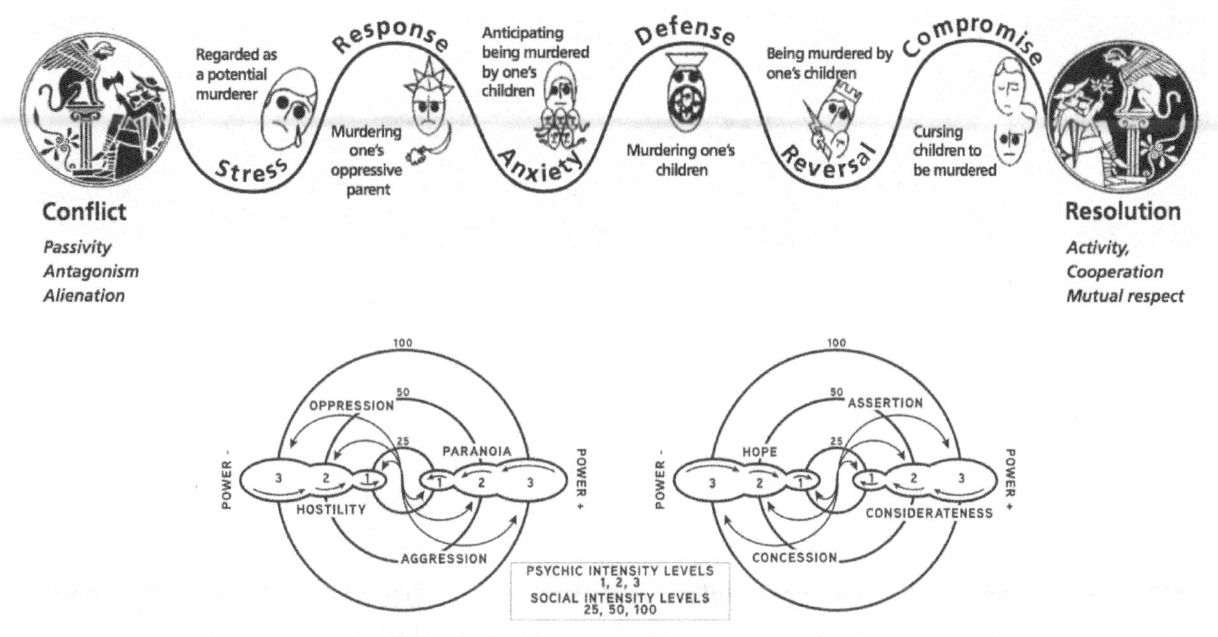

*The unconscious becomes a natural science phenomenon with a graphic representation consisting of a sine curve illustrating the six-role state sequence, and a normative field, social reality as a concentric circles system, with vectors identifying four relational alternatives. The individual thought process unwinds in a spiral with a vector in the circular normative circumference pointing to the alternatives of power, attitude, and intensity. *

Clockwise vectors represent cooperation; counterclockwise vectors represent antagonism.
The unconscious is a syndromal dialectic of six emotions leading to four alternative paths of conflict resolutions, determined by the formal operations. We recognize four relational modalities wellness personality types as physical energetic and formal entities. All processes have measurable physical and relational dimensions.

2. Wellness diagnoses

This unconscious mechanism connects six emotions as a syndrome transforming energetic ideas dialectically, resolving conflicts following the three formal operations. These lead to four alternative power and attitude choices the four wellness personality types: dominance and subordinacy each along two opposite attitude variations, cooperative and antagonistic, leading to four relational modalities.

We recognize the unconscious as a syndrome of interrelated emotions leading to four types of conflict resolutions as four relational modalities. Syndromes and modalities are wellness diagnoses departing from DSM 5 illness diagnoses as clusters of symptoms.

Diagnoses: The Theory introduces wellness diagnoses, a personality typology, as syndromes and four relational modalities, the alternative types of resolving conflict. These diagnoses clarify psychopathology as generated through the decompensation of the relational modalities and therapy as the process of the correction of the modalities.

The unconscious became the unit order of the social sciences revamping the concept of diagnosis. The unconscious consists of both a syndrome and of a set of four relational modalities. Six-role states represent the syndromal sequence leading to resolutions as the four types of relating. These are four wellness diagnoses, the relational modalities. They are wellness diagnoses, consisting of syndromes. The formal operations of reciprocity and negation allow variations in responses to a stressor. These responses correspond to the four alternative relational modalities manifested as diagnoses of the person as a wellness personality typology, and of religions as four types of conflict resolution, the moral monopolies. The three operations restore the rest state, resolving conflicts but following alternative choices as the set of four relational modalities: dominance and subordinacy, each modified by antagonism and cooperation.

SOCIAL SYNDROMES

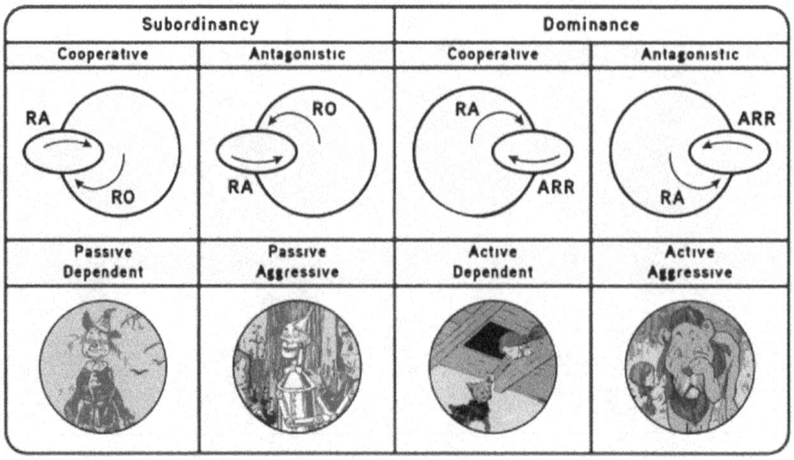

Subordinancy		Dominance	
Cooperative	Antagonistic	Cooperative	Antagonistic
RA RO	RO RA	RA ARR	ARR RA
Passive Dependent	Passive Aggressive	Active Dependent	Active Aggressive

The Formal Theory identifies a wellness personality typology as syndromes of six-role states leading to the four alternative types of conflict resolution; these are wellness diagnoses that everybody should know in dealing with one's emotions. The relational modalities are syndromes of resolving conflicts as four wellness personality types well depicted in the Wizard of Oz characters.

3. The Conflict Analysis Battery, CAB, a diagnostic, and therapeutic self-assessment

The unconscious can be readily measured with a self-assessment, the Conflict Analysis Battery. It identifies the emotional process, a syndrome, and the alternative relational modalities. The battery serves to make a person conscious of the unconscious. It is educational, diagnostic and therapeutic without requiring professional services.

Contemporary testing use personality inventories to identify traits and symptoms, and projectives like Rorschach to identify relational patterns. The instruments identify variables independently from each other. Current assessment technologies are non-theortical. They miss the evaluation of the totality of the process as a syndrome and as relational modalities; inventories and projectives examine arbitrary distinctions on the process and on personality differences.

The practical value of a theory is in its applications. The new unconscious is an entity that may be readily identified. The Formal Theory allowed the development of an assessment instrument, the Conflict Analysis Battery, CAB, which combines a diagnostic inventory identifying modalities and therapeutic projective creativity tasks, metaphors, used in reconstructing the six-role process as a syndrome and learning about how to optimize its resolutions. The inventory identifies the relational modality diagnosis, and the samples of personal conflict resolutions are analyzed as reflecting a person's pattern. Thus the CAB utilizes the creative process in identifying the unconscious for both diagnostic and therapeutic objectives.

The CAB, representing the clinical application of the Formal Theory, integrates the inventory with the set of projectives to identify the two components of the unconscious. The inventory measures the alternative ways of resolving conflict and the projectives, a set of metaphor creation tasks, lead to the reconstruction of the syndrome as one's personal way of resolving conflict. The two tests are complementary: The inventory is diagnostic; it identifies the person's relational modality and the projectives are therapeutic. They identify the innate syndromal sequence and the type of resolving conflicts as a relational dialectic of six formally interrelated emotions as interrelated role states. The completion of the tests generates an emotional cathartic therapeutic experience.

Through the battery, we readily learn about ourselves. We identify our wellness personality type as a diagnosis responsible for symptom development, and we also identify the thought process unfolding as a sequence of six interrelated emotions and behaviors as a syndrome, a predictable conflict resolution pattern. The prompts of the tests generate actionable insights. The test taker identifies attitude and power management changes to optimize one's conflict resolving skills. The battery includes an introductory essay. It is a didactic segment explaining the nature of the unconscious as a scientific totality.

The CAB self-assessment is an effective standardized treatment method
The CAB self-assessment is didactic, diagnostic and therapeutic. It leads to self-discovery and self-help reducing the need of professional services. Associations, thoughts, emotions, evolve spontaneously in the course of a story transforming energy and one's attitude from a state of conflict to one of resolutions. The unconscious transforms discomfort, illnesses, to comfort or wellness. Resolutions improve the state of wellness and provide relief by spontaneously transforming conflict identified as passivity, antagonism alienation to resolution defined as a state of mastery, cooperation and mutual respect according to the formula of the equilibrium scale. It is thus easy to become conscious of the unconscious and to guide one's awareness to deliberately identify optimization-changes. The battery is completed and interpreted by the test taker. The self-assessment may be introduced both in psychotherapy and in education as a concise program of emotional education. The assessment represents a manual driven didactic, diagnostic and therapeutic modality. It is available online and yields automatically seven reports on the process.

The CAB is presented in the case studies of the volume. We are appending a statistical analysis of responses evaluating the online delivery version and also statements from these non professionally served individuals. We are also appending statements of patients and interns, who completed the assessment, in its brief and extended versions, upon clinical and non-clinical deliveries. Also appended is a typical computer generates report consisting of the six reports. The reports of the assessment make a person conscious of the unconscious in one's own symbolic system accounting for the rational integration of the fragmented experiences of one's emotions and thoughts.

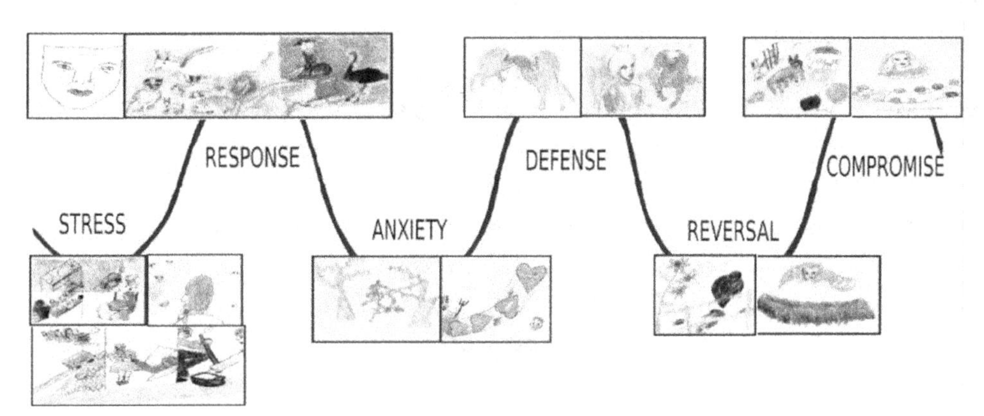

The metaphor profile, one of the six computer generated reports, reconstructs a test taker's artwork as the six-role conflict resolution process

4. On religions: Moral Order as determined by the unconscious conflict resolution process
The formal thesis identified this innate process, resolving conflicts, as the origin of all moral thought correcting relational deviations by helping the person to adjust their relational choices according to normative systems, that is roles acceptable to the prevailing culture. The unconscious is in the business of transforming conflict energy to social adjustment as moral growth. This transformation is like photosynthesis in the plant world; the mind transforms emotional conflict energy as psychosynthesis. The person grows emotionally by resolving conflicts, and intuitively conforms to social norms. Cultures grow by the human mind transforming conflicts into moral consensus captured in all creativity, be that poetry, art, stories, psychological theories and religions.

This energy may be summed up as moral philosophies, religions, works of art, and new normative systems as civilizations. The process helps to change social reality, to pursue normative change wrestling with inequities or injustices. The scientific analysis of the process integrates religions as sociological conflict resolutions. They evolved improving the family institution and increasing abstraction and universality in the definition of the divine. Religions are psychological phenomena of intuitive nature as alternative types of conflict resolution. Prophets sanctified and mystified the process inspiring conflict resolution moral paradigms, communal synergy in creating alternative civilizations.

Discussion of the disciplines presents the conceptual advantages in formalizing psychological phenomena as measurable, meaningful, predictable and manageable. The unit is a self-correcting process integrating psychology and sociology as an energetic continuum. The theory examines normative / moral systems, religions, as differing along the four modalities, bound by a dialectic of self-correction to becoming the Moral Science.

Energetic transformation coincides with moral developments defining the unconscious as a scientific moral order phenomenon. The two formulas, energy and formal operations, demystify psychology as morality bound, by analyzing the creative process, accounting for the plot of stories having a conflict resolution structure ending with wisdom. The Formal Theory understands religions as normative institutions that may be integrated as the evolution of conflict resolutions in improving the family institution and in clarifying the nature of the divine as the optimal role model in conflict resolution. The Moral Science integrates religions into a scientifically founded moral consensus facilitating their mission in inspiring peace and inner harmony.

The sociological evolution of cultures has been explored with an educational game, identified as Moral Monopoly. It uses the structure of the deck of cards to analyze the evolution of cultural stories as discoveries of the alternative relational modalities as complementary discoveries of the four relational modalities. The game consists of stories arranged like the suits of a deck of cards; There are two stories for each suit, one from mythology and one from the history of the culture. Each suit of the deck presents a conflict resolution sequence, introduces continuity between the four suits progressing to effectiveness. The four signs imply an evolutional process as four phases in completing social growth to justice for all, and evolving from conflict symbolized by the spade to resolution symbolized as the heart.

Players examine stories as consisting of six episodes leading to the alternative resolutions. They detect how the four cultures retrace the evolution of religions as generated empirically improving the family institution by increasing fairness in family role relations and abstraction on the nature of the divine. The game is a paradigm for the critical integration of the disciplines of psychology into the cohesive Moral Science. Religions are analyzed as natural science measurable phenomena that have attributed to the divine the characteristics of the unconscious conflict resolution mechanism. Science reclaims the attributes of the divine for the unconscious process and completes the merger of religions into the Moral Science as an enlightened psychology.

The four disciplines of psychology integrated through the unconscious process into the Moral Science: Epistemology/Methodology, Diagnoses, Assessment, and Morality

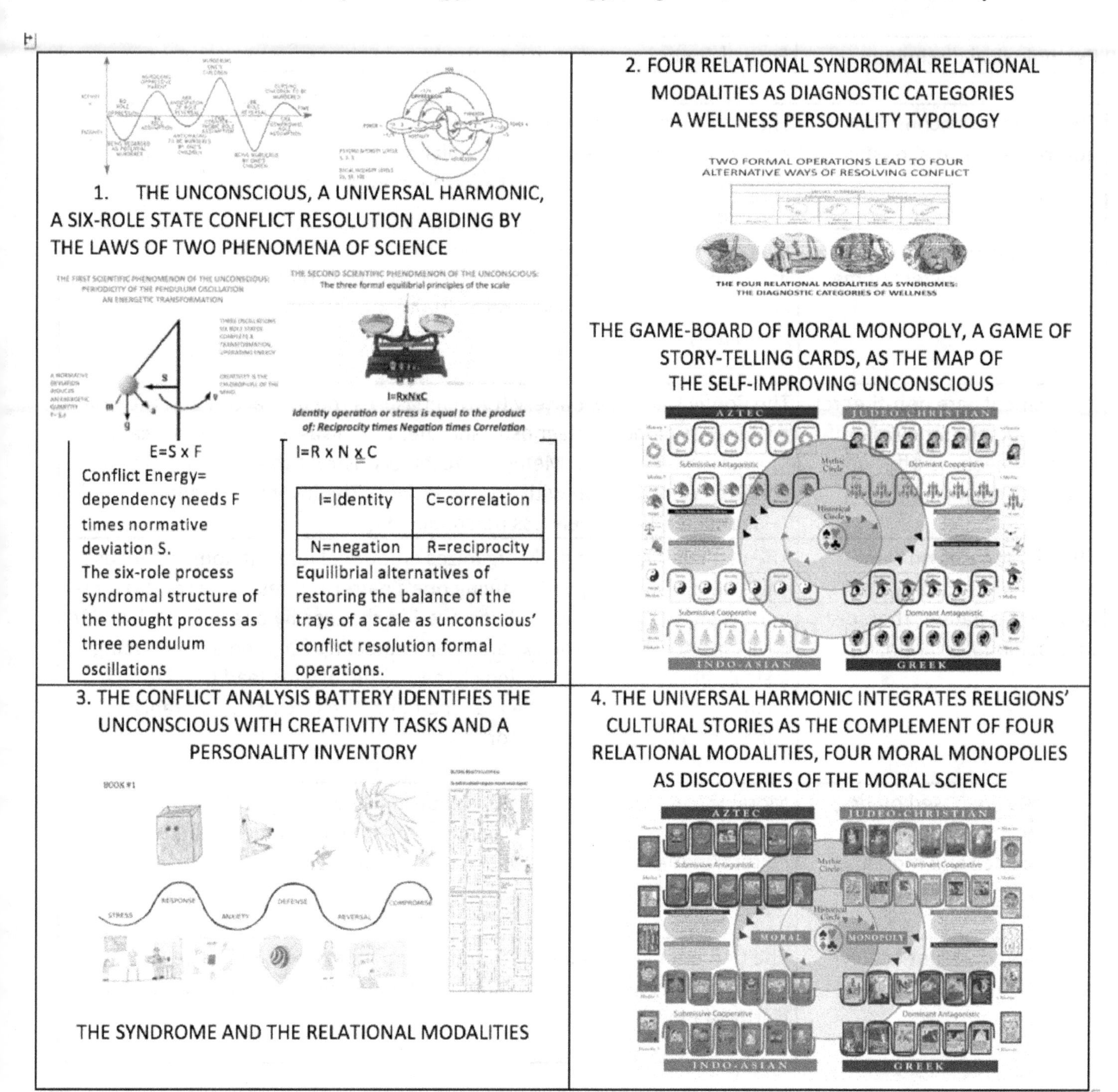

Summary of Moral Science's Conceptual Innovations

1. *Defining the unconscious as a scientific mechanism*
2. *Recognizing the alternative relational modalities on the gameboard of Moral Monopoly*
3. *Identifying the modalities as having dimensions using the self-assessment*
4. *Using the cards of the Moral Monopoly, in analyzing cultural stories, religions, as discoveries of the alternative ways of resolving conflict* (Levis, 2016).

Table: The Creative Process Reflecting the core paradigm, the Unconscious as a Conflict Resolution Natural Science Phenomenon integrates the currently divided disciplines

Psychological disciplines	Formal Theory's validation into the Moral Science
The Freudian unconscious is non-rational and agnostic.	The unconscious is rational and morality bound; it consists of two phenomena of science: Pendulum oscillation as a syndrome and the scale's relational operations leading to four relational modalities.
DSM Diagnoses are illnesses, clusters of medical symptoms	Four wellness diagnoses consisting of two components. Syndromes, six emotions predictably leading from conflict to resolution and four personality types based on power and attitude, the relational modalities.
Assessments are non-theoretical inventories, they identify traits; projectives offer unintegrated insights.	The Conflict Analysis Battery (CAB) measures the modalities and the syndrome; it is didactic, diagnostic and therapeutic as emotional education, 'power management'. Metaphor tests reconstruct the syndrome from a conflict to a resolution with art and insights The inventory identifies one's relational modality, wellness personality types.
Therapy focuses on symptoms, choice therapy is CBT, and on the patient therapist interpersonal relationship.	The test taker meaningfully organizes emotional information. The focus is on relational pathology identifying one's pattern of resolving conflicts, releasing energy blocks, identifying needed changes by oneself. The battery is an emotional cathartic experience, connecting fragments, developing insights and identifying needed changes. The insights lead to relational changes, power and attitude management. The role of the therapist is changed to that of an educator.
Religions are based on dogma. Psychology is separate from science and morality.	Moral Science examines religions evolving as complementary conflict resolutions and reconciles religions as psychological theories studying cultural stories recognizing relational modalities integrating religions into the Moral Science.
Education does not achieve its three objectives.	The CAB is an emotional education, moral literacy; it meets the three objectives of education: Integration of art and science, self-knowledge and clarity of moral values.

CHAPTER SEVEN: INTEGRATION OF FREUD'S CONCEPTUAL MODELS
Conceptual parallels between the theories of Freud, Jung, and Levis

The conflict resolution concept on the nature of the unconscious integrates Freud's axiomatically advanced perspectives into a cohesive and meaningful natural science relational entity (Freud, 1955). The advantages of the formalization of the unconscious are reviewed by applying the relational method in reconciling the multiple propositional Freudian hypotheses into the cohesiveness of the formal theoretical analysis:

Unlike the Freudian biological conflict evoking unconscious, the formal theoretical one is a natural science measurable entity, a dialectic/syndromal continuum of six emotions evolving predictably from a conflict to its resolution following three formal operations. The Oedipus Complex is interpreted as the conflict resolution process—dramatic process beginning with a transgression: hubris or arrogance as normative deviation, corrected with the punishment of the transgressor and normative change.

The psychoanalytic assumptions on the primacy of sexuality and aggression are methodologically propositional arbitrary speculations that have misled psychological research. Formal analysis examines libido and Thanatos as the dichotomy of opposite relational forms—those of cooperation and antagonism. Freud's pleasure principle related to sexual pleasures is interpreted as motivation propelled by the need for reduction of psychic tension through conflict resolution. Freud's structural model, the descriptively defined triad of the id, ego, and superego, finds a psychodynamic integration in Formal Theory's cyclic six-role state syndromal entity: stress/response, anxiety/defense, and reversal/compromise.

The descriptive psychoanalytic defense mechanisms (Vaillant, 1992; Freud, A., 1992), such as denial, projection, repression, reaction formation, and sublimation, are accounted for by the six-role process interrelated by the three formal relational operations of the systemic equilibrium of the trays of a scale. Denial and Repression correspond to the role states of Stress and Response, as Role Oppression and Role Assumption. Projection corresponds to the role state of Anxiety as Anticipations of Role Reversal. Reaction Formation corresponds to the role state of Defense, also identified as Counterphobic Role Assumption. Sublimation corresponds to conflict resolution identified as Compromise, or Compromise Role Assumption.

The developmentally determined Freudian transference is clarified as referring to the relational wellness diagnoses of personality typology of four syndromal relational modalities: innate alternative ways of resolving conflicts readily identified and precisely measured with a personality inventory and metaphor creation tests without the need for a laborious therapeutic relationship.

Freud's therapeutic technique of free associations generated on the couch through long-term psychotherapy is modified and simplified by Formal Theory's projective creativity-based assessment tasks, which the client analyzes for insights and corrective changes by oneself.
Freud's *energetic* concepts of cathexis and sublimation are understood with Formal Theory's six-role mental process energetic transformations. Energy is conserved and transformed from chaos to negative entropy.

Freud's theory of Oedipal tribal dynamics, and their role in evolving moral objectives as advanced in Moses and Monotheism (Freud, 1939), is countered by Formal Theory's understanding the unconscious need for conflict resolution as the psychological origin of all moral thinking. Religions are viewed as evolving by resolving conflicts improving social justice. The types of resolution advanced by religions reflect the personality type of the respective prophet. Religious philosophies represent the sanctification of the complement of the alternative ways of resolving conflicts. Their function is the normative structuring of societies to alleviate societal inequities (Freud, 1955).

Methodology: Freud's and Jung's methodology is based on axiomatic distinctions without support by science as opposed by Formal Theory's relational method allowing the introduction of laws of scientific phenomena.

Table: Differences and similarities between psychoanalysis and the Moral Science

Criteria examined	Psychoanalysis	Formal Theory
The Creative Process as the object for the study of the unconscious	'Repetition in all its literary manifestations may in fact work as a "binding," of textual energies that allows them to be mastered by putting them into serviceable form within the energetic economy of the narrative.' (Brooks, 1977),	The creative process consists of six-role states. Stress is energy generated by a normative deviation in a magnetic field. This energy is processed with a system of six formally interrelated role states guided by three formal operations to a normative conciliation.
The unconscious is an energetic entity: arbitrary choices versus consensus on reduction of tension.	"Energy stems from drives whose aim is death. We are given an evolutionary image of the organism in which the tension created by external influences has forced living substance to diverge ever more widely from its original course of life and to make ever more complicated detours before reaching its aim of death" (Brooks, 1977)	Psychic Energy is defined as emotional tension characterizing the polarization between ideas in a normative or symbolic universe. The unconscious needs to reduce tension by upgrading order through restoring one's rest state, reaching emotional balance in the normative field defined in the context of one's symbolic system. Personality types seek the alternative deviations.
Closure	Closure is implied by recognizing periodicity.	The closure is in the circumscribed structure of stories captured in every sample of creativity and in the binding of the metaphors of the CAB assessment as interrelated into the personal drama.
Formalization of constructs	The drives: libido and thanatos are not formally related. The id ego and super ego are not connected into an energetically conserved process.	The drives libido thanatos are equated to the formal operation of negation connecting cooperation and antagonism. The six- role process is about transformation of unstable psychic energy to stable social order.
Diagnostic Typology	Analysis of transference pertains to developmental experiences recreated in the therapeutic relationship.	Relational modalities are wellness diagnoses qualified as a spectrum of diagnosable conflict resolutions. They are innate and measurable with CAB's inventory and projective tests.

Table: The Moral Science integrating Theoretical Models

Construct definitions	Freudian analysis	Jungian analysis	Formal Theory
The unconscious as the object of study	The Oedipal complex unconscious	The personal and collective unconscious	The creative process represents the moral and natural science unconscious, a homeostatic conflict resolution process, a syndrome, a chain reaction transforming psychic energy as conflict to social adjustment as four types of resolutions.
Motivation	Sexual needs but also positive, constructive energies	Psychic energy	Physical origin of the psychic energy: Psychic energy is generated in the mind as a pendulum's deviation in the normative field: E=S x F, resolution is geared to reduction of tension and restoration of inner balance.This energy experienced as conflict is resolved automatically; changes abide by two phenomena of science: the SHM and the formal operations of the equilibrial scale. The innate mechanism is graphically portrayed as a sine curve with vectors in concentric normative circles. The configuration is portrayed as a sperm-like diagram.
The unconscious transformation process	Id/ego/ superego	Individuation through archetypes	The Conflict resolution process is a six-role energetic transformation, a syndrome, guided by three attitude modifying operations: I=R x N x C
Process analysis	Developmental model	Archetypes and personal issues	One key behavior as the role is emotional energy transformed symbolically along three formal attitude modifying operations, reducing conflicts; this process abides by natural laws, their constructs, and formulas.
Components of the process	Defense mechanism Denial, Repression, reaction formation, projection, sublimation	Persona, shadow, animus, anima, And self	Conservation of energy establishes continuity between the formally interrelated energetic states: stress, response, anxiety, defense, reversal, compromise. The six roles correspond to Freud's defense mechanisms as relational operations, establishing continuity between them. The six roles states correspond to Jung's archetypes binding them as formally interrelated role states.
Personality distinctions and typology	Transference relations are determined from early developmental experiences and fixation in oral, anal, and phallic stages	Distinctions are arbitrary as Introvert/ extrovert, feeling/ intuition, thinking/ sensing	Four relational modalities determined by formal alternative approaches to conflict resolution varying according to their distinctions: Reciprocity leading to passivity versus activity, negation to cooperation versus antagonism, correlation to alienation versus mutual respect: four types as Dominance subordinacy, Cooperation antagonism Intensity in both psychic and social systems. The syndromal structure integrates Freud's defense mechanisms and formalizes Jung's archetypes.

DIAGNOSIS AND THERAPEUTIC ASSESSMENT

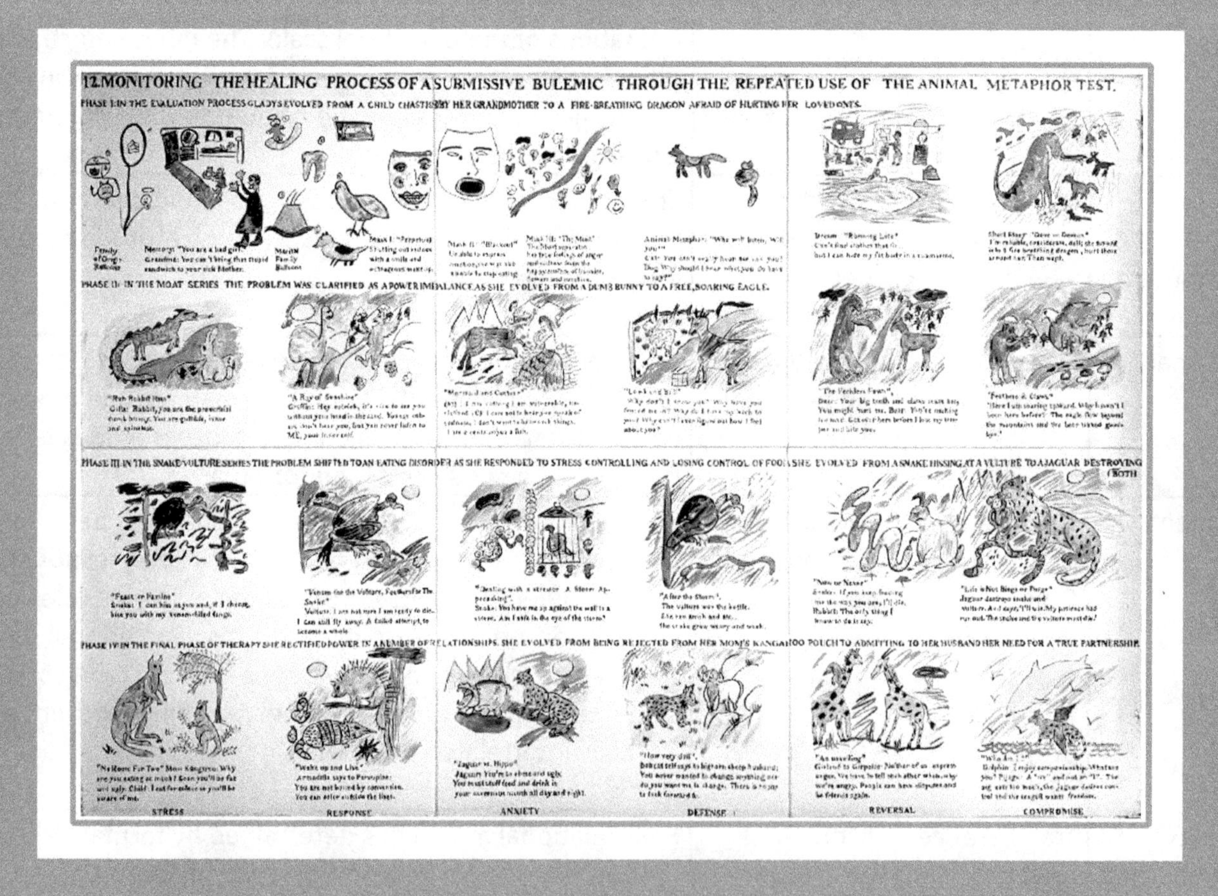

Volume Nine

Albert J. Levis M.D. & Maxwell Levis

Normative Publications

DIAGNOSIS and THERAPY

Relational modalities are pivotal to making changes in therapy

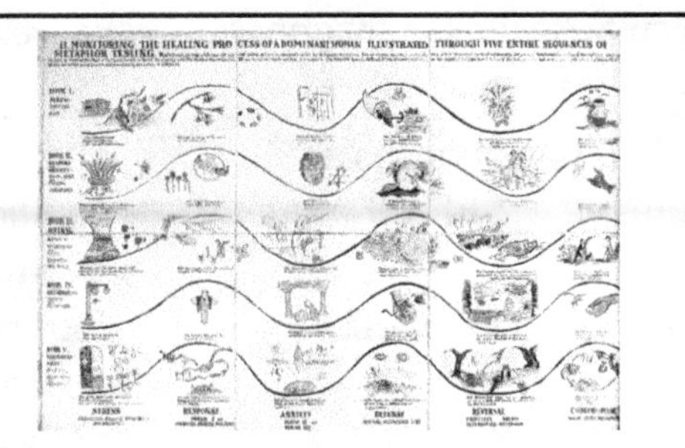

Relational syndromes evolve changing power, attitude and intensity reducing conflicts

BOOK TWO: DIAGNOSIS AND THERAPEUTIC ASSESSMENT

CHAPTER ONE: IDENTIFYING DIAGNOSES AS THE ALTERNATIVE TYPES OF CONFLICT RESOLUTION AS A WELLNESS PERSONALITY TYPOLOGY AND USING THE CONFLICT ANALYSIS BATTERY AS A DIDACTIC, DIAGNOSTIC AND THERAPEUTIC INTERVENTION

The principle application of the Formal Theory is in providing the distinctions of the unconscious the four relational modalities as syndromes in differentiating diagnostic categories. This chapter begins with a differentiation of modalities as diagnostic categories provided metaphorically by the characters of the Wizard of Oz story. The chapter also introduces the use of the Conflict Analysis Battery self-assessment instrument to measure the unconscious conflict resolution process.

The Battery is a theory based self-assessment that identifies the two aspects of the unconscious, the modality and the syndrome. Case studies illustrate the use of the assessment delivered online and as a workbook in two formats, as a brief evaluation and as a therapeutic emotional education program.

The exterior wall thus presents the well-known Oz characters as the prototypes of the four wellness diagnoses and pathologies for which the heroes of the story seek help from the wizard. The study of the panels also introduces the use of the battery. Following extensive discussion of diagnoses and of the assessment we illustrate the modalities with several case studies using the assessment; four are illustrated in the three murals of the second wall, but many more cases are examined to amplify the concept of the relational modalities as wellness diagnostic categories and of the use of the assessment for diagnostic and therapeutic ends.

We highlight the dramatic differences between the two major diagnostic categories, dominance and submissiveness alternatives. We recognize their differences both for the emotional education of the well public but also for the appropriateness of therapeutic interventions.

Thus, the second wall of the Sanctuary addresses issues of diagnosis, assessment and therapy.

Table: DSM 5's psychiatric illness diagnoses versus Relational Modalities as wellness personality types

DSM 5 psychiatric illness diagnoses are clusters of symptoms They do not identify psychodynamic explanation of patterns. They do not recognize personality types as wellness relational syndromal diagnoses.	The Formal Theory identifies the unconscious as resolving conflicts along a syndromal psychodynamic sequence of six interrelated emotions. The syndromal process leads to four types of relational modalities based on three formal operations transforming passivity to its reciprocal: activity, antagonism to its opposite: cooperation, and alienation to its correlative: mutual respect. These represent a wellness personality typology accounting for illness.
Pathogenesis is attributed to chemical imbalances and to neurological impairments.	Pathogenesis is caused by the relational factors, such as intensification of psychic tension and intensity in social responses. Modalities are genetically determined and developmentally modified.
Pathologies are not psychodynamically determined. Symptoms are not related to each other.	The four relational modalities lead to psychopathologies as formally interrelated emotions. Dominance evokes anxiety, paranoid fears, defensiveness, controls, and reversals as social setbacks. Submissiveness leads to hostility and depression, escapist conducts in dealing with stressors.
Illness is accounted for in medical neurotransmitter terms. Medical analysis does not avail abstract and graphic psychodynamic illustration of emotions and social parameters.	Relational modalities can be graphically portrayed in relational terms: The syndromal structure of emotions is presented as the sine curve of the six-role state process. Modalities are graphically presented as vectors in the normative concentric circles.
Therapeutic modalities differ along alternative interventions: Cognitive Behavior Therapy focuses on controlling emotions. Psychodynamic focuses on insights through analysis of transference. Behavior modification focuses on changes through a variety of exercises.	The key intervention is the Conflict Analysis Battery as an emotional education and as an integrative therapy focusing on learning about psychology, identifying one's relational modality pattern, and by identifying actionable insights as managing one's power and attitude.

The murals of the second wall illustrate four case studies utilizing the Conflict Analysis Battery. The four case studies show how metaphors have diagnostic and therapeutic value. Two case studies in one mural present the educational delivery of the assessment to two well college students with the opposite personality types. Their essays validate the insightfulness evoked by the assessment. Two clinically diagnosed patients in separate murals, (# 11, #12) illustrate the two dominance and submissiveness modalities, utilizing the assessment as long term therapeutic interventions. All four studies clarify the diagnostic and therapeutic differences between the two modalities.

The diagnosis, assessment and therapy book presents multiple case studies highlighting the art of the testing and summaries of the exchanges illustrating the six-role state syndromal conflict resolution process reflecting the relational modalities diagnoses. The studies confirm the scientific features of the unconscious as syndromes and modalities, and the effectiveness of the technique of metaphor interpretation. The case studies represent evidence of the intervention making persons conscious of the unconscious helping them to correct relational pathologies. The Conflict Analysis Battery is demonstrated exposing the unconscious generating actionable insights thus reducing the need for the therapist's interpretations and interventions. The test taker develops insights, becomes aware of counterproductive patterns, and identifies the needed attitude and power management changes by oneself. The therapist's role is modified to that of an educator and a support person facilitating the processing of creativity generated insights, explaining symptoms as generated by the syndromal relational thinking.

Table: Case Studies reported in this section of the book utilizing the Conflict Analysis Battery

Case studies	Type of delivery	Type of instrument used	Diagnoses	Duration of therapy
Four cases representing the four modalities	Online delivery	The brief assessment	Four modalities	Insights from brief evaluations
Exemplary online report	Online delivery	Full battery	Individual report	Self-evaluation
47 well people	Online delivery without professional services	Full battery	Feedback through query responses and personal statements	Average 4 hour self-evaluation
12 case studies of therapeutic interventions	Clinical delivery	Utilizing the entire battery as a workbook	Contrasting two sets of submissive and dominant patients	on average six sessions
Two college students	Mural 10 Educational delivery	Utilizing the workbook	dominant versus submissive types	Educational internship
Four clinical case studies in long-term therapy	Murals 11 and 12 Clinical delivery with professional services	Utilizing the battery in monitoring progress	2 dominant and 2 submissive case studies	16-40 sessions

There are differences between the traditional delivery of therapeutic services. Wellness education as well as therapy hinge on educating the patient/student with information about the unconscious resolving conflicts along four relational modalities and along a six-role state syndrome; the self-assessment generates self-awareness, insights and guidance for changes.

Table: Advantages of Therapeutic Assessment

	Current trends	Formal Theory's CAB
Diagnosis	DSM 5	Four wellness relational diagnoses, personality typology
Assessment	Assessments identify traits and symptoms Projectives are non-theoretical	CAB, self-assessment is diagnostic and therapeutic offering insights, catharsis, identification of changes, monitoring of outcome
Therapeutic modalities	Multiple therapies focus on cognitive, dynamic and behavioral models.	Power Management using the CAB, integrating therapies and monitoring progress
Therapists' role and interventions	Therapists, seek cognitive education, emphasize analysis of interpersonal relations as alliances and ruptures, focus on the control of symptoms.	The role of the therapist changes to that of an educator focusing on patient's relational wellness diagnosis, insights and choices of changes; The CAB reduces the need for an intense patient therapist relationship.

CHAPTER TWO:
PANELS ABOUT THE FOUR HEROES OF THE STORY

Panels # 4, 5, and 6
The four Wizard of Oz heroes as metaphors of the syndromal relational modalities as wellness diagnoses, a personality typology

Panel #4: The unit of conflict resolution, the unconscious, as a syndrome, a sequence of six formally interrelated role states, as a dialectic of interrelated emotions.

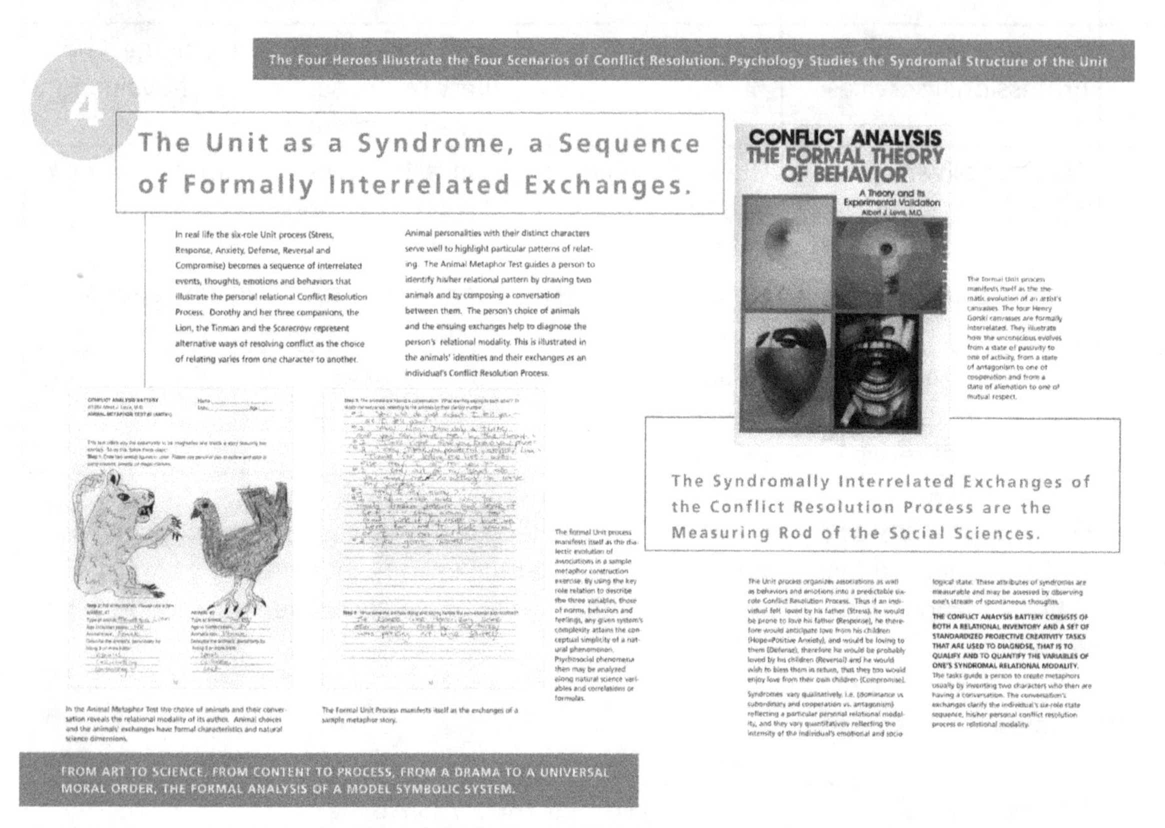

In real life, the six-role unit process (Stress, Response, Anxiety, Defense, Reversal, and Compromise) becomes a sequence of interrelated events, thoughts, emotions, and behaviors that illustrate the unconscious as the personal, relational Conflict Resolution Process. Dorothy and her three companions, the Lion, the Tinman, and the Scarecrow, represent the unconscious as four alternative ways of resolving conflict; the choice of relating varies from one character to another.

The fourth panel introduces the Animal Metaphor Test: It begins with drawing two animals identifying their traits and composing a conversation between them. The conversation's exchanges clarify the individual's six-role state sequence, his/her personal conflict resolution process, exemplifying one's relational modality.

The animal choices and the animals' exchanges have formal characteristics and natural science dimensions. The person's choice of animals and the ensuing exchanges lead to the manifestation of the person's relational modality, as well as its syndromal unfolding as the six-role pattern. The test guides a person to identify his/her relational pattern as the types of animals and their six-role state exchanges reflecting the dialectic between them. !00% of test takers identify themselves and their partners with their metaphor animals. The six-role process manifests itself as the exchanges between them as recorded in the sample metaphor story.

The interpretation of the testing identifies the key action, the role relation describing the process's three variables: those of norms, behaviors, and feelings. Thus, any given system's complexity attains the conceptual simplicity of a natural science oscillatory energetic transformation phenomenon. Psychosocial phenomena then may be analyzed and graphically illustrated along the natural science variables of the respective phenomena.

The formal unit process, syndrome and modality, manifests itself as a symbolic system with thematic consistency, and relational evolution. The four Henry Gorski canvasses on the jacket of the textbook are formally interrelated. The four images illustrate how the unconscious evolves to conflict resolution from a state of passivity to one of activity, from a state of antagonism to one of cooperation, and from a state of alienation to one of mutual respect; the canvases of the jacket of volume 4, Stealing the Fire, reflect the creator's modality unfolding as a syndrome. One can detect the modality in the syndromal process. In Gorski's case particular relational preference is that of a submissive cooperative and antagonistic person troubled by social oppressive circumstances and by his sensitivity to personal transgressions. The assessment duplicates the artist's creative work by the test taker completing a series of tasks identifying the six-role process.

The Exchanges of the Conflict Resolution Process are Interrelated as a Syndrome

The unconscious process organizes associations as behaviors and emotions into a predictable six-role Conflict Resolution Process. Thus, if an individual felt loved by his father (Stress), he would be prone to love his father (Response). He, therefore, would anticipate love from his children (Hope=Positive Anxiety) and would be loving to them (Defense). Therefore, he would be probably loved by his children (Reversal), and he would wish to bless them in return, that they too would enjoy love from their own children (Compromise).

Syndromes vary qualitatively, i.e. (dominance vs. subordinary and cooperation vs. antagonism) reflecting the particular personal, relational modality, and they vary quantitatively reflecting the intensity of the individual's emotional and sociological choices. These attributes of syndromes are measurable by the battery and may be assessed observing one's stream of spontaneous thoughts and by examining the intensity of responses in the inventory assessment as well as the intensity of conflict between the characters of one's metaphors.

Panel #5: The Four Relational Modalities as the Alternative Specific Responses to Stress

The Four Heroes Illustrate the Four Scenarios of Conflict Resolution. Psychology Studies the Syndromal Structure of the Unit

5

The Formal Range of Four Relational Modalities as the Alternative Specific Responses to Stress and the Related Distortions of Reality.

Individuals differ in the way they resolve conflicts. Their differences may be identified as qualitative distinctions along the two key principles of relating. Accordingly in dealing with stress usually an individual unconsciously chooses to be either passive or active, and either antagonistic or cooperative. His/her relational choice determines a person's expectations or anxieties and subsequent defenses, reversals and compromises.

Dorothy and the Lion illustrate the dominant-cooperative and the dominant-antagonistic modalities, the Scarecrow and the Tinman, the submissive-cooperative and the submissive-antagonistic relational alternatives. The Oz heroes exemplify the four relational syndromes.

Their respective role choices entail different passivity states, hence expectations and distortions. Dorothy who chooses to be a thinker (activity) saw Oz as an enormous head (her passivity or anxiety state). The Lion who threatened others with his roar perceived the Wizard as a fierce fireball. The Scarecrow who was kind perceived Oz as a kind lady. The Tinman who could not love, perceived Oz as a most terrible beast. (see Panel #11)

Eventually confronting their passivity or anxiety states, their relational distortions, helped the Oz heroes to overcome their weaknesses, to see reality without distortions, thus to transform their conflicts into true resolutions.

RO: Role Oppression Stress
RA: Role Assumption Response
ARR: Anticipated Role Reversal, Anxiety or Distortions

SOCIAL SYNDROMES

	Subordinacy		Dominance	
	Cooperative	Antagonistic	Cooperative	Antagonistic
	RA, RO	RO, RA	RA, ARR	ARR, RA
Diagnosis	Passive Dependent	Passive Aggressive	Active Dependent	Active Aggressive
Transactional Analysis	Child	Adapted Child	Nurturing Parent	Critical Parent
Formal Relating	RO-Accommodating RA-Trusting	RO-Withdrawing RA-Hostile	RA-Demanding CPRA-Nurturing	RA-Controlling ARR-Distrustful
New Situation	Looks forward to	Resigned to	Afraid of	Paranoid in
Degrees of stress				
Degree 1	Happy Follower	Reluctant follower	Social Leader Fights for Oppressed	Individualistic Leader Limit-tester
Degree 2	Blames self. Holds negative feelings in. Apologetic.	Blames the leader.	Blames others. Portrays self as victim.	Blames everybody. Denies hurt feelings.
Degree 3	Seeks help	Is tense but helpless	Manipulates Threatens to abandon system	Abandons system

Each Oz hero illustrates a particular type of syndromal relating or modality of resolving conflict.

FROM ART TO SCIENCE, FROM CONTENT TO PROCESS, FROM A DRAMA TO A UNIVERSAL MORAL ORDER, THE FORMAL ANALYSIS OF A MODEL SYMBOLIC SYSTEM.

The ways of dealing with temptation differ from culture to culture. Parallel cultural moral paradigms involving the apple metaphor illustrate four relational alternative choices. Mural #6 illustrates how cultural paradigms evolved progressively upgrading interpersonal effectiveness. The Formal Theory's Unit Conflict Resolution Process represents the science-based, malleable paradigm of moral order.

The Formal Range of Relational Modalities Constitutes the Spectrum of Normal Personality Categories.

THE FORMAL THEORY DISTINGUISHES FOUR PRINCIPLE RELATIONAL MODALITIES ACCORDING TO HOW A PERSON RESOLVES CONFLICTS ALONG THE PRINCIPLES OF RECIPROCITY AND OPPOSITION.

Along the principle of reciprocity a person may unconsciously choose to be dominant or submissive, and along the principle of opposition one may choose to be antagonistic or cooperative. The combination of the two relational alternatives leads to four relational modalities or syndromes; the dominant cooperative and the dominant antagonistic, also the submissive cooperative and submissive antagonistic. These modalities may vary along a third relational principle: correlation, according to whether a person chooses to be alienated vs. affiliated or respectful.

Personality differences along the dominance-subordinancy way of relating seem to be genetically determined. The other two qualifying distinctions seem to be determined by one's developmental experiences and cultural values. Cultural systems, like individual personalities, differ along the syndromal range of formal relational modalities. This is demonstrated by contrasting four culturally distinct variations of dealing with temptation as conveyed by relational variations of the metaphor of the apple of temptation.

Relational modalities as deviations along the resolution sequence may be regarded as incomplete conflict resolutions spontaneously evolving toward increased conflict resolution. This evolutional determinism manifests both in one individual, also in one culture and cross-culturally. It may be detected by observing consecutive samples of creativity as in the four Gorski canvases on the jacket of the volume *Conflict Analysis The Formal Theory of Behavior*, (Panel #4) and as in the four cultural solutions of the "forbidden fruit" as illustrated in Mural #6.

Individuals differ in the way they resolve conflicts. Their differences may be identified as qualitative distinctions along the two key principles of relating. Accordingly, in dealing with stress, usually, an individual unconsciously chooses to be either passive or active, and either antagonistic or cooperative. The relational choice determines a person's expectations or anxieties and subsequent defenses, reversals, and compromises. The Oz heroes exemplify the four relational syndromes. Dorothy and the Lion illustrate the dominant-cooperative and the dominant-antagonistic modalities, the Scarecrow and the Tinman, the submissive-cooperative, and the submissive-antagonistic relational alternatives.

The modalities correspond to different distortions of reality
Their respective role choices entail different passivity states, hence expectations and distortions. Dorothy, who chooses to be a thinker (activity), saw Oz as an enormous head (her passivity or anxiety state). The Lion, who threatened others with his roar, perceived the Wizard as a fierce fireball. The Scarecrow, who was kind, perceived Oz as a kind lady. The Tinman, who had no heart or love, who was a hostile person, perceived Oz as a most terrible beast.

Eventually, confronting their passivity or anxiety states, their relational distortions, helped the Oz heroes to overcome their weaknesses, to see reality without distortions, thus, to transform their conflicts into true resolutions. In the image of facing the wizard as a failing human they are wearing glasses symbolizing their capacity to be objective by overcoming their subjectivity as distortions of reality.

The Formal Theory's Unit Conflict Resolution Process represents the science-based, malleable paradigm of moral order. The ways of dealing with temptation differ from culture to culture. Parallel cultural, moral paradigms involving the apple metaphor illustrate four relational alternative choices. Mural #6 illustrates how cultural paradigms evolved, progressively upgrading interpersonal effectiveness.

The formal range of relational modalities constitutes the spectrum of a wellness personality typology
The Formal Theory distinguishes four principle relational modalities according to how a person resolves conflicts along the formal operations of reciprocity and opposition. Along the principle of reciprocity, a person may unconsciously be dominant or submissive, and along the principle of opposition, one may be antagonistic or cooperative. The combination of the two relational alternatives leads to four relational modalities and syndromes; the dominant cooperative and the dominant antagonistic, also the submissive cooperative and the submissive antagonistic. These modalities may vary along the third relational principle: correlation, according to whether a person is alienating versus affiliated or respectful. This variable determines the intensity of psychic tension experienced differentiating wellness from illness.

Personality differences along the dominance-subordinacy way of relating are genetically determined. The other two qualifying distinctions are likely determined by one's developmental experiences and cultural values. Cultural systems, like individual personalities, differ along the syndromal range of relational modalities. This is demonstrated by contrasting four culturally distinct variations of dealing with temptation as conveyed by relational variations of the metaphor of the apple of temptation, mural # 6.

Relational modalities as deviations along the optimal resolution sequence may be examined as a progression improving conflict resolutions. The alternatives evolve spontaneously toward optimal resolution. This evolutional determinism manifests both in one individual, also in one culture, and cross-culturally. It may be detected by observing consecutive samples of creativity as in the four Gorski canvasses on the jacket of the volume: Conflict Analysis-The Formal Theory of Behavior (Panel # 4) and as in the four cultural solutions of the "apple metaphor" as illustrated in Mural # 6.

Panel #6: Complete Conflict Resolution as a Paramount Objective

The Four Heroes Illustrate the Four Scenarios of Conflict Resolution. Psychology Studies the Syndromal Structure of the Unit

6

Complete Conflict Resolution as a Paramount Objective.

Relational modalities, as attitudes, are modifiable by completing the entire conflict resolution process, that is by outgrowing one's relational limitations through confronting one's fears or anxieties. Pursuit of complete conflict resolution and personal transformation guided the four Oz companions to encounter the Wizard of Oz who challenged them to kill the Wicked Witch of The West.

To acquire the desired qualities of courage, a heart, a brain and going back home the companions had to pursue a new six-role journey. Along this journey they transformed the Stress of their needs, to a Response, their new adventure. They overcame their fears, (Anxiety), by taking risks, and thus defeating the Wicked Witch, (Defense). Empowered by this victory, they were able to confront Oz, demystify his identity and reverse roles with him, (Reversal). Oz departed from the Emerald City and the companions succeeded him by assuming his roles of leadership (Compromise). Along this six-role-process our heroes were able to resolve their conflicts by transforming oppression to mastery, antagonism to cooperation and alienation to mutual respect.

Risk taking is the means to overcome one's fears.

"Giving a great spring, he shot through the air"

The Continuum of Psychopathology and Health

The Evolution of the Patient-Therapist Relationship

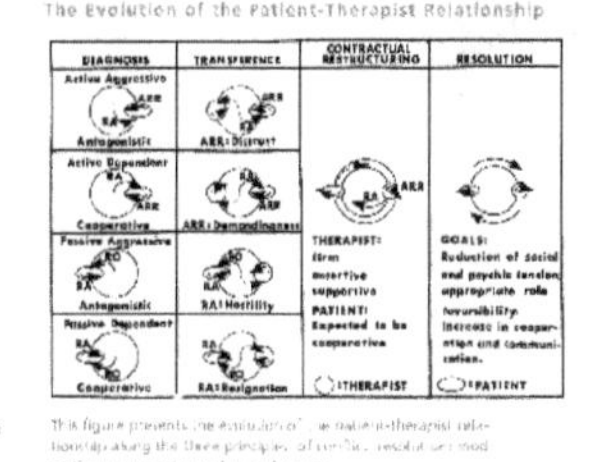

Therapy and Psychoeducation as the Deliberate Pursuit of Complete Conflict Resolution.

RELATIONAL MODALITIES DIFFER IN THE DEGREE OF INTERPERSONAL EFFECTIVENESS THEY CONFER. Individuals and cultures increase their effectiveness by spontaneously evolving across the spectrum of relational modalities toward increased conflict resolution. Incomplete conflict resolution leads to psychopathology and sociopathology. By contrast, complete conflict resolution leads to wellness and may be attained by deliberately pursuing the principles of conflict resolution. Cultures reinforce and regulate resolving conflict through their educational, legal, artistic, spiritual and psychotherapeutic institutions.

THE STUDY OF CREATIVITY ATTESTS TO THE FACT THAT BOTH INDIVIDUALS AND CULTURES INCREASE THEIR EFFECTIVENESS SPONTANEOUSLY PURSUING THE THREE OBJECTIVES OF CONFLICT RESOLUTION: MODERATION, COOPERATION AND MUTUAL RESPECT. This moral determinism may be detected at the cultural level by observing the evolution of the world moral paradigms and at the individual level by observing the evolution of an artist's spontaneous creations. This determinism may be easily validated experimentally by monitoring a testee's or patient's conflict resolution strategies in the course of one's education or therapy by using the Conflict Analysis Battery (See Murals 7-12).

FROM ART TO SCIENCE, FROM CONTENT TO PROCESS, FROM A DRAMA TO A UNIVERSAL MORAL ORDER, THE FORMAL ANALYSIS OF A MODEL SYMBOLIC SYSTEM.

Relational modalities, as power and attitudes, are not readily influenced as they are genetically determined. The intensity though is modifiable. The assessment, by completing the entire conflict resolution process, generates insights and elicits directives for changes. Test takers outgrow their relational limitations through confronting their fears or anxieties. The pursuit of complete conflict resolution and personal transformation was evoked by introducing courage to the four Oz companions by giving them permission to challenge a dreaded figure, by killing the Wicked Witch of The West.

To acquire the desired qualities of courage, a heart, a brain, and going back home, the companions had to pursue a new six-role journey starting with confronting the witch. Along this journey, they transformed the Stress of their needs to a Response, their new adventure. They overcame their fears (Anxiety) by taking risks and thus defeating the Wicked Witch (Defense). Empowered by this victory, they were able to confront Oz, demystify his identity, and reverse roles with him (Reversal). Oz departed from the Emerald City, and the companions succeeded him by assuming his role of leadership (Compromise). Along this six-role-process, our heroes were able to resolve their conflicts by transforming oppression to mastery, antagonism to cooperation, and alienation to mutual respect, hence as self-respect. Risk-taking for completion of self-discovery is the means to overcome one's pattern of established solutions.

Therapy and psychoeducation as the deliberate pursuit of Conflict Resolution

Relational modalities differ in the degree of interpersonal effectiveness they confer. Individuals and cultures increase their effectiveness by spontaneously evolving across the spectrum of relational modalities toward increased conflict resolution. Incomplete conflict resolution leads to psycho- and sociopathology. By contrast, complete conflict resolution leads to wellness and may be attained by deliberately pursuing the principles of conflict resolution. Cultures reinforce and regulate resolving conflicts through their educational, legal, artistic, spiritual, and psychotherapeutic institutions.

The study of creativity attests to the fact that both individuals and cultures increase their effectiveness spontaneously pursuing the three innate objectives of conflict resolution: moderation, cooperation, and mutual respect. This moral determinism may be detected at the cultural level by observing the evolution of the world's moral paradigms and at the individual level by observing the evolution of an artist's spontaneous creations. This determinism may be easily validated experimentally by monitoring a testee's or patient's conflict resolution strategies in the course of one's education or therapy by using the Conflict Analysis Battery.
(See Murals 7–12).

CHAPTER THREE
FORMAL THEORY'S WELLNESS DIAGNOSES AS SYNDROMES OF FOUR RELATIONAL MODALITIES VERSUS DIAGNOSTIC STATISTICAL MANUAL 5'S MENTAL ILLNESSES DIAGNOSES

The concept of diagnosis in the realm of behavior is about identifying predictable behavioral entities relevant in connecting pathogenesis and psychotherapeutic correction. The Formal Theory innovates the field of diagnosis introducing two components in the analysis of diagnostic categories, syndromes and relational modalities. These are the components of diagnostic categories. They are of psychodynamic nature accounting for pathogenesis, psychopathology and meaningful for psychotherapeutic adjustment. Of course, we recognize the medical nature of certain major psychopathologies independently of the relational psychodynamic make up of wellness diagnoses.

The syndromal mechanism is modified by the four relational modalities
The Formal Theory defines the unconscious as a physiological processor of energy; the six-role process converts conflict energy into emotional and social adjustment or personal growth. The function of the unconscious process is homeostatic; it reduces psychic tension by converting conflict or displeasure, maladjustment, through attitude change to order as rest as normative relational adjustment. This energetic transformation unfolds as a syndrome, a constellation of emotions and behaviors existing as a circumscribed pattern consisting of six-role states: stress, response, anxiety, defense reversal and compromise guided by three formal attitude-modifying formal operations to four alternative types of relational modalities.

Thus the unconscious is a conflict resolution or moral order equilibrial phenomenon that has energetic, physical and formal, relational dimensions allowing its qualitative and quantitative measurement. The six-role state emotional continuum predictably unfolds upon any stressor as associations in one's mind as well as through interpersonal exchanges as three emotional oscillations guided by the three formal equilibrial operations seeking restoration of emotional balance as relief of tension. The three formal operations transform passivity to its reciprocal, activity, antagonism to its opposite, cooperation, and alienation to its correlative: mutual respect.

The four relational modalities
The unconscious resolves conflicts as a syndrome guided by the three formal equilibrial operations of the restoration of balance to the trays of a scale. Accordingly, the unconscious self-adjustment, the conflict resolution process, propels the individual one directionally to increased inner order, transforming stress energy into internalized and externally reinforced organization of behaviors along three formal operations each having a dichotomy. The first operations is reciprocity; it introduces two distinctions passivity versus activity; the second, negation, distinguishes the alternatives of cooperation and antagonism; these two formal operations lead to four conflict resolution modalities, which vary along the formal distinctions of passivity versus activity and cooperation versus antagonism. The psychic, emotional load, intensity of responses is addressed by the third operation: correlation, whose dichotomy is alienation versus mutual respect. Alienation, as increased intensity, may manifest with clinical symptoms as illness.

Accordingly, the formal operation of reciprocity determines two alternative responses: the dominant and submissive relating; the formal operation of negation qualifies each one of the two reciprocal responses along the opposite directions of cooperation and antagonism. The change in the operation of correlation corresponds to alienation, versus mutual respect corresponding to high versus low psychic tension, wellness versus illness. We recognize four relational modalities unfolding as syndromes. They represent a personality typology, a new set of wellness diagnostic categories.

The four relational modalities are viewed relationally as power distinctions: dominance and subordinancy and attitude distinctions: as their cooperative and antagonistic variations. These four entities represent four wellness diagnostic categories. The third formal operation, correlation, reflecting how the individual relates to the public, as alienated versus mutually respectful, allows the quantitative measurement of the individual's psychic tension, reflecting the intensity of conflict experienced as maladjustment or neuroticism. The Conflict Analysis Battery measures the modalities and also the psychic tension with the mental status scale, pertaining to the intensity of conflict experienced. The tension variable is independent of the four relational modalities. While operations may be viewed as qualitative distinctions, they are also modified to reflect intensity of responses, as the quantitative determination of dominance, submission, cooperation, antagonism and psychic tension. Submissive antagonism coincides with high alienation and increased psychic tension and symptoms.

The unfolding of the syndromal process

The resolution of conflicts follows the six-role process modified by the three relational attitude-modifying formal operations. The alternative ways of resolving conflicts depend on the three relational operations transforming conflict to resolutions. The operations determine the formal range of relational modalities as the degree in which passivity is transformed to activity, antagonism to cooperation and alienation to mutual respect. According to how the person resolves conflict along the three formal operations we distinguish relational modalities. As mentioned above, the third dimension pertains to addressing the intensity of unresolved conflict as psychic tension or neuroticism.

All six emotions and actions are in formal and systemic relation to each other. The four relational modalities modify the six-role emotional syndrome. Social deviations evoke balancing corrective psychological forces. The modalities differ as systemically interrelated choices of power and attitude. The new diagnoses of wellness understand psychopathology purely psychodynamically in the context of increased social and psychic tension affected by one's wellness relational diagnosis. The formal distinctions understand clinical symptoms as generated by relational choices and intensity leading to disturbances of wellness. The diagnoses entail the corrective relational interventions on modalities that impact the management of emotions and the automatic reduction of symptoms.

The modalities unfold as dialectic sequences of conflict resolution, as syndromes in one's symbolic language. The assessment captures them with creativity exercises as metaphors of the conflict resolution process. We identify clinical variations qualifying wellness, while allowing a dynamic understanding of illness. The distinctions of modalities provide alternative clinical wellness and illness profiles along the dichotomies of passivity versus activity, and cooperation versus antagonism. We identify four diagnostic categories, the syndromes of dominance and subordinancy with the subcategories of cooperation and antagonism. Distinctions are made along the modalities, compounded by the third relational operation of alienation versus mutual respect or affiliation, which pertains to the psychic tension or distress level.

The Formal Theory introduces the four alternative ways of resolving conflict the relational modalities as wellness syndromal diagnoses. These are the dominance and subordinacy cooperative and antagonistic modalities respectively identifying a simple personality typology that explains the psychodynamic development of both wellness and most psychopathologies. Clinically identified case studies show that therapy-resistant patients diagnosed with DSM 5 symptom criteria, find effective treatment when diagnosed as relational modalities. The relational modality diagnoses are pivotal criteria as treatment interventions hinge on the modalities rather than the type of clinical symptoms.

The significance of the syndromal diagnosis

The relational diagnostic categories are useful in predicting the type of syndromal organization of emotions and behaviors. The personality types are of importance because they determine the syndromal nature of adjustment profiles. Decompensation of the wellness state can lead to distinct patterns of psychopathology and it is important that the suffering person recognizes the pathogenesis and the respective relational interventions to restore the state of wellness.

The four relational personality modalities are wellness distinctions, not stigmatizing psychiatric diagnoses. The relational modalities are genetically determined qualifiers of wellness. Yet these wellness states account for psychopathology, illness. The formal structure of the syndromes establishes a cause effect interrelation of emotions and behaviors. This personality typology clarifies individual emotional perceptions and distortions, as well as choice of behavioral responses. The formal connection of emotions intensified by stressors explains pathogenesis. Thus, the diagnostic categories account for the etiological formulation of pathology. Dominance may lead to anxiety and defensiveness, while submissiveness may lead to depression and hostility. This interrelation accounts for psychopathology as the intensification or polarization of relational responses, defensiveness and hostility, experienced intra-psychically and interpersonally. The psychic tension unlike the rest of the inventory generates clinical symptoms as intensification of wellness relational states.

About the shortcomings of the DSM

The relational diagnoses explain behaviors and emotions, wellness and illness, along the syndromal organization of emotions. They educate and inform the individual as able to make choices determining her/his emotional condition. The DSM illness diagnoses instead present the individual as helpless, victim of a chemical imbalance, or a brain anomaly and present the solution in medical management of one's condition. The success of insight and power management of one's relational condition through the self-assessment approach informs the person how to deal with one's emotional experiences by managing her attitude and power.
Self-awareness of the relational diagnostic categories eliciting symptoms reduces the perception of helplessness and passivity in dealing with one's emotions.

The patient as a well person, realizing the syndromal interconnection of emotions, assumes responsibility for the adverse experiences and seeks to correct them. Relational diagnoses entail assuming responsibility in making relational changes to reduce symptoms. Self-awareness of one's relational modality entails the individual becoming self-aware of her/his emotional and social experiences. To reduce symptoms and conflicts one understands why s/he must modify one's attitude, his/her relational disposition. The aware person seeks to address the social interactional power-managing component affecting one's state of distress.

Graphic portrayal

Identifying the psychic and the social system as a natural science entity confers to behavior the constructs and the formulas of the natural science harmonic and scale phenomena and allows the graphic representation of the process. The harmonic's cross-section allows to place the individual within the normative social system as an ellipse with two types of vectors. The first vector within the circle illustrates behaviors while the second vector within the ellipse indicates emotions in reciprocal position to the sociological vector. We may place two ellipses in the normative system to indicate interacting positions within the psyche as well as to represent interacting parties within one system.

Table: The graphic representation of relational modalities

Submissive Cooperative	Submissive Antagonistic	Dominant Cooperative	Dominant Antagonistic
Clockwise Directed to Powerlessness	Counterclockwise Directed to Powerlessness	Clockwise Towards Power	Counterclockwise Towards Power
Hope for love	Hostility	Trust	Distrust paranoia

SOCIAL SYNDROMES

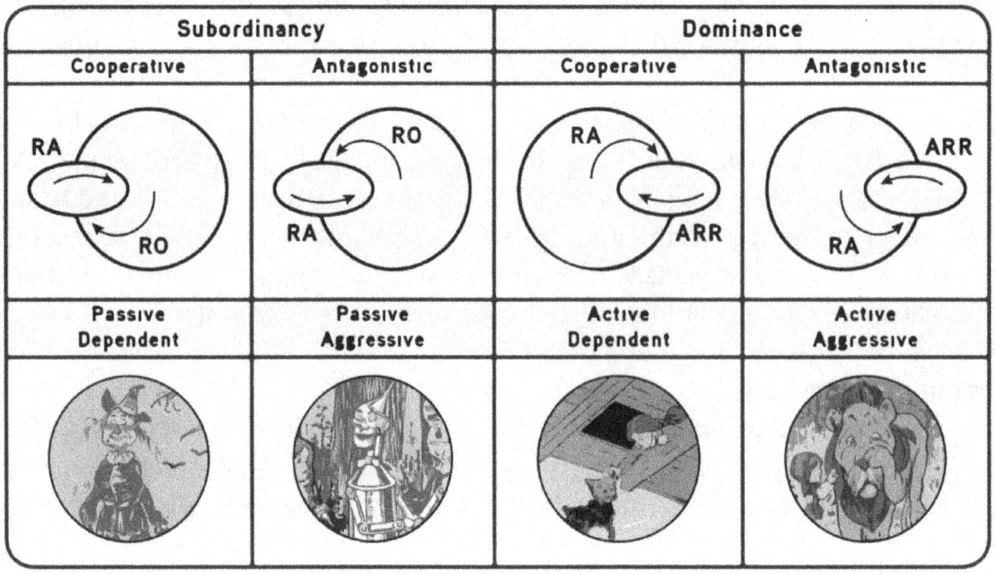

Subordinancy		Dominance	
Cooperative	Antagonistic	Cooperative	Antagonistic
RA RO	RO RA	RA ARR	ARR RA
Passive Dependent	Passive Aggressive	Active Dependent	Active Aggressive

The Genetic Origin of Modalities

We recognize relational modalities as genetically transmitted personality types. They manifest upon the beginning of one's life. Individuals are born with their relational modalities like computers bundled with their software. We speculate that the antagonistic qualifications are environmentally and culturally determined; we do not know the level of hereditary transmission of the antagonistic distinctions. The public needs to know this personality typology as the diagnoses determine the personal emotional strengths and weaknesses in interpersonal relationships potentially leading to minor and major psychopathologies.

The sanctification of conflict resolutions

The rest state is a pleasurable end. This end psychological accomplishment has sociological impact. Resolutions from personal conflict support social norms or alternatively question them. From personal discoveries of rest, patterns may evolve to spiritual, socially celebrated norms. The emotional creation of order and its periodic occurrence have inspired the creation of religions as the sanctification of particular conflict resolving approaches of conflict resolution. The Bible identified the concept of conflict resolution attributed to the Creator, or God. It identified the syndromal process as Genesis, a six-part event leading to Sabbath, the seventh day as the day of rest or resolution. The optimal way of resolving conflicts was ascribed to the Ten Commandments. The alternative modalities were identified as the four attitudes of children asking 'what is special about the Passover night celebration?'

Relational Modalities as Normative Alternatives

The formal typology, four relational categories, applies in the formal analysis of cultures. Relational diagnosis detects the syndromal organization of emotions and behaviors as manifestations of the unconscious equilibrial, homeostatic syndromal response.

Four Alternative Cultural or Normative Ways of Dealing with Temptation, the Apple as Symbol of a Desirable Object. Judea represents the dominant cooperative paradigm, Greece the dominant antagonistic counterpart. India represents the submissive cooperative modality and Mexico the submissive antagonistic disposition.

Wellness diagnoses as syndromal relational modalities

Recognizing one's relational modality explains the personal experiences, as emotions as well as symptoms, constituting parts of a totality, the relational modality syndrome. Dominant people are vulnerable to become both overactive and anxious, while submissive people readily repress feelings and evolve hostility and depression. One's sensitivities, actions, reactions, anxieties, defenses, reversals and resolutions or compromises are components of the syndrome. The relational diagnoses connect disparate personal and interpersonal experiences by explaining their connection as interrelated emotions, defenses, reversals, following the underlying pattern of the six role states. This structure of one's relational pattern entails the direction for assuming corrective intervention in power and attitude-management as making responsible changes in dealing with stressors, averting helplessness. Relational diagnosis provides the direction of emotional behavioral changes in terms of what one can do to change one's emotional maladjustment.

Table: Relational Modalities key Features

Submissive Antagonistic syndrome

Role model: Tin Man

Relational characteristics

- **Communicational Restraint, Worthlessness, Inferiority**

Assessment questions

- I don't know how to express myself without upsetting people
- I keep my anger under control. I don't let myself fly off the handle, hold everything in
- I brood about things that bother me, If I have a complaint, it takes long time for me to bring it up
- Frequently, I am mad and I don't let anyone know it, I am an extremely private person
- People don't care about what I think and how I feel

Relational modality Evaluation Scale

Submissive Cooperative Syndrome

Role model: Scarecrow, Charlie Brown

Relational characteristics, pleaser, accepts norms, gets depressed, develops hostility, escapism, dependencies

Assessment questions

Compassion, Considerateness, Respect for Limits ....I respect and obey rules and regulations

- **Cooperation, Trust** ....I never express my anger. People think that I am very modest
- **Recessivity**....I am a non-assertive person
- In my relationships, I am usually dominated by others
- I am not rebellious, I find it futile arguing, I do things to please others rather than myself

Dominant Cooperative Syndrome

Role model: Dorothy

Relational characteristics, challenges norms and rules

- **Leadership Competitiveness and Dominance**
- **Personal Discomfort and Sensitivities, anxiety disorders, performance anxiety, scared.**
- **Defensiveness and Compassion**

Assessment questions

- I get my way more than I give into others
- I am a dominant person, I have a comment all the time, I am easily frustrated when I don't get my way

Dominant Antagonistic Syndrome

Role model: The Cowardly lion

Relational characteristics

- **Distrust Provocativeness Dominance Intensity In Sensitivities and Responses Explosiveness**

Assessment questions

- I hardly ever compromise
- You are wise not to trust people
- I have a tendency to provoke people
- I attack people with little or no provocation

Consequences of the DSM diagnostic categories, the medicalization of wellness
There has been a trend in the medicalization of mental diagnoses, identifying symptoms as caused by non-relational factors. This move has deliberately shifted from psychodynamic formulations, toward neurobiological causation and chemotherapeutic and cognitive alleviation of symptoms. This diagnostic philosophy favored by contemporary psychiatry is codified in the Diagnostic Statistical Manual, DSM; it establishes emotional conditions as illnesses described by clusters of clinical symptoms. The formal theoretical perspective opposes the medicalization of diagnoses and of related set of therapeutic interventions and considers it as institutionalized malpractice. It places emphasis on the psychodynamic understanding of wellness as the alternative ways of resolving conflict being responsible for pathologies, and manageable primarily with psychodynamic educational guidance.

Formal Theory's premise is that symptoms, as behaviors and emotions are generated by relational choices. The relational modalities determine the syndromal organization of emotions and behaviors, the six-role state psychodynamic sequences departing from a conflict and leading to its resolution generating symptoms. To reduce pathology therefore we need to manage relational choices: power and attitude. So instead of managing symptoms as medical independent states, we view them as determined by relational choices and instead of seeking cognitive suppression and meds to control them, we address them by modifying power and attitude.

The objective of wellness is in managing relational choices, beginning by recognizing syndromes and modalities identified with the self-assessment, the CAB. The inventory identifies the modality and the projective testing, creation of metaphors, identify the syndrome.

The medical versus relational formulation of diagnoses
The Formal Theory defining the unconscious as a syndrome of six emotions guided by the four relational modality diagnoses challenges the illness-based model of the Diagnostic Statistical Manual, which diagnoses symptoms without comprehending their psychodynamic generation and the importance of psychodynamic interventions required for their elimination. The formal theoretical analysis of wellness diagnoses recognizes the needed psychotherapeutic interventions as relational power and attitude management choices. The proper relational diagnosis therefore is of critical significance for the effective reduction of psychopathology.

Diagnostic categories of wellness identify the two aspects of the unconscious: first, the person's relational modality and second, how this unfolds syndromally, psychodynamically, along the six-role process. The relational modality diagnoses identify the psychodynamic formal relational and syndromal nature of emotions and behaviors and depart from the clinical-symptom-oriented focus of DSMs. The formal method represents a completely different approach to diagnostic and psychotherapeutic interventions.

We understand wellness diagnoses decompensating under stress to specific psychopathologies. The diagnosis of emotional conditions as isolated clinical symptom clusters, misplaces importance on what is the cause of distress and which are the corrective therapeutic intervention. Symptom-focused-diagnoses stigmatize the sufferer, while inflicting on the person improper and ineffective treatments. The misdiagnoses of relational modalities as 'chemical imbalances' or cognitive impairments entailing cognitive behavior modification programs accompanied by medication-regiments represent improper and ineffective diagnoses and treatments. Cognitive therapies seek to suppress emotions rather than to extinguish them by modifying the underlying relational communicational power and attitude behaviors that evoke them.

Stigmatizing medical labels and focus on chemotherapies with their side effects reinforce the person's sense of helplessness, worthlessness and state of medical disability. They reduce a well person to the status of suffering from a chronic mental illness. The relational wellness diagnoses entail understanding clinical symptoms as generated by power and attitude mismanagement that are corrigible by making the appropriate relational changes. Several case studies in this book demonstrate the successful relational interventions where CBT and meds management therapies had failed.

Measuring personality, the assessment of the relational modalities and syndromes

The nature of the conflict resolution process is identified by the Conflict Analysis Battery, a self- assessment. It combines a personality inventory with a set of projective tests. The relational inventory is based on identifying one's formal operations thus identifying the modalities and the psychic tension as wellness personality types. The modalities are measurable through the relational inventory test, which also includes the psychic tension mental status questionnaire. The formal distinctions pertain to the normative deviations of the individual in the social system. The variables are graphically portrayable on the template of one's symbolic universe clarifying the diagnostic categories as wellness personality types attributed to two relational alternatives: the reciprocal dominance versus subordinancy and the opposites of cooperation versus antagonism. Intensity of unresolved conflict, quantitative variations of conflict, are attributed to the correlative distinction: alienation versus mutual respect. Sociological relational modalities intensity deviations may signal relational modality pathology choices.

The metaphor tests identify the syndromal six-role state chain of emotional events by using creativity for self-discovery. The creativity tasks present the syndromal psychodynamic integration of emotions and behaviors identified by the inventory. The associations and interactions of life experiences are reflected in one's biographical and creativity tasks as a roller coaster of formally interrelated emotions and behaviors revealing the particular power and attitude choices in engaging the environment leading to specific predictable, self-fulfilling outcomes. The therapeutic significance of the battery assessment is in generating insights for the test taker, who can readily identify the relational syndromal continuum, a psychological sociological self-fulfilling dramatic process unfolding from a conflict to its resolution along the measurable relational dichotomies. The assessment information is pertinent to the person as self-knowledge and accordingly preparing the individual to cope with adversity by knowing her pattern of responses.

The diagnostic categories are of great predictive value, identifying strengths and weaknesses of the person, health and potential pathologies. The online delivery of the battery provides the information to the test taker without requiring professional services. The relational diagnoses of wellness, dominance and submissiveness, and the assessment instruments identifying them, help the well persons and patients to recognize by themselves the cause of their problems as relational modality generated symptoms and to address their problems with appropriate power and attitude management changes. In the case of submissiveness, the relational intervention is assertiveness, improving the communication of feelings and reducing intrapsychic conflicts and dysfunctions. In the cases of dominance, the intervention is self-restraint, admission of vulnerabilities and the reduction of dominant antagonistic, controlling, defensive, guilt, paranoia, and anxiety evoking behaviors.

The CAB self-assessment is didactic, diagnostic and therapeutic.

Psychotherapy begins by determining the client's syndrome and modality using the assessment, to evolve both diagnoses but also to identify therapeutic objectives. The CAB assessment leads a test taker to become conscious of the unconscious. The completion of the assessment constitutes an emotional cathartic experience, while developing insights in one's pattern and identifying the required interventions in managing attitude and power appropriately. The completion of the assessment evokes an emotional transformative experience; it leads to developing insights in one's pattern and identifying the requisite approaches in managing attitude and power appropriately.

The significance of the self-assessment is in identifying the relational diagnoses providing the client/patient with insights, which spontaneously generate actionable relational intent. The assessment reconstructs the six-role state sequence of emotions, chain-reaction manifesting as a syndrome reducible to the formal variations of one key activity. The chain reaction may unfold intra-psychically as thoughts or associations and interpersonally as a system of reciprocal interpersonal transactions. Syndromes then consist of the constellation of the six formally interrelated role states as emotions and behaviors bound together as a perfect totality, a relational pattern, elicited upon dealing with a stressor. The relational choices being innate, they unfold unconsciously.

The self-assessment makes a person conscious of the unconscious as a syndrome and as a relational modality. It is hence both diagnostic and therapeutic.

The test taker identifies the modality and pattern by oneself entailing the recognition of the needed changes. The therapist reinforces the client's spontaneously articulated insights and directives for change. The therapist clarifies the relational diagnosis, syndrome and relational pattern, and encourages the client to adhere to the identified changes. There is benefit in the analysis of the manifestation of the pattern. Classical interpretations of transference are appropriate as additional therapeutic interventions that can be insightful.

The significance of the relational diagnoses is in providing the client/patient with insights, utilizing the self-assessment, which spontaneously generates actionable relational insights. The insights guide the test taker to the needed therapeutic relational changes. The insights are in identifying one's relational modality with the inventory and metaphorically, through one's stories, metaphors, identifying the syndromal pattern as organized thought systems. The assessment reconstructs the six-role state sequence of emotions as the conflict resolution unconscious.

The emotions and behaviors are like a chain-reaction manifesting as a syndrome; they are reducible to the formal variations of one key activity. The chain reaction may unfold intra-psychically as thoughts or associations and interpersonally as a system of reciprocal interpersonal transactions. Syndromes then consist of the constellation of the six formally interrelated role states as emotions and behaviors bound together as a perfect totality, a relational pattern, elicited upon dealing with a stressor. The relational choices are innate and unfold unconsciously. The self-assessment as diagnostic and therapeutic makes a person conscious of the unconscious as a syndrome and as a manageable relational modality.

Completing the assessment the test taker identifies the modality and pattern by oneself entailing the recognition of the needed changes. The therapist reinforces the client's spontaneously articulated insights and directives for change. The therapist clarifies the relational diagnosis, syndrome and relational pattern, and encourages the client to adhere to the identified changes. There is benefit in the analysis of the manifestation of the pattern. Classical interpretations of transference are appropriate as additional therapeutic interventions that can be insightful.

Table: DSM 5, illness diagnostic categories versus the four relational modalities as wellness personality types

DSM 5 diagnostic categories identify clusters of symptoms as classes of illness. They eliminate psychodynamic explanations and do not recognize wellness relational patterns.	The Formal Theory identifies four relational modality diagnoses as a wellness personality typology that also accounts for illness caused by relational as well as psychic intensity leading to syndromal pathology.
The etiology is attributed to chemical imbalances and to neurological impairments.	Modalities are genetically determined. Two components of wellness diagnoses: the relational modalities and the related syndromal unfolding of emotions as six interrelated role states lead to the respective diagnoses.
Personality diagnoses characterize pathologies, not wellness typology, they are unrelated to each other differing descriptively according to sets of symptoms.	The wellness personality typology represents alternative formally interrelated responses to stressors. We identify them according to the three formal operations of passivity activity as reciprocal, cooperation versus antagonism as opposites, and alienation versus mutual respect as correlatives. The modalities as syndromes are the crucial element of diagnosis. They may manifest with many symbolic or symptom presentations. The symbolic distinctions are irrelevant therapeutically. Psychopathologies are determined by the modality and not by the symptoms. Dominance evokes anxiety, paranoid fears, defensiveness, controls, reversals as social setbacks. Submissiveness may lead to hostility and depression, dependence, escapism in dealing with stressors.
Illness is determined by chemical and neurological factors.	The relational modalities are genetically determined as a range of innate relational responses in dealing with stress. Psychopathology is determined by the relational modality as decompensations in dealing with stressors, intensity variations, antagonism, alienation.
No graphic illustration of the illness is possible; alternatively, illness is identified in chemical neurotransmitter terms and therapeutic interventions interrupting them.	Relational modalities may be presented graphically as a position in the normative field, and as a sine curve dialectic pertaining to the sequence of personal emotions. The relational behavior is presented as vectors and the syndromal structure of behavior as the sine curve of the six-role state energetic transformation process. The circumference or set of concentric circles allows to illustrate the power position of the individual in the system, and to qualify vectorially the cooperative and antagonistic modalities and to illustrate the social and psychic tension quantitatively.
Therapeutic modalities differ along several alternative interventions: Cognitive behavioral focus on controlling symptoms, emotions or behaviors. Psychodynamic interventions focus on insights through transferential dynamics. Behavior modification uses exercises of relaxation and other techniques	The Conflict Analysis Battery represents a model integrative therapy focusing on learning about the unconscious as an emotional dialectic and the four relational modalities, then identifying the psychodynamic organization of emotions pattern using the testing generated insights. Power management is the key therapeutic modality as behavior modification interventions that modify one's attitude, the emotional and sociological experience.

Psychology of Relational Modalities

In this volume we present case studies featuring the Conflict Analysis Battery as the diagnostic and therapeutic intervention. We differentiate cases along the relational syndromal distinctions of dominance and submissiveness and how these differ in their respective social and psychological adjustments. All case studies validate the relational distinctions combining the inventory and the projective tests cross-validating each other, thus demonstrating the correctness of the formal relational distinctions.

The case studies assessment protocols clearly identify the relational modalities as four major wellness diagnostic categories. While a person may score high at several modalities, usually individuals score high on one set of scales and score low on the reciprocal ones. Dominant individuals are not submissive and vice versa. The testing rediscovers four factors as relational modality diagnoses and a fifth factor, alienation versus mutual respect, reflecting the intensity of conflict coinciding with neuroticism.

The case studies are organized under the headings of two key distinctions, the alternative personality types of dominance and subordinancy. Nuances of cooperation and antagonism are discussed where appropriate. Dominance and subordinancy determine a person's responses, which have not been identified by the DSM classifications. Freud identified relationship issues as transference but he did not identify relational diagnostic categories. Jung identified extroversion versus introversion, but neither as relational nor as syndromal. The Formal Theory identifies the relational modalities as syndromes and introduces their measurement and modification bound to scientific distinctions with the Conflict Analysis Battery. The Simple Harmonic Motion model is applied to the analysis of the metaphors.

Both natural science models allow the introduction of the rigorous constructs and formulas of the two scientific equilibrial phenomena into the analysis of the personality characteristics. The tests of the assessment measure the unconscious as alternative ways of resolving conflicts along one of the four relational modalities. The formal analysis profile, FAP, identifies ten levels for the analysis of symbolic systems.

- In the dominance cases individuals assume leadership roles. They also act out impulsively, manipulatively, occasionally conduct antisocial and limit testing behaviors. Emotionally they experience the syndrome of anger, arrogance, but also on the reverse side they experience fears of reversal of roles as anxiety, paranoia, guilt, leading to performance anxiety, and social phobias.

- The submissive individuals present relational perseverance versus withdrawal, resilience under stress alternatively escapism, acting out behaviors such as dependencies, eroticism and eating disorders, self-mutilation and hostile acting out.

The two major types of personality diagnosis are complementary compatible opposites and as such individuals with opposite modalities pair themselves in social and spousal selection. Such relations decompensate leading to pathologies; dominance turns to abuse of power and submissiveness to escapism, anxiety, hostility and depression. The case study of the judge, case #1, in the section of subordinancy, describes the decompensation of the spousal self-selection in graphic detail.

CHAPTER FOUR: MEASURING THE UNCONSCIOUS WITH THE CONFLICT ANALYSIS BATTERY (CAB)

The conceptual problem for psychology to become a science has been the lack of a measurable natural science object. This has been addressed by the Formal Theory by identifying the creative process, reflecting the unconscious, both as an energy transformation and a conflict resolution mechanism abiding by the laws of two phenomena of science. The Formal Theory identified the unconscious as a homeostatic energetic transformation mechanism reducing psychic tension, emotional energy, while enhancing social adjustment. Energy, experienced as conflict, unpleasant psychic tension, generated upon a normative deviation, is transformed to the conflict's resolution through attitude change as pleasant social adjustment and sociologically manifested as a normative conciliation. The premise of the Formal Theory is that this conflict energy transformation through attitude modification is a natural science phenomenon abiding by two phenomena of science, the Simple Harmonic Motion and the three formal operations of the equilibrial scale restoring its balance.

The formal unconscious is a structure that has two measurable components, the syndrome as a universal dialectic role sequence, and a set of wellness diagnostic categories, the four relational modalities. The natural science analysis of the creative process, a sequence of six emotions, and four types of resolution, the relational modalities, provide dimensions for the accurate measurement of the unconscious. Understanding the creative process as a well-defined measurable entity reflecting the unconscious allowed the development of an assessment. The Conflict Analysis Battery, CAB, a self-assessment, combines an inventory and creativity tasks measuring the two components of the unconscious. The inventory identifies one's relational modality diagnosis, while the projectives identify the syndromal structure of the process as a six-part conflict resolving dialectic. The unconscious transformation of energy occurs as three pendulum oscillations guided by the three formal operations. The process is validated readily as we show it manifested in most sample stories as six formally interrelated exchanges whose in*itial state stress*, is in formal relation with the end state, *compromise*. Examining these states we detect that they are reciprocal, opposite and correlative to each other thus validating the formal thesis.

There have been no batteries of psychological assessments measuring both personality types and projective patterns. Conflict Analysis, The Formal Theory Of Behavior, published in 1987 along with a workbook, the Conflict Analysis Training, contained the Conflict Analysis Battery, CAB, a self-assessment instrument founded on the theoretical premise of the unconscious as a natural science measurable entity, an innate homeostatic conflict resolution process phenomenon. The battery evolved from its inception in the 70s at a clinical psychiatric practice to its online delivery in 2014 by Maxwell Levis Ph.D., who computerized the assessment into a software application. A brief version fulfills evaluation objectives; here is a link to the brief assessment:
https://cab.co1.qualtrics.com/jfe/form/SV_3mGg2O8hjLmxBWd

The entire battery has educational, diagnostic and therapeutic functions which can be found here:
https://cab.co1.qualtrics.com/jfe/form/SV_d0xwLFs9l3C3Y45

The Conflict Analysis Battery (CAB), self-assessment, unlike all assessments, has two distinct scientific parameters for measurement: the six-role process syndromal conflict resolution entity and the four relational modalities. The combination of a personality inventory and the projective testing are complementary instruments. They are founded on the same theoretical position on the nature of the unconscious.

The inventory consists of four relational modality questionnaires and a psychic tension scale. The projective tests consist of numerous creativity tasks, only 12 tasks in the online version. These tasks begin with free-form drawings, followed by the composition of stories, and their interpretation by the test taker. The online battery generates a real time interactive collaboration and a report. The self-administering CAB takes on the average four hours to complete. The projective tests are designed to elicit both factual biographical and clinical information but also information about one's relational makeup. Thus the assessment provides material to conduct a comprehensive evaluation of an individual.

The battery has been used in its two type of deliveries: the online and the workbook based versions. It has been used in conducting therapy and also as a wellness emotional education delivered to the general public. The assessment is user-friendly and cost effective as it is self-administered and self-interpreted communicating the findings directly to the test taker without requiring professional services for its delivery and its interpretation. Of course, the assessment is of even greater value combined with professional services.

Material generated from the CAB can be interpreted systemically. Insights from this testing are actionable; they pertain to both diagnosis and treatment. They constitute the thorough psychological analysis of the individual psycho-dynamic structure. Scientific analysis of the data may be pursued along the ten levels of the Formal Analysis Profile.

While inventories have been delivered readily through online processing, the traditional projective tests, like Rorschach, are not self-managed computer interpreted instruments, they require elaborate methods of delivery and interpretation of data; hence they have been of limited clinical diagnostic and therapeutic value. The online delivered CAB standardizes the assessment as a concise program of emotional education. The online delivery of the complete assessment combines an introductory essay explaining the concepts of the unconscious and of the wellness relational diagnoses, with an inventory and 12 metaphor creation tasks and with the outcome report. Test takers learn about psychology as a science, through the introductory essay; they learn through the assessment about themselves and also about suggested changes in how to manage power and attitude to reduce conflicts. They receive a report summing up their insights and the changes for the optimization changes at the end.

The interpretation of the projective tests is completed by the test taker in a real time interactive collaboration. A seven point report is generated upon the completion of the online delivery. The self-administering CAB takes on the average 4 hours to complete. The online delivered CAB standardizes the assessment as a concise emotional education. Test takers learn about psychology as a science with the introductory essay, they learn about themselves completing the assessment by identifying their personality type, they enjoy an emotional cathartic experience, and identify how to manage power and attitude to reduce the experience of conflicts. The battery has been used in conducting therapy, but also for its educational wellness function with the general public.

The battery's two instruments

The CAB battery combines two instruments each measuring a component of the unconscious: The Relational Modality Evaluation Scales, RMES, is an inventory of relational statements with which we determine the structure of an individual's relational modality and psychic tension. The dichotomies identify the equilibrial alternatives of the Kleinian set of transformations. We distinguish reciprocal alternatives: power versus powerlessness, opposite alternatives as cooperation versus antagonism, and correlative alternatives: alienation versus mutual respect. The inventory is a 200-item personality test, The inventory has five scales. Four scales correspond to the four modalities and the fifth to a wellness versus illness dichotomy reflecting the psychic intensity as degree of illness. The inventory identifies one's personality type as a single relational modality, or a combination of features of the four personality types.

The five factors are determined by the three equilibrial operations of the scale; two operations, reciprocity and negation, determine four types of resolving, the personality types; the fifth scale based on the third formal operation, correlation, identifies the psychic intensity differentiating wellness from illness. Through the test we can make clear distinctions along the dimensions of submissive and dominant, cooperative and antagonistic relational modalities and we can measure the degree of psychic conflict tension or pathologies experienced.

Formal Theory's inventory has been researched. The results, validity, reliability, factor analysis, scale item analysis, test acceptability, are impressive: reliability of the RMES, 0.96-8.6; average acceptability of the combined battery tests 9/10 as compared with 5/10 for TAT and 3/10 for Rorschach. Traits strength along the six-role process in each modality are evaluated by the computer and reported in the analysis of the inventory online. There are several variation of the inventory instrument: the Spectrum Profile, examines four types of relational responses to 20 statements. The report identifies the chosen responses, while also identifying numerically the relational composition of a person's personality types. Another version reduces the items of each scale to seven instead of 40.

Conflict Analysis Battery's creativity tasks consist of a series of self-administered exercises designed to elicit material to reconstruct the six-role syndromal process. The multiple creativity tasks combine starting with a drawing, then composing a dialogue and then analyzing the pattern captured by the story through self-reflection. There are different topics in these creativity exercises. The autobiographical tests, *Conflictual Memories Test (CMT)* identify the stress role state of the syndrome. The traumatic experiences have formative role or reinforce the development and intensification of an individual's relational pattern. *Current Conflict* tests encourage the subject to focus attention on current problematic situations and assist the subject to develop self-awareness and mastery over relational dispositions. Similarly the two *Sociometric Tests, Balloon Portraits and Story, of Family of Origin as well as the Marital Family,* provide us with information on the individual's formative normative influences as well as information on the individual response relational pattern through transactions with the marital, and peer group systems. Contrasting parental and marital systems, one may detect areas of particular conflicts inception, facilitation, and perpetuation of mastery responses. The balloon tests examine both stress and the response role states.

The *Transparent Mask Test (TMT); and the Feelings Mask,* and *What is in your Heart* reflect the response and anxiety role states of the syndromal process. The *Metaphor Tests, Animal Metaphor (AMT,) and the Fairy Tale Test, (FTT)* reflect defense role state responses. There are nuances in symbolic parallels in the *Metaphor Tests,* Animal Metaphor: spontaneous version #1, intensified conflicts #2, conflict resolution #3, specific relationships and patterns #4, *Short Story Metaphor, Hero and Villain, Fairy Tale,* etc., they capture their author's conflicts and resolution patterns. These tests convey a great deal of information by constructing a mini-structure of the person's relational choices in very simple metaphorical languages; the samples of creativity reveal the individual's dimensions of the conflict resolution unconscious. The *Dream Analysis Tests (DAT)* protocol and *the Intensified Metaphor Test, (IMT),* focus on the reversal role state of the relational pattern. The *Short Story Test, (SST) reflects the compromise role state.*

The assessment's metaphor profile achieves the gathering and organization of art work illustrating the continuity of emotions in a pattern revealing a meaningful transparent dramatic continuum. Again the symbols and themes of all tests may be viewed as providing a thematic continuity in the process. Conflicts, mask, metaphors, dreams reflect one's universal pattern of relating. The tests are relevant in the formulation of the thematic continuity throughout the personal conflictual dynamics.

The 12 exercises of the complete online battery assessment connect memories, family portraits, imaginary animals and fairy tale figures, dreams short stories into a conflict resolution continuum. The composition entails an emotional release as well as motivation to pursue actionable insights into modifying the pattern one repeats throughout one's life. The battery helps a person to become conscious of the unconscious as well as how to steer it to free oneself from repeating a pattern that causes unwanted consequences, emotions, adversity and symptoms.

Table: Creativity tasks arranged to reconstruct the six-role process

	ROLE	EXPERIENCE	EXERCISE
1	STRESS	Experiencing conflict, the first *passivity position*	Conflictual Memory Tests and Parental Family Portrait
2	RESPONSE	Reacting to stress, the first *activity position*	Transparent Mask Test and the Marital Family Portrait
3	ANXIETY	Fears of reversal of fortune, the second *passivity position*	Hidden Mask and What is in your Heart?
4	DEFENSE	Offsetting anxiety, counter-phobic choice through defense, the second *activity position*	Animal Metaphor and the Fairy Tale Metaphor Tests
5	REVERSAL	Experiencing real loss of power, the third *passivity position*	Intensified Animal Metaphor Test and the Dream Metaphor
6	COMPROMISE	Resolving conflict transforming passivity to activity, antagonism to cooperation and alienation to mutual respect, the third and final *activity position*	Short Story Test and the Letter to Oneself

Interpretation of the assessment along the Formal Analysis Profile, the scientific analysis of the conflict resolution process

The workbook format of the battery includes protocols for the client to conduct analysis of the pattern, such as the *Cyclic Pattern Analysis,* the *Know Thyself* statement, and self-monitoring forms. The online delivery provides automatically generated reports extracted by the test documents. The significance of the testing is in that it performs a physiological function, reducing psychic tension, while also leading the person to a cognitive and a relational sociological change, social adjustment, by developing a positive attitude in dealing with adverse emotions and circumstances. This six-role process is the innate dynamic progression, which acts like a roller coaster leading the mind spontaneously from stress to compromise.

In the evaluation of the pattern the computer and the test taker unite all artwork meaningfully. Of interest to us is to recognize two aspects of the process:
(1) The conflict begins as a clear distinction in the realm of personal developmental experiences and it is usually depicted in the Conflictual Memories Test protocols. There are three memories to be identified beginning the battery; also the family balloon portrait; the four tests reflect the consistency of traumatic experiences usually reflective of a person's way of responding to stressors. These tests correspond to the initial, formative role experience determining the person's symbolic currency.
(2) The spontaneous mental process of overcoming conflict corresponds to the balance of the six roles of the Conflict Resolution Process, CRP: role assumption, anticipation of role reversal, counter-phobic role assumption, role reversal and compromise role assumption. The CRP is confirmed as a triple formal reversing of the original passivity experience. The individual reacting to the initial oppression chooses a role assumption, which creates anticipations of role reversal, which elicit defenses and eventually lead to one's role reversal, the self-fulfillment of fears evoked by one's defensive stance. The reversal leads to conflict resolution, attitude changes as the compromise role assumption, the person's conflict resolution revised identity. While the conflictual memory indicates the pivotal distinction, the Short Story represents the compromise.
Statistical analysis of Short Stories demonstrates their reflecting conflict resolution. It is important to understand the nature of Short Story writing as consistently leading to happy endings, conflict resolutions. The reason is that unlike all other metaphor tests, the Short Story writing begins without artwork. This reflects that

the conscious mind captures reality and is less influenced by unresolved unconscious conflicts. The conscious mind is prone to be realistic rather than empathic. The Conflict Analysis Battery thus captures the entire sequence of the unconscious process.

The Formal Theory introduces the unconscious as a scientific phenomenon abiding by laws of nature, first the laws of the SHM clarifying the process as an energetic entity second, abiding by the laws of the Kleinian group as a scientific phenomenon abiding by the laws of formal principles of the set theory. The formal analysis of the testing examines the assessment variables: emotions, behaviors, deviations, with the variables of the established formulas of physics and logic, the laws of scientific phenomena making the testing measurable. The formal personality inventory identifies four personality types based on the dialectic of three formal operations, the two formal dichotomies as reciprocal and opposite, the third differentiates wellness from illness as neuroticism or high psychic intensity. The Formal Theory identified five factors in the analysis of the inventory items as four alternative types of conflict resolutions, the relational modality syndromal diagnoses and the psychic tension differentiating wellness from illness as question of intensity of conflict. The formal operations uniting the process are easily understood as symbolizing the equilibrial principles, formal operations of the balance of the trays of a scale bound by a formula and corresponding to attitude modifying operations. Passivity is turned to activity, antagonism to cooperation and alienation to mutual respect. Statistical evidence validates the postulation by the inventory scales identifying clearly profiled personality types and degree of neuroticism versus wellness.

The metaphor tests capture the syndromal structure of the conflict resolution process, from stress/trauma to healing bound by the choice role behavior as the common theme; the sequence completes the symbolic universe reflecting the person's relationally determined perception of reality. The symbolic system begins with the Conflictual Memory Test as passivity, antagonism, alienation and is completed with the Short Story Test as activity, cooperation, and mutual respect. The formal alternative states in the creativity tasks validates the conflict resolution or moral nature of our unconscious as a psychological sociological phenomenon guided by the innate relational principles leading to moderation, cooperation and mutual respect in improving a person's social emotional adjustment.

The tests' interpretation follows a rigorous methodological process, the Formal Analysis Profile, FAP. Rigor reduces interpretive errors and facilitates the objectivity of the assessment. The FAP identifies ten levels of equivalence of the social science phenomenon with the two natural science ones. The parallel conceptual methodology of the physical and social realms is summarized in ten levels of parallel abstraction of natural and behavioral phenomena examining aspects of the organization of emotions as energy transformation.

The information is identified as the dynamics of stigma representing the emotional symbolic universe of any conflict.

Level 1: Universe of stigmatization includes that of positive stigma, praise or honor.
Level 2: The constructs-variables of the particular stigmatization process: S, v, a, m.
Level 3: Stigma as a process of a conflict energy and its components: $E = F \times S$.
Level 4: Conservation of energy and its transformation into energetic modalities: E1, E2, E3.
Level 5: Types of stigma conflict: Stigma is a relation of emotions reciprocal to deviation:
$a = -1/2\ KS$.
Level 6: The processing or overcoming of stigma; conflict resolution, distinction of six role state syndromal stigmatization process.
Level 7: Graphic representation.
Level 8: Conflict experienced differently according to normative systems, personality types and sensitivities.
Level 9: Quantification.
Level 10: Conversion of stigma conflict into insight, resolution.

At Formal Theory's Level 1, we discuss any phenomenon or conflict as consisting of a symbolic universe of formally related ideas or elements. These are examined in their relationship to each other, such as opposition and reciprocity. Accordingly conflict energy is considered as part of a symbolic system in context with its formal variations: reciprocal: activity/passivity, and opposite: cooperative/antagonistic, variations. Conflict may be seen, for instance, in the context of the two formal distinctions i.e. as stigmatizing (active) and becoming stigmatized (passive) at the antagonistic end of the relational spectrum, and in the context of praising, honoring, and being praised or honored at the cooperative end of the formal spectrum. These formal variations may be presented graphically as the counterclockwise and clockwise, diametrically opposed vectors within a circumference that represents the entirety of the symbolic universe of a role choice.

At Level 2, we identify constructs that enter into the experience of engineering conflict as a physical energetic phenomenon. We recognize the equivalence of concepts of the emotional system with the concepts of physics' Simple Harmonic Motion. The physics' variables are therefore introduced into in the psychological domain:
First, we recognize Simple Harmonic Motion's displacement from the state of rest as equivalent to behavior's social status deviation or normative deviation, activity and passivity (S, 1/S).
Second, we recognize SHM's velocity (v) to be equivalent to behaviors (v and 1/v, active and passive respectively).

Finally, we identify physics' acceleration (a) with behavior's emotions or motivational forces (a or 1/a, active and passive).

Unlike what is done in physics, in behavior we will refer to the +/- signs in the context of opposite relation. The designation of the plus (+) or minus (-) in front of the variable or constructs will represent cooperative and antagonistic forms respectively. With these notations, physics' variables of S, v, a will serve to identify any shift of an individual within the normative continuum and qualify that deviation quantitatively. Another crucial physics variable pertaining to the description of the experience of conflict is the construct of mass (m). This characterizes the individual's dependency needs or that of her/his emotional investment. The force of acceleration (a) will be in relation to the construct of the individual dependency needs (m), determined by another variable, the normative or cultural gravitational pull on the individual (g).

At Level 3, we are considering the experience of stigmatization (or, inversely, praise) according to the formula of physics:
$E = F \times S$, which corresponds to energy as the product of dependency or gravitational needs of the individual and their displacement from the normative state of rest. We define the experience of conflict or stigmatization as one of energetic nature quantitatively determined as the product of, first, a normative deviation (S), transgression (-S), or oppression (-1/s), of the individual within the normative continuum, second, of the emotional needs of the individual (F) defined by the gravitational pull (g) and on his dependency needs (m).

At Level 4, we consider the principles of thermodynamics, conservation of energy summed up in the formula: Etotal = Epotential + Ekinetic + Emomentum. This formula indicates that the energy of stigmatization is conserved but also transformed along a number of energetic modalities during the oscillatory manifestations of the Conflict Resolution Process as the stigmatized individual experiences shifts from states of passivity to such of activity and vice versa. During these oscillations, energies are transformed from psychic tension (dynamic energy) to social action (kinetic energy) to such of psychosomatic excitement (momentum energy). This entails that a person who has experienced a stigma has to contend with an energetic excitement, a state of conflict or stress, which somehow will affect the individual's emotional, social, and psychosomatic well-being, especially because the stigmatized individual does not communicate with others about his/her social disgrace and related embarrassment. The onus of stigma becomes a barrier to expression and therefore discharge of conflict energy. Alternatively, stored up energy is manifested in one or all of its forms, psychopathology in the realms of feelings, intense acting out behaviors, and with stimulated psychosomatic states.

In physics, Level 5 pertains to the correlation between force of acceleration (a) and of displacement (-S), a = -1/2KxS. In behavior, the correlation is between emotions (a) and normative deviation. The formula from physics signifies in the realm of behavior that a person experiences emotions which are the reciprocal to the displacement of the individual within the normative continuum. (In this case, the minus sign corresponds to the reciprocal rather than the opposite state.) According to this formula, the experience of stigmatization may be qualified by the range of possible insults to the person's balance as the deviations from the rest state, which can occur along a great number of particular nuances. We may formalize these nuances in two ways: in terms of formal-pure definition of power and in terms of the symbolic presentation of power. Along the latter, the person may be a deviant and hence stigmatized in the context of ethnic and racial distinctions, but also in the context of what is culturally acceptable or normative sexual behaviors, body image, ethical standards in political donations, classroom behaviors, etc. Norms of behavior, morality, are culturally and legally defined, but also by the person's definition of what is acceptable. In any case, the individual's emotions will be symbolically focused on the area of the normative deviation and will be in reciprocal form. For instance, the person who is oppressed will experience hostility and the person who transgresses will experience guilt, be the deviations and emotions in the sexual, political, religious, or body image set of norms. But whatever the symbolic fixation of the individual, the formula a =-KxS indicates a correlation of great relevance.

In physics, Level 6 corresponds to the trigonometric variations of the key constructs S, v, a corresponding to the cyclic or the oscillatory nature of the SHM. In behavior, Level 6 pertains to the essence of the circumscribed nature of the Conflict Resolution Process as the psychic unit phenomenon, that of the six-role state process. The relevance of these six states is manifold in the discussion of overcoming stigma as a process of conflict resolution. Here we must clarify what we mean by stigma as we differentiate one type of stigma state from another because from this perspective, stigma is a six-role sequence of passivity/activity cyclical transformations: role oppression-role assumption (RO-RA), anticipated role reversal-counterphobic role assumption (AAR-CPRA), and role reversal-compromise role assumption (RR-CRA).

In the first cycle, Role Oppression-Role Assumption stigma is seen as the duality of a norm (that is, a definition of acceptable behavior, Role Oppression) and the shift of the individual breaking the norm passively (RO,- 1/s), or actively (RA-S) within the polarized normative context. The role assumption (RA) corresponds to the transgression, in the case of the individual engaging in an active deviation within the system (-v). The definition of the stigma coincides with power process in which the role oppression or passivity is indicative of what is unacceptable (-1/s) to the individual and its reciprocal, a state of activity, role assumption, which seems desirable (-S) to the individual but unacceptable to the community and/or the individual at a later phase. In the case of voyeurism during the first cycle the individual feels the norm of the prohibition of genital exposure, feels traumatized if he has been seen naked and feels excited and guilty when engaging in voyeuristic activity.

The second cycle consists of the role states of anxieties and defensiveness of exaggerated distortions and desperate attempts to control things (ARR-CPRA). In the case of the transgressor, during this cycle the voyeur anticipates passivities of the stigmatizing behavior in the form of reciprocities from others (where S transgression seeing, then – 1/a is fear of being seen, the reciprocal of the active state of transgressing, -a), hence, with little stress, the voyeur feels totally naked and defensively controls his own vulnerability, buttons himself up and draws blinds down to avoid the anticipated passivity. In this cycle, we categorize the psychological experience of stigmatization as an ongoing mental state of anxiety and defensiveness which, instead of alleviating suffering for the individual, is responsible for the eventual setback, the actual loss of control--the fulfillment of one's own prophecy about being stigmatized, the actual stigmatization, the necessary outcome of any defensive process.

The third cycle consists of the setback, reversal, and the compromise (RR-CRA). The individual is experiencing stigmatization in a public way as defined by himself in an inevitable social embarrassment consistent with the early definition of stigma. Accordingly, a person is socially recognized as a deviant by the chorus of public opinion, the ethics committee, associates, and family. For instance, the voyeur is caught with his pants down, the abused woman who is afraid of becoming abusive loses control of herself and becomes an abuser. The person obsessed with weight control becomes excessively overweight. The person who is avoiding being controlled by her mother is imprisoned by her employer or her husband. The homophobic becomes homosexual. The person who is agoraphobic has a panic attack. Stigma is experienced in the symbolic system merely as a loss of the desirable role or power in the symbolic currency or praise that counts for the individual as bankruptcy, loss of face. The person attains his meaningful downfall and feels depressed. The individual's response to a role reversal may consist in a resolution, a compromise, a development of a new identity and an attitude. The resolution may lead to growth and freedom from conflict, in the case of a stigma, provided the person is willing to free herself from the energetic quantity that is entailed in the stigmatization. Because as long as the individual is experiencing a secret and the related conflict, s/he will be driven to ongoing defensive processing of this energy and will remain captive to the oscillatory process.

In the case of Alcoholics Anonymous approach, the stigma of alcoholism is resolved first through the communication to others of the problem and the admission of humility, of powerlessness, of helplessness, that is, through the assumption of a cooperative role and implicitly restructuring of authority relations. The individual recognizes a caring authority defined in a religious context as God, feels cared for +RO(+1/S). He is willing to care in his role assumption, anticipates being cared for, ARR (+1/a), and counterphobically only cares more (+v, +1/S). As an outcome, the individual is cared for, RR (+S), and he is willing to identify with the caretaker (+S -- +1/S), somebody who grants power to others. The basic restructuring of alternatives may be so powerful as to disengage the individual from the rigidity of the prior symbolic fixation of the obsession of stigmatization and free the person from circular counterproductive thinking.

According to the six role distinctions enumerated above, we may distinguish stigmatization according to the following alternative aspects of the sequence.
1. Through RO: the infliction of untenable, restrictive norms engendering the obligatory commission of a transgression (RA) related to the setting and breaking of norms.
2. The predominant group of suffering results from self- stigmatization, the psychological reality of the second cycle. ARR, anxiety, and CPRA, defense, lead the individual to agonize between feeling stigmatized by loss of control and by controlling a behavior defensively and losing control of the dreaded behavior and suffering distress. This category of suffering may be assisted through therapy to overcome stigma.
3. The third category of stigmatization pertains to the sociological distinction of deviating simply by being a member of a minority group. In this grouping also belong the stigmatizations afflicted to sociologically different groups, e.g. the minority as identified in terms of groups differing from the majority in terms of status, ethnic, sexual preference, physical intactness, political beliefs, etc. This stigma may not be dealt with psychologically but through social change.

At level seven we address the graphic representation of the syndromal process as a sine curve and of the relational modalities as vectors within the concentric circles defining the dimensions of the normative system. There are differences between the graphic presentation of formal theoretical alternatives as diagnostic relational modalities categories versus the descriptive depiction of Circumplex traits as personality types. Graphically the formal operations are illustrated by a normative field in which we may clearly identify the three formal operations reflecting power, attitude and intensity.

The circumplex is a flat depiction that does not distinguish the separate formal operations, power, attitude, intensity, which are clearly graphically illustrated in the formal normative model, which identifies

- Psychological and sociological context, circles versus ellipses.
- Relational alternatives of cooperation versus antagonism
- Power differential submissive versus dominant
- Reversibility of roles, variations identified as alienation versus mutual respect

The circumplex illustration misses the dyadic interactive component and misses the accurate portrayal of personality types. Traits are static states of mind. Circumplex traits are typically mapped as a circle, the axes of power and communion dividing this space into four equal quadrants. Each quadrant's location is formally related to the other quadrants, corresponding to the axial continuum.

In physics, Level 8 pertains to alternative directional rotations of the flow of energy or of the swinging of the pendulum ball. In behavior, we distinguish alternative relational modalities which lead to valuing alternative, structural outcomes. Relational modalities attain personal significance as types of personality and culturally as types of religious and political philosophy. Accordingly, what is a personality variable universally has been adopted regionally as the acceptable philosophy: In India, subordinancy and cooperation, in Greece, dominance and antagonism, dominance and cooperation in Judea, and subordinancy and antagonism in Mexico. In terms of the experience of stigma, deviation from the cultural value judgments or normative distinctions (what is acceptable behavior within a setting) will affect the individual's experience of conflict. The Greek person pursuing apples will feel like a deviant in the Judaic world of the forbidden fruit. Authoritarian, Victorian, or Catholic upbringing generates intense guilt and oppressive lack of openness. This culture creates and fosters stigma in the conduct of otherwise normal or acceptable behaviors and exacerbates the guilt generated from any deviance. Sexual practices may generate an intense system of stigmatization, anxiety, and defensiveness depending on what the individual learned from his culture. In our contemporary times of body image consciousness and wide prevalence of weight control programs, individuals are extremely prone to feel the stigma of deviation and the need to conform and excel in terms of body image. Any deviation from the norm engenders a polarized magnetic field within which susceptible individuals will develop an oscillatory pattern of behavioral excess toward either extreme pole.

In physics level 9 we examine the quantification of the process along the intensity of the relational modality scores of the five factors, the relational modalities and the psychic tension.

In physics, Level 10 pertains to the capacity for utilization of energy conveyed as the fraction of useful energy over total energy made available to the system. In behavior, efficiency qualifies health as the capacity to resolve stigma or conflict through the conversion of conflict to resolution, that is, the capacity of the individual to effectively pass from crises to identity formation and growth. Inversely, pathology is determined by how inefficient or handicapped a person is in resolving conflicts, reaching compromises and assuming appropriate identities. Health is facilitated as the environment assists the individual to proceed through the tasks of each developmental phase. The formal perspective contributes to recognizing the conceptualization of the desirable process, i.e., the optimal structuring of authority relations, the significance of attaining insight, the relevance of freedom of expression. In the case of stigma, we consider the ease with which a person resolves conflicts in general. Accordingly, we must recognize the possibility of facilitation of resolution along the directions that diminish induction of conflict and promotes its resolution.

Here lies the overall relevance of emotional education, an education that fosters emotional literacy as opposed to the traditional literacy. This objective entails the following: 1. Education to increase awareness of the orderly nature of sociological and mental phenomena. 2. Educationally enhancing awareness of cultural normative biases and personal developmental sensitivities in the shaping of conflict. In particular, youth must be educated in recognizing the significance of personal relational tendencies and of exaggerated dependency needs as contributing to becoming conflicted. 3. Providing recognition of the importance of openness and the function of creativity for the communication of feelings and the importance of availability of support systems for the reduction of suffering for the traumatized, the self-stigmatizing, and the socially stigmatized individuals. 4. Finally, the public should be aware that the system too may be modified so that it does not induce conflicts by inflicting discriminations. The individual should have recourse to change the social norms and culture, the system, so that individuals and groups may not be victimized by the defensiveness of cultural short-sightedness, prejudice, and totalitarianism.

Test Delivery and the computer generated report

In contrast to traditional assessments that typically require professional services for the delivery of the testing and its interpretation, the online tool is designed to help clients interpret and contextualize results by themselves with diminished need for professional services by identifying diagnostic categories and their syndromal configuration and predictability. (Mitchell, Stanimirovic, Klein, & Vella-Brodrick, 2009). The online version includes a report with seven tables. These personalize feedback from the inventory, RMES, and relevant excerpts from narrative responses that help identify the core relationship pattern as a diagnostic relational modality exemplified in its syndromal unfolding with twelve meaningful metaphors that can be integrated into a single dramatic conflict resolution totality. The Battery thus measures the unconscious both as a personality type diagnosis and as a syndrome, a mechanical energetic psychodynamic transformation resolving conflicts. The battery clarifies insights and then guides the person to making deliberately adjustments to resolving conflicts. Thus, the experience is educational, diagnostic and therapeutic.

There are two approaches to taking the testing: completing a workbook processing the information with a counselor, therapist or educator, versus completing it by oneself online. The workbook completion needs assistance from a therapist to maximize insights and to achieve changes. The online delivery leads to a report generated upon completion of the testing that is meaningful to the test taker without requiring professional services. The computer organizes the assessment generated information automatically. There are seven tables of feedback information, generated upon the completion of the testing; the interpretation of the assessment does not require professional services, but such are welcome increasing the meaningfulness of the record. Training is suggested and is available for therapists utilizing the testing. The record leads the test taker to self-knowledge and healing. The projective tests introduce the syndromal unfolding of one's relational modality. The artwork symbolism and texts confirm the relational modality diagnosis conferred by the inventory.

Results from the RMES and creativity exercises are automatically compiled at the end of the CAB in seven tables:

1. The inventory results: A first report presents the RMES scores based upon item selection identifying the personal relational modality diagnosis via a five-scale questionnaire corresponding to the four relational modalities as diagnostic categories and a fifth identifying psychic tension. Traits are identified for each modality.
2. The art work profile: It integrates all drawings reconstructing visually the six role process starting with the Memory of a Childhood Conflict and ending with the image of the Short Story. The metaphor pro file sums up visually the emotional experiences into the continuum of the conflict resolution process template. This sequence connects the drawings as a logical cause effect emotional dialectic, illustrating the personal drama.
3. Insights report: This segment excerpts insights generated in most tests.
4. Changes report: It excerpts statements about optimizing relations, power and attitude changes that the test taker identified during completion of 5 creativity tasks.
5. Reflections about emotions generated by the assessment experience.
6. Query responses evaluating the qualities of the assessment.
7. Transcript of the total CAB output.

The CAB's two instruments are complementary. The inventory identifies the unconscious as relational modalities and the projectives as a psychodynamic syndromal process.

Three functions of the testing

The tests have didactic, diagnostic and therapeutic functions. The diagnostic function includes determining one's relational modality, the state of one's psychic tension, past and current conflicts, relational structure of one's family and other social systems. The assessment also reflects the individual's intellectual functions, prognosis, capacity for insight, willingness to change, and receptivity to be in therapy.

The tests have a therapeutic function. They are meaningful to the testee: (1) They provide considerable insight into one's conflicts and their resolution through the comprehensible language (a) of animal and other metaphors and (b) of the formal constructs applied in the self-evaluation of the test documents, e.g., three of the six pages of the AMT are devoted to the extraction of insights from the metaphor and to the articulation of changes that need to be made. (2) The CAB tests offer emotional release through the communication of repressed material. (3) The CAB tests represent a personal mastery experience in the creativity elicited from the testee and (4) unlike any other psychological tests they place the client in assuming active role in the soul searching endeavor. The testee creates the documents, extracts insights from them, and proceeds to recommendations for change.

Discussion of assessment literature

The ultimate validation of a psychological theory lies in the effectiveness of its applications. Psychoanalysis failed to provide measurable and testable parameters in spite of the persistent need to demonstrate its validity as a theory that explains the unconscious and its effectiveness as a therapeutic modality. Psychoanalysis has been hindered in this development by the limitations of its phenomenological, propositional methodology. It has been impossible to integrate information about its constructs along any number of instruments, inventories and projectives. For example, measuring the entities of ego, as in reality testing and ego strength scales, has not been interfaced with measuring superego intensity or authoritarianism of the F scale.

Inventories

Regarding inventory literature: Psychologists have studied personality differences with the development of inventories. These differ in the dichotomies identified in analyzing personality characteristics. Current inventories identify traits as unrelated from each other.

The assessment literature has explored multiple dichotomies to identify personality types. The dichotomies are mixed between formal distinctions such as reciprocals and opposites but also non relationally connected such as love hate, hot cold, sensing feeling, judging, labeled as traits and acronyms, etc. The classic inventories identify 5 factors as unrelated traits. Researchers have agreed on a five-factor grouping of traits and these factors have been given names of key traits by their creators which are memorable by their acronyms, instead of being formally interrelated and bound by an equation of formal equilibrial operations. Research has confirmed by the statistical features five factors but as traits not as relational modalities. There is absence of a theoretical model to integrate assessment findings in a meaningful and efficient way relevant for clinical work.

DiSC and Myers Briggs inventories are informational but atheoretical. Their distinctions and traits are unrelated to each other and do not diagnose personality types. The CAB inventory identifies the five factors as diagnostic categories that represent power and attitude management formally interrelated wellness diagnoses, which potentially lead to pathologies that entail the needed changes as relational, power and attitude alternatives. Circumplex model of personality, an interpersonal taxonomy theorizes that personality traits are interactive, existing in formal relationship to each other but in reality, they are non-related factors. RMES scales differ from the Circumplex model of personality. RMES interpersonal taxonomy are interactive, existing in formal relationship to each other, as opposed to non-related factors (Costa & McCrae, 1989). Many psychological inventories have identified trait information about personality, but have not identified a personality typology. Trait findings pertain to unrelated variables, which have not been formalized. Constructs such as agency and communion are not explicitly relationally connected. Warm and cold, love and hate, power and powerlessness are not formal distinctions. OCEAN, DiSC and Myers Briggs initials of dichotomies, identify traits that are not formally connected. They do not identify actionable personality dimensions. Projectives like TAT and Rorschach have provided insights on dynamics of relating without identifying cohesive syndromal entities, or diagnostic categories founded on orderly modifiable patterns.

Regarding projective testing: Formal projectives provide insights into the conflict resolution process. The interpretation of projectives like Rorschach and TAT is a very elaborate technical procedure, identifying fragments of the psychodynamic process. The insights generated in a report bypass the test taker's awareness. Formal testing yields insights to the test taker. Current tests do not generate insights for changes as the information pertains to traits instead of identifying relational patterns entailing relational changes.

Projective tests

The literature has explored alternative theories about the unconscious without understanding it as energetic and as seeking conflict resolutions. Several approaches in literature seek to identify the process with elaborate technologies. Independently of the atheoretical Rorschach and TAT instruments process research (Luborsky, 2000) identified a central relationship pattern as the key component of psychotherapeutic case formulations. Barber and colleagues described the central relationship pattern to correspond to internalized schemas associated with important childhood relationships and experiences (Barber et al., 1998). Brenner identified these patterns as developmentally determined compromise formations helping individuals resolve incipient conflict and adjust to expected roles (Brenner, 2002). These patterns, although necessary for managing life stressors, are not always adaptive and may limit well-being.

Recognizing the clinical importance of identifying such patterns, researchers have established an array of central relationship assessment tools such as the:
Core Conflictual Relationship Theme (CCRT; Luborsky & Crits-Christoph, 1998), the Consensual Response Formulation (Horowitz & Rosenberg, 1994), the Plan Formulation Method (Curtis et al., 1994), and the Idiographic Conflict Formulation (Perry, 1994).

Graphically they do not fit on the Cartesian dichotomy, a variant of the agency and communion axes model of interpersonal behavior (Bliton & Pincus, 2020; Ghaed & Gallo, 2006; Hopwood et al., 2008; Locke, 2000; Moskowitz, 1994). Agency and communion are descriptive concepts not formally related abstractions. Reciprocity broadly corresponds with agency, while negation broadly corresponds with communion, but they are descriptive distinctions. The bi-polar continuum of elevated agency (dominance) and reduced agency (submissiveness) has been widely studied (Alden et al., 1990; Leary et al., 2001; Russell et al., 2007). While dominance has been linked with positive affect, attention to rewards, and uninhibited behavior, submissiveness has been linked with negative affect, attention to threats, punishment, and others' interests, as well as inhibited social behavior (Keltner et al., 2003).

This continuum has been found to be relatively enduring over time (Locke, 2000) and across situational contexts (Moskowitz, 1994). The bi-polar continuum of elevated communion (cooperativeness) versus reduced communion (antagonism) is similarly well explored (Alden et al., 1990; Barford et al., 2015; McCrae & Costa, 1989). Referenced by a variety of other labels, this axis is often referenced as warm versus cold (McCrae & Costa, 1989), distant versus self-sacrificing (Hopwood et al., 2008), or love versus hate (Wiggins, 1995)

While cooperativeness has been linked with positive affect and openness to interpersonal exchange, antagonism has been linked with negative affect and hesitancy towards interpersonal exchange (Smith et al., 2010; Wiggins, 1995). Each of the formal operations corresponds to a descriptive distinction. The abstract concepts are formally interrelated and lead to diagnostic categories, the relational modalities as wellness personality types that are meaningful, graphically portrayable and actionable.

Table: The theoretical premise of the Conflict Analysis Battery

The unconscious has measurable dimensions: it is a syndrome leading to four relational modalities
The Conflict Analysis Battery self-assessment is diagnostic with an inventory and therapeutic with its analytical metaphor creation tests.

Table: Equivalence between formal and propositional distinctions

Reciprocity, as adding an equal weight on the other tray. Graphically portrayed as polarities of the normative circles	Reciprocity achieves balance by shifting passivity to activity	Reciprocity broadly corresponds with agency, but agency is not a formal concept	Elevated agency (dominance) and reduced agency (submissiveness)
Negation, removing the weight, graphically portrayed with vectors in opposite direction	Negation transforms antagonism to cooperation	Negation broadly corresponds with communion. Communion also is not a formal distinction	Elevated communion (cooperativeness) versus reduced communion (antagonism)
Correlation, shifting the weight on the fulcrum. Graphically portrayed with concentric circles	Correlation is associated with the change from alienation to mutual respect	Neuroticism scales are non-relational pathology identifying psychic intensity, conflict	List of symptoms

Table: Relational Modalities diagnoses versus descriptive trait distinctions

Dominant Cooperative (DC),	elevated agency (dominance)	elevated communion (cooperativeness)	Warm, self-sacrificing
Dominant Antagonistic (DA),	elevated agency (dominance)	reduced communion (antagonism)	Cold, distant
Submissive Cooperative (SC)	reduced agency (submissiveness)	elevated communion (cooperativeness)	Warm, self-sacrificing
Submissive Antagonistic (SA	reduced agency (submissiveness)	reduced communion (antagonism)	Cold, distant
The Psychic Tension (PT) subscale items deal with emotional intensity	NEUROTICISM Items are symptoms of pathology		

Table: Differences of traditional assessments and the Conflict Analysis Battery

Variables	**Traditional assessments**	**Formal Theory's Conflict Analysis battery**
Object of assessment	Traits and symptoms	The unconscious is a syndrome, and four relational modalities We note variability in psychic tension.
Theory	Non-theoretical testing, separate inventories and projectives	Theory bound distinctions identified by both the inventory and the projective tests.
Administration	Professional services needed	Professional services are not needed for the delivery and interpretation of metaphors.
Interpretation	Inventories and projectives are interpreted along unrelated distinctions	Distinctions along the formulas of two scientific phenomena as syndromes of six-role states and three formal operations.
Function	Diagnostic	Completing the battery is educational, diagnostic, and therapeutic.

Table: Contrasting features of traditional assessments to those of the Conflict Analysis Battery

Current psychological instruments are non-theoretical. They are inventories compiled with arbitrary distinctions, and projective tests with art that is standardized like a set of inkblots and dark, dated pictures. The House Tree Person test uses personal original art work but it does not utilize a standardized use of prompts in processing information.	The Conflict Analysis Battery is theory based. It identifies the unconscious studying personal creativity as a scientific conflict resolution measurable phenomenon that identifies the personal six-emotions pattern, a syndrome, leading to four types of conflict resolution, the relational modalities. The syndrome and the modalities represent wellness diagnostic categories.
Psychological assessments are either personality inventories like Myers Briggs or projectives like Rorschach, TAT and the House, tree, person. They are not evoking emotions or actionable insights.	The CAB measures the two aspects of the unconscious. An inventory identifies the person's relational modality as a wellness personality type, and a set of projective metaphor creation tasks, with original art, and personal analysis of the syndromal relational pattern generating insights and guidance for changes. The completion of the battery represents a therapeutic emotional experience.
Current inventory tests identify traits as five unrelated factors of personality, held together with acronyms like OCEAN corresponding to five unrelated traits: Openness to Experience, Conscientiousness, Extroversion, Agreeableness, and Neuroticism. DiSC as Dominance, Influence, Steadiness, Conscientiousness. Myers Briggs has four dichotomies leading to 16 four letter personality types.	The CAB inventory identifies one's relational modality choices along a set of formal distinctions: states of passivity versus activity, cooperation versus antagonism and alienation versus mutual respect. The projective tests identify the syndromal six-interrelated emotions and behaviors, a psychodynamic pattern that entails the development of symptoms and provides actionable insights for relational changes to reduce them.
The current inventories and projectives are not therapeutic; they do not connect emotions and behaviors as actionable insights entailing relational adjustments.	The combination of cognitive information, tests evoking emotions and observation of continuity in one's emotional experiences, clarify changes to reduce inner conflicts. The tests have enormous therapeutic value.
Psychologists' professional services are needed to deliver and to interpret projective tests. Results are technical. They are conveyed to the therapist and not to the patient.	The online delivered CAB yields a 7 segment report delivered directly to the test taker. The report has numbers for the inventory's modalities. It has six tables: reconstructing the personal pattern, summing up insights, and suggested changes, a self-report on the experience and finally a complete transcript of the assessment.
Traditional tests are not didactic, diagnostic of wellness and not therapeutic. They identify illnesses. They provide distinctions as traits that are not actionable and insights that are alienating instead of being meaningful.	The CAB is a concise, personalized program of emotional education that is didactic, diagnostic and therapeutic yet without requiring professional services. It may be used both as a routine self-evaluation and in the context of training and therapy. It may be delivered in the classroom and the boardroom. The testing is an emotional learning experience preparing a person for life's challenges.

Discussion and conclusion

Inventories provide personality traits and projectives provide insights in a very fragmented fashion. The interpretation of personality inventories can be complex as well with many traits considered independently from each other. The interpretation of projectives like Rorschach and TAT is a very elaborate technical procedure and it bypasses the test taker's awareness of the significance of the findings. These test do not generate insights for changes as the information pertains to traits instead of identifying patterns as relational syndromal actionable diagnostic categories.

The CAB contains an inventory, which is more meaningful than Myers Briggs inventories, which are atheoretical, and which identify distinctions and traits that are formally unrelated to each other. The DiSC inventory identifies four factors. The REMS diagnostic categories represent power and attitude management diagnoses and that entail the needed changes as relational management issues. The set of projectives identify the psychodynamic nature of the relational diagnosis informing the test taker on how the pattern is structured and how it can be restructured to eliminate pathology.

Assessment literature has evolved measuring the unconscious but has failed in understanding it as a measurable entity. This is the objective of the CAB identifying both process and the relational modalities binding the process and relational modalities as interrelated variables of equations, formal distinctions, which are translated in clinical syndromal and relational diagnoses.

1. The Formal Theory identifying the scientific analysis of the process and of the modalities contributes the missing theoretical model linking both types of assessment, but it also places both approaches of assessment on a scientific foundation clarifying the difference between what is process, SHM energetic transformations, and what are the relational modalities, relational equilibrial principles. It addresses the current lack of objectivity in assessment literature by introducing the creative process as the measurable object for the analysis of the unconscious. It identifies it as both a circumscribed energetic and relational process leading to well identified relational modalities as syndromal diagnostic categories.

2. The Formal Theory introducing the CAB measures accurately the conflict resolution process as a syndrome and the modalities as relational diagnoses. The pattern is a circumscribed energetic phenomenon having a beginning middle and closure, abiding by scientific constructs and formulas of the SHM, yet differing from purely mechanistic equivalents. We identify the relational principles, the formal equilibrial operations of the scale united by a formula and providing the clear variables in measuring personality differences along these criteria to examine relational alternatives.

3. The Formal Theory contributes the graphic portrayal of the process and of the modalities.

4. The CAB assessment identifying the unconscious is clinically very meaningful helping the test taker to become conscious of the unconscious and recognizing how to modify the syndrome intervening in the six-role cycle towards improving its outcome by actively and deliberately modifying power and attitude.

5. The CAB mends the missing clinical relevance of the traditional assessments making the assessment user friendly and affordable, useful not only for clinically diagnosed patients but available for the well public in the context of a concise program of emotional education developing meaningful insights and guidance for changes. The CAB testing provides insights that are well received by the test takers. The assessment is educational, diagnostic and therapeutic merely by tapping creativity online leading to self-discovery and potentially healing.

Overview of the Conflict Analysis Battery's innovations

The Conflict Analysis Battery differs from traditional assessment instruments. It represents a radical breakthrough in assessment technology. It provides an accurate record of one's unconscious. Compared to other tests, the interpretation of the CAB is relatively easy and simple. The CAB has the following differentiating characteristics:

1. The assessment is theory based

The online assessment begins with an informative essay on the Formal Theory's concept of the creative process unconscious and its two components, the modalities and the syndrome. The test taker is educated on the outset on the procedure and the objectives of the assessment, utilizing an inventory for determining the relational modality and metaphors for the reconstruction of the syndrome.

The test taker understands that the battery measures the dimensions of the unconscious as a natural science conflict resolving psychodynamic entity with physical and formal dimensions. The premise of the Formal Theory is that the unconscious resolves conflicts along a six-role sequence guided by three formal operations. The CAB instruments measure the unit of the unconscious as a relational diagnosis and identify the physical and formal structure as a natural science conflict resolving syndrome.

2. The battery is a self-assessment

The battery is a self-assessment: the testee completes the inventory, constructs metaphors beginning with artwork, interprets them following a structured questionnaire and integrates them as the conflict resolution sequence to identify the personal relational pattern and how to modify it to improve one's social adjustment. The self-assessment addresses both the generation of the art and its interpretation leading to insights and changes without requiring professional services for the test's delivery and its interpretation. The self-assessment represents a new way of collecting, organizing and interpreting information based on the Formal Theory measuring the physical and formal dimensions of the unconscious as a natural science conflict resolving entity identifying a new set of diagnostic categories, along a wellness personality typology.

3. The object of study of the battery, the creative process, is a natural science phenomenon

It is identified with the circumscribed totality of a story as an energetic transformation. This entity is examined as a conflict resolution phenomenon with the constructs of the physics of the SHM organizing the syndromal dialectic of emotions and the formal operations of the scale as three relational dichotomies, directing conflict resolution to four alternative modalities and the intensity of the person's psychic tension.

4. The battery combines two types of tests

A personality inventory identifying one's relational modality diagnosis and a set of projective tasks measuring the modality's syndromal organization as a six-part conflict resolving process. The two tests are complementary in evaluating two different aspects of the unconscious: the relational modality and its syndromal unfolding. The personality inventory measures the three formal operations; the projective techniques identify the six roles of the dialectic process as syndromally interrelated emotions. The relational operations identified by the inventory are illustrated by the projective tests. The inventory test identifies the test taker's relational modality abstractly and the metaphors confirm it and clarify it as an emotional chain reaction integrating episodes of one's life.

6. The diagnostic categories are formal relational wellness diagnoses

The personality inventory uses the constructs and formulas of the equilibrial scale identifying relational distinctions of reciprocity, opposition and correlation. The personality typology along these formal operations identifies four relational syndromal modalities and the psychic intensity. Modalities are interrelated as subordinancy versus dominance, antagonism versus cooperation, and they are measured quantitatively in terms of the dichotomy of alienation versus mutual respect.

7. The projective tasks measure the syndromal organization of emotions
These are the physical energetic dimensions of the Simple Harmonic Motion. They identify the six interrelated emotions: stress, response, anxiety, defense, reversal and compromise integrated into an overarching order reflecting the unconscious need for conflict resolution leading to inner balance. The metaphors guide a person to create a conflict, then to personalize the pattern, to see it as organizing one's personal experiences, to rethink how one deals with conflicts. Insights evolve recognizing one's pattern, leading to conclusions about how to make changes.

8. The inventory and the projective tasks complement and cross-validate each other. The relational operations identified by the inventory numerically, abstractly are illustrated pictorially and emotionally by the projective tests.

9. The battery has three functions
The CAB is didactic, introducing the theoretical concepts about the unconscious and the diagnostic categories, it is diagnostic by identifying one's relational modality through the inventory and confirmed by the metaphors; it is therapeutic as the metaphors guide the test taker to deal with emotions, to identify patterns, their manifestation in one's life, and to explore changes to make, in order to optimize conflict resolution. The completion of the tasks represents an emotional experience that is cathartic, insightful, and spiritual.

The assessment experience is didactic or educational, cognitive, as it clarifies several key concepts about psychology: the conflict resolving nature of the unconscious as a scientific entity, the range of relational modalities as diagnostic categories, the nature of the formal principles of the unconscious as moral values.

The relational modality instrument is diagnostic. It uses the Kleinian group of four formal transformations. Unlike other inventories lacking theoretical formulations the inventory measures precisely the inner relational distinctions, which identify modalities, subordinancy versus dominance as reciprocal to each other, and antagonism versus cooperation, as opposite to each other and as alienation versus mutual respect, correlative to each other, corresponding to low versus high psychic tension.

The projective segment of the self-assessment is therapeutic as it represents an emotional growth experience. It leads the person to create conflict resolutions projectively and then to personalize the pattern, to see it as a metaphor of personal conflictual experiences, and to start rethinking how one deals with such responses. One draws insights about oneself and arrives at conclusions about how to make changes.

10. The interpretation of the testing is provided in a lengthy factual report
It consists of seven reports template integrating the information. They identify the relational modality with numbers, the artwork of the metaphors reconstructing pictorially the process, a list of insights, a list of suggestions for changes, feedback on the experience, an evaluation of the testing experience and the transcript of all the testing.

This report integrates the testing information, clarifying the personal relational diagnosis with numbers, then illustrated as the images of one's drama, insights, changes, growth experience. This clinical record reflects the intellectual and emotional faculties of the test taker.

The report is delivered directly to the test taker, who thus readily identifies one's relational pattern. The clinical record may be meaningful without professional services, though therapists can reinforce and clarify the interpretation of the projective material. The report has a query soliciting feedback on the personal experience and information about its therapeutic impact. Query scores validate the premise of the formal theoretical assumption confirming the scientific and moral organization of the unconscious predictably resolving conflict following certain natural science laws as a purely scientific phenomenon resolving conflicts. The assessment validates Formal Theory's premise: the conflict resolution principles are attitude changers reducing conflict; hence they are moral values. Reconciling morality and psychology the unconscious process is shown as guiding the person to respect conflict resolution restructuring one's thought process and social relations.

The report is a valuable clinical record useful for the test-taker and any observers, be that teachers or clinicians/therapists. The assessment represents a standardized valid and reliable clinical record that reflects the intellectual and emotional state of the test-taker, and her/his sociometric realities. The assessment is useful to the testee, the therapist, the educator in the classroom, the coach in an organizational setting.

11. The personal unconscious may be graphically portrayed
The pattern is manifested as the power differential in every metaphor. We may graphically portray the heroes of stories on the concentric circles of a sociogram and identify the cooperative versus antagonistic interactions with appropriate vectors within the circles. We may also place the images as the succession of interrelated emotions along the sine curve timeline of the process as the metaphor profile.

12. The tests are valid and reliable
Its statistical profile scores surpass by far existing tests' validity and reliability ratings. The inventory and the projectives cross-validate each other.

13. The assessment may be repeated to monitor therapy outcome but also to monitor and enhance progress
The testing demonstrates that the unconscious mind resolves conflict as a purely scientific phenomenon; hence the information and process may be used for educational purposes in the classroom rather than be monopolized by psychologists.

14. The CAB represents a new way of collecting, organizing and interpreting assessment information
The report has a query soliciting feedback on the personal experience and information about its therapeutic impact. The overarching order is recognizing a six-role state dialectic of emotions proceeding universally to conflict resolution reflecting an inner need for justice. The assessment validates the Formal Theory's assumption on the nature of the unconscious. The assessment promotes awareness of the conflict resolution principles as moral values.

15. The assessment is an emotional education program
Creativity and Power Management can be delivered independently of the program. The assessment is an emotional experience and as such leads to the release of repressed feelings, while organizing meaningfully a person's lifetime experiences illustrating a psychodynamic syndromal pattern.

16. It has many applications in a variety of counseling, evaluation, and educational settings.

17. The assessment is cost-effective
The information is generated by the test taker and is delivered directly to the test taker who readily identifies her relational modality. The clinical record is meaningful to the test taker without professional services; trained assistants' knowledge can reinforce and clarify the personal impressions. The self-assessment being meaningful to the creator the test bypasses the need for an interpreter. The assessment is a self-empowering exercise of creativity.

Evidence
Two volumes of case studies, Creativity And Power Management, A Concise Program Of Emotional Education Demonstrate how the Battery helps patients and educates students and online test takers. The assessment demonstrates the validity of the theory identifying the unconscious as a conflict resolution phenomenon, and hence morality as a science.

The assessment illustrates and validates the Formal Theory into the Moral Science bridging the great divide of our times: the division between science and the humanities by studying the creative process as a scientific conflict resolution mechanism. The battery introduces science and morality into psychology and changes the fields of assessment, education, therapy, and politics.

The notion of the conflict-resolving unconscious as a scientific phenomenon is good news for the perplexed world. Morality is a psychological sociological normative phenomenon, not a metaphysical one. The Moral Science reconciles religions and agnostic psychology, the intervention is making a huge difference in both revamping religions and psychology by introducing their merger into a believable and functional understanding of morality thereby freeing the public from the limitations of either. The Moral Science addresses the fragmentation of knowledge.

The Conflict Analysis Battery, CAB, represents a concise program of emotional education that is didactic, diagnostic and therapeutic. The beneficiary is the test taker but also the therapist. The experience is educational as it teaches about the nature of the unconscious as resolving conflicts along four relational modalities and a six-role syndromal process.

It is diagnostic as a person identifies one's relational modality as a wellness diagnosis and its unfolding as a six part psychodynamic syndromal entity.

It is therapeutic as it has a profound emotional cathartic function, as it provides insights on one's pattern, and as it helps a person to identify changes to reduce one's conflicts. It serves self-discovery enhancing a therapeutic experience but it also has a therapeutic function without a therapist.

SOUTHERN CONNECTICUT STATE UNIVERSITY New Haven,

I conducted Item Analysis, Reliability, and Validity Studies of the Conflict Analysis Battery which was constructed by Dr. Albert Levis.

The reliability study of the battery indicates that the different scales have high reliability coefficients to be used in individual diagnosis. The Dominant Cooperative, Dominant Antagonistic, Submissive Cooperative, Submissive Antagonistic, and Psychic Conflict Tension scales have reliability coefficients which range from .88 - .96. The Antagonistic/Cooperative Scale has a reliability coefficient of .79. This is due to the fact that it is the shortest scale. It has only ten items. The different reliability coefficients are much higher than those of the MMPI scales.

The different validity studies of the battery indicate that the scales have enough evidence of validity for its purpose.

In addition, factor analysis was conducted on the battery items. The factors which were extradited highly overlapped the original scales. The results of factor analysis are indicative of the factorial validity of the different battery scales.

The battery is comparable to the best available personality inventories in construction, reliability and validity. Also, it measures important personality dimensions based on Dr. Levis' Theory of Behavior. By continuing research, the battery will gain prominence in personality assessment.

F-Karas

Shawky F. Karas, Ed.D.
Professor & Director of the Research & Measurement Program

Reliability
As far as the reliabilities of the scales are concerned, the Conflict Analysis Battery scales are much better than the MMPI scales. "Several studies among psychiatric groups have reported coefficient within the range of .11 (Welsh, 1952) to .96 (Winfield, 1952)." (Kleinmuntz, 1967). The reliabilities of the Conflict Analysis Battery scales are comparable to the carefully constructed the California Psychological Inventory scales whose reliabilities are generally high, "in the upper .80's and lower .90's (Kleinmuntz, 1967). The Conflict Analysis Battery scales reliabilities are generally higher than those of the Guilford-Zimmerman Temperament Survey scales whose split-half reliabilities range from .75 to .87 (Kleinmuntz, 1967).

Validity
A of the "Conflict Analysis Battery" has a significant correlation with SA of the "Interpersonal Check List." The correlation is noticeably a high correlation (.778). While the correlations between SA of the "Conflict Analysis Battery" and other scale in the "Interpersonal Check List" is not significantly higher than zero. This is a very clear evidence of the concurrent validity and discriminant validity of SA.

Factorial Validity
To find the factorial structure of the Conflict Analysis Battery items, the intercorrelations among the items were computed, factor analysis of the correlation matrix was carried out using the Principle Component method, and the factors were rotated using the Varimax method. Three factors were extracted using the criterion that the sign values should not be less than one. The items of the three factors are highly overlapping with the items of the major three scales. When six factors were extracted, the six battery scales were almost reproduced. The results are clearly indicative of the factorial validity of the six scales of the battery.

Conclusion
There is enough evidence of the construct validity of the battery scales besides its ability to discriminate between the clinical groups. While "the greatest limitation of the MMPI, as critics have repeatedly indicated (Adock, 1965; Lingoes, 1965), is its lack of sensitivity in discriminating within abnormal or normal group themselves" (Kleinmuntz, 1967).

The Conflict Analysis Battery scales were constructed around the framework of a new theory and have enough evidence of reliabilities and construct validity for each scale to identify clinical groups and discriminate among them. While the Conflict Analysis Battery is theoretical the MMPI is atheoretical. In addition, the Conflict Analysis Battery scales have enough high reliabilities to be used for the interpretation of individual scores; and enough evidence of construct validity for the purpose of each scale.

Report on the projective tests
The Structure Of The Testing:

Professor Donald Mosher's Description of the Entire CAB Upon a Copyright Infringement Suit
I will begin with a general description of Levis' Conflict Analysis Battery. The CAB was copyrighted in 1984, and has a lengthy and detailed manual, The Conflict Analysis Battery: Theory and Tests.

It consists of three chapters:

(1) The Formal Analysis Profile (70 pp.), (2) The Diagnostic Inquiry for the Determination of Relational Parameters (80 pp.), and (3) Testing (approx. 99 pp.) which contains the CAB itself.

The Formal Analysis Profile presents an original scientific theory of behavior and a detailed discussion of ten levels of analysis applied to the CAB:

(1) Relational, (2) Variables, (3) Induction, (4) Energetic Transformation, (5) Conflict, (6) Syndromal, (7) Graphic, (8) Relational Modality, (9) Quantitative, and (10) Efficiency.

After discussing its functions and advantages, Chapter 2 relates the ten levels of analysis to specific psychometric indicators on the CAB. Its rationales and procedures are unusually explicit and detailed.

The CAB, itself, contains:

(1) Personal Data and Biographical Information,
(2) the Relational Modality Evaluation Scale,
(3) the Animal Metaphor Test,
(4) Balloon Portraits and Stories, the Family of Origin, and the Marital Family, Peer Group/Fellow workers,
(5) Conflictual Memories Test (Childhood, Adolescence, and Recent),
(6) Chronological List of Outstanding Conflicts,
(7) Intensified Animal Metaphor Test AMT #2,
(8) Transparent Mask Test,
(9) Report of Dream Analysis,
(10) Adapted Scribble Metaphor,
(11) Short Story Metaphor,
(12) Adapted Rorschach Response Process,
(13) Adapted TAT Response Process,
(14) Lifetime Repetitions of the Metaphor Cycle,
(15) AMT #3, Resolution of Conflict Test,
(16) Letter to Yourself, Know Thyself Statement,
(17) AMT #4, Exploring Special Relationships and/or Patterns,
(18) Hero and Villain Metaphor Test,
(19) Fairy Tale Metaphor Story,
(20) Adapted House-Tree-Person Test,
(21) AMT #5 Beyond the Obsession, and
(22) AMT #6, Special Relations Protocol

In addition, several other forms are included in the manual:

(1) Conflict in Psychodrama,
(2) Psychodrama Metaphor Analysis,
(3) Power Struggle Protocol (per-termination),
(4) Formal Analysis of Individual Therapy Session,
(5) Evaluation Format,
(6) General Feedback Information,
(6) Release and Feedback Form, and
(7) The CAB Supplement which is a form used to help convert insights into behavior modification in a specifically developed Formal Analysis Training Program.

The functions of the CAB include:
(1) determining the structure of an individual's psychic and social systems, namely, degree of psychic tension, and relational modalities,
(2) measuring the person's conflicts and their resolution patterns,
(3) measuring sociometric and normative patterns, and
(4) assessing conflicts, both past traumatic and recent conflicts, and as reviewed and changing in dreams.

The manual lists the following advantages of the CAB as a testing instrument:
(1) the CAB's interpretation follows a rigorous methodological process, The Formal Analysis Profile,
(2) the CAB has a comprehensive diagnostic function,
(3) the CAB has a therapeutic function--(a) provides insight, (b) offers emotional release, (c) creates a personal mastery experience, and (d) places client in role of responsibility,
(4) The CAB is cost effective,
(5) the CAB has multiple applications,
and (6) when used with therapy, achieves insight and behavior modification in a few sessions. In addition, the manual contains information about reliabilities and validity of the RMES.

From my study of the CAB, it is an innovative, useful, and significant test battery in my opinion as an expert on psychological tests and assessment. It integrates a thorough test battery with a formal theory and method of test analysis. Particularly noteworthy is Dr. Levis' process analysis--a set of questions designed to elicit psychological information about the drawing process itself. Also innovative is Dr. Levis' therapeutic use of questions that provoke insight, elicit adaptive strategies, and contract for change.

I would characterize the CAB most favorably as a state-of-the-art or state-of-the-science psychological test battery.

As one example of the level of sophistication involved, Dr. Levis systematically relates a model of simple harmonic motion taken from physics to the repetition of relational patterns across five generations of Greek cosmogony. Physical variables are assigned parallel psychological constructs, for example, displacement of the pendulum is equated to normative deviation. Further, normative deviation is related to location of animals from the AMT. Energy equations from physics are used to make predictions. Both graphic and sine wave systems are used to model psychological states and behavior.

CHAPTER FIVE: EVALUATION OF THE SELF-ASSESSMENT

BRIEF ONLINE BATTERY DELIVERY'S FUNCTION AS A DIAGNOSTIC INSTRUMENT

Four case studies as diagnostic evaluation with the brief battery

The four cases which follow exemplify the use of the brief battery's function as a diagnostic evaluation instrument useful for the test taker but also for the therapist, trainer. The Brief CAB uses an abbreviated personality inventory of 20 items each providing four relational modality alternative choices along the distinctions of power and attitude. The test-taker chooses one response per item. The twenty items chosen are analyzed by the computer along the relational modality choices.

The averages reveal one's personality type as a spectrum of relational choices; the chosen items can be read as a report on one's personality type, first, per modality and then per numerical composition along the two separate dichotomies, overall power distinctions and overall attitude choices. The figures reflect one's personality type as the composition per modality and per combined relational variables giving a score on overall power and overall attitude choices.

The Brief CAB uses only one projective test, the Animal Metaphor, which consists of a set of prompts guiding a person to construct a metaphor story and then to analyze it along its personal relevance generating insights and awareness of changes to be made to improve one's pattern of resolving conflicts. Additional prompts seek the evaluation by the test taker of the emotional relevance of the assessment experience.

Four case studies generated with the online delivery to a non-clinical cohort, of the brief assessment are presented below to illustrate the use of the brief testing. The cases were chosen to reflect the differences between the four modalities identified both with the inventory scores and with examples of interpersonal manifestation of the relational pattern.

The studies exemplify the instrument's function in identifying one's personality type numerically and in its syndromal unfolding. The cases also examine the value of the assessment as insights generated creating self-awareness and as statements reflecting the receptivity, of the test taker for relational emotional growth. This information is useful in the evaluation of a person's personality type and for the emotional readiness for a more complete exploration of her emotional makeup.

1. Submissive cooperative: the Peacock and the Dog

Gender	*Male*
Age	*60*
Ethnicity	*White European-American, English-Irish descent*

RMES Spectrum Selected Items:
The following chart shows the RMES spectrum items that you selected.

Items	Selection
Leadership Style:	I am easy going and do not make many demands.
Rules:	I respect rules and regulations.
Dominance:	I am a supportive friend and partner.
Leadership and Partnership:	I enjoy partnership more than leadership.
Likability:	I am liked by everyone.
Self-Worth:	I am modest; I don't expect much in return for my dedication.
Ability to Communicate:	I am very good at being supportive, but have difficulty asking people to consider my needs.
Dealing With Anger:	I tend to hold my feelings to myself. Even when I am mad, I don't let anyone know it.
Giving Criticism:	I do not like being critical. I like being patient and supportive.
Receiving Criticism:	When criticized I feel very hurt and resigned and ready to run away from things.
Need for Approval:	I have a tendency to doubt myself.
Determination:	I am comfortable not being the winner.
Respect:	I respect authorities. I am modest and unassuming.
Expectations:	I work hard to please others, and typically they are happy with my initiatives.
Self-Respect	I am modest about my accomplishments.
Vulnerability:	I feel vulnerable, but hide my feelings.
Praise:	Criticism feels like a personal attack.
Sense of fairness:	I strive for fairness in my relations, but I do not let others take advantage of me.
Prevailing:	I am easily frustrated when I don't get my way.
Help:	I have difficulty asking for help.

Dominant Cooperative	*2*
Dominant Antagonistic	*1*
Submissive Cooperative	*12*
Submissive Antagonistic	*5*

dominance	3
submissiveness	17
cooperation	14
antagonism	6

Creativity Template

This table reviews a sample of your creativity and identifies how, within this sample, you resolved conflict.

Items ***Animal Metaphor***

Image

Animal Metaphor

Members

Peacock 3 years old, Male

1. Likes to show off. 2. Is very proud 3. Does not think others are as smart as self. 4. Tries to out-do others.

Dog 8 years old,, Male

1. Very loyal friend. 2. Pretty easy-going most of the time. 3. Likes to make others happy. 4. Has a long fuse but when it burns all the way down, watch out!

Conver-sation

#1. Aren't my feathers the most beautiful thing you have ever seen? #2. They are very colorful and lovely. #1. But don't you think they are the most beautiful thing you have ever seen? #2. They are very nice and they are beautiful but I am not sure they are the most beautiful thing I have ever seen. #1. If I pulled them all off and sold them I could get one million dollars for them! #2. Wow, that's very nice. #1. Everyone would love to look as beautiful as I do. #2. Yeah, right.

Conflicts

The peacock tends to be a bit obnoxious and wants everyone to always look at him and admire his beauty. He is always bothering others and fishing for compliments. The dog prefers people that are humble and unassuming. He dislikes listening to the peacock's boasting but he puts up with it because he wants to be polite and nice. The dog really dislikes the peacock because he is such a narcissist and he would rather not talk to him but it is hard for him to avoid that without being rude or nasty and he does not want to act that way,

Reflecting on your experience completing this program, what have you learned about yourself? Has your experience been meaningful and/ or beneficial?

It is interesting to have some of my beliefs about myself "confirmed" with this study. I really cannot say I learned anything about myself that I did not already know. In that case, it does not seem all that meaningful to me. It may be somewhat beneficial since it influenced me to consider certain aspects of my personality and behavior that I should probably work to change somewhat for my own good.

Insights Template

The following table presents relevant information collected from your responses. The goal of this table is to help you identify your patterns and how they are present in your different stories.

Item	**Animal Metaphor**
Identification	*Animal #2, the dog. I often find that I should be more assertive and I do things for people that I really do not want to do. I tend to not value myself as much as I should. I am loyal to my friends and sometimes I may be too loyal and let things slide that I probably should not have. I have a neighbor named Frank who loves to brag to other people and make it seem like he knows more than he does. He wants others to be impressed with the things he claims to know about.*
Pattern	*I ran into Frank once not too long ago and he told me that some of our neighbors are big drug dealers and that the police had set up a secret camera to monitor their activities. I knew that was false because one of my other neighbors has a son who is actually a narcotics detective and he would know if that were the case. I patiently listened to Frank and pretended to believe him just to be nice when I really did not want to listen to him at all.*
Pertinence	*I sometimes run into my neighbor Frank (even though I usually try to avoid him) and then I end up listening to his stories, which are most likely all fabricated or at least greatly embellished. I dislike listening to his silly stories and I would rather just get away from him.*
Responsibility	*I am too polite and too concerned about what others think of me. I do not want to be seen as unkind or impolite. I let myself be drawn into things sometimes because I do not want to be seen as unkind by saying "no."*

Insights that have developed through this process.

It has helped me to think more about the things that I should work on to change myself.

Suggested Changes Template

This table presents information selected from your responses, identifying your willingness for change and growth.

Items	**Animal Metaphor**
Personal Change	I hope that I could become more assertive and learn to say "no" to people at least some of the time. I also might be a bit more overt in my effort to avoid people (like Frank) and perhaps they will get the message and not bother me.
Willingness for Change	The peacock should be more humble and realize that he is really no better than others. He should spend more time appreciating others and less time obsessing about his own greatness. The dog should be more assertive and realize he can do that without being mean. He needs to learn to push back on others when he feels like they are asking things of him that he really does not want to do.

Reflecting on the table above and on your experience completing the Power Management Program, please identify the changes you are willing to make.

I should make an effort to be a bit more assertive for the sake of my own peace of mind and to save myself some time listening to people or dealing with people I would rather not.

2. **Submissive antagonistic: Two dogs**

Gender	*Female*
Age	*54*
Ethnicity	*Caucasian*
Education	*College*

RMES Spectrum Selected Items:
The following chart shows the RMES spectrum items that you selected.

Items	**Selection**
Leadership Style:	I am easy going and do not make many demands.
Rules:	I comply with rules reluctantly.
Dominance:	I am deferential, conscientious, and reliable.
Leadership & Partnership:	I enjoy partnership more than leadership.
Likability:	People either admire me or hate me.
Self Worth:	I do not feel sure of myself even though I know that I am as good as others.
Ability to Communicate:	I am very good at being supportive, but have difficulty asking people to consider my needs.
Dealing With Anger:	I don't easily get angry, but when I do, I let people know exactly how I feel.
Giving Criticism:	I do not like being critical. I like being patient and supportive.
Receiving Criticism:	I am understanding and patient when criticized.
Need for Approval:	I have a tendency to doubt myself.
Determination:	I am comfortable not being the winner.
Respect:	I challenge authorities and rules.
Expectations:	I expect too much of other people and of myself.
Self-Respect	I am self-critical.
Vulnerability:	I do not allow myself to show weakness.
Praise:	I expect criticism and disapproval.
Sense of fairness:	I strive for fairness in my relations, but I do not let others take advantage of me.
Prevailing:	I give in to others overtly but quietly do what I want.
Help:	Having to ask for help makes me feel like a failure.

Relational Modality Spectrum Scores
The following table shows your scores from the Relational Modality Spectrum. Scores are tallied by adding the scores for the respective selections. The Relational Modality which has the highest score is indicative of your relational modality.

Relational Modality Spectrum	***Score (Mean)***
Dominant Cooperative	*6*
Dominant Antagonistic	*1*
Submissive Cooperative	*6*
Submissive Antagonistic	*7*

dominance	7
submissiveness	13
cooperation	12
antagonism	8

Creativity Template
This table reviews a sample of your creativity and identifies how, within this sample, you resolve conflicts.

Items	***Animal Metaphor***
Image	
Members	*dog 35, male quiet, tough, strong* *dog 35, male boastful, not very smart, annoying*
Conversation	*#2- Hey Doggo! What"s up this morning?; #1 Not much, same shit different day.; #2 Well I have a big day planned and I wondered if you wanted to come with me? #1 No. Your schemes and plans always turn out to be a clusterfuck and I am not going this time. I'm gonna dig a hole under the tree and sleep in the shade while you go screw up something again and make the humans yell.; #2 Are ya sure? It'll be fun.; #1 yeah, I am very sure. Get away from me.*
Conflicts	*#1 doesn't like #2 because #2 has created drama in the household before and #1 doesn't like conflict, yelling, and drama.*
Changes	*#2 should quit trying to lure others into his schemes and maybe #1 could be a bit more tolerant*
Identification	*#1. I'd rather be left alone most of the time and really don't like tagging along on someone else's activities. Wasn't ever an only kid but watch the dynamic with dogs I had some years ago. Most of the rest of humans I have to come in contact with*
Pertinence	*Mirrors similar events that happen with some regularity in everyday life*
Changes	*Be more tolerant of some people and better at staying away from potential situations where someone is trying to persuade me to do something I don't want to because eventually I'll mouth off if they don't back down after I've said no more than once*
Pattern	*My neighbor constantly asking me to take her here or there*
Responsibility	*I avoid people. If I go around too many people, they will piss me off, I will insult them, and it's better if I stay away.*

Reflecting on your experience completing this program, what have you learned about yourself? Has your experience been meaningful and/ or beneficial?
I learned I cannot draw and I am about to have a goddamn breakdown trying to finish this hit

Insight Template *The following table presents relevant information collected from your responses. The goal of this table is to help you identify your patterns and how they are present in your different stories.*

Identification	*#1. I'd rather be left alone most of the time and really don't like tagging along on someone else's activities. Wasn't ever an only kid but watch the dynamic with dogs I had some years ago. Most of the rest of humans I have to come in contact with*
Pattern	*My neighbor constantly asking me to take her here or there*
Pertinence	*Mirrors similar events that happen with some regularity in everyday life*
Responsibility	*I avoid people. If I go around too many people, they will piss me off, I will insult them, and it's better if I stay away.*

Discuss the insights that have developed through this process.
Screw people. They lie and only want something from others instead of bucking up and handling their own shit

Growth: Suggested Changes Template

This table presents information selected from your responses, identifying your willingness for change and growth.

Items	Animal Metaphor
Personal Change	I've made my world pretty small already as far as humans I let in and past experiences have taught me to expect to be screwed over and lied to so I don't know what else to do but stay away as much as possible, limiting interactions to the few people I trust.
Willingness for Change	#2 should quit trying to lure others into his schemes and maybe #1 could be a bit more tolerant

Reflecting on the table above and on your experience completing the Power Management Program, please identify the changes you are willing to make.

I'm staying away from people always

3. **Moderate dominant antagonistic: Dog Fish**

RMES Spectrum Selected Items:

The following chart shows the RMES spectrum items that you selected.

Items	Selection
Leadership Style:	I am very critical of people who do not cooperate with me.
Rules:	I test limits, rules, and norms.
Dominance:	I get my way more than I give into others, but I do try to listen to others' concerns.
Leadership and Partnership:	I have always been a leader and enjoy initiating and taking charge.
Likability:	People either admire me or hate me.
Self Worth:	I feel other people would do a better job under my supervision than on their own.
Ability to Communicate:	I am very private about my needs and feelings. People have to pry things out of me.
Dealing With Anger:	I get angry easily and don't hold my feelings back.
Giving Criticism:	I have no difficulty being critical.
Receiving Criticism:	When I am criticized, I become defensive and blame others.
Need for Approval:	I have a tendency to doubt myself.
Determination:	If I want to do something, I do it.
Respect:	I am reliable, but I tend to resent authorities and quietly undermine them.
Expectations:	I demand loyalty.
Self-Respect	I am proud of my accomplishments and personal achievements.
Vulnerability:	I do not allow myself to show weakness.
Praise:	Criticism feels like a personal attack.
Sense of fairness:	I strive for fairness in my relations, but I do not let others take advantage of me.
Prevailing:	I am easily frustrated when I don't get my way.
Help:	Having to ask for help makes me feel like a failure.

Relational Modality Spectrum Scores

The following table shows your scores from the Relational Modality Spectrum. Scores are tallied by adding the scores for the respective selections. The Relational Modality which has the highest score is indicative of your relational modality.

Relational Modality Spectrum	***Score (Mean)***
Dominant Cooperative	*11*
Dominant Antagonistic	*2*
Submissive Cooperative	*7*
Submissive Antagonistic	*0*

dominance	13
submissiveness	7
cooperation	18
antagonism	2

Creativity Template

This table reviews a sample of your creativity and identifies how, within this sample, you resolved conflict.

Items	Animal Metaphor
Image	
Members	*Dog 20, Male Friendly, outgoing, optimistic, extroverted* *Fish 25, Male Friendly, shy, reserved, sincere*
Conversation	*Dog #1 would be telling fish #2 all about his day and how excited he was to play ball and go to the dog park. Fish #2, although quiet, would be enjoying dog #1 presence's very much and listening intently to his fun stories.*
Conflicts	*The dog, if hungry enough, would probably try to eat the fish, so the fish would be a bit concerned and having second thoughts about the dog.*
Changes	*The dog could assure the fish he shouldn't fear him because he would never eat another animal since he is well fed by his owners.*
Identification	*I identify the most with the fish because he is friendly but has his reservations, he is unable to completely trust others, like me.* *I identify my wife with the dog because she is very friendly and outspoken like him, she is the kind of person who loves to tell stories and others love to listen to her.*
Pertinence	*I guess sometimes I feel deep down that I should not trust my wife completely and should keep my guard up, even though I really love her and love her company.*
Changes	*I would need my wife to constantly assure me that she would never betray me in any way and I can trust her 100%.*
Pattern	*Just yesterday my wife was telling me some stories about her new job and I was listening to it intently, enjoying her account of it very much, even though I didn't really add anything to the conversation.*
Responsibility	*I guess I might unconsciously distance myself from people when I'm being more reserved and quiet, which is not something I actively want to do.*

What have you learned about yourself? Has your experience been meaningful and/ or beneficial?
I have learned I'm more introspective than I assumed and I think it's beneficial because it helps me to recognize a flaw I have and hopefully work on it.

Insight Template *The following table presents relevant information collected from your responses. The goal of this table is to help you identify your patterns and how they are present in your different stories.*

Item	**Animal Metaphor**
Identification	*I identify the most with the fish because he is friendly but has his reservations, he is unable to completely trust others, like me.* *I identify my wife with the dog because she is very friendly and outspoken like him, she is the kind of person who loves to tell stories and others love to listen to her.*
Pattern	*Just yesterday my wife was telling me some stories about her new job and I was listening to it intently, enjoying her account of it very much, even though I didn't really add anything to the conversation.*
Pertinence	*I guess sometimes I feel deep down that I should not trust my wife completely and should keep my guard up, even though I really love her and love her company.*
Responsibility	*I guess I might unconsciously distance myself from people when I'm being more reserved and quiet, which is not something I actively want to do.*

Reflecting on the table above and on your experience completing the Power Management Program, please discuss the insights that have developed through this process.

I identified that I'm more introspective and quiet than I assumed, and that does bother me deep down, so it's something I want to work on.

Growth: Suggested Changes Template

This table presents information selected from your responses, identifying your willingness for change and growth.

Items	**Animal Metaphor**
Personal Change	I would be willing to take an effort in trying to be more trusting and open with others, and try to be more active in conversations instead of being the passive listener who does not add much.
Willingness for Change	The dog could assure the fish he shouldn't fear him because he would never eat another animal since he is well fed by his owners.

Changes you are willing to make.

I'm willing to be more open and trusting of others.

4. **Dominant cooperative: Lion Fish**

Gender *Male*
Age *35*
Ethnicity *Black*

RMES Spectrum Selected Items:
The following chart shows the RMES spectrum items that you selected.

Items	Selection
Leadership Style:	I demand that others cooperate with me.
Rules:	I respect rules and regulations.
Dominance:	I get my way more than I give into others, but I do try to listen to others' concerns.
Leadership & Partnership:	I am a great leader and very confident about my ability to take charge.
Likability:	People admire me or respect me.
Self Worth:	I feel other people would do a better job under my supervision than on their own.
Ability to Communicate:	If I have a thought, I say it loud and clear regardless of other people's feelings.
Dealing With Anger:	I don't easily get angry, but when I do, I let people know exactly how I feel.
Giving Criticism:	I do not like being critical. I like being patient and supportive.
Receiving Criticism:	I am understanding and patient when criticized.
Need for Approval:	I try to please others and get their approval.
Determination:	If I want to do something, I do it.
Respect:	I challenge authorities and rules.
Expectations:	I expect too much of other people and of myself.
Self-Respect	I am modest about my accomplishments.
Vulnerability:	I do not allow myself to show weakness.
Praise:	I welcome compliments as well as criticism.
Sense of fairness:	I strive for fairness in my relations, but I do not let others take advantage of me.
Prevailing:	I always make concessions out of consideration of others.
Help:	Having to ask for help makes me feel like a failure.

Relational Modality Spectrum Scores
The following table shows your scores from the Relational Modality Spectrum. Scores are tallied by adding the scores for the respective selections. The Relational Modality which has the highest score is indicative of your relational modality.

Relational Modality Spectrum	*Score (Mean)*
Dominant Cooperative	*11*
Dominant Antagonistic	*2*
Submissive Cooperative	*7*
Submissive Antagonistic	*0*

dominance	13
submissiveness	7
cooperation	18
antagonism	2

Creativity Template

This table reviews a sample of your creativity and identifies how, within this sample, you resolved conflict.

	Animal Metaphor
Items	
Image	
Members	*Lion 25 Male Fearless, protective, leader* *Fish 18 Male Fast, smart, Independent*
Conversation	*#1 Hey fish how is going? #2 Everything is good. You? #1 Not much besides ruling the jungle, you know how that is. About to go find something to eat. How's the family? #2 They're great. At least I think they're great, haven't seen them in a while. Trying to do my own thing. #1 I can't relate to that. My family is large and I feel responsible for all of them. Well hope everything works out for you. Hope to see you soon #2 Yea it was good seeing you too. Well not the part where you almost ate me but everything else*
Conflicts	*One almost ate the other*
Changes	*The fish should remain as cautious as possible and the lion should keep leading and watch out for other lions*
Identification	*The lion. I too have a large family that I feel responsible for.* *The average person just trying to survive and make a living.*
Pertinence	*Although I relate more to the lion I feel like my life is more like the fish. Just trying to survive and make a decent living for myself and family.*
Changes	*Keep working and striving for the best and progressing in my career.*
Pattern	*I had an idea at work and I pitched it to my supervisor. He tried pitching the idea as his own. The bigger and more powerful people always try to eat the smaller ones for lunch.*
Responsibility	*As a fish i think we all have experienced something like this in life. We all most likely have experiences with a larger entity trying to infringe.*

Has your experience been meaningful and/ or beneficial?

I learned there are somethings I can do differently and when I do become more of a leader in my organization to support and help progress my subordinates instead of stepping on them.

Insight Template *The following table presents relevant information collected from your responses. The goal of this table is to help you identify your patterns and how they are present in your different stories.*

Identification	*The lion. I too have a large family that I feel responsible for.* *The average person just trying to survive and make a living.*
Pattern	*I had an idea at work and I pitched it to my supervisor. He tried pitching the idea as his own. The bigger and more powerful people always try to eat the smaller ones for lunch.*
Pertinence	*Although I relate more to the lion I feel like my life is more like the fish. Just trying to survive and make a decent living for myself and family.*
Responsibility	*As a fish i think we all have experienced something like this in life. We all most likely have experience with a larger entity trying to infringe.*

Please discuss the insights that have developed through this process.

I have a better understanding of the situation I went through and what I would do differently.

Growth: Suggested Changes Template

This table presents information selected from your responses, identifying your willingness for change and growth.

Items	**Animal Metaphor**
Personal Change	Standing up for myself and keeping good ideas closer to the vest.
Willingness for Change	The fish should remain as cautious as possible and the lion should keep leading and watch out for other lions

please identify the changes you are willing to make.

I change by not being so open with my ideas and helping boost coworker up.

COMPUTER GENERATED REPORT OF THE COMPLETE ONLINE DELIVERED BATTERY

The following is a transcript of the online delivered complete battery

Relational Modality Scores

The following table shows your overall RMES score profile. The relational modalities correspond to alternative models of resolving conflict, all of which have strengths and weaknesses. You might score higher in one or several scales. The highest score reflects your Relational Modality type as one of the four characters of the Wizard of Oz story. The types differ according to the mode of pursuing power versus powerlessness qualified as antagonistic/ competitive, the Lion and the Tin Man, versus cooperative/collaborative alternatives, Dorothy and the Scarecrow.

Relational Modality	***Scores***
Dominant Cooperative	***2.83***
Dominant Antagonistic	***2.42***
Submissive Cooperative	***3.68***
Submissive Antagonistic	***1.97***
Psychic Tension	***2.73***

Relational Modality Sub scores

The next charts review in greater detail each of the four relational modalities and the six accompanying sub-scores. The sub-scores correspond with more nuanced qualities that characterize the relational modality. Each of these sub-scores are characterized by a descriptive label as well as by a position with the Stress, Response, Anxiety, Defense, Reversal, Compromise dialectic. This pattern is a useful template to chart psychological responses to conflict, allowing you to identify specific areas to work on making changes.

a. ***Dominant Cooperative Scoring Profile***

Relational Modality	***Weighted Average***	***Demanding (Stress)***	***Leadership (Response)***	***Competitiveness (Anxiety)***	***Determination (Defense)***	***Invulnerability (Reversal)***	***Outspokenness (Compromise)***
Dominant Cooperative	*2.83*	*3.8*	*3*	*1.67*	*4.5*	*1*	*1.33*

b. ***Dominant Antagonistic Scoring Profile***

Relational Modality	***Weighted Average***	***Irreverence (Stress)***	***Territorialism (Response)***	***Explosiveness (Anxiety)***	***Self-Righteousness (Defense)***	***Insubordination (Reversal)***	***Independence (Compromise)***
Dominant Antagonistic	*2.42*	*1*	*3.71*	*2.17*	*2*	*3.71*	*4*

c. ***Submissive Cooperative Scoring Profile***

Relational Modality	***Weighted Average***	***Trustworthiness (Stress)***	***Selflessness (Response)***	***Flexibility (Anxiety)***	***Non-Confrontational (Defense)***	***Considerateness (Reversal)***	***Compliance (Compromise)***
Submissive Cooperative	*3.68*	*3.67*	*5.5*	*4.33*	*2.79*	*4.5*	*5*

d. ***Submissive Antagonistic Scoring Profile***

Relational Modality	***Weighted Average***	***Disinterestedness (Stress)***	***Hostility (Response)***	***Passivity (Anxiety)***	***Privacy (Defense)***	***Resignation (Reversal)***	***Self-Restraint (Compromise)***
Submissive Antagonistic	*1.97*	*1.5*	*1.67*	*2*	*2.79*	*1.8*	*2.75*

e. ***Psychic Tension Scoring Profile***

Relational Modality	***Weighted Average***	***Degree of Conflicts***	***Duration of Conflicts***	***Depression***	***Self-conscious Symptoms***	***Specific Conditions***
Psychic Tension	*2.73*	*1.83*	*3.57*	*3.46*	*1.83*	*2.92*

Creativity Template

The following table presents your drawings organized along the six-step process, each story revealing one of the links in the chain reaction. This table groups your artwork in relation to each other as the set of six emotions. The images integrate the fragments of the personal experiences into one's conflict resolution pattern encrypted in a symbolic language. The table identifies how your personal pattern fits into a dialectic, evolving from conflict to resolution and progressing from passivity states or emotions to activity states or behaviors.

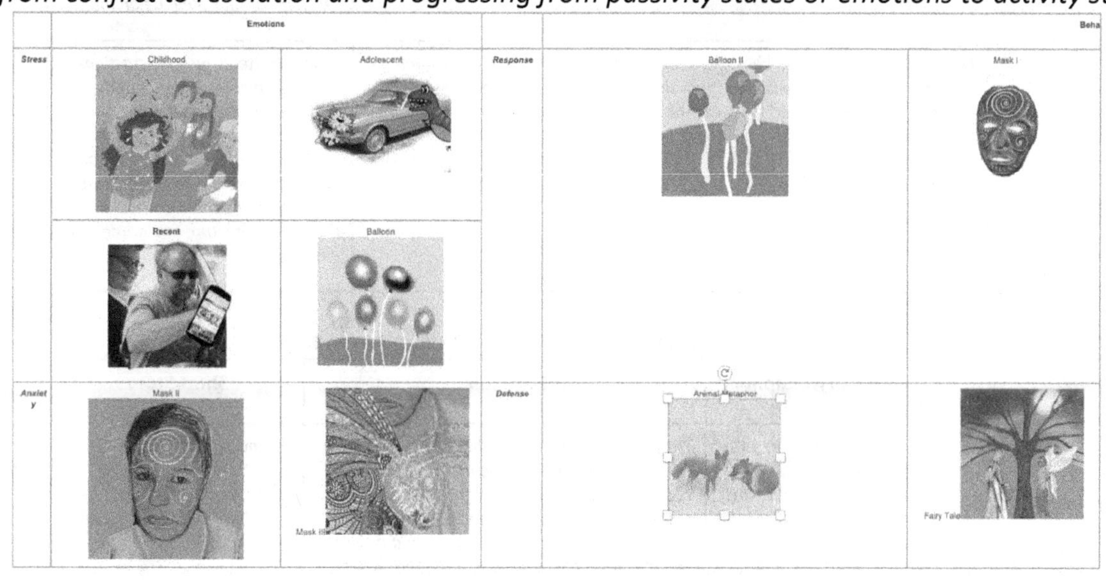

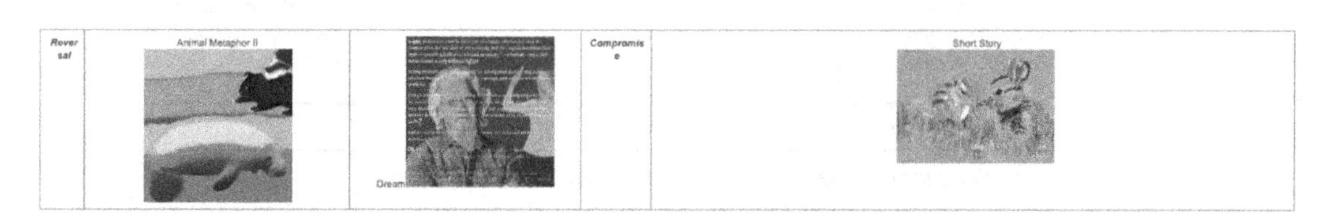

Insight Template

The following table presents relevant information collected from your responses. The goal of this table is to help you identify your patterns and how they are present in your different stories.

	Mask	Animal Metaphor	Fairy Tale Metaphor	Short Story
Identification	*Open heart*	*I am the domesticated coyote. Roxy has had some rough times, but she's getting her strength back and is ready to take on the world and be part of her community in a good way. She sees the kindness in other animals even if they don't see it yet and hopes that if we are just kinder to each other that we can heal some past hurts.*	*Esmé, she is a generous farm-girl that just wants to be in a place that is beautiful with people she loves.*	*I am the chipmunk. I am eager to have fun each day and I get easily bored if I'm not experiencing fun new stuff*
Pattern	*The mask that represents strength and courage is a fight to stay on track because there is sadness and beauty in life, (the transparent mask) the mask is the armor for the heart which is strong and resilient but bears scars from past battles.*	*I may see her as someone who needs a friend, but so do I. I will approach this relationship as equals.*	*I think I may have a bit of an unrealistic ability to wish that things will magically change with my past loves and that they will wake up and realize what they missed, that we will someday get back together when we are old and wise and they will appreciate me.*	*My husband Randy can make fun into a chore. He seems more familiar with this idea that just lazing around eating strawberries in the sun isn't fun. I'd like to be with a partner who really values the fun in life and doesn't make everything into a chore.*

Pertinence	*She tries to move on when it seems like the right thing to do and keeps her heart open.*	*It pertains to e because I am starting over again to a certain degree. Finding my community and learning to trust people again.*	*As I age I realize what is most important to me which is to surround myself with people that are kind.*	*We used to pick berries a lot as a child, as we were often told not to eat them all. My brother was very clumsy and adorable and would often squish them by stepping on them by accident. I think we were expected to be sort of productive and fun was secondary, but I have switched this for the little animals.*
Responsibility	*It feels accurate.*	*I can just be open to folks being who they are and not jumping in with too many ideas - hard for me to do. I need to let them be part of the process.*	*Whew, I think I need some help with this part. Stop trying to save people. Don't look for drama. Look for a sense of humor and a sense of kindness first and foremost.*	*I can admittedly be a procrastinator, when a chore is particularly boring or mathematical, it is hard for me to get motivated. I also don't like to exercise unless it's an adventure, like a bike ride or a walk in a beautiful place. I particularly like the architecture and gardens in a nice city like Saratoga.*

Growth: Suggested Changes Template

The following table presents information selected from your responses, identifying your willingness for change and growth.

	Mask	Animal Metaphor	Fairy Tale	Short Story
Personal Change	*When someone deems them self hurtful and untrustworthy, keep them at a safe distance and don't try to fix them, that is up to them. Show kindness and compassion where it is possible and not to the deficit of staying safe.*	*They should agree to be honest and real, that kindness will guide their relationship.*	*They should stop fearing what people will think. They should be with people that love and support them and leave behind the closed-minded judgmental ones that are apt to keep them small. Hopefully, by living a happy and fulfilling life, they will show others to stop fearing one another too.*	*Let my kids have this kind of fun and not make fun into a chore, work and fun can be together, but fun should just be fun.*
Willingness for Change	*I will just try to keep my heart open and find someone to share my heart with that is kind and sweet and has a sense of humor.*	*I can just be open to folks being who they are and not jumping in with too many ideas - hard for me to do. I need to let them be part of the process.*	*I am willing to stay away from red flag people and orange, and yellow. I think. I just wish there was a litmus test.*	*I would like to focus more on being healthy and doing things sometimes that I need to, whether it's a boring task that needs to be done (paperwork) or fun that is meant to be fun!*

Letter to yourself summary

Relational Modality	*Does it appear that I am a scarecrow? Kind of along for the ride. I'd like to be the good witch if I could choose.*
Six-Role Process	*My best guess is that some of my relationships, like with my origin family and husband represent stress, trust issues and betrayal. As time goes by I find others that I can trust, that are cooperative and equal in partnership with me.*
Insight	*Issues such as trust and boundaries (?) come up repeatedly. I will be interested to see what you and my therapist think.*
Changes	*This one is great! It is all the things I am really working on to be a happier healthier person. Thank you for affirming that!*
Feelings	*It was amazing, a lot of work and it took me a couple of days to get through it. I loved the drawing prompts and the stories that were remembered from them. I used sort of a digital collage method on my iPad for the most part which helped me get the imagery that I wanted quickly. I felt like they just kept getting more interesting, the drawing themselves, and that was a lot of fun, very cathartic, and sometimes made me really emotional. It was a powerful experience. I am grateful for the chance to do this.*

Outcome Evaluation

The Conflict Analysis Battery was informative about the concept of the unconscious as a conflict resolving entity.	Agree
The Conflict Analysis Battery provided clear information about relational modalities as wellness categories.	Agree
I felt the Conflict Analysis Battery helped me gain understanding about the nature of the unconscious as an orderly conflict resolution mechanism.	Agree
The program was diagnostic. It helped me to identify my relational pattern.	Strongly Agree
Identifying my relational pattern helped me to better understand myself.	Strongly Agree

Which one of the following relational modality type do you identify with? A for Dorothy, dominant cooperative, B for the Lion, dominant antagonistic, C for the Scare Crow, submissive cooperative, and D for the Tin Man, submissive antagonistic?	Type C
The Conflict Analysis Battery helped me understand the conflict resolution process as a sequence of six emotions: stress, response, anxiety, defense, reversal and compromise.	Agree
This program helped me to identify changes to improve my relational adjustment.	Agree
I found that the six-role template, combining images and text, integrated fragments of my life into a meaningful conflict resolution pattern.	Agree
Completing the creativity component was an emotional experience.	Strongly Agree
I identified with one or both of the characters in the narrative stories that I created.	Agree
This program offered me new information about myself.	Agree
I was surprised by the personal relevance of the creativity component.	Agree
The creativity component was therapeutic; the metaphors helped me to better understand myself and to also think of making changes.	Strongly Agree
I was surprised by how much insight I gathered.	Strongly Agree
This program helped me identify how to better manage power.	Neither Agree nor Disagree
I think that this survey would be useful for high school students.	Agree
I think that this survey would be useful for clinical evaluations.	Agree
After taking this survey, I feel more motivated to make changes in my life.	Agree
The program offered me both diagnostic and therapeutic information about myself.	Agree
The suggested value for taking this program should be:	$100

ONLINE VALIDATION STUDIES

The self-assessment validates Formal Theory's premise on the nature of the unconscious and its clinical impact in becoming conscious of the unconscious. Validations are provided in the identification of one's modality of the projective tests integrated in the syndromal sequence. Clinical relevance validation is offered by one's comments in the query along the didactic, diagnostic and therapeutic impact to the test taker but also in the clients comments about the testing's emotional cathartic experience.

The personality inventory (Relational Modality Evaluation Scale) identifies the modality. The metaphor exercises complete a resolution in six exchanges.
The two instruments: the inventory and the projectives identify the unconscious.
The assessment experience is a meaningful emotional cathartic experience for the test taker.
The assessment validates the theory confirming the premise by capturing the person's relational modality with the inventory and by identifying the syndrome as the correlation of the six role states as the continuum completed by the metaphor tests, departing from a conflict, stress and ending with a compromise being in formal relationship to each other defined by the three formal operations.
The subject and the observer analyst of the protocol can identify the interrelation of the inventory diagnosis and that imparted graphically with the metaphors. The information validates the theoretical premise both subjectively by the test taker's comments but also objectively in identifying one's relational modality diagnosis

using the inventory, and by identifying one's syndromal process as a six-role conflict resolution mechanism. The metaphors may be connected into the syndrome of a six-part emotional dialectic: Stress identified by Conflictual Memories Test, Balloon Portraits, Response as the Transparent Mask Test, Anxiety as the hidden emotions. Defense as the Animal Metaphor Test and the Fairy Tale Metaphor Test, Reversal as Dream Analysis and Intensified Animal Metaphor test, Compromise as Short Story Metaphor.

While we seek the technical evidence of the process examining the associations generated as a mechanical, scientific mechanism, the syndrome and the relational modalities, we also examine the clinical benefits, insights generated by the assessment. The test taker experiences clinically emotional relief and insights about one's unconscious pattern through the assessment. S/he identifies one's personality type as a relational modality resolving conflicts, and also identifies changes that can reduce discomfort or maladaptive adjustment.

QUERY RESULTS CONFIRM THE EFFECTIVENESS OF THE ONLINE DELIVERY OF THE BATTERY AS AN EMOTIONAL EDUCATION PROGRAM THAT IS DIDACTIC, DIAGNOSTIC AND THERAPEUTIC

The introductory essay of the battery explains the nature of the unconscious and of the relational modalities a relational modality and as a conflict resolution process integrating meaningfully the fragments of the battery into dramatic totalities. Does the testee recognize his modality and its syndromal unfolding? Does he thus become conscious of the unconscious and motivated to modify it?

The query survey below documents the impressions generated by the online delivery of the complete battery self-assessment along the three functions of the testing. The questions of the query examine sequentially the effectiveness of the assessment in fulfilling the program's three objectives: didactic or cognitive, diagnostic by identifying one's psychodynamic relational pattern, and therapeutic by learning from the insights and seeking changes to optimize one's way of dealing with conflicts.

1. The principle function of the inventory is the diagnosis of a relational pattern. The inventory is diagnostic of the relational modality. It validates the hypothesis that the unconscious proceeds resolving conflicts along the three formal dichotomies. The diagnosis of the relational modality explains the particular syndromal unfolding of emotions and behaviors.
2. The metaphor testing is therapeutic because the tests allow the test taker to become conscious of the manifestation of the unconscious pattern validating the fact that the mental process proceeds along the six-role emotional transformative sequence to complete a resolution. The metaphors besides presenting the pattern confirm the relational modality diagnosis identified by the inventory test. Thus the testing results are complementary.

Is the relational modality diagnosis from the inventory confirmed and also illustrated in its psychodynamic manifestation through the metaphor testing? Are the metaphors integrated into a conflict resolving dialectic?

Do the two types of tests validate the thesis of the natural science moral unconscious that conflict resolution process occurs guided by three formal operations and that it unfolds along a six-role state dialectic?

A computer generated report compounds the parallel discoveries of both types of testing. The analysis of the relational items is relatively simple. It is a matter of automatic processing of the answers to the inventory scales. The analysis of the series of metaphors is more complex. The report compounds information by summing up all answers to parallel questions across the testing. A single narrative presents the factual choices of characters and their attributes. The next narrative accumulates the insights about one's conflicts. Another narrative places together the changes a person wants to make. The several narratives confirm the relational modality diagnosis as characterized by one's choices in the inventory.

The report combines the relational modality diagnosis from the inventory with its clinical manifestation through the metaphor testing. The Insights table reinforces understanding the relational psychodynamic organization of one's emotions, while the Changes table identifies relational changes in power and attitude to reduce conflicts experienced. Along the modality the test takers suggest changes: distressed dominant individuals experience anxiety and seek moderation, while submissive individuals experience depression and hostility identifying their need for assertiveness.

Conclusion from the testing

The query results of the online delivery of the testing yield statistically evidence that we have a didactic, diagnostic and therapeutic instrument. The results are of theoretical significance attesting that the Formal Theoretical hypothesis on the nature of the human unconscious is correct.

The assessment is successful because the unconscious is a measurable natural science entity. It has the scientific attributes of a formal and energetic structure with a moral or adjustive function; it entails that the diagnostic categories of the four relational modalities are correct. It confirms that the unconscious is spontaneous in its relational choices but that once the person becomes conscious of the unconscious s/he will make the correct relational or moral choices.

We may conclude that the CAB or 'Wizard' assessment is a simple cognitive machine that readily helps the test taker to identify her his relational modality diagnosis and to arrive to corrective behavioral power management choices. The software of the assessment generate information that delivers insights to the student and the patient without a therapist's participation. The testing alone produces significant educational objectives and also a clinical record that is useful in documenting an evaluation and also examining therapy outcome.

Comments of test takers upon completing the online self-assessment

354. Reflecting on the program as a whole, please share your thoughts and feelings about this learning experience.

It really makes you look at yourself and asses what's going on in your life, it was a good experience and I hope I can improve my quality of life by making gradual changes to how I think about things

It's been an interesting experience! **I feel like I've learned some new things about myself, and had the chance to look at myself in a new way.** I definitely feel emotionally exhausted, so I think my emotions and inner self got a good workout in!

I thought this experience was very unique. I am surprised I was able to learn so much about myself that I didn't realize. I never knew that events from my past really shaped the life I have now. You don't really see the connections as you are going through them, but see the pictures and what I wrote laid out in a sequence was eye-opening.

It was fun but very strange.

I think it was a great program to find out about oneself. It was kind of like digital meditation. I was able to recall and think about past memories and visualize them with the drawings.

This was a wonderful take on my life and the way I think about things. I am very thankful for the opportunity because it has shined a new light on what I'm willing to say and do in order to make things more enjoyable for me in life... Thank You.

This helped get a lot of feeling out. i learned somethings about myself like i'm not a good drawer, but i digress. this was a fun and interesting way of learning those things. i feel like some weight has been lifted.

I think this was a fun way to force myself to look inwards, both implicitly and explicitly, to learn about my inner workings and motivations in life.

It was hard at times, but **there was a reoccurring theme throughout my life that became more apparent as the study progressed**. I will continue to be kind to myself, and to protect myself from people that are not healthy for me.

It's interesting to see everything come together and explained.

This was very interesting! I did not know what to expect going in, but I actually had a lot of fun participating. **I knew a lot of these things already, but some of my drawings really surprised me when I was asked to talk more in depth about them.**

It has been interesting and enlightening!

I really enjoyed it. I am not very good at the drawing part of it but i enjoyed trying and thinking about the different scenarios

It is impressive to me how things from different exercises came together to form a coherent statement about the way I handle myself and other people. At first, some of the drawings and the point of them was slightly confusing because I didn't know how it was going to come together in the end. **However, the farther I went, the more it made sense and gave me an interesting insight into my own head.** Not only did I have to confront some less than pleasant memories, but I was able to handle them in a way that gave me creative freedom to express it as I needed to. Exaggerating some things and downplaying other things. It tells me that I've been hiding in a turtle shell for goodness knows how long and seem to have forgotten how to come out of it. I am already making some small, manageable changes to try and attain the things I want out of social relationships, but they are baby steps. This gives me an idea of how I can continue and where I can go with it. The better I know myself, the better I can be at showing others who I am.

I am kind of saddened. I see a lonely person who has shut herself out. I don't know if I am over reading it. IT is a lot of information but it seems like the information combined is familiar to me even though this is my first time reading it. I wish I had more information of what it all means and advise on how to address issues I think I see in it.

It was very interesting and provocative.

I need to talk about how I feel

It exhausted me. The drawings are a lot of work. My mind keeps flashing the drawing of my mom and I holding hands in the bedroom on the last night I saw her 28 years ago, and not in a good way. It just keeps flashing and making me sad. Sometimes I hoped to have put behind me just weeks ago after I came out of being depressed. It made me incredibly upset and sad to draw it. but maybe there's a reason my mind latched onto that one picture. Perhaps seeing it often in my head will make that memory fade more. I don't know, that was a pretty huge memory. **Again, I think writing it out helped on one level, and I probably needed that.**

I have been given an insight to my character that I had not realized before. As much as I was trying to avoid it, I was becoming like my mother and father. I wanted to control my finances and blame my husband if things did not work out the way I wanted them to. I need to be less controlling and not bottle up my feelings. I need to be more understanding and listen to my husband's wants and desires as well. I need to experience life and not be afraid of it. I need to meet new people and be open to new friendships. Life is always changing and I need to accept the changes and either move with it or move beyond it.

It's been very confusing and took a long time.

I am happy with the experience. It was great to go through.

This has helped me to change the way I think and to let go of old news and to better myself for the future

I feel like it opened my eyes to seeing how I react to certain things and situations. I have been able to pinpoint feelings that I have had or see myself in other's situations. I can tell how I have been acting and how I actually should be acting when it comes to certain situations or feeling different emotions.

I think it was a great way to explore yourself

This was a great learning exercise. It is very thorough and covers a lot of ground. I love that in the end I can see my scores and how everything came together and was related in the end. Very interesting indeed.

I learned a great deal about myself. I went into the program thinking that drawing a bunch of pictures was going to be useless. I thought it was just a glorified art project. I was very wrong. **Sketching out the ideas helped me put a picture to my thoughts and feelings. When I looked at the pictures I was able to articulate feelings I didn't even realize I had. I feel like I was able to see how I truly am. This was great because it allowed me to see areas I can improve in. Like a cat, I am a solitary animal. I shy away from people and am self absorbed. I now realize that I can have more fulfilling relationships by opening up to people.**

It was interesting experience to know myself more as a whole. After the writing process I noticed that what I answered in the bubble questions were not so accurate.

This was an amazing experience. It's sad but if I hadn't been paid via mTurk to try this I wouldn't have. Now I can't imagine not doing it. It's been so long since I allowed myself to doodle or play with ideas. I needed to do that though to get in touch with that other aspect of myself. **I will be using what I learned here in the future.**

It opens up my mind and lay my life out for me in a path that I can see and understand, I now know the importance of the steps that I went through in my life. All are important and are steps for me to complete my life and have a proper path. Without writing it down, it is all a jumbled mess. I am glad to participate in this project, it helps me with my healing process.

It was long and tiring. By the end of it, I think my brain is really hurting and I cannot retain a lot of the information. I think It requires a lot. I would have a hard time doing it just for fun.

It did help explore my inner-self and try to find the roots of my problems and why I am the way I am. By focusing on the root, I can find the solution to lessen its impact on me and use it to sprout up great fruit for the future.

It has been exhausting to be honest. **I realize as I read through everything I wrote that I have a serious issue with trust. I have been so afraid to trust people that I do not tell them how I really feel and this has hurt me. I have mentioned conflict and trust in my previous relationships so many times that I realize I have put up a wall and that only I can take it down and free myself from the restrictions I have placed on revealing my true feelings to people. I need to not be so afraid to be myself completely. It has taken a long time to go through this process (nearly 9 hours!) but it has been insightful.**

That I wish I had more to write about but at least I got to reflect a bit and realize a bit more what I have to do.

It was nice to really pinpoint where my character flaws were and come up with a plan to fix them.

I never really thought of how my Dad leaving affected me to the point where I have to protect my Mom and never say no but also enable my Dad because I am afraid he will leave again. **I realize how I live my life for others and not myself and how I don't think i am as important as other peoples needs**

I can see some things that I need to change.

This was really neat. I was confused at times but I got it together. I have been told I need to make changes and from this I can tell I need to as well.

I think it can be rare to reflect on your life. It allowed me to analyze my experiences and trust in my decision making process.

This was a really fascinating learning exercise. I've not often thought about aspects of my personality in the context of my entire life, or with how I handle conflict. As someone who loves literature and film, it's easy for me to escape into a fictional world, but I think the real draw for fictional worlds, to me, has always been how they reflect certain aspects of our real lives, and of humanity. These exercises have given me not just a better understanding of myself, but of how I process real life situations through the lens of fiction.

I like this program, but I could have done without the art portion. I tried my best to be creative; however, art is not my strong suit. Having to draw reaffirmed my beliefs that I am horrible at it, but **the program overall was a pleasant experience that I believe I will carry with me and use to make myself a better person.**

Summary of statistics on the group of 47 test takers regarding the assessment experience as educational, diagnostic and therapeutic

The program was didactic

1. The Power Management Program was informative about the concept of the unconscious as a conflict resolving entity. Agree: 91%
2. The Power Management Program provided clear information about relational modalities as wellness categories. Agree: 77%
3. I felt the Power Management Program helped me gain understanding about the nature of the unconscious as an orderly conflict resolution mechanism. Agree: 87%

It is diagnostic

The program was diagnostic.

4. It helped me to identify my relational pattern. Agree: 86%
5. Identifying my relational pattern helped me to better understand myself. Agree: 87%
6. The Power Management Program helped me understand the conflict resolution process as a sequence of six emotions: stress, response, anxiety, defense, reversal, and compromise. Agree: 76%
7. This program helped me to identify changes to improve my relational adjustment. Agree: 83%
8. I found that the six-role template, combining images and text, integrated fragments of my life into a meaningful conflict resolution pattern. Agree: 75%

The program was therapeutic

9. Completing the creativity component was an emotional experience. Agree: 83%
10. I identified with one or both of the characters in the narrative stories that I created. Agree: 96%
11. This program offered me new information about myself. Agree: 79%
12. I was surprised by the personal relevance of the creativity component. Agree: 70%
13. The creativity component was therapeutic; the metaphors helped me to better understand myself and to also think of making changes. Agree: 70%
14. I was surprised by how much insight I gathered. Agree: 80%
15. This program helped me identify how to better manage power. Agree: 70%
16. After taking this survey, I feel more motivated to make changes in my life. Agree: 85%
17. I think that this survey would be useful for high school students. Agree: 75%
18. I think that this survey would be useful for clinical evaluations. Agree: 89%
19. The program offered me both diagnostic and therapeutic information about myself. Agree: 83%

COMMENTS BY STUDENTS AND PATIENTS COMPLETING THE SELF-ASSESSMENT

We have presented the theoretical concept and the technology for its measurement.
We have illustrated the brief assessment capturing the structure and function of the testing in leading to meaningful and actionable insights generated simply by the brief assessment. This information prepares the reader to examine the validation of the unconscious as a scientific measurable phenomenon, its diagnostic capacity in identifying the personality types and the relevance of the assessment in delivering a concise program of emotional education to the general public but also as a therapeutic modality that is effective in promoting wellness as articulated by test takers own words. We are appending here samples of three types of testimonials about the personal experience of completing the full assessment.
We already reviewed the responses to a query of 47 online completions of the assessment without any additional therapeutic or counseling services whatsoever. A group of seven patients from an outcome study.
A group of 4 interns, well individuals, completing the workbook without therapeutic services in an educational setting, This information attests to the function of the assessment in confirming the educational and therapeutic value of the assessment of the unconscious while also validating the assessment and its theoretical premise the nature of the unconscious, and on the diagnostic distinctions._The statements validate the effectiveness of the battery as a concise program of emotional education that by itself without professional services leads to meaningfulness.

INTERNS' REVIEWS OF THEIR SELF-ASSESSMENT EXPERIENCES

A college student's comments upon completing the brief self-assessment battery

My immediate reactions after completing these two tests were those of wonder and insight. These tests challenged me to really think introspectively. The first test, the survey, (the personality inventory identified as the Relational Modality Evaluation Scale, RMES), was a very good explicit test that was interesting and very detailed. I think that it kind of sets the scene to try to make one seem all good and wonderful to a viewer's eye, whereas the Animal Metaphor Test, challenges one to think in a different perspective in a more artistic sort of way. I found the Animal Metaphor Test to be an especially interesting implicit test. I have never done a test like this but have definitely read about them through psychology courses. I think that it has its own special spin to it though that really encourages one to put effort and thought into each response. The artistic aspect accompanied with the narrative allows one to really express their inner selves in a way that simply talking or brain imaging cannot detect. I like the way that it forces one to address some inner conflict in their current lives and then at the end, how to take immediate action for the betterment of life and resolution of conflicts. The section, where it explains that we repeat ourselves and to describe a situation, where the certain conflict has happened, really puts into perspective our own actions. Most times we are either unaware or reluctant to admit when we are causing conflict, which can bottle up inside and disrupt at a given moment. Since the person is recognizing their flaws and conflicts themselves, and not hearing it from a friend or therapist, they will do much more to change these flaws. I also like the concept of drawing an animal to represent oneself. With so many different varieties to choose from, an animal representation is a really interesting way to gain insight to a person's personality. Overall, I though the tests were very interesting and informative to both the person taking the test and the experimenter distributing the tests.

Intern's comments about completing the workbook twice

There currently exists no mode of psychological testing that serves as both a diagnostic and therapeutic tool. Many might ask how such a balance or confluence of these traditionally separate categories would or could ever be achieved in a consistently reliable form. Projective testing is primarily understood to be of diagnostic value. In tests like the Rorschach and Thematic Apperception Test (TAT), visual stimuli are directed at an individual with the intent to analyze their responses and then statistically classify their interpretations in order to place them into a particular diagnostic category. Creative assessments in which someone is asked to draw certain subject matter or compose their own stories in a less rigidly structured way, like tests used in art therapy and narrative therapy, are less focused on strict diagnostic data and more on the actual creative content of those drawings or stories. Analyses of such test results rely heavily on the supervision and observation of thoroughly trained professionals. Creative and projective tests used in art therapy and narrative therapy touch on diagnostic and therapeutic facets, though limit the involvement of artists in the analysis of their own work. Analyses of such pieces of art rely on the counselor or therapist's interpretation of the presence or absence of certain elements and the orientation of certain images on a page. Such tests can be used to help in a diagnosis and may eventually provide therapeutic benefit to the patient receiving professional feedback and commentary on his or her own work. While creative and narrative testing seems much more effective in the therapeutic sense, providing the patient with insight and opportunities for emotional growth, such insights cannot be achieved without the highly specialized input and analysis of the professional administering the test.

Narrative therapy seems to provide consistently evocative therapeutic experiences, and to be applicable across cultures and ages. However, the lack of standardization in such testing prevents them from being easily accessible to a wide range of people without the access to or means for mental health services. If engaging in the creative process of making art and telling stories can serve as a therapeutic tool of expression that allows a therapist to help patients better understand themselves, might there be a way to create a tool which allows this creative, individual work to occur without so much dependence on the interpretation of a second or third party? Surely the artist would have more insights than a therapist who played no role in the imaginative and cognitive processes triggering the fabrication of the personal narratives in that artist's work. Perhaps so, you might say. But we would need a creative assessment tool which provided a structured venue for people to draw insights from their own creative work without the supervision of a specialized professional. If such testing could be easily interpreted by the artist him or herself, in a format that encouraged and directed a methodical yet cathartic self-assessment, such testing could be administered in a consistently quantifiable form, which would then permit statistically useful diagnostic data. Such testing could also make therapy more efficient and valuable, helping to target main areas of concern and work towards a resolution more quickly.

Dr. Albert J. Levis believes the human unconscious naturally falls into a pattern of emotional and behavioral trends that attempt to resolve conflict. During the creative process, our unconscious predilection for conflict resolution presents itself pictorially for interpretation by the artist. Dr. Levis has developed a series of projective and self-analytic exercises that utilize this therapeutic and diagnostically relevant method. These comprise his assessment booklet of emotional education, the Conflict Analysis Battery, which allows an individual to gain personal insight with very little input or interpretation from a therapist. This eliminates the risk of a therapist's projecting certain problems onto the patient without proper evidence, and further accommodates any distorted portraits of reality in the mind of the patient, whose creative process and creative interpretation will be entirely his or her own. The way someone remembers a conflict and feels about it, regardless of how others might describe the event, will speak powerfully to this person's perception and experience of stressors and threats. Therefore, these creative exercises provide invaluable emotional and behavioral cues in a consistently helpful way.

Dr. Levis has an extensively research-supported theory of conflict analysis, what he terms the Formal Theory, which provides an outline for an individual to understand his or her own creative work, unresolved emotional conflicts, and behavioral patterns. However, whether one is familiar with the intricacies of Levis' theory or not, the art and personal commentary of test takers alone often demonstrates remarkable continuity and consistent personal insights over the course of the testing booklet. One can draw out common threads of tension and emotional themes with little effort in witnessing the progress an individual can make, completely on his or her own, by completing this progressive assessment booklet.

The series of creative, projective assessments outlined in Dr. Levis' conflict analysis workbook compile a figurative inventory that speaks to the way one responds to stress and tries to resolve emotional imbalances by symbolically representing one's relational patterns and cognitive processes. Each exercise, considered on its own, may provide significant insight into dominant and overarching conflicts one struggles with. However, when all of the exercises are examined as elements of one coherent narrative, the six stages of conflict resolution may be identified and provide a framework to understand the assessments in a new light.

Considering the dominant themes, tensions, and even the graphic layout or artistic patterns within one's workbook as a symbolic whole brings continuity to the process of recognizing cyclical patterns and recurring details or tones that, together, highlight deeper underlying conflicts which can be considered on a simplified and less daunting plane. The different exercises can be plotted out along the resolution curve in an order which illustrates the conflict resolution process in its six steps: A *Stress* triggers a *Response* which gives way to *Anxiety,* prompting a counteractive *Defense*, eventually leading to the final two phases of *Reversal* and *Compromise*.

THE UNIVERSAL HARMONIC: THE MENTAL OSCILLATION

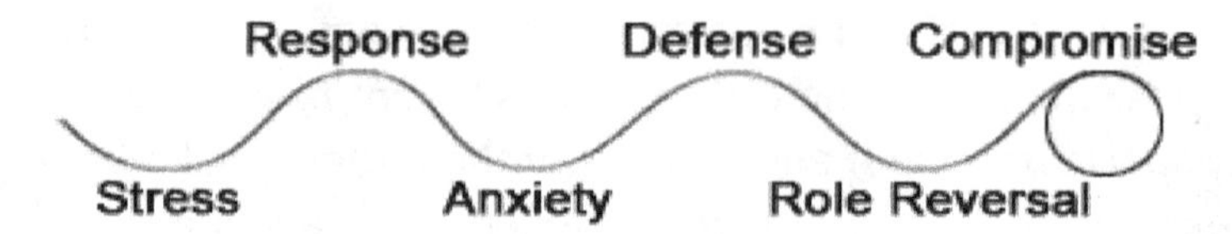

The *Conflictual Memory Test* tends to represent the initial Stress *phase*; the *Response* and *Anxiety* phases are then illustrated by the *Transparent Mask Test*: the first mask speaking to the face of *Response*, and the next two communicating the Anxiety harbored in the wake of responding in that certain way. The *Animal Metaphor Test (AMT)* and the *Fairy Tale Metaphor Test* illustrate the components of the Defense phase, speaking to one's attempts to rationalize or reframe the uneasiness and worry of the prior phase of Anxiety and prepare oneself for the imminent *Reversal* phase which will illustrate another potential setback. This *Reversal* can be assessed in examining the second animal metaphor *Intensification of Conflict Test* and the *Dream Analysis.* The *Short Story Metaphor* test will tie everything together, bringing about some form of *Compromise*, a conclusive force, which reconciles the ebb and flow of stresses and responses to those stresses.

The natural oscillation of the human unconscious towards resolution and compromise can also be assessed on a smaller scale, evident within individual tests. Mapping out one's artwork along the six-step roller-coaster curve of conflict resolution does not necessarily provide a clear quick-fix solution to finding the ideal balance or compromise one is looking for, but certainly makes the path leading to the healthiest course of action much less convoluted and overwhelming.

Before commencing work on the creative exercises, the Conflict Analysis Battery requires the patient to complete a self-report inventory, called the Relational Modality Evaluation Scale. This inventory of almost 200 questions provides visual and diagnostic feedback which is very useful in evaluating someone's means of relating. The four modalities are broad and universal: providing space in which every human being can be placed. Having this extensive self-report scale at the beginning of the booklet can very quickly give one a sense of what category best describes one's general patterns of relating. This test can help gauge whether someone is Dominant or Submissive, and whether he or she tends to approach conflict on a continuum between adaptive collaboration versus inflexible animosity. The four relational categories are: Dominant Cooperative or Dominant Antagonistic and Submissive Cooperative or Submissive Antagonistic. As a reference point, Dr. Levis uses the main characters from the Wizard of Oz as archetypes of the four relational modalities. Dorothy is Dominant Cooperative; the Cowardly Lion is Dominant Antagonistic; the Scarecrow is Submissive Cooperative; and the Tin Man is Submissive Antagonistic.

A scattering of scores across the various relational categories is common, especially when the patient presents with higher levels of psychic tension, which is minimally assessed in the relational modality questionnaire as well. The number of positive and negative scores in different categories will immediately provide one with visual feedback, helpful in determining one's relational modality. This test does not provide "deep insight", but it does create a certain plane or contextual reference point with which to continue the assessments with a more informed initial understanding of things. The Relational Modality test would appear to be the most strictly diagnostic tool in this workbook, but I hope to demonstrate that it is one greatly enhanced by the seemingly less traditional creative assessments following it.

To assess underlying sources of stress and identify central themes recurring throughout an individual's booklet, the conflictual memory exercises serve as an effective place to begin the analysis of each case study. It is unlikely that anyone has one self-defining memory, but, as Dr. Levis has found, the underlying conflicts and emotions connected with any conflictual memory will likely indicate someone's behavioral and emotional patterns, whether the memory is truly significant or not. In searching for someone's personal pattern of unconscious conflict resolution, the conflictual memory usually falls into place as an initial stressor, which can serve as a reference point in relation to the following five stages which work towards some sort of compromise. If the conflictual memory includes members of one's immediate family, it can be beneficial to look at the memory and juxtapose it to the family balloon exercises, which often indicate certain familial hierarchies and notable emotional bonds.

Theories about the unconscious, in general, have been dismissed as unscientific and have been criticized to the extent that skepticism and doubt cling to our verbal associations with the term. Freud presented the unconscious as a conflicted adversarial unit working to conceal and stifle unresolved conflict and inappropriate feelings while also deeply wanting to act on strong impulses that it attempts to resist for moral reasons.

The notion of the unconscious as a conflict resolution mechanism, therefore, is one at odds with the Freudian model. In sharp contrast, Levis in his Formal Theory presents the unconscious as an energized mechanism constantly working towards resolution and compromise rather than working to protect an individual from conflicts, he or she unconsciously deemed too painful to process fully. This is not to say that the unconscious according to Levis is always successful in resolving conflict. Indeed, if it were there would be very few problems in the world, and very few reasons for me to write this paper.

In saying the unconscious is predisposed to resolve conflict I mean that human emotions, behaviors, morals and values are all contingent on striking some sort of balance, finding some middle ground—on resolving conflict. Levis considers the evolution of religion as evidence of this Moral Science. Believing in something greater, having faith in forces that can reconcile disputes and misunderstandings, whether this is a faith in God, in Science, in the Supernatural or in Modern Medicine—this need to trust, believe and be guided towards a deeper understanding seems to be an inextricable component of the human condition.

I would like to clarify that the creative assessments referenced and summarized throughout this paper are not intended to serve as clear cut evidence or confirmations supporting what a therapist suspects based on his or her other cases, social prejudices, or flair for creating conflict where there is none (which psychoanalysis and projective testing has somewhat of a reputation for). Rather than clear-cut evidence, the assessments in Dr. Levis' Conflict Analysis Battery can serve as informative and educational guides for the test taker and the therapist. The workbook provides one with a visual metaphorical arc of one's emotional and behavioral patterns which can clarify areas of weakness that one personally needs to work on.

Someone's behavioral patterns and relational modes develop and change over time, influenced by one's surroundings, relationships, and life experiences. In gaining insight into personal patterns and recurring themes in one's life, it is highly likely that one will end up drawing parallels to the traits and behaviors of those people who most heavily influenced and guided the development of one's moral, social, and behavioral modes of operation. Because the self is a fabricated composite or living collage of one's experiences, emotions, memories and perceptions of those memories, the self cannot be effectively separated and examined as an isolated entity. Thus, in attempting to understand one's self, one must also gain insight into those persons who have deeply impacted and shaped the self-one has become.

Whether a family is particularly "close knit" or not, there exist common threads of emotional and behavioral trends, related stances and proclivities which unconsciously tie any family together (whether in a neat web or tangled, knotted mess). With this in mind, I would like to examine four booklets of one family with nothing but an open mind and eye for patterns and an ear for personal discoveries. In going through the workbooks of this family one may also look for the integrated therapeutic and diagnostic value of self-expression combined with self-assessment and self-discovery.

Intern's essay following completion of the workbook

"And when you gaze long into an abyss the abyss also gazes into you". This metaphor by Fredrich Nietzsche perfectly sums up my experience with the Conflict Analysis Training, CAT, book. We often forget to look within ourselves, to our internal abyss, the darkest part of our subconscious, which has no boundary or limit. It rules behavior and influences our relational patterns. Due to the pace of life we have become accustomed to, we rarely take the time for introspective thought. American culture supports and enforces this pattern of ignoring what's inside and only dealing with external stimulus. The solution to this issue is not an easy one and requires creativity. But through this creativity we are introduced to a whole new world of healing and enlightenment.

Far from the literal sense, darkness here is used in the most abstract of ways. The darkness is that which we have become unfamiliar with. The natural state of human nature is one of balance. There must be a harmony between the two sides of being. Lean too much to one side and the equilibrium is thrown off. Resolving conflict becomes a Sisyphean task and we are placed in a state of dis-ease. Even the simplest of conflicts can't be resolved. Once this state of imbalance is reached problems aggregate, entangling themselves making life unpleasant and complicated. Surely, there must be a solution, a way to undo the damage, avoid the self-inflicted suffering. Our unconscious mind is a powerhouse that has been underutilized, swept under the rug as we indulge in fruitless distractions. But what would happen if we were to forgo these interruptions and engage in a serious exercise of introspection looking deep into the abyss, embracing the unconscious and letting it take the wheel. Even if only for a moment this can undoubtedly prove beneficial.

The Conflict Analysis Training book is the key to regaining equilibrium. It pushes you towards self-realization through a series of projective exercises. What I found most interesting about these exercises is the reversal of unconscious to conscious. The conscious mind is distracted while it attempts to comprehend the series of questions. But in this occupation the unconscious mind takes over. The stories flow naturally, characters are created and before you know it you've finished the exercise. When you take a closer look at the story it strangely resonates with you on a different, highly profound level. This is the genius of this theory and method. The latent content of the metaphor stems from life experiences. This was my experience with the Conflict Analysis Training workbook. With creativity as the filter my unconscious gradually became conscious. My metaphors represented sources of major conflicts in my life.

The depiction of my mother's funeral in the conflictual memories test set the stage for my pattern of achieving and maintaining power. As a young child, your mom as your primary care giver constructs your world. She determines what you are introduced to and according to her experience your worldview is determined. Take this tremendous force in development away and I was left to discover the world for myself. Grasping concepts and dealing with life was difficult. I often times felt like I had no control. As I grew older I learned how to maintain power. Not only over myself but also in the world I created for myself. Self-control became the prism with which I categorized the world. It was my motivation, the catalyst to accomplishing my heart's desires, and conquering the unknown.

However, fear of the unknown is inherently part of consciousness. It is the reason animals retreat while crossing the street when a car approaches. It is how we justify ordering the same thing at a restaurant every time we go. Familiarity rests within our comfort zone. This was also one of my emerging patterns illustrated in multiple metaphor tests. There's a great degree of comfort in the familiar. But I have a burning desire to venture off of the familiar path. The unknown calls to me but I still long for the sense of safety that normative behavior yields. I could follow the path of my father, which has been proven to have a profitable return. Or I could blaze my own trail, explore a new frontier and see where I end up. I tend to oscillate between the two. Seeing the clear benefit of playing it safe while at the same time knowing the adventure that awaits me in the uncertainty. The radiance of creating my own path in life seems like the only way but the conflict stands strong. Hinting at the possibility of failure or merely being a flash in the pan. This insight would have been hard to decipher without the help of the CAT. It made my inner thoughts more understandable.

Through continued work I saw how my metaphors fit into the six stages (stress, response, anxiety, defense, setback, and resolution). The pattern evolved before my eyes; it materialized and became real. It was no longer just words on a page. It shed light on my relational patterns. I saw how I tend to place myself in a leadership position, calling the shots, teaching and helping those who needed help. But it also showed my ineffective patterns of repression and avoidance. These morals were all evident in the plot of my metaphors. Shrouded in depictions of aged samurai warriors, ninjas and the way of the sword. My reference point was clear and substantially interesting. The main tenets of many forms of martial arts are self-control and discipline. These tactics empowered me. Facilitating growth beyond my fears of failure and inadequacy. Giving me confidence and the will to courageously move on.

My pattern of resolution grew from a dim flicker in the first animal metaphor test to a full-blown torrent of high-powered solar energy in the short story metaphor. The CAT was revealing my true self. At the same time it enabled me to step outside of myself and see how others perceive me leading to a feeling of totality, wholeness and peace. Culminating in the "Know thyself letter" the journey was dynamic and extremely influential. The CAT, much like inception, was a dream inside a dream, inside a dream. The individual essays showed my pattern of conflict resolution within a specific situation. These specific situations in each metaphor built upon themselves and the whole book provides a grander perspective of my pattern. Providing multiple looks at how I relate to others.

The personal growth occurs in stages. Each level is heavily dependent on the structure and strength of the previous one. Stage two can't be reached without first establishing the basis of stage one. Remove stage three and stage four crumbles into a confusing mess of emotions and chaos. Completed in an orderly fashion the result is monumental and for this I am truly grateful. The CAT is definitely a life altering and enlightening experience. I plan on incorporating it into my life as yearly reviews to ensure progress and growth toward being a more whole person. I looked deep into the abyss and found that it was in fact looking back at me. But the face looking back at me was familiar. It was welcoming me back like an old friend. Arms open and smiling, eliminating the fear which once separated us. I owe this reunion to the CAT and look forward to further improving my relational patterns.

PATIENTS' REVIEWS OF THE BATTERY BASED THERAPY

Therapy is simplified by recognizing the science of conflict resolution, the importance of the syndromal connection of emotions and of the impact of one's personality type, one's relational modality diagnosis. The principles affirmed by these case studies is first, the importance of connecting one's emotions as a syndrome, explaining anxiety, such as fears, as symptoms handicapping one's life with recognizing their origin in one's own behaviors, role assumption choices that create anxieties as anticipations of role reversals and related defensiveness, which leads to the fulfillment of one's fears.
Second, recognizing the importance of one's relational modality, as dominance, aggressiveness hurting others and as submissiveness holding feeling in and suffering self-doubts, hurting oneself.

Patient#1 Threatening as a stepchild and feeling threatened by her stepchildren
Hostility at one's step mother backfiring as anxieties in encountering step-children
Patient #2. Insomnia, Seeking control and fearing losing it upon going to sleep
Patient #3. The mad postal employee's dominance elicited by a setback, being fired and experiencing rejection by wife leading to tremendous anger thinking of murdering family and committing suicide.
Patient #4. Passive aggressiveness building walls around one's heart and afraid of them collapsing resolved by reaching out.
Patient #5. Competitiveness and the fear of failure, as emphasis on success that brings about failure to a college student cured simply by becoming aware of the syndromal cycle of emotions.
Patient # 6. Submissiveness, holding back in sharing, and losing sleep, corrected by opening up and sharing feelings with the family.

Patient #1. Threatening as a stepchild and feeling threatened by her stepchildren This patient wrote an essay about her therapeutic experience upon the completion of two books of tests; the original was for a four-session evaluation, the second was completed during a group therapeutic phase. One of her Animal Metaphor Tests, two animals and dialogue, is transcribed on the Oz Panel #4. Her completed battery is presented as a Metaphor Profile integrating all testing on Oz Panel #8. This patient identified as "The Turkey who became a Terrier", reports on the completion of and interpretation of the second battery of tests.
Patient: a 33 year-old anxious woman suffering from panic-attacks and depression Diagnosis: Axis I Depression - Anxiety
Personality type: Dominant-cooperative
Length of Therapy: 4 Sessions evaluation completing one set of tests, followed by ten sessions in group therapy.
Comments:
"As a 33 year-old woman, I went through this therapeutic evaluation to find the cause of my panic attacks and my severe anxiety I began to experience whenever my boyfriend's children would come to visit him at our shared apartment. I was no stranger to therapy. In fact for at least 20 years (perhaps more?), I have suffered from depression, two suicide attempts, hospitalizations, fragmented interpersonal relationships, hypochondria, migraine headaches, asthma and a host of other no doubt psychologically related maladies.
The first battery of tests, allowed me to bring forth through a sequence of revealing drawings and statements, my innermost fears, traumas and conflicts. After completing the testing, I felt a sense of mastery realizing the rational nature of my conflicts in a non-threatening way. By drawing the metaphor exercises I came to realize my problematic tendencies manifested in images and dialogues.
In my first book, I made illustrations of a strong predatory animal and one which gets preyed upon: Mouse and a Hawk, Red-Riding Hood and The Wolf, a Shark and a Sea fish, A tired Greyhound dog and Three mocking Alley Cats. During the training that followed, the structure of my relationships repeated itself in the second battery series: a Mountain Lion and A Turkey, Jack Jumping over the Candlestick and A Basking Shark and tiny Plankton and finally a Terrier and a Buffalo.

The implications of my exercises were meaningful in looking at myself. The integration of the testing revealed that, the anxiety I experienced from encounters with my step-children as illustrated in the tired Greyhound derided by three Alley Cats was related to the hostility I felt against my own stepmother. The artwork and commentary helped me to realize the deep seated anxieties about my step children as the mirror image of my hostile unexpressed attitude at my stepmother (Mouse vs. Hawk in the first series) and (Turkey vs. Mt. Lion in the second).

Adjusting my feelings toward my Father as in the Short Story of 'The Terrier and the Buffalo,' helped me to feel less threatened by my boyfriend's children's visits. I felt less threatened by them. After the second testing experience I felt more resolved in my relationship with my Father and my Stepmother.

The two self-studies provided me with an overview of my present in the context of the past. I depicted my immediate family, their characteristics, strengths and failings. The drawings helped me to review my past family life and my subsequent responses, anxieties and defenses in a logical, rational progression instead of solely as non-connected emotional outpourings as it occurred in other therapies I have experienced. I now recognized my underlying hostile and antagonistic disposition whereas I always felt victimized, "devoured", preyed upon in relationships. And all this information about the past and about my perceptions came to bear on my current interactions with my parents as well as my boyfriend and his children. It explained how I perceived them as hostile and demanding like I had felt as a restrained stepchild.

Some of my behavior/s had been touched upon in prior therapy programs ---- but none of them made connections, never so quickly and concisely as in this experience. What I have achieved is a clearer and better springboard from which to either continue therapy or work some conflicts out on my own. Without these insight-generating diagnostic instruments and change-generating processes I would not have been able to identify the sources of my current conflicts so easily, quickly and logically. These insights helped to modify my attitude and to experience less anxiety. Medication alone would have postponed dealing with the conflicts as opposed to dealing and permanently trying to resolve them.

I used anti-depressants for a while but I experienced the brief exposure to the Power Management therapy as a 'user-friendly, psychological education which allowed me to diagnose myself and to work towards evolving a clear understanding of connecting my past attitude and my current fears. It is a positive program for self-realization that is needed in order to change attitudes and overcome symptoms. I wish I had had an opportunity to work through my conflicts early in life before my personality developed into inescapable life patterns, which sadly followed me into adulthood."

I recommend bringing Power Management into the classroom, the school system, where it might provide a 'User-Friendly', systematic, psychological venue in which to diagnose and work towards resolution of conflicts in today's youth. It is a positive program for self-realization and young people need self-realization in order to master their feelings early on in life. Before their own personality conflicts cripple or fix them into inescapable life patterns, which would sadly follow them into adulthood.

Patient #2. The owl and the puppy dog, controlling and losing control

This case is a testimony of the power of insights generated by the testing. A single test led to profound personal insight that evoked a radical attitude change, which eradicated severe psychopathology in the shortest period of time.

Patient: a 29-year old male college student

: Axis I, severe chronic Insomnia-Depression,

Axis II Relational Diagnosis Dominant-Cooperative relational modality.

Length of Therapy: seven visits.

Outcome: The insomniac patient was able to sleep without medications.

History: This college student had suffered from severe chronic insomnia for 15 years. He had been on a variety of medications, none of which appeared to be successful. He came to the Center requesting to be hospitalized because he had been deprived of sleep for a week. Seven weeks later the patient was able to sleep without medication and he experienced a dramatic psychosocial adjustment, a remarkable personal transformation, after having been dysfunctional for years.

Patient's first essay

Picture this, a very dark day begins. It's 7:30 AM. The sun is shining, the birds are singing and the dew is rising off the trees but not for me. For me this is just another extension of a day that has not ended. For several days it is painful to see the sunrise, for it means I have not slept for another night. Barely having the strength to continue, I move forward in what seems a worthless life, which I wish I could leave. Pain is all around me, my head hurts, my body aches, my eyes so heavy that I do not understand why they will not stay closed. Every minute I welcome death. I will not take my life but I wish for death to either come or go away. My life is a living hell. No one understands and people say things like 'you just need to work a little or be more tired'. Little do they realize I have physically and mentally worked straight with no sleep for more than four days. My sanity slowly comes and goes. I worry about what I will do sometimes but I must remember to remain strong. The sun sets for another day. I am petrified, for this signals the beginning of my personal hell. Days aren't so bad, but nights are extreme pain, every minute slowly ticking by and me wondering 'can I make it through another night?' Tears begin to swell in my eyes as I know this will be another sleepless night. This is painful to write. I had to hide it after I wrote it. It represents so much pain. I let my fiancée' read it. Last few nights the hopelessness is not there. I am close to being able to sleep on my own, but yet it seems far.

Patient's second essay #2

When I first came to see Dr. Levis, I was not sleeping and I had a sense of hopelessness. Dr. Levis used some drawings I had made to unlock the meaning of my animal metaphors. The first drawing I made, a picture of an outdoor setting with an owl and a puppy dog. The owl was my grandfather and the puppy was myself. My grandfather had died about a year and a half ago and Dr. Levis pointed out that I was following my grandfather like a puppy and when my grandfather passed away I had become the owl in the picture and that I was controlling everything around me and that I needed to stop controlling and start trusting people. I immediately could see that I had become the owl and that I was controlling people. As I left the office that day I felt tons lighter and saw things differently.

It did not take me long to start to realize I had been controlling all the people in my life. I did not like this and I started to trust people and not control them. I must admit, it was a huge difference in the way I looked at the world. Instead of trying to control events around me, I would just let them happen and trust. I realized for many years I was controlling my younger brother. My brother had died several years ago in an auto accident. So one person I could never stop controlling was him because he is gone. Dr. Levis knew I was controlling my brother by another picture I had drawn. In this drawing I was much younger and was getting out of my bed to shut a light off that my brother had turned on earlier. Back and forth my brother and I would compete and me always trying to control him. I would do things like break his collarbone when he beat me at a soccer game, smash him in the face for touching my truck and on and on. I wish I could apologize to him.

I knew I would have to talk to my parents and fiancé' about the ways I was trying to control them. It wasn't easy but I confronted them one at a time to let them know I am sorry and I am another person now. My father was the least receptive. He was angry and said 'everyone has problems' and continued to unload on me. But I knew this would happen because I had not been honest with him in the past. Although he was angry, I felt better because I told him. At the same time, I went into relapse Thursday and Friday. I did not sleep at all. Saturday I got drunk and slept a few hours. Sunday and Monday I had not slept at all and Tuesday I was exhausted. During these sleepless nights I cannot say it wasn't difficult. But something was different. I did not feel as hopeless and I came very close to sleeping but just could not go that extra inch or two needed to fall asleep.

Wednesday I came to see Dr. Levis and explained to him about the relapse. I wrote some things down on a piece of paper and I was instructed to sit down in the chair and kick back and relax. It took a few minutes but then I felt myself fall into the grasp of the comfortable chair. I was told about a pendulum on a clock and the ocean waves coming in and out. This was extremely relaxing and a breathing pattern began to emerge, a different pattern from before, a more relaxing pattern. As I awoke I felt much better and I think another piece to my puzzle has been put into place.

Patient #3. The mad postal employee, aggression, paranoia and more aggression

The patient's comments tell of the significance of the testing for evolving insights and for better understanding the need for changes.

Age 49, Postal employee fired for committing theft of a tape.
Diagnosis: Hospitalized following a suicide and thoughts of murdering his family.
Axis I- Schizo-Affective Disorder.
Relational Modality: Dominant/Antagonistic.
Length of Therapy: Three visit-evaluation.
Outcome: the three visit evaluation was successful
Patient comments: "I would like to reply to the test given by Dr. Levis. I have seen the doctor three times and when I was working on the test and drawings I found it to be very helpful in dealing with my aggression attempting suicide and thinking of harming my family.
The Balloons have helped me deal with my childhood and realize that aggression started in my younger years. This testing is a much better way of dealing with a patient as one could sit and talk to the doctor and never get to the scope of the problem. This is also a very good way to get to the problem much quicker. This type of testing will also help decide the exact type of therapy, which will be most beneficial to me, the patient.
I have never had this type of therapy before and have found it to be very helpful in getting to my problem sooner. This test also helps one to analyze oneself.
I did feel under pressure with thoughts as I really did not want to release feelings, but the drawings helped even though I do not like to draw. I have been through therapy before and it did not work with just talking to the doctor as I was not able to reveal my true feelings. I would like to see this test expanded to other patients as it has started me to think positive and less negative. This test has also given me a different outlook on life as SUICIDE is not the answer."

Patient #4. Building walls around one's heart and afraid of them collapsing
This case illustrates the thematic continuity between the metaphor drawings helping to establish insight into a consistent relational pattern.
Patient: a 40 year-old divorced nurse.
Diagnosis: Axis I Chronic Depression,
Axis II Relational Diagnosis: Submissive-Antagonistic Personality
Length of Therapy: Total of 5 Sessions
Outcome: Symptom free and also able to pursue life goals.
Comments: "Therapy here is different, it is more structured. It is not just winging it. There is a beginning, a middle, and an end as opposed to free flow of comments like "what is going on this week? and trying to raise the self-esteem of the patient by making things that have happened look better."
"The focus is what YOU have to do better to relieve symptoms rather than 'I did the best I could do at the time.' It is not about what makes you feel better for the moment like an ice cream cone. It is not instant gratification. It is about what to do to feel better in the long run".

Patient #5. Competitiveness and the fear of failure
The patient was a college student who quit school several times in anticipation of failing grades. After four weekly sessions the patient did not feel paralyzed by her fears of failure, she was able to enjoy peer relations and feel good about herself.
Patient's comments:
"I've gained more insight on my own doing the drawings. It brought out a lot of hidden meanings. I am able to be more aware of how to gain inner peace by making an effort. I realize that there is a build-up of experiences throughout my life that show how I conducted myself being competitive, obsessed with grades and how I got constantly depressed. I have caused myself to be that way."
The patient's parents' comments:
"Dear Dr. Levis,
I wanted you to know how grateful we are to see our daughter's progress and her happier and more confident disposition. In a short time you have already given her some valuable and long-lasting "tools" to use throughout life. Thank you for your professional interest in our daughter and your courtesy to us. Appreciatively,

Patient #6. Losing trust and trusting again

This case reveals the facilitation of the program in enhancing openness and the development of trust. The patient is a 56 year-old business man who suffered from insomnia for the last 30 years, ever since his first wife left him for another man. He had been in therapy and on a variety of sleeping and antidepressant medications several times. After five visits he terminated feeling secure about his recovery and the improvement of his sleeping pattern.

Diagnosis: Axis I: Chronic Insomnia and also panic for inability to sleep.

Axis II: Relational modality, Dominant Cooperative

Length of Therapy: Five Visits

Outcome: Relief of symptoms, able to sleep without dependence on medications, self-confidence.

Patient Comments:

"This time I opened up a lot more--- not only here but to my wife, my children and others. I have talked to them about my difficulty sleeping, whereas before I kept it from them. When I went to my family doctor, then a psychiatrist, they gave me pills to make me sleep. Here I learned to become self-reliant rather than depend on somebody else's authority and advice to fix me. I have learned to be communicative... it is all right to talk about my feelings... insomnia is not an insurmountable thing. "

"I did the artwork when I was feeling bad and it helped me to express feelings that I otherwise wouldn't have faced. I am happy to have made this progress. I feel confident that I can handle my fears of insomnia from now on without panicking. I am having more and more good nights and days without medication." "I have to trust people more. Not to be too careful. Let it happen."

THE TRAINING PROGRAM

Research on the Formal Theory evolved in 50-years of experimentation in my psychiatric practice and at the VT educational retreat; over the years the concepts and technologies matured. My interest in promoting awareness of the creative process led me to the creation of the Museum of the Creative Process, a Training Center and the publication of a number of studies. The mission has been to deliver evidence of the creative process as a scientific conflict resolving mechanism as the common denominator of all stories, of all creativity. The unconscious as a scientific and conflict resolving phenomenon reconciled psychology and religions into the Moral Science.

Psychology as a science is useful for people in therapy but also useful for well people as emotional education_ for all. The science allows it to be introduced into the classroom. The science has far reaching relevance in our contemporary world with multiple psychological and sociological moral problems. The new concepts and technologies represent new wisdom helpful in the optimization of resolving conflicts at the individual and of the cultural levels.

The world needs insights into behavior as a science and one helping to understand religions as moral paradigms that have evolved as discoveries of science but, which have not completed their evolution to fairness and to abstraction. They are all metaphors of conflict resolution seeking justice, peace in the world but instead they are divisive, perpetuating conflicts. The scientific understanding of behavior reconciles now psychology and religions. The Formal Theory identifying the unconscious as the origin of all moral thought reconciles psychology and morality and places them both on the same scientific foundation.

The Formal Theory qualifies to heal the person and the world with the help of its two technologies based on the study of the creative process unconscious; the CAB and Moral Monopoly. The first is a perfect emotional education technology, while Moral Monopoly serves to understand the evolution of religions and to reconcile them into the science.

DISCUSSION OF THE ASSESSMENT EXPERIENCE

The consensus of the test takers confirms that the assessment is didactic, diagnostic and therapeutic with and without any professional services. The structure of the assessment offers insights with minimal need for professional work. This advantage makes it a very cost-effective instrument available at the click of a link. Literature on case studies is provided with several publications and beta testing information. It represents a technological breakthrough as it is an online deliverable inventory and projective assessment with automatic processing of information fed back to the test taker hence avoiding the need for prohibitively expensive professional services.

Target populations, potential users: schools, clinics, hospitals, practitioners, the general public, special populations, prisons, military, clergy, police force training.

The testing format may be modified along the needed application and population considered. The abbreviated format should be used at the medical office for a quick evaluation of a person's emotional status facilitating a doctor's understanding a patient's personality type, psychological status and intellectual functioning. It can be used as a screening tool for any patient as well as a pre-employment evaluation beneficial for the test-taker and for the recruiter. The lengthy version is an educational, diagnostic and therapeutic instrument that should be delivered to patients in therapy, for addicted populations, the training of personnel, the rehabilitation of prisoners, the screening of military, police and pilots, and the education of college students. The lengthy version could serve for psychiatric evaluation expediting therapy.

The assessment represents a concise wellness emotional education program that could be delivered yearly in the classroom and repeated twice for each student every year. It may be used as educational, as diagnostic, as therapeutic as it evokes insights to the person, as it helps to identify changes, and to monitor progress. Psychiatric patients will benefit. But the principle target population is the well public. The assessment is a concise program of emotional education that should be introduced in the classroom for all students on a yearly basis to enhance the attaining the three objectives of education: bridging the humanities and the sciences, self-knowledge, clarity of values as the principles of conflict resolution: moderation, cooperation and mutual respect.

The program is a must for the completion of therapy and training, for coaching clients, as it helps the person to identify one's wellness diagnosis, the features of these modalities, with their strengths and weaknesses as well as understanding changes for self-optimization in dealing with emotions.

The program can be used for screening cohorts prior to admission to special programs. It detects pathology and examines evolution and resolution of conflicts. It may be repeated periodically monitoring therapy outcome.

It can be used for inmate populations as a tool for training and insight development.

Normative comparisons and additional research

It is good to apply the testing on various groups, i.e. couples to identify the incidence of personality complementarity and marital compatibility. We can use studies of particular populations and the beneficial impact of the training at addiction centers, group settings, such as schools and organizations, jails and military groups. The validity is guaranteed by the complementarity of the inventory detecting the relational modality and the projectives reflecting the modality with autobiographic testing and projective information. Reliability is extraordinary as repetition of the testing reflects sameness and also changes that identify progress on the therapy's outcome; repetition of the testing is recommended.

The psychic tension scale reflects pathology. The intensity of relational modalities may also reflect pathologies. The intensity of agreement with scales reflects intensity of personality type. Moderation is virtue.

EMOTIONAL EDUCATION

The Formal Theory rethinks the disciplines:

- Psychology has lacked a scientific and moral foundation.
- Religions have lacked understanding of psychology and science.
- The arts have been misunderstood as study of aesthetics and dispensable in education upon cost cutting budgetary situations
- Science has had no relevance for the humanities religion and psychology.

The Formal Theory integrates psychology and morality, art and science. Its findings target education's objectives: The integration of the humanities and the sciences, self-knowledge and clarity of values.

- Psychology becomes the science of conflict resolution and embraces morality as generated in the unconscious. Science is shown to provide the insights to the unconscious as an energetic transformation guided by formal attitude transforming operations, which are the moral values.
- Art is not decorative skills, aesthetic exercises in beautifying our environment. Creativity is the path to integration of the humanities and the sciences, the path to emotional education of the public; creativity is the most meaningful language to access our emotions, organized into patterns of conflict resolution. Art is the x-ray of the unconscious. Religions are introduced as discoveries of science and psychology of conflict resolution, identifying the human need for morality as the foundation for psychology.
- Finally, card games are not just for entertainment. The Moral Monopoly provides information on the structure of the unconscious, to social psychology, to anthropology, the history of civilization retracing the moral evolution of humanity as well as the integration of the humanities and the sciences.

This knowledge now must be presented to the students as the topic of wellness and of moral wisdom. This is the function of the training programs based on the Formal Theory. The key path to wisdom is the study of the creative process. The fact that behavior becomes a science allows briefing the student population about the Moral Science and its personal relevance. Part of the message is imparting scientific information but also talking of moral values as principles of science and stressing the value of sacrifice and mutual respect as the means of resolving conflicts.

Emotional Education (abbreviated EE) is the wellness alternative to AA's recovery from addictions relying on the concept of a higher power. We wish to explore the delivery of EE, as a peer supported public resource. We are developing Emotional Education peer supported conflict resolving workshops. We welcome the public to learn about behavior and themselves. The Emotional Education workshops fulfill the three objectives of education: Integration of art and science, self-knowledge, and clarity of moral values. This new knowledge should be made available in the classroom, for training of the general public and for the education of professionals.

Emotional Education studies creativity as a science, and utilizes creativity for self-discovery and moral growth. The experience shows that psychology is a natural and moral science. Psychology and morality are integrated and applied to serve the personal need for self-awareness. The concepts and technologies improve education, and expedite psychotherapy by introducing the wellness diagnoses and the self-assessment as diagnostic and therapeutic; the education demystifies religions as complementary discoveries of the Moral Science and focuses on creativity as the path to healing.

We wish to introduce EE into the classroom, into the school curriculum and into the public domain. The education begins with the study of the process as a scientific mechanism changing psychology into an exact science; we learn about the unconscious as a scientific, measurable, graphically portrayable entity, about the alternative types of resolution as diagnostic categories of wellness, about the assessment as the measurement of the unconscious and how to apply the assessment for self-discovery. We also play the game of Moral Monopoly for the study and integration of religions as discoveries of science.

THE EMOTIONAL EDUCATION CURRICULUM

My long term vision is to create awareness of the scientific study of behavior shifting the focus of education from encyclopedic knowledge to learning about the Science of Conflict Resolution. It is important to recognize how our emotions affect our perception of reality, and how understanding our perceptions can improve communications and reduce personal and interpersonal pathology. Psychology, education and religion integrated can reduce conflicts and make the world a safe place for all.

Emotional Education is a well-structured educational program founded on the analysis of the creative process as a conflict resolution scientific mechanism. The curriculum represents a concise program of science-based emotional education suitable for the classroom, useful for patients as well as for the training of professionals and the general public. EE, Emotional Education workshops study the unconscious as a scientific conflict resolving entity based on the analysis of the creative process.

The Emotional Education curriculum attains education's three objectives in three phases:
1. Educational Phase: An essay introduces the core principles of the Formal Theory of Behavior, clarifying psychology's concepts of the unconscious, diagnoses, assessment, therapy, and notions on morality. The Formal Theory premise is that the mind resolves conflict unconsciously. This process is an energetic phenomenon that abides by the principles of physics and logic. The Formal Theory identifies that this process consists of a six-role-emotions dialectic leading to four types of conflict resolution.

The study of the science and its applications departs with inspection of the art exhibits of the Museum of the Creative Process. We show the paradigm shift in examining what is universal in all stories, their plot as the creative process, a scientific phenomenon, transforming energy of emotions to societal order. The exhibits illustrate how religions evolved alternative types of moral paradigms coming close to the abstractions of science. The new psychology studies the creative process as a scientific conflict resolution phenomenon integrating physics, psychology and morality into the Moral Science.

Workshops study art exhibits to learn about the Moral Science:

- **The welcome center exhibit provides an overview of the exhibits** clarifying the concept of the creative process as a scientific conflict resolution phenomenon, reflecting the unconscious as the sperm configuration.
- **The sculptural trail in the history of love** retraces the evolution of religions deifying alternative conflict resolutions as a progression of covenants, such as the discovery of the marital vows in Greece, of the father-son covenant in Judea, and of the mother-child alliance by the messianic faiths. This exhibit on the evolution of religions clarifies the unconscious as both scientific and as morality or love bound.
- **The Sanctuary of the Wizard and of Wisdom** combines the study of metaphors of the Wizard of Oz with metaphors created by completing the Conflict Analysis Battery. We learn about psychology's four disciplines and how using the battery anyone can become conscious of the unconscious
- **The Gorski Retrospective introduces a new way of looking at art** as reflecting the emotional growth of the artist resolving lifetime conflicts to spiritual resolutions.
- **Moral Monopoly is a game studying of stories of religions**, to recognize the scientific nature of morality integrating the religions of the world as complementary discoveries of the Moral Science. The game clarifies moral values as the formal operations guiding the unconscious to conflict resolution: mastery, cooperation and mutual respect.

2. The self-discovery phase is a workshop dedicated to completing the brief self-assessment, the Conflict Analysis Battery, for self-discovery, to identify one's wellness diagnosis or relational modality as one's personality type. **The completed battery is identified as the power management phase** to evolve actionable insights and the pursuit of emotional growth.

Completing the Conflict Analysis Battery identifies the six-role psychodynamic process which explains and predicts emotions, and identifies changes to modify power management choices. After completion, a report is presented that organizes all tests, insights and suggestions for changes. Feedback is excerpted from the metaphor writing and answers. This feedback guides to actionable insights to modify managing power by turning passivity to activity, transforming antagonism to cooperation, and reducing alienation by encouraging mutual respect.

The experience is diagnostic: The first exercise of CAB is the Relational Modality Evaluation Scale, (RMES), a multiple-choice personality inventory that uses a wellness-based relational approach to evaluate individual patterns of resolving conflict. Instead of emphasizing illness-based symptoms, the RMES identifies enduring life patterns, the relational modalities measuring power (dominance vs submissiveness) and attitude (cooperation vs. antagonism). The inventory also assesses the intensity of experienced conflicts, the Psychic Tension.

The assessment is therapeutic: CAB features creativity based self-discovery tests, whose prompts invite the test taker to draw art and compose stories, then reflect on the stories as metaphors of one's conflict resolution pattern as well as options on how to improve it. The CAB's tests are integrated into a meaningful continuum that highlights one's syndrome of emotions along the person's relational modality.

3. The Moral Science phase provides clarity on moral values by integrating religions as partial and complementary discoveries of the process.

We understand psychology as scientific and humanistic, addressing the notion of the psychic need for conflict resolution as the origin of moral motivation, manifested in all samples of creativity as the scientific structure of the thought process. The universality of religions is evidence for the recognition of psychology as the science of morality.

Moral Monopoly is a game of cards, integrating religions' cultural stories as discoveries of the science. The game retraces the history of religions as partial and complementary discoveries of science clarifying Formal Theory's process and establishing the field into a cohesive, holistic continuum completing religion's mission for happiness and world peace.

At the end of the training program I anticipate the creation of three tiers of workshops: one for young people 12 to 20 years old, another for couples, and the third for counseling individuals with alternative pathologies.

Opposite: Advertisement for the Educational Phase Workshops

MUSEUM OF THE CREATIVE PROCESS

257 Wilburton Drive, Manchester, Vermont 05254 | 802-379-6350
Museumofthecreativeprocess.com
Confirm your interest in participating with an email to moralscience@hotmail.com

Upon the publication of ***The Moral Science Primer***, introducing the scientific analysis of the creative process, and upon the upcoming Columbus Day weekend, Dr. Albert Levis is launching **Wellness Emotional Education (WEE)** Weekend Workshops as a series of guided tours of the museum's art exhibits to learn about the nature of the unconscious as the integrative paradigm.

Paradigm Shift: From Art to Science

KICKOFF WEEKEND FREE OF CHARGE!

Friday: 7:30-9:30 pm

Viewing the *Silver Fence exhibit* illustrating the creative process unconscious as consisting of two phenomena of science transforming energy from a conflict across a dialectic of six emotions to a resolution as attitude change.

The physical structure of the unconscious as three emotional oscillations, a syndrome, leading to four types of conflict resolution, the relational modalities, as wellness diagnoses

Science Integrates Religion and Psychology

Saturday: 10am-12pm

Viewing the *Sculptural Trail and the History of Love*, we learn how religions evolved from matriarchy through patriarchy, to asceticism and finally monotheism, as discoveries of the four types of conflict resolution thus improving the family institution.

Odysseus bound on the mast of his boat to listen to the sirens without losing control; he is the hero of power management concluding his journey to Ithaka celebrating the concept of the marital vows, loyalty of spouses to each other.

Healing the Person:

Saturday: 2pm-4pm

Viewing the *Metaphoria Murals of the Sanctuary of the Wizard* to learn about tapping the creative process completing the Conflict Analysis Battery, available online. It is a self-assessment identifying the unconscious as a wellness diagnosis, a relational modality, and as actionable insights.

Mural #4, My Metaphors Myself, generated by completing the Conflict Analysis Battery reflecting my struggle to deal with metaphors by understanding the underlying science of conflict resolution as spelled in Conflict Analysis, the Formal Theory of Behavior

Healing the World:

Sunday: 10am-12pm

Playing *Moral Monopoly* integrating religions' cultural stories, as the complementary discoveries of conflict resolution, merged into the Moral Science.

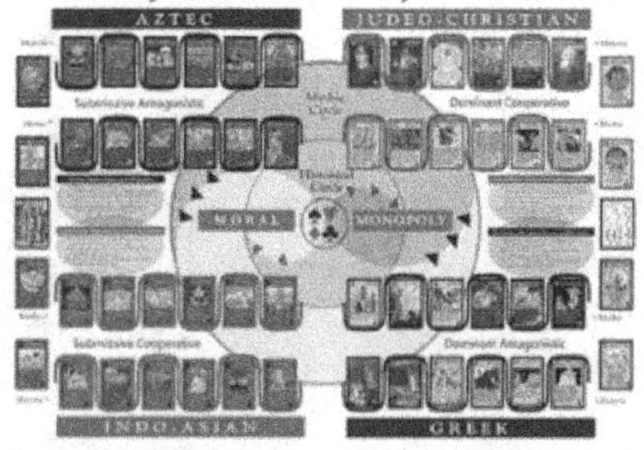

The gameboard of Moral Monopoly, featuring cultural stories retraces the evolution of religions as discoveries of the four relational modalities by redefining the role model divine, and by increasing fairness in family role relations.

CHAPTER SIX : MURAL #10
THE EVERYDAY PSYCHOPATHOLOGY OF THE DOMINANCE AND SUBORDINANCE RELATIONAL MODALITIES ILLUSTRATED BY THE WORKBOOK GENERATED METAPHOR PROFILES OF TWO INTERNS

In 1992, two college students, a philosophy major from Princeton named Chris and a theater major from Brown, my daughter Melissa, participated in a summer training program in Vermont. They were my first interns, college students attending classes at the Museum of the Creative Process. The education consisted in viewing art exhibits, discussing them and competing the assessment. Chris and Missy completed the workbook and evolved insights from their metaphors. This delivery represents the concise program of emotional education using the workbook delivered to two college students. Mural #10 evolved from that experience and it highlights the differences between the two major relational modalities.

Melissa was clearly a dominant person and Chris the submissive counterpart. The mural contrasts the two relational modalities exemplified with Chris' passive aggressive dynamics and Missy's dominant competitive ones. The mural presents the typical profiles of the two key diagnostic categories. Their profiles illustrate the syndromal differences of the two modalities as wellness diagnoses that the public and psychology need to recognize in order to treat patients and educate students.

The significance of this study is that it illustrates clearly the differences between the relational modalities as diagnostic categories of paramount importance in conferring insights and pathology as well as reflecting the value of the learning experience as therapeutic. The study offers compelling evidence of introducing emotional education in the classroom a learning experience that can be delivered by educators to students.

The program is educational helping to understand the new concepts of psychology as a natural science, including the unconscious, the relational modality diagnoses, and religion as scientific measurable phenomena. The program utilizing the assessment becomes diagnostic and therapeutic. An essay presents concepts and then it applies them in generating personal actionable insights validating the conceptual knowledge in a laboratory fashion.

It is education's elusive objective to integrate the humanities and the sciences, contribute self-knowledge, 'know thyself', and to clarify values. The three objectives are reached by learning about psychology as a science and then learning about one's psychological emotional pattern by completing the assessment in the classroom. The interns' essays illustrate the personal significance of this program as a routine emotional education.

Chris's essay is included here in its entirety to demonstrate the significance of the assessment as a meaningful learning experience. The essay provides the reader an introduction to the concepts revamping our notions of psychology. It begins examining the differences between propositional and relational method, then introducing the concepts of the unconscious as consisting of a process, a syndrome of six emotions, and of four relational modalities, then the use of the assessment to reconstruct the six role process as a single dramatic continuum with a beginning and a resolution, applied to understanding oneself.

Chris's conceptual analysis is accompanied by sensitive and honest analysis of his own emotional make up. Chris and Melissa were able to understand patterns, themselves and also how to seek to correct their patterns. Melissa is very clear that her dominance has affected her life experiences, her happiness and though she is knowledgeable about herself and the theory, she has had to struggle with the issues of power and competitiveness throughout her life.

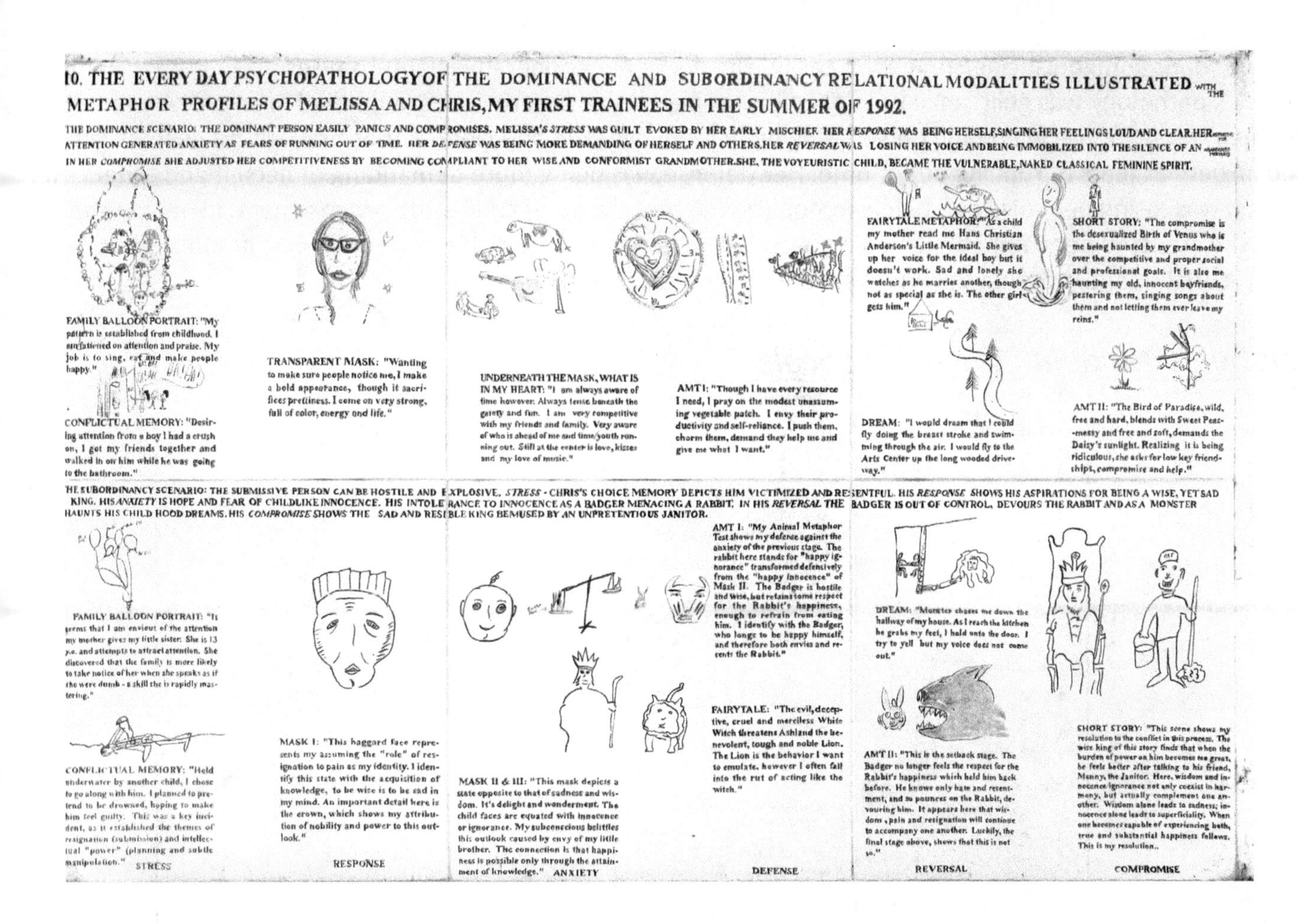

Images of the metaphor profiles of the two interns and their transcriptions along with essays illustrate the differences between the two relational modalities as the opposite ways of resolving conflicts.

Intern #1 Melissa: The dominance scenario: Reflections on my metaphors

The dominant person easily panics and compromises. Melissa's stress was guilt, evoked by personal exuberance and competitiveness and well reflected in one early memory of mischief. Her response was being herself, singing her feelings loud and clear. Her competitiveness and major aspirations for success and attention generated anxiety as fears of running out of time. Her defense was being more demanding of herself and others. Her reversal was losing her voice and being immobilized in the silence of an abandoned mermaid. In her compromise she adjusted her competitiveness by becoming compliant to her wise and conformist grandmother. She, the voyeuristic child, became the vulnerable, naked classical feminine spirit. In reality she had a great voice and built a career around it as a singer.

Melissa completed five books over the years on her own and detected clearly the continuation of a pattern. She observed the ease of rediscovering the pattern in her testing and the difficulty of making changes. She recognized the consequence of her intense **dominance** and **competitiveness** generating anxiety. Her dominance syndrome was resistant to change but insights on the pattern helped her to manage her impatience and distressing pressure to succeed. The insights were helpful in moderating her anger and in reducing her fears. The knowledge from the testing had an impact in her career. She opted to become a playwright and musician specializing in emotional education for kids: Moey's Music Party. Kids have loved her exuberance. She has been written up as the Pied Piper of NY City's Central Park. One of her compositions has been kids' use of fairy tales as metaphors modified to learn about conflict resolution and kids' empowerment.

The dominant antagonistic person panics easily. The dominant cooperative compromises.
Melissa's pathology was guilt, anxiety, evoked by her aggressive nature. It is exemplified in an early memory of mischief. Her response was being herself, singing her feelings loud and clear. Her aspirations for success generated anxiety as fears of running out of time. Her defense was being more demanding of herself and others. Her reversal was losing her voice and being immobilized in the silence of an abandoned mermaid. In her compromise, she adjusted her competitiveness by becoming compliant to her wise and conformist grandmother. She, the voyeuristic child, became the vulnerable, naked classical feminine spirit.

Relational Modality Evaluation Scale

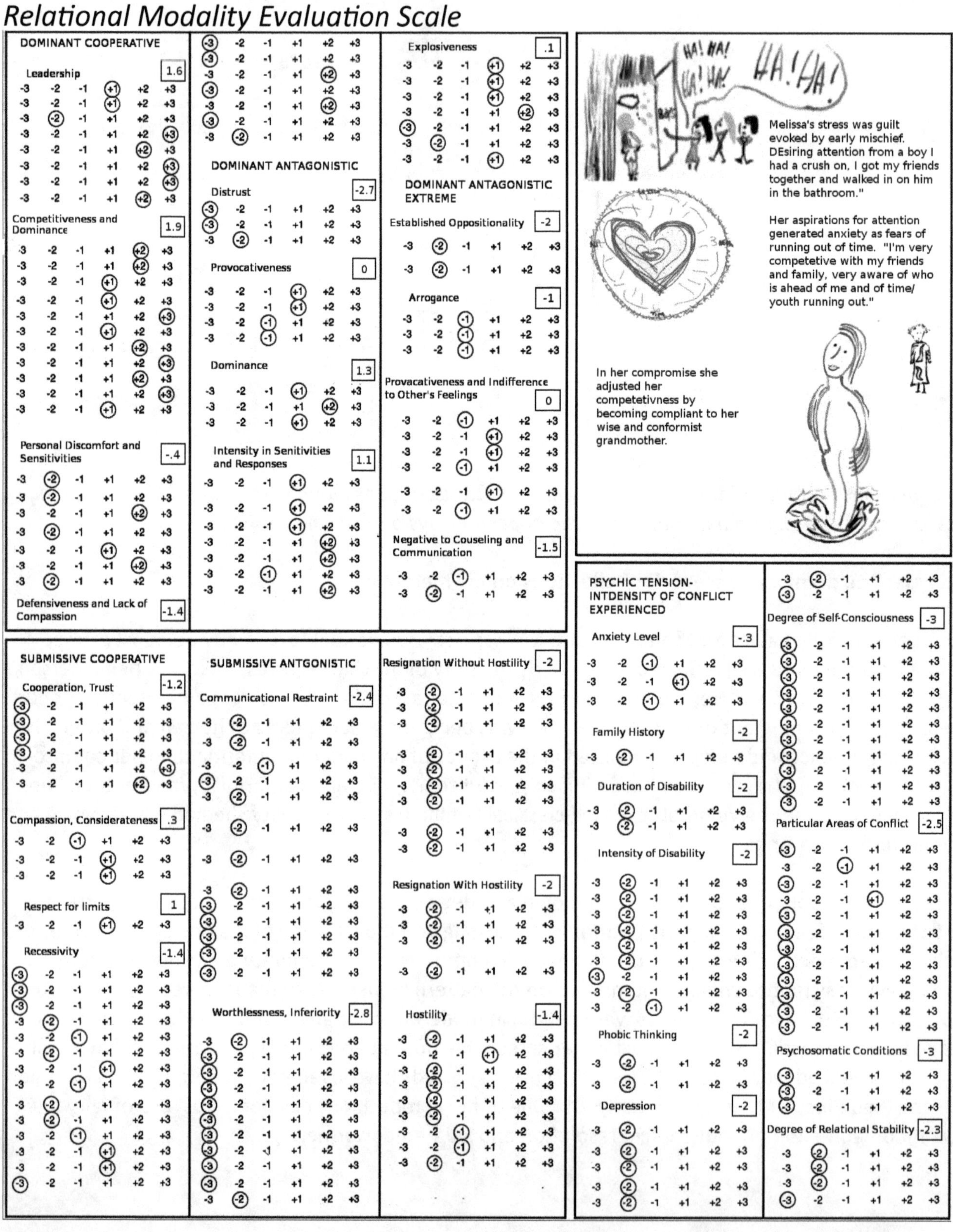

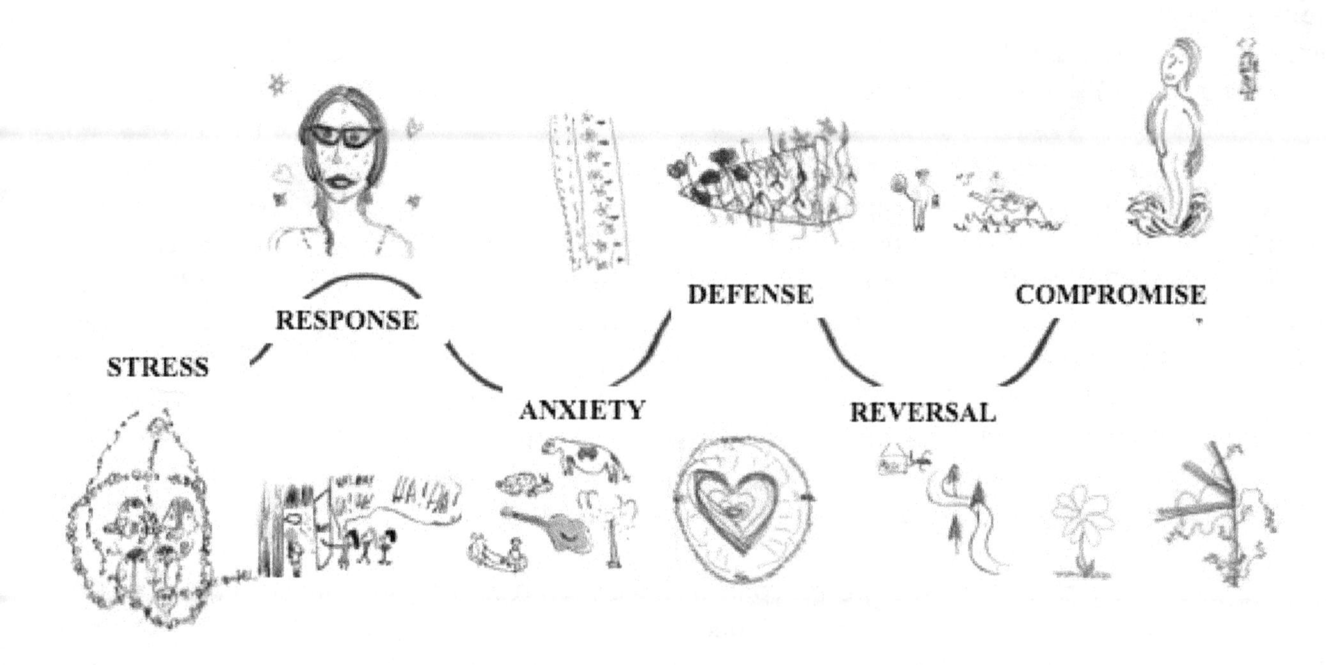

STRESS- FAMILY BALLOONS	RESPONSE - MASK I	ANXIETY - MASK II	DEFENSE- ANIMAL METAPHOR	REVERSAL - AMT II	COMPROMISE SHORT STORY
"My pattern is established from childhood. I am fattened on attention and praise. My job is to sing, eat and make people happy." Second conflict "Desiring attention from a boy I had a crush on, I got my friends together and walked in on him going to the bathroom."	"Wanting to make sure people notice me, I make a bold appearance ... though it sacrifices prettiness. I come on very strong, full of color, energy and life."	"I am always aware of time however. Always tense beneath the gaiety and fun. I'm very competitive with my friends and family. Very aware of who is ahead of me and time/ youth running out. Still at the center is love. Kisses and music is my love."	"Though I have every resource I need, I pray on the modest unassuming vegetable patch. I envy their productivity and self-reliance. I push them, charm them, demand they help me and give me what I want." FAIRY TALE"As a child my mother read me Hans Christian Anderson's Little Mermaid She gives up her voice for the ideal boy, but it doesn't work. She is sad and lonely.	"The Bird of Paradise, wild, free and hard, blends with sweet peas—messy, free and soft. She demands the daisy's sunlight. Realizing it is being ridiculous, she asks for low key friendships, compromise and help." DREAM "I would dream that I could fly doing the breast-stroke and swimming through the air. I would fly to the Art Center up the long, wooded driveway." -------------------- She watches as he marries another, though not as special as she is. The other girl gets him."	"The compromise is the desexualized Birth of Venus who is me being haunted by my grandmother over the competitive and proper social and professional goals. It is also me haunting my old, innocent boyfriends, pestering them, singing songs about them and not letting them ever leave my reins."

Reflections on my metaphors
By Melissa Levis, March 20, 2012
Melissa: Running Out of Time/Jealous Flowers

It's been 20 years since I completed my first Conflict Analysis Training Workbook, and I am in awe of how consistently and accurately these tests have captured my personality and internal and external struggles at critical junctions in life. It is almost like these tests are a magic crystal ball. They reliably predict my pattern of relating and show me like a flashlight into the dark where I will get into trouble next if I don't stay mindful of the three tenants of Power Management – living with moderation, cooperation, and mutual respect. Alas, though I am my father's daughter and have grown up hearing of these ideas, I am innately wired to be dominant and aggressive. I recklessly power through life and get myself in trouble by not heeding the Power Management mantra enough. I have turned to these workbooks throughout my life to give me clarity and insights during times of personal crisis: leaving home at 22, deciding on a career at 27, struggling with my marriage and young child at 35, and facing financial and professional fears at 42.

Though two decades have passed and the specific conflicts have been resolved, what has stayed exactly the same is my dominant, aggressive score on the Relational Modality Scale. It clearly shows that I am a leader. I am a plus three on all the questions that involve dominance and being assertive. These qualities have helped me in some good ways. I have envisioned, written, and produced a million dollar award winning Off-Broadway musical and personally raised $500,000 from investors. I created a business writing and performing songs for governors, prime ministers, movie stars and business tycoons. I started a singing group with fortune 500 Hamptons Moguls as my backup band. I created a business writing songs for children and performing annually at 60 concerts and 240 classes for over 10,000 kids a year.

These are positive examples of how my dominance and confidence and aggressive personality has helped me, but exactly as the Formal Theory predicts, I suffer in direct proportion to my strength. The Formal Theory is based on the idea of balance and reciprocal emotions. So, was I less aggressive, I would also be less scared. If I were less intense, I would be more peaceful and joyful. If I weren't so competitive, I wouldn't feel like I was always in such a race against time. This test has given me wisdom, but alas I am so recklessly racing through the day and years in a rush to get everything done, I am not mindful enough of moderating my power. Thus I do get into trouble. And I suffer because of it.

My dominant personality makes me want to be the center of attention, and when I'm not, I feel incredibly frustrated and angry. My conflictual memory test is of waking up from naps and hearing my parents downstairs and being in a fury, and launching into a temper tantrum. My parents tried to soothe me, but of course they had no idea that really what made me cry was the feeling that the world was going on without me, while I was taking a nap and I had missed out on all the fun. Another conflictual memory was of not getting into the private high school that my sister went to. The rejection was especially hurtful because I felt excluded, I was missing out. Now as an adult, I have terrible conflicts around the stock market. I feel like I am missing out on all the action and profits and it's too late to get invested. I've missed it. The run on Apple computer stock kills me. Literally, I fear I am aging my body from the stress that I put on myself about having missed buying the stock at $150 a share and watching it creep up to $600 a share and feeling like it's too late to get in now because I missed the window. My temper tantrum is to not watch the TV, to refuse to play the game, and of course, all it does is punish myself. I am getting in my own way.

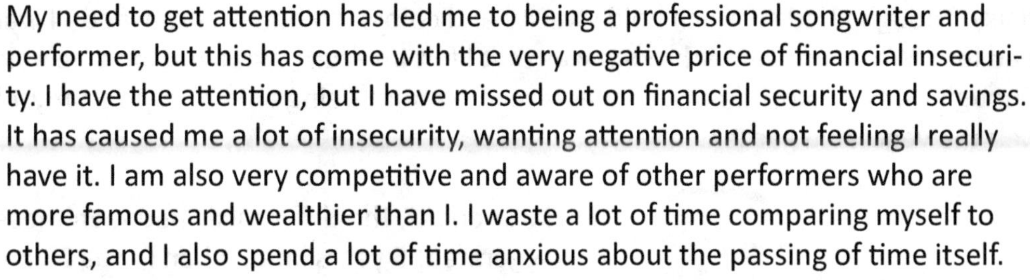

My need to get attention has led me to being a professional songwriter and performer, but this has come with the very negative price of financial insecurity. I have the attention, but I have missed out on financial security and savings. It has caused me a lot of insecurity, wanting attention and not feeling I really have it. I am also very competitive and aware of other performers who are more famous and wealthier than I. I waste a lot of time comparing myself to others, and I also spend a lot of time anxious about the passing of time itself.

It's interesting to note that my first test in 1992 already foreshadowed my preoccupation with time. The mask test of my heart was open singing/kissing lips surrounded by a colorful heart, encircled by a clock of time, with my 4 best friends' names written at 12:00, 3:00, 6:00, & 9:00 around the dial. I was very aware of what my friends were up to in the professional and personal lives. I was competing with them and pressuring myself to keep up and excel, especially in relation with them. In my most recent book, time has become my nemesis. Three characters in my most recent animal metaphor and story tests are the Time Keeper, Father Time, and the hourglass. My heart races and aches with the pressure of trying to slow down time or cram in more things to beat time. I identify with Cinderella cramming to get everything done before the clock chimes 12:00 at the ball.

I am terribly afraid I am going to be the ultimate loser in life and die early, burn out early because I want too much – too much attention, too much success and recognition, too much power. I wonder if that's what happened to my two famous aunts and legendary businessman uncle who all accomplished great success but died by age 60. On the opposite side, I have an Aunt Chris who is slow and steady, consistent, calm, and measured. She is the absolute opposite of me: shy, passive, ordered, composed. Though she has no roar of the lion, she is actually much more internally centered and strong. She epitomizes the tortoise and is probably the ultimate winner in life. She will certainly live the longest and in the best health. (She is famous for ordering an "unstuffed" sandwich at a deli, as opposed to me who piles on everything and crams every last ingredient in the proverbial sandwich of life.)

Being so aggressive also has its drawbacks because I am scared. When I wanted to get a boy's attention, I did it in negative ways. I walked into the nursery room bathroom of a little boy peeing. Or I kicked 10-year-old boys in the shins when I really wanted him to give me a kiss. I think 30 years later with my husband, I still struggle with being able to ask for attention and love in a normal, nice, kind way. Coming from a place of vulnerability is hard for me. I am much more comfortable with coming from anger and demanding – but that only gets me in trouble as is evidenced in my animal metaphor tests.

In exploring the polarity of my choices of animals, I consistently chose a flashy, dominant, colorful, bossy, demanding, exuberant and internally scared animal with a more subdued, subtle, quiet, and stable small animal. In my first book in 1992, I drew myself as the overgrown, colorful flower patch that demanded extra sunlight and nourishing melons from a productive, orderly, modest vegetable garden. In the intensified animal metaphor test, I saw myself as a wild snapdragon entwined with the bird of paradise that demanded extra sunlight from the modest, unassuming daisy. Though I had so much bold vivacity and colors, I didn't feel satisfied - I wanted more from those who had less. What also came through was that I felt insecure that I wouldn't be able to nurture and sustain myself. Though I was a colorful flower, I was insecure about being able to support myself and provide basics like food i.e.: the vegetable garden.

In later books, the differences between these characters became even more exaggerated. 5 years later, when I was 27 and at a professional crossroads – to settle down and study psychology or continue with the insecure but more fun life of a singer, I drew a bull butting my horns in a tree with a wise owl and a dragon roaring and breathing fire at a kindly wizard. The bull and dragon are scary, powerful, dominant characters that are reciprocally frightened and helpless inside. Despite all their noise and power, they feel insecure and that they are incomplete inside themselves. My father has repeatedly been the owl—wise, patient, generous and kind. He is stable and all knowing. I am the younger, headstrong animal who fights him, only to tire myself out and come to some sort of compromise position.

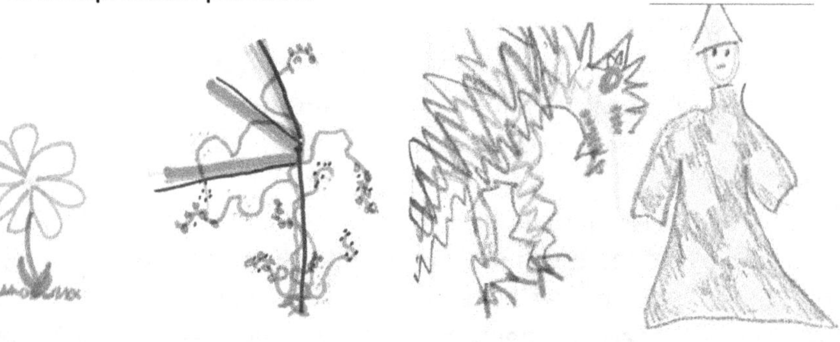

In my 3rd book, seven years later, I was in the midst of another crisis. Now I was married with a young child and struggling with my marriage and career. The insecurity of my choice to be a professional songwriter meant I still did not have financial comfort and security. And the prince, who I thought would rescue me in the tower, was fed up by me. Although he was a kind man, he was sick of the bossy, demanding, insatiable princesses.

He was very close to not wanting to rescue her any more. The animals in my metaphor were again a complete dichotomy: an aggressive, 'foxy' fox and the silent modest newt. The newt survives by blending in, keeping quiet, being unassuming. The fox gets in trouble for her flashy tail. The hunter is also the hunted. My second pair of animals in my intensified animal metaphor is a lion and a mouse. Though the lion is powerful, he is not happy, though in this metaphor I did not wish to be the mouse. (There is a limit to how meek I want to be! I know I must reign in my power, but I still do not really want to be mousy...).

In my 4th book and final animal metaphor, 20 years after the first test, I drew two new stories, one with a dove and a puffer fish and another with Athena and the Hourglass. My life has resolved earlier conflicts and found resolution—finding a partner, compromising and staying happily within the limits of a marriage and parenthood; however, the career and financial uncertainty remains. Now the dove is my husband – kind and patient, much like the wizard, the owl, the vegetable patch, the daisy, the prince, and the newt. The puffer fish is me – aggressive, defensive, prickly, and tough. (And who epitomizes an aggressive character more than Athena, decked out in her armor, ready for battle? She may have pink rhinestones on her javelin, but she is still a warrior.) But now the ultimate opponent isn't my father or my husband, it's time. The hourglass or father time is kind; it's not loud or aggressive. It is steady and constant. It is what it is. It is an enemy I can never battle and triumph over. It is my task to surrender and make peace with it, for all I am doing is upsetting myself by butting my horns and trying to change it.

The good news is that I have stayed married. I have accepted and embraced compromise with my husband and with my career. I have one child rather than more. I sing for kids rather than Broadway audiences or Madison Square Garden. I have made peace with certain things. I do need to finally make peace with time, because I know it is the ultimate winner. I need to make peace with the golden three of Power Management – they are the ultimate golden mean and best advice too.

Intern #2, Chris: Badger vs. Rabbit, the subordinacy scenario:

Chris was a 20 year-old college philosophy major; he discovered his submissive antagonism as the badger exploding at a kind naïve rabbit. Chris' stressful memory depicts him victimized and resentful. His response shows his aspirations for being a wise, yet sad King. His anxiety was hope and fear of childlike innocence. His defense was intolerance to innocence as a badger menacing a rabbit. In his reversal the Intensified Animal Metaphor presents the badger out of control. He devours the rabbit. In his Dream Metaphor, a monster pulls him away. His compromise presents a resolution: it shows the sad and risible King bemused by an unpretentious and cheerful janitor.

Upon his graduation from the summer internship program, he composed a lengthy essay in which he explained the Formal Theory and his findings through the formal interpretation of his testing. He presented the key concepts of the Formal Theory and exemplified the theory with a detailed analysis of his personal metaphors. I have enjoyed his essay as a model introduction to the theory and its clinical application. He, a novice intern, understood and could explain the concepts and technology of the new grand theory of psychology. He also was able to clarify its relevance for self-discovery. I have recommended his essay as the preparatory reading to the new interns.

The submissive person can be hostile and explosive.
Stress- Chris's choice of memory depicts him victimized and resentful.
His response shows his aspirations for being a wise, yet sad King.
His anxiety is hope and fear of his sibling's childlike innocence.
His defense: Animal Metaphor is intolerance to innocence as a badger menacing a rabbit.
In his reversal, the badger is out of control, devours the rabbit, and in his dreams he is scared of monsters.
His compromise shows the sad and risible king bemused by an unpretentious janitor. Conflict resolution is validated in the cycle that begins with sibling rivalries, escalates with violent resentment but that ends in a reconciliation as the big brother, a king, feels compassionate to the unpretentious Manny the Janitor.

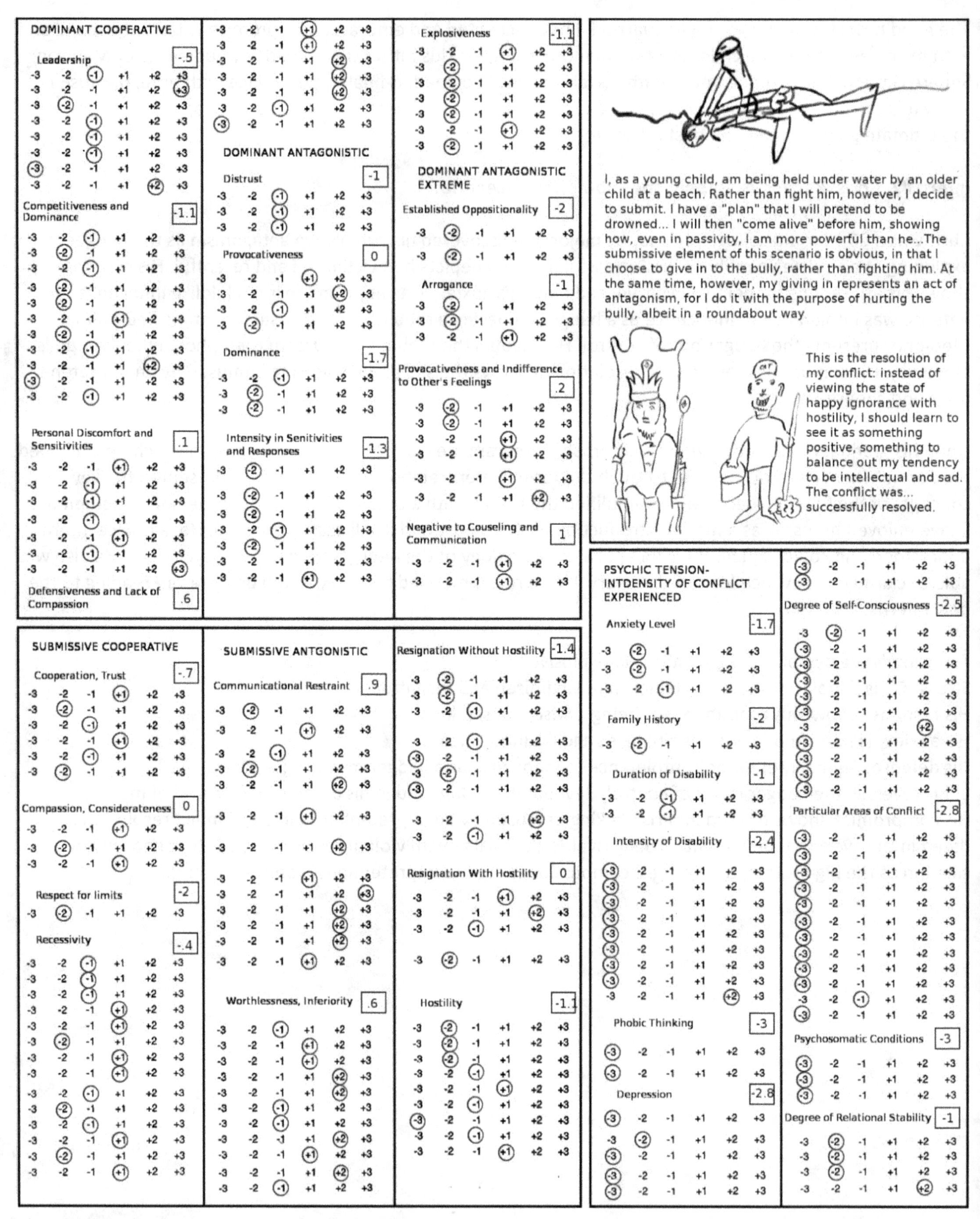

The relational modality scores reflect elevation in the submissive antagonistic scale

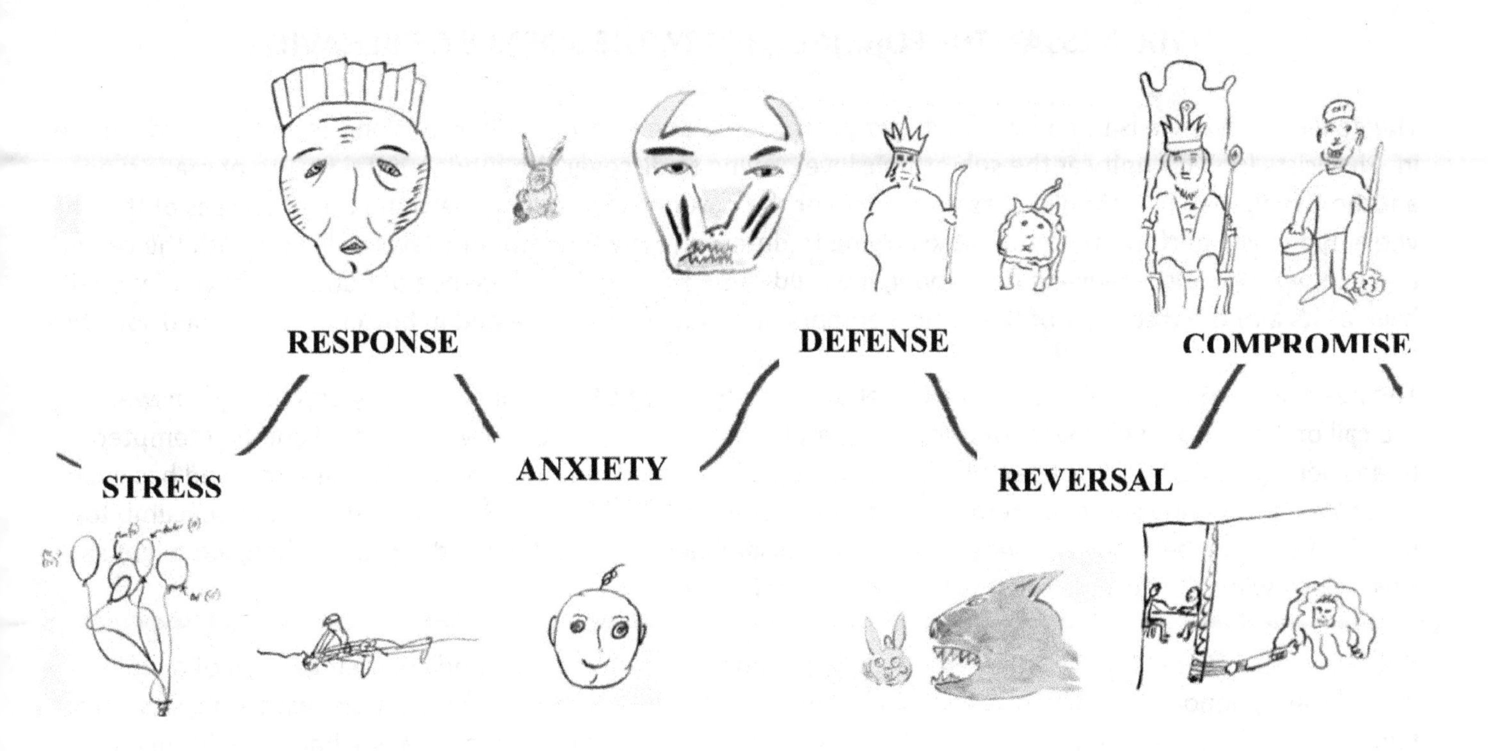

Family Balloons: "It seems I am envious of the attention my mother gives my little sister. She is 13 y.o. and attempts to attract attention. She discovered that the family is more likely to take notice of her when she speaks as if she were dumb—a skill she is rapidly mastering."

Conflictual Memory: "Held underwater by another child, a chose to go along with him. I planned to pretend to be drowned, hoping to make him feel guilty."

Mask I: "This haggard face represents my assuming the 'role' of resignation to pain as my identity. I identify this state with the acquisition of knowledge; to be wise is to be sad in my mind. An important detail here is the crown, which shows my attribution of nobility and power to this outlook."

Mask II: "This mask depicts a state opposite to that of sadness and wisdom. It's delight and wonderment. The child's face is equated with innocence or ignorance. My subconscious belittles this outlook caused by envy of my little brother. The connection is that happiness is possible only through the attainment of knowledge."

Animal Metaphor Test: "My AMT shows my defense against the anxiety of the previous stage, the rabbit here stands for 'happy ignorance' transformed defensively from the 'happy ignorance' of mask II. The badger is hostile and wise, but retains some respect for the rabbit's happiness, and refrains from eating him. I identify with the badger, who longs to be happy himself, and both envies and resents the rabbit."

Fairy Tale: "The evil, deceptive, cruel, merciless White Witch threatens Aslan, the benevolent, tough, noble Lion. The Lion is the behavior I want to emulate; however, I often fall into the rut of acting like the witch."

Dream: "Monster chases me down the hallway of my house. As I reach the kitchen he grabs my feet, I hold onto the door. I try to yell but my voice does not come out.

Animal Metaphor #2: "This is the setback. The badger no longer feels respect for rabbit's happiness which held him back before. He knows only hate and resentment, and so pounces on the rabbit, devouring him. It appears that wisdom, pain and resignation will continue to accompany one another. Luckily, the final stage shows that this is not so.

Short Story: "This scene shows my resolution to the conflict in this process. The wise king of this story finds that when the burden of power becomes too great, he feels better after talking to his friend, Manny the Janitor. Wisdom, and innocence/ignoran ce not only coexist in harmony, but actually complement one another. Wisdom alone leads to sadness; innocence alone leads to superficiality. When one becomes capable of experiencing both, true and substantial happiness follows.

CHRIS' ESSAY THE FORMAL THEORY, THE SCIENCE OF BEHAVIOR

The goal of all science is to find unity and simplicity in the apparently incongruous and complex world we live in. Physicists look for unity at the sub-atomic level, trying to discover the fundamental nature of matter; on another level, they find simplicity as they discover the natural laws which determine the processes of the universe. Biologists perform the same tasks, trying to determine the fundamental laws of life on both the cellular and ecological levels. Following this model, it would seem that any true "science of human behavior" would have as its aim the discovery of the basic elements of behavior as manifested in both individuals and societies.

The nearest thing we have to a science of behavior is psychology. Does contemporary psychology answer the call of science, the discovery of unity and simplicity? One might well survey this field and feel tempted to answer "yes". Psychology, after all, has diagnosed and labeled hundreds of mental ailments, and has even succeeded in treating some of them. Perhaps it is just a matter of time before these sicknesses succumb to the march of science, before man conquers the many disabilities to which his mind is prone. Then, we might say, psychology will truly deserve the label "science of behavior".

But is this really true? Is a "science" which attempts only the identification and characterization of a multitude of disparate phenomena truly worthy of the name? Would we be satisfied, for example, with a physics which had one "law" for the motion of a falling brick, and another for the motion of a falling ball? Would such a body of knowledge be a "science"? The answer, of course, is "no". The goal of science, again, is to find unity and simplicity. This means that the scientist must understand phenomena as they relate to one another, and, through induction, as they illustrate general laws. A true science of behavior, then, cannot end with the identification of behavioral ailments. Rather, it must theorize as to the fundamental rules which lead to these various ailments. When these laws have been discovered, and their truth validated through experimentation, then we will have a truly useful system, a system which shows us the universality of behavior, and is therefore valuable to everyone, whether psychologically "sick" or "healthy." We will have a science of behavior.

The Formal Theory of Dr. Albert Levis is an attempt at creating just such a science. Within the Formal Theory, a basic unit of behavior, called the "Conflict Resolution Process", is identified. The discovery and application of this unit allows us to understand behavior in any form, whether "normal" or "pathological", and at any level, from the individual to the societal, as manifestations of a universal behavioral process. Obsessive-compulsive disorders, Buddhism, mild depression, and Christianity are all understood in the same way: all are particular ways in which the basic unit of the mind, the Conflict Resolution Process, is expressed. No longer must particular behaviors be seen as unrelated and distinct. The Formal Theory of Behavior provides the unity and simplicity which is the goal of science.

Before going into the details of the Formal Theory, it is important that we recognize just how important the construction of a science of behavior is. We live in a world of jihads and racism, of international tensions and domestic strife. All over the world, women are habitually oppressed and racial and religious minorities persecuted. Why is this? Why do we persist in doing things which we know to be wrong? The answer is that we cannot help it. We are, all of us, under the power of religious, moral, and political doctrines which exhort us to perform these unjust actions. We cleave to these dogmatic dictates as if they were absolute truth, and so find ourselves doing and believing things we know to be wrong. Whether in the explicit form of religion, or the more subtle form of established social structures, we "learn" to act and think in immoral ways every minute of our lives. The lack of a scientific, abstract understanding of behavior leads us to accept uncritically these lessons. The results are hate, anger, tension, violence, and unhappiness. In turn, we do our part in perpetuating this cycle by passing our prejudices and uncriticized attitudes down to our children. We make steps toward solving our problems, such as those of racism and sexism, but find that, so hard as we might try, we are unable to truly understand and eradicate them. Perhaps the passage of time will wear away these remaining prejudices. Or perhaps they will persist forever, having diminished to a level many consider "tolerable".

Rather than give in to our weaknesses, however, why do we not attack them? Our prejudiced outlooks and immoral moralities have a hold on us only because we do not attempt to understand them. Previously, we have been unable to do this: we lacked the tools to dissect dogma and understand it in the light of science. The Formal Theory provides us with these tools. If we can learn to see our personal and social strife in a scientific way, then these attitudes can no longer grip us and drive us to unjust actions. Reason can take the place of unquestioned bias, and undermine the foundations of illusion just as illusion undermines the pursuit of happiness and peace. We need to understand where our attitudes come from, so that we can distinguish between constructive and destructive alternatives. We need to see that no particular religion or moral system should be accepted uncritically and accredited an absolute value. Theories, religions and moralities are valuable only in so far as they promote insight and justice, a concept, which can be defined scientifically in relation to the fundamental construct and universal laws of science. When we are able to see ourselves through the eyes of science, when we can understand our behaviors, attitudes, and opinions scientifically, then we will be on our way toward achieving justice. The Formal Theory will help us to do this.

The methodology of the Formal Theory: The six-role conflict resolution process and the four relational modalities as wellness diagnoses.

When Freud wrote of the workings of the human mind as he saw them, he postulated that certain urges were common to us all, and that these urges and their repression could explain many of our problems. In logical terms, Freud made a proposition: he said that the Oedipal impulse was present in all male children. A proposition is a statement, which asserts an absolute factual condition. "Ducks can fly," "Fire engines are red," and "Young boys have the urge to kill their fathers and seduce their mothers" are all examples of propositions. Propositions are rigid; they attempt to describe a definite aspect of the world with no ifs, ands, or buts. Because of this, many propositions turn out to be false. Find one duck without wings, and the proposition "Ducks can fly" never leaves the ground. When this happens, when a proposition doesn't hold up after it is compared to experience, we often try to moderate it. In the case above, we might say "most ducks can fly". Such an effort, however, invariably leads to ambiguity. What, exactly, does "most" mean? Does it mean "more than one-half"? "eighty percent"? Or something else? As soon as we try to resolve this ambiguity by attaching a definite meaning to the word or phrase at issue, we are caught again in the initial trap of rigidity. Clearly, propositions are difficult to work with, and potentially dangerous to any attempt at establishing knowledge. When Freud established the Oedipal impulse as fundamental to human behavior, he was taking a risk. For, if it could be shown that even one person did not have this impulse, then Freud's theory could no longer be considered a valid, universal one. In fact, modern psychology has largely abandoned the Freudian model. We have seen that, while the impulses Freud described are present in some people, they are by no means universal ones. The propositional nature of Freud's work made it too rigid and static to endure.

Unfortunately, modern psychology continues to look at the mind with much the same logical method that Freud did. Psychologists identify various pathologies and describe them, perhaps speculating as to what their causes and cures might be. Descriptions and diagnoses are revised and discarded as new evidence makes the old descriptions obviously incorrect. This is not to say that psychology makes no advances. Its successes, however, are slow and painstaking. A psychologist constructs a description of a mental illness and speculates as to its cause. He searches for a cure. If he is "successful", then his work will endure until its inadequacy is exposed. If he is lucky, this might take quite some time. What is obvious, however, is that his work will not remain acceptable. The reason why this is so is that psychology now recognizes hundreds of supposedly different and distinct pathologies.

This might seem to be quite an achievement, until one remembers the obvious: that all of these pathologies affect the same thing, the human mind. Isn't science supposed to show us the unity of things behind the apparent complexity? Is it possible that the currently accepted descriptions of mental illness represent all the unity that is to be found in the human mind? Modern psychology appears to have forsaken the quest for simplicity, for it spends very little effort in searching for the unifying forces of the mind. Instead, psychologists turn to studying the multitude of concrete biological phenomena.

Psychologists today study the brain, and not the mind. They associate certain physical conditions in the brain with certain mental illnesses, and stop there. This is not the search for simplicity, which characterizes science, but rather mere description. A true science of the mind would aim at discovering and describing the universal laws of behavior, which produce these physical conditions and their associated symptoms. Modern psychology does not do this, but instead approaches the physical conditions as if they were given, and then attempts "band-aid" medicinal cures. Psychologists today largely ignore the fact that mental illnesses, whether viewed from a behavioral or biological perspective, stem from the mind's basic laws.

Psychology has turned to biology out of disappointment with the propositional method of describing the mind. The nature of the human mind can never be described propositionally, as Freud tried to do. Our experiences and characteristics as individuals are simply too diverse for any one description of what the mind is to be adequate.

There is, however, another possibility. Instead of trying to describe what impulses drive the mind, we might look and see how the mind works with the impulses, which are put into it. Instead of trying to come to a conclusion about the universal content of the mind, we might look instead for the basic process of the mind. This other way of viewing the mind uses a relational logic, instead of a propositional one. Instead of saying "Boys have the Oedipal impulse which results in. . .", we might say, for example, "An impulse X (here inserting whatever impulse is at issue) is transformed by the mind into an opposite impulse."

Such a way of describing the mind is much more flexible. This method looks at the structure and dynamic activity of the mind, or its form. Then, when we have discovered this basic structure, we can see specific instances of behavior as the mind's form taking on content. Such a theory of the mind would not be committed to any specific content, as was Freud's, but would rather propose a model of the mind's processes in abstraction from any content, i.e., "If x, then y", where the meaning of the variables depends on the experiences of a particular individual. Once such a model has been established, it is applied by examining the influences in a person's life and seeing how these influences have been transformed and rearranged by the mind according to its basic, universal nature. The Formal Theory presents such a model.

The primary discovery of the Formal Theory is the Conflict Resolution Process unit. This unit represents the fundamental level of the mind's activity; it is the way in which the mind performs its function of transforming conflict and stress into resolution and order. This transformation is what makes man into a moral being, able to reconcile conflicting urges and responsibilities.

The unit is composed of six steps, which are logically and intrinsically related to one another. No one step can be isolated or removed from the process. Each is really a particular aspect of a continuous, dynamic process of mental activity. The Conflict Resolution Process in its theoretical form is without content: it is a series of logically related steps, which can be applied to the particular influences of any individual. Through these steps, the Conflict Resolution Process transforms submission into assertion, antagonism into cooperation, and alienation into affiliation, or mutual respect. The relationship between the two elements in each of these word-pairs can be described according to the rules of logic: submission and assertion are related as logical "reciprocals", antagonism and cooperation as "opposites", and alienation and affiliation as "correlatives".

Through this system, the Formal Theory avoids the trap of asserting the existence of universal impulses or drives, as did Freud. The Formal Theory simply asserts that whatever impulses and influences are present in an individual will be transformed by the mind according to the three relational steps of the Conflict Resolution Process: mastery, cooperation, and mutual respect. A psychologically healthy mind, according to the Formal Theory, is one, which is able to complete this transformation. A "sick" mind fails to do this, to a degree, which corresponds to the severity of the "sickness".

Dr. Levis discovered the Conflict Resolution Process while reading ancient Greek cosmogony myths. In these myths, five successive generations of parent and child are locked in violent relationships. The general structure of each generational conflict is this: the parent sees its child as threatening; the parent attempts to do away with the child; the child reacts by injuring or killing the parent; the child in becoming a parent itself fears its own children and perpetuates the cycle.

The content of this particular story is perhaps so violent that we cannot relate to it. The Formal Theory, however, is not concerned with the myth's content. Dr. Levis saw in the cosmogony myth not the evidence of some universal impulse or desire, but rather the evidence of a universal formal transformation that characterizes all mental activity. What follows is an outline of the Conflict Resolution Process, with the Greek myth used as illustration. While the process is described as six steps, it is important to note that it can also be seen as consisting of three stages, each of which contains two steps. Each stage represents the transformation from passivity to activity.

1. **Role Oppression (Stress):** This step initiates the Conflict Resolution Process. Here, environmental influences cause a person to feel that he is viewed in a certain way, or that he is expected to act in a certain way. In the Greek cosmogony myths, the Role Oppression stage for each child is that he is viewed by the parent as a potential murderer, and oppressed according to that perception. The father of the Olympian gods, Kronos, swallows his children, except Zeus, because he believed that they will murder him.

2. **Role Assumption (Response):** Here, the role established in the preceding stage is, in fact, taken on by the person. This is the active counterpart of the passive first step. In the Greek myths, the child viewed as a potential murderer of his parent actually attempts patricide; he assumes the role oppressed on him. Zeus leads his siblings in killing their father, Kronos. They thereby "assume" the role of father-murderers, which was "oppressed" on them by Kronos himself.

3. **Anticipated Role Reversal (Anxiety):** In this step, the individual experiences an anxiety relating to his assumed role. Often, this is the result of the person seeing his role as a sort of universal rule of making distinctions. For example, in the Greek cosmogony, the child who murders his parent begins to believe that all children murder their parents, just as he did. Therefore, he becomes anxious that his own children will kill him. The old saying that "Thieves lock their doors more tightly than honest people" is another example of this anxiety.

   Another, more general, way in which this anxiety may take form is that a person assuming a powerful role anticipates the loss of power in the future. The essence of this stage is that the individual fears that her role will be inverted. In the Greek cosmogony, the murderer of his parents fears becoming the victim of his own children. Zeus, for example, becomes paranoid of his wife, Metis, as soon as she becomes pregnant. In everyday life, people who hold power over others fear that others will come to hold power over them. This step is emotionally passive; the individual experiences an emotion about how the world will evolve to affect him.

4. **Counter-Phobic Role Assumption (Defense):** In this stage, the person undertakes positive action to ward off what he perceives as a future threat. Just as the Role Assumption stage is the active counterpart of Role Oppression, so this stage is the active counterpart of the previous one. The person experiences an anxiety relating to her role status and attempts a defense. In the Greek system, Zeus, the parent viewing his child, Athena, as a potential murderer tries to incapacitate or kill the child by swallowing her mother before Athena is even born. In real life, political dictators, fearing that their positions of total power will be destroyed, try to exterminate opposition through such actions as censorship of the press and persecution of perceived enemies.

5. **Role Reversal (Setback):** This is the step of the self-fulfilling prophecy. Here, the person's efforts of the previous stage are shown to be counter-productive. In the Greek myths, for example, the parent's attempt at defending himself by neutralizing his children leads to the children's actually trying to murder the parent. Athena grew to maturity inside Zeus' body, nearly killing him until she sprang, fully armed and ready for combat, from his opened head. In the case of a dictator, his efforts to eliminate any opposition lead the population to be less willing to tolerate him; in trying to eliminate illusory enemies, he creates real ones. This is another passive step; the person is a victim or beneficiary of others' actions.

6. **Compromise Role Assumption (Resolution):** In this final step, the individual attempts to reconcile his initial role with that established in the role reversal. This is the attempt at finding a middle ground, or a resolution, between two opposed roles. This step is therefore the active counterpart of the passive role reversal. The mythic Greek parents "resolved" their conflict by cursing their children to be murdered in turn. In this case, the conflict was not completely resolved in any one case; it persisted through five generations, with the intensity of the parent-child conflict gradually diminishing until it ended with Athena and her son. A political dictator might make a more adequate conciliation by attempting to court support from his country's population, instead of exterminating them.

These are the steps of the Conflict Resolution Process. These six steps can also be viewed as comprising a three-stage process, each stage of which consists of a movement from passivity to activity. In order to emphasize the character of each step, I have used examples, which are highly conflictual. This does not mean, however, that this process only applies where there is violence or great tension. In fact, this process is the way in which we all subconsciously react to the many influences and demands on us which we encounter in everyday life.

Conflict is a daily occurrence for all of us, albeit to a lesser degree than in the Greek cosmogony (hopefully). Our responses to the conflicts we experience are what define us as individuals. If we are successful in reconciling our many opposed experiences, if we create good resolutions to our conflicts, then we are happy and healthy. If, on the other hand, our attempts at resolution leave too much tension and opposition behind, then we are sick: we become racists, or schizophrenics, or psychotics, or generally unhappy, hateful people.

The particular brand of mental pain we experience due to unresolved conflict depends on the character of the original conflict. Some types of pain are completely debilitating. These are the ailments which modern psychology diagnoses and attempts to treat or contain. Other types of pain are less obvious, and so allow us to lead the semblances of "healthy" lives. Hateful racists, tyrannical sexists, arrogant anti-Semites, scared homophobes, and countless others are all examples of those who suffer from various varieties of unresolved conflict, although they are rarely labeled as mentally "sick".

The Formal Theory recognizes that mental "health or wellness" is really a matter of degree, a relative measure of how successfully an individual's mind resolves conflict. Modern psychology creates the illusion that there is a definite boundary between "health" and "sickness" by concentrating on the categorization of artificially distinguished mental illnesses. Its work is therefore useless for most of us, we who resolve conflict well enough to avoid these illnesses. But why should this be so? Shouldn't a true science of behavior be helpful to anyone, whether only mildly dissatisfied with life or completely suicidal? The fact that most of us benefit very little from psychology is a telling one. It exposes the unscientific, not universal, un-simplified nature of modern psychology. The Formal Theory, with its relational unit of behavior, gives us a truly scientific tool, which is like a measuring rod as applicable to the well public as to the chronically institutionalized.

Another of the Formal Theory's discoveries is that this unit of mental activity can be related to the rigorous sciences of math, logic, and physics. The transformation, which occurs throughout the Conflict Resolution Process can be described in terms of the Kleinian group theory in mathematics. The three essential relationships of the Formal Theory are defined in the strict terms of logic. Also the movement of the role status in the Conflict Resolution Process is remarkably similar to the simple harmonic motion of a pendulum in physics. These connections between the Formal Theory and these three strict sciences show us two things: first, that the methodology of the Formal Theory is, in fact, scientific in the strict sense, and, second, that our knowledge in the fields of math, logic, and physics can help us to study and understand the workings of the mind. The similarities between the Formal Theory and math and logic are useful largely for ensuring that the methodology of the theory remains rigorous. The correlation between the simple harmonic motion of physics and the Conflict Resolution Process adds a more practical benefit, in that we can use the formulas and diagrams of physics to help us see more clearly the movement of the process.

In order to make this relational unit of the Formal Theory truly useful, however, we need to become even more practical. We begin with a framework which has great potential because of its universal validity, but which is difficult to use. There must be a way of making this general model more particular, of fleshing out, to a certain extent, our theoretical "skeleton". The Formal Theory responds to this need with its four "Relational Modalities". Each Relational Modality represents relationally a more specific way in which the Conflict Resolution Process unfolds. The entirely general and universal unit of behavior is thereby lent greater particularity and applicability. The all-encompassing theoretical unit descends into the realm of the practically useful through the introduction of the Relational Modalities.

One might feel tempted to object here that the Formal Theory, in its categorization of behavior under four distinct labels, is really doing the same thing as all psychology, that is, forgetting about the goal of science. This is not so, however, for two reasons. The first reason is that the four Relational Modalities are not independent of the universal Conflict Resolution Process. Rather, they are simply more particular ways in which this process occurs. Behind every Relational Modality still lies the universal unit of behavior. Universality is therefore preserved: the Conflict Resolution Process is the universal unit, while the Relational Modalities are simply practical categories into which the specific manifestations of this universal unit are placed.

There is a second reason why the Relational Modalities of the Formal Theory are justly labeled "scientific". The four categories of the Relational Modalities are the result of the possible combinations of two formal alternative responses. They represent the logically connected alternatives, opposites and reciprocals. What this means in simpler language is that the four Modalities are defined such that, taken together, they do not exclude anything.

A psychologist might attempt to make a list of all known types of behavior. In the fashion of modern psychology, he would begin, say, with "Attention Deficit Disorder" and proceed to write down every behavioral pattern he could think of. When he was done, he might have an impressively lengthy list. He would not, however, have created a universally inclusive system of categorization. Some behavioral patterns are bound to have been left out. The reason why is that this approach is unscientific. Instead of trying to create a simple, universal system of categories, he settles for creating a new category every time he observes a new behavior. Perhaps, eventually, he might succeed in giving a name to every possible behavioral pattern, but by this time, his system of classification would be composed of so many labels as to be completely useless.

There is, however, a better way of categorizing behavior. The Formal Theory uses labels, which are logically defined so that they include all possible behavioral patterns. It does this by "bracketing" behavior through the use of logically inverse forms. In order to make sense of this concept, let us consider an analogous example.

Suppose a "scientist" were given the job of classifying a large bag of marbles. After examining a few of the marbles, he notices that, while all are spherical glass objects, they are of many different colors. He has a general notion as to the character of the group he must classify. He must now settle on a method of classification. Suppose that this scientist is an unemployed psychiatrist. His method of classification would be this, analogous to the method of modern psychology: he would remove a marble from the bag, and examine its color. He would then construct, on the basis of that marble's color, a category. If, for example, the first marble is red, he would write in his notebook the heading "red" and note that one marble so far fits in this category. For each marble he pulls from the bag, he will repeat this process. If he removes another red marble, then he will make another mark in the "red" column. If, however, the marble is of a new color, he will construct a new category. If all the marbles turn out, say, to be red or blue, then he will have a simple, elegant, system of classification.

What if, however, he discovers that the "marble world" he is observing is not so simple? What if, in addition to the common colors of red, blue, and green, there are such oddball variants as fuchsia and burnt umber? In this case, his system will no longer be so elegant. He will have a lengthy list of categories, some of which apply to many marbles, others to only one or two. Not only will this list be inelegant, but, because of its haphazard construction, it will be unstructured and disorganized. This is not a very scientific way of classifying: it does not yield simplicity and unity.

Suppose, however, that a scientist acquainted with the Formal Theory attempts this project. She will then recognize the need for a logically structured system of classification. She will create classifying labels not in response to isolated observations, but rather according to logical rules. She might, for example, select as her starting points the two labels "primary colors" and "non-primary colors". Under the heading "primary colors" she will note all marbles, which are red, blue, or yellow. Under the other heading will come all other marbles. In this system, because of the relationship between the two labels she has chosen, every marble will fit in one of the two categories.

This system is simple and elegant. If she wants greater precision in her classification, she can continue by breaking down the "non-primary" colors according to what primary colors they contain. This method is much like that used in biology, where organisms are classified according to categories like "vertebrate", meaning that the animal has a spine, and "invertebrate", meaning that the animal does not have a spine. When she is done, she will have a system, which is structured, simple, elegant, and all-inclusive. The other scientist only has a bunch of unrelated labels.

The Formal Theory uses this logically-minded method of classifying behavioral patterns. The Relational Modalities are the results of the combination of two logically inverse word-pairs. The first pair consists of the words "Dominant" and "Submissive". These two words are related as logical reciprocals. Mathematically, their relationship is expressed in the formula $A \times 1/A = 1$. Essentially, what this means is that "dominance" and "submissiveness" are two actions that are balancing each other out, like placing a weight on the tray of a scale and then balancing it out adding the same weight on the other tray. Dominance is the assumption of power, submissiveness the giving of power. Dominance is the active expression of power, submissiveness the passive yielding counterpart.

The labels of the second word-pair of the Relational Modalities are related as logical opposites. These are the categories "Antagonistic" and "Cooperative". Their relationship is expressed mathematically by the equation $(A) + (-A)=0$. Antagonism and cooperation are like two masses of equal weight on the one pan of a scale: the addition of one is cancelled by its subtraction producing a net effect of zero, or balance.

The Formal Theory takes these two word-pairs and combines them in order to describe four types of behavioral patterns. The four Relational Modalities are "Dominant Cooperative", "Dominant Antagonistic", "Submissive Cooperative", and "Submissive Antagonistic". These four are the only logically possible categories resulting from the initial word-pairs. This is because the inverse relationships between the words of each word-pair prevents their combination. Someone cannot, for example, be described as "Dominant" and "Submissive" at the same time, in the same context. This is logically invalid.

The importance of the four Relational Modalities is that they make the abstraction of the Conflict Resolution Process into a practical tool. When we discover, through testing, what someone's life-time Relational Modality is, it becomes much easier to see the functioning and relevance of the Conflict Resolution Process. Each Relational Modality corresponds to a characteristic method of conflict resolution. Someone who is submissive and antagonistic, for example, tends to resolve conflicts with others in a sneaky, spiteful way. Someone who is dominant and cooperative, on the other hand, looks to eliminate conflict in an open, considerate manner. Taken alone, the Relational Modalities are not of great value; they merely form a logically valid system of classifying behavior. They are, however, of tremendous importance when applied to the universal unit of behavior, the Conflict Resolution Process, for they give us the ability to capture in two words the various ways in which this universal pattern occurs.

One might feel compelled to question the methodology of the Formal Theory here. It might seem that the four categories of the Relational Modalities are too general, that they do not account for the tremendous range of human behavior. Surely, one could say, there is more to humanity than an abstract process and four labels. The answer to this accusation is that, yes, there is much, much more to humanity than this. In all the billions of people who live, have lived, or will live, there will never be two minds exactly alike. This, in fact, is why the Formal Theory stops classifying where it does.

The Conflict Resolution Process and the Relational Modalities are the two tools of the Formal Theory, the tools, which are applied to the substance of the individual mind. To attempt to create a theory which describes every little behavioral quirk in the world is not only impossible, but pointless. The Formal Theory establishes the universality of a mental process, without reference to the actual content that process works on. In order to employ the theory, we need to discover the actual content of an individual's mind, the way in which the individual makes distinctions regarding his personal sensitivities. No amount of theorizing or classification can ever predict this. This is where theoretical science enters the laboratory, where abstractions become concrete. How this is done is the subject of the next section.

III. Creativity and the Mind

As was mentioned earlier, Dr. Levis first discovered the Conflict Resolution Process in Greek creation myths. One might well wonder how this was possible. The Conflict Resolution Process, after all, is supposed to be the fundamental unit of human behavior. Greek myths, however, do not detail the activities of real people, but are rather fictional creations. How is it that these unreal characters themselves obey the laws of behavior?

The answer provided by the Formal Theory is that the Greek myths, or, in fact, any creative works, are not simply fiction. It is important to remember that art and creativity, whether in the form of myth, drama, sculpture, or religion, does not simply spring into being. Art is the product of the human mind. Art expresses our concerns and desires, our conflicts and dreams. Because of this, art reflects the workings of the artist's mind. Since the mind of the artist functions according to the Conflict Resolution Process, we can see this same process occurring in the artist's creations.

As evidence of this, let us examine the ancient Greek view of the tragedy. In his Poetics, Aristotle wrote of the structure of the drama as a "teleion holon", or perfect totality. The three stages of a play, the beginning, middle, and the end, taken together form a complete unit. Each stage is an intrinsic part of the whole; it has value only as a part of this whole, and the whole loses its effectiveness if any part of it is removed. The structure of the play is a fundamental unit in which one action, or praxis, is transformed according to necessary connections.

What Aristotle was describing was the movement of the Conflict Resolution Process as it occurs in dramatic art. The Conflict Resolution Process, too, is composed of three stages, the first stage being "Role Oppression—Role Assumption", the second being "Anticipated Role Reversal—Counterphobic Role Assumption", and the third being "Role Reversal—Compromise Role Assumption". These three stages form a perfect totality, or unit, such that the individual stages are of significance only as they relate to the whole. Additionally, as with a play, a single event, or "role" in the terminology of the Formal Theory, is transformed through this process according to logical rules of necessary connection. The whole of the process is immersed in a definite purpose, which is the result of the combination of the universal process with the particular event or role. Aristotle even noted the importance in drama of the relation between the active states, or drasis, and the passive states, or pathos. Just as the three stages of the Conflict Resolution process each represent the transformation between passivity and activity, so the three stages of a play each consist of a movement between drasis and pathos. Once we recognize that creativity is a product of the mind's subconscious workings, we can use the tools of the Formal Theory to bridge the gap between art and science.

This connection between creativity and the unconscious is the cornerstone of the Formal Theory's practical method. In order to utilize the theoretical tool of the Conflict Resolution Process, we need to discover what themes and concerns are relevant to a particular individual. The Formal Theory's "Conflict Analysis Battery" is a series of self-administered tests designed to do this. The tests of the Conflict Analysis Battery are essentially creative exercises with a minimum of structure and few restrictions. The test-taker is asked, for example, to draw two animals and characterize them. He then creates a dialogue between the animals. Finally, he answers a series of questions concerning his attitude toward his creation. These questions gradually expose the relevance of a particular creation for the individual. The characterizations and dialogues created through the Conflict Analysis Battery are, like all art, in no way random. They reflect in a very evident way the problems, conflicts, and successes of their creator.

The test-taker, in her role as an artist, creates art, which reflects her psychological fixations. The animals, fairy tales, and balloons of the Conflict Analysis Battery are the means by which the subconscious concerns of the test-taker become apparent. These concerns are the key issues relating to the individual mind's function, the creation of order and the stabilization and upgrading of psychic energy. The mind strives, through the Conflict Resolution Process, to take the myriad influences, which it feels and transform their randomness and conflict into order and affiliation. The technical term for this process is "endelechy", inner order.

In the purely physical, mechanical world, energy is normally dissipated and reduced in order through a process called "entropy". An example of this is the motion of a pendulum: in the real world, the pendulum must eventually stop, because the energy imparted to it gradually becomes useless heat through the force of friction. Living organisms, however, are able to do the opposite of this. They take disordered energy and infuse it with order. Like the plant which takes in the jumbled rays of the sun and makes them into useful energy, the mind of man works on the random inputs it receives and orders and reconciles them. The creative testing of the Conflict Analysis Battery lets us discover exactly which influences are of the greatest relevance for each individual's attempt at producing endelechy, or ordered energy. The series of tests exposes an individual's personal symbolic system, a system which corresponds to the actual experiences and influences which are most relevant for a particular individual.

This exposure of one's unconscious concerns is interesting and valuable in itself. The Formal Theory, however, promises and delivers more. In addition to realizing on a conscious level her particular sub-conscious issues, the test-taker also sees how these factors are transformed according to the Conflict Resolution Process. The tests of the Conflict Analysis Battery are designed such that each pertains to a distinct step of the Process. By viewing the tests as indications of the status of a particular conflict at various stages, the test-taker comes to see, through the evidence of her own mind, how behavior really is predictable according to the model of the Formal Theory. She can also discover, in the case of a psychic tension, how a poorly resolved conflict leads to mental pain or disability. The test-taker, armed with conscious and specific knowledge of her particular problem, can then take steps to alleviate this tension. The mind of a healthy, happy person resolves conflict smoothly and efficiently. The minds of others do not do so; they get stuck at a particular step or create a "resolution" which is polarized and tense. The Conflict Analysis Battery lets us examine the workings of our minds. This knowledge enables efficient minds to remain so, and inefficient ones to improve.

The Formal Theory does not purport to be able to solve our problems for us. Any significant change in one's behavioral pattern is bound to involve much effort and will inevitably require a great commitment on the individual's part. Our behavioral patterns are largely automatic; each of us has a way of responding to conflicts, which we use out of habit. If this manner of response is satisfactory, that is, if it leads to happiness, then we are justified in maintaining it. If it is not, then we need to improve it. In order to improve it, we must first become conscious of how, exactly, we respond. The Formal Theory lets us attain this consciousness through the application of the Conflict Resolution Process model to one's creative testing.

One obvious criticism of the Formal Theory is that it seems to reduce behavior to a mechanism. We do not like to think of ourselves as machines. It is difficult, therefore, to accept a model of behavior, which is as scientific and apparently lifeless as that of the Formal Theory. This reluctance, however, is due to a misunderstanding. The fact that behavior can be explained according to a logical, scientific model does not make us machines. As human beings, we have the ability to change ourselves. We are machine-like only in so far as we act out of habit and ignorance, responding according to a settled behavioral pattern, regardless of whether this pattern produces happiness. We express our humanity in so far as we are able to transform energy of conflict to resolution an upgraded form of order. We understand our automatic behaviors, and evaluate, criticize, and alter them.

That we should have these automatic patterns is unavoidable and necessary; they represent the "auto-pilot" which enables to make day-to-day decisions without becoming paralyzed by thought. But we owe it to ourselves as dignified people to seek to understand our patterns, and create new ones where old ones are inadequate. The Formal Theory helps us to do this. In making the mechanistic side of human nature understandable and predictable, it frees us from uncritical bondage to the unconscious machine. It allows us to consciously alter our unconscious response patterns, so that we become whole people. It is not an act of dehumanization to recognize our predictability; this realization allows us to transcend our machine-like side, and create ourselves anew, should this be necessary. If the essence of humanity is its ability to create, then what could be more fundamentally human than the act of self-creation? By making our behavior understandable and identifiable, the Formal Theory lets us engage in this most important of artistic endeavors.

IV. From Art and Religion to Science, Definitive Normative Changes

Our knowledge in the "hard sciences" of physics, biology, and chemistry has led to an immense understanding of our world, from the furthest reaches of the universe to the cells of which we are made. The result has been an ever-increasing level of material comfort and mastery of nature. But where the physical world ends, and our real lives as thinking beings begin, we have made very little progress. We still fight and kill one another without really knowing why, accepting without question the moral and religious dogmatism of our societies. We still lead lives that range from mildly unsatisfying to intensely miserable, and rarely stop to ask why this is so. While further advances in the material sciences are not to be scorned, it is clearly time that we focus our energies on understanding our lives as thinking people. No car, house, medicine, or pacemaker can ever give us meaning or anything but the most fleeting happiness. Only an understanding of the human mind can help us achieve the truly substantial satisfaction we all desire.

The potential of the Formal Theory is not confined to its application to the mind of the individual. Since the Formal Theory presents a universal model of human behavior, it can also help us gain insight into situations where the issue is human nature in general, and not the nature of any particular human. Religions and other moral and mythic systems are examples of human nature showing itself on a general level. These systems are metaphors of behavioral patterns; they tell us, in a symbolic way, how we should resolve our conflicts. As metaphors of behavior, they can be examined and understood with the Formal Theory. The benefit of this ability is that we can gain a better awareness of why we act in the way we do, through a critical examination of the religions and moralities we often accept unthinkingly.

We first need to recognize that religions and moralities are essentially paradigms of conflict resolution and power structuring. They purport to show, either symbolically or literally, the correct way of dealing with psychic energy. If we are to evaluate these systems, then, we must do so according to how effective each is in upgrading energy and structuring power. A system, which leaves much relational tension, or disordered energy, is ineffective. One, which leads to smooth, non-conflictual relationships between people is effective. With regard to religion, the dogmatist simply accepts one vision of God and man as the ultimate one, without considering the consequences of this vision. The scientist considers all of the alternatives, judging each with regard to its effectiveness in promoting endelechy, and has total faith only in the ideals of justice and equitable relationships.

The history of religion is the story of the evolving effectiveness of moral paradigms. The religions of Mexico and ancient Greece, for example, were ineffective in creating order or endelechy. Both promoted violence and domination of the strong over the weak. Violence as antagonism and domination are not effective relational choices. Rather than allowing energy to be channeled into productive relationships, these moral ideals allow disordered, unproductive energy. By espousing conflict, they insure that no conflict will be resolved. If man is a moral being in so far as he orders energy by resolving conflicts, then these normative standards do not deserve the name of moralities.

Modern religions are much more effective paradigms. Religiously advocated violence is less common than before, and the espousal of relationships of domination and submission has diminished. This does not mean that we have arrived at perfect religion. Most religions still advocate, to a certain extent, the domination of men over women. The absolutist character of most religions still leads to inter-religious violence and hatred. These problems, of domination and violence, are the same ones man has always faced. The evolved effectiveness of religion, espousing moderation, cooperation and mutual respect however, has led to a great reduction in oppression and unproductive energy. In order to continue on this path toward efficient normative orders, it is important that we remember the real nature of religion. While some religions require an absolute, unquestioning faith in their tenets, we must learn to see morality beyond them and be able to evaluate our religious beliefs in terms of their relational effectiveness.

Absolute, unquestioning faith is dangerous. When we accept in an unqualified manner any belief system, we expose ourselves to the shackles of fanaticism. The fanatic is one who has given himself over completely to a cause. He is no longer an autonomous human being with the potential to create, but rather one devoted solely to the dictates of his belief system. In attempting to serve blindly his God, or his morality, or his nation, he has lost the most important element of his humanity, the potential to live creatively. Religions, which promote or require fanaticism are immoral: they do injustice to their followers by oppressing and stifling them.

The Formal Theory does not say that religion is without value. On the contrary, it sees in religion much of the beauty, elegance, and spirit of human nature. What the Formal Theory requires is simply that we seek to understand, to contemplate, and even to criticize our own beliefs. The goal of all this is not to convert believers into agnostics or atheists, but rather to preserve that creative, independently moral core of humanity, which is often smothered by religions. Should we lose this core, should we give in to religious fanaticism, we are no longer moral, creative beings, but rather pawns of monolithic, rigid, belief and unexamined relational systems.

We are exposed to these belief systems in many different forms and intensities throughout our lives. It is inevitable that we will accept some of them; like our unconscious "auto-pilot", they make life easier for us. What we need to do, however, is consider them with the critical eye of the scientist before we take them to be true. In this way we can weed out what is bad and hold on to what is good. We can see that the racism which permeates our culture is clearly unjust, a matter of channeling hatefulness into arbitrary, irrelevant distinctions. We can see that traditional attitudes about gender roles are unjustly limiting, archaic remnants from less enlightened times. We can see that violence in the name of a belief, solely to preserve that belief, is the result of uncritical acceptance, and is therefore wrong. Many distinctions will be less obvious than this, and will require much more effort on questioning an individual's part. While this effort may often be painful, as belief systems we have grown attached to, are seen to be invalid and unjust, the end result is the expression of one's true self as a thinking, creative, autonomous human.

This is truly the goal of the Formal Theory: that, through a relational understanding of ourselves and our beliefs, we might transcend our weaknesses and create in their place new strengths, based on an awareness of justice and a devotion to love. Like any worthwhile undertaking, this critical analysis of oneself and one's belief systems is bound to require much time and effort. The tools of the Formal Theory, however scientifically important, cannot provide us with the energy this task requires. It is up to each of us to look our dissatisfaction, our unhappiness, and our hate, and recognize how these stem from our mechanical acting out of behavioral patterns and belief systems, which we have never questioned. This recognition alone should provide the impetus to embark on a journey of self-analysis, self-transformation, and ultimately, self-creation. Once we have committed ourselves to beginning this journey, the discoveries of the Formal Theory will show us the way.

A Self-Analysis and Validation of the Formal Theory

The conduct of analysis of religions and also of the personal relational effectiveness may be pursued utilizing formal relational analysis. The personal analysis utilizes an assessment analytical approach, the Conflict Analysis Battery. It consists of a series of creative exercises designed to expose themes of psychological relevance for the test-taker. It is here that the theoretical tools of the Formal Theory become practically useful for the individual. The Conflict Resolution Process and the four Relational Modalities are used to expose the inherent coherence of the mind's activity as revealed through these creative tests. By applying these tools to the results of the testing in the manner prescribed by Dr. Levis, the test-taker gains insight into the way he unconsciously resolves conflicts by managing power or relations. This realization of how one structures one's psychological reality allows the test-taker to alter the relational patterns to increase one's effectiveness in resolving conflicts. Relational changes result in diminishing psychic tension, and strengthening social adjustment, effectiveness alleviating tension in interactions.

I hope in this paper to accomplish a two-fold objective through an examination of my own testing in the light of the Formal Theory. First, I will show how the Conflict Resolution Process and Relational Modalities expose the predictable nature of the unconscious mind as manifested in the symbolic system of my testing. While this study does not represent a scientifically conclusive validation of the Formal Theory, I hope that the reader will be intrigued enough with this limited evidence to pursue the theory further. Having applied the theory to my own testing, I will then discuss as my second objective the personal relevance of this analysis. By exposing the unconscious activity of my mind, the Formal Theory has led me to an awareness of the need for certain changes in my relational pattern.

Testing Analysis

The tests of the Conflict Analysis Battery can be studied on two levels. On the "micro" level, each test stands alone as a manifestation of the Conflict Resolution Process, displaying an internal predictability and coherence. In order to illustrate this aspect of the battery, I will analyze my "Animal Metaphor Test" in this way. On the "macro" level, the tests can each be viewed as individual steps of a more general manifestation of the personal Conflict Resolution Process. As evidence of this, I will show how my tests, when arranged in a specific manner, display the unity and logical relationships of this process. The "micro" level of validation gives detailed insights into the individual steps of the more general "macro" analysis. The two modes of analysis, then, are not independent, but rather interdependent. Like the steps of the Conflict Resolution Process itself, they form a coherent whole.

Formal Analysis of a Metaphor Profile: Personal Case Study Report

In this section, I will attempt to construct a Formal Analysis of my Animal Metaphor testing. The Formal Theory analyzes "forms" in terms of four relational modalities. These are the four groupings yielded by the possible combinations of the logical pairs "cooperative" and "antagonistic" as opposites, and "submissive" and "dominant" as reciprocals. Thus, the four relational modalities are "dominant cooperative", "dominant antagonistic", "submissive cooperative", and "submissive antagonistic". Each category is supposed to represent a different method of conflict resolution.

General Role Analysis

Within the exchanges of the AMT, the Formal Theory's conflict resolution process was the crucial analytical tool, as it allowed the dynamics of that conflict to be made quite transparent. The Formal Theory holds, in fact, that the dynamics of the conflict resolution process should be observable at any level, in any situation. Where the pattern of the conflict resolution process was applied previously to a creative microcosm, it will now be used to identify the links between a series of distinct tests, so that a more general picture of my relational pattern becomes visible. Each of the tests in the conflict analysis battery is identified by Dr. Levis as corresponding to a particular stage in the CRP.

The first stage in the conflict resolution process is that of "role oppression", or "stress". This stage represents the initiation of a conflict, and it is here that the particular conflict of the CRP is determined. The CRP in abstraction is sterile and completely general, its individual stages abstractions themselves. When applied to a specific case, the focus and content of the CRP are provided in this first step. In the conflict analysis testing battery, the test which corresponds to this first step is the "Conflictual Memory Test". Here the test-taker is asked to illustrate and describe incidents of conflict in his or her childhood, adolescence, and adulthood. In addition to the factual descriptions of the incidents, the test-taker also describes his or her feelings during the incident. For the sake of brevity, I will examine only my childhood conflictual memory.

The memory I chose to portray is one where I, as a young child, am being held under water by an older child at a beach. Rather than fight him, however, I decide to submit. I have a "plan" that I will pretend to be drowned, whereupon he will be shocked and frightened. I will then "come alive" before him, showing how, even in passivity, I am more powerful than he. This plan is foiled, however, when I hear my mother shouting. She has seen what is happening, and is frightened. In response to this, I push the other child off me. This incident has always stood out in my mind, because I have always felt it to be representative of a strange behavior which I could not understand.

The Formal Theory has helped me to recognize that this behavior, in fact, should not seem so alien to me. In fact, the type of behavior occurring in this incident is actually quite representative of my normal relational patterns. The submissive element of this scenario is obvious, in that I choose to give in to the bully, rather than fighting him. At the same time, however, my giving in represents an act of antagonism, for I do it with the purpose of hurting the bully, albeit in a roundabout way. Perhaps I should identify with this memory as symbolic of my relational pattern rather than viewing it as strange, for it certainly exhibits the submissive antagonistic behavior which I commonly employ. Another important aspect of this memory is that I choose my reaction to the bully in a very calculating, "intellectual" way; rather than react in an instinctive, physical manner, I plan ahead, hoping to "outwit" the bully, as it were. The importance of thinking and the intellect in this memory carries through the series of tests, as does the submissive antagonistic modality. This fact is predicted by the Formal Theory, which holds, as was stated above, that the "role oppression" stage introduces specific areas of concern in the Conflict Resolution Process.

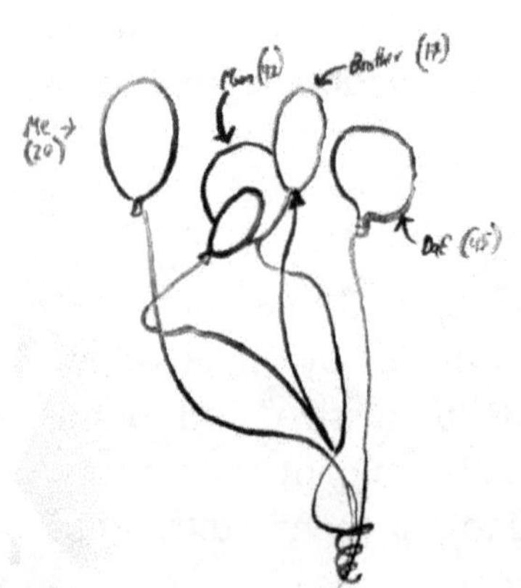

Family Balloon Portrait:
"It seems that I am envious of the attention my mother gives my little sister. She is 13 y.o. and attempts to attract attention. She discovered that the family is more likely to take notice of her when she speaks as if she were dumb - a skill she is rapidly mastering.

The next step in the CRP is the "role assumption" or "response" stage. This is the stage where the individual actually assumes the role impressed on him in the first stage. In order to proceed, it is important to clarify what exactly this role is in my CMT. An adequate description of this, I believe, would convey the elements of victimization, submission, and hostility as stemming from an over-intellectualized approach to life. According to Dr. Levis, these elements should be displayed in the first mask test.

My mask is entitled "hanged man" and depicts a sorrowful, aged face. I described the mask as conveying the emotions of "defeat, peaceful resignation, [and] an almost pleasurable sorrow." Without a doubt, the elements of defeat and resignation depicted here are present in the CMT. The mask wears a crown-like hat, symbolizing for me power and wisdom. This equation of wisdom and power with sorrow and resignation is perhaps the most important aspect of my testing. From the initial intellectualized resignation of the Conflictual Memory Test, it is gradually transformed through the Conflict Resolution Process into a more satisfactory association, as I will show.

After the assumption of the role in the second stage of the CRP, we proceed to the anticipation of role reversal, or anxiety stage. The test which corresponds to this stage is the second mask test. My second mask depicts the face of a baby, wide-eyed and smiling. The mask conveys the emotions of "wonder, happiness, excitement, anticipation, amusement, [and] levity." It is titled "Don't lose sight." The essence of the ARR stage is that it represents an anticipation on the part of the subject that the role assumed in the second step will be inverted. My role is that of desiring wisdom and power. At this point, however, I feel that the cost of attaining wisdom is sadness and resignation. The anticipation of this stage is that attaining happiness would require a return to child-like innocence and ignorance. The conflict presented in my testing, then, is between what I perceive initially as two mutually exclusive characters. The first is that of wisdom coupled with sadness, and the second is that of ignorance accompanied by happiness. According to the Formal Theory, the balance of my testing should display my subconscious mind's attempts to reconcile these two polarities.

The next stage in the CRP is the "counter-phobic role assumption" or "defense" stage. Here, the mind attempts to ward off the role reversal anticipated in the previous stage. The test which corresponds to this stage is the Animal Metaphor Test. In this test, the rabbit represents the happy ignorance of the anticipated role reversal.

My AMT consists of two animals, a rabbit and a badger. The rabbit is five years old, male, and characterized as "somewhat ignorant, but friendly and generally happy." The badger is 40 years old, male, and characterized as "very cunning, but also self-interested, potentially vicious." The rabbit, for which the entire animal is drawn, takes up approximately one-fourth the room of the badger, for which only the head is drawn.

Both animals face forward. This arrangement is said to represent anxiety and self-consciousness. The dialogue is essentially an exchange where the rabbit attempts to engage the badger in conversation. The badger refuses this, insulting the rabbit in a way the rabbit cannot understand, after restraining an urge to attack the rabbit. The rabbit finally gives up, but on a positive note, saying "I'll see you later". The badger has already turned away at this point.

The dialogue as it appears in Chris' workbook:

Rabbit – "Hello there, how are you?"

Badger – "I am fine" (does not return interest, but rather remains closed, sizing up the rabbit).

Rabbit – "Why so quiet? Aren't you happy?"

Badger – (Badger does not respond—for a moment he seems about to springing at the rabbit, but then decide otherwise.) "Of course I am happy—I am happy that I am not possessed of your dim-wittedness."

Rabbit – (looks puzzled, but smiles) "I like you—you're funny. I'm going to get some carrots, would you like to come."

Badger – (badger is frustrated.) "No, I don't eat vegetables. Now get out of here before I do decide to eat something."

Rabbit – "Okay—I'll see you later."

Badger – (Has already turned away himself.)

In characterizing the rabbit formally, it is obvious that he is "cooperative", in that he approaches the badger in a friendly manner. Since he is the one who initiates the conversation and attempts to continue it, he appears to be the "dominant" member of the pair. I have labeled the rabbit "dominant" within the context of the exchange because he is the one who initiates and pursues it. However, with regard to actual power in the situation, it would seem that the badger would have to be labeled "dominant". While the rabbit is in control of the conversation, it is the badger who holds power over the rabbit's life, and not vice versa.

In the context of the exchange, then, the badger must be labeled the submissive one, or less powerful in the social system, or interaction. He yields power to the rabbit but only superficially so. He yields to the rabbit to the extent that he replies when spoken to, although he does not wish to do so. He does not, however, give in to the rabbit to the extent of acceding to the rabbit's request that the two spend time together. While only mildly submissive, it is clear that the badger is quite hostile or antagonistic. He replies to the rabbit in scorn, and turns away before the rabbit can say a pleasant good-bye.

One more difficult element to fit into this analysis is the badger's urge to kill the rabbit, which he restrains. The urge is obviously attributable to the badger's antagonism; this much is clear. It appears that the badger's social submissiveness defines the ways in which he becomes emotionally hostile and eventually socially aggressive. He will eventually act out his antagonistic attitude. To attack the rabbit physically would be an act of overt domination. The badger, being socially submissive, cannot act in this way. Under this hypothesis, it is as if the badger had the predatory instinct of a wolf, but the external docility of a sheep. We then distinguish social power choices and compensatory emotional equilibrial forces.

Although he feels, on some level, a very real urge to attack the rabbit, the badger is incapable of carrying out this urge: he submits to some more powerful urge, the desire to avoid confrontation. In fact, the way in which the badger actually expresses his hostility is a very nonconfrontational one: he insults the rabbit in a way the rabbit cannot understand. The badger's behavior relative to the rabbit, then, is quite well described as hostile, "submissive antagonistic".

The confrontation illustrated in this exchange is therefore one between a "socially dominant cooperative" rabbit and a socially "submissive" but emotionally "antagonistic" badger. Before proceeding to a role analysis of this exercise, I feel that it is necessary to emphasize a few relevant elements, which are not captured by these labels. As I wrote previously, while the rabbit may be termed "dominant" socially in light of his role in establishing and maintaining the conversation, he, in fact, is depicted as the less powerful of the two.

While the badger is characterized as “cunning”, the rabbit is described as “somewhat ignorant”. The badger is a predatory hostile animal; the rabbit is naturally prey, powerless and vulnerable. It seems that the relationship, which one would expect with regard to dominance and submission has been inverted. The badger, who is more powerful than the rabbit both mentally and physically, would seem the natural candidate for the “dominant” position. As I have shown, however, he does not assume this post. This fact may well be the cause of the tension, which occurs in the dialogue, a role analysis which will be later discussed.

Role Analysis as a Six-Part Process Illustrated in the Animal Metaphor Test
In this section, I will attempt a “role analysis” of the conversation in the AMT. I will attempt to identify the six stages of the conflict resolution process as they occur within the dialogue. The first of these stages is called the “role oppression”, or “stress” and represents the initial conflict, which carries through the process. In this case, the role oppression must be the rabbit’s attempt to talk to the badger. This action creates a conflict because the badger does not wish to speak with the rabbit. In the terminology of the Formal Theory, the badger is “regarded as a potential power player or partner in a dialogue or conversation”.

According to the Formal Theory, the next step in the process is the assumption of this role on the part of the badger. This does, in fact, occur. The badger, although unwilling to converse with the rabbit, makes a terse reply. The badger has “assumed” the role with which he was “oppressed”, issuing a response, which fulfills the rabbit’s expectations of him.

The next step in the process is the “anticipation of role reversal” or “anxiety”. The rabbit, feeling encouraged by even the badger’s curt response, now feels as though the badger wishes to speak to him. The rabbit was the initiator of the conversation; his interest in the dialogue was evident from the beginning, while no such judgment could be made with regard to the badger. Now, however, the rabbit’s continuation of the exchange shows that he regards the badger as an active, interested partner in the dialogue. The badger’s role, initially that of only a potentially interested partner, is on the verge of being transformed, at least in the rabbit’s mind, into that of an active may be hostile participant. This is the rabbit’s state of anxiety, that he will be somehow taking a hostile initiative in their conversation.

The initial stress on the badger was that he was regarded as one who would potentially respond to a friendly inquiry. The anxiety occurring here does represent a sort of role reversal for the rabbit. The badger is now expected to attack.

This role is secondary to the badger’s initial role oppression. The badger now attempts a defense, or a counter-phobic role assumption. His goal is that the rabbit should no longer regard him as a partner in conversation. To this end, he issues an extremely rude reply to the rabbit, in an effort to make the rabbit dislike him. The Formal Theory predicts that this defense should fail, or even that it should have a result opposite to the intended one. This, in fact, is what occurs. Where the badger had hoped to anger or cow the rabbit, he actually encourages him, to the extent that the rabbit expresses affection. This is the “role reversal” or “setback” stage.

The final stage is the “compromise role assumption”, where the conflict is either solved or perpetuated. In this case, the conflict is clearly perpetuated. The “compromise” which is reached in this case is only a temporary one, since the scenario ends with the badger frustrated and angry and the rabbit looking forward to the next meeting of the two.

Ideally, the two would reach a compromise, which would leave both parties satisfied and the conflict settled. Here, however, both the badger’s frustration and the rabbit’s eagerness have been raised in pitch, such that their next meeting will obviously be an even more conflictual one. This judgment is validated in the Intensified

Animal Metaphor Test, where the rabbit again approaches the badger in a friendly manner, but is this time devoured. At this point the conflict is "resolved" with finality, but in an unhappy manner.

Having established that the conflict, which occurred in this scenario was resolved unsuccessfully, it is important to discover what led to this unfortunate outcome. It is clear that each party contributed in to the negative result. The rabbit's dominant cooperative attitude, coupled with a good dose of ignorance, led him to pressure the badger excessively. The badger, however, must be twice faulted for failing to respond to this pressure in an appropriate manner. In the initial sequence, he is overly submissive, and fails to let the rabbit know about his displeasure. This withheld anger leads him to "snap" in the second test, where he eats the rabbit.

The greater share of blame, then, must fall on the badger. The rabbit is guilty mostly of simple-mindedness, a trait, which cannot be overcome. The badger's fault, however, is one of a poor relational style, which leads to hostility, resentment, and, eventually, the victimization of the partner, the rabbit. It is unrealistic to expect that the badger should be able to transform his antagonism into cooperation. Such an attempt would undoubtedly lead to only a superficial appearance of friendliness, a facade whose positive value would not be outweighed by the high degree of internal hostility, which would accompany it. Instead, the badger should have asserted himself more directly, in a more "dominant" manner. The badger's rudeness in the first AMT is a patently submissive ploy, since he has good reason to suspect that the rabbit will not understand it for what it is. Had the badger expressed his anger in a way, which the rabbit could understand, the conflict might have been resolved in a less violent manner.

Fairytale:

"The evil, deceptive, cruel and merciless White Witch threatens Aslan, the benevolent, tough and noble Lion. The Lion is the behavior I want to emulate, however I often fall into the rut of acting like the witch.

Intensified Animal Metaphor Test

The fifth stage of the process is the "role reversal" or "setback" stage. Here, the defense created in the previous step is shown to be counter-productive. The test, which goes with this stage is the Intensified Animal Metaphor Test. In my intensified AMT, the rabbit approaches the badger in a friendly manner and is immediately devoured. The badger is unable to control his hostility any longer, and so kills the rabbit. This "setback" is the direct result of the "defense" attempted in the previous stage. The badger's attempt to distance himself from the rabbit actually encouraged the rabbit and made the badger angrier. As a result, the next meeting of the two is a violent one. That this stage represents a setback is obvious: if the conflict resolution process were to end here, my relational pattern would consist of long periods of intellectual brooding and sorrow, broken only by intervals of lashing out at those I perceive as happy and ignorant.

The transcribed interaction between the Rabbit and Badger:

"The animals are not having a conversation. The badger is about to devour the Rabbit. The Rabbit cannot move as he is so scared—he always feels a strange but powerful interest in his death, which he realizes is to be now."

The badger is the character I identify with: he is wise, cunning, and powerful, but also bitter, sad, and hostile. The badger represents the same attributes as in the "role oppression" and "role assumption" stages. The badger is hostile toward the rabbit, but also respects and envies him, as is evidenced by his restraint. The defense initiated in this stage is the badger's attempt to distance himself from the rabbit. He hopes that, by pushing the rabbit out of his life, he will no longer be forced to witness that animal's happiness when he himself is so sad.

Dream: "Monster chases me down the hallway of my house. As I reach the kitchen he grabs my feet, I hold onto the door. I try to yell but my voice does not come out.

Compromise Role Assumption

Fortunately, my mind has created a more satisfactory resolution, as is predicted by the Formal Theory. The final stage of the Conflict Resolution Process, the "Compromise Role Assumption", establishes this resolution. The "Short Story Metaphor" test illustrates this resolution.

In my Short Story, A wise king is faced with a difficult decision. He fears that whatever decision he makes will hurt some members of his community. This fear leads him to feel resigned to hurting others and himself because of his power and wisdom. He is sitting alone in his throne room, brooding over his problems, when a janitor enters and happily shouts out "Hiya king-o!". The janitor's happy innocence jolts the king out of his sorrow and gives him happiness, too. This is the resolution of my conflict: that, instead of viewing the state of happy ignorance with hostility, I should learn to see it as something positive, something to balance out my tendency to be intellectual and sad. This is a marked contrast to the case of the badger and rabbit, where I, in the form of the badger, lash out at the happy, ignorant rabbit. Here, I have learned to accept and benefit from the rabbit. Alienation has been transformed into affiliation, hostility into love. The conflict was, in the end, successfully resolved.

Here, wisdom and innocence/ignorance not only coexist in harmony, but actually complement one another. Wisdom alone leads to sadness; innocence alone leads to superficiality. When one becomes capable of experiencing both, true and substantial happiness follows. This is my resolution."

Summary: The Subordinancy Scenario

The submissive individual can be hostile and explosive. Chris' stressful memory depicts him victimized and resentful. His response reflects his aspirations for being a wise, yet sad King. His anxiety is hope and fear of childlike innocence. In his animal metaphor, a general intolerance for innocence is demonstrated by a badger menacing a rabbit. In his reversal the badger is out of control, devours the rabbit, AMT II, and a monster haunts his childhood dreams, Dream Test. His compromise shows the sad and risible King bemused by an unpretentious janitor.

CHAPTER SEVEN: CASE STUDIES ILLUSTRATING THE INTERPRETATION OF METAPHORS AS SYNDROMES AND AS RELATIONAL MODALITIES

Psychiatric Versus Relational Diagnoses

The relational modality diagnoses depart from the traditional clinical-symptom-oriented focus of DSM 5 by identifying instead the psychodynamic relational and syndromal nature of the unconscious. This approach examines the formal organization of emotions and behaviors and entails a completely different approach to diagnosis and related psychotherapeutic interventions.

Diagnostic categories of wellness identify two items: first the person's relational modality and second how this unfolds syndromally psychodynamically along the six role process. In the following case studies we identify the subordinacy and dominance syndromes, the relational modality diagnoses, as underlying a variety of symptom-based disorders. Submissiveness and dominance are wellness conditions that under stress may manifest as multiple symptoms diagnosed as clinical psychiatric diagnoses.

Here we must understand that the relational modalities under stress may decompensate from wellness to illness. The diagnosis of these conditions as DSM clinical symptom categories represents misdiagnoses stigmatizing the sufferer, while inflicting on them improper and ineffective treatments. The clinical diagnoses of relational modalities as 'chemical imbalances' or cognitive impairments entailing focused cognitive behavior modification programs accompanied by medication-regiments are ineffective treatments. Cognitive and behavior modification therapies seek to suppress emotions rather than to extinguish them by modifying the underlying power and attitude related difficulties that evoke them. Stigmatizing labels and chemotherapies with their side effects reinforce the patients' sense of helplessness and defectiveness.

The relational wellness diagnoses entail understanding clinical symptoms as generated by power management behaviors that are corrigible by making the appropriate psychodynamic relational changes. Several conditions in the following pages have been addressed successfully with relational insights and power management patient-identified interventions. The diagnoses of wellness, dominance and submissiveness, with the CAB self-assessment help the patients to identify their problems as relational modality generated symptoms and to address them with appropriate interventions. In the case of submissiveness the intervention is assertiveness by improving the communication of feelings.

In the cases of dominance the intervention is the opposite, self-restraint, admission of vulnerabilities and the reduction of dominant aggressive controlling, defensive behaviors. The path to changes begins with understanding the alternative modalities and their syndromal manifestation. It continues with cathartic emotional progress facilitated by the creation and then the analysis of the assessment's metaphors. The creator develops insights into one's pattern and identifies following the prompts of the test the need for changes in the area of power and attitude.

The significance of the relational diagnoses is in providing the client/patient with insights that s/he identifies through the completion of the self-assessment guiding the test taker to the needed therapeutic relational changes. The test taker with the help of the assessment recognizes one's relational modality and its syndromal repercussions as a pattern organizing one's life experiences and intuitively identifying and consciously suggesting the needed changes. The therapist reinforces the client's spontaneously articulated insights and directives for change. The therapist can clarify the relational diagnosis syndromal pattern and encourage the client/patient to adhere to the identified changes.

There is benefit in the analysis of the manifestation of the pattern as transference and as resistance in pursuing the identified changes. These interpretations are appropriate as additional therapeutic interventions that can be helpful as needed.

ABOUT THE SUBMISSIVENESS RELATIONAL MODALITY

Submissiveness as a syndromal relational modality diagnosis entails the psychodynamic treatment of assertiveness. This diagnosis is a preferable alternative to attributing the problems to a clinical stigmatizing and alienating illness that is beyond the patient's control. Power Management Therapy addresses relational psychodynamic restructuring of behaviors and emotions, attitude changes, as the means to combat the clinical symptoms.

Submissive people have difficulty expressing their feelings out of consideration of other people's feelings. They have difficulty pursuing power positioning by being assertive. They keep their feelings to themselves rather than expressing them. Consequently they suffer of a sense of alienation translated into feelings of self-doubt, worthlessness leading to resignation.

To compensate for this deficit in self-assurance and esteem they seek approval and attention by readily conforming and pleasing, but secretly resenting authorities. The submissive individual is vulnerable to authority figures; s/he feels easily respect and dependence to powerful secure people. They become depressed if they do not get this support or recognition. Alternatively they may seek escapes and also assume antagonistic defiant, self-defeating negative attention-seeking behaviors.

Thus while these individuals give in to parental and marital authorities rather than express their feelings appropriately they may silently defy their partners by tenaciously escaping them seeking secret pleasures, multiple escapes or self-defeating, and self-destructive patterns inflicting harm to themselves. They also may become resentful and hostile, negative, depressed, and suicidal.

Some of the secret ways for achieving pleasure and some negative attention getting behaviors are illustrated in this cohort of patients: depression, self-indulgence with food, sexual escapades, active phantasies like foot-fetishism, and alternatively expressing anger through self-mutilation self-destructive patterns. At some point these patterns of escapism fail. The submissive persons get overwhelmed with the consequences of defensive behaviors going out of control. Patterns and fantasies backfire and these individuals lose control over their behaviors with ensuing anxiety, guilt, depression, embarrassment, hopelessness and alienation. Their fears of worthlessness become self-fulfilling.

Unlike Cognitive Behavioral Therapy focusing on the clinical symptoms the focus in all clinical diagnoses is the underlying relational modality deviation.
The following case studies reflect the effective use of power management as the means of restoring wellness. The Power Management therapy combines the administration of the self-assessment battery with its cognitive educational component, explanations on the syndromal nature of the relational diagnoses. Gradually through the emotional release elicited through the artwork and insights generated by the therapeutic self-evaluation, alternatively through long-term individual or group therapy utilizing creativity for self-discovery, these patients are relieved of their patterns through relatively short-term therapeutic interventions. Recoveries have occurred in the span of six sessions, varying from 3 to 16 sessions, though long-term therapy cases are also recorded here.

The treatment of choice has been consistent in the following studies:

1. The diagnosis is established with the inventory test, reinforced with the metaphor therapeutic tests, generating insights about one's relational modality.
2. Personal empowerment is facilitated through improved communication of feelings both through encouraging creativity for self-discovery and through relational guidance.
3. The evidence of the effectiveness of this treatment is in the swift reduction of protracted symptoms upon utilizing the self-assessment.

These case studies illustrate the range of conditions that have benefited from learning to cope with communicational-relational difficulties and as a result recovering self-confidence, self-esteem and feelings of wellness. The studies demonstrate how the submissive patients' problems are offset by expressing their thoughts and feelings and by understanding their wellness diagnoses and their symptoms as these diagnoses' decompensation.

The relational diagnoses are made with the Relational Modality Evaluation Scale, RMES; the relational diagnosis is confirmed through the patients' Animal Metaphor Choices. It is of significance that the patients in this study are given names based on their animal metaphor tests making the relational diagnosis more meaningful to the test taker.

These metaphor identified names, present their respective relational identities. They reveal their problematic relating and entail their therapeutic changes:

1. 'The caribou falling behind the herd and the predatory wolf' is about a very submissive judge, who suffered from a chronic dysfunctional marital relationship with a very dominant spouse. He suffered symptoms of chronic depression.

2. 'Trying to survive as a dog' is about a man suffering of gastrointestinal symptoms secondary to stress experienced in a marital relationship again with a very dominant spouse.

3. 'The anteater and the lion' is about depression and personality damage caused to a young vulnerable submissive woman by a protracted incestuous relationship with her dominant grandfather.

4. 'The horse that wanted to jump a fence' is about a woman suffering of panic attacks, anxiety and depression following escapist tendencies related to a very dominant and abusive husband.

5. 'The wolf and the bird with the broken wing' is about a submissive antagonistic self-mutilating and suicidal woman overwhelmed by a very dominant mother.

6. 'The vulture and the snake' is about a woman with a serious chronic eating disorder since childhood elicited by difficulties in expressing her feelings to her noble but indifferent father and then husband.

7. 'The foot fetish' or 'The explosive Lion and the withdrawn Dog' is the story of a young submissive man with a compulsive conduct disorder. The animal metaphor below shows his relational diagnosis, the lion is his wife:

Sample metaphor:

Type of animal: Lion

Age in human years: 24

Sex: Female

Describe the animal's personality using 3 or more traits: Unpredictable, explosive, distraught.

Animal #2

Type of animal: Dog

Age in human years: 26

Sex: Male

Describe the animal's personality using 3 or more traits: Withdrawn, uncomfortable, confused.

Step 6: Give a title to the story. "The Rock Meets Hard Place"

Note what these case studies' metaphors have in common: the identity animals are victims of powerful counterparts. Submissiveness is about feeling overpowered and victimized.

Review of the Seven Case Studies

Case Study 1: *The Caribou Falling Behind the Herd and the Predatory Wolf*

'The caribou falling behind the herd at the mercy of a wolf'-*a simple evaluation without therapy* is the story of a submissive judge, who could not stand up for his rights. He was compelled into a marriage by a manipulative and demanding girlfriend, who 'had gotten herself pregnant'. He stayed married feeling like a prisoner, avoiding relations with his wife, while she was unfaithful and unabashedly promiscuous. He did not have the courage to either confront his wife or the freedom of starting his life again without the church's approval. He was evaluated utilizing a workbook to examine if he qualified for the Catholic Tribunal's criteria for terminating a marriage.

The submissiveness of the judge shows throughout his testing. His pattern determined his lifetime adjustment. The memories included early life self-sacrifice, a shotgun wedding, and recently an attack in public by his new girlfriend. The mask portrayed a judge, an authority; behind the mask was a scared and innocent lamb. In his Animal Metaphor Test he is a caribou falling behind the herd at the mercy of a wolf. The insight on the caribou's conduct was that he 'was willing to accept this fate of being sacrificed in the service of improving the species'. In his Fairy Tale Metaphor he was the pig relating to the proverbial wolf. The wolf is trying to reassure the pig, 'Trust me', while we see a knife up his sleeve. In this case study we see the dysfunctional social adjustment of submissiveness. The evaluation was completed and the judge added his personal letter to the Tribunal explaining his submissive personality's difficulties dealing with a very difficult dominant spouse.

See complete case study transcript

Case Study 2: *Trying to Survive as a Dog*

Surviving as a dog with a lion biting his head off' was the metaphor of a 57 year old professor of art. He was consulting me for protracted gastrointestinal problems. In an 8 sessions therapy he managed to produce a lengthy testing record recognizing his submissiveness successfully addressing a better management of feelings. The professor emerged to become self-aware and more confident. He was able to correct many perceptions and become secure in relationships. He completed therapy and was more comfortable with people and feelings and less preoccupied by his gastrointestinal complaints.

Summary: Metaphor Profile

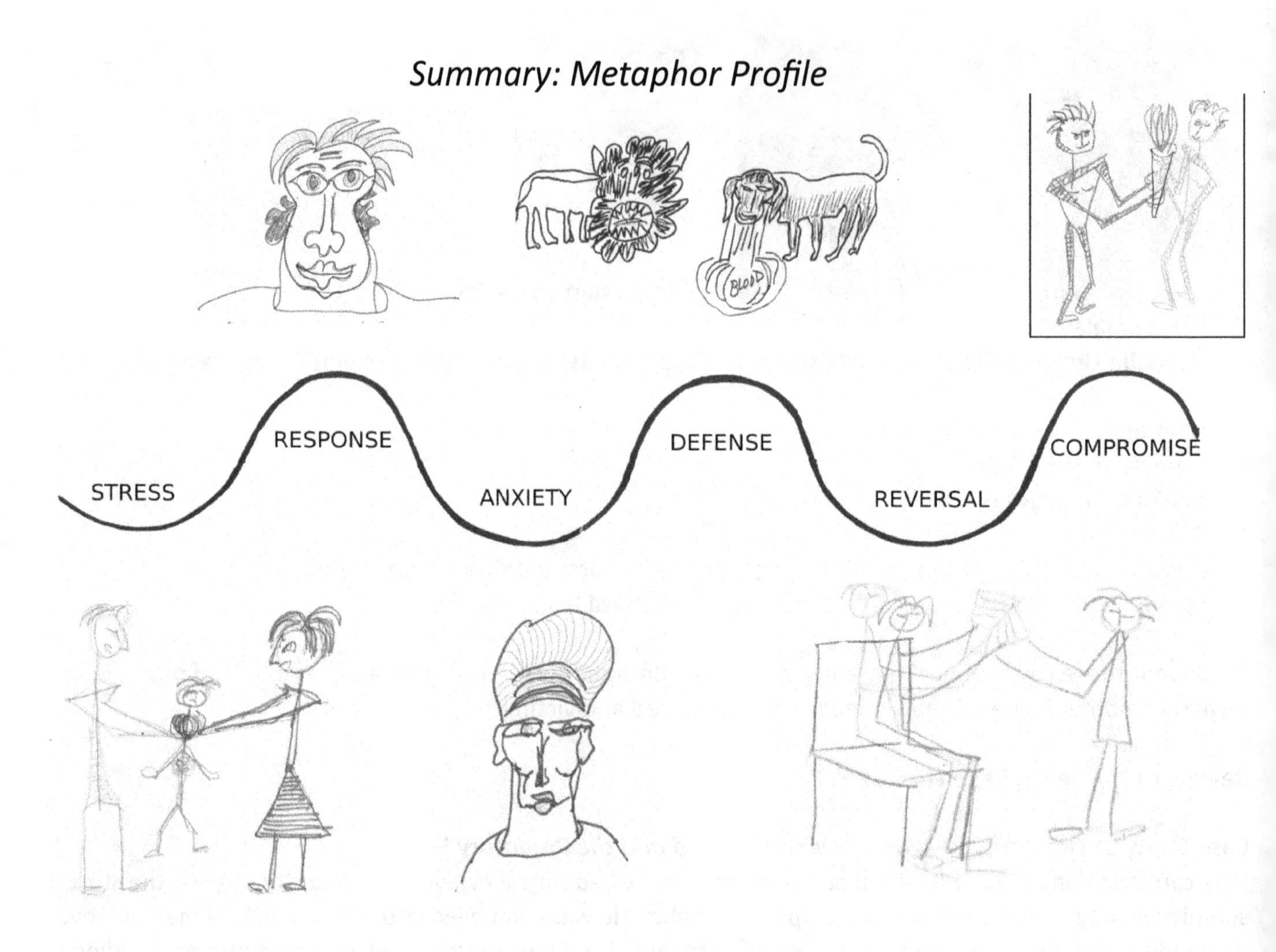

Stress:	**Response:**	**Anxiety:**	**Defense:**	**Reversal:**	**Compromise:**
Throughout his childhood, he watched from the sidelines as his parents constantly fought.	His mask, titled "Mr. Dynamo," is bold and confident.	Underneath the mask, the face is confused about its true identity.	A lion bites off a dog's head. He identifies himself with the dog and his ex-wife with the lion.	A dream, in which a woman prevents him from reading at his own pace.	The experienced character teaches the inexperienced character.

Case Study 3: *The Anteater and the Lion*

'The Ant Eater and the Lion' is the evaluation protocol of a 23-year-old woman, who had been victim of sexual abuse by her grand-father for many years. She had submitted to his demands until she confided to a girlfriend, then she finally protested at the abuse. 'The Ant Eater and the Lion' completed a self-evaluation, without any therapist interpretation or intervention; the inventory revealed the young woman was a very submissive co-operative person. She illustrated the abuse by her grandfather in her conflictual memory. In her Animal Metaphor she is disfigured into an anteater admiring a lion. In her quest for recovery she had great aspirations and wished to become herself a lion, at least pretend being one. She concluded her book of self-revelations with a metaphor of assertiveness as a unicorn battling a dragon. The letter to herself discusses her new insights.

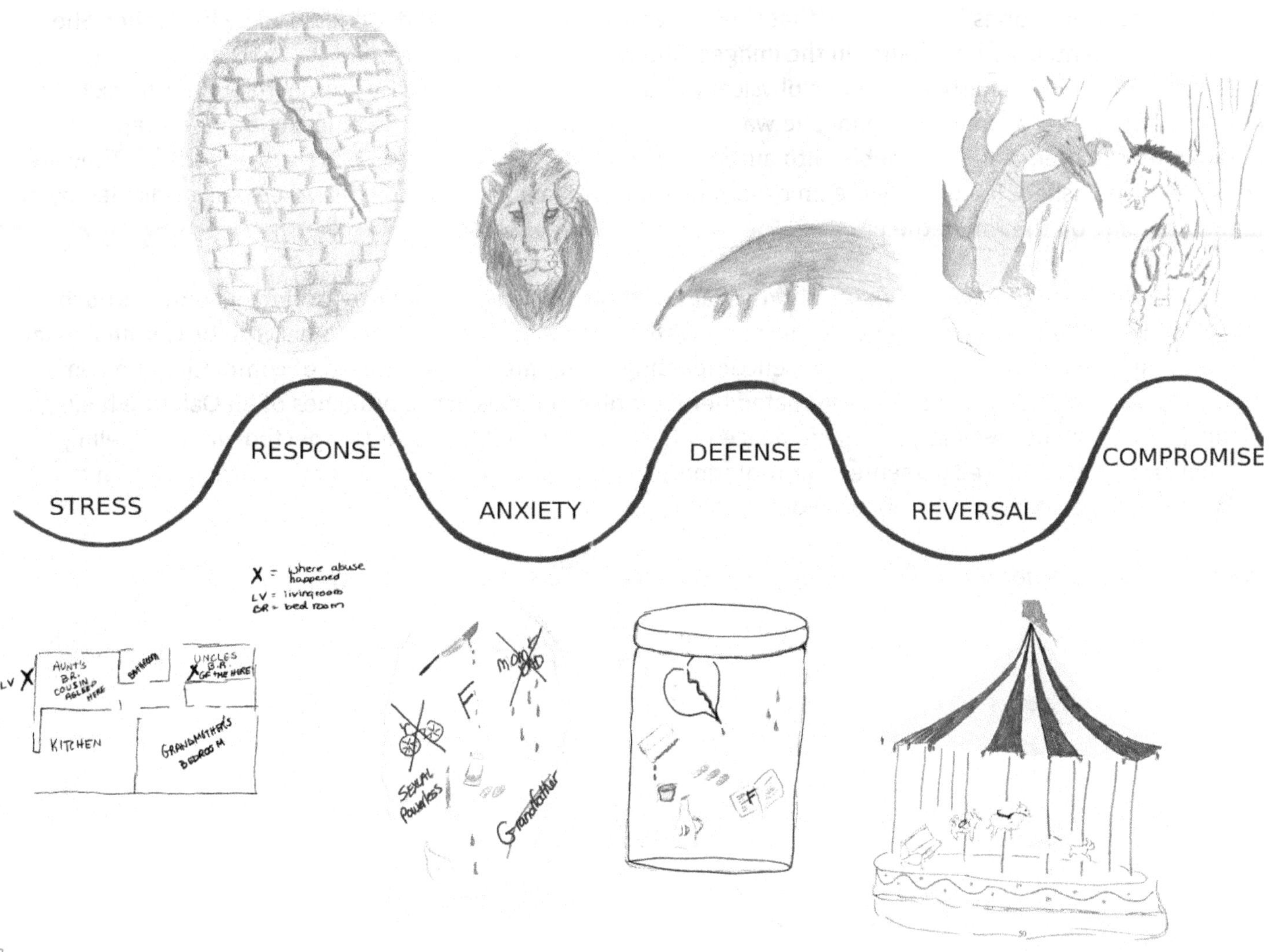

Stress:	**Response:**	**Anxiety:**	**Defense:**	**Reversal:**	**Compromise:**
She relates the first time she was sexually abused by her grandfather.	Her mask is a brick wall.	Under the mask, the face and heart are filled with pain, rejection, failure, shame, self-mutilation, and her grandfather.	A submissive anteater wants to be beautiful, and confides in a "Powerful Beast."	Dream in which she encounters her grandfather and forgets to bring her daughter on the merry-go-round.	A Unicorn and a Dragon fight: Innocence versus Experience.

Case Study 4: ***The Horse That Wanted to Jump a Fence, also identified as The Wise Oak***

'The horse that wanted to jump a fence' was a submissive cooperative married woman in her thirties. She had rebelled by having an extramarital relationship and upon that she experienced multiple anxiety attacks followed by medical interventions. She was trying to escape a controlling cruel very dominant husband, while she did not have the strength of seeking divorce. She completed three workbooks in a therapeutic relationship. Two of them derived from an initial period in therapy and then a third book many years later. Her conflicts are depicted across her several workbooks. The books were her therapy. She was very creative and used the creativity to unfold her troubled youth and complicated adult emotional life.

Her Conflictual Memories Tests portray that she was abusively punished and intimidated by her father. She is helpless presented without hands in the images. She was the 'blondie, the child that was an accident, and who did not fit'. In her marriage she was physically abused and manipulated by her husband. Her mask hides her emotions. In her Animal Metaphor she was a horse that wants to jump the fence. In other metaphors her animals got predictably in trouble with authorities, or alternatively sought to please authorities. They are consistently punished. In her early dream experience she had fallen in a pit full of snakes being ridiculed by her family standing on the rim of the pit.

In therapy she learned how to manage her marriage without generating conflicts for herself with her husband. As she grew confident she saw her cruel husband with compassion but set limits to his cruelty. Her final essay was accompanied by the image of an oak, encompassing all her metaphors instead of completing the conflict resolution six-cycle poster. She accommodated her metaphor animals in the branches of an Oak tree feeling reconciled with all her feelings; she made peace with herself, she felt loved and respected without feeling divided and guilty. The tree presented her rootedness in the marriage. She compromised staying put in her difficult marriage content with her cruel but reliable husband.

Book 1: *Testing the normative limits in the pursuit of love and experiencing anxiety*

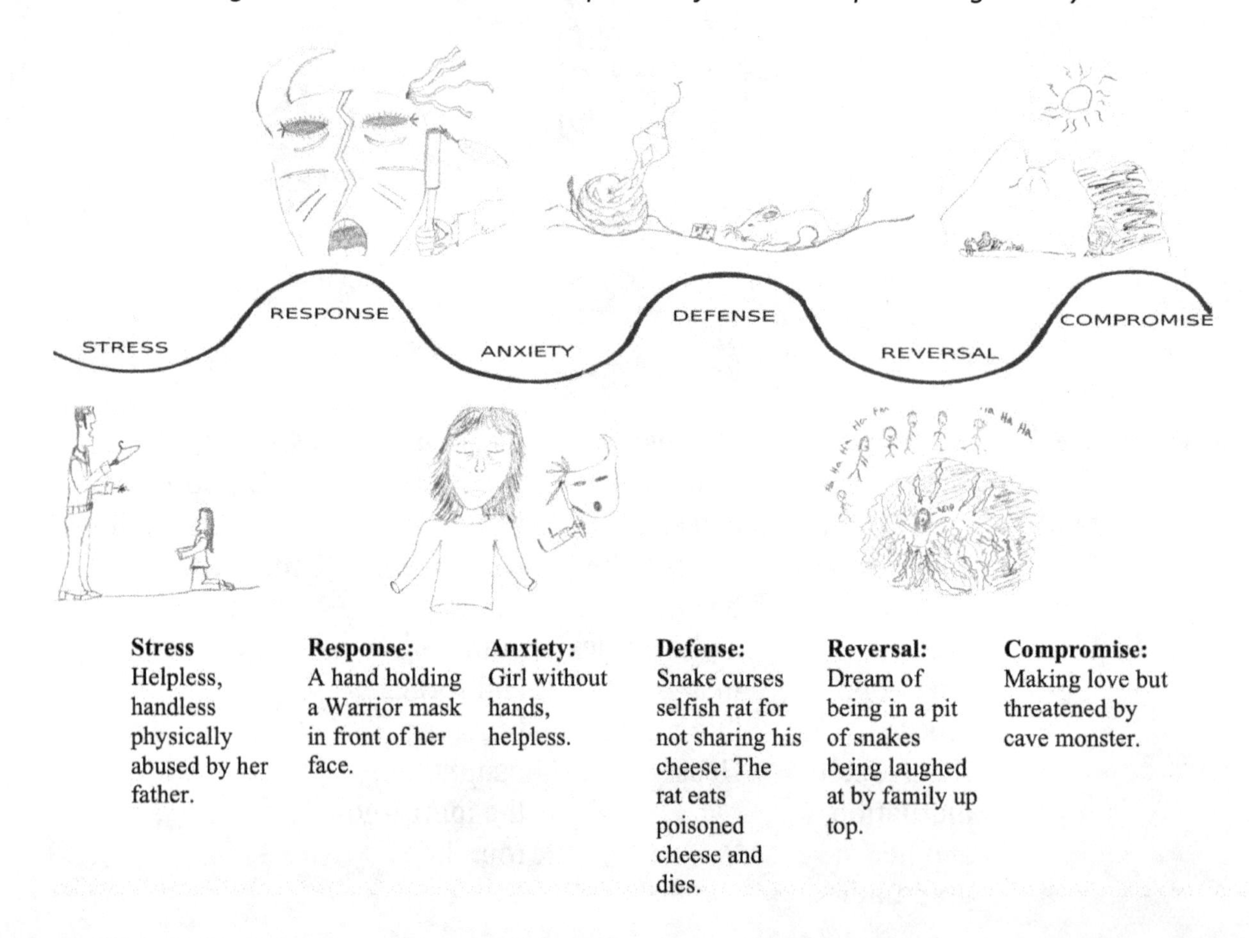

Stress Helpless, handless physically abused by her father.

Response: A hand holding a Warrior mask in front of her face.

Anxiety: Girl without hands, helpless.

Defense: Snake curses selfish rat for not sharing his cheese. The rat eats poisoned cheese and dies.

Reversal: Dream of being in a pit of snakes being laughed at by family up top.

Compromise: Making love but threatened by cave monster.

Book 2: Learning about limits in her quest for love

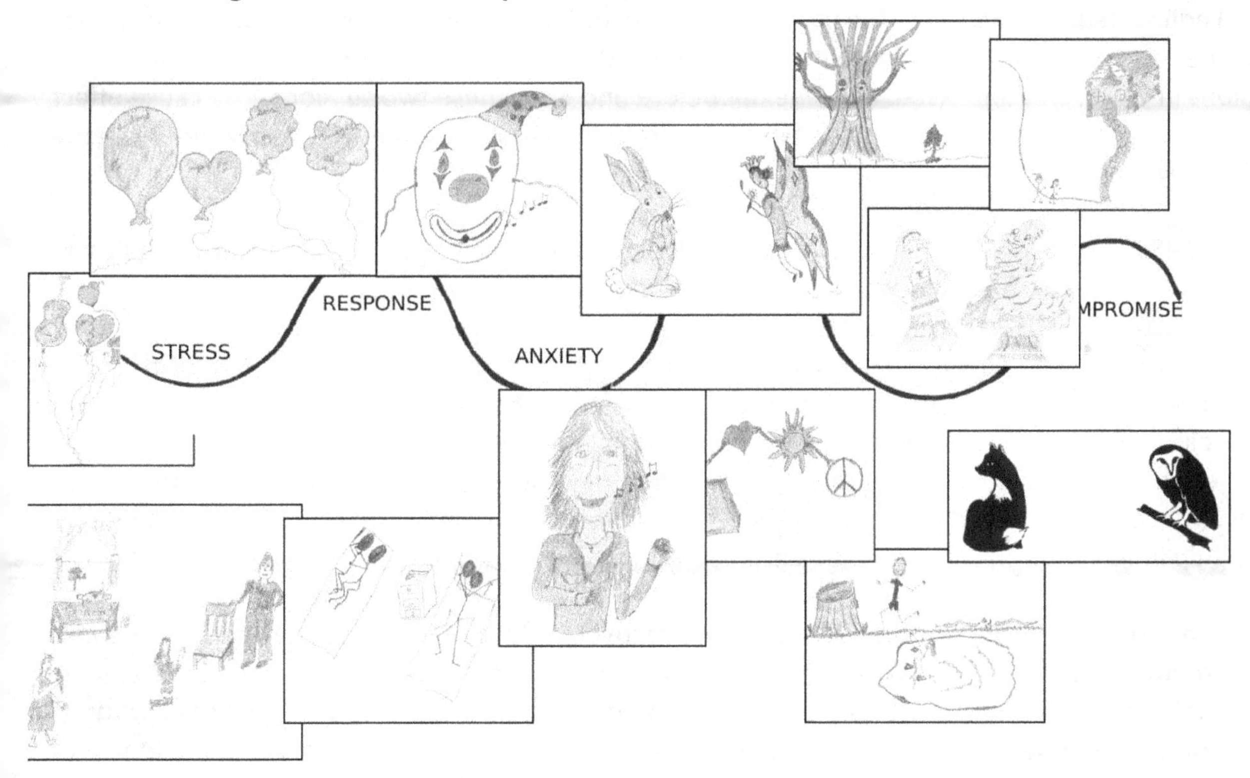

Healing testimony, cured of the need for love and attention from me

Second book: Outcome

Stress: The girl who was seeking attention that was not given to her by the family, sought to find love by passers by. She and her friend got raped, were taken advantage of by older men.

Response: She learned early to distance herself from her family, holding her feelings of hurt and anger inside but kept a positive outlook and her mask shows her as a whistling not speaking clown.

Anxiety: The hidden face now is a beautiful person weighted down by a ton of depression but inspired by uplifting peaceful feelings.

Defense: A number of stories now tell her to stop seeking attention to not get in trouble and not get flattened by traffic. The oak tree tells the sapling to trust growing and developing roots and branches caring for creatures.

As Alice she knows how to resist the temptations of the wonderland.

Reversal:

She is rewarded and she has a dream of emerging from the pit of snakes and walking out of feeling rejected by her family and friends.

Compromise: Indeed she is able to have attention without bribing the owl. The two are engaged now to catch a mouse to feed each other.

The errant flying kite is no longer victim of the winds about to be ruined but is tethered to a magic carpet bound to success. Remarkable keeping herself at a distance from the playful owl

Case Study 5: *The Wolf and the Bird with the Broken Wing, case reviewed in therapy outcome chapter.*

This very troubled woman was bent to self-destruct. 'The wolf and the bird with the broken wing', also identified from another metaphor as the 'Troll burned by the Sun' was a 35 year old teacher, married for second time, with a long term history of self mutilations and suicidal attempts; she was a 'cutter', who had been hospitalized multiple times for suicidal attempts, without therapeutic success. She was unstoppable in cutting herself upon any frustration. She kept a journal of incidents in parallel with taking multiple medications.

She completed in 16 sessions two workbooks, stopped cutting herself, stopped using medications and progressed to social adjustment. She represents a stunning rapid recovery after years of in and out patient therapeutic failures. The recovery because of the treatment is reflected in art work generated upon the end of her initial two sessions in which she contrasted how she felt before and after these two sessions. The cause effect connection of therapy and healing is also reflected in the rapid reduction of self-mutilation episodes as recorded between biweekly sessions.

Her relational modality diagnosis was clearly that of a submissive antagonistic person. The pattern manifested across the personality inventory and all her creativity tests. The conflictual memories present punishments and losses. The family portrait shows the sense of self-discrimination and feelings of lack of status suffered in her divided family. The masks reflect cover-ups of many wounds underneath. Her original metaphor was that of a bird with a broken wing in front of a wolf's open mouth. The wolf thought she was not even worth eating. In her second book's intensified animal metaphor she was a bunny encircled by a boa constrictor threatening to eat her. She begs him to get her out of her misery. In her dream we see a glimpse of her hoped for recovery: she was portrayed successful running a special education musical class. The first book Short Story Metaphor is of a troll burning up in flames at the sight of the sun.

The second sequence of metaphors reflects evidence of her recovery. Her metaphors present transformation across the same themes as in the first book. Transformation is evident by contrasting the new set of metaphors with the original set. Her many improvements, are summed up in the same symbolic choices reconfigured: reflected in memories, masks, animal metaphors etc. In the second book the principle metaphor presents her as a turtle on the way of a lion and moving on as fast as she can. Finally the short story presents the theme of the sun and the burning troll transformed to the Sun and the Moon. Her skittish troll in flames becomes the self-assured moon lighting the sky at night. She was the princess of the night, the moon, instead of feeling downtrodden and antagonistic she became respectful and collaborative.

The transformation of a self-mutilating woman from a scared fragile troll hiding from the Sun to a luminous moon was associated with her complete rehabilitation from her obsessive self-mutilation to functioning in the real world at home and in an upstart family business. In 16 sessions, she had completed her therapy. She had been able to stop completely hurting herself. Her recovery is recorded with the gradual cessation of her cutting episodes. Upon termination of therapy, she had stopped her multiple medications, and had assumed responsibilities in real life challenges. She also composed a short essay reviewing her progress.

Case Study 6: *The Vulture and the Snake, case reviewed on the therapy outcome chapter*
Gladys was a 50-year-old married woman in a long-term therapy with myself. Her case study is recorded as multiple animal metaphors. Clearly a submissive antagonistic person, the record of her therapy is shown as a series of phases consistently evolving to resolutions as the convoluted path of her finding her identity and her voice. She summed up her transformation, as how the "we" becomes an "I" overcoming inner conflicts and addressing her world of relations.

She ended her long journey of many soul searching bold poems asking in a metaphor: 'Who am I?' She answered it with the Pijasu: the "we" that becomes an "I": The pig that eats too much, the jaguar, who desires control and the seagull, who wants freedom. In another metaphor these multiple identities are united to become a Dolphin that enjoys companionship and is not embarrassed to talk of feelings, argue and be friends again.

Case Study 7: *The Foot Fetish Youth*
A young married man was referred for an evaluation. He completed the workbook and all his documents reflected his deep preoccupation with women's feet. The record explained the history of the development of his obsession, which manifested in the daytime but also was troubling him at night in his dreams. The assessment identified his relational modality as submissive cooperative. Fetishism had evolved as a pattern of inner asser-

tiveness. The problem was that he lost control of his escapist conduct. He experienced guilt and embarrassment reinforcing his feeling of worthlessness and furthering his social withdrawal.

The assessment was therapeutic in the sense that he recognized his vulnerability to approval by his parents, who were deceased, and that he could feel good about himself without their approval since he had achieved certain accomplishments that attested his being successful along their criteria. The assessment helped him: first, by understanding his problem as one of a relational modality diagnosis; he developed insights about the logical connection of his personality pattern of submissiveness, compensated by his aggressive attention-getting escapism, which elicited his embarrassment as reversals as losing control to overpowering rejecting women. Second, he experienced cathartic release from guilt by revealing his secret preoccupations.

Characteristics Of Submissive Persons' Artwork, Animal Metaphors And The Transparent Mask Sequence

Submissiveness Demonstrated by the Animal Metaphor Tests

We recognize substantial polarization between animal choices with asymmetry of the animals' power positions. The asymmetry reflects severe conflicts where one animal is presented as a victim of a violent partner, i.e. one is a hunter the other is hunted.

- The test taker identifies with the weak vulnerable animal, usually being neglected, and occasionally abused.
- The identity animal features signs of defect or injury, handicap, like a broken wing, his head being in the mouth of the dominant animal, her face deformed like that of the ant eater.
- The underlying difficulty in communications is reflected in the positions and the placement of the animals, such as turning their backs to each other and the viewer.
- The identity animal is usually positioned on the right side of the field reflecting the stance of depression, guilt and introspection rather than impulsivity and extroversion.

Case Title	Picture	Who Do You Identify With?
Case Study 1 *A Caribou Falling Behind the Herd and the Predatory Wolf*		"[I identify with] Caribou: his world exploits his weakness. He is naïve and bewildered...as a young man, I was 'behind the herd' of my peers in areas of self-esteem and self-confidence as well as sexual sophistication."
Case Study 2 *Trying to Survive as a Dog*		"[I identify with] the dog – all he needs to do is to learn to live the life he has been given. He's never going to be a tiger! [This is] simply just a scenario between me and the strong people in my life."

Case Study 3 *The Anteater and the Lion*		"[I identify with the] Anteater, because I want to run a lot, [and] believe that [the] ony way to deal is to run...I'm afraid of what others think of me...I want to be powerful and beautifull ike the lion."
Case Study 4 *The Wise Oak*		"[I identify with] both. I am the little bunny, because as a child I missed getting loved and whenever I was getting attention, it was usually because I had done something wrong. The tree fairy is...my conscience."
Case Study 5 *The Wolf and the Bird with the Broken Wing*		"I want to fly away from my problems, but can't. I feel I can't help myself...I feel like my problems will not go away, leaving me helpless to defend myself from those who don't accept me."
Case Study 6 *The Vulture and the Snake*	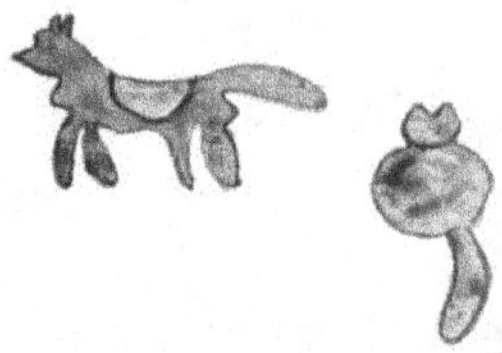	"[I identify with] the dog...perhaps I'm bored/lonely since husband started working in the city...when under pressure, or feeling sorry for myself, I plan on over-eating and drinking as a reward.

Submissiveness' Transparent Mask Test
While the first mask presents power and strength, the second mask reflects the true feelings of helplessness, failure, sadness, guilt and often hostility. The third mask, the heart, encompasses the duality of feelings as the prevalent conflicts and resolutions.

There are distinct differences for the dominant and submissive sets of masks.

The front mask may present deceptive symbols of power and authority, like the Judge, or defenses, like a wall, and also a warrior attitude or anger, like Mr. Dynamo.
The second mask presents hurt feelings, images of traumas, and words identifying hurt feelings. It presents the weaknesses of a person's identity, like behind the powerful judge we have a vulnerable lamb, confusion, lack of identity, and the loss of control.

The third mask, the heart encompassing the totality of conflicts, traumas encapsulated, hiding the hurt feelings reflecting alienation and social withdrawal. The submissive person shows more attention to inner feelings than outward interpersonal conflicts. It shows also the difficulty communicating feelings, like the impediment of a moat dividing the heart in halves. The heart is empty; it has a hole, another is totally encased in a jar, 'completely unrevealed'.

Case Title	Mask	Feelings	Heart's Inner Conflict
Case Study 1 *The Caribou Falling Behind the Herd and the Predatory Wolf* *The Judge and the Lamb*	*Judge in a Wig* Power, authority vs. insecurity. [This mask represents a] hiding place... [a] vehicle to project controlled images to the world – an image of power and control.	*Lamb in the Meadow* Vulnerability. [An] actor without costumes or props.	*My Heart* Everything is pushed in, encased from the world... [a] bubbling cauldron of conflicts that is hidden from everyone.
Case Study 2 *Trying to Survive as a Dog*	*Mr. Dynamo* Artistry, confidence, boldness, trust...stability, immunity, firmness.	*Who Is This Man?* Confusion. I'm not sure who is behind the smiling mask...it seems to be the start of conflicts. The always happy face I thought was my true face is removed.	*Heart Under Siege* Threats to the heart, confusion...this represents a heart that is in danger.
Case Study 3 *The Anteater and the Lion*	*Unknown* Power, strength, no fear, tough...need to be powerful instead of being weak. Don't let anyone get close to me.	*Unkindly Thoughts* Pain, anger, rage, fear, hate, rejection, failure, hurt, relief, shame. Let down walls and show what's there.	*Completely Unrevealed* A lot of times I feel that I am not okay. Anger, hate, failure, wanting to stay alive but bothered by suicidal thoughts."

Case Study 4 *The Wise Oak*	*The Warrior* 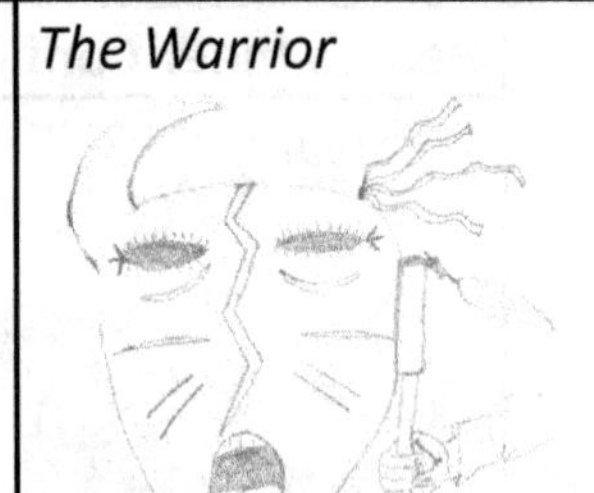 Strength, fearlessness, power, free to scream... [but] someone other than the warrior is holding her mask.	*Seeking Control*  Peace, no anger, no control, emotions, sadness, happiness someone else is controlling her mask... this person needs help making decisions for herself.	 *Mixed Emotions* Most of the heart is full of love, a small portion is anger, then confusion...on how to feel, and when.
Case Study 5 *The Bird with the Broken Wing*	*Put a Bag Over Your Head*  Embarrassment, worthlessness, ugliness. I don't want the world to see my bad characteristics. I'll come out when it's safe	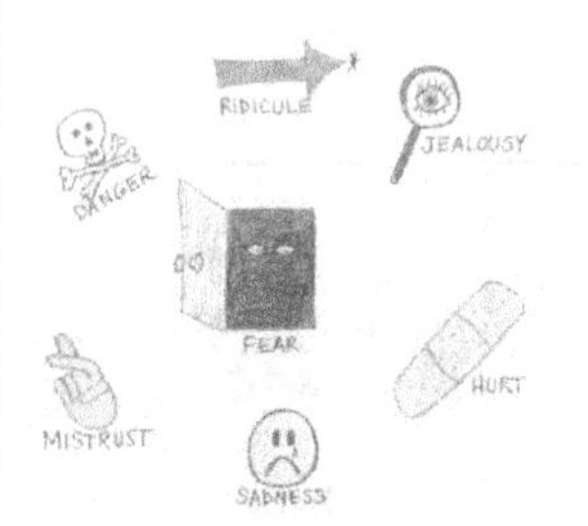 *My World* Fear of: danger, ridicule, jealousy, hurt, sadness, mistrust. I can't deal with conflicts, real or imagined – I fear confrontations [and[negative feedback.	 *Hole in My Heart* I feel incomplete, unfinished, not a whole person. I need to find what I am missing.
Case Study 6 *The Vulture and the Snake*	 *Perpetual Smile* False happiness. Self-deceit, mockery. Shutting out sadness with a smile.	*Blackout* 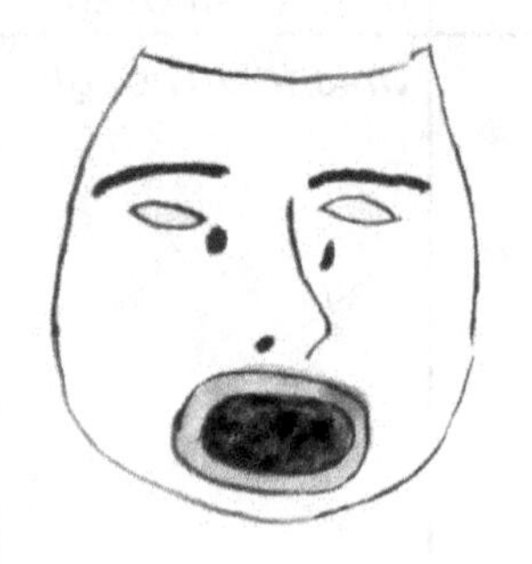 Dejection, rejection, unwillingness [and] inability to express her feelings, and being preoccupied with eating.	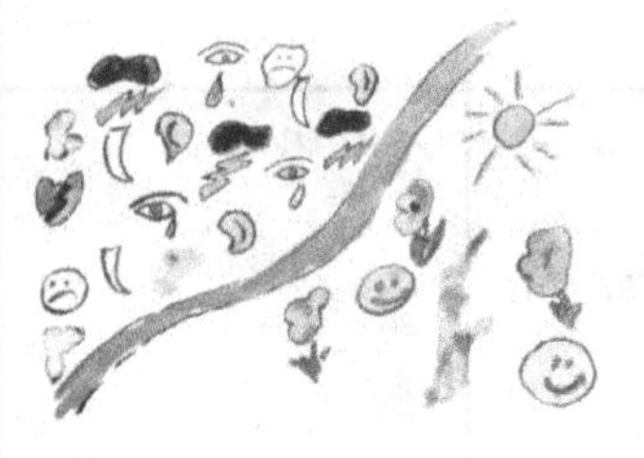 Double Image. Discord Two facets are separated: happiness on one side; hidden feelings, anger, sadness, fear [and] shadows are there, but they are constantly being repressed.

Submissiveness Case Study

Psychiatric Evaluation of a Judge, "The Sacrificial Lamb"
Alternatively, "The Caribou that Falls Behind the Herd"

Introduction and Discussion

This is the evaluation of a judge, referred to me by his priest regarding annulment of his marriage to be granted by the Tribunal based on his entering the marriage using his free will versus being coerced. I saw the judge for five sessions and evaluated him using the Conflict Analysis Battery. His case is reviewed here because it illustrates very clearly the profile of the submissive personality across the range of the battery testing. This study also illustrates the educational, diagnostic and therapeutic value of the assessment as demonstrated in the patient's self-report.

The submissiveness relational profile is equally pronounced across all the projective tests.
To the question of '*How do you relate with others, and how do you get yourself in trouble?*' He responded saying: "I surrender my own wants and needs to avoid conflicts. To avoid making the other person mad or upset, I give in. Later I resent the other person and hate myself."

The Personality Inventory

The personality inventory scores present his relational modality as both submissive cooperative and antagonistic. The metaphor testing is integrated along the conflict resolution template of six emotions, reflecting his choices along the syndromal sequence of passivities and activities leading him to the resolution of his conflicts showing the end of his marital relationship.

His RMES scores were uniformly -3 across the dominance items and +3 across the submissive scales informing us that his relational modality was clearly submissive. He scored high on both the submissive cooperative and the antagonistic scales. The judge's inventory choices reflect consistently the submissive relational modality. The scores are less consistent in the subscale of hostility. He is angry but he has difficulty communicating it, consistently holding his feelings to himself and experiencing the need to avoid conflict rather than confront his counterparts. There is elevation of psychic tension in the area of depression.

Projective tests confirm the inventory's findings of submissiveness.

Summary of the projective tests:

- The drawing of his parental family shows that he felt manipulated by his powerful mother like a puppet.
- His childhood conflictual memory is about not protesting when he wasn't treated equally with his siblings.
- His later life memory is about his shotgun wedding; he is getting married at gun point; he is wearing a prisoner's striped outfit, ball and chain on his feet; next to the church is a jail.
- The image behind the mask of a judge is a lamb.
- His two metaphors are about being a victim of a misleading wolf. In the animal metaphor he is the caribou that falls behind the herd and in the fairy tale metaphor he is the pig being reassured by a wolf with a hidden knife.
- He reports a significant dream about getting shot by a disgruntled criminal whom he had given a sentence.
- His short story is about a voyage with a selfish partner that ends with parting company.

The record confirms the submissiveness relational pattern clearly across all his metaphors: The projective material, the autobiographical tests, family portrait, memories and dream test confirm this as the relational pattern that affected his decisions throughout his life. His metaphor stories corroborate this deviation by presenting a consistent preference for self-sacrifice out of concern for the welfare of others.

Stress is presented with the family portrait and three conflictual memories

- The family portrait reveals that while his father is sitting in a chair slumped over a table with a bottle of wine at a distance, his mother is portrayed as a puppeteer of her children. Unlike his siblings cutting off the puppet strings held by his mother the judge is going off into the world still controlled by his mother holding on to his strings. Strings still attached to his image show the ease of his being manipulated and his powerlessness in making decisions in relationships.

- His childhood conflictual memory presents an episode of self-sacrifice: the judge recalls a time that his father sent him to buy ice cream with only enough money for three rather than four ice cream bars. He recalled not asserting himself; he rationalized his reaction by deciding that he simply did not desire to have any ice cream.

- In the conflictual memory from his adult life, he presented his wedding. It reveals a shotgun held at his head. Behind the church is a jail. The bride is presented as pregnant. His father in law was an officer, his warden. He wore a striped suit like a prisoner and was held in place by a ball and chain. He explained that he was coerced by a manipulative, willful and selfish promiscuous woman into marriage against his will by her deliberately getting pregnant. He was not ready for marriage. He had wanted to go to law school but when she got pregnant he consented to marry her. He did not tell any of his college friends about getting married, and did not invite any of them to the wedding and later to his home. He recalled getting drunk the night before and having an accident on the way to renting his tuxedo. He avoided his bride during their honeymoon and there was little interest in sex in their relationship; in fact, he chose to have vasectomy after a few years of marriage. His wife was unfaithful but he did not confront her. She undermined his authority with their children, sabotaged his finances, and competed with his professional interests.

***Response* and *Anxiety* is presented in the triple mask test**

- He drew a mask of a judge, but when the mask becomes transparent we see the client's true identity, that of a lamb. His heart is well-encapsulated identifying only positive feelings. In his third mask he portrayed love--no hostility or anger at the suffering he experienced over the years. He indicated love for his new lady friend, and his children and duty for his profession.

***Defense* is illustrated in the animal and fairy tale tests**

- In both his Animal and Fairy Tale metaphors, his counterpart appears to be a willful and deceptive wolf.

- In the Animal Metaphor he identified with a caribou falling behind the herd. In his comments he accepts surrendering without fight as the predicament of improving the species. He yields cooperatively, sacrifices his interests and avoids fighting or attempting to defend himself, and these choices show his lack of assertiveness.

- In the Fairy Tale metaphor the proverbial pig seeks to erect a house to protect himself from the deceitful wolf knocking on his door saying: 'trust me', while carrying a knife in his sleeve.

***Reversal* is presented in the dream metaphor:**

- He suffers of a recurring nightmare in which he is haunted by the image of a gunman targeting his shotgun at him. He is afraid for his life and safety. The conflictual memory of his shotgun wedding also featured a gun like his recurring nightmare. One may connect the two and conclude that the judge is suffering from guilt, which inhibited him from speaking his mind and from asserting his rights as a person and as a judge.

***Compromise* is illustrated in the short story metaphor**

- The Short Story exercise presents him upon the end of a dangerous journey by boat. His companion has betrayed him and as soon as the voyage ends, the two companions will part ways forever. The test reflects his bitterness toward his wife and his deep-seated desire to extricate himself from his spouse of many years.

Information on a Second Workbook

I asked the judge to repeat the assessment with another workbook to detect an evolution in his disposition following the completion of the evaluation. The judge misunderstood my instructions and instead copied the testing, using colors and a more legible handwriting. He used a pen instead of a pencil. In the second set of images he presented more clearly his mother's powerful manipulation of the family. He presented the Judge and lamb masks, but altered the symmetry of the animal metaphors, making the caribou into a dot in the distance, the little pig was eclipsed while the wolf stands up alone in the picture obviously hiding a knife in his sleeve saying 'trust me'.

This censorship reinforced the impression that the judge's subordinacy is problematic deferring to dominant, inconsiderate, and manipulative partners in his life in a consistent manner, censoring his own image and interests while attending to the demands of others. Indeed in the first book he related a recent conflict pertaining to his current relationship; the new lady in his life had recently physically attacked him in public in a fit of rage over his supporting his son's education. In the second book he left this memory out of the book altogether. His suppressing his thoughts and feelings and unpleasant emotions reflected the problematic dimension of his relational modality.

Diagnostic Impression

The clearly submissive pattern of the inventory test, corroborated by the projective tests, confirms his vulnerability to being coerced. He consistently presented himself as a person willing to be intimidated, manipulated, and abused. This relational pattern determined his lifetime decisions and it was the factor leading him to his wedding. This information leads us to conclude that coercion, not free will, was the reason he entered into his marriage of 24 years.

The battery findings and his self-assessment report reveal a consistent pattern of extreme submissive cooperation, which under moderate stress transforms into submissive antagonism, his default modality in resolving conflicts. His testing reveals this submissive way of relating prior to, during, and after his marriage. This approach to resolving conflict has led him to yield to authorities or circumstances in his life without expressing any resistance.

His submissiveness has magnified external factors in making decisions out of a sense of moral obligation to conform by surrendering his own interests to societal expectations. He experienced this submissive disposition toward many authority figures, in particular his mother and his father. Completing his duties as a judge was one of the items in the drawing of his heart. Finally this submissiveness is demonstrated in his compliance to the requirements of Church's authority.

There is no doubt that the judge, not having the capacity to express his feelings, was compelled to make concessions and suffer in a Christian manner. Deprived of the skill to communicate his feelings effectively and identifying with Christian values he did not have the means to be directed by personal choices. This deferential approach deprived this devout person of the freedom to choose.

But this pattern of surrender did not serve him right in his relationship with his ex-wife as resentments increased. He felt victimized and coerced into the marriage. He felt manipulated by her from the outset of their relationship. He perceived her during their marriage as consistently abusing power at his expense. He defended himself from her by withdrawing since the inception of their relationship. He was willing to be a lamb led to slaughter, a caribou that had to be sacrificed to the wolf, to the pig trusting the words of a wolf knocking on his door. Thus he built resentments like the helpless pig whose house is going to be blown away by the calculating wolf. In his marriage, resentments ran his life rather than love. It was a miserable relationship and it was terminated as untenable. At some point in his life's journey he decided to seek a divorce for lack of a meaningful and fair partnership. His divorce was a preferable alternative to living at home behind a brick wall protecting him from a wife whom he perceived as a wolf constantly threatening him with emotional extinction.

This development in a relationship is not unusual, except in its intensity. Frequently through a pattern of spousal self-selection, opposites often attract and marry. But couples displaying extreme relational power management modalities often fail in their relationships for two reasons:
First, the submissive person, like the judge, holds his feelings in, experiences excessive resentments, and instead of seeking to actively repair the relationship, chooses to avoid further conflicts building defenses/walls to protect himself from abuse. The battery findings reveal a consistent pattern of extreme submissive-cooperative relating which, under stress, has been transformed into submissive-antagonistic relating as the default modality of resolving conflicts.

His excessively submissive mode of relating led to his being oppressed and feeling exploited and betrayed. The judge's submissiveness, reinforced culturally by his being a devout Christian embracing the spirit of self-sacrifice, manifested upon the inception of this marriage conceived because of an unwanted pregnancy. External social and internal psychological factors forced him to yield to a union in spite of his own preference. He experienced this marriage as serving a sentence. With this disposition he has been feeling resentful towards his partner and justified in seeking termination of this relationship.

Second, concurrently his dominant wife expressed anger, and engaged in limit testing, self-righteous and sometimes unconscionable acts. His withdrawal facilitated his wife's taking liberties and testing the limits of the marriage, which in turn intensified his perception of her as selfish and self-righteous, demanding and controlling, judgmental and dismissive. His submissiveness and her dominance led to mutual suffering and the failure of their relationship.
This pattern of alienation compounded their marital strife and led to psychopathology and incompatibility. This course of events has been the scenario of this marriage.
The psychological profile of the judge and the alleged social profile of his wife should have been considered enough of a justification to annul the marriage on the basis of incompatibility and well established alienation. The church's tribunal considered his report and mine but rejected his application.

I recommended therapy for the judge to specifically develop self-confidence and skills to effectively express his feelings. This skill could help him avert his being a victim and his becoming resentful and self-loathing in future relationships.

Personal Essay

The Judge Composed The Following Letter To The Tribunal At The End Of The Evaluation

To: The Tribunal
Please consider this letter as a supplement to the marital summary that I provided as part of my application for annulment.

I am asking this Tribunal to declare my marriage to T. T. on June 21, 1972 a nullity because the evidence proves, to a standard of moral certitude, that the "marriage" was the result of a gross defect in consent. I realize that there are many forces working against me in this effort. These include:

1) A general disapproval by the Church hierarchy in Rome to the number of annulments granted in the United States.

2) The 24 year length of my marriage

3) The opposition by my spiteful ex-wife

4) The New York Tribunal's conclusion that they could not conclude to a nullity in my case.

Despite these obstacles, I intend to persevere with my petition now pending. I am doing this because:

1) I firmly believe in the rightness of my cause and know in my heart that my marriage was not bound by God;

2) I do not wish to live my life as an "outlaw" in the eyes of the Church but rather as a full member of the mystical body of Christ; and

3) I want to remarry within the Church and in that way have a good and holy marital relationship with my new wife.

Given the realities of my situation, I have endeavored to learn about myself and about human personality and behavior so as to present the most complete and persuasive case to the Tribunal.

In this regard, I offer the following:
The modern approach groups human personality types into generally two categories: dominant and submissive. Within these basic groups there can be antagonistic and cooperative features. So a person may be dominant antagonistic, dominant cooperative, submissive antagonistic or submissive cooperative. Or, have a combination of traits from the various groups. While, from a scientific point of view, no one group is "good" or "bad", personality profiles that are strongly dominant or submissive create problems for the person in interpersonal relationships. These problems can, in turn, result in coping strategies that are undesirable and destructive.
In my case, the above information on human personality is of more than mere abstract academic interest. Indeed, I gave up a quarter century of my life because of my inability to surmount the barriers to happiness imposed by my personality. Psychological testing has demonstrated quite clearly that I am a submissive personality type. As such, there is a strong feature of my personality that is willing to subvert my own interests in order to avoid conflict. This subversion results in adverse behaviors at the same time.

a. Adopt positions inimical to my happiness but are perceived as necessary to avoid stress and conflict; and,

b. Allows the unfulfilled feelings to fester within creating resentment, unhappiness and despair.

The experience of the psychological testing has also shown me that my former wife is very much a dominant personality. As such she thrives on conflict, insists that her feelings be accepted, exalts her wants and needs over everything else, is prone to anger and uses anger as a behavioral response to get her way. As detailed in the Marital Summary, my account of the circumstances of my wedding and marriage are replete with examples of this dominant behavior. A few instances are as follows.

a. T. T. tumultuous and rebellious relationship with her father that involved her violent arguments with him as a young teenager and his corresponding several efforts to tame his wild daughter [this stands in stark contrast to my experience of being an overly dutiful and conforming son for my parents].

b. T. T.'s experiences with sex. She started dating GI's when she was 13 and continued in numerous relationships ever since. She was sexually promiscuous as a teenager in part to satisfy her own sexual interests and in part to disrespect her father. This promiscuity continued even after her marriage as evidenced by her numerous extra marital affairs. [Again, this is just the opposite of my experience, which involved no dating whatsoever as a teenager, no sexual experience before T. T. and no significant experience with women at all].

c. T. T.' s reaction when faced with the certain prospect that our relationship would end when I entered law school in the fall of 1971. Her dominant personality and desire to get married and get away from her tyrannical father was responsible for her getting herself pregnant so as to trap me into marriage. This was accomplished by her aggressively making our relationship sexual when it had previously not been that way. For my part, once she became pregnant with the attendant scandal, I felt I had no choice but to marry her despite the fact that I did not love her.

d. Her slothful behavior during the marriage as manifested by her refusal to work in the face of economic need. Her anger, which flared regularly when she would not get her way. Her extra marital affairs that fed her sexual needs that were unsatisfied in our loveless marriage.

e. Finally, her conduct during our divorce as shown by her mercenary and greedy attempts to destroy me, because I had finally rejected her. Her purchase of a new dining room set, new car, credit card purchases and house all were efforts to aggrandize her lifestyle at my expense. She further demanded that I am fully responsible for the educational needs of our two children.

The benefits of these personality insights are twofold:

First, they show quite clearly why and how I could be forced into a loveless marriage. I saw my options through the prism of my submissive personality that refracted away any self-interest in favor of avoiding scandal to my family at all costs. On her side, it shows the ends that she would go to get what she wanted- a ticket out of her dysfunctional home and a meal ticket for life.

Second, the personality insights provide a measure of self-knowledge that will inform my future conduct and relationships so as to avoid the destructive decisions I've made in the past. I look to the future with clarity I never had before.

Thank you for considering the above,

Very truly yours, Judge ABC

Transcription of the Judge's Metaphors

STRESS

CHILDHOOD CONFLICTUAL MEMORY

Step 1: Draw a conflictual childhood memory:

Step 2: Describe the incident: I was about 9 years old. We went to hockey game with my two cousins. My father sent me to an ice cream vendor to buy 4 ice cream bars (two for my brother and me and two for my two cousins.) I ordered four bars from the vendor, but only had enough money for three. I was not sure my father had more money and did not want to embarrass him. I bought three bars and told everyone that I did not want any ice cream. It was very embarrassing.

Step 3: How did you feel about this person? I was angry at my father but also felt bad for him. I did not want him to look bad in front of my uncle. **How did this person feel about you?** My father had no idea I was short of money.

Step 4: What were the conflicts? [left blank]

Step 5: What happened before? [left blank]

Step 6: After? [left blank]

Step 7: Your share in this conflict? Not talking about the problem.

Note: Remainder of questions in this test are left blank.

Adolescent Conflictual Memory

Step 1: Draw a conflictual adolescent memory:

Step 2: Describe the incident: Shotgun marriage. I did not assert my own interests. My tuxedo is the stripes of a convict--front door church, back door jail.

Step 3: Effect on life: It ruined my life for 24 years.

Recent Conflict

Step 1: Draw a recent conflictual memory:

Step 2: Describe the incident: Fight with girlfriend, she ripped his shirt in a public dispute.

Step 3: Effect on life: Introduced doubt that I can maintain a loving and happy relationship.

Balloon Portrait and Story

Family Origin

Step 1: Draw a balloon portrait of your family of origin:

Step 2: Identify each individual:
Father, postal clerk, distant insular, silent passive.
Mother, extrovert, domineering, control, distant.
Me, intelligent, first-born, hardworking, withdrawn.
J., brother, extrovert, rebellious, drives Mercedes Benz.
M., sister, kind, scatterbrained
J., brother, even-tempered

Step 3: What are they saying? The balloons do not talk together.

Step 4: What happened before? [left blank]

Step 5: After? [left blank]

Step 6: Title: "Trailblazer."

Step 7: What are the conflicts? I have to forge my path in the world alone. Brother is cutting the strings of control.

Step 8: What changes should be made to resolve these conflicts?

RESPONSE

Mask I

Step 1: Draw a mask:

Step 2: Answer the following questions:

Title: "Judge in a Wig."

Age: 48 **Sex:** Male

Emotions conveyed: Power, authority.

Step 3: Conflicts represented: Power vs. Insecurity.

Step 4: Resolution of conflicts represented: Hiding Place

ANXIETY

Mask II

Step 5: Draw what is behind the mask:

Step 6: Fill in the blanks and answer the questions:

Title: "Lamb in a Meadow"

Age: ? **Sex:** ?

Emotions conveyed: [left blank]

Step 7: Conflicts represented: Vulnerability.
Step 8: Resolution of conflicts: None.
Mask III
Step 9: Draw what is in the heart:
Title: "My Heart."
Step 10: Items and themes represented: A witches brew of love, guilt and duty.
Step 11: Feelings and conflicts represented: Everything is pushed in, encased from the world.
Step 12: Resolution of conflicts? Handle these things yourself in your <u>own</u> way.
Step 13: Title of the sequence: "Free to the World; Face; Gut."
Step 14: Summarize the sequence of transformations:

Mask = vehicle to project controlled image to the world – an image of power and control.
Transparent Mask = actor without costume or props.
Heart = bubbling cauldron of conflicts that is hidden from everybody.

Step 15: Conclusions about the way this person resolves conflicts: Internalizes everything.
Step 16: Does this relate to how you handle feelings: All things are directed inward.
Step 17: What changes should be made: Although changes are desirable, they are possible.
Step 18: What changes are you willing to make: I am not sure.

DEFENSE
ANIMAL METAPHOR TEST #1
Step 1: Draw two animals

Step 2: Fill in the blanks

Animal #1 Type of animal: Wolf
Age: 20 **Sex:** Female
Personality: Ruthless, cruel, survivor.
Animal #2 Caribou, Age: 20 **Sex:** Male
Personality: Peaceful, kind, friendly
Step 3: What are they saying?

#2: "Wolf, why must you attack me? I will do you no harm, I just want to live in peace with my herd."

#1: "I need to eat in order to live. You are weak and unable to keep up with your herd. I make the herd stronger by hunting the weak members. There is nothing personal in this – but I need to survive."

#2: "Wolf, why can't you survive on the grass and plants like I do? Why must you kill me? I want to live too. I may be weak and slow, but I do not want to die. I cannot survive your attack, but you can find other kinds of food."

#1: "I do not want to debate this. It is not a matter of logic or fairness, it is survival!"

Step 4: What happened before? The wolf was chasing the herd and the caribou fell behind and was about to be attacked.

Step 5: After? The wolf attacked and killed the caribou.
Step 6: Title: "Improving the Herd."
Step 7a: Conflicts between themselves: "Improving the Herd."
Step 7b: Conflicts between them and the world: The wolf's world required her to be ruthless and exploit the weakness of others. The caribou's world provides him peace and community, but exposes him to a violent death.
Step 8: What changes should they make to resolve conflicts? The wolf should "look outside the dots" to find a way of survival that does not involve killing. The caribou should be more wry and wily and protect itself more and not submit to death. He must see the world as it is--dangerous and hostile, and act accordingly.
Step 9: Which animal do you identify with: Caribou: his world exploits his weakness. He is naive and bewildered. **Other animal:** Ex-wife: She is shallow and ruthless, selfish and domineering.
Step 10: How does this pertain to you? As a young man, I was behind the "herd" of my peers in areas of self-esteem and self-confidence as well as sexual sophistication. My ex-wife got herself pregnant and trapped me into marriage. She "hunted" me and devoured me. I, like the caribou, did not assert my rights effectively.
Step 11: What changes should you make? I must assert my own wants in situations where others are trying to infringe on those rights.
Step 12: Present a similar incident: Shotgun marriage; student loan for son.
Step 13: How do you relate with others, and how do you get yourself in trouble? I surrender my own wants and needs to avoid conflicts. To avoid making the other person mad or upset, I give in. Later I resent the other person and hate myself.
Step 14: What changes are you willing to make? Although I understand the problem from an intellectual point of view, I am not sure that I can make the needed changes. I usually prefer to withdraw than to engage in conflict. It is not worth it to me.

Fairytale Metaphor

Step 1: Draw two fairy tale characters:
Step 2: Fill in the blanks

Character#1: Pig **(not presented in the drawing)**
Age: 20 **Sex:** Male
Personality: Industrious, cautious, vulnerable. **Character#2:** Wolf
Age: 20 **Sex:** Male
Personality: Cruel, aggressive, persistent, smooth, attractive, persuasive.
Step 3: What are they saying?

- **#2:** So pig, I see that you are going to build a brick house, why are you doing that?
- **#1:** Well, I'm not saying that you would do me harm, but a pig cannot be too careful these days.
- **#2:** Oh pig, I'm disappointed. Don't you trust me? If you were any kind of a decent pig, you would not think badly of your fellow creatures. What have I ever done to you?
- **#1:** You blew down the straw house of my younger brother and the stick house of my older brother. So, I'm not taking any chances!
- **#2:** Who said I did those things? Don't believe everything you hear. I never blew down anybody's house. Trust me. Now, put away those bricks and let's take a walk and have dinner together.

Step 4: What happened before? The pig was building a brick house to protect himself from the wolf. The wolf was stalking food.
Step 5: After? I'm not sure. If the pig believed the wolf, then maybe they went for a walk and the pig felt guilty for mistrusting the wolf. If the pig did not believe the wolf, then the pig kept building--fast.
Step 6: Title: "Trust?"
Step 7a: Conflicts between themselves: The pig wants a barrier between himself and the threats, the wolf wants to remove barriers to achieve his wants and needs.
Step 7b: Conflicts between them and the world: The pig feels vulnerable and needs protection from a danger-

ous world. The wolf needs to dominate resisting world.
Step 8: What changes should they make to resolve conflicts? Sincerity that leads to mutual trust. The pig must protect himself first, then open his heart to maybe trusting someone. He cannot run the risk of blind trust.
Step 9: Which character do you identify with: I am the pig, attempting to protect myself from a hostile world.
Other character: [left blank]
Step 10: How does this pertain to you? I see myself as naive. I see the world as hostile. I want a "brick wall" around me.
Step 11: What changes should you make? Unsure. Maybe this is a conflict that should not be "resolved". It may be that a state of conflict simply exists and one must accept it.
Note: Remainder of questions in this test are left blank.

Dream Analysis

Step 1: Choose a dream: Past dream.
Step 2: Draw the dream:
Step 3: Describe the dream: I am walking from the courthouse--am shot and killed by a gunman inside the car.
Step 4: Describe the participants:
Me: working, trusting, naïve.
Gunman: brazen, angry, killer.
Step 5: What are the conflicts? Life/Death.
Step 6: What occurrences preceded the dream? Not sure.
Step 7: Explanation of the dream: Death may be the final escape from the pains of life.
Step 8: Do you dream a lot? No.
Step 9: Other dreams: I rarely recall dreams.
Step 10: Connections or patterns in dreams: My job makes me the object of people's frustration and anger.

COMPROMISE *Short Story*
Step 1: Write a short story:
Jack and Tom were sailing around the world in a 40' sailboat. When they reached the southern tip of South America they encountered a terrible storm. Help was over one thousand miles away, so they had to manage the problem themselves.
Jack wanted to abandon ship but Tom insisted that they stay. Jack felt that the lifeboat would have a better chance of making it to the rocky shore. Tom did not want to abandon the boat because he had a lot of money invested in it.
Jack agreed to stay. By reefing the sails and staying awake for 3o hours they rode out the storm and continued on their voyage. But Jack resented the fact that Tom put the value of the boat over Tom's safety.
Step 2: Illustrate the story:
Step 3: Fill in the blanks:
Character#1
Character name: Jack
Age: 30 **Sex:** Male
Personality: Sensible, considerate, submissive, naïve, silent.
Character#2
Character name: Tom
Age: 35 **Sex:** Male
Personality: Mercenary, selfish, aggressive, materialistic, verbal.

Step 4: What happened before? The two had bought the boat and planned the trip for years. They thought themselves to be close friends.
Step 5: After: They continued to finish the voyage, then parted together.
Step 6: Title: "Lifeboat."
Step 7: Conflicts between themselves: Jack values his safety over money. Tom values money over safety.
Step 8: What changes should they make to resolve conflicts? Consider the others views; understand the value system each is operating on.
Step 9: Which character do you identify with: Jack. **Other character:** Ex-wife.
Step 10: How does this pertain to you? I want to escape the stormy seas of my life.
Step 11: What changes should you make? Not sure.
Step 12: Present a similar incident: [left blank]
Step 13: How do you relate with others, and how do you get yourself in trouble? Too submissive.
Step 14: What changes are you willing to make? [left blank]

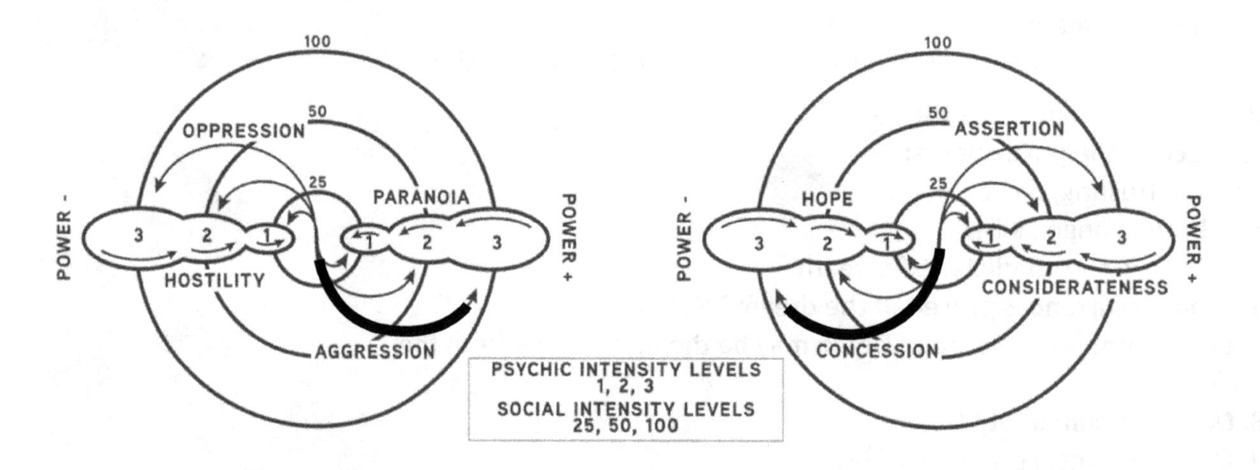

Ex-wife depicted as wolf, ruthless, selfish and domineering; dominant antagonistic relational modality.

Self: depicted as a lamb and as a caribou falling behind the herd; submissive cooperative and antagonistic relational modality, as reflected in the scores of the personality inventory on the opposite page.

Step 9: Which animal do you identify with: Caribou: his world exploits his weakness. He is naive and bewildered. **Other animal:** Ex-wife: She is shallow and ruthless, selfish and domineering.
Step 10: How does this pertain to you? As a young man, I was behind the "herd" of my peers in areas of self-esteem and self-confidence as well as sexual sophistication. My ex-wife got herself pregnant and trapped me into marriage. She "hunted" me and devoured me. I, like the caribou, did not assert my rights effectively.
Step 11: What changes should you make? I must assert my own wants in situations where others are trying to infringe on those rights.

UNDER THE MASK: THE LAMB

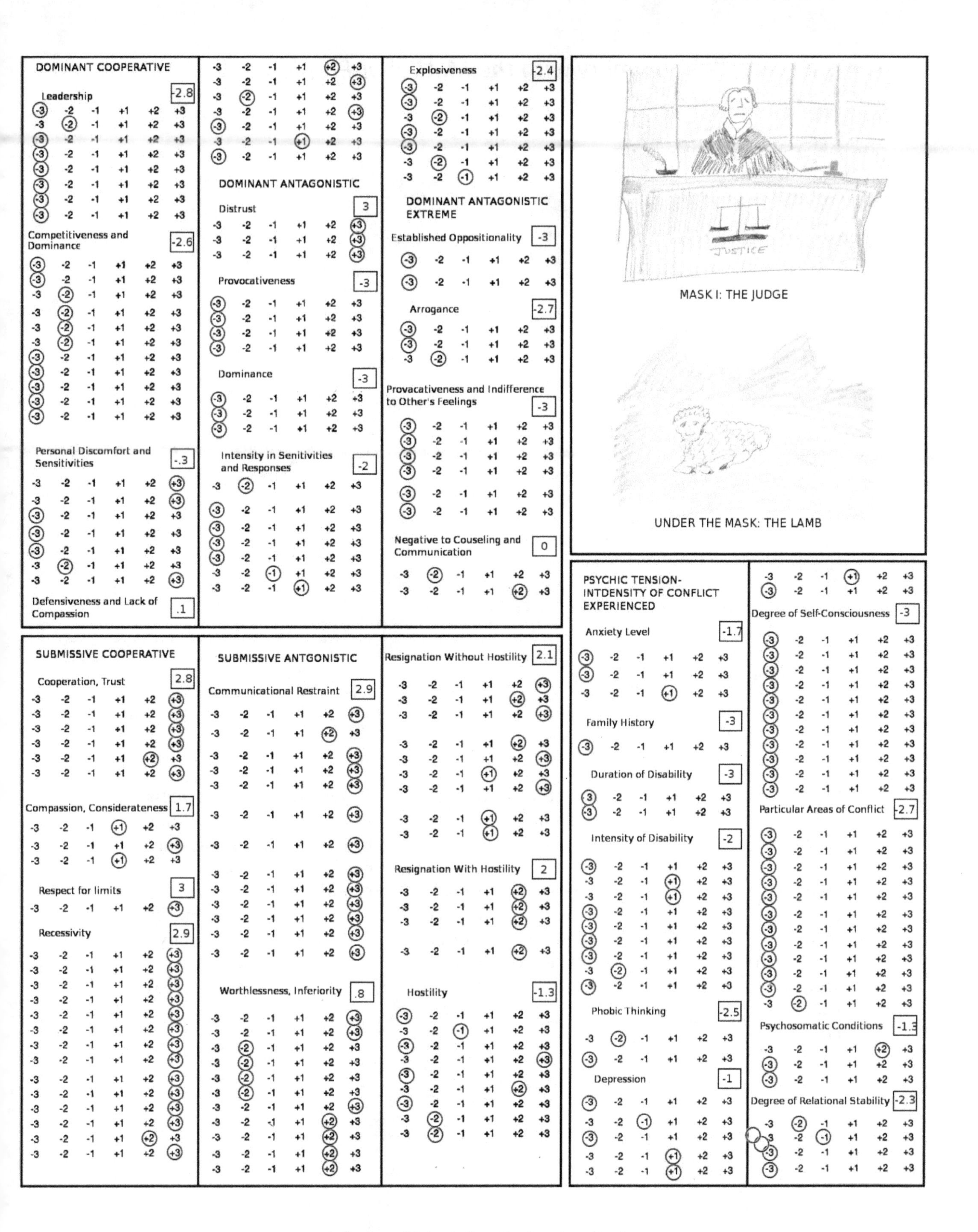

DOMINANT COOPERATIVE

Leadership -2.8

Competitiveness and Dominance -2.6

Personal Discomfort and Sensitivities -.3

Defensiveness and Lack of Compassion .1

DOMINANT ANTAGONISTIC

Distrust 3

Provocativeness -3

Dominance -3

Intensity in Senitivities and Responses -2

Explosiveness 2.4

DOMINANT ANTAGONISTIC EXTREME

Established Oppositionality -3

Arrogance -2.7

Provacativeness and Indifference to Other's Feelings -3

Negative to Couseling and Communication 0

SUBMISSIVE COOPERATIVE

Cooperation, Trust 2.8

Compassion, Considerateness 1.7

Respect for limits 3

Recessivity 2.9

SUBMISSIVE ANTGONISTIC

Communicational Restraint 2.9

Worthlessness, Inferiority .8

Resignation Without Hostility 2.1

Resignation With Hostility 2

Hostility -1.3

PSYCHIC TENSION-INTDENSITY OF CONFLICT EXPERIENCED

Anxiety Level -1.7

Family History -3

Duration of Disability -3

Intensity of Disability -2

Phobic Thinking -2.5

Depression -1

Degree of Self-Consciousness -3

Particular Areas of Conflict -2.7

Psychosomatic Conditions -1.3

Degree of Relational Stability -2.3

Relational Modality Evaluation Scale

Summary with the Metaphor Profile

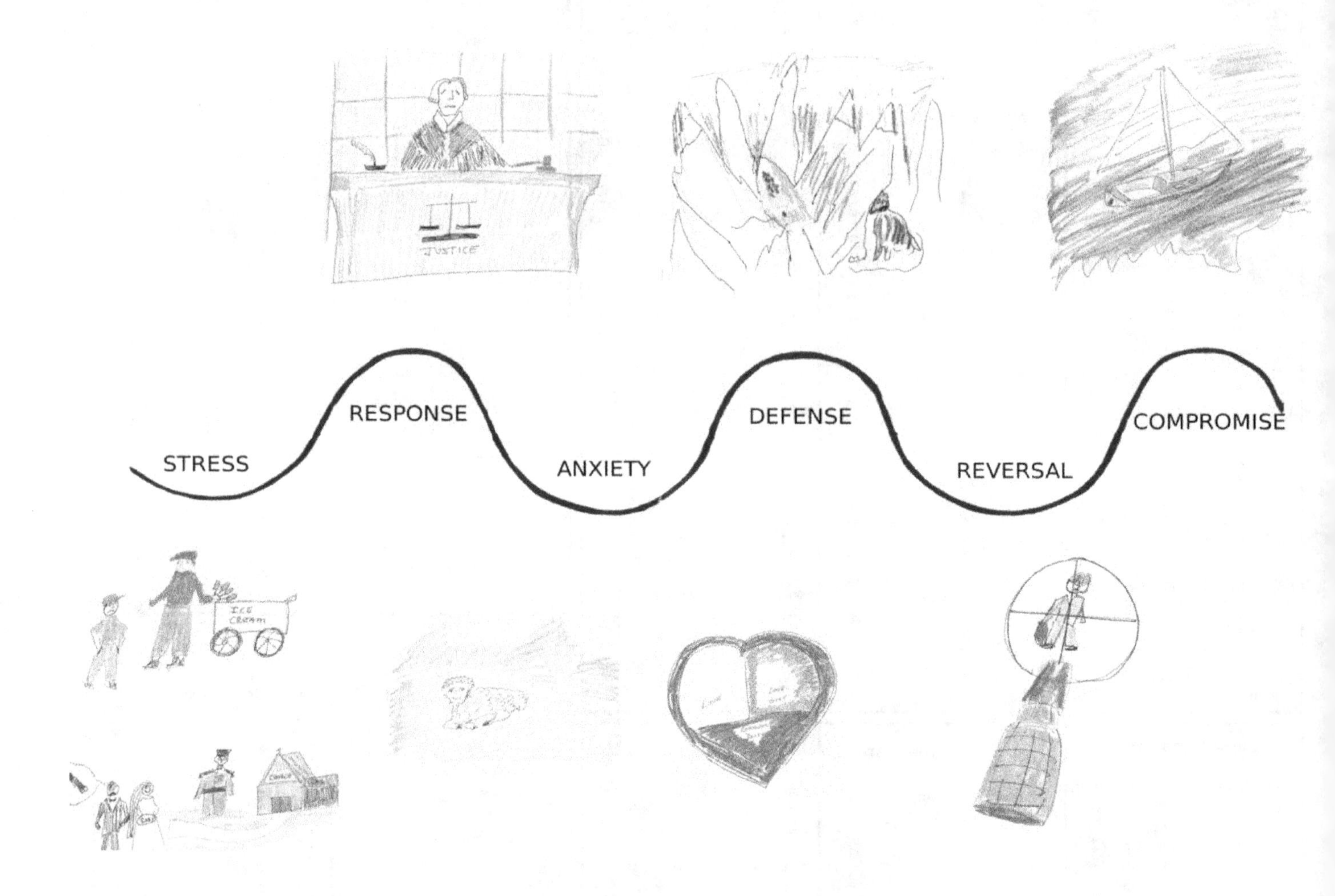

Stress:	**Response:**	**Anxiety:**	**Defense:**	**Reversal:**	**Compromise:**
Told to buy ice cream he sacrifices his own share. Trapped in shotgun marriage to dominant wife.	Judge as a mask.	Under the mask is a scared meek lamb. His heart is full of love for kids and fiancé.	Caribou falling behind the herd doomed to become prey to ruthless wolf	Being shot at by criminal outside the courthouse	Boat drifting in high seas in conflict with materialist companion. They survive to go their separate ways

ABOUT THE DOMINANCE RELATIONAL MODALITY

Introduction And Definition Of the Dominance Relational Modalities

In this chapter we focus on the clinical delivery of Power Management to patients of my psychiatric practice diagnosed with dominant relational modalities. We examine the wellness syndromal characteristics of this diagnosis and its decompensation to illness. The patients in these case studies illustrate the psychodynamic genesis of clinical symptoms and the psychotherapeutic value of the power management intervention. They demonstrate the effectiveness of the self-assessment battery in helping to develop insights and to generate directives for behavior modification. The studies demonstrate the diagnostic and therapeutic effectiveness of the assessment in eliminating or at least diminishing psychopathology.

Traditional DSM 5 psychiatric diagnoses focus on symptoms and overlook the psychodynamic origin of pathology. Each of these dominance cases would have been ascribed a clinical symptom focused diagnosis. The study observes psycho- and socio-pathologies in the seven cases in exclusively psychodynamic terms. The clinical symptoms for dominance include a whole range of symptoms. Anxiety is pervasive, manifested through a variety of clinical symptoms and social dysfunctional adjustments. It is experienced as phobias, panic disorders, paralyzing emotions that can be disabling in many aspects of one's life, such as performance anxiety, but also discretely as insidious emotional resistance, a defense to vulnerability and a pervasive lack of trust reinforcing one's readiness to overreact.

There are two types of pathology: The first is generated by experiences of passivity intensified as anticipations of role reversals: anxiety conditions, reaching the intensity of panic attacks, or alternatively festering as paranoid fears, emotional apprehension, distrust.

The second is generated by states of activity: Interpersonally we encounter social problems secondary to the behavior of aggressiveness: counterphobic provocative or defensive activities leading to conflicts in relationships, domestic and professional, potentially escalating to suicidal and homicidal thinking and actions. Two individuals in this study of seven patients got in trouble and were fired from their employment positions. One upon being fired and also rejected by his wife was close to murdering his wife and two children and also committing suicide.

The relational wellness diagnosis of dominance entails recognizing the pathogenetic role of aggressiveness, anger, uninhibited expression of feelings as the normative deviation towards power positions. This may be graphically portrayed with vectors towards the power polarity in the concentric circles power=field sociogram. Antagonism is portrayed with counterclockwise vectors, while cooperation with clockwise ones. The response to the power positioning induces in the person psychic tension experienced as anticipations of role reversal; the person anticipates becoming the recipient of her/his aggressiveness. Freud identified the state of anticipation of role reversal as 'projection'. The projected emotions may be graphically portrayed in the peripherally positioned ellipse representing the psychic system of the individual as vectors, forces, countering aggressive power positioning in the social system. These forces in the aggressive person, are experienced as paranoia, eliciting the ensuing escalation of defensiveness, of social conflicts and, which eventually leads to the social role reversal of the individual, the self-fulfillment of one's fears.

In the metaphorical language of the Wizard of Oz the dominant antagonistic modality is illustrated in the image of being a lion that is cowardly. Examining the feelings of the Lion or the aggressive individual we may recognize the evolution of the dominance syndrome along the six-role process:

Stress is the position of personal disturbance.
Power as role assumption is the response state as aggression, depicted by being a lion.
This response generates anxiety as anticipations of role-reversal; this is reflected in the lion becoming anxious or cowardly.
In turn anxieties elicit defensiveness as counterphobic responses. The lion roars and shows his teeth.

Defensiveness eventually leads to role reversals; the lion loses control to the hunters; s/he is in panic; s/he is rescued by the proverbial mouse, the submissive spouse.
The reversal elicits compromises; the lion is grateful to the mouse, who rescues him. The mouse is the lion's submissive partner. Lions seek out mice; these are the only persons lions are comfortable with. Dominant individuals marry submissive partners.

The dominance diagnosis entails the therapeutic intervention of realizing one's own transgressive display of power as the origin of fears, anxieties, and disabilities. With this realization the patient becomes aware of the need of power management as reduction of his / her angry disposition. The case studies reflect this consistent psychodynamic pattern: intense power positioning, be it cooperative or antagonistic, as responsible for the generation of paralyzing emotional and social, personal and interpersonal states of discomfort. The patient realizes that the restraint of power is the secret in healing oneself from the disabling symptoms.
Note that five of the seven patients in this cohort chose in their animal metaphors the identity of a lion, while most of their metaphors are power plays between the two metaphorical figures.

Case #1: *Holocaust Survivor Lion Versus Lion, Mural 9 reviewed in Book #3*

Two lions in conflict over an antelope, the spoils of the hunt, was the Animal Metaphor title of a 65-year-old **dominant cooperative** woman, whose problems were related with having been a Holocaust survivor. She was troubled by her unresolved guilt feelings from misdeeds that occurred in her childhood.

In a single workbook completed in a three-session therapeutic evaluation she presented her dominance pattern. Her aggressiveness was reflected in her Animal Metaphor Test, 'two lions in conflict over a dead antelope' reflecting her need for control. Her mask labeled 'Inscrutable', reflected on her emotional defensive stance. This seeming coldness covered up her deep sense of self-doubt, illustrated in a tree with poison fruit revealed underneath the mask. She was able to admit her self-blame for the sense of relief she had experienced as a seven-year old girl upon the deportation of her overprotective grand-parents. The dream metaphor illustrated her reunion with her beloved grandparents. She was also able to check her transgressiveness manifested in a number of metaphors like her Short Story.

The healing effect of the experience was in her being able to emote and mourn the loss of her grandparents upon the celebration of an anniversary of the creation of Israel. She sent me a letter containing art and text of a metaphor test that she constructed herself to thank me for making progress in her emotional life. In this letter she informed me of her making a fool of herself, breaking down and crying in a pubic setting. She was no longer 'inscrutable' or emotionally frozen.

Case #2: *The Ant And The Flea*

The Flea and the lame Ant, was a 45-year-old male pianist, with performance anxiety. With the help of four workbooks completed in as many sessions, the performance phobic pianist was freed from his anxiety by recognizing the role of his dominant personality. He identified his arrogance in his conflictual memory as defiance of his mother. He had been self-pleasuring obsessively, in spite of his mother's reproaching him of this conduct. His early sexual rebelliousness had caused him to feel worthless and self-conscious. The self-consciousness was the underlying factor in his performance anxiety. His metaphors evolved from his diminished self-identity as a lame ant and a damaged flea into his final image of a rehabilitated lion and high flying wounded eagle, coinciding with the cure of his performance anxiety. His emotional evolution becomes dramatically obvious utilizing in parallel to the battery the House Tree Person test modified by the test taker completing a set of questions qualifying the standard images.

House-Tree-Person Test

These four HTP tests illustrate a clear transformation. In the first, the images are somewhat generic and the responses are positive. The second book presents a drastic change: the house, tree and person are all dead, and the responses are negative – the only thing he likes in this sequence is the fact that the man is "dead and free of pain." The images in the third book are very simple and broken down to basic shapes. Lastly, the fourth book presents a positive point of view.

House	**Things you like about the house:** Fireplace, lots of windows, trees, quiet and cozy. **Things you don't like:** [left blank]	**Things you like about the house:** [left blank] **Things you don't like:** cold, violated, empty.	**Things you like about the house:** it's there, gives security. **Things you don't like:** unfinished, not grounded.	**Things you like about the house:** cozy, beautiful, just right, warm and comfortable. **Things you don't like:** [left blank]
Tree	**Things you like about the tree:** green, smell, age, shadow. **Things you don't like:** [left blank	**Things you like about the tree:** [left blank] **Things you don't like:** dead, cut down, unfulfilled.	**Things you like about the tree:** it's alive. **Things you don't like:** it's crying?	**Things you like about the tree:** large and stately, green, beautiful, wise. **Things you don't like:** [left blank]
Person	**Things you like about the person:** nice body, nice clothes. **Things you don't like:** big nose	**Things you like about the person:** dead and free of pain. **Things you don't like:** no life, can't do any good.	**Things you like about the person:** [left blank] **Things you don't like:** no hands or face.	**Things you like about the person:** smart, talented, hardworking, determined. **Things you don't like:** neurotic, lacks focus under pressure, gets too involved with details.

Book One **Book Two** **Book Three** **Book Four**

Case Study #3: *Captive as a Circus Elephant versus Free Like a Butterfly*

A 28-year-old artist was referred to me by her mother to consider administering an antidepressant. She was angry with her mother and had chosen to live far away from home. A two-session single workbook evaluation provided insights into her well-established dominance. This manifested in her scales and also in her metaphors.

The dominance pattern had determined her abrasive family interactions. The workbook helped her to understand her sensitivities and anger manifested across her metaphors: She identified many conflictual memories of anger at others. The anger at her mother was illustrated in the jagged family balloon of her mother, the anger at her step-father was depicted in a recent conflictual memory upon him trying to embrace her. Her phobic sensitivities showed in her two metaphors as the dilemmas of a bride: the first was captured in her Animal Metaphor between a slaving circus elephant versus feeling free like a butterfly, the second was captured in the Fairy Tale Metaphor as Beauty loving the Beast versus Cinderella looking for a prince.

The young woman suffered of general apprehension, anxiety and depression manifested in hesitations in getting married lasting several years for fear of trusting him as a partner. In the third mask, presenting what is in your heart, she made sure that her heart is very well defended; the heart had three layers of protective encapsulations. In her Dream image, a nightmare, her heart is broken in two halves. Her fears of his breaking her heart caused her to resist getting married. Her counter-phobic defensiveness resolved itself in her Short Story Metaphor with the image of a couple trusting each other and kissing.

The insights into her pattern of dominance enabled her to look at her self, identify her anger at her relationships starting with her mother and also manifesting in her relationship with her boyfriend of three years. She got married soon after the evaluation. I heard from her mother that the marriage lasted only three months. Her hopes of happiness soured, as she soon perceived her husband as the hurtful beast. Fears are self-fulfilling. The dominant person is guided by her fears rather than by reality. She divorced the husband and returned to being the Butterfly-Cinderella looking for a prince.

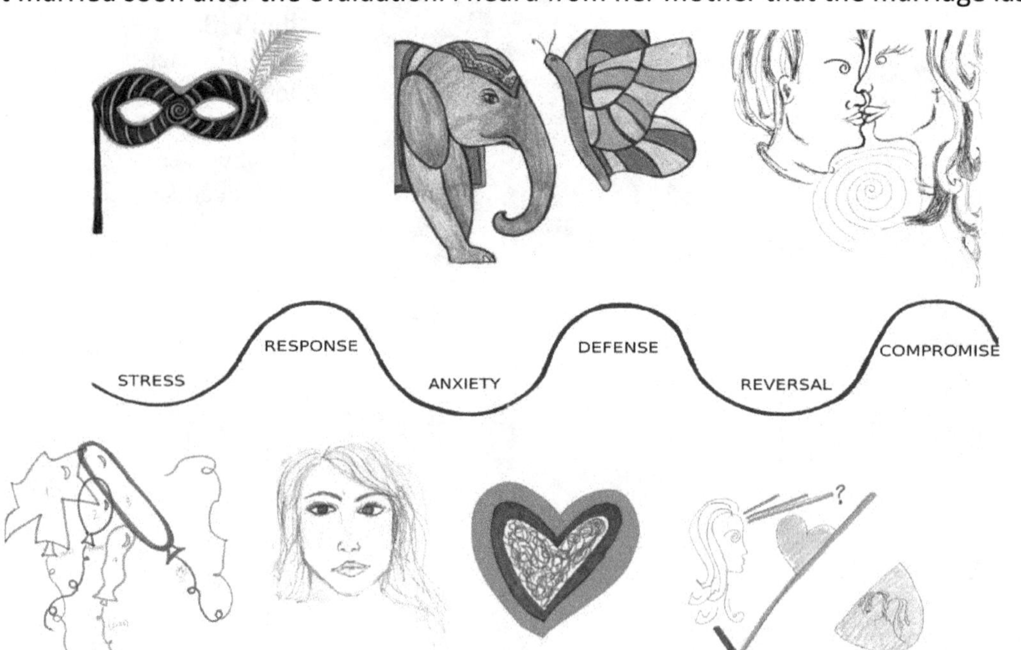

Stress:	**Response:**	**Anxiety:**	**Defense:**	**Reversal:**	**Compromise:**
Caught between parents' fights Mother as prickly balloon threatening to pop daughter's balloon.	Ballroom mask.	Self-portrait presents clear intense feelings. Heart is contained in a series of shells.	Trapped circus elephant versus free and scared butterfly. Trapped as Beauty and the beast vs. free as playful and scared Alice in the wonderland.	Dream in which her heart is broken by lover who betrayed her.	Love story happy ending in a carefree union.

Case Study #4: ***The Dragon and the Unicorn, case fully transcribed below***
The dragon and the unicorn, a 22-year-old college student, married woman, experienced panic elicited upon her anticipation of delivering a paper in her literature class. An eight-session therapy helped her to comprehend her performance anxiety by understanding her dominance syndrome. Her limit testing behavior had caused her self-consciousness, which manifested clinically as performance anxiety.

Her extraordinary dominant personality was the origin of the anxiety as anticipations of reversal. She identified her dominance as the cause of her social phobia and tried to learn to contain her over-reactions. Her art work helped her to realize this anger manifested in all her very beautiful images: these included her conflictual memories as an intense need for reassurance, her intense responses at being left out of a family funeral, her devastating responses at feeling neglected, her acting out with young people prior to her marriage. She realized that her Mask identity was that of a Lion. It covered a very angry lion underneath. Her heart was tethered illustrating the anxiety as unacceptable restraints to her intense emotions.

Insights in her pattern of angry responses led to restraining her emotionality that successfully resolved her anxiety and fears of performance. Her paranoid, and paralyzing fears dissipated and she was able to prepare herself for the presentation. She completed therapy with a lengthy Short Story illustrated in a massive drawing. The story reflected her anger transformed into leadership and commitment for success: A brave unicorn rescued her father's nation by single handedly battling the enemy, a devastating dragon. Her winged unicorn, probably presenting her passion for success and recognition, overpowered the fiery demonic dragon threatening her father's kingdom; the dragon, her tethered personal powerful anger was harnessed in the service to her family as caring leadership. In the story she was triumphant rescuing her clan and her brother who was defeated in the battle with the dragon. She saved the kingdom and her sense of safety in the leadership position thus also dealing with her sibling rivalry feelings. This case is discussed in its entirety below.

Case Study #5: ***The Turkey and the Mountain Lion***
The Turkey and the Mountain Lion was a 35-year-old attractive woman experiencing severe anxiety around her boyfriend's three children. She composed in four sessions her first workbook, the evaluation. This was followed up with two months of group therapy during which she completed a second workbook. She understood how her dominant relational pattern caused anxiety and chronic depression.

In her first workbook's Short Story Metaphor, she was the humbled greyhound upset by three alley cats; she realized the connection between her fear of her boyfriend's three children as the anticipations of a role reversal: she projected her aggressiveness directed against her own stepmother to her boyfriend's children. Because of these fears she was intolerant of his three kind children. This insight helped her to moderate her defensive responses. Her anxiety and depression diminished. She recovered her self-confidence. Self-aware she was able to settle down and get married to her friend after a six-year long engagement. This marriage lasted several years.

In the second workbook she found comfort recognizing the source of her feelings in her relationship with her father. She had reacted angrily at experiencing abandonment by her father who had left home abruptly. She resolved her agitation at him as she composed a story between 'a nervous terrier upsetting a beefalo'. She was the nervous terrier circling around a beefalo driving him dizzy with her antiques. She recognized in the big animal her annoyed father and became emotionally ready to be reconciled with him.

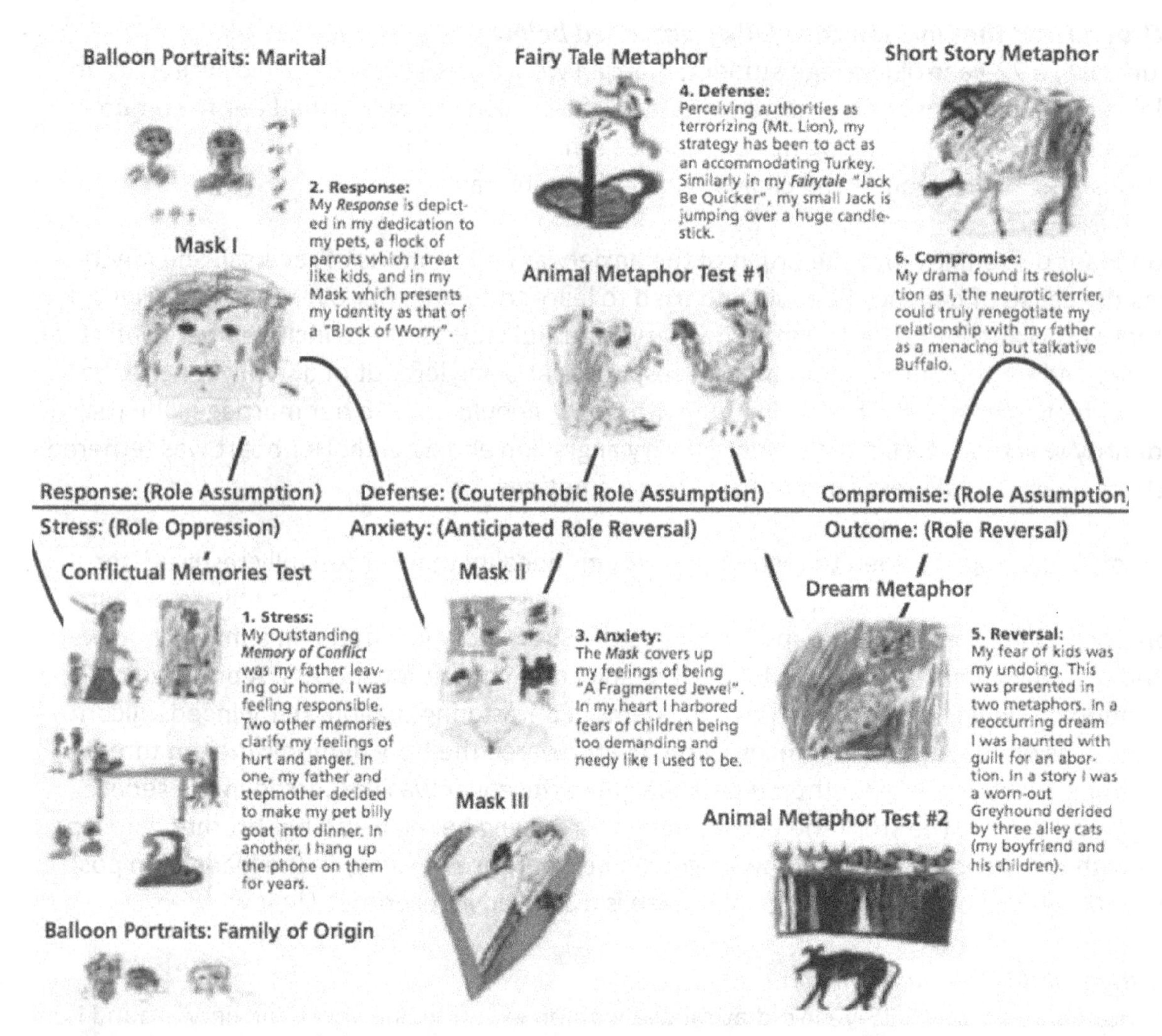

Case Study #6: *The Cheshire Cat and the Pit-bull*

Cheshire Cat versus Pit-bull, was the story of a 40 year-old male teacher, a cooperative dominant person, who was very depressed for being fired from his school for insubordination. In a six-session therapeutic evaluation he completed two workbooks, which he then used to sum up his life episodes meaningfully explaining the pattern of his dominance. In his self-evaluation he clearly explained his dominant pattern evoking social and emotional conflicts.

His dominant cooperative personality diagnosis manifested in his mask as the Cheshire Cat's ear to ear grin. In the first book the individual recognized the significance of his defense and how the crisis at his school system reflected a reversal for his controlling pattern, identified with the smiling Cheshire Cat. In his Animal Metaphor his cat was pinned down by a Pit Bull. His self-confidence collapsing led him to cry in his Short Story Metaphor. He was able to recognize his Cheshire Cat smile as a defense to being hurt and was able to let himself feel good for breaking down and crying for the first time in his life. But his compromise illustrated in the first book did not change his dominant personality; he swiftly recovered from his depression fighting back the school system and winning the battle of his dismissal.

The second book portrayed his recovery from the state of depression as he used his wit to outsmart the school system. Instead of being fired for insubordination he was able to get out of the school system with a compensable disability. His humor was a powerful defense but also the key factor in his social conflicts, which led to his reversal of fortune; it had precipitated insubordination and the end of his career, accompanied by an emotional breakdown. His faulty survival tactic reflected his self-defeating power struggle; he was trying to change the system rather than himself. His dominance resisted therapy but he was able to become self aware of his troubling emotional dynamic. He admitted that he could also be a pit-bull.

Case #7: *The Bull and the Cow Versus the Lamb and the Bear*
This middle-aged dominant man was fired because of stealing an article from the place of his employment. His dominant antagonistic behavior manifested in both the work environment and his domestic relations. He was very mad at being fired from his work and rejected in his advances by his easy-going wife. This loss of standing almost led him to the ultimate abuse of power; he came close to murdering his family and committing suicide. Awareness of his being out of control drove him to seek help.

Therapeutic Insights
Therapeutically it is important that the test taker realize the syndromal relational nature of the process as the cause effect relation between aggressiveness and the experience of anxiety. Evolving insights into the anxiety as secondary to one's own aggressive conduct is the first step to making relational attitudinal corrective changes. This connection has been the key interpretation throughout the case studies. Following up on these insights with personal self-restraints has led the ensuing excellent therapy outcomes. We observe rapid recoveries in the seven clinical case studies presented under dominance. Anxiety may manifest as anticipations of aggression from others.

Power Management entails a shift in interventions from cognitive focus on controlling irrational emotions to the simpler alternative of managing behaviors.
Unlike cognitive behavior therapies the focus in Power Management is not in dealing with distressing emotions like anxiety and depression, but in dealing with the *behaviors* responsible for the generation of the unpleasant *emotions*. One can readily experience relief of these emotions, be those anxiety, depression or paranoid distortions, defensiveness and real social setbacks handicapping one's adjustment by addressing one's own inappropriate aggressiveness.

Therapy begins with education on the syndromal nature of relational modalities and ends with identifying one's modality diagnosis. The diagnosis of dominance is made in the metaphor tests by the test taker and so is the insight for making concessions. It helps to understand the condition of the Cowardly Lion as the aggressiveness projected to others eliciting anxiety and more defensiveness. Once a person understands the price of being a lion s/he will modify one's behavior. Thus learning about the psychodynamic origin of anxiety, as a relational modality diagnosis and recognizing its manifestation in one's inventory and metaphors, the person becomes comfortable in making changes. Knowledge delivers reassurance and the testing delivers insights. These are the tools for the individual to identify the problem and to moderate power behaviors, which in turn diminish the level of apprehensiveness, floating anxiety, and reduce the need for defensive aggressiveness.

The insight on the relational diagnosis goes hand in hand with understanding the difficulty of a dominant person to respect the two problematic aspects of this relational modality: First, restraining one's tendency to abuse power. Second, the difficulty the dominant person has in listening to criticism, hence surrendering power.

Characteristics Of Dominant Persons' Artwork

Below one can see the images reflecting the profiles of dominance in both the Animal Metaphor Tests and also the three Masks; we recognize there the conflicts of the dominant modality and the insights generated by the metaphors.

The images frequently present fights and conflicts. The metaphor identity animal frequently is that of a lion. It is so in five of the seven patients including the Animal metaphor and the Mask Test.

- Two equally powerful animals confront each other.
- The test taker identifies with the most powerful animal when there are differences between the two.
- The identity animal has difficulty accepting responsibility.
- The test taker realizes the pattern of dominance and suggests changes by restraining one's controlling tendencies.
- The test taker accepts making changes or compromises.

A reminder of the alternative images reflecting the submissive individuals' metaphor choices.

Substantial polarization between animal choices such as one animal is presented as a victim of the violent partner. Asymmetry of power positions: one is a hunter the other is hunted. The person identifies with the weak animal. An animal will feature signs of damage, defect or injury, handicap, like a broken wing, a ring around one's neck where one's head is being bitten off. The positions and the placement of the animals show lack of communication between them. The animal of choice is in a posture showing remorse, guilt and quest for forgiveness.

Case Title	Picture	Who Do You Identify With?
Case #1: *Holocaust Survivor Lion Versus Lion*		"[I identify with Lion] #1, since he did the killing and the spoils belong to him. However, he is not willing to share even a small piece with the other lion, who is also needy."
Case #2: *The Ant and the Flea*		"[I identify with the] llama – out of place, lonely, sad and worthless – so much and yet so little. Unlike her, though, I don't 'take it as it is.'
Case #3: *The Elephant and the Butterfly*		"I can move like [the elephant] in terms of analyzing feelings and emotions and understanding how one needs to deal with responsibilities. You can't just keep on flying."
Case #4: *The Dragon and the Unicorn*		"[I identify with] Piglet. When I was young, I'd always blame something else for my wrongdoing. I denied my own responsibility."
Case #5: *The Turkey and the Mountain Lion*		"[I identify with] the Turkey. My modus operandi is 'flight, not fight'...it's a manifestation of a scenario I know well: myself being weaker than a more controlling dominant person."
Case #6: *The Cheshire Cat and the Pit-bull*		"I am the Cheshire Cat. I used to be the happiest 'cat' I know. I really wish I could disappear from my current situation, or at least use my climbing ability to climb out of the pit I'm in. I want my ear-to-ear smile back."

Dominance Case Studies' Three Masks

Dominant Masks

The first mask presents one's powerful emotions as in authority, resistance to weakness and emotions. The feelings mask presents self-portraits realistically and with feelings of determination and defiance. The heart mask shows the conflicts with external forces rather than internal conflicts. The heart is suffering in alternative ways and also affected by guilt feelings rather than anger and depression.

Reminder of submissive masks

There are distinct differences for the dominant and submissive sets of masks. The first mask may present power and authority, or defenses, like a wall, and also a warrior attitude or anger, like Mr. Dynamo; these are deceptive symbols of power. The second mask presents hurt feelings, images of traumas, and enumeration of hurt feelings and mishaps. It presents the weaknesses of a person's identity, like behind the powerful judge we have a vulnerable lamb, confusion, lack of identity, pursuit of control, and the loss of control. The heart is traumatized and encapsulated, hiding the hurt feelings. But it shows also the difficulty communicating feelings, like the impediment of a moat, a hole in the heart, encasement, a state of being 'completely unrevealed'.

Case Study	Mask	Hidden Feelings	Total Picture What Is In Your Heart
Case #1: *Holocaust Survivor*	 "'Inscrutable.' Some worry, but well controlled...a non-committal posture."	 "'Perfect Looking Poison Fruit.' Suspicion, impulse ... take things at face value... flawless fruits which are poison, things are not what they seem."	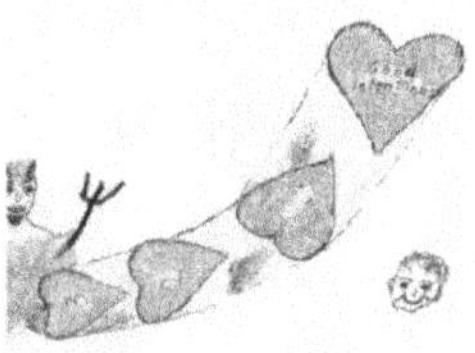 "'A Heart Full of Good Intentions, and What it Paves the Road To.' Laughing at emptiness, pain, confusion...humor helps in the solutions of difficult problems."
Case #2: *The Ant and the Flea*	 "'Venetian Rendezvous.' Expectation, anxiety. Lust vs. spirituality, fear vs. confidence. "	 "'Determined.' Persistent determination [and] absence of doubt.	 "'Bleeding Heart with Halo.' Deep sadness and despair. Helplessness and great goodness of spirit."
Case #3: *The Elephant and the Butterfly*	 "'Infinity.' An eternal sense of being strong, hiding any conflict that may be in this person. [The mask represents] truth."	 "'Jillian' Motion, Beauty, Intensity, Mystery. Seeing the beauty and strength, insecure person who wears the mask. "	 "'Amazing Grace.' Abnormality [and] sensitivity – not a perfect heart. The heart is complicated...[it] has layers for protection. What is really inside the

Case #4: *The Dragon and the Unicorn*	 "'Phoenix the Cat.' This mask became handy…whenever she got angry, upset, suspicious. Learn to control your emotion."	 "'Phoenix the Mad Cat.'[This is] the girl's true color. The girl could get aggressive when the mad cat was let out of his cage. Two cats lived inside her."	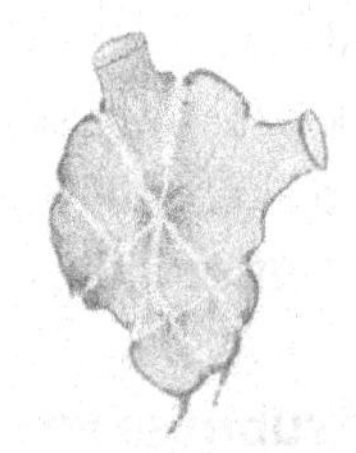 "'Heart in Chains.' She restrained herself to avoid getting in trouble…she could not express her love."
Case #5: *The Turkey and the Mountain Lion*	 "'Block of Worry.' Stress, confusion, sadness, frustration, fear, indecision."	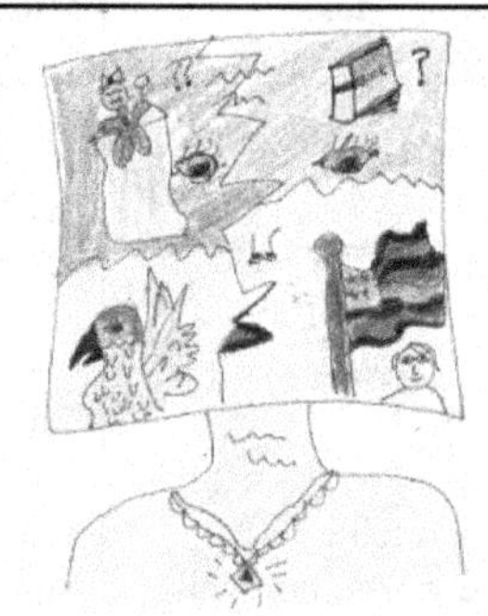 "'Fragmenting of the Perfect Jewel.' Fragmenting of energies, dissipation of dreams. Not knowing where to focus."	 "'Hope and Fear.' The struggle to maintain my own goals against other desires, biology, etc…maybe there will be time for all in its due course?"
Case #6: *The Cheshire Cat*	 "'The Ever-Smiling Cheshire Cat.' Perpetual happiness…I want to return to this face/mask…I thought [it] was my true face."	 "'Who Is This Man?' Confusion…I'm not sure who is behind the smiling mask."	 "'Heart Under Siege.' Threats to the heart, confusion. This represents a heart, which is in danger.

Dominant Case Study Four

The Dragon and the Unicorn

Introduction And Discussion: Before And After Images

Interest of this case is in illustrating the dominance related sense of anxiety or paranoia

A 24-year-old married woman from an Asian country, a student at a local college, sought help because of her disabling social performance anxiety; she was in an utter panic about making a presentation to her college class. I detected her condition as a typical panic attack that could be explained by her relational modality, that of a very pronounced dominant personality. She was the cowardly lion; indeed this was the image of her mask. The aggressiveness of the lion is presented graphically with the angry open mouth of the lion and the consequence to that is revealed in the heart image, a heart bound tightly by a rope, representing how she was expected as an angry child to contain her anger. This relational modality explained the fears, anxiety, stemming from projecting her very aggressive disposition to the environment of her classmates.

Therapy lasted 10 sessions structured by completing the Conflict Analysis Battery, which helped her to identify her massive aggressiveness, manifested in her childhood, continuing into her adolescence and currently in conflicts with her husband. Her dramatic disposition had alienated her mother, a beautiful model, and had generated for her the closeness to a beloved second grandmother. The loss of this grandmother had elicited renewed manifestation of her immense anger.

The patient recognized her angry disposition. She talks about herself in her essay in is confirmed in a 'before and after therapy image'. It portrays her with a whip of mastery in the place of the original alienation and panic.

The patient's essay about her therapeutic experience clarifies the benefit contributed by the battery tests as insights in the relational nature of her fears. The Short Story metaphor reflects her turning around by reconciling herself with her family assuming the leadership role in the service of her father though still competing with her brother; it reflects her capacity to feel comfortable in social situations instead of being paralyzed by fears.

Before and After Images

Therapy's outcome illustrated with a before and after therapy drawing:

"How I perceived myself when I had to make a presentation
[Before I talked to Dr. Levis]. 'Joker Clown.'
[After]. 'Same Clown, but this time he's holding a whip!'"

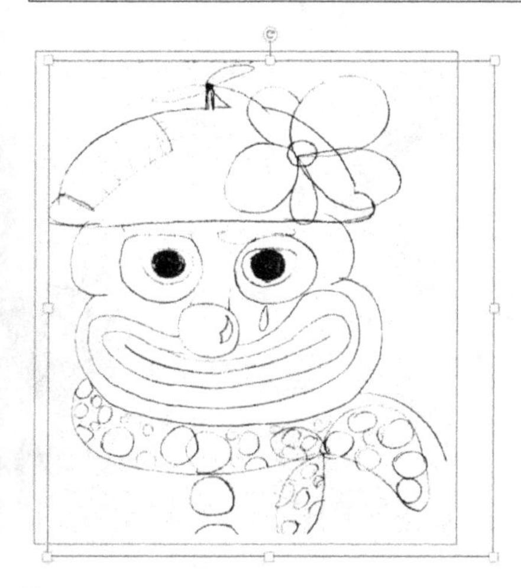

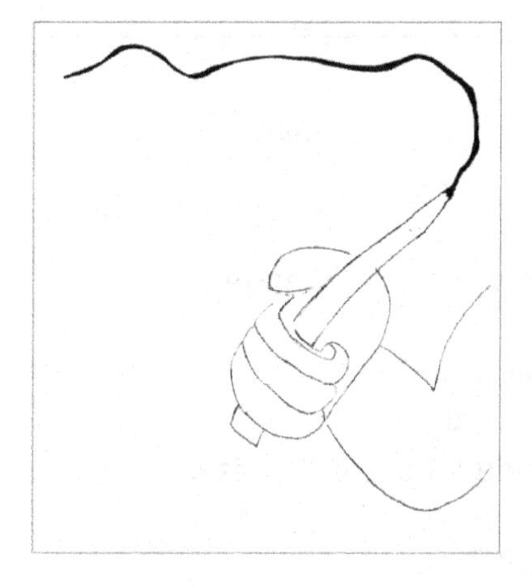

Transcription of the case study

Stress

Conflictual Memories

Childhood Memory

Please sit next to me and listen to a story about a girl who was born with a massive box full of anger. There are several ways to hurt a girl, especially the one with anger in her pocket. Either to smack, to slap, to pinch, or just simply choke her with hurtful words. A stubborn brat deserves occasional painful punishment in which she must accept it silently. There was nothing but the big "ID" coming out of that tiny human being and everyone seemed to have enough for her. She had been told a million times how much everyone loved her and yet they appeared to act in the opposite direction.

Mom kept disappearing every Monday and reappeared like a magician every Friday. How did she manage to be invisible for so long? Dad, too, traveled around and worked very hard with high ambition.

The girl's real grandmother could not walk, so her second grandmother was in charge of looking after her while her parents were away. You see, my mother has a mother and a stepmother because her father had two wives. The second grandma unintentionally became the girl's second mother. Grandma never went away, and besides, she was there when the girl cried. Grandma knew best. She knew things that scared her step-granddaughter. God forgave her for smacking her granddaughter when she was crying. Too bad, the girl loved to cry. What a shame to be born from a beautiful mother who wholeheartedly wished her first child to be as pretty as she was, but her wish has ever been granted. It was such disgraceful for her to live with all the criticisms among friends and relatives. "Why don't you look like your beautiful mother?" "Why your mother was so mean that she did not grant you just a speck of her beauty?" "How could she disappoint her loving and caring parents?" However, Grandma's never complained. Instead, she even liked having her step granddaughter smile.

When the girl turned 18, her mother took her to see a plastic surgeon. Why? Mom just needed some advice about having a face-lift. However, it all ended up with the girl was asked to see the plastic surgeon and within a couple of weeks after, the girl had her nose reconstructed. The girl was happy. Everyone including grandma were happy. Dad did not notice the change of his daughter until mom told him. Dad made no comment. New nose and what's next? Eyes, yes we almost forgot bout the eyes. No, you cannot have those pair of eyes that look like you are sleeping all the time. Why don't we make them look bigger? Just wee bit bigger. That would do. Why the girl become so self-conscious? Why she hated her looks so much? Why she believed that she was so ugly that she could even stop a clock? You have everything now, my dear. You look fine now. Mom was happy and the girl was happy. The caterpillar had made the transformation.

Adolescent Conflictual Memory

Step 1: Draw a conflictual childhood memory.

Step 2: Describe the incident. Me, my friends, and the temptations of the outside world.

Step 3: How did you feel about this person? I loved them, hated them, and could not live without them.

How did this person feel about you? My friends thought I was crazy.

Step 4: What were the conflicts? We were too wild.

Step 5: What happened before? We flew around the magic garden with 20 unicorns.

Step 6: After? We got bitten by the snake.

Step 7: Your share in this conflict? I was lost.

Step 8: Effect on life: I have a bad attitude for society. It is a sick sad world that we live in.

Step 9: Have you been repeating yourself? No.

Step 10: Has this conflict been resolved in your mind? No.
Step 11: Resolved in this relationship? No.
Step 12: What changes should be made? I would return to my nest and help my mom go through tough times.

Recent Conflict

Recent episode of intense angry reaction illustrated both in the dark image of this memory and in the story about this reaction.

"The Loss"

Grandma was the first one who cried on the day the girl got married. Later on the girl realized that none of her pictures that were taken with her step grandmother carried the smile. The girl forgot to ask her grandmother to take a photo with her. Grandma waited until most of the guests were gone before she asked the girl for a picture. How could she forget all about her grandma? How did she do that to her beloved grandma? May she burn in hell forever for disregarding her grandma. What the girl forgot to tell her grandma was how she hated being the center of attention and how difficult it was for her to pretend that it was not her wedding day.

It is too late. Grandma died just a year after the girl's marriage. Dad did not want to break the news because he did not want the girl and her husband to travel all the way from the States just for attending grandma's funeral. It's too much of the trouble you see. No, dad would not let the family business interfere with the girl's in-laws. Respect others and always put them first. How well the girl remembered her dad's teaching. Grandma's death was just another sad news that reflected the facts of life. You have to live and learn and try to cope with those facts. You may cry until your eyeballs pop out but it won't bring grandma back. The girl took the next available flight back home. She cried all the way home. It's O.K. Grandma did not suffer. She had been blessed. We respect those who did not suffer before they died. People kept telling the girl that everything was okay. Grandma was very lucky because she passed away in her sleep while she was at the hospital. Did the girl want to hear that fact? Yes she did. Did the girl want to see her grandma while she was alive at the hospital? Yes she did. Why then someone did not inform her? That's the way her dad wanted it to be. No need to tell her. She's too busy and too far away, anyway. Oh. How angry the girl became. The girl was betrayed. She was disappointed with her family. She hated them all. She hated her in-laws. She hated her husband. They were the reason that kept her dad from telling her, from letting her know that grandma was very, very ill. She wanted her in-laws to die. She wanted them to cry, to suffer, to fall apart.

Zoo Portrait and Story

Family of Origin

Step 1: Draw a zoo portrait of your family of origin.
Step 2: Identify each individual.

Dad: hard working, enjoys good food and wine, plays golf every weekend
Mom: loves animals, has a salty tongue but she is kind, always worries.
Me: likes to argue with Mom, has too many boyfriends, always changes her mind
My Brother: kind, independent, very bright.

Step 3: What are the conflicts?
Not sure. May be lack of communication?

Step 4: What changes should be made to resolve these conflicts?
Get together more often. Joke more, and laugh more.
RESPONSE

Transparent Mask: Mask I
Draw a mask.
"Phoenix The Cat"
It all began from just a minute of uncontrollable urge for attention, together with the rampages power of dominant characteristics; the girl has turned into a baby-sitter's nightmare. To tame this wild creature, physical punishment seemed to speak louder than words. Her father smacked the girl and she was not allowed to cry. She was smacked until she agreed to stop crying. Learn to suppress your anger, my dear child. Learn to control your emotions because there's no room here for such thing. We still love you. The mask became pretty handy for the girl whenever she got angry, upset, suspicious, or hurt. She could not express her emotions. People became too scary especially when she 's angry. She got hurt even if she had no intention to hurting the people. Why is life so complicated?

ANXIETY
Mask II
Draw what is under the mask.
"Phoenix The Mad Cat."
Phoenix the mad cat was the girl's true color. Phoenix's hair was red, purple, shocking orange, pink, and maroon. When he spoke, the girl had to cover her ears with her hands because his voice was so loud. The girl could get very aggressive whenever she let the Phoenix, The Mad Cat out of his cage. He was amazingly unpredictable. However, things were not as bad as when the girl was very young. Because now, she knew that there were two cats living inside her.

Mask III
The Heart
Make a drawing of what you see in this person's heart.
"Heart In Chains."
The girl became used to how she restrained herself in order to avoid getting into troubles with her parents and other people. She was upset when she could not express her love to her step grandmother. Once she recalled of bringing home a box of cake for her grandma, but she was told not to let her mother know because she would get jealous. How could she tell her mother not to worry? How could she explain to her mom that her step grandma meant so much to her? How could she stop her step grandma from moving out of her house? How could she tell her not to love her real grandchildren as much as she loved the girl? How to ask a person if he or she really loved her?
What is love anyway?

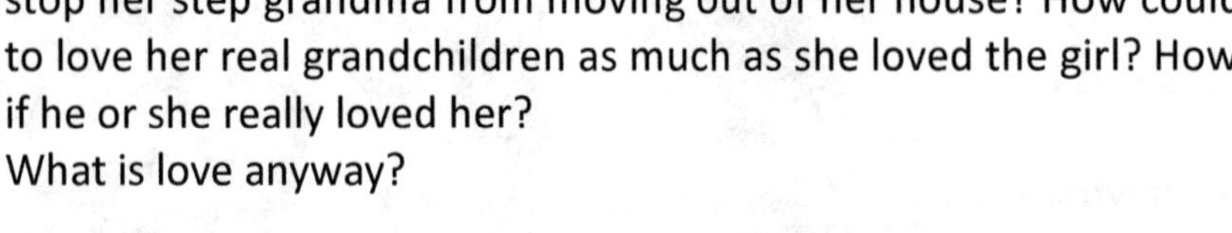

Defense

Animal Metaphor #1

Step 1: Draw two animal figures in color.

Step 2: Fill in the blanks

Animal #1

Type of animal: Piglet with rainbow tail

Age: 11 **Animal's sex:** Male

Personality: Loves to sing and dance; loves to bake cakes and muffins; does not like thunderstorms.

Animal #2

Type of animal: Owl with eyeglasses

Age: 97 **Sex:** Male

Personality: Very wise and kind; loves to read and experiment; very happy all the time.

Step 3: What are they saying?

#1 – "Hello Owl! How are you today?"

#2 – "Hello, my little one! I am absolutely fine. What can I do for you today?"

#1 – "I 've received a new recipe for Apple Muffin from Grandma yesterday."

#2 – "Then?"

#1 – "You see, last night there was a thunderstorm and I got really scared."

#2 – "Uh-ha. So what does it have anything to do with your Grandma's recipe?"

#1 – "I talked to her on the phone and forgot to write it down on a piece of paper. I thought that I could remember everything easily."

#2 – "Let me guess. This morning you can't remember what your grandma said, can you?"

#1 – "That's correct but it was not my fault. It was the storm's. It made me forget everything."

#2 – "No, no silly little one. It's because you did not write it down on a piece of paper. Don't blame the storm. Come on, let's have a cup of tea."

#1 – "Okay Owl. Can I have some cookies too?"

Step 4: What happened before? The owl was working in his laboratory at his house**.** The piglet was trying to recall his grandma's recipe for apple muffin

Step 5: After? They both sat down at the owl's greenhouse under the beautiful fig tree and enjoy their cup of tea and cookies.

Step 6: Title: "The Storm, The Piglet, and His Lost Recipe."

Step 7a: Conflicts between themselves: Piglet is too young to accept his own fault, in other words, he does not want to blame himself when things go wrong.

Step 7b: Conflicts between them and the world: Piglet is young and has a lot to learn. Owl is very old. His days are counted. However, he's never stopped learning, discovering, seeking for answers.

Step 8: What changes should they make to resolve conflicts? For piglet only time can help him. Hopefully, when he grows older, he will become wiser and more responsible. Still, he needs a good adviser.
For Owl, he should take some time off from his work and projects because he is getting very old. He has spent all of his life seeking the answers. He did not realize that more answers he discovers, the more questions will arise.

Step 9: Which animal do you identify with: The owl also represents myself at the present time. I am forever looking for answers for every question that comes into my head. The more I want to know the reason, the more I become puzzled. I also identify with Piglet. When I was young, I'd always blame somebody else for my wrong doing. I denied my own responsibility.

Step 10: How does this pertain to you? There is conflict within myself.

Step 11: What changes should you make? Don't know. Maybe the best solution is to end everything.

Reversal

Dream Analysis

Step 1: Choose a dream: Significant childhood dream.

Step 2: Draw the dream:

Step 3: Describe the dream:

– two-faced monster
– me running away
– voice over
– mysterious woman with no face
– swing chair

The voice over always belongs to a woman. It says "How pity." The mysterious woman has a kind of wheezy, high pitch voice. She has no face. All I could see was her long, dark hair that covered most of her face. She sat so close to me and bent down to me so that I could hear her voice. The swing chair in the playground. I used to dream of myself sitting on the swing chair, playing and humming a song. It's very windy. Just like the storm was approaching. But I kept swinging on that chair.

In most dreams I try to run away from things or events that scare me. But I just can't get away from those scary things. It's like running on an exercise mill.

Step 4: Describe the participants: Most of the participants are strangers who I have never met before.

Step 5: What are the conflicts? Arguing over something; threatening to kill me; accusing me of being dumb and ugly.

Step 6: What occurrences preceded the dream? [left blank].

Step 7: Explanation of the dream: No idea.

Step 8: Do you dream a lot? Yes

Step 9: Other dreams:

1. Dreams about the death of someone close to me i.e. Dad, Mom, my dog, my brother.
2. Dreams about the death of myself.
3. Dream of taking a shower in the middle of a basketball field.
4. Dream of worms.
5. Dreams of listening to the orchestra but the music was too loud and I could not tell them to stop playing. It always wakes me up.

Step 10: Connections or patterns in dreams: No clue.

Dreams are related to each other.

Do you see any pertinent connection or patterns in your dreams? No clue.

Compromise

Short Story

The phobic patient completed her therapy presenting me with an oversize illustration of her last test, a short story in which she vindicated herself as a unicorn rescuing her father's kingdom from a dangerous dragon.

She was successful in presenting her work in the classroom without experiencing any anxiety.

Step 1: Choose two imaginary characters and write a short story about one of their adventures.

Once upon the time in the island called Neverland, there was a group of flying unicorns living peacefully with other animals on the lost island. Since there are plenty of food available everywhere for everyone, all the animals are healthy and strong. The strongest flying unicorn in the group has been elected to rule the land and to fight with the dragon that lives in the cave by the sea. On every full moon; he will leave his cave for hunting. The dragon wants to kill all the unicorns in order to overtake the island; therefore, he is the most troublesome of all the unicorns' enemies. There have been fighting events between the Unicorn and the dragon for many decades and the Unicorns have lost so many members of its group.

One day, the King of all Unicorns has called for his daughter and son to discuss about how they would fight against the dragon on the incoming full moon. The King's daughter's name is Sierra. She is a very powerful unicorn that can shoot the fire from the tip of her wings. She has no fear of anything and always wants to go out in the battle with her father on every full moon but her request has always been denied. Her father knows that the anger is his daughter's weakness and is too afraid that he might lose her in the battle. On the other hand the King's son, Pegasus, is more mature and calm even if he is much younger than his sister. Pegasus is not as strong as Sierra, however, he uses his wisdom and intelligence to combat the troubles. Today will be his 20th birthday which in the unicorns' tradition, enables him to join his father in the battlefield.

The King asks Pegasus what he would do if he were to fight with the dragon. Pegasus replies "Father, I would set a trap outside his cave and bait him with fake animals. I would cover those fake animals with raspberry juices and fish blood. Once he sets his feet outside his cave, he would smell the blood and run into the trap. We will dig the trap so deep that he would not be able to climb up and when the tides come in, he will be drowned." The King nods his head and turns to his daughter. "What about you Sierra? What would you do if you were to fight with the dragon?" Sierra stamps her hoof loudly and replies " Father, I am a war-unicorn and I have zero tolerance with that dirty beast. I shall bring my troops and slay him with hundred horns and burn him up with my fire before he even wakes up." The King then asks " Don't you know that the dragon has a very keen nose? What if he could smell you as you enter the cave and there is no room for all of your troops to flee if the dragon wakes up?' The King then adds " My dear daughter, I rather lose my own heart than let you into that cave". The King then decided 'Sierra, would you agree with me if I rather chose your brother's suggestion?' Sierra became so upset once she heard her father's decision that she galloped off into the wilderness.

The full moon is here and every unicorn is ready to capture the dragon according to Pegasus's plan. The wind is so strong and tonight seems to be the perfect night for the end of the beast. The tides crash into the nearby cliff spraying the water all over the rocks. The stars are so bright and seem like they are getting ready to celebrate the victory. Everything is in order, the trap that is so deep, the raspberry juices are so red, and the fish bloods are so rich. All the unicorn troops are waiting on the cliff above the cave's entrance. There is no sign of Sierra and her troops. The wind starts to build up and carry the rich smell of fish blood into the cave. Yes, this will wake up the dragon quicker. Pegasus watches the cave's entrance with unblinking eyes. His wings flapping around with excitement. Suddenly, the ground beneath their hooves starts shaking violently. The dragon is awake.

The dragon's roars sound like thunder. The unicorns start standing on their hind legs and kicking their front legs in the air. " Here it comes!" Pegasus whispers in his throat. He thought he was shouting. The dragon must have smelt the blood and rushed out of the cave to find the first pray of the night.

"KA-BLAM!!!" Without delay, the dragon fell into the trap and left behind the echo angry roars in the air. All the unicorns dance around with joy and salute the King and Pegasus." The dragon is dead. The dragon is dead. Hail the King."

But, wait! The trap is too dry. The tides are still too low to reach the trap. The dragon has managed to climb up by digging its claws into the ground. Panic. The King orders his troops to get ready to attack. Pegasus cries out loud. "Oh ! No, the trap could not hold him" He shouts to the King" Father, please call back your troops, I don't want anyone to get killed. "The dragon is extremely angry with us and he is heading for our city." Please send the messengers to tell all animals to evacuate their home and gather around the foothill". The King orders his messengers to carry the emergency message to all animals and orders his troops to try to stop the dragon. "I think I will stop him myself. Pegasus, go to the foothill and guard all the animals". The King left the cliff with his order to his son. "No, father, you are too frail to fight. Please come with us," Pegasus shouts back but it's too late.

The King tries to stop the dragon by distracting him from heading towards the city. The dragon rises his tail and hits the King. The unicorn soldiers rush to him and protect him with their wings. The land is covered with dead unicorn soldiers and blood is everywhere. The trees catch fire and it spreads out rapidly. The dragon left the King and his unicorn soldiers behind as they head for the city.

Suddenly, the sky is blackened by hundreds of unicorn soldiers and the leader of the troops has a pair of fire wings. Sierra appears from the back of the mountain with her wings ready to fire. She orders her troops to round up the dragon and wound it with their extra sharp horn. The dragon cries in pain and confusion. Sierra flaps her wings and releases the giant ball of fire into the dragon's eyes. The dragon roars for the last time. The city and all animals are back to normal again but this time everyone seems to look happier than before. The King announces his retirement and proclaims that his son and his daughter shall rule the kingdom together. Sierra bows to her brother and Pegasus bows to his sister. "From now on, I will respect your ideas as much as mines. I know that I would have been dead by now if I had led my troops into the cave". Sierra speaks calmly to her brother and father. And Pegasus replies to Sierra, "I should have thought about having you and your troops stand by because we never know what could possibly go wrong." The King smiles and says "Use your power wisely and use your wisdom powerfully."

Discussion of the case study
What a beautiful case study in content and also with the artistically perfect illustrations of her dramatically intense emotions! So much need for love and so much sense of pain; so much anxiety and intense defenses; such beautiful healing accepting responsibility instead of being paralyzed. I am very touched by this young woman's need for love and her sensitivity for rejection, her fiery emotions as Phoenix the Mad Cat and the subtle containment of her anger in the tethered heart. What an interesting journey from her paranoid suffering about making a presentation in her college class to her recovery as masterfully leading the unicorns to save her father and collaborate with her brother.

The dynamics of the dominance syndrome:
This case study illustrates well the dynamics of dominance and its treatment. We see here the syndromal nature of the dominance relational modality, as well as its correction with simple proper management of power by transforming passivity to activity, antagonism to cooperation and alienation to mutual respect. This study provides ample evidence on the topic of the dominance relational modality as a disposition that drives a person to express massive anger or to seek power in the system. How sensitive in her experiences of rejection and how intense her responses! The images and the words demonstrate the range of her intense responses to life's stressors. She was aware of these angry and norm testing behaviors and she had awareness of trying to moderate them.

Patient Note
"I am screaming for attention, then they give me love and attention. Then I reject it. Why don't you give me love from the beginning? Last night I had dinner with my husband he said there is improvement. It takes time. When I have anger, I manage it."

Therapy Outcome:
Therapy started for dealing with the panic prior to a class presentation. It was concluded following her masterful presentation at school and the completion of her Short Story.

Stress: Intense hurt being rejected by her mother, feeling loved by her grandmother.
Response: Her lion with anger contained, for fears of overwhelming her father with her screams.
Anxiety: Losing control of her anger as the lion unleashed, as thundering anger balanced out by her heart being tethered.
Defense: She was the piglet blaming others unable to accept responsibilities.
Reversal: This is the phase of her panic attack upon performance behavior. Her dreams too show multiple instances of loss of control, fears, running away and being stuck.
Compromise: Her conflict resolution is presented in her Short Story battling the Dragon threatening her community. Her power is now in her fiery wings and horns blinding the overpowering dragon.

She did not talk about her clinical problem that drove her to ask for help other than in her before and after images of how she felt before the therapeutic intervention and after it. This case illustrates the dynamics of anxiety related to dominance relating. Anxiety as anticipations of reversals handicapped her capacity to deliver a paper, to face the class. Therapy helped her to understand her fears. She developed insights and moderated her behaviors. She processed the power management problems in her life at multiple situations. She recognized her problem of anger. And now she accepted responsibility for modifying it and not blaming others. What a clear evidence of outcome in the images of before and after therapy. She presents here her transformation from a scared clown to a masterful tamer with a whip in hand.

She emerged in reality learning about herself and making a great presentation to her peers. She also healed from her tendency to overreact becoming aware of the need to moderate herself in her family relations. She made changes; she felt less angry and less scared. She concluded therapy with her short story with the statement: "Use your power wisely and use your wisdom powerfully.

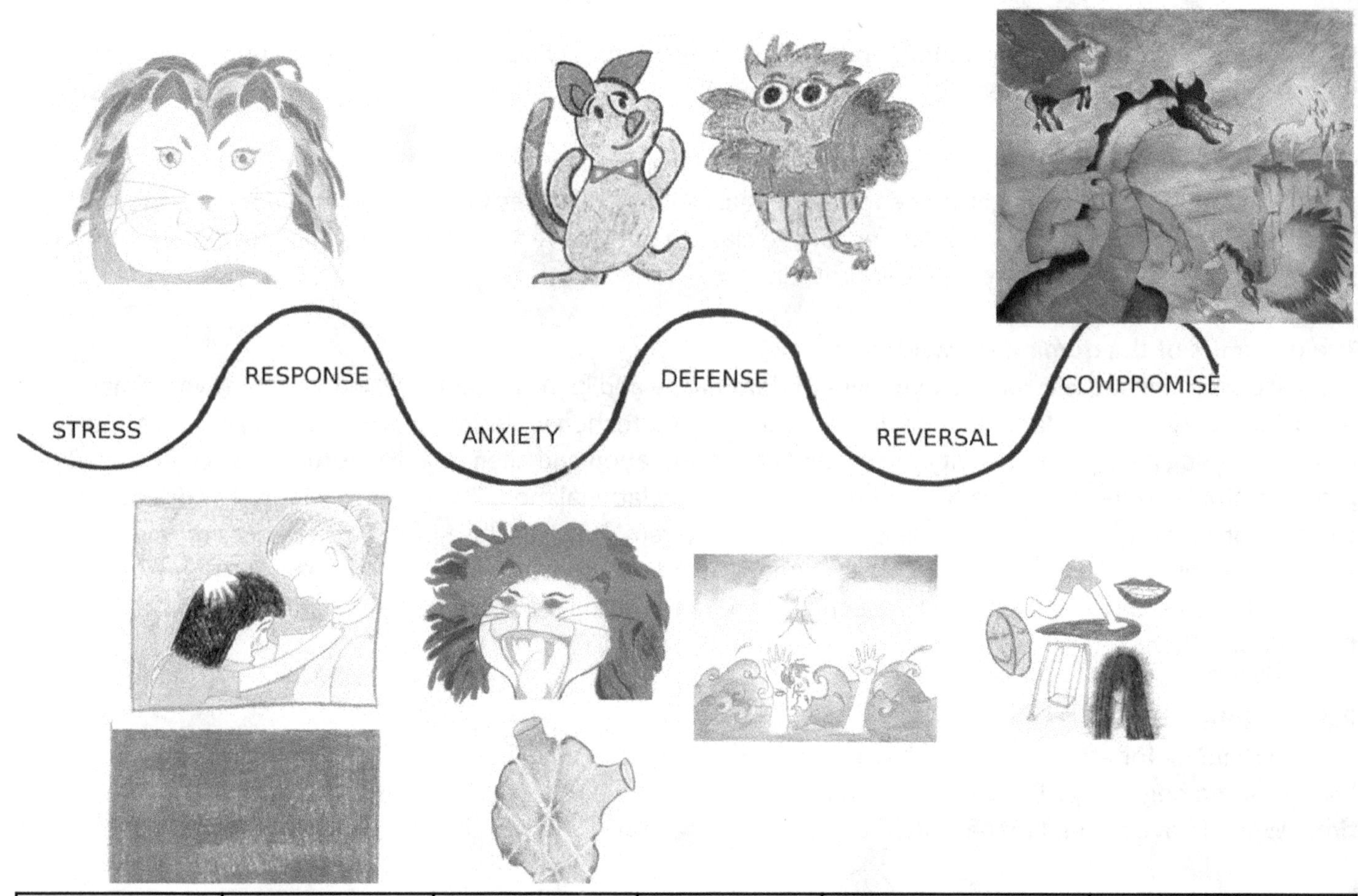

Stress:	Response:	Anxiety:	Defense:	Reversal:	Compromise:
She had a strong relationship with her grandmother, but wasn't told about her death.	Her mask is "Phoenix the Cat." She wears it when she is "angry, upset, suspi-cious, or hurt."	"Phoenix the Mad Cat" is the true face. Her heart is wrapped in chains.	A wise owl teaches a young pig to be responsible for his actions.	Dream: A two-faced monster, a woman with a face obscured by hair, hands reaching out of the ocean, hold-ing a fruit filled with worms.	A unicorn makes peace with its family in order to defeat a dragon, and learns to "use its wisdom powerfully and it's power wisely."

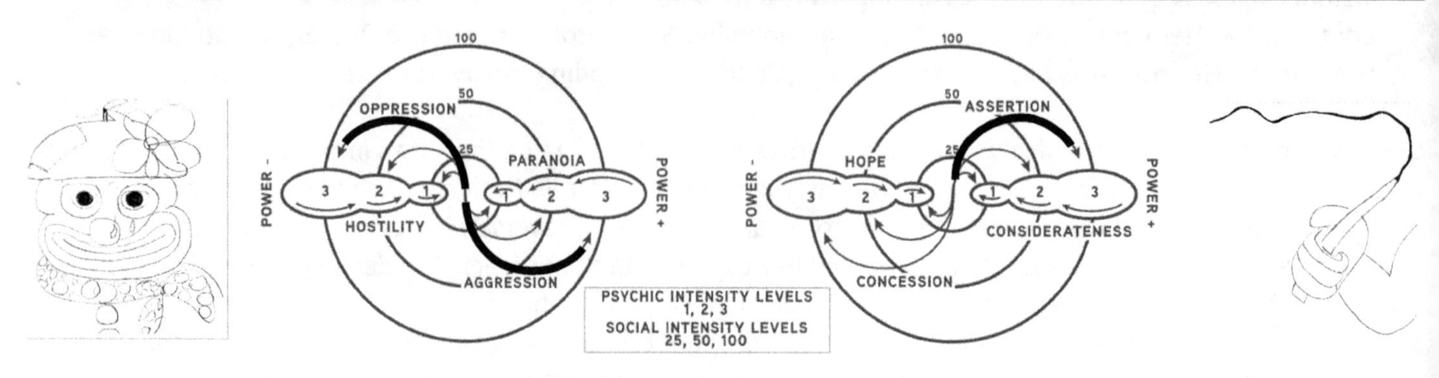

Inception of Therapy (paralyzed by fears due to her dominance); elevated inventory scores indicate both submissive and antagonistic qualitites. Intense hurt and anger at the loss of her grandmother, reflecting a submissive and hostile attitude, eliciting a response as a double lion.

Therapy Outcome (release of anxiety and empowerment) inventory scores indicate dominant cooperative qualities accounting for her healing. Identifying as a unicorn fighting and winning over the dragon threatening her family, reflecting her dominant cooperative disposition as the phase of healing.

DOMINANT COOPERATIVE
Leadership 0
Competitiveness and Dominance -1
Personal Discomfort and Sensitivities 1.3
Defensiveness and Lack of Compassion 1.7
DOMINANT ANTAGONISTIC
Distrust 1.7
Provocativeness -1
Dominance .3
Intensity in Senitivities and Responses -.7
Explosiveness 2.7
DOMINANT ANTAGONISTIC EXTREME
Established Oppositionality 2.5
Arrogance -1.7
Provacativeness and Indifference to Other's Feelings -1.7
Negative to Couseling and Communication 2
Phoenix the Cat -- Phoenix the Mad Cat -- Heart in Chains
The Mask
The True Face
The Heart
"The Dragon and the Unicorns"
Her father knows that the anger is his daughter's weakness. Sierra bows to her brother and Pegasus bows to his sister. " From now on, I will respect your ideas as much as mine."
SUBMISSIVE COOPERATIVE
Cooperation, Trust .8
Compassion, Considerateness -1
Respect for limits 1
Recessivity .9
SUBMISSIVE ANTGONISTIC
Communicational Restraint 2.7
Worthlessness, Inferiority 2.7
Resignation Without Hostility 1.7
Resignation With Hostility 1.8
Hostility 1.2
PSYCHIC TENSION-INTDENSITY OF CONFLICT EXPERIENCED
Anxiety Level 3
Family History 3
Duration of Disability .5
Intensity of Disability 1.7
Phobic Thinking 2.5
Depression 2.6
Degree of Self-Consciousness -1.5
Particular Areas of Conflict -1.4
Psychosomatic Conditions .3
Degree of Relational Stability 1.8

CHAPTER EIGHT:
RECORDING THE COURSE OF THERAPY AND ITS OUTCOME UTILIZING THE CONFLICT ANALYSIS BATTERY

The Formal Theory departs from the axiomatic methodology of arbitrary determinations of psychological phenomena and norms and introduces the relational method revamping psychology from a medical, agnostic specialty focused on illness, non-dynamic diagnostic categories, neuroscience, avoiding the concepts of the unconscious and of morality, by applying relational method in the study of the creative process, reflecting the unconscious as a scientific, psychodynamic energetic conflict resolving phenomenon. The unconscious is defined as a homeostatic conflict resolution or morality-driven periodic phenomenon, the unit of the social sciences. Its homeostatic function is catharsis, as the transformation of unpleasant psychic energy into personal attitudinal growth and sociological adjustment. The unconscious is thus viewed as a scientific moral order phenomenon binding art and science, biology and sociology, psychology and morality. Psychotherapy is viewed accordingly as a facilitated and accelerated experience of conflict resolution. This study documents therapeutic changes in the transformation of modalities of resolving conflict with a record generated by the use of the Conflict Analysis Battery.

Reviewing the Formal Theory's key hypothesis conflict resolution is energy and attitude transformation abiding by two scientific phenomena: the Simple Harmonic Motion and Klein's set theory. Conflict, a normative deviation, is an emotional energetic load transformed through normative compliance to moral growth. This process consists of three pendulum oscillations, as a six-role syndromal entity guided by three formal operations, the equilibrial operations of the scale, restoring balance within any symbolic system. The three formal operations transform passivity to activity, antagonism to cooperation and alienation to mutual respect. The redefined unconscious reduces behavior to the purely abstract concepts and formulas of physics' energy and logic's forms. The unconscious becomes a scientific, measurable, graphically portrayable phenomenon.

The formal operations lead to four types of conflict resolution identified as a set of wellness personality diagnoses: dominance, subordinancy and their attitudinal, cooperative, antagonistic variations. Evidence validating the theory is in completing the Conflict Analysis Battery self-assessment. The battery identifies the relational modalities with an inventory and reconstructs the syndrome of six emotions through several metaphor creation tasks. Completing the online delivered battery takes four hours to identify one's personality type and to generate insights on one's syndromal pattern. The assessment provides evidence demonstrating the unconscious as a scientific conflict resolution phenomenon, the integrative paradigm, the software of the unconscious, revamping psychology into the Moral Science.

Formal Theory's conceptual distinctions identified by Conflict Analysis Battery's technology
The Moral Science reconciles epistemology, diagnosis, assessment, morality leading to the delivery of therapeutic services through using the Conflict Analysis Battery, a self-assessment. The battery combines cognitive information, delivers a diagnosis, therapeutic insights and guidance for changes. The program delivered as 'Creativity and Power Management' is basically a wellness emotional education utilizing the generation and interpretation of metaphors, targeting the analysis of the personal way of resolving conflicts.

The Conflict Analysis Battery self-assessment standardizes therapy as a concise program of wellness emotional education. Therapeutic change is facilitated and recorded by utilizing the battery. We identify pathology along the relational modality wellness diagnoses, dominance and subordinancy as syndromes of conflict resolution. The battery records diagnoses and therapeutic changes. Four case studies are presented here identifying pathology based on relational diagnoses, and using the CAB in streamlining psychotherapy, generating a visual record monitoring the progression of changes.

Relational diagnoses wellness and pathology

Formal relational modalities represent alternatives types of relating and communicating that pertain to wellness psychology. The wellness typology under stress leads to particular modality related pathologies. The battery helps to identify diagnostic criteria and evaluate wellness and pathology in terms of types of sociological deviations and intensity of emotions. With the battery we examine the course of therapy and judge therapy outcome observing the artwork and companion comments to detect improvement of the relational dispositions.

Dominant individuals clearly seek power as demands for love or support. Dominant people are very sensitive, jealous, very easily hurt and angered, very demanding from the therapist. Their conflicts are with other people. Submissive people are afraid to ask power or attention. They are deferential, easily embarrassed, guilt ridden and very self-conscious. Their conflicts are internal.

The CAB generated records clearly illustrate the developments in the course of therapy for both the dominant and the submissive individuals. One of the dominant individuals presented, Segmet, recognized her problem as anger at her mother. She evolved in all her relations. In particular instead of feeling threatened by her mother as a vicious dog and being afraid and angry at her, she evolved in understanding her and experiencing her as a dachshund leaking her face.

Gladys, one of the submissive individuals, consistently presented her inner turmoil as seeking food but also as seeking to control her eating habits. She evolved to be able to voice her feelings becoming a poet. Using her creativity, we witness her gradually being able to address feelings with her mother, boss, and husband. She told her mother her need to eat was because she felt emotionally starved, feeling abandoned by her to another sibling. She was also able to talk about anger and ask her husband for companionship.

Advantages of the Conflict Analysis Battery

The Conflict Analysis Battery creating art generates a visual and text record of symbolic representations that are interpreted by the test taker as measurable relational entities. This record offers objectivity in examining the emotional transactions confirming the relational diagnosis and reconstructing the conflict resolution syndrome. The ongoing use of the testing captures the journal of the therapeutic developments; this record can be analyzed objectively by the patient and the therapist to identify changes in the patient's attitude in a number of relationships reflecting the issues dealt with during therapy including that of the therapeutic relationship. The visual record can be readily interpreted and graphically illustrated, reflecting the conflicts as well as the changes experienced in dealing with them. This visual record, and the companion narratives, reflect the evolution of problematic relations towards their respective resolutions. The testing records portray clearly the evolution in key relationships with imagery, which is analyzed by the patient for its personal relevance. The patient identifies with metaphors how she feels and also examines the connections of the images illustrating the evolution of feelings and attitude.

The focus in therapy is in the correction of deviations within the person's emotional system. Therapy addresses modifications along the relational principles: modifications in power, reducing relational extremism, and furthering cooperation and mutual respect. The objective with dominant persons is reduction of the quest for power and antagonism manifested as anger, blame, alienation, ridicule of others, whereas with submissive people the objective is seeking power as assertiveness, as courage to share one's feelings with others, reducing psychic tension, and the experience of antagonism and alienation. Effective changes in the respective modalities reduce the emotional intensity, leading to resolution of conflicts, and elimination of symptoms.

Sample of the formal analysis method by observing two images illustrating the process of change and capturing it conceptually and graphically

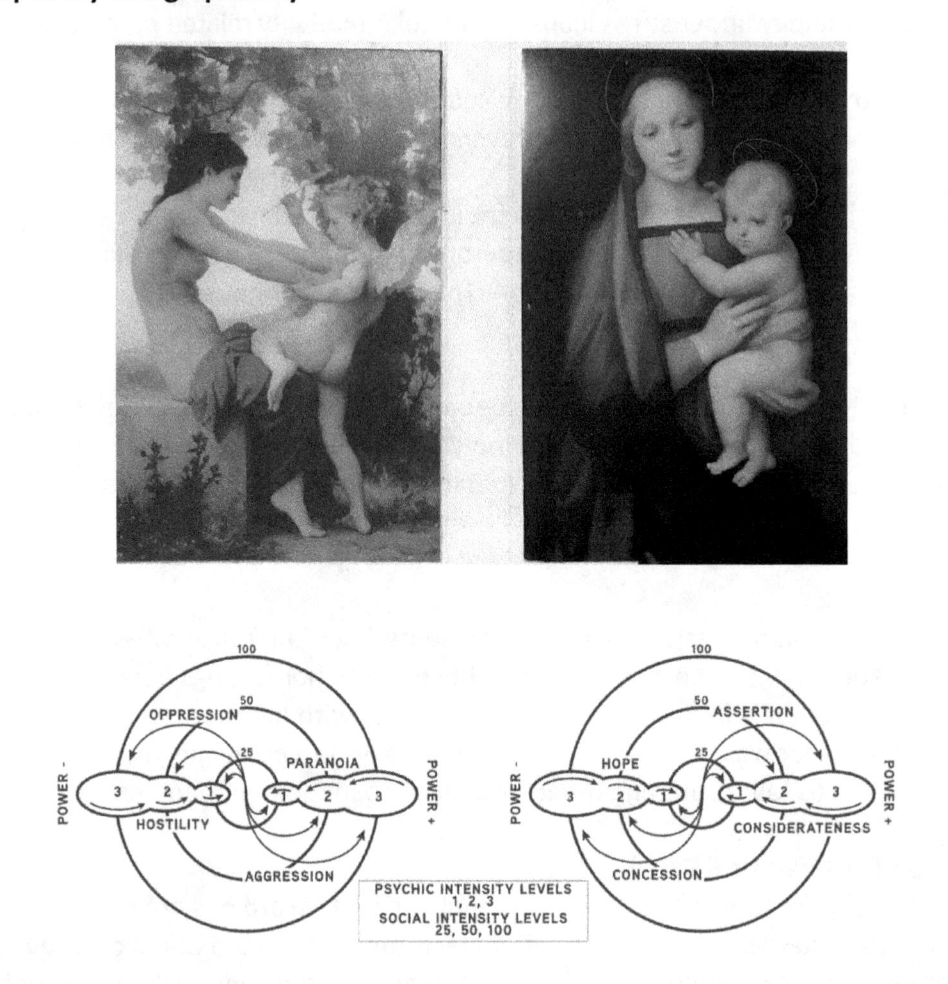

The images illustrate the formal analysis of two alternative types of relating as having measurable graphically portrayable natural science sociological and emotional dimensions. The two images: a naked voluptuous woman battling Eros with an arrow in his hand, a playful antagonistic system, versus the Virgin holding a happy loved child may be viewed as reflecting measurable progress in therapy. The art is interpreted below with graphically conveying dimensions along three formal distinctions: the dichotomies of power, attitude and intensity, the relational alternatives of the unconscious process in resolving conflicts. The diagrams depict the social and personal opposite emotional social alternatives; the first, depicting conflict as antagonism, counter-clockwise vectors, and the second, presenting conflict resolution with clockwise vectors denoting cooperation.

This sample analysis is the key to the simplicity of translating transactional phenomena from concrete imagery to abstract science by utilizing the concepts of the Formal Theory and the technology of the Conflict Analysis Battery, (CAB) self-assessment. The scientific interpretation of metaphors serves both diagnostic and therapeutic work. The battery generates art tasks, qualified metaphors, identifying insights on the personal emotional pattern and also into the relational diagnoses, reflecting emotional growth occurring during therapy.

An additional exercise of creativity helps to evaluate progress by asking the patient to illustrate the progress by drawing images on how she felt at the beginning of therapy as compared at its conclusion. The Thai princess evolved from being scared to holding a whip, as illustrated in the case above (page 233).

The deck of cards as the template of orderly therapeutic transformations

We introduce a model of scientific relational analysis of changes, the systematic organization of information, as spelled metaphorically in the structure of the deck of cards as an orderly system of transformations. We recognize the order of the deck of cards representing symbolically a progression of conflict resolutions. The components of the order identify every suit as a conflict resolutions process; it identifies the four suits as four relational modalities, the four signs, alluding to changes from the black spade, an upside down stabbed heart evolves through the expanded black stabbed club to the red diamond and finally the bright red upright heart reflecting a cyclic evolution of modalities, a progression in the quality of resolutions.

This model is used in evaluating therapeutic changes occurring spontaneously in the course of therapy by observing the creative process. This model is exemplified in the formal analysis of an artist's retrospective, but also in examining the evolution of religions as the spontaneous search for improvements in the family institution. This model is also exemplified in developing an educational game Moral Monopoly, using cultural stories reflecting religions as discoveries of the alternative relational modalities evolving predictably improving the family. The retrospective and the game introduce the spontaneous evolution of attitudes in resolving conflicts in the course of therapy. Examining the structure of the deck of playing cards, the template of the game becomes a map of the unconscious organization of the emotions present in life, but also expedited through therapeutic work.

Moral Monopoly introduces cultural stories exemplifying the relational modalities

The template of the deck of cards identifies relational modalities differing as degrees of effectiveness in resolving conflict. The template retraces the evolution of religions as moral paradigms identified as changes of the family institution in terms of power and attitude in the gender relations. We observe the evolution from Matriarchy as the submissive antagonistic phase in the development of family relations manifested both in Greece but prevailing in the Aztec cultures. Matriarchy evolved to dominant antagonistic patriarchy in Greece promoting the concept of marital vows for women.

In the structure of Moral Monopoly we see two levels of growth

In each culture we recognize two phases illustrated respectively by two stories, one from mythology of the culture's principle conflict, and one of a historic era, which shows the cultural conflict's resolution.

At another level we identify four cultures as a series of four relational modalities and how cultures evolved through history by discovering the modalities as improvements in gender relations. This gradual transformation exemplifies the evolution of personal dynamics during therapy; a person starts with a conflict, based on her relational modality. Therapy begins as submissive antagonism; it proceeds to explore alternative resolutions. The person remains diagnosed along a modality but s/he evolves from the conflictual phase to the optimal resolution, upon termination of therapy.

Psychotherapy outcome research

The prototype of the deck of cards illustrated with the evolution of cultures along the four relational modalities is applied in the analysis of metaphorical imagery produced by patients in the course of therapy utilizing the CAB. The card game template presents the model of reference in examining progress in therapy along the four modalities. Utilizing the CAB as a journal in the course of therapy, generating metaphors, we observe the evolution of the personal pattern as relational phases in the course of therapy. Relationships are predictably evolving along the four relational modalities. We see the progression in the art generated by the metaphor testing in the course of therapy as phases of conflict resolution.

This deck as a template of relational changes is used in evaluating therapeutic changes visually as manifested in the evolving imagery captured by the CAB's metaphors.

1. Every suit of the deck exemplifies the conflict resolution process captured by the sequence of personal metaphors reflecting the emotional evolution of the patient resolving conflicts.
2. The sequences of conflict resolutions are examined relationally as relational modalities evolving in the course of therapy like the four suits reflecting the four relational modalities.
3. The relational modalities evolving in the course of therapy are examined along the deck's signs qualifying the progression in therapy as a model of cyclic improvements as a continuum of relational transformations.

This pattern of relational improvements recorded by the use of the metaphorical constructions of the battery is observed in the course of therapy with four patients, two dominant and two submissive. The actual diagnosis as a relational modality does not change but persons evolve through phases in dealing with their respective conflicts. The therapeutic process duplicates the spontaneous course of relational transformations.

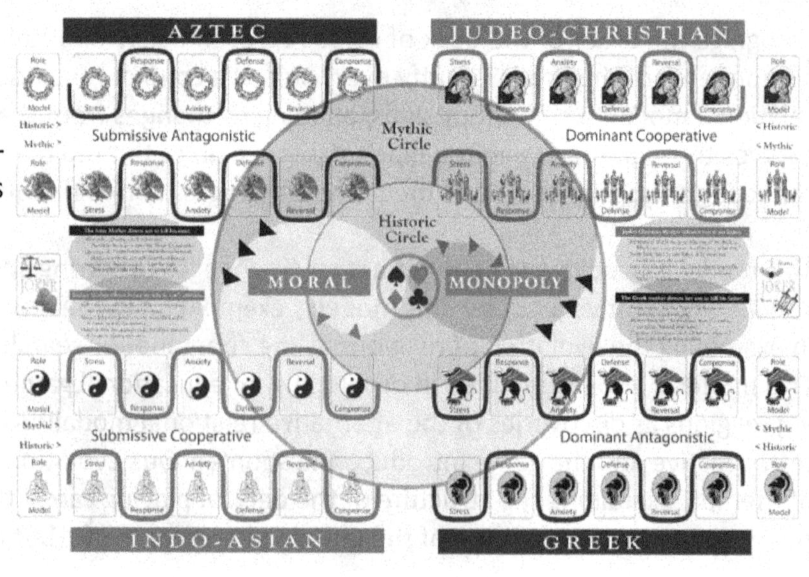

The Gorski Retrospective as an example of the spontaneous evolution in resolving conflicts

The Gorski Retrospective at a glance examines the two phenomena of science illustrated by the evolution of the symbolic imagery of the canvases. First examining the three formal operations establishing formal continuity in the images of the mouth, occurring in the course of the six role states of the syndromal continuum. Then the overview presents the cyclic evolution of imagery as such unfolded in the retrospective illustrating this progression through alternative cycles of symbolic choices: mouthlessness, kisses, sports paintings and that of institutionalized individuals.

The Gorski canvases illustrate this progression as the artist is shifting from the original phase of submissive antagonism, of mouthlessness, and abandoned bodies, to assertiveness as political criticism during the Vietnam era, then a phase of sexual risk taking, as dominant cooperation, leading to his crucifixions expiations; in the phase of sports paintings his heroes struggle but are blocked revealing submissive antagonism; the artist's work is completed as a phase of submissive cooperation as he focused on images of the institutionalized disabled people, one of them being his son, as the heroes of the culture, who though disabled express their feelings, both joy and anger. In this phase the masks that prevailed in his work are now removed showing empowerment of the disabled. The overview examines the phases of his art work as the three acts of a play, a formal conflict resolution continuum. The artist personality diagnosis remained submissive throughout the relationally diverse phases as depicted in all his canvases.

- The play begins portraying his autistic son as 'the child of darkness' and ends with depicting disabled people as the heroes expressing joy and anger.

- He evolved from submissive antagonism the mouthlessness experiencing alienation, pain, abandonment and hostility to multiple relational resolutions.

- He enjoyed assertiveness expressing political advocacy during the Vietnam era denouncing the politicians as in the canvases named 'the Committee' and 'Five percent'.

- He evolved through erotic risk taking, dominance, with the phase of kisses, which ended with his transgression, the 'Rape of the Rose' leading to 'Nowhere to Hide' resolved to being crucified at the end of this phase.

- Then he focused on sports heroes, muted assertiveness, but his athletic heroes always wear masks; he evolved in this phase to safe spirituality with 'Winner take all' and 'Love triangle', a kiss that was implying liberation yet spirituality alluding to Christian values.

- His final phase are disabled people, who though handicapped, express their emotions of joy and anger. They are not wearing any masks.

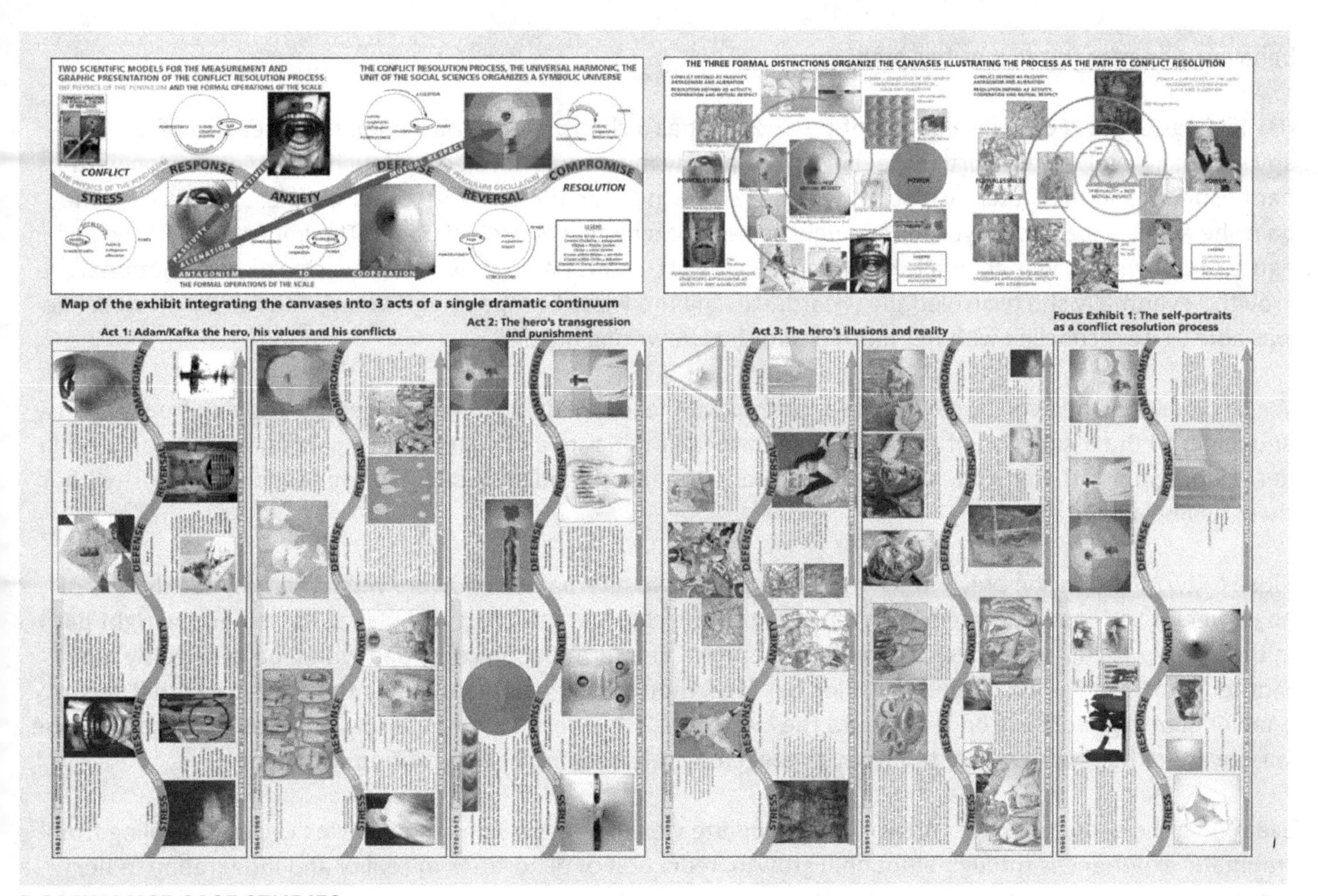

DOMINANCE CASE STUDIES

Dominance is a modality whose six-role syndromal sequence evolves from stress to anger, generating paranoia, eliciting strong defensiveness, setbacks as social strain that brings a person to therapy. Compromises as resolutions are very hard to come by. Two patients are presented here. Segmet was a teacher in conflict with the school and parent-teacher relations. Kathy was in personal distress, restless and needy, unable to function as a mother, not feeling good about herself. Emotionally deprived in her early childhood, she had a lifelong experience with therapies that left her confused and traumatized.

Segmet, the mighty black cat

Segmet, (name of an Egyptian black cat personifying dominance,) is a good example of the pathology of dominance and of the difficult course of healing as this unfolds in therapy. We are presenting the evolution of her therapy as a cycle of relational developments. These are documented by art and commentaries summed up by the patient, who describes the emotional significance of the developments in the course of her therapy.
S. was a 47 year old, married, school teacher, with no children. Her case is unique as a record of developments because in her metaphors she consistently identified critical figures in her life as the same characters diligently executed during the course of her therapy. She presented herself as a black cat, the therapist as a wizard, her husband as the Siamese cat and her mother as a dog.

In the course of therapy we observe the evolution of her relationship with her mother, the origin of intense conflicts during developmental experiences. The original extremely troubled relationship was transformed in the course of her therapy. Mother was originally portrayed as a rabid vicious dog with the black cat in her mouth; at the end she was transformed upon termination to a dachshund licking her face.

We observe her relationship with her husband in the beginning magnified as a loving support person. This relationship evolved through multiple crises to portray him finally as her victim, as an observer of her madness, her pathology, her anger portrayed as fires; upon termination she was accepting responsibility for this odd behavior. She recognized it as her problem.

Her feelings of exaggerated valuation of the therapist as a charismatic wizard upon the inception of the therapy gradually evolved as I hurt her feelings by relatively minor acts of rejection, such as a joint session with her husband, and then later by placing her as a couple in group therapy with other couples. We observe the pain she experienced portrayed as feeling stepped upon by the wizard's slippers. The importance of the loving figure of the wizard, was gradually reduced to a gray cat, I considered it as a positive sign of her emotional growth, eventually she overruled the wizard, stealing the wizard's cape, magic wand, and building a wall. She was able to be reconciled with her mother and thus 'rewriting history'.

We also observe the evolution of her relationship with fellow patients in group therapy evolving from jealousy and anger to the expression of gratitude accepting their criticism and support. In a parallel way she evolved in her relationship with her students from being very threatened and controlling to experiencing comfort with them having a good time.

Close to termination she presented herself in front of two alternatives: flowers versus flames, her choices of anger versus self-restraint; she became aware of these choices in relating and placed herself on the right path in the crossroads of independence from the therapist. The termination coincided with feeling loved by her mother, portrayed as a dachshund leaking her face, though with darts landing on the dog's back; that security enabled her to go forward on her path to the classroom, while terminating therapy. She was not cured but she was aware of her problem, the tendency to feel easily rejected and becoming livid with anger.

Examining the evolution of her artwork we recognize viewing the sessions the evolving cycles of healing from traumatic experiences through emotional growth, reduction of distortions of reality and moderation in her responses. The art shows sessions resolving the key conflict, her excruciating sensitivities. She is a person who wishes to be loved like a cat, but who readily feels hurt and like a cat arches her back, hisses at the stressor, and withdraws to protect herself. We see six cycles of overcoming the tendency to hiss and run away and instead be able to endure the pain and instead of distorting experiences as too hurtful to become able to deal with them. This growth process is well illustrated in the table of cycles of conflict resolutions generated in the course of two years in therapy: 12/3/83-2/27/86.

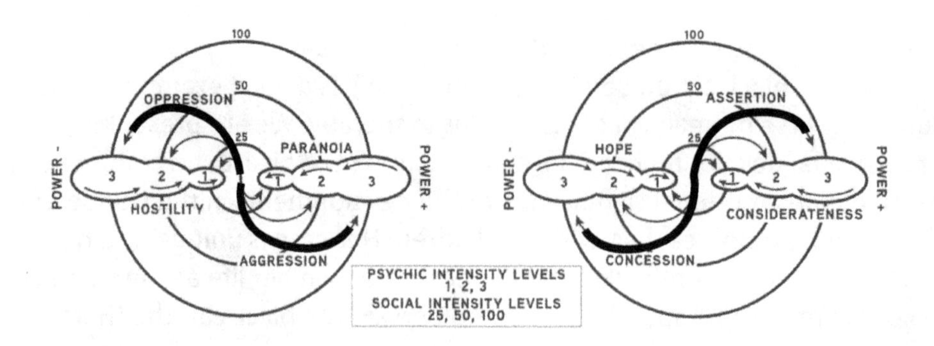

Her original emotional state was based on feeling invalidated by her mother, portrayed as a vicious dog engulfing her as a black cat and perceiving the therapist as the rescuer as a loving, caring wizard, reversing her state of depression and anger.

See corresponding images on page 254.

In the course of therapy she asserted herself by sharing her anger at her mother, who was transformed into a loving dachshund licking her face. She also reduced her need for a loving authority by transforming him into a gray cat and stealing his wand and cape. She identified her anger, which needed management and that she could grow from a needy child to a responsible adult.

STRESS

Images illustrate her stress as her need for love

SIX CYCLES OF CONFLICT RESOLUTION in the COURSE OF THERAPY

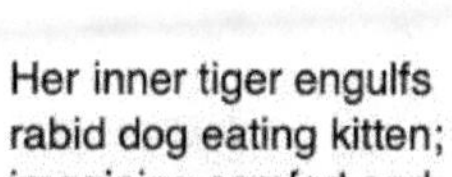

COMPROMISE

Resolution as empowerment in overcoming need for love

12/3/83 Kitties in Love

Loved and embraced by husband

Her inner tiger engulfs rabid dog eating kitten; imagining comfort and safety with wizard

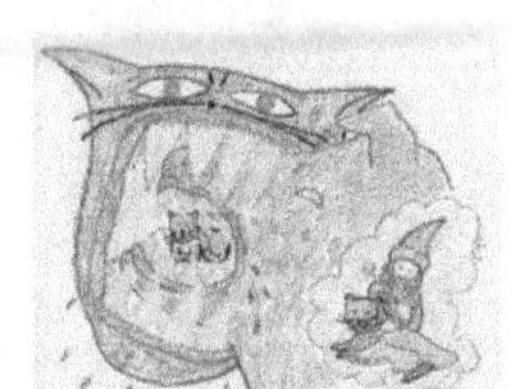

10/04/84 Who's Who

10/15/84 Yes You May

Feeling loved, kissing wizard, sees him as silver cat in the bubble, i.e. similar to herself

She is able to handle rejection by silver cat wizard, who holds cat with friendly dog; rabid dog is exiting the scene

12/07/84 Agape/ Nurture

01/01/85 Off the Hook

Feeling self-acceptance by doctor reviving her from grave where she felt buried by parental rejection upon the birth of sibling at age four; feels "taken off the hook" by doctor

She experiences growth in surviving rejection felt by the alliance of husband and doctor

03/13/85 Through the Cracks

04/04/85 The Circus

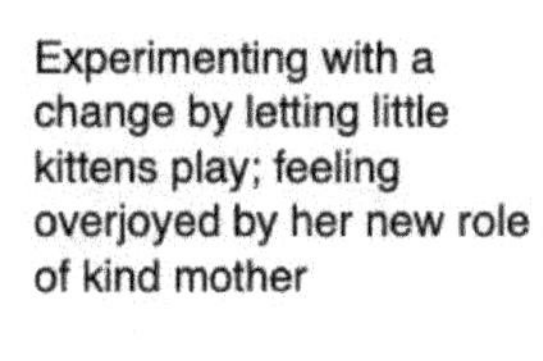

Experimenting with a change by letting little kittens play; feeling overjoyed by her new role of kind mother

Achieves reversibility of roles as she takes on the power of the caring doctor

06/21/85 Deep Is My Power

10/02/85 30 Second Count-down

Self-awareness of her escalation of anger; she begins to understand its dynamics and takes responsibility for angry episodes

Achieves individuation: acknowledges her ability to choose between anger and love: she chooses the good (love)

01/01/86 Moment of Choice

01/06/86 Dawning of an Age

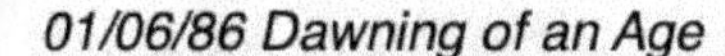

Rewriting history feeling loved by mother, which enables her to act responsibly

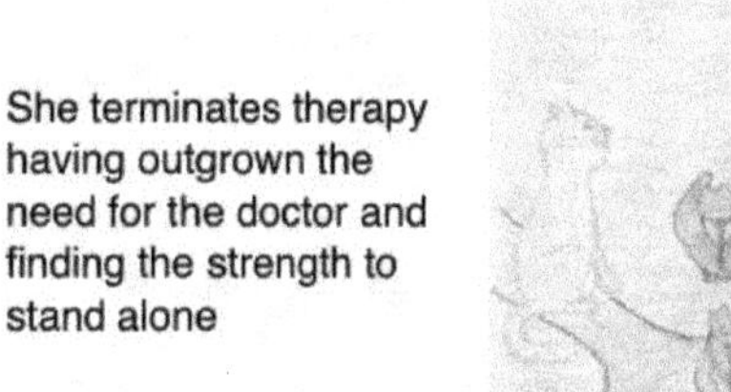

She terminates therapy having outgrown the need for the doctor and finding the strength to stand alone

02/27/86 The Dream Fades

RESPONSE

STRESS

12/03/83 *Kitties In Love*

Black cat and Siamese cat on pillows; loving, happy, content. Siamese protective of black cat who had been treated roughly by other cats (school principal, other authorities). Black cat had received magic mouse meat from two senior cats, had felt her troubles melt away and had retained the magic.

2/15/84 *Keys*

Black cat and Siamese cat on boat in Hawaii, embracing, tails entwined. Golden key in "bubble" inset. Black cat had been to necromancers for resolving psychic problems. Sees future as brighter because "only the invisible is changed and therein lies the universal key." Black cat feels ruinous evil thoughts can become a pattern, one which can be "unlearned".

ANXIETY

6/1/84 *Who's Who?*

Black cat and Siamese cat "in the same place at the same time". Wizard in background with magic wand. Black cat asking wizard to separate the cats and put them in almost the same place, being capable of reversing. Black cat feels guilty if she is in a better position; angry if she is less comfortable. She does not believe that the Siamese cat "doesn't mind". Conflict of guilt/anger toward mother; neediness; repressed assertiveness becoming hostility.

DEFENSE

6/84 *Try or die, and if you don't try hard enough you'll die anyway*

Black cat in mouth of vicious dog. Two wizards in background, one going "wrong way" off page, also, small figure with whip and indicated swear words. Dog: "More! Not enough!" Cat: "I tried! Pleeeze!" Dog identified as mother and/or father (rabid/psychotic). As a child she was constantly pushed beyond what she felt were her capabilities. Double wizard, fear he had abandoned her twice when she was demanding and possessive regarding therapy.

REVERSAL

6/15/84 *The Last Tears*

Rabid dog flogging weeping black cat. Wizard with wand coming to rescue with the Siamese cat who is bringing a pair of golden wings to the black cat. Repeat of mother's demanding injunctions about grades in school. Wizard shown "going in right direction" toward black cat to help her "utilize substitute experiences to make her whole". Issue of hostility covered up by politeness when anger at injustices or abandonment is repressed. Issue of birth of younger brother and Betsy's abandonment by mother through denial of affection.

COMPROMISE

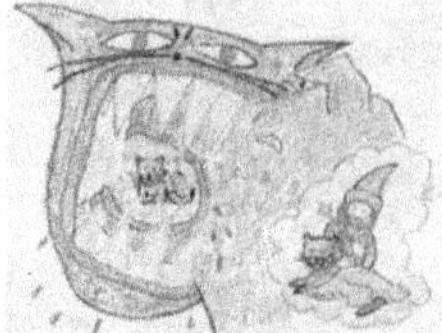

10/04/84 *Who's Who?*

Black cat in mouth of rabid dog whose face is superimposed on an angry black cat with huge teeth. "Bubble" insert shows black cat seeing wizard with herself on his lap, protected. "Eat or be eaten" theme as cat turns into fierce panther, defeating the vicious dog. Black cat not caught in "generational curse" of viciousness because she has a loving heart. She returns to the wizard and the Siamese cat.

RESPONSE

STRESS

10/15/84 and 10/22/84
Yes You May

Black cat kissing wizard. "Bubble" insert of wizard with cat; question mark over cat's head. "Double place" trick of wizard being on pedestal yet with cat. Wizard now seen as beautiful silver gray cat, less awesome. Cat challenged wizard about "magic potion" (medication) but felt accepted by him; wants to kiss him but "dares to hope she won't be kicked".

11/14/84 *Mind Warp*

Wizard's feet in golden shoes kicking black cat and Siamese cat over flames of volcano. Pele, goddess of the volcano sketched in background. The cats tried to buy plane tickets but were kicked out by "a stranger in expensive shoes." Cats "are a gang of two and should stay that way". (Betsy and Richard)

ANXIETY

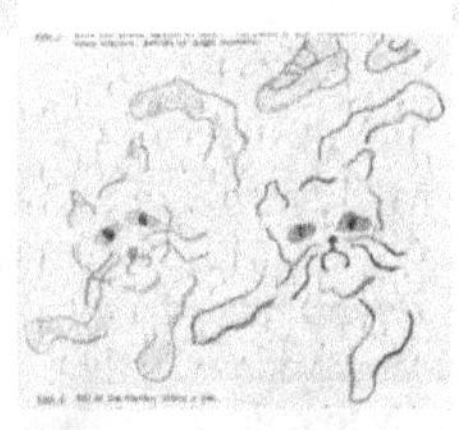

11/14/84 (2) *Costly Shoes Do Not A Magician Make*

Wizard's feet in golden shoes. Black cat and Siamese cat in rain or water, bedraggled, kicked out of wizard's garden. Hostility toward wearer of shoes. "Self-sufficiency is the best bet but I never learn."

DEFENSE

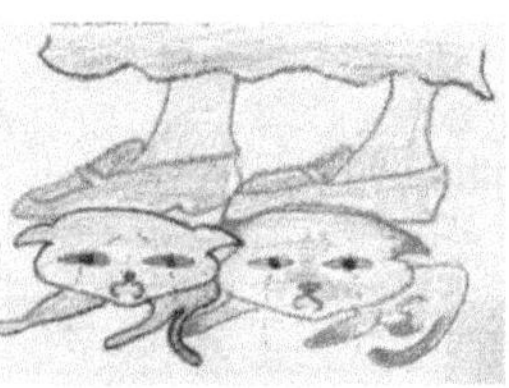

11/15/84 *No, You May Not!*

Black cat and Siamese cat crying, being stepped on by wizard in golden shoes. Black cat had brought a gift of blossoms but the wizard was allergic to them and annoyed and unappreciative. Continuing hostility toward wizard. "They should have relied only upon other cats."

REVERSAL

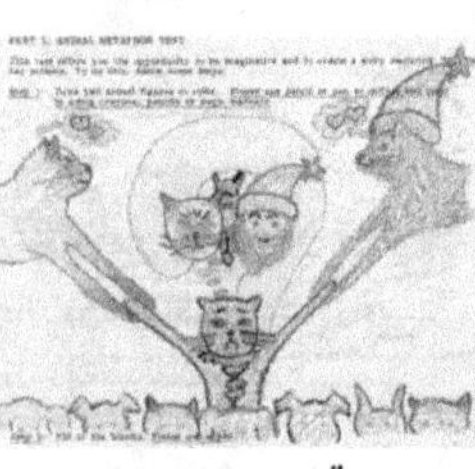

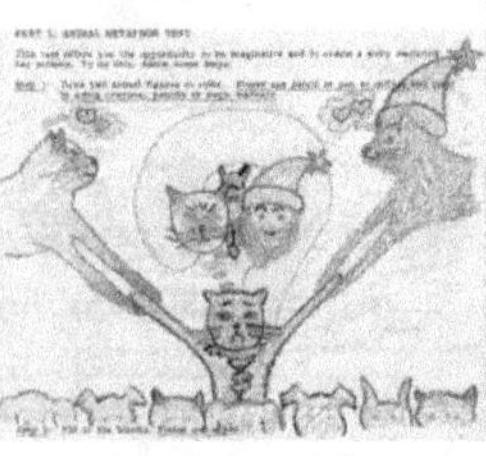

11/26/84 *The "Club"*

Siamese cat and silver cat (wizard) pulling black cat in two directions, but with love (hearts). "Bubble" inset shows black cat thinking of wizard, Siamese and herself all together, but with a question mark. Figures of other animals below symbolizing group members. Controversy between Betsy and Richard about attending group. He does not wish to, thus going against the wizard. Black cat torn between husband and therapist. Members of "club" (group) shown as dogs making cats uncomfortable, "no matter how small and apparently friendly."

COMPROMISE

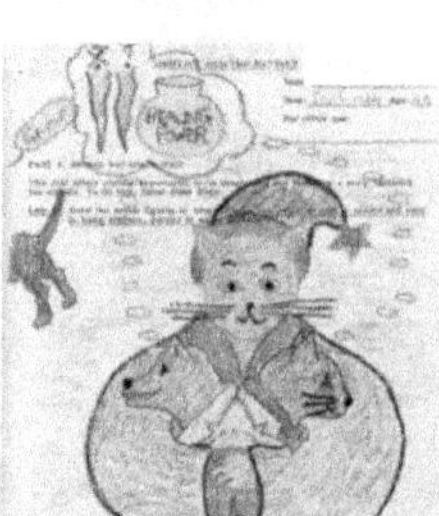

12/07/84 *Agape/ Nurture*

Wizard (now silver cat) wearing magenta robes and holding black cat and friendly dog. Vicious dog going out of picture. "Bubble" insert showing jar of healing power, teeth from rabid dog. Black cat's capacity for love helps tame the dog, through the wizard/ cat who is capable of loving both of them. Wizard seen as more humanized: episode of Dr. Levis putting his coat over Betsy and introducing her to his mother. This session followed by Christmas gifts with relevant, artistic messages, home made bread and butter.

STRESS

01/01/85 *Off the Hook*

Silver cat (wizard) helping black cat down from a hook. "Bubble" insert of black cat in grave with stone saying "Betsy, 12/23/43, age 4, broken heart" (time of birth of her brother and withholding of love by mother. Black cat now has gifts for the wizard instead of the unappreciative dog. She sees the appreciation and "must take lessons from the wizard cat who is a masterful; dog-trainer." Reconciliation with therapy rather than

RESPONSE

1/15/85 *Eight Hour Marathon*

Siamese cat and black cat together with image of wizard/cat behind them, filling the page. Siamese cat is angry and hurt over supposed "sins" of wizard. Black cat feels Siamese is jealous over her love for the wizard and is distorting any supposed slights. She wishes to assist the Siamese but doesn't want to be called controlling.

ANXIETY

1/23/85 *Pandora's Box*

Vicious dog in box under table, partially trapped by carpet. Black cat pawing at carpet. Large broom to sweep things under the rug. Arm and hand (silver paw) of wizard with wand. Pot of "healing power" on table. Black cat afraid to let dog out but does not want to cause death by closing box. Waited for wizard to let the dog out and discovered it had no teeth. Observation that dogs need training. "The patience and love of the wizard will flow into the

DEFENSE

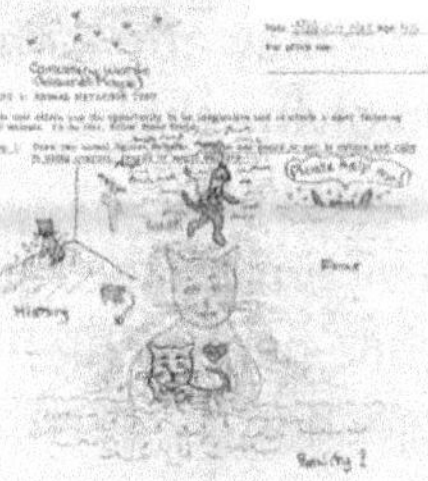

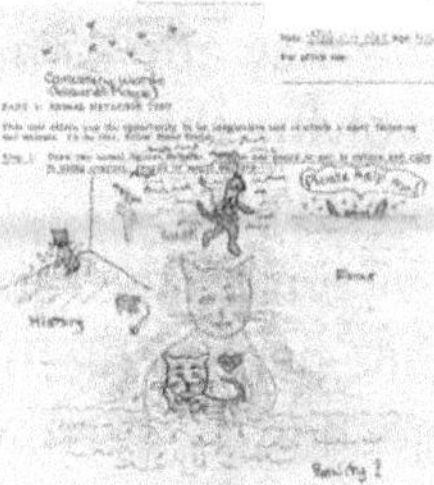

2/20/85 *Release*

Multiple drawing: "fear", cat drowning saying "please help me"; "history", cat in corner of room crying, taboo sign as cross; "luck" cat with book walking; pond with "caressing words (wizard's magic); "reality?" silver cat holding black cat above deep water. Black kitten felt the presence of the cat/wizard as "a long-lost caress". Hard cold pain was dispersed with tears, releasing her feelings from childhood. She sees therapy as "a much wished-for second chance". Realignment with the wizard as he wraps her in a magenta towel to dry her.

REVERSAL

3/06/85 *Dance of Death*

Black cat with devilish horns killing the vicious dog (mother and/or father) with the silver cat (Dr. Levis) looking on. The vicious dog is also shown departing in the upper right corner. A newt in the lower right holds the scales of justice signifying permission for the patient to be free from guilt.

COMPROMISE

3/13/85 *Through the Cracks*

The siamese cat and the wizard have become inflated by a capricious sprinkling of golden dust and have entered into a new alliance with each other. In order to escape suffocation, the black cat escapes through a crack in the floor.

STRESS

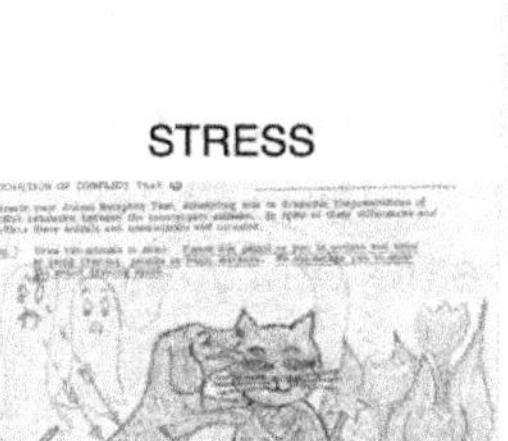

01/06/86 *Dawning of an Age*

The black cat has had a breakthrough by realizing that she can rewrite history, or change her relationship to the past. The copper dachshund represents her mother who thinks of history as "carved in stone." Nonetheless the mother is giving the black cat her blessing. The black cat can accept the coexistence of hateful behavior and love coming from the dog. This is a good way for her to resolve the past and to let go of the feeling of being overly critical of herself.

RESPONSE

01/28/86 *Paths of Destiny*

The black cat is faced with the choice of which path to take to reach her ideal, future self. In her mind she has her mother's blessing, symbolized by the dog inside the thought bubble. Feeling this she is able to navigate a combination of paths and arrive at her destiny, shown as a teacher before her students.

ANXIETY

01/29/86 *Fire Without a Cause*

The black cat has been hurt by a stray dart that hit her when the other animals were just playing around. They are mystified by her extreme reaction. She thinks that they hurt her purposely. Because she feels so small, she reacts to her hurt and vulnerability by puffing herself up and flying into flames.

DEFENSE

02/27/86 *The Dream Fades*

The patient has chosen to end therapy. She perceives a change in her relationship with the doctor. She thinks that he is being too harsh with her by playing practical jokes on her, and persisting in doing so even though she has asked him to stop. She feels that the covenant between them has been broken beyond repair. She feels that if she continues to argue with Dr. Levis and to try to change him, she degrades herself, so she must walk away. The many flowers on her path belie a happy ending and perhaps signify that she has outgrown her therapy because she has been healed.

Four phases in the healing process
Examining changes through the therapy we may adopt the format of the deck of cards by analyzing the transformation of her attitude and power as evolving through four phases by placing her art sequences in the quadrants of the four corresponding relational modalities.
1. Therapy began identifying herself as a victim of her very critical and demanding school principal. She also portrayed her mother as a vicious dog while perceiving the therapist as a magical loving wizard. Soon afterwards she showed her vulnerability to rejection by portraying the wizard's shoes stepping upon two cats, herself and her husband. The trauma was sharing me with her husband in a session and later with fellow patients in group therapy. She felt betrayed. Thus the first phase was experiencing submissive antagonism in both her traumatic relationship with her mother and in the inception of a relationship with myself.

2. Staying in therapy dealing with her sensitivities of dependence, rejection and anger she entered the phase of dominant antagonism, which began by admitting the hurt she experienced upon the birth of her brother at the age of 4. This phase began with her emerging from her grave delivered by the wizard; during this phase she expressed her massive anger at her mother, killing her as the rabid dog and burying her under the carpet. The phase was completed as she tolerated rejection upon the alliance of her husband and myself transformed to a silver cat. She illustrated this rejection and compromise as 'falling through the cracks'.

3. The next phase of personal growth is marked by ongoing confrontations with the therapist in a phase of dominant cooperation. She examined critically her hurts and reconciliation with the doctor yet consistently robbing him of his power. She also learned about moderating herself.

4. The last phase was one of submissive cooperation during which she was able to feel loved by her redefined mother and was able to confront her own problematic reactions of anger. She was the cat in flames, while her mother, the dachshund, her husband, the Siamese cat, and the doctor, the grey cat, were helpless bystanders watching the cat enraged, by both expanding her body and surrounding herself with flames. She terminated therapy, accepting responsibility for her feeling readily hurt and becoming excessively angry. We agreed that her therapy was a course of immunization shots in dealing progressively with rejections, learning about restraining her sensitivities, and restraining her massive reactions to hurt.

This case study addresses first, the importance of a relational diagnosis, the dynamics of dominance; the relational modality explained her behaviors and her anxieties, her distortions of reality as paranoia associated to her aggressiveness. She was cooperative when feeling loved and antagonistic upon feeling hurt. The tendency to claim power and the fears of others taking it away from her evoking belligerent reactions and the consequences.

The second point: the method of metaphors helps to became conscious of the pattern of sensitivities and anger, by establishing a visual and text analytical record that is easily translated into viewing a pattern. The choice of a cat explained her identity as an animal that is sensitive to love and to rejection. The patient enjoyed this approach and she became aware of her vulnerability to emotional setbacks; she visualized the pattern of her exquisite sensitivities as traumatic experiences and her predictable overreactions, including my seeing her jointly with her husband and feeling upstaged in her seat, feeling stepped upon by being in group therapy, the sense of dying upon the birth of her brother at the age of four, upon realizing that she was not unique, her sensitivities to criticism by her mother. She learned to overcome these feelings of rejection by reducing her dependency needs for an exclusive relationship with a magical authority. She was able to terminate therapy feeling reconciled with her mother, whom she had experienced as a sadist.

The third point to observe is examining her therapy as cyclic developments along four types of relating utilizing the template of the deck of cards. We clearly recognize four relationally distinct phases in the course of the therapeutic relationship following the pattern of the four modalities marking the emotional evolution of her personal growth in learning how to deal rationally rather than emotionally with stressful realities.

Four phases of growth in the course of therapy.

Phase 1: Submissive antagonistic

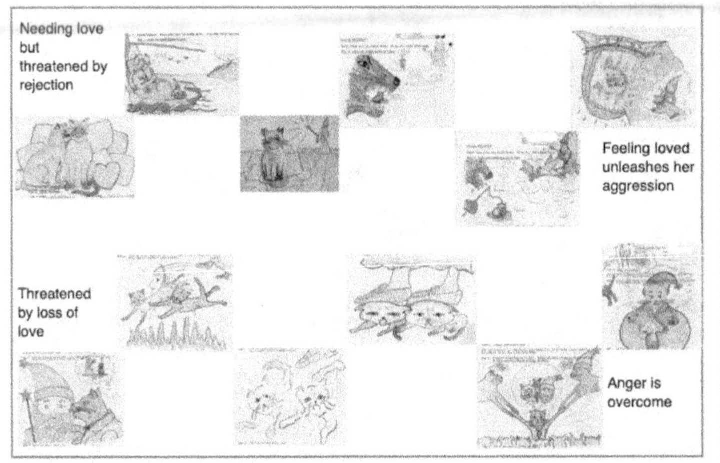

Phase 3: Dominant cooperative

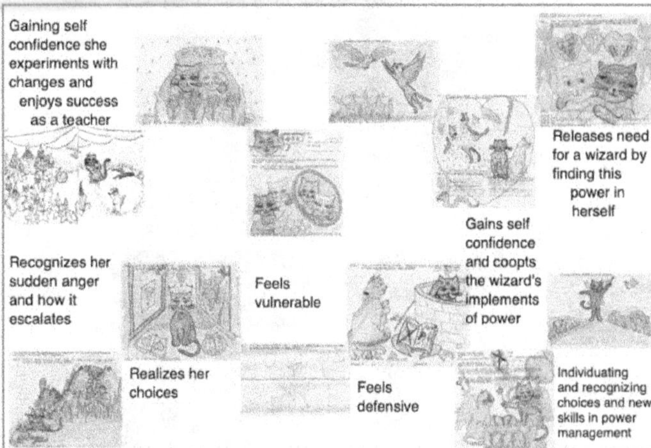

Phase 4: Submissive cooperative

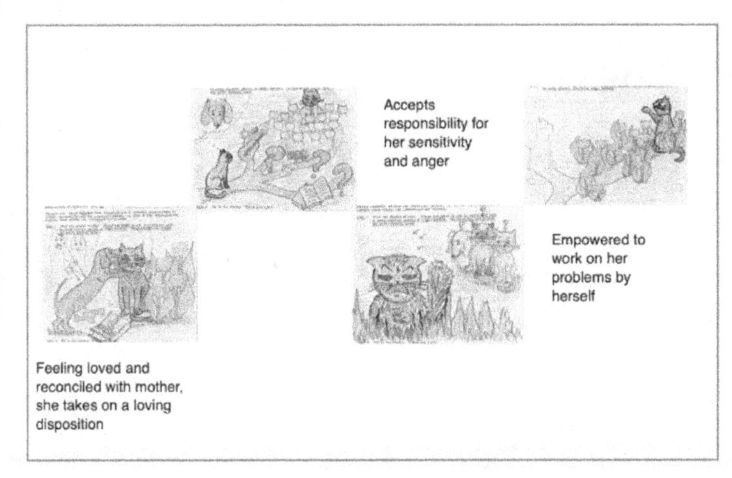

Phase 2: Dominant antagonistic

This image illustrates the four distinct cycles of conflict resolutions in the course of her therapy.

Four phases in the healing process

Below we are examining the evolution of her responses to a number of relationships, first her relationship with her mother, second recognizing her problematic anger responses, third her relationship with the therapist, among many others, such as her relationship with the group members and the relationship with students.

1 Depiction of conflicts	2 Second phase
3 Third phase	4 Resolutions

For more information review the corresponding session narration by the patient following dates identified in the images and those of the narratives composed by the patient.

Evolving relationship with mother

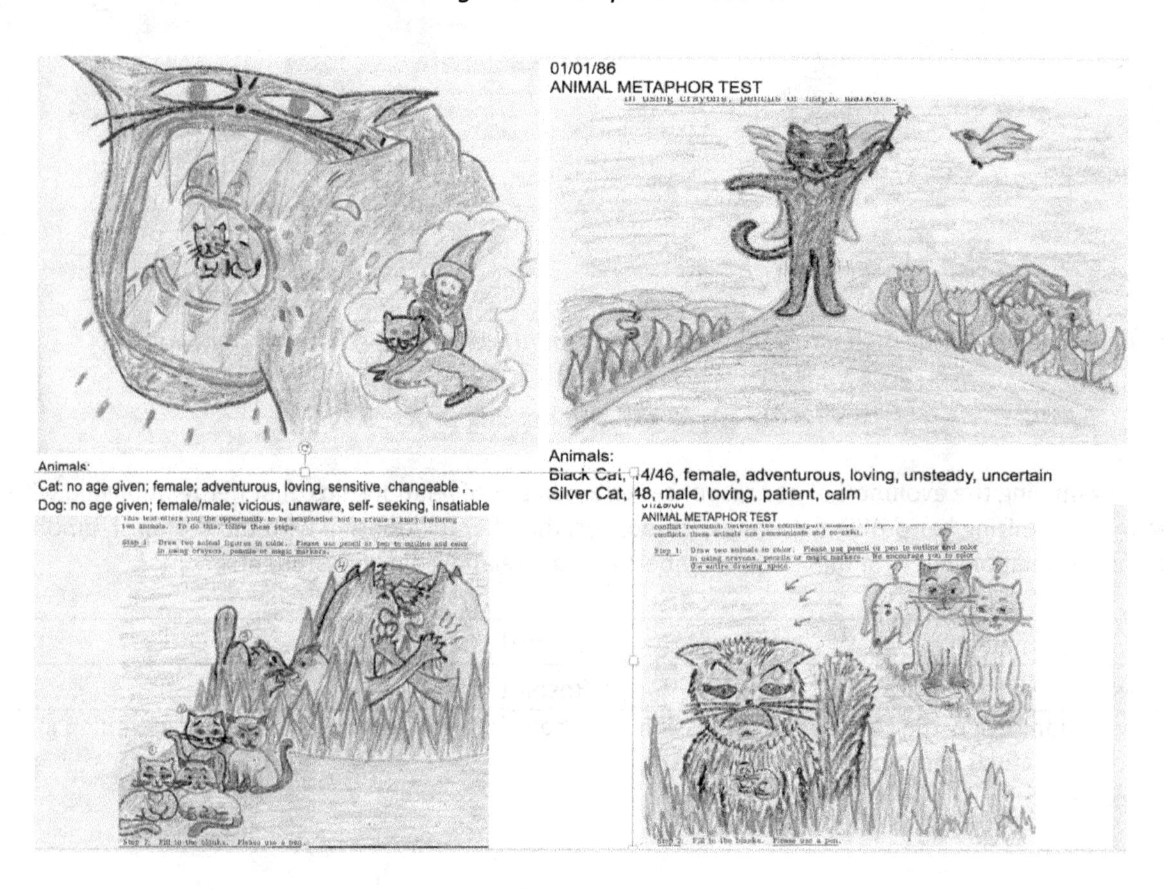

Evolving relationship with self, with husband, doctor, mother recognizing her anger generated by her own reactions independently of others but also recognizing that she has choices in the alternatives

Evolving relationship with her therapist, myself from a wizard, to a silver cat, to a fading grey cat.

Patient's essay

These drawings illustrate a four-year-old child's search for a mother who will love and accept her and help her to rejoice in the tasks of growing up. It is the heartwarming story of a second chance, symbolic and compressed in time, to recapture the magical world of an exuberant four-year-old and to nurture that love of life until it reaches the full bloom of maturity.

In retrospect, I would say that my life was perfect until I was four. At that point my brother was born and my mother, unable to cope with two children, began a series of illnesses (psychosomatic). During my school years I was an excellent student, but mother was never satisfied. Father withdrew into alcoholism as did mother. By the time I was fourteen our upper middle-class home was chaotic, although material supports were plentiful. After graduating near the top of my high school class college was a near disaster due to constant conflict with mother about grades. Since college I have been married, divorced, and remarried and have worked mainly as a teacher. I have felt that I could never do enough for my students and have been in a number of scrapes with school officials and other teachers. In December 1983, I sought psychiatric help because of constant anxiety, intense anger, and real questions about where my life was going.

At the beginning of therapy, I had a very poor concept of how it could work for me and was interested primarily in drug treatment. The animal metaphors captured my imagination because I saw a chance to make believe I was a child again. What I did not see is how these metaphors would help me tap inner resources that were alive and well but thoroughly hidden. Each picture and story are the conscious expression of unconscious feelings, but the "cuteness" of the animals makes the feelings easier to express and share and lends a sense of safety to a transaction that could otherwise be too dangerous to attempt. The expression and sharing of love and tenderness through the metaphors makes these feelings "bigger than life" so that they can be held and cherished rather than drowned out with hate and fear. And love that can be held onto (internalized) is the fabric of the joy of life.

Kitties In Love 12/3/83

In this initial metaphor I show myself (black cat) and my husband, Anubis (Siamese cat), in a loving position. The story mentions some other people (attacking cats) who have caused me trouble. Dr. Levis (grey cat in story, but not in picture) is a minor character who shares a bit of "magic mousemeat" (drugs) with the kitties. At the end of the story the two kitties are able to continue in their present lifestyle, which is quite luxurious and filled with friends. The quality is improved because the drugs ("magic mousemeat") cause my troubles to melt away without effort.

The seeds of resolution are present even in this story, however unrecognizable. The main problem, excessive self-demands and explosive anger is present but projected onto outside forces. The helper is present, but in a non-related and "magical" way. The solution is present but only as something to passively ingest, rather than actively work upon and integrate.

2/15/84

The picture shows me (black cat) and Anubis (Siamese cat) on an anticipated trip to Hawaii. After the months on medication I am feeling better, a fact which is attributed to Dr. Levis (mentioned in the text as a necromancer or wizard). In the text I recognize superficially that enjoyment or trouble is caused by learned attitudes which can be unlearned: "After a visit to the lair of the necromancer the Kitty Girl's soul emerged from the dungeon of the evil spirits. It's the power of the mind," mused the Kitty Girl.

I am starting to see conflict as mainly internal, but the solution will depend upon a wizard who is beneficent but still mainly unrelated and inaccessible.

Who's Who? 6/1, 6/11/84

This is the first drawing showing Dr. Levis (wizard). He is shown with myself (black cat) and my husband (Siamese cat) occupying the same place at the same time by virtue of his magic.

The conflict was precipitated by my husband taking more attention than I thought he should have and relates to childhood preoccupations with sibling rivalry that was set off and perpetuated by a needy and domineering mother. The question is how to share mother's love without losing out.

The metaphor is significant because (1) it represents Dr. Levis as a magic person with curative powers, (2) shows a love triangle with sibling rivalry, and (3) by its very subject matter shows my deepening involvement in the transference aspects of therapy. Dr. Levis is still distant, but now very relevant. The text shows that the "trick" he will perform will be psychic in nature because he cannot transcend the laws of physical reality. From this point forward Dr. Levis will become increasingly important as I take full grasp of a second chance to grow up.

Interim Notes (after 6/11/84)

Shortly after this Dr. Levis made a daring move. He asked if his 15-year-old daughter could sit in on one of my individual sessions. I was uneasy but obliged him, so Melissa listened, and I talked with him becoming less and less self-conscious about her presence. At the end of the session he put his arm around me and said, "You have shared your session with Melissa and Melissa has shared her Daddy with you."
As I walked away, I saw the two cats in the same place at the same time, being petted simultaneously on the head by the wizard's hand. This, in a microcosm, was sharing mother's love without losing out.

6/14/84

Try or Die, and If You Don't Try Hard Enough You'll Die Anyway

Mother is shown twice here: as the vicious dog and as a swearing human figure with a whip. I (black cat) am about to be devoured for failing to meet the elusive standards of the vicious dog. The dual position

(approach-retreat) of Dr. Levis (wizard) is my fearful response to his being initially unavailable in a major emotional crisis. Will he or won't he rescue me from the cruelty of the vicious dog: can he be trusted?
The question of trust is explicitly raised because of my deepening involvement hinted at in the previous metaphor (6/1/84). The fact that the wizard is shown in a dual position is key: I felt abandoned by Dr. Levis but am still hoping that this is only apparent or momentary but not real and permanent. My deepest wish, for love to be preserved, is first expressed here and will become the central theme in all of the metaphors to come.

The Last Tears 6/15/84

Here I (kitten) am being beaten to shreds (figuratively) by the vicious dog (mother). Nothing I did was ever good enough for her; love was conditional. This pattern I have internalized since my teen years. Dr. Levis (wizard) and my husband (Siamese cat) are coming with a pair of wings so that I can fly away from the vicious dog. In this way Dr. Levis is portrayed as a vital step in breaking this pattern of hate, frustration, and conditional love. The text of my story predicts that "The wizard will help the kitten to leave the vicious dog in her place. This will be possible because the kitten will receive a redirection of energy from the wizard."

Who's Who? 10/4/84

This picture is a portrayal of my sudden outbursts of anger. The pattern is always the same: I (kitten) try to please someone (dog) who does not appreciate (or appears not to) my efforts. I then make a vicious counter-attack (panther) which is much more intense than the situation calls for.

The bubble inset is the first illustration of Dr. Levis (wizard) in an explicitly loving and caring (motherly) role, representing movement from magic to love, from hocus-pocus to an openly caring, human relationship. In retrospect, this part of the picture is a request for permission to love and be loved. I symbolically asked Dr. Levis to accept my love as that of a perfect four-year-old child. His warmth and acceptance during the session showed that he symbolically granted permission. This is a milestone in the drama of a little girl's wish for a mother. The drama and its resolution are symbolic and compressed in time.

Yes, You May 10/15, 10/22/84

This drawing shows two important elements: reduction of distance between me (cat) and Dr. Levis (wizard), and the intensification of warm feelings and acceptance.
In the main part of the picture I am kissing Dr. Levis, while being protectively covered by his jacket. I have moved toward him in an open, loving expression, whereas earlier pictures show him moving toward me with a "magic" touch.

The bubble inset shows Dr. Levis on his "wizard's pedestal" but I am (hesitantly and questioningly) on the pedestal with him. I am beginning to see him in more human terms. The impetus for this is the memory of his acceptance, months earlier, of my refusal to take certain medication. I sensed after the fact his distaste for challenges to his authority. Thus, I saw him as more human (subject to conflict) and also as more loving (accepting my choice).

11/84

During the fall of 1984 my husband and I entered group therapy with Dr. Levis, while I continued individual therapy. Frequently things did not go well. In group there was constant conflict and/or disappointment with other members. I was in a situation of intense sibling rivalry with other group members and my husband was fearful of being controlled by Dr. Levis. My husband was also increasingly jealous of my very intense relationship with Dr. Levis. By mid-November the strain had reached an unbearable pitch. A misunderstanding about fee payment prompted three metaphors of rejection and aggression. In the first, the wizard is shooing the two cats out of his garden. They are wet and bedraggled, as if beaten and thrown into water. The second metaphor shows the wizard kicking the two cats into a volcano that has a fire-goddess above it. The story text indicates that the cats get revenge: "They made an offering of gin and pork to Pele, goddess of the volcano. Gratified, she turned the lava flow so that it engulfed the shoes. This made a "cast" out of their wearer, which is now a tourist attraction near the fire pit."

The third metaphor shows the wizard stepping on the cats. The "vicious dog" theme appears in the text in disguised form: the black cat brought a gift to the wizard, but the gift was not appreciated, and hate was given in return for the gift. She believes she can prevent further problems by having her vocal cords cut! (self-punishment). These metaphors represent history. The wizard (Dr. Levis, the new mother) distributes love to people other than myself and does nothing when these others (group members) hurt me. My efforts (fee payment, and it was his office's error, not mine) are not enough so he scolds me. My reaction is rage.

The Club 11/25/84

Here I (black cat) am caught in a conflict between Dr. Levis (silver wizard cat) and my husband (Siamese cat). The issue is group therapy which both of us disliked due to a series of frustrations and disappointments vis a vis the members' response to us. I preferred to give the group one more try to please Dr. Levis, but my husband had serious reservations (underlying jealousy) about Dr. Levis and wanted no further part of group therapy.

During a joint therapy session nothing was resolved between my husband and Dr. Levis. In addition, I was deeply hurt when Dr. Levis accused us of not wanting to "deal with real issues". Feeling battered, I reluctantly wrote a letter of termination stating: "I feel ambivalent about that group, not totally negative. If it were only me, I'd probably try it again for you. Nevertheless, Anubis is against it. I have to live with him and not with you, so my choice has to be with him." I had hoped that either my husband would soften of his own accord or Dr. Levis would succeed in disarming him. Note that when these possibilities did not work out, I was unable to assert my wish to continue with Dr. Levis in the face of my husband's rage and jealousy. Perhaps the most noteworthy element of this metaphor is not even noted in the story text: the wizard has become another cat, albeit still with the magic hat of the wizard. In a sense the wizard has become more accessible, more like me—no small development in a story which is essentially a quest for love, acceptance, and self-acceptance.

Agape/Nurture 12/7/84

Here is the pivotal metaphor, the turning point between hesitant, tentative, unbelieving affection and the intense, trusting devotion of a four-year-old child.
The wizard cat (Dr. Levis) chases the vicious dog (mother, internalized rejecting) away. He lovingly holds a two-headed creature, both dog and cat. This creature is my loving self (cat) and a tame version of my vitriolic self (dog). The healing power cream is linked with this loving scene. The distant, unpictured necromancer of the first metaphors is at last transformed to a loving, accepting cat much like myself— accessible, comprehensible and truly present.

In the text I recognized for the first time that the power of therapy comes largely from myself. I saw this in terms of love, which is the power behind all growth and development: "The love which she (cat) can feel and express becomes real; the wizard cannot put love in her. He can only receive it lovingly, with a caressing spirit, and therein lies his power...But I have love, although it was side-tracked when I was only four. It remains to rediscover that love through expression, and the receiving will take care of itself."

Off the Hook 1/1/85

At Christmas I brought homemade bread and butter for Dr. Levis which he appreciated enormously. Later I realized that he had not commented on the quality of the food.

This experience took me "off the hook" of my experience with mother. Nothing I did for mother was quite right, nothing was perfect simply because of the love it symbolized. Mother neither received nor gave love unconditionally. For the first time the love that I gave was valued above the gift itself, unconditionally.

The story text predicts that the silver cat (Dr. Levis) will help the black cat (me) tame the vicious dog (mother). In this way the black kitten will gradually outgrow the need to re- experience the critical rejection of the vicious dog. This will be entirely symbolic; there is no real dog because my mother is dead.
The inset at the top of the page shows the black cat emerging from a grave. She died of a broken heart when brother was born, and mother's love became scarce. A spiritual resurrection will take place as I "re-learn what to expect from myself and others...I will accept a symbolic substitute experience, compressed in time."

Eight-Hour Marathon 1/15/85

This story deals with the ongoing conflict between Anubis(Siamese cat) and Dr. Levis (wizard cat in background).Anubis has felt rejected by Dr. Levis and also jealous of my strong positive relationship with Dr. Levis. I am caught in the middle. I spent countless hours with Anubis trying to encourage him to reconcile with Dr. Levis and help him see that our own relationship is in no way compromised by my love (agape) for Dr.Levis.

Eventually these problems were resolved. Anubis confronted Dr. Levis with his "sins" and subsequently saw that no real sins had been committed. He saw that my love for Dr. Levis did not compromise my love for him. I, in turn, came to accept the fact that Anubis did not need the extremely close, dependent relationship with Dr. Levis that I wanted and needed. Consequently, I did not push him to lean on Dr. Levis in the way I leaned on Dr. Levis.

Pandora' s Box 1/23/85

Here memories of my mother are shown as a vicious (but toothless) dog emerging from a box that may be a coffin. I (black cat) am struggling to keep the box shut and hidden under the rug. The wizard cat (Dr. Levis) will guide me in looking at my feelings about mother and me.

My anger and guilt in relation to my mother were never a secret, but they were never resolved in any way, either. Showing the dog without teeth expresses a willingness to consider that perhaps mother never was as mighty as I had given her credit for, and also that perhaps she did not intend all the evil that seemed to emanate from her. The wizard will help the cat tame the dog. I am here preparing to accept a symbolic solution to the hate and guilt that has plagued me for years.

Release 2/20/85

In this story the black cat (me) is crying so many tears that she is almost drowning in the puddle that formed. The silver cat (now shown without the wizard's hat) (Dr. Levis) holds her up so she doesn't drown.

This is the beginning of the symbolic solution hinted at in the last story. I am anticipating that I will share my feelings of guilt, loneliness, fear and grief in a public setting (group therapy). The group will listen, and I will accept this as a symbolic resolution. In this metaphor I test the idea out with Dr. Levis, to see if my anticipated behavior will be "safe" (i.e., not rejected).

The small pictures represent an enormous burden that I was forced to carry alone starting at age 13. It was diabetes. Neither mother nor father could face telling me what was wrong. As a result, no one really told me; I caught on by making inferences when I was hospitalized. The insulin kit is shown as a lighted but as yet undetonated time bomb. Luck allows me to march along with everyone else for over thirty years, but the unshared, unexpressed fear of "complications" remains to this day. Sharing this metaphor with Dr. Levis made me feel that it would be safe to really let out some of these feelings in group therapy.

Dance of Death 3/6/85

Shortly after the previous metaphor I shared some of my deeper (guilt, loneliness, grief, frustration) feelings in group therapy. We did a psychodrama in which several of the women played the mean, rejecting and perfectionistic roles of my mother. I was myself, and one of the women played a strong, healthy alter-ego for me. I could see from the play that my mother deserved neither the power I gave her nor the guilt I felt in relation to her.

The metaphor shows me (black cat with horns) joyously but devilishly finishing off the death of the vicious dog, with the silver cat (Dr. Levis) pervading the scene and giving an "O.K.". The vicious dog is also shown departing in the upper righthand corner. The newt on the right holds the scales of justice, symbolizing permission for me not to feel guilty anymore, specifically for (1) arriving in Arizona three hours after mother's death instead of beforehand; (2) not really caring that mother was dead; (3) not really wanting mother's company; (4) not wanting to help her or be inconvenienced in any way. The cat and the brick wall (another woman) made me see why I had these feelings and how they were really quite natural, considering how rejecting mother had been over the years. Since that evening I have given almost no thought to these four points of guilt.

In retrospect, this picture contains the seeds of future development. The dog which I am joyously killing here can be seen not only as a release from guilt but also as the beginning of a release from mother's standards for me. These internalized standards were always forbiddingly high and have made me unable to accept and enjoy many of my own real accomplishments.

Through the Cracks 3/18/85

This metaphor shows a partnership between the Siamese cat (R) and the wizard (Dr. Levis) with the black cat (me) being left out and lost through the cracks in the floor. I want Anubis to be close to Dr. Levis, but when it happens, I'm afraid of losing out, as I did almost forty years ago when my brother was born.

The Circus Tent 4/4/85

This is a metaphor of myself with my class on the playground. Many of the "clown cats" (students) are angry and generally not about 'behaving themselves." Usually in real life I feel anxious about classroom control (my performance) and am consequently never satisfied with the children's behavior. This is a legacy from mother, whom I could never please. In this metaphor I consider alternative behavior; instead of being tense or angry, I make light of a situation which in reality was not all that bad anyway. The devil's horns express my uncertainty about the "rightness" of altering my stiff standards for myself.

Together 5/9/85

The picture, showing both cats crying with arms around each other, is a metaphor for a real happening. At the last session before Mother's Day I planned a symbolic gift: four flowers to symbolize the first four perfect years of my life. The previous evening at group therapy I felt that Dr. Levis had "talked over my head" and possibly betrayed a confidence, so I was in a state of turmoil. Consequently, I added a knife to the box with the flowers and invited him to cut up the flowers. In the story and in real life the silver cat (Dr. Levis) shook his head sadly and said, "Your love is very real and so is your hate." I suggested he could choose either the flowers or the knife as a gift, but he chose to accept both.

For the first time hate did not drown love out, or vice versa. The gift of flowers and a knife represents both sides of my ambivalence expressed simultaneously in one gesture, the essence of wholeness, completeness.

Never before have I received sadness in exchange for any of my behavior. It has always been anger or hate, *or* joy or love, and that is all I have ever given on a deep level in response to someone else. Sadness is a deeper feeling because in a sense it combines anger and love; sadness can be anger tempered with love.

The tears are falling like a spring rain that makes flowers bloom, and I will hold tight to this experience and never let it go.

Group Encounter 5/18/85

On this day our therapy group showed loving concern for me around a devastating incident in my professional life.

A child was absent on the day of the class play. Accustomed to the highest respect from the parents of my students over a period of seventeen years, I was incredulous that this child's mother failed to phone me at home as requested. The class saw my anger and used it against the absentee when she returned to school. I was further outraged that her mother lodged a complaint about this because that parent normally showed no cooperation or interest in the school at all.

The group spent most of the session trying to show me that it was in my interest to protect the child. They made me see the child's need for my love, even as I needed their love and the love of Dr. Levis.

After the session I saw that I could make a success or a failure of the group according to whether or not I used their love to help myself. I chose to accept their love, to let it flow into me and then from me to my students. I affirmed the love of the group rather than negating it.

I drew a picture as a gift for the group, a symbol for my acceptance of their loving concern the previous week. Note that Dr. Levis (silver cat) is shown as the same size as the other group members. He is "just another cat." The next metaphor celebrates this breakthrough.

Magic Mirror 5/30/85

It was Dr. Levis who pointed out that he was "just another cat" in the previous picture. At first, I resisted accepting what I intuitively knew: there is no wizard, only another cat like myself. The previous picture is a "snapshot" that the cats are discussing. The black cat (me) is uneasy and resistant and the silver cat (Dr. Levis) is both pleased at the marvelous change and a bit wistful about losing his power. This is the moment of awakening that he has hoped for and tried to make happen. In the story the cats happen to glance in a mirror and see themselves reflected, but the colors are reversed. In real life there will be a greater sense of equal partnership, more reversibility in the therapeutic relationship.

Flight of Fancy 6/12/85

The picture shows a winged cat aspiring to fly with a bird, which symbolizes ideals. There is a double interpretation intended: either Dr. Levis (cat) is shown aspiring freely toward his ideals (bird); or I (cat) am striving to identify with the free qualities of Dr. Levis (bird). It is a metaphor of ideally becoming one's self.

Here is an explicit statement of ideas introduced in the previous metaphor, "Magic Mirror". With the knife and the roses, the searing contradiction of love and hate was in a certain sense brought to a close. From here on I will be more free to consider ideals (identity) and less bound up in the search for love. I have leaped a decade from the concerns of a little girl to the wider world of a teenager. The question now is not how to get love, but how to be.

Shattered Wings 6/20/85

This metaphor represents a setback. The silver cat (Dr. Levis) has his back turned on the black cat (me), whose heart (and wings) are broken.

The precipitating cause was the arrival of the snarling dog (hated other patient) at group therapy on my last night before a long vacation. I felt betrayed because I could not cope with this person, and angry because Dr. Levis had angrily tried to guide my behavior toward her. I was also deeply disappointed because my hate and fear of the situation made it impossible to give warm feelings to the rest of the group. In the text my tactic is to see Dr. Levis later and to wait and see if he can still be trusted. Note that I did not jump to the conclusion that Dr. Levis could never be trusted again; I will wait rather than run away.

Deep Is My Power 6/21/85

This is the resolution of "Shattered Wings". The black cat (me) "waited" to see what the silver cat (Dr. Levis) would say about the incident at group therapy. His reply: "I thought you could handle it, but I guess you couldn't...I guess I expected too much from you." No more than that.

In these words, I heard his disappointment, and, in his tone, I heard him set these expectations aside. I felt him accept me as I was instead of being angry, because I had not met his hopes for me. He should not have had these expectations at all, but with his leadership it was easy not for me to put my love for him above what he should or should not have done. I accepted him as he accepted me.

This drama parallels countless episodes from my life with mother, but the ending is different. Mother could not set her disappointment aside when I was unable to produce (grades) up to her expectations for me. Therefore, most of my encounters with her were filled with unresolved anger and frustration, because I followed her lead and did not "understand" her behavior as she did not "understand" mine.

I could see from this that mother probably did love me, even though I have mainly doubted it! Dr. Levis (like mother) loves me and wants the best for me, which led him to expect too much. He underscored his love for me by setting his expectations aside. Mother was unable to do this, so I lost sight of the love.

Concepts, diagnoses and technology introducing self-awareness and responsibility

The creation of art and its analysis by the patient illustrates a new concept in the practice of psychotherapy. The key element in all cases presented in this book, but in particular with this study is the concept of a role relational change in the patient therapist relationship. The therapeutic relationship becomes a growing partnership, where the patient analyses the transference, her relating with the authority of the therapist, in the context of awareness of her dominant personality diagnosis and the context of restructuring relating based on the valued principles of conflict resolution: moderation, cooperation and mutual respect.

Segmet overestimated the role of authorities, of both the badness of her mother and of the goodness of the therapist as a wizard. The therapist redefined the power system in relations structuring roles of support, empowerment and tolerance for her failures. The therapist being supportive and reassuring, permissive and yet limit setting, redefined healthy role relating, allowing her to feel good about herself but also to experience setbacks as immunization to feelings of rejection. She identified her dominance and paranoia in relations catching her own transgressiveness and prompted to learn gradually to let go of anger; power management led to reduction of her fears. The original power imbalance projectively identifying myself as a wizard and her mother as a vicious dog, evolved. She gradually humanized me during an ongoing power play with the wizard. The power play is well illustrated with the imagery of reducing the Wizard first, to a silver cat and finally, into a gray cat, with her usurping the symbols of magical power, cape, wand, wings, identifying the power as her own. My indifference and support of her doing so clarified that power is not necessary in feeling good about oneself, and that power is in feeling self-ware, evolving insights and ability to manage it, that is learning to be responsible.

She grew emotionally and we see the evidence of that in the fact that she was able to change her attitude towards her mother, towards her own self by identifying her problematic outbursts as reflecting a personality relational problem.. The implication of this development validates the conceptual premise of the Formal Theory about the unconscious, about wellness diagnoses, and the suitability of the technology as creating a partnership in roles of patient and therapist reenforcing the principles of moderation, cooperation and practicing mutual respect. The method allowed the patient to be active in creating and observing the emotional experience objectively, to experience her growth in emotional strength, aware of the wisdom of her creative process. This role is an advantage over being passive to the analytical insights pronounced by an expert.

Her evolution in attitudes in all relationships is clear. The value of this record is that the patient created it as art and as insights by herself, thus enhancing her identity by assuming responsibility in observing imbalances and managing them responsibly both in her private and her professional relations.

Dominant patient number two:
Kathy's creativity weaving healing from multiple traumatic experiences

Kathy's sequence of five workbooks illustrates conflict resolution at each book starting with a conflictual memory and ending with a resolution portrayed in a short story. The sequence of the books illustrates progress in therapy as the workbooks evolved to portray her relational growth.
Reading the summaries of the succession of books one can detect the consistency of therapy as emotional healing and personal empowerment.

Kathy was a 40-year-old married mother of three in a desperate search for acceptance. Her problems started as an adopted child, from a foundling home, where she had been emotionally deprived during the first six months of her life. Her pictorial journey records her rollercoaster odyssey as five interrelated cycles of self-discovery and personal transformation. Her books are interrelated as a dialectic continuum of soul-searching departing from a serious sense of feeling damaged with a fragile self progressing to a solid sense of identity, feeling part of a loving well connected family system. To get an idea of her growth simply read the captions transcribed as the summary of her metaphors. The metaphorical images attest to a radical emotional transformation. We observe the evolution from the beginning of the therapy to termination as a sequence portraying her attitudinal growth. Her workbooks recorded this transformation from a fragile twig of a crystal tree to solid affiliation with the family, portrayed with husband and children connected to each other into cycles of interdependence and emotional solidarity.

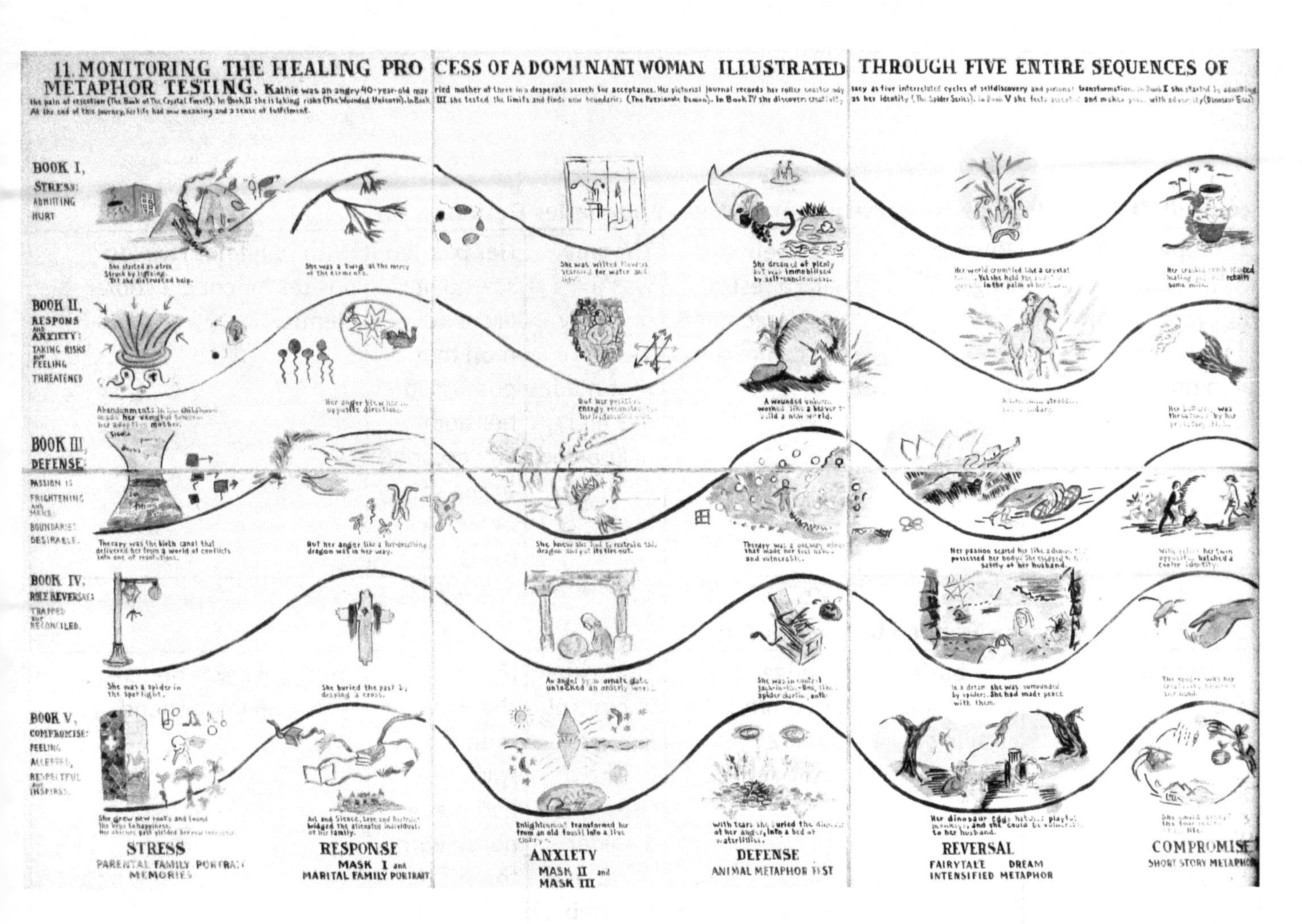

Book I, Stress: Admitting Hurt					
She started as a tree struck by lightning. Yet she distrusted help.	She was a twig at the mercy of the elements	She was wilted flowers yearning for water and light.	She dreamed of plenty but was immobilized by self-consciousness	Her world crumbled like a crystal forest. Yet she held the secret of growth in the palm of her hand.	Her cracked crock started healing and could retain some milk.

Book II: Response and Anxiety: Taking Risks but Feeling Threatened.					
Abandonment was her childhood. It made her feel vengeful towards her adoptive mother.	Her anger blew her into opposite directions.	But her positive energy reconstructed her fragmented self.	A wounded Unicorn worked with a beaver to rebuild a damaged dam.	A horseman straddled the boundary.	Her new self as a butterfly was threatened by a predatory fish.

Book III: Defense: Passion is Frightening and Makes Boundaries Desirable.					
Therapy was the birth canal that delivered her from a world of conflicts into one of resolutions.	But her anger like a fire-breathing dragon was in her way.	She knew she had to restrain this dragon and put its fire out.	Therapy was a one-way mirror that made her feel naked and vulnerable.	Her passion scared her like a demon that possessed her body. She escaped to the safety of her husband.	With relief her twin opposites hatched a cooler identity.
Book IV: Role Reversal: Trapped but Reconciled					
She was a spider in the spotlight	She buried the past by draping a cross.	An angel by an ornate gate unlocked an orderly world.	She was in control like Jack-in-The-Box, like a spider darting on the web.	In a dream she was surrounded by spiders. She had made peace with them.	The spider was her creativity hidden in her hand.
Book V: Compromise: Feeling Accepted, Respectful and Inspired					
She grew new roots and found the keys to happiness. Her obscure past yielded her new innocence.	Art and Science, Love and Restraint bridged the alienated individuals of her family.	Enlightenment transformed her from an old fossil into a live embryo.	With tears she buried the dinosaur of her anger into a bed of waterlilies.	Her dinosaur eggs hatched playful monkeys and she could be vulnerable to her husband.	She could accept the four seasons of her life.

The formal analysis of Kathy's five workbooks of metaphors examine the evolution of her emotions contrasting the inception of the therapy in the first book with its completion in the fifth.

We examine vertically the evolution of her conflictual memories to the corresponding short stories reflecting sequences of resolutions. We examine her transference in the third book.

Analysis of the five books reflects well her evolution in therapy as a sequence of resolutions progressing to healing as evidenced in contrasting the summaries of the six roles of the first book to those of the fifth book contrasting equivalent metaphors. The initial book presents her at a state characterized as passivity, antagonism, and alienation. The fifth book presents the healing with equivalent metaphors illustrating mastery, cooperation and mutual respect.

Book I, Stress: Admitting Hurt					
She started as a tree struck by lightning. Yet she distrusted help.	She was a twig at the mercy of the elements	She was wilted flowers yearning for water and light.	She dreamed of plenty but was immobilized by self-consciousness	Her world crumbled like a crystal forest. Yet she held the secret of growth in the palm of her hand.	Her cracked crock started healing and could retain some milk.

Book V: Compromise: Feeling Accepted, Respectful and Inspired					
She grew new roots and found the keys to happiness. Her obscure past yielded her new innocence.	Art and Science, Love and Restraint bridged the alienated individuals of her family.	Enlightenment transformed her from an old fossil into a live embryo.	With tears she buried the dinosaur of her anger into a bed of waterlilies.	Her dinosaur eggs hatched playful monkeys and she could be vulnerable to her husband.	She could accept the four seasons of her life.

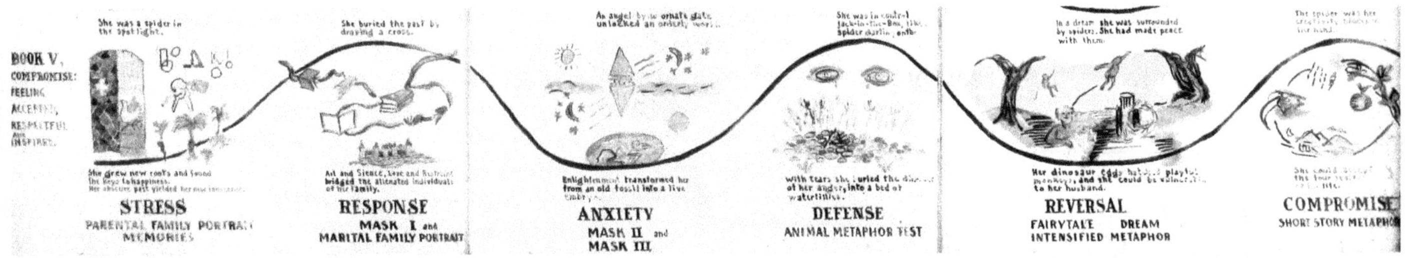

Reading vertically we identify the evolution in her conflictual memories and the evolution of her resolutions as the Short Story Metaphors representing her compromises. The books are interrelated to each other as a conflict resolution sequence: the first book identifies the stress state; the second is the response to the stress and related anxiety. The third corresponds to the defense state. The fourth is the role reversal state in the sequence, while the fifth corresponds to the resolution as a state of compromise.

Book I, Stress: Admitting Hurt
She started as a tree struck by lightning. Yet she distrusted help.
Book II: Response and Anxiety: Taking Risks but Feeling Threatened.
Abandonment was her childhood. It made her feel vengeful towards her adoptive mother.
Book III: defense: Passion is Frightening and Makes Boundaries Desirable.
Therapy was the birth canal that delivered her from a world of conflicts into one of resolutions.
Book IV: Role Reversal: Trapped but Reconciled
She was a spider in the spotlight
Book V: Compromise: Feeling Accepted, Respectful and Inspired
She grew new roots and found the keys to happiness. Her obscure past yielded her new innocence.

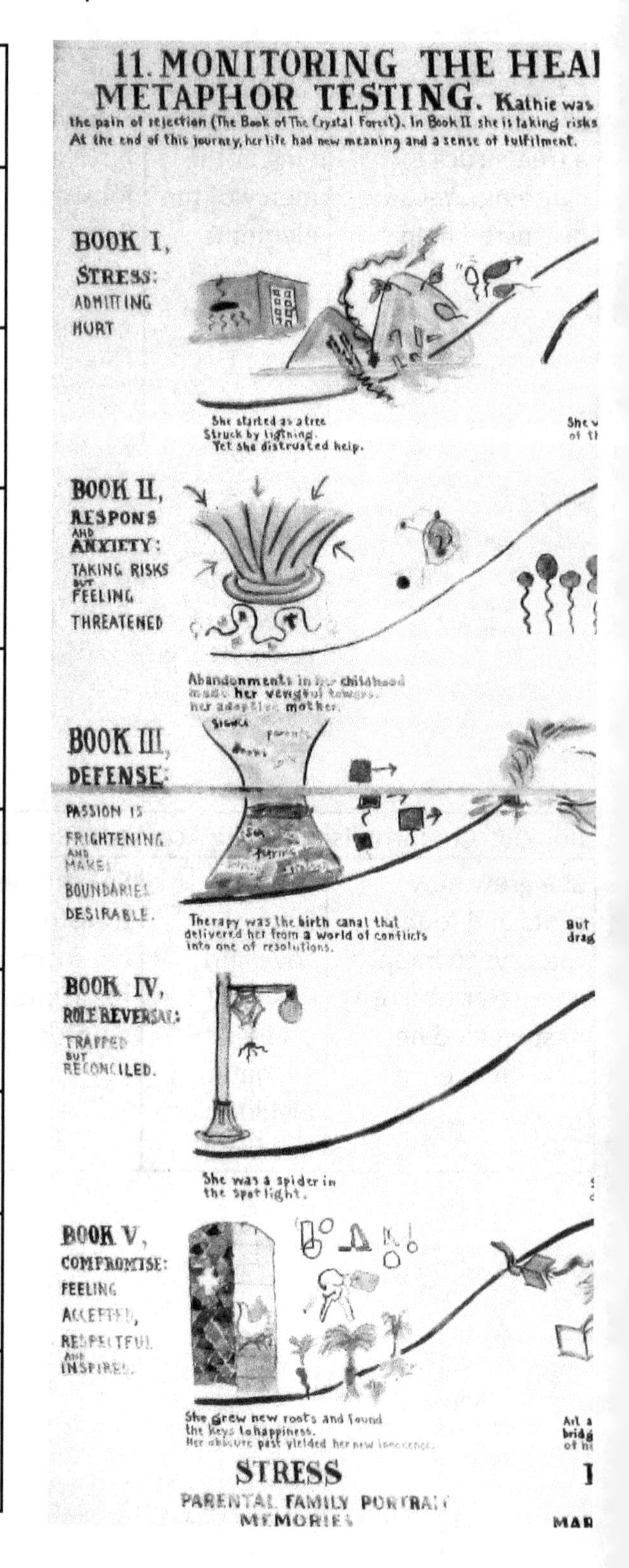

Reading vertically we identify the evolution of her compromises as a sequence to healing

Book I, Stress: Admitting Hurt	
Her world crumbled like a crystal forest. Yet she held the secret of growth in the palm of her hand.	Her cracked crock started healing and could retain some milk.
Book II: Response and Anxiety: Taking Risks but Feeling Threatened.	
Her new self as a butterfly was threatened by a predatory fish.	
Book III: defense: Passion is Frightening and Makes Boundaries Desirable.	
With relief her twin opposites hatched a cooler identity.	
Book IV: Role Reversal: Trapped but Reconciled	
The spider was her creativity hidden in her hand.	
Book V: Compromise: Feeling Accepted, Respectful and Inspired She could accept the four seasons of her life.	

The third volume reflects her transference relationship as seeking recognition by the therapist and having feelings that scared her, to which she reacted by reinforcing her commitment to her husband. 'Her passion scared her like a demon that possessed her body. She escaped to the safety of her husband.' She dealt with her dependency needs by reconciling her opposite aspects in her mind as twin opposites, the antagonistic versus the cooperative selves. The twin identities pertain to the evolution of the personal conflict in feeling vulnerable to the therapist. 'With relief her twin opposites hatched a cooler identity.'

Book III: Defense: Passion is Frightening and Makes Boundaries Desirable.					
Therapy was the birth canal that delivered her from a world of conflicts into one of resolutions.	But her anger like a fire-breathing dragon was in her way.	She knew she had to restrain this dragon and put its fire out.	Therapy was a one-way mirror that made her feel naked and vulnerable.	Her passion scared her like a demon that possessed her body. She escaped to the safety of her husband.	With relief her twin opposites hatched a cooler identity.

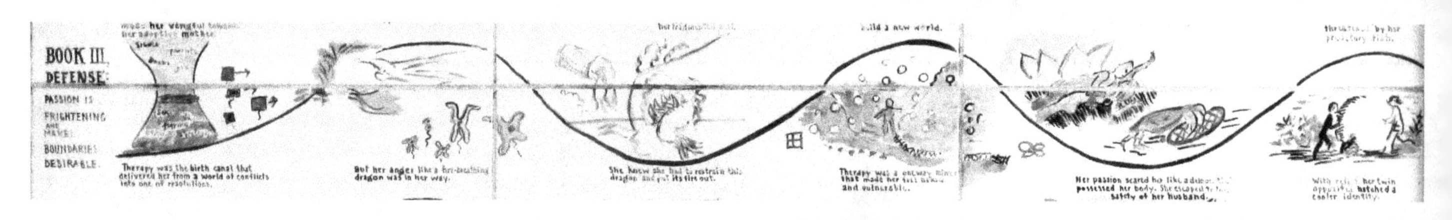

In the fourth book she grew self-confidence, she identified the healing in her own creativity as being a spider in the spotlight:

Book IV: Role Reversal: Trapped but Reconciled					
She was a spider in the spotlight	She buried the past by draping a cross.	An angel by an ornate gate unlocked an orderly world.	She was in control like Jack-in-The -Box, like a spider darting on the web.	In a dream she was surrounded by spiders. She had made peace with them.	The spider was her creativity hidden in her hand.

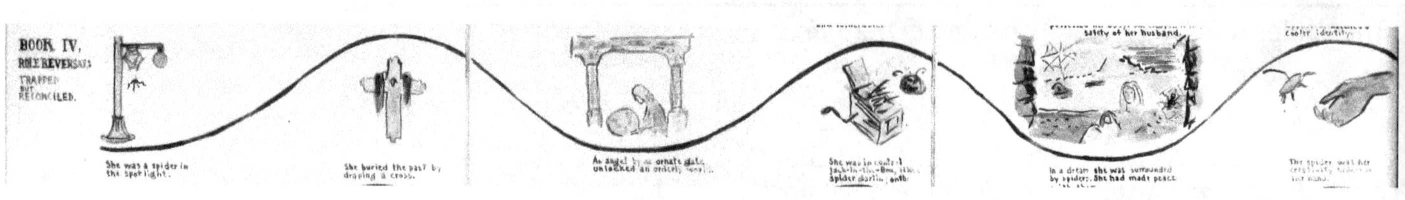

So, this case study reveals well the evolution of therapy in the dialectic of the evolution of her metaphors. How about the quaternity of the deck of cards? We may identify the evolution beginning with submissive antagonism, in the first book as a victim resenting the world.
The second book presents submissive cooperation. 'A wounded Unicorn worked with a beaver to rebuild a damaged dam'. The third book presents dominant antagonism as erotic fantasies in a relationship with the therapist.

Therapy was a one-way mirror that made her feel naked and vulnerable.	Her passion scared her like a demon that possessed her body. She escaped to the safety of her husband.

Books four and five illustrate her willingness to be submissive cooperative and dominant cooperative with good control over intensity of role assumptions.

Book IV: Role Reversal: Trapped but Reconciled					
She was a spider in the spotlight	She buried the past by draping a cross.	An angel by an ornate gate unlocked an orderly world.	She was in control like Jack-in-The -Box, like a spider darting on the web.	In a dream she was surrounded by spiders. She had made peace with them.	The spider was her creativity hidden in her hand.
Book V: Compromise: Feeling Accepted, Respectful and Inspired					
She grew new roots and found the keys to happiness. Her obscure past yielded her new innocence.	Art and Science, Love and Restraint bridged the alienated individuals of her family.	Enlightenment transformed her from an old fossil into a live embryo.	With tears she buried the dinosaur of her anger into a bed of waterlilies.	Her dinosaur eggs hatched playful monkeys and she could be vulnerable to her husband.	She could accept the four seasons of her life.

SUBMISSIVENESS CASE STUDIES

Submissiveness represents a very different pathology illustrated in two case studies below.
The pathologies were misdiagnosed determined as medical symptoms: self-mutilation and eating disorders. The patients from the formal theoretical perspective were diagnosed as suffering of the submissive relational modality, a wellness diagnosis. Both patients had difficulty asserting themselves feeling angry inside but unable to deal with their feelings. The one was expressing her anger with cutting herself and attempting suicides. The other responded to criticism and feelings of rejection by secretly binging and using alcohol. The first patient was cured from cutting in 16 sessions attested with forty years remission. The second evolved gradually with the communicational correction by becoming a poet and a therapist.

Alicia, how the scared troll became the moon

Alicia was a 30 year old married teacher who had sliced systematically her entire body in spite of therapy and three hospitalizations during the past four years. From a chronic condition, resistant to cognitive therapy, she was cured in 16 sessions. The changes are recorded in two workbooks summed up below. We observe the evolution of Alicia's portrayal of herself from one set of workbook images to the second detecting the evolution of all tests of the battery showing growth and reflecting her recovery. The artwork and comments identify changes in each symbolic system, reflecting her interpersonal relations along the six key tests of the battery as recorded in two workbooks a few weeks apart. The personal growth in relating to others is clearly depicted in contrasting the Short Stories Metaphors of the successive workbooks. She evolved from a troll hiding from the sun, that gets burned upon interacting with the sun, to one of being the moon taking turns with the sun in illuminating the earth.

The patient's Relational Modality Inventory provides a clear diagnostic profile of a submissive person. She scored +3 across all items of the submissive cooperative and antagonistic relational modality scales (validated by the contrast that she scored -3 in most of the two dominant modality scales), with elevated scores in the realm of psychic tension. "I brood about things that bother me" and "do not let others know when I am angry". Her submissive antagonism made her helpless and resentful.
Conflict Analysis Battery's Inventory: the Relational Modality Evaluation Scales, reflecting an intensely polarized submissive cooperative and antagonistic relational profile with elevation of psychic tension. The two images above right contrast the Short Story Metaphor Tests of the two consecutive workbooks reflecting the patient's emotional growth (A. Levis J. & Levis, 2016).

She completed one workbook (the evaluation record) and a few weeks later she completed a second workbook, (the therapy outcome record). Her metaphor testing confirmed her relational scores of a very polarized Submissive Cooperative and Antagonistic modality. Her Conflictual Memories and Family Balloon Portrait present the intense stress of her developmental experiences. She was caught between her feuding parents. The Mask Test is 'wearing a paper bag over her head'. Her Animal Metaphor Test was a 'wolf's open mouth and a bird with a broken wing', her Short Story was about a Troll avoiding the Sun but burning up upon an unavoidable encounter; each test depicting herself in a helpless position.

The Psychic Tension was changed mildly in the second workbook. There were only subtle changes in her relational inventory from Book One to Book Two, but there were striking changes reflected in her projective tests. The Mask Test reflected growth with eyes and mouth, half her heart was full of little hearts, her Balloon Portrait evolved from a broken one underneath her father's umbrella to a square balloon like her father's rising above the family's balloons; the Animal Metaphor of the bird with the broken wing changed to portray a lion respecting a turtle moving slowly in front of it; her Short Story transformed a Troll afraid of the Sun into the collaborative self-confident Moon. The Short Story tests of the two workbooks reflect her transformation as how the patient evolved from feeling like an ugly Troll hiding from the sun to feeling like the wise Moon looking forward to a bright day. Her record demonstrated the growth along the three relational operations: she evolved from a state of conflict defined as passivity, antagonism and alienation to a state of wellness and mental health defined as mastery, cooperation and mutual respect.

She terminated therapy with full recovery from her depression and her compulsion to cut herself. She had already returned to a well-functioning state of mind and employability. She did not return to be a teacher, but she was able to assume the responsibility of running a new store and resuming her life as a wife and mother in a new location.

The study contrasts the corresponding tests of the two consecutive workbooks a month and a half apart illustrating her emotional growth and the change of her emotional disposition. The first book served as the record of her evaluation upon intake. It reveals her relational modality as a submissive cooperative and antagonistic personality. The second, or recovery, book completed upon the next few sessions reflects her emotional growth as modifications in the themes of the respective tests.

Upon the completion of each of her two workbooks she composed a short essay about her state of mind. At the end of a few sessions she completed the first workbook and composed the summation of insights as recognizing the syndromal psychodynamic unfolding of her emotions along the six role-state process reassuring herself. "I must learn to reconcile this duality and find a balance, which is psychologically healthy in order to reclaim my mental health."

The essay upon termination of therapy describes her emotional travesty leading to recovery. It confirms her successful social adjustment and her positive outlook as compared to the original suicidal profile. Her emotional growth in attitude and in relating is confirmed with the end statement: "I am still learning to live with myself, but I think I can, I think I can, I think I can".

The two workbooks are an accurate record of her progress. They document the effectiveness of this therapeutic modality in identifying and addressing the problem as one of a relational modality rather than a DSM5 illness diagnosis (McWilliams, 2017).

Conflict Analysis Battery, Book one:
the metaphor profile upon the evaluation phase of therapy

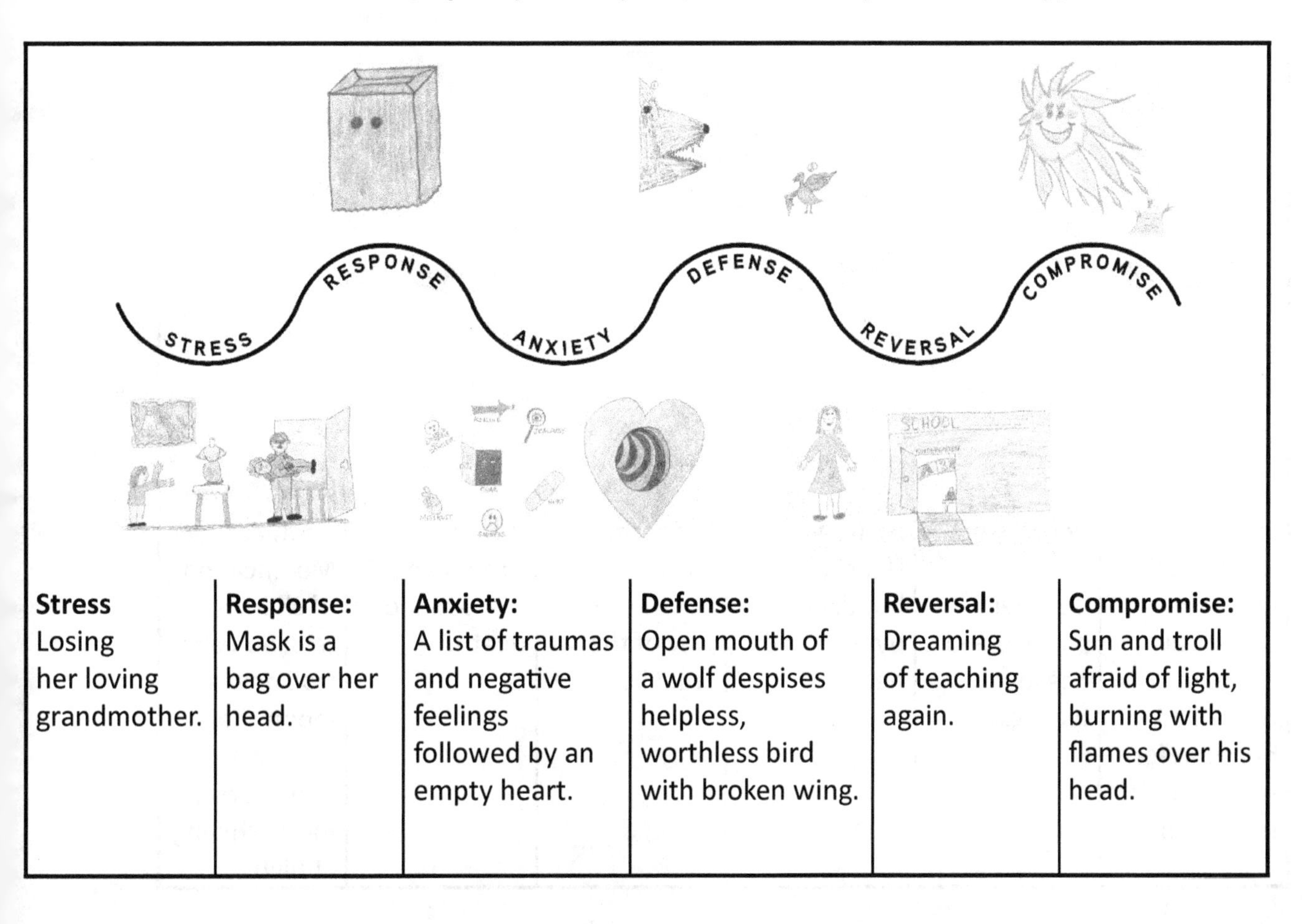

Stress	Response:	Anxiety:	Defense:	Reversal:	Compromise:
Losing her loving grandmother.	Mask is a bag over her head.	A list of traumas and negative feelings followed by an empty heart.	Open mouth of a wolf despises helpless, worthless bird with broken wing.	Dreaming of teaching again.	Sun and troll afraid of light, burning with flames over his head.

First Essay Following, the Completion of the Evaluation, 1/15/97 Patient's comments completed after her fourth visit on insights generated by the first workbook as a psychodynamic sequence of six emotions and behaviors, a system of role states as a dramatic continuum:

> **Stress:** The stressors I have identified through my drawings and writings center on themes of intensity, worthlessness, insignificance, and fear.
>
> **Response:** I have identified my typical response to stress as running away from, hiding from, or otherwise eluding stressful confrontations.
>
> **Anxiety:** The anxiety I feel comes in several forms, but all relate to fear, 1) guilt (fear of having done the wrong thing), 2) death (fear of dying), 3) shame (fear of social "death"), 4) anger, (fear of my inability to make appropriate responses).
>
> **Defense:** The defenses I have identified are two-fold: one is a very hostile and aggressive reaction to a perceived threat, the other is to just give up and admit my worthlessness and inability to help others.
>
> **Reversal:** In the reversal exercise, some positive elements are apparent, including the ability to help myself and show love.
>
> **Compromise:** The compromise aspect revealed a duality of personality – the ability to exhibit traits, which are in direct conflict with one another. One side is a dark, worthless, troublesome entity, while the other is a caring, giving, responsive entity. I must learn to reconcile this duality and find a balance, which is psychologically healthy in order to reclaim my mental health.

Table 2: Conflict Analysis Battery, Book two:
The metaphor profile reflecting many changes in the equivalent tests

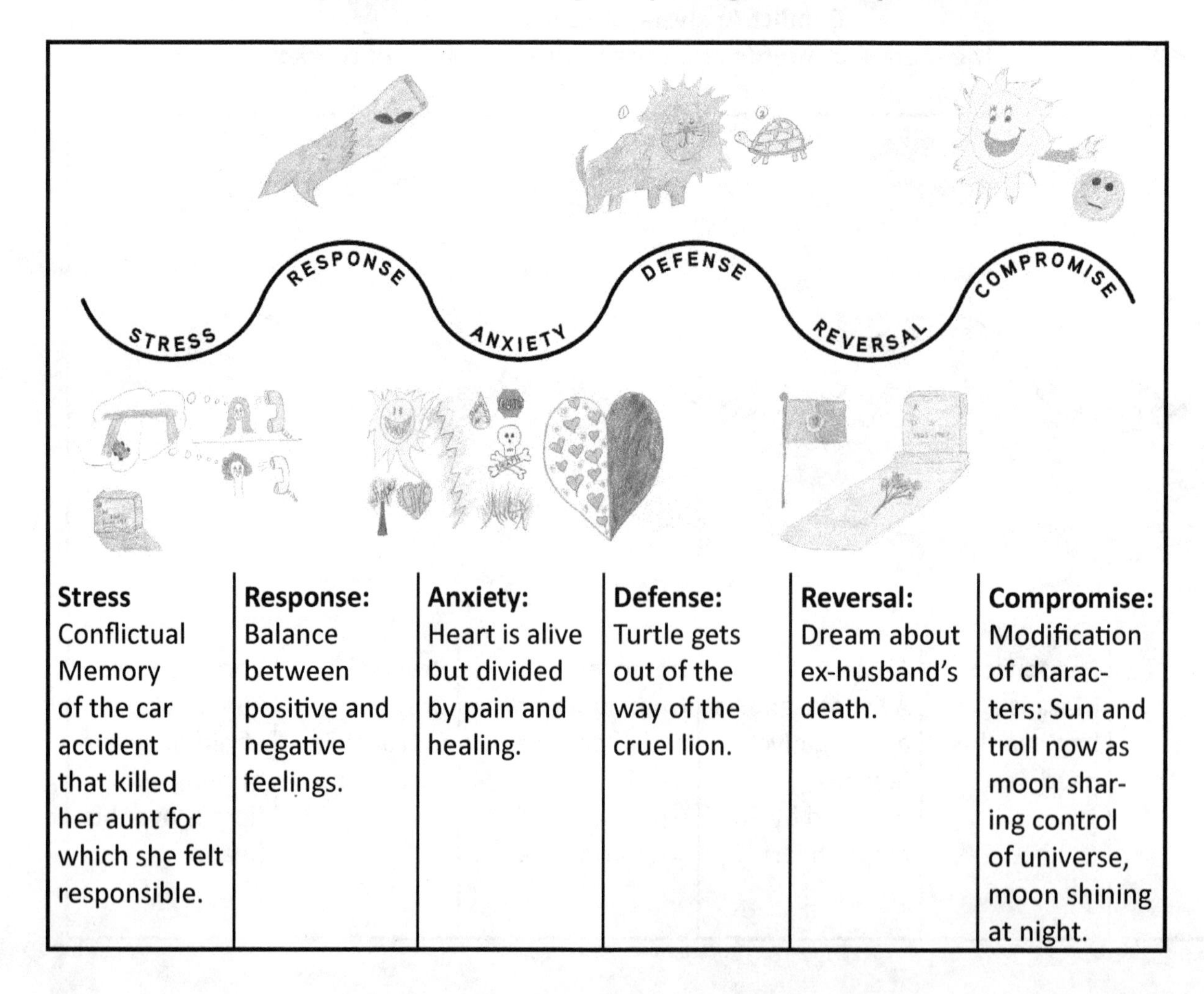

Stress	**Response:**	**Anxiety:**	**Defense:**	**Reversal:**	**Compromise:**
Conflictual Memory of the car accident that killed her aunt for which she felt responsible.	Balance between positive and negative feelings.	Heart is alive but divided by pain and healing.	Turtle gets out of the way of the cruel lion.	Dream about ex-husband's death.	Modification of characters: Sun and troll now as moon sharing control of universe, moon shining at night.

Second Essay, end of therapy in March, 1997.
'Towards recovery', four months later.
Looking back at the past few years of my life, it seems as if I were a different person from who I once was, and almost the opposite of who I would hope to be. The horrible things I have done to myself have reinforced my self-loathing and have left emotional scars on my family. I am sickened and embarrassed by my behavior: screaming tantrums, cutting and scarring my skin, biting myself, hitting myself, suicide scenarios and quasi-attempts to kill myself, fleeing and hiding from my family, swearing, throwing knives at the wall, tying my hair in knots, refusing to bathe. Who was that person, and how did she get that way?
During my therapy, I have been able to identify contributing factors to my state of emotional distress. Some of these were: a controlling mother, a critical father, self-perceived guilt for the death of my aunt, an uncommunicative step-father, a criticizing grandmother, a marriage of false pretense, a series of rapes, a severely mentally ill mother-in-law, failure to attain the job I had planned for and an extremely stressful work environment.
The feelings arising from my responses to these factors in my life have created the horrible monster I became. If asked to describe myself, I would say bad, stupid, lazy, ugly, fat, mean, bitter, unwanted, worthless and a burden to those around her – better off dead.
So, after five hospitalizations for suicide, a series of medications and countless therapy sessions, has anything changed?
Yes – in degrees. I have not cut myself in a while, and think of it infrequently. I do not believe that I would actually kill myself, nor seriously threaten to, again. I am becoming more involved in my daily family life and responsibilities. I am able to take care of my young step-daughter, niece and nephew. I am not becoming overwhelmed by the major changes in my life – moving to a new home and opening a store. I am looking forward to my new job.

I am still learning to live with myself, but I think I can, I think I can, I think I can...

Gladys, How Pijagu: The pig that eats too much, the jaguar who desires control and the seagull who wants freedom become a Dolphin, who enjoys companionship or How a "we" becomes an "I".

Personal Essay: An Autobiography Illustrated by Metaphors
Gladys was a 45 year old married woman suffering of an eating disorder throughout her life. Her real pathology was being a submissive cooperative/antagonistic person with her pathology in the area of eating behaviors. She had chosen to be in the weight-watchers business.
We observe the evolution of her therapy through the diagnostic phase, conveyed in the evaluation workbook. This phase is followed by the use of the ongoing creation of a diversity of animal metaphor protocols, which we identify as a sequence of three phases of inner growth.

The evaluation book presented her chronic condition of submissive antagonistic life adjustment of a person seeking to please but angry and rebellious inside. She was deprived of communications and was scared of losing control of her anger. Her mask presented a face with a 'perpetual smile'. The hidden image depicted her mouth as the black hole. Her heart presented a moat dividing good feelings and hidden sadness and distress. Her animal metaphor presented a dog and a cat turning their backs to each other and the viewer. Her dream was hiding her body, submerged in a submarine; her Short Story was about herself as a mouse burned by dragon to a crisp, but it could be interpreted as she herself being the dragon, afraid of losing control of her anger and hurting her family.
The second phase was submissive cooperative establishing dialogues with people across the moat but consistently finding herself in the submissive cooperative phase.
The third phase presented inner conflicts as submissive antagonistic phase by confronting her binge eating vulture assuming the snake self-starving identity. This phase was elicited by her trying to impress a fellow therapist, seeking her approval, by reversing her binging pattern, prevailing as an anorexic snake. The inner struggles ended by addressing the ineffectiveness of communications along the eating dichotomy as the vulture and the

snake were devoured by a tiger. She finally broke through the wall of silence by actually dealing with her feelings and honestly telling people in a civilized manner her feelings honestly. In this final phase, dominant cooperative relating, she evolved to truly express her feelings. She evolved from the initial Animal Metaphor Test to the final phase by asserting herself in dialogues with the important people in her life. She presented in a series of metaphors two animals of equal size facing each other communicating her grievances with all parties with whom she had experienced anger that was never dealt with. Her mother was a kangaroo, who had rejected her from her pouch, she told her employer that she could take initiatives of her own, she told her husband that they could air their differences and still be friends, she asked for companionship.

Upon the inception of the therapy her two animals turned their backs to each other and the viewer. Her comments, 'what do I care about your feelings?' Upon completion she addresses her husband 'We can argue and still be friends'. The final metaphor establishes her identities in transition: 'I am a we not an I'. Expressing her feelings she became comfortable in relations and less obsessed about her looks and her eating disorder. She excelled in becoming a poet and also a therapist.

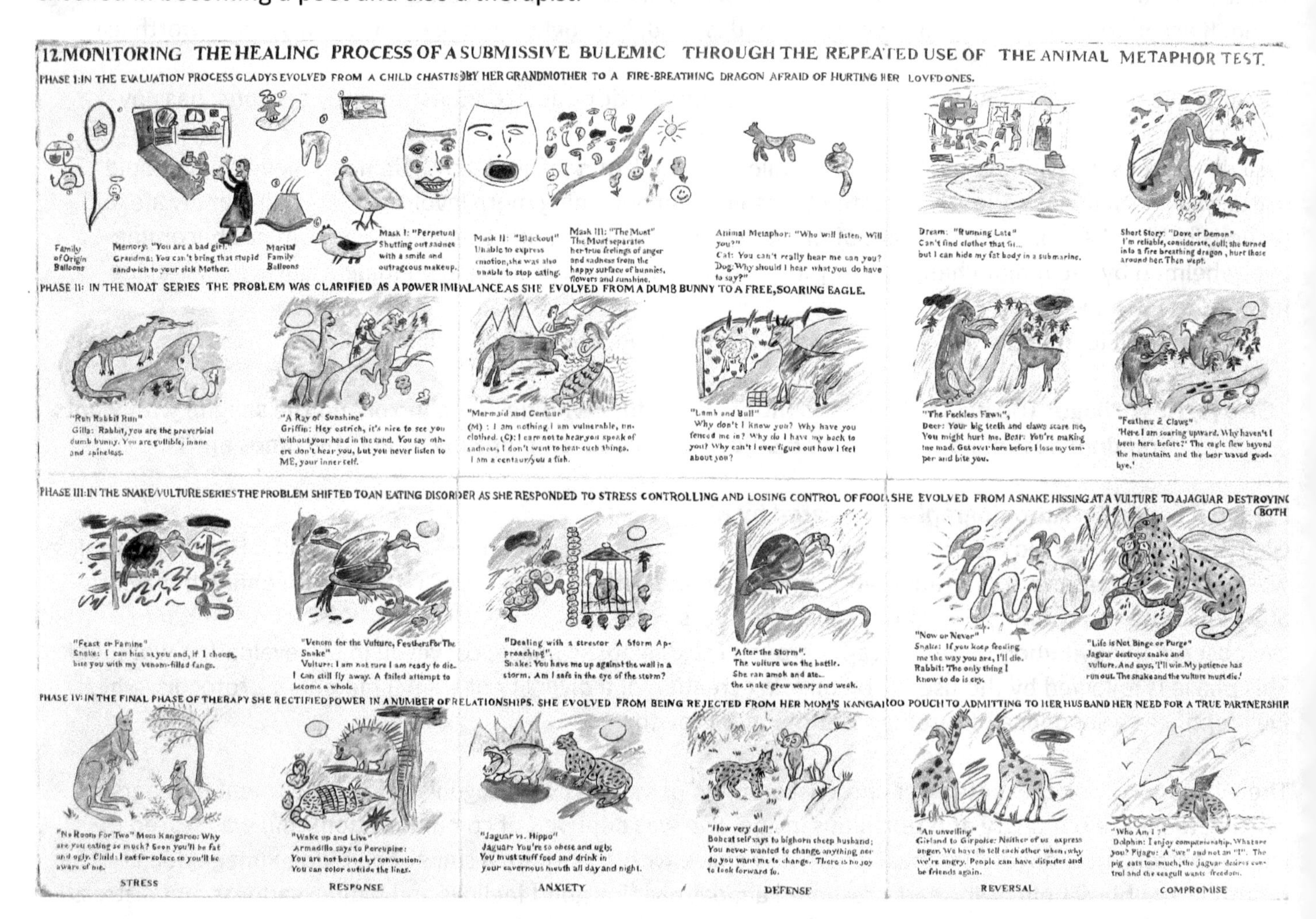

PHASE I

In the evaluation process, Gladys connected being chastised by her grandmother to having a black hole for a mouth, as well as becoming a fire-breathing dragon afraid of hurting her loved ones. In the process she admitted her problem of repression of emotions: 'Express rather than repress.'

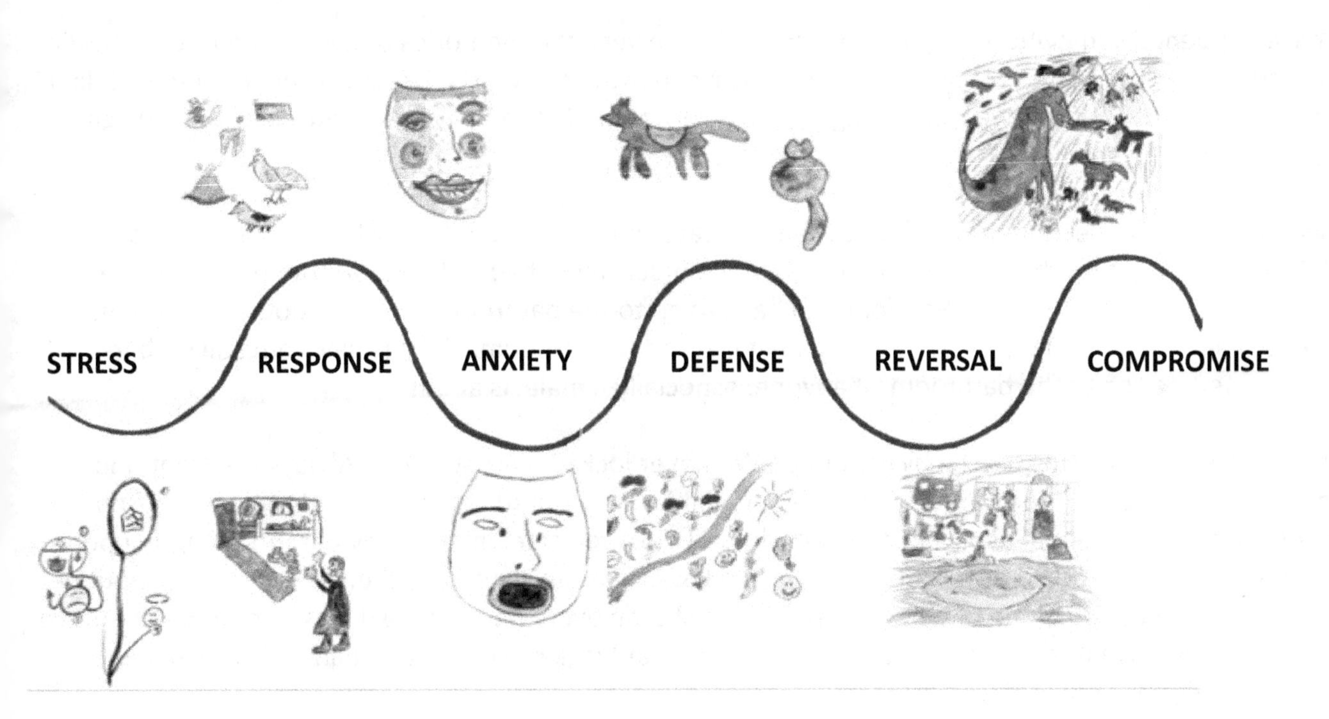

FAMILY OF ORIGIN BALLOONS & CONFLICTUAL MEMORY: Grandma: You can't bring that stupid sandwich to your sick mother.	MARITAL FAMILY BALLOONS & Mask I: "Perpetual Smile." Shutting out sadness with a smile and outrageous makeup.	Mask II: "Blackout." Unable to express emotion and being preoccupied with eating. Mask III: The moat separates her feelings of anger and sadness from the happy surface of bunnies and sunshine.	ANIMAL METAPHOR: "Who Will Listen, Will You?" Cat: You can't really hear me, can you? Dog: Why should I hear what you have to say?	DREAM: "Running Late." Can't find any clothes that fit... but I can hide my fat body in a submarine.	SHORT STORY: "Rage and Fear." I'm reliable, considerate, dull. She turned into a fire-breathing dragon and hurt those around her. Then she wept.

Personal Essay:
An Autobiography Illustrated by Metaphors and Progress Accomplished Through Poetry

I was not born fat. But I spent most of my life fat. Fat consumed me. Fat made me hide. Fat made me lie. My entire life was ruled by fat with but one desire--to be thin.

It must have happened somewhere in grammar school. I have very few memories of ever being not fat. My Girl Scout uniform was a "Chubette." I looked like a green wave in my camp shorts. Usually a very obedient child, I ran from the classroom that day we were being weighed. How could I live if my classmates knew my weight? Such degradation. Such shame.

Shame was instilled in me early on. (The "toxic" shame that John Bradshaw speaks of.) How do we "learn" shame? By an unthinking mother. My brother (2 1/2 years older) and I had a childhood friend, Billy. In the midst of our playing one day, I said, "Wait for me, I have to go to the bathroom." Mother pounced on that. "You never tell anyone, especially boys, that you are going to the bathroom." To this day, I am still embarrassed, or shamed, to "go to the bathroom" if anyone, especially a male, is about.

Shame was also etched into my psyche by my father. We never locked our back door. Always the front door, never the back door. Alone in that large, old house one night, I was scared. Strange sounds emanated from cellar to attic. Could I be so bold as to lock the back door? I did. I felt safe. Imagine my parents' chagrin upon reaching home and being locked out! None of us carried keys. I was awakened by their knocking and shouting. Father asked me, "Were you afraid of being stolen?" Such shame overwhelmed me. I was unfit to be the brave daughter of this god, my father. On the rare occasion today that I lock the back door, I am still swallowed in a sea of shame. The front door is always locked.

Brothers can activate shame. Again involving our friend Billy. After Billy moved away, my brother and I were invited to spend a weekend with his family. It was late winter. My mother packed my clothes. Eddie, my brother, and Billy were in the bedroom while I unpacked. Eddie drew from the suitcase a pair of woolen, almost-to-the-knee "undies." He held them up (they were peach colored--I still dislike that color) at arm's length and chortled. Billy also chortled. I wanted to evaporate.

My mother was still at it even after I was a wife and mother. Mother was an excellent cook. We often "went to Grandma's house" for holidays. The extremely caloric and delicious-looking dessert was always presented with a flourish. Mother would pause, look at her only daughter and proclaim, "You, of course, don't want any." Shame on you, daughter dear, you are fat--you cannot share my offering, was, of course, the message I received. Engulfed in shame, I would eat everything in my house when I got home.

Shame was most insidious when I deposited it on myself. The better part of my life was spent trying to impress and please my father. Although in many childhood areas I think I did this. I was the baseball nut, not my brother. I had a regulation score book and scored the NY Giants games whilst listening to the radio. The Mets get my attention now. Baseball was one of the few topics I could safely discuss with my father. Many of his opinions were drivel to me. But, of course, I could not dissent. That would be shameful.

My grammar school grades were great. Graduated salutatorian. My brother, with his lousy grades, was sent away to prep school. Did I envy him his glamorous military school life away from home? My high school grades plummeted to the ocean floor. My memories of those four years are: fat, shame, rebellion, fat, hate for my parents, hate for me, and more fat and shame.

During my teenage years there was scant exchange with my parents. After dinner, I immediately withdrew to my room, my Maginot Line. It too was violated. After my clandestine visits to the bakery shop, I would stash the empty boxes in a drawer, waiting for a chance to discard the evidence of my eating, my shame. Upon reaching my haven one day, I was stunned by an overwhelming sight. These "binge boxes" were piled on the floor in the middle of the room. My mother did this and never said a word to me about this sin of sins. If shame could kill, I died.

Never let it be said my not-fat mother and father were not in touch with my fat. Many dollars were fed to various doctors in an effort to rid me of my fat. These efforts were all abysmal failures.
Innumerable diets were spawned over the ensuing years. At times I was almost "normal" in weight. But never quite. This was elusive. Many times I nearly grasped it, only to have it slip away with the tide.
I married. A most aloof and uncommunicative person, such as I. He was MAN, I was woman. He now shared the pedestal with my father. There were two gods to please.

As my weight bounced up and down, he never disparaged me. No remarks were ever made about my eating. Of course, most of my eating, and certainly all of my binging, was done in solitude.

As was most of my thinking. We were both unto ourselves. Meaningful, intimate, heart-to-heart talk was rare. Not surprising, it was a continuum of my rearing.

From this lopsided union, three sons were born. The eldest to die before age twenty-and-one in an auto crash. Our third son was born two days before our first son's fourth birthday. I was not child-oriented. My vague, far-off plan had been to someday have two children, a he and a she. It was both shocking and dismaying to be pregnant. I loathed every month. I was misshapen, fat again and again and again. But they were mine and life went on.

Until a clear, cold day in February when our first-born died. The puppy-size rift that existed between my husband and I rapidly matured into mastiff-size. It was as though we had all died. All four of us grieved unto ourselves. Each created their own barrier to pain and disbelief. We accepted not, we shared not.

At the time of the accident, I was relatively thin for me. I was just completing one of the better-known weight loss programs. Seventy pounds were shed. Within the next year or so, I gained ninety. Again, I was fat. Again the travail of losing and gaining and finding the diet that would work. I found it. I became almost-thin. I delighted in it. My husband never said a word during these whopping losses, gains and losses. But I did please the other god. My father was enthused with my thinner body.

Within eighteen months of becoming an almost-thin person, I did something totally out of character. I bought a franchised weight loss business. My husband went along with me, my father was appalled. "You must be dumb to leave your job with all those great benefits." At the same time, he loaned me money to buy the place!

This step toward independence proved to be dangerous. In my new business, I was surrounded by food. Food and fat-people-wanting-to-be-thin pervaded my waking hours. It permeated my dreams. It drove me to eat. It drove me away from the scale. It haunted me. It nearly destroyed me. A weight loss counselor may not be fat. I was becoming fat again. The parent company would slap my hand and say, "Shame on you. You must be thin." This Is How I Got Where I Was At. It led me to therapy.

My Mask, My Cloak

My reason for seeking professional help was, you guessed it, my fat. Give therapy a few weeks and I'd be that thin person I always yearned for.

Each passing week brought forth pain, confusion and bleakness, but given at the start of my therapy, no thinness. It became apparent, via the tests given at the start of my therapy, that my fat was but my insulation, my buffer zone, against the world. Of deeper significance, was my perpetual smile and happy mien presented to the outside world. This defense had been in place for many years. Fat and complaisance were my bed partners. As a fat person I could not draw attention to me. A low profile was essential. Smile, Smile. Anger must be hidden at all cost.

I was asked to draw a mask, the Transparent Mask Test. I did. It was my perception of the face I presented to the world. A clown's face. A smiling face. I dubbed it "Perpetual Smile". The emotion conveyed was my way of self-deceit and mockery. I shut out my sadness with a smile and outrageous make-up -- like a clown.

The underside of this mask, the transparency, I called "Blackout". It showed my dejection and feelings of rejection. The eyes were closed but they wept. The mouth a blank, a black hole. Communication was nil. Nothing came forth. But everything went in. Anger, food, hate, food, hostility, food, guilt, food.

With my eyes closed, I could ignore all that was hurtful. My mother's illness and death; my five-year old niece's illness and death. Conversely, no one, even those closest to me, could see my inner emotions, both good and bad.

Next up was my drawing depicting what I saw in my heart. It was called "Double Image". A moat separated two sets of feelings. On the one side there were the sun, flowers, smiling faces. My mask to the world. On the other side of the moat was my inner self: tears, black clouds, a broken heart, grim faces, and the ears to show that no one ever listened.

My title for the sequence: "Deceit, Reality and Discord". Through this soul-searching test, I concluded that I was constantly running away from life; I relegated conflicts to the rear of my mind. It became obvious that I had to express rather than repress. My two fragmented selves had to be integrated into a whole.

To express my feelings, both hateful and loving, would only draw attention to me. People would see me -- and my fat. Create no waves, be a good child, be a good wife. True anger was only expressed as a mother. I could yell and scream when my children substantially aroused my ire. In all my life, I only exploded, publicly, in front of my children.

My children suffered due to my taciturnity. They were often left undefended. I could never allow myself to show emotion or the chutzpah to even speak up for my own children. Only dogs get mad. A daughter and wife do not.

One of my high school teachers referred to me as imperturbable. My favorite aunt would make unseemly statements in an effort to break through my coat of calm. A neighbor once stated he'd like to be with me during an atomic attack -- I was always so placid. The caption in my high school yearbook: "As merry as the day is long." I was indeed a fortress. Nothing could erupt this volcano. Total control. So important to me. Present a smile to the world, be unflappable and I would be safe.

In 34 years of marriage I can recall but one verbal argument -- this only a year or so ago. My feelings were never let know, I ate them. My life was a constant binge not only with food, but emotions as well. My outside grew larger, my inside shriveled.

In the AMT my animals turned their backs to each other and the viewer of the images. In the story I recognized a pattern. When under pressure, or feeling sorry for myself, or lonely I plan on over-eating, drinking as a reward. It seems to be something to look forward to.

Disclosure of self was incomprehensible to me. No one was allowed to see the shriveled inner me, not even I. I was a Dorian Gray. This made therapy extremely painful and slow-paced. How could I reveal my innermost feelings and fears to another being? A psychiatrist, fine, but still a body with two ears. These ears would listen and hear, not like others in the past. These ears would know me for what I was. A nothing. A sham. A mask with a perpetual smile. A chunk of ice. So painful. My principal fear was being seen for who I am. A dream as a metaphor reflected my fears of being seen as fat. The dream gave me the perfect hideaway, a submarine.

Dragon / Mouse

A modicum of self-destruction is appearing through the pen. This was an early statement of self-hate. I didn't like me, but I had the power to self-destruct me. I also had the power to change me. My wall separating me from humanity showed up in this early AMT, a dragon and a mouse.

Needless to say, I am the Mouse -- the rest of the world a Dragon. Such a fierce, colorful, aggressive Dragon. Living in secure and mighty mountains. Someone to be admired. The epitome of control and power. The Mouse existed in a drab, colorless, nothing world.

The Mouse was in the Dragon's way and the Dragon threatened to burn the Mouse to a crisp. Or, being the Mouse was so inconsequential, the Dragon thought it easier to just step on and squash the Mouse. She wasn't worth the Dragon's breath. The Mouse was totally intimidated and in awe of the Dragon. She allowed the Dragon to slay her. She didn't even have the prudence to flee.

Here was verification of me, The Mouse. Don't object, don't argue, don't defend myself. Do not open my mouth. Be in awe of the world. Be a willow tree, bend and bend some more. Do unto others, never unto myself. These lessons leak well, came forth via the pen.

Poetry

One day my hand started to write. Sheer gibberish to me, but a less painful avenue to expression. I was mortified and ashamed after presenting my writings. Eventually they were dubbed as "poetry". This I refused to believe since I was a creative-less clod. But the pen had free rein. It wrote what I couldn't say.

Early on in my writings, I discovered Sylvia Plath. Her poetry and life consumed me. I read every book I could find by her or about her. I affiliated with her in so many instances, e.g., "When there is no one around to make you feel wanted and appreciated, it's sort of easy to talk yourself into feeling worthless." "I am obsessed by wanting to escape from that course." (I too had such an obsession.): "Sometimes I feel so stupid and dull and uncreative that I am amazed when people tell me differently." She killed herself. My early readings did not indicate how. I called the library -- gas from her stove. I was mesmerized and infatuated with her life. I admired all she did.

I equated with Sylvia. So many of my thoughts intermingled with hers. Both warped and not so.

My Poem:

Sylvia

A mask was her downfall, it was always in place.

Hostility must remain caned as a beast in the zoo.

Alas, it crack'd, she fell apart.

Too gutless for the razor, the sea regurgitated her.

Forty pretty pills almost did her in

But the bitch goddess said, "Nay, I shall not die"

The inner being was strong and won.

Only for a decade, though.

The storm clouds are moving ever so swiftly

I wish they wouldn't go, they are my friends.

They cloak me from my fears

Nay, they reinforce my fears

But they are ever so comforting.

They seem to hide me from the world.

I hide behind them as I hide behind my glasses.

It is said the eyes are the mirror of the soul

I must be hiding my innermost self

Is that self so bad it needs to be held in secret?

Do I fear it will erupt like Dorian Gray?

His soul became warped, his body remained pure

His was a life of duplicity and, yes, fear

Alas, mine is so too.

My fears of being uncloaked show up here.

Breaking up of the clouds alarmed me –

the world would then see me as I truly was -- a sum of nothing:

I'm always worried about what others may think.

I am compulsed to be well-behaved and fall in place

I must please, please, please.

All must be perfect, perfect, perfect.

Do not create waves my dear, Be quiet and demure.

I don't, I am. What a waste.

How did I grow to be a pleaser?

I was brought up to be sweet and kind

You must never be rude - it's not nice

Others always come first,

that must be so I don't remember the lessons,

But I did learn very well

Otherwise, why am I so?

Uselessity

I must have been born docile and pliable

Indelible impressions were cast on me.

Squished and squashed.

Mother was teacher, Father was god

Force did not exist, words did their job

Why must I be perfect? I'm certainly not.

Memories are so rare, is that repression?

Or a defense mechanism to maintain my sanity?

Again an "ity" - mediocrity, stupidity, on and on

Tonight is me - uselessity.

There was no time for me to be me. I spent my life in pursuit of happiness -- other peoples'. My dues for walking this earth were perfection. Nothing else would do. I expressed it so:

Perfection Only May Exist

Mediocrity, you may not, nay, cannot, exist

You reek with hollowness, you are unfulfilled.

To be perfect is to be supreme

You are as trash and not to be stood

Contamination, putrification, stagnant, imperfect

You are to be scorned and slain again and again

Mediocrity, you are death.

Perfection exacts a heavy toll. To be perfect is a state of apartness, aloofness. To a fat person, it's akin to hiding in a tent dress. Should any one see the rolls of fat, I would be imperfect. Not to be allowed. My separation from the world of reality may be likened to the operation that separates Siamese twins. A wall, a moat, a fence always enabled me to keep my distance from others and to pursue my path to perfection.

The building of the wall was exacerbated by non-hearing ears. When I did communicate with others, I was ignored. Pull back, pull back. Don't let them hurt me again. If they shan't listen, I shan't speak. Another binge--stuffing myself with anger:

Run, rabbit, run.
Hurry away into the sun.
Run to the forest, the trees are tall
The pine needles are soft, the moss is cool.
They can't hear you when you speak.
They don't see you when you are there.
So, hide, rabbit, hide, it's good for you.
The rabbit's ears are back.
Hurray, he's getting mad.
He's not a he, he's a she, he's me.

But why didn't people hear me?
Why, didn't they listen to what I said?
K's burn was treated so lightly
The vet ignored the poor ill dog.
Husband never heard me about the meeting place.
Was it my serenity in the face of adversity?
Did I not speak loud enough?
I guess I don't speak since no one hears.

The three references in this poem, my son's burned arm, the vet not hearing me for months about my dog's worsening condition, and my husband's failure to know where to meet me after graduation for my Master's degree, were all meaningful to me. Yet, they were ignored.

Dogs bark, cat's meow, birds sing, elephants bellow
They express their anger and their fears.
People talk softly at times, they also shout at times
They express their love, their anger and their fears.
Why am I mute?

I was even jealous of animals expressing emotions.

Still asking that question: "Why am I mute?"

I love you, I hate you

You are mine, do I want you?

I can throw you away

I can keep you if I want

I despise your weakness

I hate your quietness

You are mute, you are dull

I don't like you, you are me.

A modicum of self-destruction is appearing through the pen. This was an early statement of self-hate. I didn't like me, but I had the power to self-destruct me. I also had the power to change me.

Bravado

The rain is on the windshield all blotchy and dull

It softens the light.

Turn on the wipers, clear it away.

You are a raindrop on my soul.

I love you not, I think tonight.

If you were to die, I'd miss you not.

I know your secret.

You are bravado, a machine programmed well

Once taught, that is the end

You could not change, can you now?

A pile of putty you were born

Thence molded into a piece of quartz.

A free thinker not, once taught, cast in concrete

You should be pitied, your brain was stifled

Parenting was poor, it ruined a soul

No free thinking, no creativity, imagination none.

You were programmed and that was that

The spark was squashed, she ruled your head

You might as well be dead.

My Anger, My Moat, My Quiet:

As downtrodden and mouse-like as I felt, it became obvious that anger seethed beneath my mask. But anger was undesirable. To be angry was naughty. An awareness of my anger cropped up in a very few lines:

It must be easier as well as safer

To wear an almost constant smile.

It's a mask to hide me from the world

If I smile I can't be angry

At least not so anyone knows

However, I know.

I was also in deep fear of expressing my anger:

I cannot cry, I cannot rage

To cry is uncontrollable, why can't I?

To rage is controllable, and had always been

If you learn to control an emotion entirely

Why can't you learn to give it leeway?

Is rage too strong a word?

Rage must be over-expressed anger

If anger has been so long suppressed

Will rage run rampant and just explode?

Anger, and especially rage, were almost never allowed to surface through my mask. Indeed, I created a river, a moat. One side was cool and calm – the other ferocious and furious. This dichotomy was so rigid, I often didn't even know when I was angered:

It's not just a matter of expressing anger
Although that I don't know how to do
More important than expression of anger
Is knowing indeed when you are angry.

Anger scared me. Anger awed me. Oh, to be angry. I was overwhelmed when someone, anyone, expressed anger. I was jealous. Why didn't the world cast aspersions on these people. How could they not alienate those who received their outbursts of anger? How could anyone still like them? Anger terrified me to such an extent that I overcame it. I made it surrender to my power. The power of control. I imprisoned it so deep in my soul that it couldn't erupt. This dung heap was nurtured over the years. It fed upon itself. A cancer dissipating my spirit. As it intensified, it warped my mind.

When my first son was five years old, my anger unloosed itself. To a proportion unknown to me. My child did something to upset me (I remember not what). He was on the floor. My hands seized his shoulders. I pounded his head on the floor. The scene is as vivid today as it was that day thirty years ago. I must never allow my anger to take control ever-again. What had I done? This was my son. I, no, my anger, was a monster. It was omnipotent. It attacked with fearsome speed. Something snapped in my head. It was me. The horror of what I was capable of immobilized me. Shame and fear espoused one another. Guilt was spawned.

Guilt and shame intermingle such as the tendrils of a morning glory. The longer they are allowed to flourish, the more difficult they are to untangle:

Guilt comes in many shapes and forms. It is most tremendous when people die:

My grandmother died -- I didn't like her, but I caused her demise

My mother died -- I was impatient with her.

My son died -- did I cause it?

It also attacks in other ways

It builds up and almost envelops me.

My guilt for these past offenses hung heavy. It impacted on my present existence -- it clouded the future. More from Sylvia Plath: "The hardest thing, I think, is to live richly in the present without letting it be tainted and spoiled out of fear for the future or regret for a badly damaged past."

Guilt was heaviest regarding the death of my son. We had lived in a small village in Westchester County during K's growing up years. He loved the village, he loved the house, he loved his friends. He loved life. While he was going to college, a local school, we moved to Connecticut. The main reason being the company I worked for relocated to CT. Everything considered, we deemed it beneficial to leave our home of twelve years for another in CT. None of the boys were ecstatic! K. was outraged! He ultimately found an apartment, went to school and worked at three jobs to support his apartment. When one or two of his jobs petered out, he was forced to move back to CT. He commuted to NY school and to see his friends.

One Friday night he almost made it home. He died in a car crash a scant ten minutes from home. K. was dead. My twenty-year-old son lay dead on a road. I was the cause. Because of me, we moved. Guilt wrapped itself around each convolution of my brain. It's message oozed from each tentacle as it grew: "Bad mother", and grew "Bad daughter", and grew "Bad granddaughter", and grew "Bad wife."

A bird flew into my car years after my son died. Guilt surged through my being. I had killed the bird.

A Poem:

They fly in the air so free

Their colors are lovely to see

They create happiness with their song

They are a joy to behold as they soar

Then they go thump and are dead.

I began to equate the myriad of dead animals I passed every day on the parkway with my son who had died:

I cry for the animals dead on the road

I cry for the animals forsaken and lone

They affect me in a manner untold

It is as though my heart is broken

Words cannot explain the effect

It is like the night Kevin died.

It is desperation

It is frustration

It breaks my heart

It is a weight so heavy I want to die.

I feel like I'm on a far-off mountain
Removed from everything – isolated
I am cold and aloof and yet a frenzy exists
I feel helpless, I feel inert, I am in turmoil. (08-20-85)

Rumblings of self-hate began to appear out of my anger, my moat, my guilt:

Love is another four-letter word nicer than most
It connotes deep feeling, pure and kind
Some love you take for granted --
You love your children, you love your dog
To be silly, you love your shoes
The word is often misused like so many others
You hate this, you hate that
Do I truly hate myself? (08-22-85)

Was this self-hate generated by years of unspoken anger, distancing myself from the rest of the world and my cancerous guilt? Menacing dread was creeping into my life:

The lights are all on, the radio too.
The air cleaner drones as I sit here alone
An eerie feeling is covering me like a shroud
There is something to be feared out there
Rather, it is something to be met
But it is a fearsome thing
I have put it off so long -- forever it seems
Am I able to bring it forth in a normal way
Or will it encompass me and blow me apart? (08-22-85)
Was the fat attack that had brought me to therapy indeed born from my anger, my moat, my guilt?

Analysis of the Relapse

In the midst of my turmoil -- my anger -- my guilt and the on-going fat, I met Sue. Sue was the psychodrama leader in a group I was invited to attend. I hesitantly agreed to go, but not to speak. I intended to blend into the background and watch and listen. Not easy to do when you are fat.
Sue fascinated me -- she was bright, attractive, outgoing, just nice – and thin. Everything I ached to be. As much as I scrunched into my chair, she found me. Not strange, since you can't hide fat. She asked why I was in the group. My reply: "I'm fat." Sue's reply: "You're not fat." How could this pinnacle of excellence not see I was fat? It shouted out from every roll: "Fat, fat, this is fat! How could I make her see the fat? Such a simple solution! I would become thin -- then Sue would know I had been fat. Pure logic. I was pleased with myself. I was determined. I was powerful. I could do it.

My expression of these feelings:

> You don't seem to understand my need
> I am not trying to please you
> I but want to make your eyes
> See me as my eyes see me -- fat.
> Fat is indeed not the main problem
> That I now know is so
> But since my anger remains hidden deep and will not surface
> The only thing I know to do is attack the fat. (08-22-85)

Sue was all-important to me. I not only needed her approval, I needed her empathy. There was no other way to make Sue's eyes see me. More significantly, to make Sue's ears hear me. This became my mission. My burning desire, my life. Sue must see me thin to appreciate that I was fat.

To be thin, you may not eat. But being highly skilled in matters of nutrition, I knew I had to eat something. Due to his job, my husband was living in Chicago at this time. He came home two or three weekends a month. I did not have to cook for another. There was no one to interrupt my plan. Although, I could eat everything in sight or absolutely nothing at all without any reaction or comment from my spouse. But it was easier being alone. My "diet" consisted of cauliflower, mushrooms, tomatoes and an occasional peach. Very occasional -- fruit is partly composed of sugar! To add a bit of variety, I'd sometimes use dietetic blue cheese salad dressing on the tomatoes. Eating was confined to dinner. Copious amounts of coffee filled my stomach throughout the day. My counseling to my dieters however was never compromised and right on target. If only I could listen to my own good advice.

> The Vulture appeared shortly after my anorexic behavior sprouted:
> I'm running scared -- it's the rabbit again.
> Or is it a dragon trying to emerge?
> Perhaps it's the Vulture wanting to consume
> Vultures eat carrion - - that I don't want
> I want to be a dragon to do as I please
> I want to be someone who will be seen and heard (09-02-85)

I was so intent that Sue would see and hear me. Whilst working on an AMT at this time my cast of characters emerged. The rotund Vulture was lazy and taciturn. The slender Snake was sharp-tongued and forward. The Vulture was surprised to see the slinky, thin Snake slither up the tree so fast. The Snake told the Vulture she had been hiding under rocks for a long time. She was growing old and fat and found it hard to slither at all. But her newly-gained thinness brought her pleasure, attention and agility. She warned the Vulture that she could kill her with her ven-

om-filled fangs. The Vulture queried the Snake as to why the Snake would want to harm her. The Snake replied that the Vulture was the epitome of a big blob. She did nothing but perch in a dead tree looking for dead things on the ground to pick at and snake added that the Vulture only attacked those dead and rotting -- no one who would fight back. The Vulture declared that the Snake was no better -- slithering along the ground and in trees to attack those living. The Vulture deemed it better to remain as she was -- silent and calm.
I was both the vulture and, down deep, the Snake. The Vulture sat and wait never acted, never allowed herself to express feelings -- a big blob. She ate and ate and became sadder and sadder. The Snake said what she wanted. But me, the Snake, was still mostly under a rock. The Snake was the me I wanted to be. She was stretching and stirring from my depths. She would be living proof for Sue. The Snake was winning the battle with the Vulture. I was losing weight. Sheer delight! Thinness was within my grasp.

But the Vulture was not annihilated! She too stirred. She came out through my pen:

> I'm afraid to eat
> I'm afraid not to eat
> I'm obsessed with the scales
> I weigh at least twice a day
> I now look in all mirrors rather than running away. It seems as though I'll lose control.
> Should I eat as I know I should
> I've been adept at excuses for almost three weeks
> It's time to stop this nonsense, so why can't I? (09-85)

More:

> Am I doing this to prove a point?
> Or is it much more than that?
> The point has been made -- I am indeed somewhat thinner
> So why do I persist in this silliness? (09-85)
> Something strange was happening. I was losing weight and should have been ecstatic. I was not:
> Sunrise is a thing of beauty
> The pinks, the dusty mauve are a delight.
> These gentle colors diminish ever so fast In their stead appears a magnificent orb
> It's brightness and magnitude overwhelm the eyes
> There was no sunrise today (09-85)

and:

> I am hurting today. I know not why.
> Sadness pervades like a dismal shroud
> I yearn to be caressed and cared for.
> Loneliness is all about me and I despair. (09-85)

At this time the Vulture and Snake made their second appearance:

The Snake was now the star of the cast. She was forward, angry, in control, assured, powerful and still sharp-tongued. The Vulture was self-recriminating, an escapist, non-expressive, distant, out of control and weak.

An Early Poem:

The conflictual memory captured my inner conflict, food as my initiative, my identity versus obedience.

PHASE II

In the moat series, the problem was clarified as a power imbalance as she evolved from a dumb bunny to a soaring eagle.

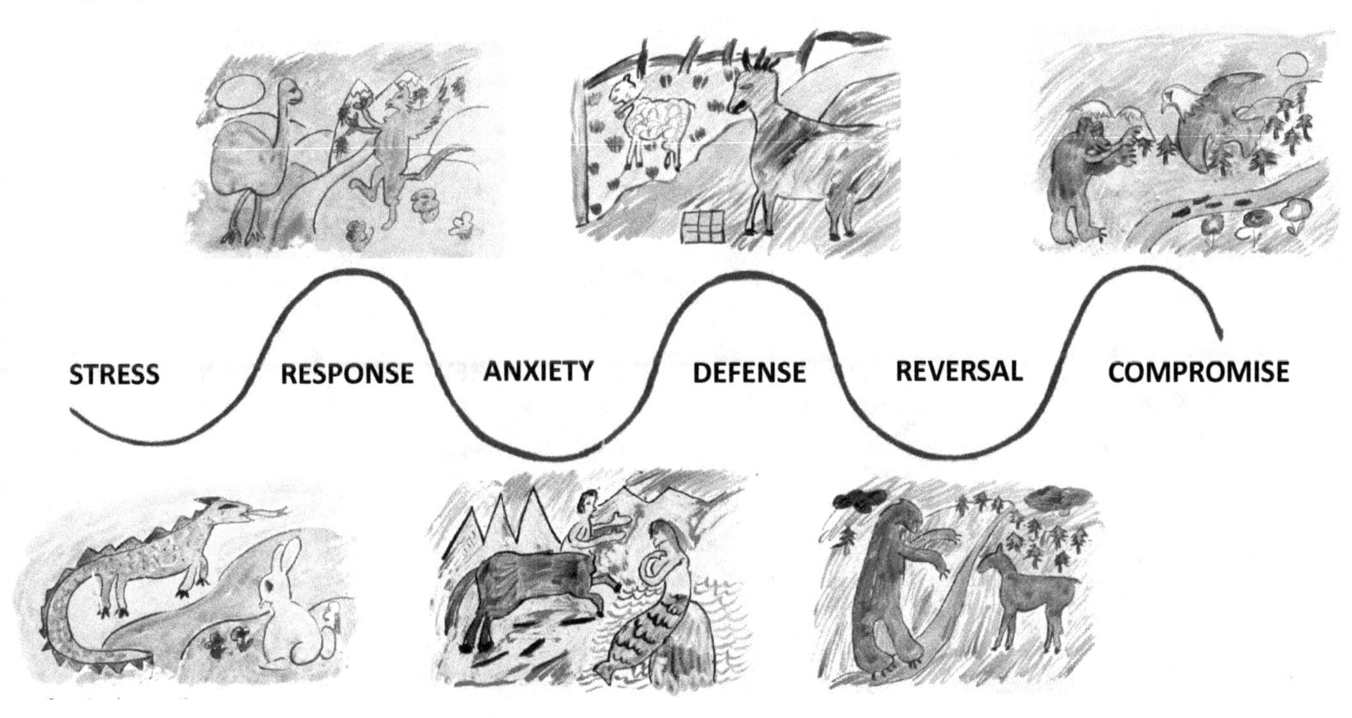

"Run, Rabbit, Run" Gila: Rabbit, you are the proverbial 'dumb bunny.' You are gullible, inane and spineless.	"A Ray of Sunshine" Griffin: Hey, ostrich, it's nice to see you without your head in the sand. You say others don't hear you, but then you never listen to me, your inner self.	"Mermaid and Centaur" (M): I am vulnerable, I am unclothed. (C): I do not want to hear such things. I am a mighty centaur. You are nothing but a fish.	"Lamb and Bull" Lamb: Why don't I know you? Why have you fenced me in? Why do I have my back to you? Why can't I ever figure out how I feel about you?	"The Feckless Fawn" Deer: Your big teeth and claws scare me. You might hurt me. Bear: You're making me mad. Get over here before I lose my temper and bite you.	"Feathers and Claws" Eagle: Here I am, soaring upward. Why haven't I been here before? The eagle flew beyond the mountains and the bear waved goodbye.

Phase III:

In the Snake / Vulture series, the problem of the eating disorder reemerged as she responded to stress, controlling and losing control of food. Her metaphors evolved from snake hissing at a vulture to a jaguar destroying both snake and vulture.

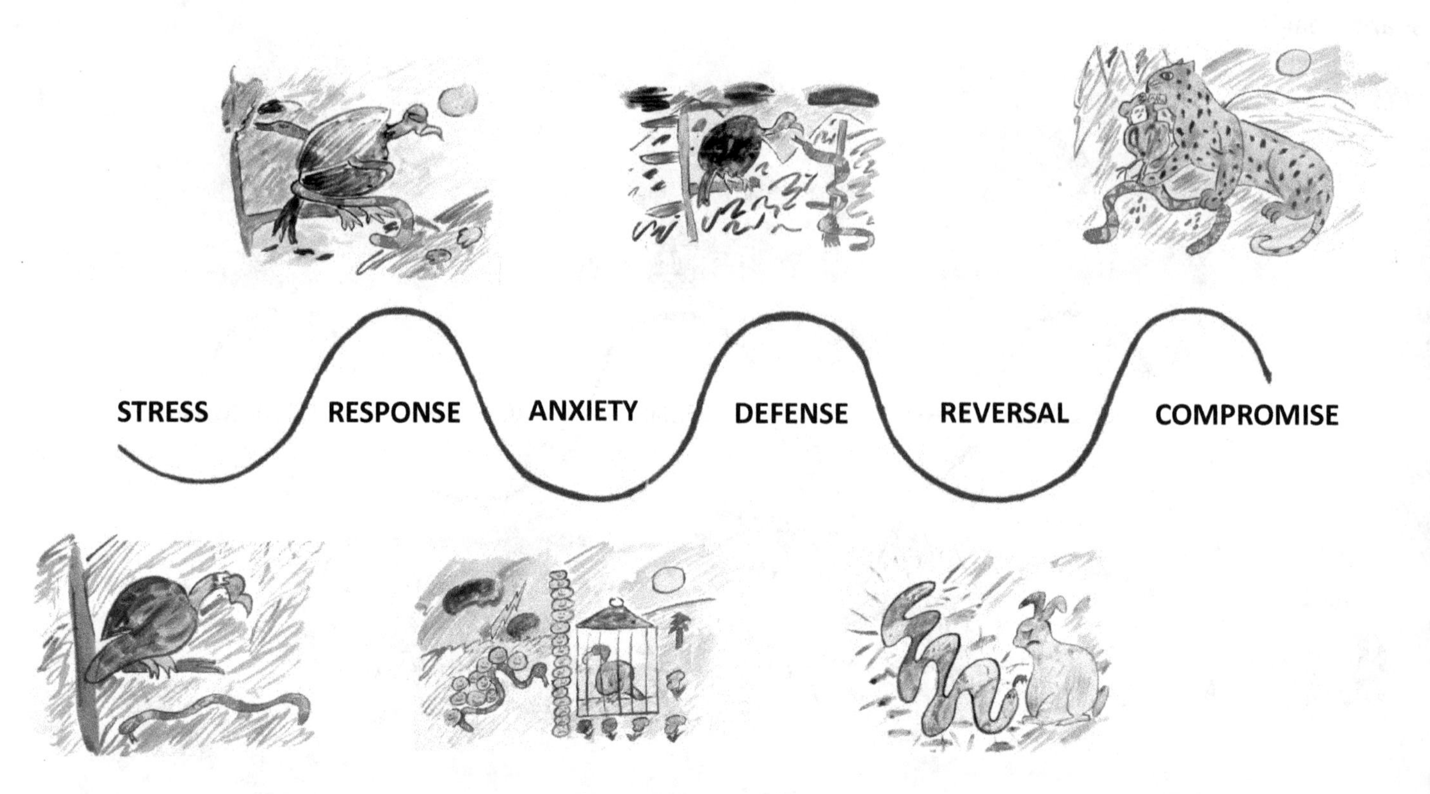

"Feast or Famine" Snake: I can hiss at you, and if I want, bite you with my venom filled fangs.	**"Venom for the Vulture, Wings for the Snake"** Vulture: I am not sure I am ready to die. I can still fly away. A failed attempt to become a whole.	**"Dealing with Stress, or, a Storm Approaching"** Snake: You have me up against the wall in the storm. Am I safe in the eye of the storm?	**"After the Storm"** The vulture won the battle. She ran amok and ate...the snake grew weary and weak.	**"Now or Never"** Snake: If you keep feeding me the way you are, I'll die. Rabbit: The only thing I know how to do is cry.	**"Life is Not Binge or Purge"** Jaguar destroys vulture and snake, and says, "I'll win. My patience has run out. The snake and vulture must die!"

Phase IV

In the final phase of therapy she rectified power in a number of relationships. She evolved from being rejected from her mom's kangaroo pouch to admitting to her husband a need for a real partnership, seeking acceptance for all parts of her many hidden identities.

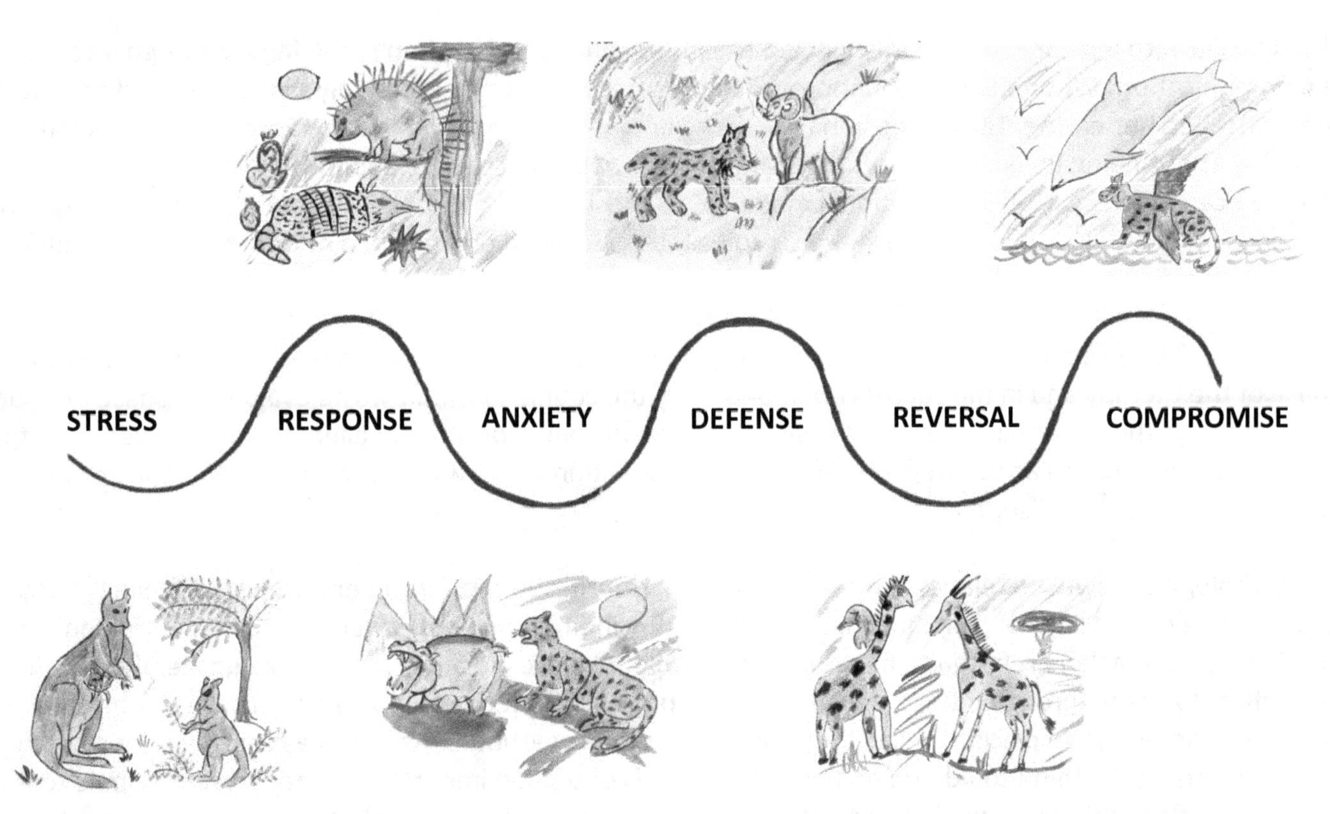

"No Room For Two"	"Wake Up and Live"	"Jaguar vs. Hip-po"	"How Very Dull"	"An Unveiling"	"Who Am I?"
Mother: Why are you eating so much? Soon you'll be fat and ugly. Child: I eat for solace. I eat so you'll be aware of me.	Armadillo says to Porcupine: You are not bound by convention. You can color outside the lines.	Jaguar: You're ugly and obese. You must stuff food and drink in your cavernous mouth all day and night.	Bobcat self says to bighorn sheep husband: you never wanted to change anything nor did you want me to change. There is no joy to look forward to.	Girland to Gir-poise: Neither of us express anger. We have to tell each other when, why we're angry. People can have disputes and be friends again.	Dolphin: I enjoy companionship. What are you? Pijagu: A "we" and not an "I". The pig eats too much, the jaguar desires control and the seagull wants freedom.

Concluding Comments

The Power Management therapy accomplished the objectives of understanding the eating disorder as a relational problem, an emotional behavioral problem originating in managing power and attitude. The crucial manifestation of her pathology surfaced with the intense need to use her eating behaviors as the means of seeking assertion, rather than deal with words talking about her feelings.

The struggle with a person in authority kindled the inner conflict **rather than resolving it through interpersonal communication. When deprived of approval she resorted in eating excessively; as she wanted approval she controlled her eating. The eating behavior was her way of being good or bad, accepting love versus rebelling at not being loved. The** case study confirms the two aspects of relational analysis: the notion of communicating feelings, along a relational modality diagnosis and the notion of the syndromal organization of emotions proceeding predictably along the six-role state syndromal organization of emotions from a conflict to its resolution.

We witness this dialectic organization in each sample metaphor, in the organization of metaphors in each phase of the therapy and in the succession of phases in the course of therapy. The evaluation phase is in formal relation to the final phase: a conflict defined as passivity, antagonism and alienation is resolved as a state of mastery, cooperation and mutual respect. Conflict resolution led to wellness as personal empowerment and cessation of the eating disorder.

The pathology is viewed in relational terms as power in refusing admitting vulnerability, hurt feelings: Power was in hiding her feelings of pain and anger by presenting indifference but rewarding herself with food. 'One of my high school teachers referred to me as imperturbable. My favorite aunt would make unseemly statements in an effort to break through my coat of calm. A neighbor once stated he'd like to be with me during an atomic attack -- I was always so placid. The caption in my high school yearbook: "As merry as the day is long". I was indeed a fortress. Nothing could erupt this volcano. Total control. So important to me. Present a smile to the world, be unflappable and I would be safe. In 34 years of marriage I can recall but one verbal argument -- this only a year or so ago. My feelings were never let known, I ate them. My life was a constant binge not only with food, but emotions as well. My outside grew larger, my inside shriveled. In the AMT my animals turned their backs to each other and the viewer of the images. In the story I recognized a pattern. When under pressure, or feeling sorry for myself, or lonely I plan on over-eating, drinking as a reward. It seems to be something to look forward to'. The last metaphors present the resolution to this withdrawal; they attest comfort in talking about her feelings: 'We have to tell each other when, why we're angry. People can have disputes and be friends again'. Submissive people experience inner turmoil instead of sharing their thoughts assertively.

Gladys' case study attests that emotions are a formally related sequence of ideas as energies, which progress obligatorily from conflict to resolution seeking power balance. Pathology consists in the manifestation of imbalance, symptomatically expressed as unresolved conflicts, leading to cycles of acting out and related guilt ridden consequences. The case study attests that the vicious cycle may be interrupted as emotions are expressed and the person achieves a sense of self-respect reducing alienation. It is important to understand the psychodynamic nature of pathology in order to intervene appropriately to achieve wellness. The solution is not in antidepressant medications to overcome the depression but in self-awareness and the development of appropriate relational coping skills.

Resolution occurred gradually as Gladys recognized her capacity to express her feelings by eloquently composing them as poetry. She had fun re-channeling her energy, redirecting emotional charges into non-conflictual emotional expression, creativity, which helped her to feel good about herself. Her poems, were honest non aggressive behaviors; artistic license allowed her the expression of feelings as a therapeutic emotional release coinciding with a sense of empowerment upon the completion of a poem. The energies processed through creativity are like waters channeled into a generator producing useful electricity rather than as wild self-destructive imploding cataclysm.

Gladys became aware of the original pattern of defiance of authority, compliance and secret rebellion. The poetry elicited by the use of the metaphors manifested in the power of her own creativity, which surpassed the limits of the testing. It served her in venting her feelings spontaneously. Creativity as art helped Gladys' volcano to explode beyond dependency on the approval of a parent or of the therapist. Indeed it helped her to question all authorities. Artfully presented, thoughts surpassed science in expressing emotions. "With poetry I am coming out of hiding. I am free. I don't want to ever be accused of being a logical person. That is my doctor's bag." Her hostile criticism represents a sign of healthy expression of feelings. It is a welcome assertion over the medicalization of creativity. Poetic license was freeing her from medical authoritarianism.

Rebelling from her 'doctor's bag' she offered me her art to chronicle the science of her therapeutic experience as a dramatic totality with a beginning, middle and a moral end. Dramatic plays resolve power issues with justice. Weak characters, victims, become protagonists as heroes, while their inner counterparts are weakened. In plays, like Ibsen's "Doll's House", we witness her dramatic exit with empowerment as she walks out on her cruel dominant husband. The "doll-wife", who was once considered dishonest, walks away from her judgmental husband Torvald and her children, accusing him of dishonesty. How could the tender, thoughtful wife of yesterday be so heartless to her husband, for whom she was committing a crime? In this play the victim seeks empowerment without compromise. In that sense she acts negatively, or in an over-compensatory way, selfishly. She resolved her personal conflicts by compounding the social one, as lack of respect for the marital union.

In therapy the desirable resolution is in a compromise, a reconciliation that reduces personal and social alienation. Therapy seeks a happy ending. Here it achieved non-dramatically personal adjustment as establishing mutual respect saving the marital union. Plath, the poet, her heroine, who committed suicide is a reflection that spontaneous creativity needs to be reined in and interpreted rather than become dramatic escalation of unresolved emotional conflicts.

Therapy, unlike theater, and drama, seeks compromises between the opposite inner sides, the tragic hero's inner conflicts. Therapy seeks to accomplish personal transformation following the principles of correcting both inner and outer systemic balance in restructuring relationships, beginning with the analysis of the dramatic metaphors as circumscribed calls for help. Her characters across the moat started communicating and eventually the moat disappeared into a power struggle between her inner identities. Then she addressed the inner conflict, the opposite aspects of the eating behaviors, eat versus not eat, the vulture versus the snake. The spontaneous resolution is the change to being vulnerable and honest. In symbolic terms she evolved to a new identity, the tiger, who killed the vulture and the snake, tired of the inner conflict, showing her readiness to confront eating patterns, by facing the outside reality. Her metaphors finally reflected improved communications based on showing her emotional hurts. She presented dialogues between herself and the real people in her life as animals in symmetrical positions. She examined all partnerships talking honestly and kindly to each other.

Gladys did not abandon her husband and home. She was able to reduce the inner conflicts, and enjoy a dignified integration by expressing herself in key relationships. The metaphors end with her becoming a happy dolphin staying at home hurt as a bereaved mother, but liking herself and her husband, admitting she 'wants companionship', that is love. She interrupted the cheating game of hiding her feelings and sneaking food, as she did when she was a girl chastised by her mother and in vain seeking to please her father. Instead of hiding her feelings and binging she was enjoying talking to her husband and no longer needing escapist outlets.

She completed therapy and enjoyed her flower garden project, loving her picket fence covered with roses. She was proud of getting angry with her husband for his messing up her knife in clearing a bush. She was able to converse with her son about his feelings and to critically review her deceased mother's disposition. She was able to deal with relations openly and honestly rather than be mad and sneak food, then pay the price by being obsessed by her looks, her image and her diet. She continued writing poetry in a book. This was the desirable conclusion to her despair. Therapy like a drama was concluded and the curtain fell with a happy ending. The patient became a poet. I asked her permission to give her credit for her poetry revealing her identity as a poet. She consented beginning a new tradition in therapeutic reporting.
Gladys' last name is Furphy.

Two dominant clinically diagnosed patients with interpersonal conflicts
The records of self-discovery proceed by the patient completing the creativity assignments and composing essays, combining art and commentary, metaphors, records of evolving insights, poetry. The studies of patients are like those of interns, literary masterpieces, like college papers. Therapy becomes like attending a college course on one's own emotional development. The therapist is a channel, an educator; the patient is an artist, a poet, a student, an explorer of her emotions. The therapeutic technique is tapping one's creativity by composing art, poetry, literature. It evolves self-awareness, wisdom in psychology. But the wisdom is learning about the science of emotions, the Moral Science. Are these cases therapy or emotional education?

The records attest to the diagnostic and therapeutic use of the metaphor analysis technique and its relevance in monitoring therapy outcome. The key therapeutic intervention is self-exploration. The therapy is a collaboration, where most of the work and writing is done by the patient rather than the therapist. The therapeutic information includes learning about psychology reading the introductory essay to the assessment. The essay addresses the topics of the unconscious as a scientific phenomenon, diagnoses, assessment, therapeutic interventions, and monitoring therapeutic changes. The unconscious as creativity is a scientific phenomenon qualified as diagnostic categories, the four syndromal relational modalities as wellness personality typology, also determining relational pathology. The CAB self-assessment technology is utilized as didactic, diagnostic and therapeutic. One readily becomes conscious of the unconscious. Therapeutic changes, are elicited and monitored by the repeated administration of the assessment or simply one of its metaphor creation tasks.

The relational diagnoses were applied to two sets of cases, illustrating the differences of pathologies between dominance and subordinancy; The assessment generates a record. The assessment records reflect the conflict resolution six-role state process and the cyclic evolution of modalities marking the course of therapy into an evolving conflict resolving continuum. The assessment records have been used to illustrate the syndromal process evolving through the cycles of the alternative resolutions.

Thus this study based on the objectivity of records gives us an opportunity to examine the therapeutic experience:
First, we identify pathology as determined by the relational syndromal modality diagnoses.
Second, we examine the evolution of changes in the course of psychotherapy as phases of a dialectic progression in attitude changes as a conflict resolution continuum.
Third, we examine these changes manifested in the patient therapist relationship as a confirmation of the patient's emotional pathology but also reflecting growth.

Review of the three points
The crucial contribution of the Formal Theory is in clarifying pathology associated with the two key relational modalities as syndromes of six interrelated emotions. We recognize modalities as the principle diagnostic criteria determining pathology and entailing the alternative corrective interventions. The case studies illustrate dominance and subordinancy diagnoses becoming relational communicational disorders that we must recognize as leading to different pathologies.

Being aggressive leads to perceiving reality as threatening, a person being sensitive and overreacting, challenging the social system and seeking help because of experiencing power struggles with others including the therapist as both an ally and as an enemy.

Being submissive leads to experiencing fears of expressing one's feelings leading to the intensification of inner conflicts; emotions held in, leading to escapist behaviors, such as hostile wishes to hurt somebody or alternatively hurting oneself, conditions of dependency, such as addictions, escapist activities of defiance, such as eating disorders and self-mutilation, generating fears of losing control.

The power differences lead to alternative distortions of reality; they must be recognized in their consequences in affecting therapeutic relationships and the respective interventions. The therapist has to address the excruciating sensitivities of dominant individuals and the need for reassurance for the submissive emotionally torn individuals having difficulty in expressing their feelings.

Table: Two dominant clinically diagnosed patients with interpersonal conflicts

Regarding reason for consultation	Segmet, seeking help to deal with anger, interpersonal conflicts. Her therapy was recorded with 40 metaphors in the story of a black cat.	Kathy, mural #11 Confused, depressed, angry, afraid of therapy Multiple prior failed therapies since childhood. She completed 5 books.
Relations, principle troubling emotions	Anger, authoritarianism, hate, jealousy, vindictiveness, paranoia, fears of rejection, fears of disapproval.	Anger, distrust, emotionally sensitive and fragile
Processing of energy	Energy externalized as anger Sensitivities as doctor's welcome power and magic versus dreaded tricks	Irritable and expressive, creative and insightful
Transference	Intense dependency needs, seeking love from therapist, while fearing rejections and expressing anger upon any hurt	Evolved through five phases in gradually trusting the therapist and restraining her need for his approval.
Course of therapy record	Autobiography of the therapy utilizing one character, self as a black cat full of needs for stroking and anger at rejections.	Monitored with five books over 2 years; books are formally interrelated as four phases of therapy.
Termination	Termination upon resolving relational conflicts, admitted her growth from a 4 year old to a teenager. Accepted responsibility of her problem of anger; she resolved key relations. Felt loved by her mother.	Successful termination upon feeling connected with her family members. She evolved interest in psychology and philosophy.

Table: Two submissive clinically diagnosed case studies: eating disorder and self-mutilation

Regarding reason for consultation	Gladys mural # 12, eating disorder, shame, guilt, self-consciousness, evasiveness, inability to express her feelings to anyone.	Alicia, anger at self, guilt, self-blame, embarrassment, cutting disorder, suicidality, repeated hospitalizations Inner conflicts.
Prior therapies	Multiple prior therapies	Therapy-resistant condition Four years of cognitive therapies and meds failed completely
Course of therapy	Energy held inside, hostile, scared of losing control in the expression of her anger. Deference to the therapist, instead dealing with inner conflicts, she never articulated any feelings about the therapist.	Recovered in 16 sessions by processing conflicts in two work-books.
Evidence	Unable to address the therapist, multiple animal identities in dialogues; massive exploration of her feelings through poetry, her own creativity.	Two workbooks Not relating to therapist but completed symbolic transformation, stopped cutting episodes. Composed personal report
	Successful termination Interest in poetry and writing, becoming a therapist. Evolution from lack of communications to being able to express self to key relations. She liked being a poet and a supportive therapist.	Successful termination. Found her own identity. Returned to teaching.

Detecting therapy changes

The second point is in detecting therapy changes evolving as a conflict resolution process along a sequence of relational phases. The case studies have demonstrated that therapy evolves through phases of the individual growing along modalities of conflict resolution. The therapist must be receptive in allowing these modalities to manifest as patients' need for alliances and for ruptures. The relational phases evolve around one's relational modality diagnosis, which remains unchanged as genetically determined.

Both dominant and submissive persons start therapy feeling in a passive aggressive phase. The distortions impact the therapeutic relationship. Dominant people are tortured by social conflicts, lack of social support in domestic and in professional environments, frequently in panic because of paranoia due to projection of their own role choices. They have issues with authorities.

Powerful Segmet perceived the therapist as the powerful Wizard. Kathy overwhelmed having been traumatized by prior therapeutic experiences was cautious. The dominant patient needs support and reassurance in an alliance with the therapist. The distressed dominant person needs support to express anger in dealing with relationships. Next, this anger is turned into a phase of assertiveness combating the therapist. Then comes the phase of termination during which the patient feels confidence and self-sufficiency seeking termination from the therapist as an unnecessary challenger. Dominant Segmet evolved emotionally through these phases. At the end of therapy she felt loved by her mother, and needed less support from the humanized magician therapist; she also felt responsible for her distortions and overreactions.

The dominant person upon successful termination becomes aware of her pathology, accepts responsibility for it, which we consider as the submissive cooperative disposition phase of therapy; the patient remains consistently dominant in spite for the cycling. It is desirable to terminate therapy with the dominant person showing respect and gratitude for the therapist. Modesty is very hard to come by. Establishing mutual respect is a criterium of successful termination; criticism and rejection of the therapist upon termination is not a good sign. Segmet had difficulties upon termination. Kathy was much more resolved.

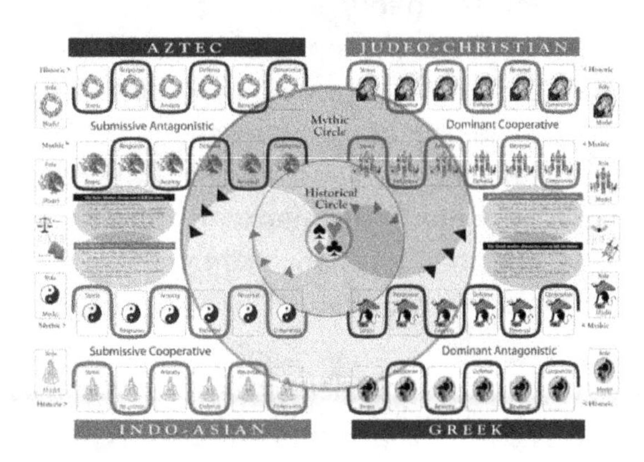

Similarly we witness phases in the course of therapy with cases of submissiveness. These individuals too evolved through the modalities. In the beginning of therapy Gladys presented herself as shadow-fighting with her inner escapist impulses, binging and drinking, staying deceptive. She evolved from hiding her emotions and behaviors, to being assertive in the moat series evolving communications; she was much more determined for changes in the anorexic snake seeking recognition by a therapist, she struggled with her bulimic vulture, finally she broke down seeking help upon failing in her eating struggles, she found the self-confidence to articulate her feelings to the persons that mattered in her life. Symbolically the inner conflicts in terms of eating behaviors were transformed to interactions with the key people. In the final phase she was able to confront the dreaded authorities. She could not totally prevail. Her identity remained fluid. Unlike Segmet's mighty cat identity throughout she was seeking alternative animal identities for herself. At the end she was a 'we rather than an I'. She was many wishes, many animals rather than a single firm voice. The modalities are stable diagnoses, but during therapy they evolve improving the way of resolving conflict. Wanting to be a dolphin was a wonderful potential identity.

The therapeutic relationship

The new diagnostic categories and the assessment technology change the therapeutic experience and the focus on the patient therapist relationship. Therapy begins with the battery. The patient reads an essay. S/he is educated on the principles of psychology as a science. S/he is becoming clearly aware of the nature of the problems as relational choices evoking pathologies. The self-assessment identifies the diagnosis and clarifies how to address it. The battery is didactic, diagnostic and therapeutic by itself. It generates readily clear insights, the patients conduct personal analysis by examining their patterns. The battery evokes a cathartic emotional experience, and it helps the test-taker to identify the needed changes by oneself. The patient gets used to the analysis of her creative process, leading to insights and changes. The pattern also manifests in the relationship with the therapist, but we recognize the transference as one of several manifestations of the pattern. The patient becoming self-sufficient, the role and work of the therapist becomes less complex, less ambiguous.

Transference manifests in the course of therapy. But the therapist's role is easy in explaining the science behind the sequence of interrelated emotions, syndromes and modalities.

There is a sociological significance in these changes in the therapeutic experience. The explicitness of the cognitive information confirmed by the use of the battery leads to the reduction of emotional investment on the part of the patient and also on the part of the therapist. Science allows educating the patient changing the therapy into psychoeducation expanding its delivery to the well public. This self-sufficiency facilitates the work of the therapist as an expert of the science; the therapist becomes an educator. This role reduces the dependency needs of the client to the therapist; it increases the challenge of learning about how to achieve self-confidence and acceptance of responsibility for one's emotions and behaviors. Thus the battery may be used by educators in the classroom and by self-managed peer support groups.

The methodological significance of the Formal Theory

Concluding, psychology is presented as the science of morality, the Science of Conflict Resolution, abbreviated into the Moral Science. This science reconciles epistemology, diagnosis, assessment, morality leading to the delivery of therapeutic services through a program of wellness emotional and moral education utilizing the creative process. The Formal Theory encompasses knowledge of the pure sciences, physics and logic with biology by identifying the unconscious as a homeostatic mechanism transforming energy, changing attitudes, resolving conflict by abiding to or protesting at/to normative conformity. The theory integrates psychology with sociology founded on art, science and biology.

The process of change embraces religions as psychological phenomena, and as normative institutions. They originate in the psyche, leading to sociological changes improving domestic role relations by sanctifying norms. Religions evolved changing norms to increase fairness in family relations and abstraction on the nature of the divine. They have settled to alternative role ascriptions to genders. Gods have been ascribed the attributes of the creative process unconscious. Science reclaims reason to moral thinking.

It is important to understand the methodological shift as the essence of this scientific breakthrough. It is a shift from the axiomatic method to the relational. The relational method departs by identifying an object of study the emotional relational structure of any story as a unit periodic entity; the story or a metaphor is examined as a closed periodic entity completing an energetic transformation with biological origination and sociological function.

The definition of the unconscious has been presented by propositional method as axiomatic definitions advanced by theorists like Freud and Jung. Freud advanced several propositions or models, such as focusing on sexuality and aggression as the motivational forces, yet he also evolved a developmental model, an economic model, the structural model, the transference model, and utilized free associations on the couch as the therapeutic method. Jung departed from the unconscious as determined by archetypes inherent to the unconscious explored through dream interpretation as alchemy. He introduced a dichotomy in thinking intuitively and empirically. He also introduced key distinction in personality typology, the distinction of being introvert versus extrovert. But this is not relational. It is about traits; it is a very different distinction from the formal alternatives of dominance and subordinancy. The Myers Briggs assessment introduced more non formal sets of distinctions. Similarly all assessments identify traits and symptoms; they use non-relational distinctions such as warmth and cold, agency and communion.

The Formal Theory relies on the relational method. It clarifies the unconscious as energy, and as relations being transformed relationally. It identifies a syndromal sequence following formal operations to the formation of four relational resolutions, the modalities. This entails clear diagnostic categories and an assessment identifying measurable relational alternatives, scientific dichotomies that allow graphic mapping of the personal and social positions as interrelated social and psychic measurable variables. These dichotomies are actionable; we need to explore power, attitude and intensity in relating. The CAB self-assessment identifies the social and emotional components as interrelated and as measurable variations according to intensity in the social and psychic realms.

The diagnostic distinctions of dominance and submissiveness are interrelated in terms of communications as flow of energy. The dominant expresses oneself readily, while the submissive channels energy internally. The dominant experiences socialization conflicts, while the submissive experiences inner conflicts. These conditions require alternative interventions and goals.

The CAB provides relational imagery. The images are meaningful through the relational analysis using distinctions in power and attitude. Analysis is based on contrasting one image with another: the original with the ones following. We can detect changes by contrasting the original image of conflict with the final. There we see the evidence of changes.

The card game symbolic signs show change in the comparison of the spade to the heart.
The Gorski retrospective presents change by contrasting the artist's conflict beginning the retrospective with the 'Child of darkness', portraying his autistic son, completed years later with the series of 'Empowered disabled figures'.

Segmet begins feeling captured in her mother's mouth, perceiving her as a vicious dog, and ends with her mother as a dachshund leaking her face.

Kathy starts as a twig broken from a tree, fire-breathing dragons and completes her therapy with her family united by bridges, seasons of the year, key chains and dragons delivering playful monkeys.
Alicia is transformed from a troll failing in hiding from the sun and getting burnt to becoming a moon illuminating the nights, a partner to the sun.

Gladys departs from the animal metaphor of two animals turning their backs to each other and the viewer to two animals facing each other and admitting that 'we can express anger but still be friends'.

The religions evolved from destructive matriarchs like Medusa, and Oedipal divisiveness to becoming wise virgins, like Athena and biblical matriarchs trusting their sons with their fathers, in the father-son covenant. So this study examining therapy delivers evidence of therapeutic change. But the study has a broader relevance. It serves in rethinking psychology from the conflict of unintegrated axiomatically defined disciplines to resolution of the conflict by adopting a clear relational methodology. Psychology thus becomes the well-documented Moral Science.

Every person has a set of metaphors that need interpretation. Most of the time there is a happy ending at the end of a therapeutic experience.

Training facility and programs
The online delivery of the self-assessment, free to the public, is supported by artwork, the exhibits of the Museum of the Creative Process, a museum volume is available, and by an educational game Moral Monopoly retracing the history of religions. The three prong program may be delivered as an emotional education that can be applied for therapeutic objectives. Seven volumes present the research on the Formal Theory. The theory has a home, the Wilburton Inn, incorporated in 1987 as the Art to Science, Inc. it is our training center. It features a mansion built in 1902 as a twin project to the Hildene, next door, the home of the Lincoln family, commemorating the history of America's deadliest conflict leading to its resolution as a critical social change. Political conflicts are generated by religions and by problematic leaders. Now we can neutralize the distortions of perceptions of reality by having a clearer understanding of the psyche and the divine.

FROM TRAUMA TO HEALING

Volume Ten

Albert J. Levis M.D. & Maxwell Levis, Ph.D.

Normative Publications

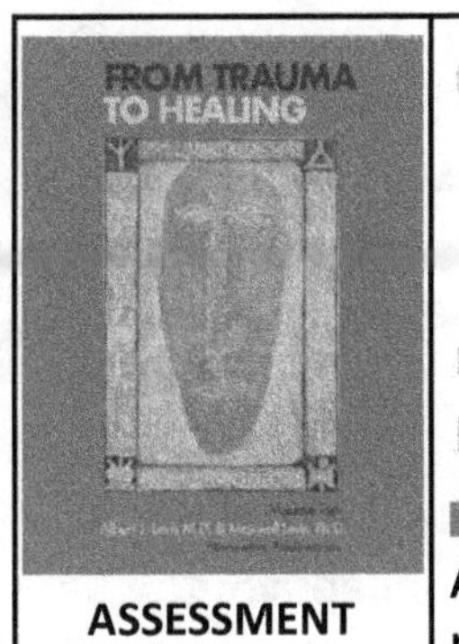 ASSESSMENT ANALYSIS	Assessment's inventory identifies the relational modalities	 Assessment's metaphors identify the unfolding syndromal unit

BOOK THREE

THE BATTERY VALIDATES THE SCIENTIFIC STRUCTURE AND THE EMOTIONAL FUNCTION OF THE UNCONSCIOUS

Overview of the third wall panels and murals

We establish the *yellow brick road* as the metaphor of the scientific and moral nature of the creative process in the first wall. We analyzed the *four heroes of the story* in the second wall, introducing diagnostic categories consisting of four syndromal relational modalities. We also use the Conflict Analysis Battery, CAB, self-assessment. The third wall focuses on the meaning of *'Killing the Witch'* as a metaphor of venturing forth to confront the science behind witchcraft, magic, by recognizing the scientific order in the world of feelings. The metaphor of killing is about the nature of emotions by recognizing rational connections behind emotions and images. The laws of science demystify the assessment experience, the emotional discomfort manifested in emotions and images entailing clarity of laws of science.

The emotional experiences are orderly symbolic transformations determined by laws of logic and those of physics. Killing the witch amounts in demystifying the testing symbolic configurations as dictated by formal operations and recognizing emotional imagery as energy transformations, portraying pendulum oscillations. It is also clarifying the magic of healing as discovering the process behind guilt and scary dreams and as a pattern of misconduct and emotions that may be broken by recognizing the scientific organization of behaviors and emotions.

The third wall confirms the Formal Theory's assessment experience as a measurable physical and emotional transformative mechanism hence utilizing the generation of metaphors for the clear understanding of a person's unconscious and for a predictable emotional transformation of therapeutic significance.

Panels 7, 8, and 9

The first panel captures the Tinman opened up surgically to examine his condition under the defense armor. This clearly implies painful self-examination. The second image is the path to insights using the testing's Animal Metaphor to reconstruct the six-role process. The third panel presents the transformation of the heroes wearing glasses viewing the Wizard apologising, admitting he is an imposter. This image presents the empowerment of insights in the person capturing the benefit of the self-examination as transforming one's attitude from passivity to activity, antagonism to cooperation and from alienation to mutual respect.

On the interior wall we examine Murals # 4, 7, 8, and 9. Mural 4 introduces the metaphor testing choices to reconstruct the syndromal process, the syndromal sequence as a dialectic departing from a conflict and ending to a resolution. The other three murals illustrate the measurable scientific parameters of the battery's metaphors and the therapeutic impact of the testing. The three murals present three case studies illustrating the scientific processing of emotions leading to healing.

The three murals of the third wall demystify the creative process as consisting of an energetic transformative function abiding by the laws of the two phenomena of science. Two murals of the third wall illustrate the scientific nature of the testing process: symbolic systems of frightening experiences are translated into conflict resolving images abiding by the laws of the two scientific phenomena, confirming the formal and physical organization of the thought process; the third mural examines the healing function of the creative process as an energetic transformative emotional experience.

Mural number seven informs on the three formal operations of the scale connecting the metaphors of the testing validating the formal structure of emotions. It focuses on the formal analysis of the concepts of the battery as happens upon repetition of the workbook representing formal continuity between equivalent symbolic representations reflecting the unconscious transforming passivity to activity, antagonism to cooperation and alienation to mutual respect.

Mural number eight informs on the directionality of art as reflecting pendulum oscillations exemplifying the manifestation of the process abiding by the laws of the Simple Harmonic Motion. It addresses the emotional experiences as following physical energetic continuity. The mental processing of conflict resolution manifests clearly as oscillations of a pendulum connecting the episodes of the six-role syndrome. The visual configuration of the emotional developments coincide with the imagery of pendulum oscillations. The story unfolds as three pendulum oscillations.

Mural 9 informs on the therapeutic function of the assessment as an emotional transformative experience freeing the person of pathology. The mural illustrates the emotional impact of the three session assessment experience confirmed by an essay composed by the patient upon completion of the consultation. The insights gave her relief from lifelong emotional distress. The patient had first a cathartic experience completing the testing, relief of guilt harbored for early misbehaviors; she also had insights about her current adjustment catching herself as a limit tester. She experienced relief of guilt for the past and awareness of the need of self-control in dealing with the future.

So killing the witch examines the assessment reflecting the unconscious as a scientific phenomenon abiding by the laws of logic and physics and the processing of emotions leading to cathartic emotional growth as an attitude transformation.

The battery metaphors are about the unconscious as a scientific therapeutic phenomenon. They generate insights and guidance for changes. The task is identifying one's wellness relational diagnosis with the inventory clarifying one's type of pathology and how to correct it through deliberate attitude and power management changes. The metaphors are shown to generate insights about the physical and emotional structure of the conflict resolution process illustrating and validating the Formal Theory, the formal and energetic organization of the thought process but also coinciding with the emotional, therapeutic and healing function of the assessment.

In conclusion the third wall panels and murals illustrate the science and the emotional function of the unconscious conflict resolution process. The CAB represents a concise program of emotional education integrating knowledge, self-knowledge, science and moral values. We identify the battery as a learning and emotionally meaningful experience. We utilize the battery as an emotional education as 'Creativity and Power Management'.

'Killing the witch' as a metaphor of emotional transformation

It is very interesting to examine the powerful witch as corresponding to the role of overwhelming conflicts with one's mother, authorities in general. It is very interesting that once a person examines the conflictual relation with one's mother, etc. conflicts clear up and a person gets reconciled with the mother/authority figure.

- Segmet's relation with her mother is a great example of the evolution of feelings recorded in the course of therapy using metaphors. In several original protocols she depicted her mother's criticisms as a vicious dog eating up herself as a black cat. She felt destroyed by her mother's constant disapprovals. At some point in her own protocols the black cat literally kills the vicious dog. Her most difficult protocol was one, she ventured to present her perception of her mother as a sadist, enjoying inflicting pain on her with an enema. Following daring admitting with great embarrassment her negative feelings for her mother's assault, her feelings for her mother changed. Her therapy was concluded with her mother transformed to a dachshund leaking the black cat's face.
- Nicolas' case study presents in his Animal Metaphor test a dead cow hit by lighting. In the fairy tale metaphor Maleficent is cursing the Sleeping Beauty to die at age 16. In his comments he admitted that at times as a child he considered his mother as Maleficent. He also reported that upon his 16th birthday he initiated homosexual unprotected sex during the beginning of the Aids epidemic.
- David presented his mother's criticism for his obsessive masturbation as a child as devastating, and traumatic.
- Alicia's balloons family portrait presented her mother as a cloud with lightning bolts, while her father was an umbrella over her own broken balloon. In the next family portrait she presented herself above all family balloons but in the square shape emulating her father's square balloon.
- Rena used to visit me on consecutive years upon mother's day with exacerbating migraines. She reported a crisis that broke her relationship with her mother upon finding her in bed with her husband. She had reacted by leaving her husband and home. In her turn she tried very hard to be a perfect grandmother to her grandchild. She committed suicide upon failing to be accepted by her daughter as a good grandmother.
- Hannah, a holocaust survivor experienced lifelong guilt feelings for having sensed as a kid relief upon her grand parents' deportation to a work camp, which she later discovered as a death camp. Her guilt feelings were overwhelming. She processed them by examining the image underneath her mask of imperturbability as a tree bearing poison fruit and a heart with good wishes that bring one to hell.
- Gladys unable to deal with feelings of anger finally voiced them as experiencing a strong rejection by her mother upon her brother's birth. She confronted her feeling expelled from her mother's kangaroo pouch.

Confronting mothers is a theme of several dramatic stories of Greek mythology. Greek culture fought matriarchy to evolve patriarchy. Patriarchy overruled matriarchy.

We identify several encounters with mother figures marking cultural transformations.

- Zeus swallowed his wife, pregnant Metis, and gave birth to Athena out of his head. He had many affairs, while his wife Hera sought to damage his escapades; one initiative was to kill his extra-marital child Hercules, placing snakes in his crib; another was transforming one of his mistresses, Ios, into a cow and giving her husband Argos Panoptes hundred eyes to guard his wife as a cow.
- Hera is perceived as a witch, with snakes, and with magic skills like turning a rival into a cow.
- Perseus killed Medusa.
- Hippolytus confronted incestuous Phaedra upon her making advances on him. The conflict led to his death. She committed suicide.
- Another tragic story is about Iocasta killing herself upon discovering her relation with her son, Oedipus.
- The Trojan War was about confronting Helen of Troy, a runaway wife for braking her vows.
- The most emotionally charged mother confrontation was by two children Orestes and Electra killing their unfaithful and murderous mother Clytemnestra.
- The Homeric epics present Odysseus dealing with matriarchal conflict-arousing sirens as sorceresses impeding his journey to Ithaca and reunion with his loyal wife, Penelope.
- Gilgamesh fighting Ishtar, a dominant female lost his beloved superman partner Enkidu. This epic is the inception of the biblical stories of Adam and Eve and Samson and Delila, as well as of the inception of the biblical father son-covenant.

CHAPTER ONE PANELS

Panel 7: The function of the CAB self-assessment as the Journey of Self-Discovery and

Killing the Witch, Confronting Evil as the Condition to Transformation and Healing.
Psychoeducation Studies Restructuring the Unit in the Pursuit of Conflict Resolution

7

Creativity & Power Management, the Journey of Self-Discovery and Personal Transformation.

The Wizard of Oz story may be seen as a sample of the Creativity and Power Management course. This course deliberately taps creativity to capture the personal symbolic system in metaphorical language for diagnostic and therapeutic objectives. The adventures of the heroes in the Oz metaphor-land herald what occurs in the Power Management training. The adventures lead first to self-discovery and then to personal transformation.

Like the book of the Wizard, the training creates awareness of the unifying central path, the roller-coaster of the Unit Process. Then it organizes along this path one's experiences and thoughts as a pattern of relating. Next it explores the restructuring of one's relating. Finally the training addresses the rethinking of morality. It departs from the static notions of an external authority figure by promoting awareness of the dynamic intrapsychic principles of conflict resolution.

Power Management differs from the Oz book merely in that it is about one's own symbolic universe and about the abstract redefinition of moral order stemming from one's very own unconscious.

"The tinsmiths worked for three days and four nights..."

THE CREATIVE PROCESS
IS THE UNIT THAT INTEGRATES ALL KNOWLEDGE
IT IS THE KEY THAT UNLOCKS ALL BOOKS

THE MUSEUM OF THE CREATIVE PROCESS

Creativity and Power Management, a Comprehensive Emotional Education.

CREATIVITY AND POWER MANAGEMENT OR CONFLICT ANALYSIS TRAINING IS A STANDARDIZED COMPREHENSIVE EMOTIONAL EDUCATION AND A BRIEF PSYCHOTHERAPY PROGRAM THAT TARGETS INSIGHT AND WISDOM THAT LEADS TO INCREASED PERSONAL AND INTERPERSONAL EFFECTIVENESS.

The program addresses three objectives:

FROM ART TO SCIENCE, FROM CONTENT TO PROCESS, FROM A DRAMA TO A UNIVERSAL MORAL ORDER, THE FORMAL ANALYSIS OF A MODEL SYMBOLIC SYSTEM.

The Wizard of Oz injunction of Killing the Witch may be seen as a very threatening injunction; one has to overcome one's dependency needs, one's hesitations to be brave and complete the assessment as the task to sample creativity for self-discovery. This is the challenge of deliberately taping creativity to capture the personal symbolic system in metaphorical language for diagnostic and therapeutic objectives.

The adventures of the heroes in the Oz metaphors herald what occurs in the Power Management training. They lead first to self-discovery and then to personal transformation. Like the book of the Wizard, the conflict analysis training creates awareness of the unifying central path, the roller-coaster of the Unit Process, which organizes one's experiences and thoughts as a pattern exploring one's relating. The testing addresses reducing the need of an external authority figure like a therapist by trusting one's own judgement in exploring the testing. Power Management requires examining one's own relational pattern. Tin-man's three days and four nights of reconstruction work are a timeframe parallel to the work in completing the Conflict Analysis Battery leading to examining critically one's relational pattern as one's own symbolic universe.

'Creativity and Power Management', a Comprehensive Emotional Education

Creativity and Power Management through the Conflict Analysis Battery is a standardized emotional education that targets insight and personal transformation leading to increased personal and interpersonal effectiveness. The educational therapeutic program addresses three objectives:

- Understanding the Unit for the integration of knowledge.
- Understanding the Unit's personal manifestation for self-knowledge.
- Identifying the principles of conflict resolution as moral values.

KNOWLEDGE- The training includes a cognitive or didactic component, an essay alternatively a series of lectures targeting understanding the Formal Theory's unit of the six-role process intrinsically connecting thoughts, behaviors, and emotions, pursuing conflict resolution, along the four relational modalities.

SELF-KNOWLEDGE- The Conflict Analysis Battery self-assessment, constitutes the experiential, insight generating component. Creativity exercises guide the trainee to identify how s/he resolves conflict. Trainees create art, compose metaphors, interpret them reconstructing the continuity between them as a process of conflict resolution, yielding insights, manifestation of meaning in their symbolic language. Ideally students compose an essay recognizing the conflict resolution principles leading to self-realization and self-improvement.

MORAL GROWTH - The training includes an interactive component targeting personal and social growth, also study of sociology retracing the evolution of religions as discoveries of the modalities improving personal and family role relations by playing Moral Monopoly, an educational card-game. Trainees practice role-playing along the cultural stories learning about conflict resolution consciously targeting the choices of mastery, cooperation, and mutual respect.

Unlike other psycho-assessment instruments, the battery is a theory-based comprehensive self-assessment that combines both an inventory test and a set of projective techniques. Both types of testing target the determination of the Unit process as one's relational modality and its syndromal deployment as a Conflict Resolution Process. While the inventory identifies one's relational modality, the projective tests reveal the formal continuity of emotions in the personal symbolic language.

The personal Conflict Resolution Process is recognized, at two levels. It manifests first through the analysis of each metaphor test as a totality of formally connected choices reflecting how a person evolves from a conflict to a resolution, second through analysis of the interrelation of the tests of the entire Battery. Both formats reflect the personal conflict resolution process revealing how a person resolves conflicts.

Accordingly, the personal Conflict Resolution pattern is reconstructed by sequencing the metaphor tests into a conflict resolving dialectic in the context of the six roles: Stress is depicted in the Conflictual Memory Test and the parental Family Balloon Portrait, Response is depicted by the Transparent Mask I and The Marital Family Balloon portrait. Anxiety is depicted in Mask II and III. Defense by The Animal and The Fairy Tale Metaphors, Reversal by the second Animal Metaphor, and the Dream Metaphor. Compromise is depicted in the Short Story Metaphor.

Panel 8: The Unit as the Superhighway to Wisdom

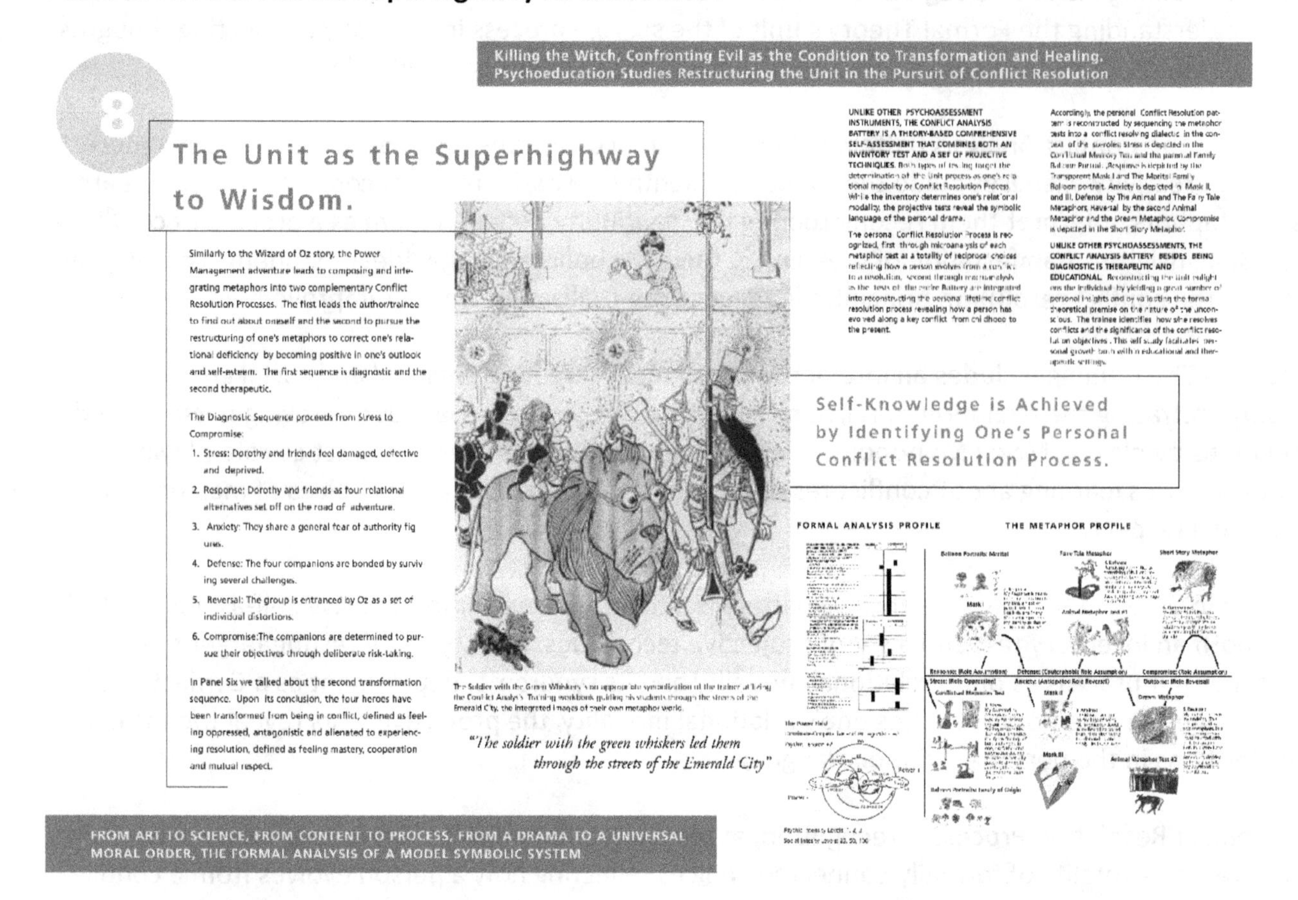

Similarly to the Wizard of Oz story, Power Management leads to composing and integrating metaphors. In brief therapy it is recommended in completing two workbooks. The first is the evaluation. The second battery illustrates transformation. The first leads the author/trainee to find out about oneself and the second to examine the evolution of one's metaphors correcting initial relational deficiencies. The first sequence is diagnostic and therapeutic. The second reflects transformation and serves as a testimony of personal growth.

In the case of the Oz story, the first sequence proceeds from Stress to Compromise:
Stress: Dorothy and friends feel damaged, defective, and deprived.
Response: Dorothy and friends as four relational alternatives, set off on the road of adventure.
Anxiety: They share a general fear of authority figures.
Defense: The four companions are bonded by surviving several challenges.
Reversal: The group is entranced by Oz as a set of individual distortions.
Compromise: The companions are determined to pursue healing through deliberate risk-taking.

In Panel Eight, we view the transformation sequence. Upon its conclusion, the four heroes have been transformed from being in conflict, defined as feeling oppressed, antagonistic, and alienated, to experiencing resolution, defined as feeling masterful, cooperative, and respecting themselves. The Soldier with the Green Whiskers is an appropriate symbolization of the trainer utilizing the Conflict Analysis Training workbook guiding his students through the streets of the Emerald City, the integrated images of their own metaphor world.

Unlike other psycho-assessments, the Conflict Analysis Battery - besides being diagnostic - is educational and therapeutic

Reconstructing the Unit enlightens the individual by its yielding personal insights and by validating the formal theoretical premise on the nature of the unconscious. The trainee identifies how s/he resolves conflicts and the significance of the conflict resolution objectives. This self-study facilitates personal growth both within educational and therapeutic settings.

Case study: Self-Knowledge is Achieved by Identifying One's Personal Conflict Resolution Process.
Stress: My Outstanding Memory of Conflict was my father leaving our home. I was feeling responsible. Two other memories clarify my feelings of hurt and anger. In one, my father and stepmother decided to make my pet billy goat into dinner. In another, I hang up the phone on them for years.
Response: My Response is depicted in my Family Balloons dedicated to my pets, a flock of parrots which I treat like kids, and in my Mask, which presents my identity as that of a "Block of Worry."
Anxiety: The Mask covers up my feelings of being "A Fragmented Jewel." In my heart, I harbored fears of children being too demanding and needy like I used to be.
Defense: Perceiving authorities as terrorizing (Mt. Lion), my strategy has been to act as an accommodating Turkey. Similarly, in my Fairytale "Jack Be Quicker," my small Jack is jumping over a huge candlestick.
Reversal: My fear of my boyfriend's kids was my undoing. This was presented in two metaphors. In a reoccurring dream, I was haunted with guilt for an abortion. In a metaphor, I was a worn-out Greyhound derided by three alley cats (my boyfriend's children).
Compromise: My drama found its resolution as I, the neurotic terrier, could truly renegotiate my relationship with my father as a menacing but talkative Buffalo.

Panel 9: The Unit Integrates Knowledge, Self-Knowledge, and Clarity of Values

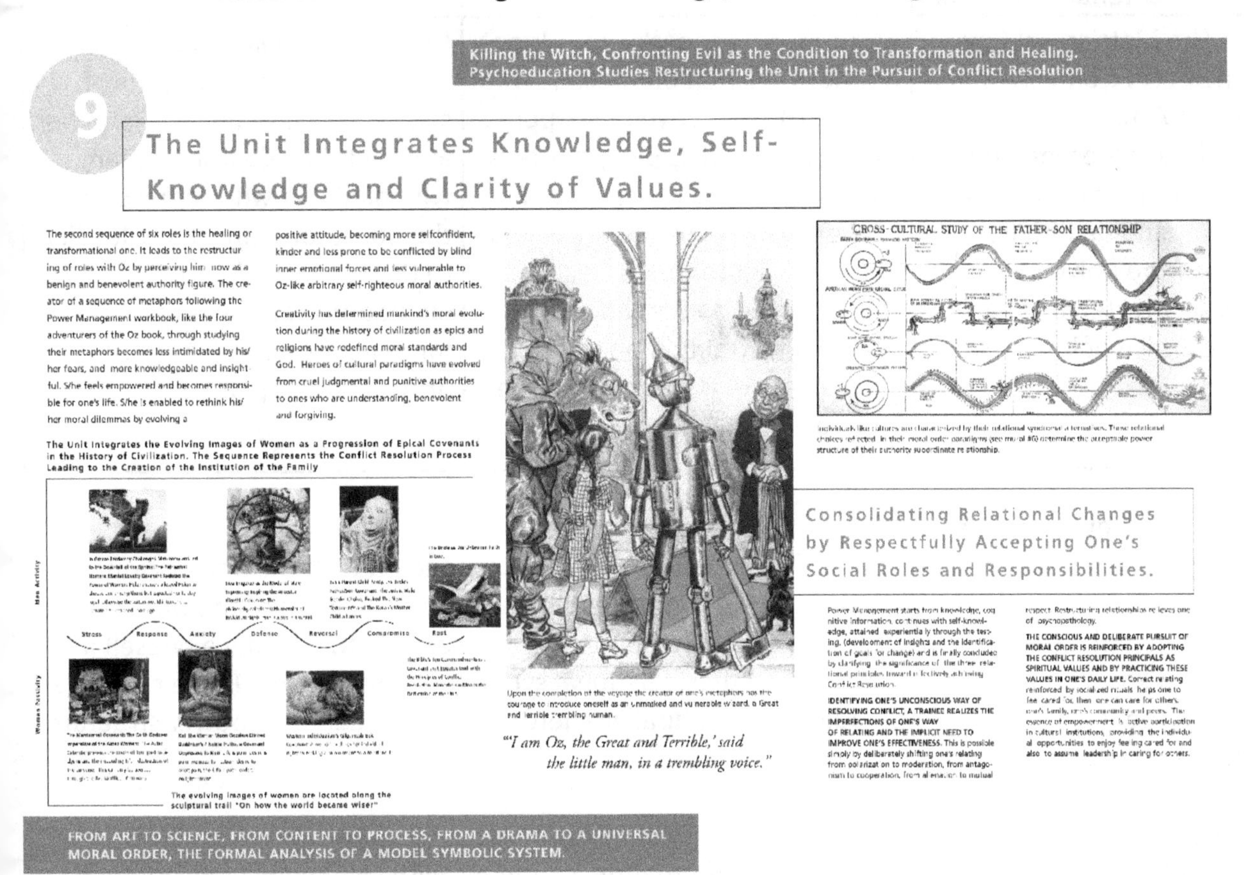

The second sequence of six roles is the healing or transformational one. It leads to the restructuring of roles with Oz by perceiving him now as a benign and benevolent authority figure. The creator of a sequence of metaphors following the Power Management workbook, like the four adventurers of the Oz book, through studying their metaphors, becomes less intimidated by his/her fears, and more self-confident, knowledgeable and insightful. S/he feels empowered and becomes responsible for one's life. S/he is enabled to rethink his/her moral dilemmas by evolving a positive attitude, becoming kinder, and less prone to be conflicted by blind inner emotional forces and less vulnerable to Oz-like arbitrary self-righteous moral authorities.

Creativity has determined mankind's moral evolution during the history of civilization as epics and religions have redefined norms as moral standards and God as a role model. Heroes of cultural paradigms have evolved from cruel judgmental and punitive authorities to ones who are understanding, benevolent, and forgiving. The Unit Integrates the Evolving Images of Women as a Progression of Epical Covenants in the History of Civilization. The Sequence Represents the Conflict Resolution Process Leading to the Creation of the Institution of the Family.

Mural 5 inserted in the assessment as a paradigm of evolution in resolving conflicts

Men in Activity	RESPONSE: In Greece Patriarchy Challenged Matriarchy and led to the Downfall of the Sphinx: The Patriarchal Homeric Marital Loyalty Covenant Reduced the Power of Women: Helen's suitors allowed Helen to choose one among them but expected her to stay loyal; otherwise the suitors would intervene to restore a threatened marriage.	DEFENSE: Men emerge as dragons, feather serpents, sun gods, powerful Egyptian male Sphinxes	COMPROMISE: Bible's Father/Son Covenant: The Judaic Male Gender Choice, evoked The New Testament's and The Koran's Mother-Child alliances.
Men in Passivity	STRESS: The Matriarchal Covenant: The Earth Goddess Imperative of the Aztec Women: The Aztec Calendar presents the doom of four past cataclysms and the impending fifth destruction of the universe. This can only be averted through the live sacrifice of humans.	ANXIETY: Kali, the Warrior Moon Goddess, Elicited Buddhism's 4 Noble Truths, a Covenant Oppressive to Men: Life is pain; desire is pain; we need to restrain desire to avert pain following the 8-fold path to enlightenment. Siva Emerged as the Model of personal restraint, man is a cog in a wheel; he is stepping on the inner child.	REVERSAL: Gilgamesh Epic A woman explores her rights of seduction, Gilagamish rejects her and finds Enkidu a superman, who died and who represents the quest for immortality leading to the concept of father son covenant and women as responsible for being expelled from Paradise or the state of peace.

The Bride as the Bible, representing the covenant with God.

The Ten Commandments as the Principles of Conflict Resolution are now connected with the unconscious as the source of the conflict resolution formal operations. Monotheism means the Deification of the Unit, monas. Upon the completion of the voyage, the creator of one's metaphors has the courage to introduce oneself as unified. Individuals, like cultures, are characterized by their relational syndromal alternatives. These relational choices reflected in the four moral order paradigms (see mural #6) determine the acceptable power structure of the respective relational modalities.

Relational Identity

Power Management starts from knowledge, cognitive information, continues with self-knowledge, attained experientially through the testing (development of insights and the identification of goals for change), and is finally concluded by clarifying the significance of the three relational principles toward effectively achieving Conflict Resolution. Identifying one's unconscious way of resolving conflict, a trainee realizes the imperfections of one's way of relating and the implicit need to improve one's effectiveness. This is possible simply by deliberately shifting one's relating from polarization to moderation, from antagonism to cooperation, from alienation to mutual respect. Restructuring relationships relieves one of psychopathology.

The conscious and deliberate pursuit of moral order is reinforced by adopting the conflict resolution principles as spiritual values and by practicing these values in one's daily life. Correct relating reinforced by socialized rituals helps one to feel cared for, then one can care for others: one's family, one's community, and peers.

CHAPTER TWO: THE MURALS
CASE STUDIES FOR THE SCIENTIFIC INTERPRETATION OF THE SELF-ASSESSMENT METAPHORS

Introduction: Murals #4, 7, 8, and 9 illustrate the battery's metaphors and their interpretation
On the interior wall three, we present three case studies illustrating the detailed scientific interpretation of metaphors of three personal profiles generated using the battery.
Mural 7 informs on the formal continuity of metaphors in symbolic systems following the three formal operations of the equilibrial scale.
Mural 8 informs on the directionality of art as reflecting physical dimensions of the conflict resolution process exemplifying the manifestation of the laws of the Simple Harmonic Motion. Mural 9 informs on the diagnostic and therapeutic function of the assessment. The case studies exemplify the scientific dimensions of the symbolic language of metaphors. The inventory is diagnostic, the metaphors are therapeutic. They generate insights and guidance for changes. The task is identifying one's wellness relational diagnosis and pathology and how to correct it. The analysis of metaphors entails actionable adjustments.

SUB-CHAPTER ONE
Mural 4: My Metaphors, Myself: 1983

Mural #4 is added to the three murals of wall three as it pertains to the study of the self-assessment. This mural presents my case study introducing the testing instruments used in reconstructing the Conflict Resolution Process through the battery.

Mural #4 introduces the use of creativity for self-discovery. The personal system of conflict resolution as a harmonic is reconstructed by the metaphor testing of the Conflict Analysis Battery. The mural clarifies the correspondence of tests and role-states, reflecting the organization of personal emotions into the dramatic totality of the creator's Conflict Resolution Process. The mural captions explain the correspondence between each role state and a specific test of the Conflict Analysis Battery.

Here, six metaphor creation tests help to reconstruct the personal six-role Conflict Resolution Process of your author. The experimentally derived sequence validates the theory by showing that parts are formally interrelated within the dramatic totality. This totality tells my story as to how I evolved from a *stress,* "The War of Metaphors," through my *response* identifying with Pinocchio, the wooden puppet lying about my identity, because during the Holocaust years, my assumed name was a lie, protecting me from being arrested as a Jew. *Anxiety* reflects the need for the puppet to become a boy, to evolve confidence on who he really is by solving the mystery of religions; anxiety was in explaining religions with a scientific mechanism, the Formal Theory; *Defense* was in validating the theory by solving the riddle of the Sphinx as expressing mutual respect between the genders, a very different explanation from the Freudian interpretation of Oedipus Complex; *reversal* was in my seeing my family delivering hospitality and emotional education to the guests of the Wilburton Inn; the resolution to my drama was in the *compromise* role state as "The reconciliation of the world religions as complementary metaphors."

This Mural Shows How the Process Integrates the Creativity Tests of the Conflict Analysis Battery to Identify the Personal Way of Resolving Conflicts.
The fourth mural illustrates how tapping the personal creativity with a series of standardized creativity exercises, the Conflict Analysis Battery (CAB) achieves two goals: The result is both a validation of the key postulation of the nature of the unconscious predictably proceeding along the formal transformations of the Conflict Resolution Process and second the assessment measures the personal way of resolving conflict.

The person tested is the author. The mural reveals how my unconscious guided by the Conflict Analysis Battery (CAB) of tests, proceeds to provide information, which then is integrated to reconstruct my Conflict Resolution Process. Because each test of the CAB provides information about each one of the six role states, e.g., the Conflictual Memories Test yields information on the personal *stress state,* the Mask identifies the personal *response*, etc. by piecing the metaphor tests into a sequence, it is easy to reconstruct the six-role personal process. Thus, the battery of metaphor exercises yields the personal story as a three-act dramatic continuum, the personal conflict resolution totality. This process entity illustrates the three formal transformations integrating the isolated fragments of each test into a dialectic continuum, identifying the personal syndromal process.

2. RESPONSE is identified by the Transparent Mask Test, which reveals a person's identity. I chose the image of the runaway Pinocchio, the wooden puppet lying about his identity, fleeing the killer whale of hot ideologies pursuing naive consumers.	4. DEFENSE is identified by the Animal Metaphor Test. Here, the Formal Theory Oedipus is offering the Sphinx an olive branch--Conflict Resolution--as the new answer to the everlasting riddle on the nature of humans.	6. COMPROMISE is identified by the Short Story Test. My Judaic passion for justice and my Greek respect for reason as the fiddler on the temple roof unites the world metaphors in the cosmic dance of a universal moral order.
1. STRESS is identified by the Memories Test. It represents my recollection of World War II as "The War of the Metaphors," the war of multiple cultural conflicts endangering everybody's survival.	3. ANXIETY is identified by the Behind the Mask Test. It presents Pinocchio trapped in the stomach of the killer whale with his creator, Geppetto. My Pinocchio is showing the Unit of the Conflict Resolution Process to Geppetto. This discovery has transformed him from a puppet into a true human.	5. ROLE REVERSAL is identified by the Dream Test. It presents the daydream of my family working as a team delivering hospitality and wisdom to fellow travelers on the patio of the Art to Science Project, the Wilburton Inn.

This is the author's own metaphor profile: the sequence of metaphors are connected by the role of metaphors: stress as persecuted by them as ideologies, responding by escaping from them, anxiety as hoping to analyze them, defense as interpreting them, reversal as delivering an educational program, and compromise as interpretation of metaphors reconciling art and science, psychology and religions.

The Conflict Analysis Battery metaphor creation tests may be integrated as sharing a common theme as one's symbolic language. The tests then are interrelated as formal transformations of each other. In parallel to the metaphors, the inventory test, the Relational Modality Evaluation Scale identifies one's relational modality, confirming one's wellness personality type diagnosis.

My story starts with my conflictual childhood memory revealing the stress or role oppression phase of the process. It identifies what I experienced as a child at the mercy of cultural conflicts, the religious distinctions. The testing sequence ends in my interpreting cultural metaphors reconciling reason and faith, reconciling my Greek propensity for logic and my Judaic need for social justice. The tests are metaphors integrated into the six-role process, validating the unconscious generation of a Conflict Resolution Process. The process reflects my predicament in seeking meaning as my healing from my childhood trauma of cultural conflicts. The testing leads to self-discovery and to emotional growth, as the imagery reveals my unconscious reasoning behind my lifelong pursuit to evolve the Formal Theory of Behavior.

There are two ways of identifying the conflict resolution process. One is in the analysis of each metaphor, illustrating conflict resolution in the dialogue between the characters in each metaphor. The second is in the manifestation of the universal dynamic structuring the unconscious, as manifested in the formal relation between the tests. We will detect this structure at the macro level as the dialectic formal integration of the battery tests to each other. The tests are examined as unfolding along the six roles integrated along the three formal operations. The mural illustrates the macro validation as each creativity task is in the predicted formal relationship to the other tests as a six-role state totality.

I. *Role Oppression or Stress is portrayed by the Childhood Memory and the Family Portrait.* These tests capture the most formative childhood experiences. Here, the image, a war memory from the year 1944, presents the author's parental family, his mother with the youngest and father with the two older boys, seeking shelter during a bombardment presenting the war of metaphors. These are the many religions and nationalities represented by a church with a cross, a synagogue with the Star of David, a Greek temple, a German tank with a swastika, a British airplane with colored circles. This childhood memory, the war of metaphors, my trauma, and personal oppression was the departure for my research career on reconciling religions and the sciences into a new theory of behavior.

2. *The Role Assumption or Response is conveyed in Mask I,* which usually reveals the person's identity. Here the author assumes being Pinocchio, the mortal, fragile wooden marionette escaping the killer whale, the whale of metaphors pursuing to devour it. In the author's world, the beast had devoured his father, his grandfather, the entire Jewish community of Greece, young and old. The beast was the divisive metaphors: the Nationalists and the Communists, the Greeks, Italian and German soldiers. The reason for the choice of Pinocchio is that I felt like a runaway puppet lying about who I was, a Jew, hiding with an assumed Christian name. The little boy was not going to be gobbled up. I was making a stand to the violation of human rights inflicted by being stereotyped.

3. *Anticipated Role Reversal or Anxiety and Hope is revealed in the Mask II Test.* The marionette is portrayed inside the stomach of the killer whale, reunited with his creator Father Geppetto. The puppet explains to Geppetto, "In order for people to stop being marionettes, they must understand their metaphors, they must find the key to knowledge and self-knowledge!" Pinocchio is holding the key—it is the Conflict Resolution Process. His face is transformed to human. Geppetto is puzzled with the wisdom of his puppet. Can his wooden child predict behavior? Can he be transformed to a free and true human? Could humankind rid itself from the confusing multiplicity of moral orders robbing the public from the freedom of thinking?

4. *The Counterphobic Role Assumption or Defense is identified by Animal Metaphor Test #1,* revealing how a person transforms passivity to activity. Here the author uses the classical metaphor of Oedipus and the Sphinx but providing a new solution to Freud's interpretation of the Riddle. Oedipus has a new answer. He restructures the power relationship between himself and the beast by offering her an olive branch and telling her, "I know the

answer to your riddle, but please do not jump off the cliff. Let us be partners. Could you take care of the sheep?" The secret to the riddle is the principles of Conflict Resolution, moderation of power, cooperation, and respect. They are the relational alternatives of the Greek structuring of relations entailing polarization, antagonism, and parental, filial disrespect as manifested in perennial polarization in the father-son relationship leading to patricide, incest, and guilt. The formal position advocates fair sharing of power between the genders and the generations. It transforms the normative Greek dominant/antagonistic and disrespectful attitude toward authority to the resolved effective structuring of relations, offering equality between the genders and across the generations. The resolution of the riddle is a conflict resolution. It leads to mutual empowerment and relational effectiveness.

5. *The Role Reversal is conveyed by the Dream Test.* Dreams evoke information about the self-fulfillment of anxieties and hopes, described as anticipations of role reversal. Here the author's dream is a vision; he wishes to evolve an educational resort where he and his family can be imparting to others the wisdom of conflict resolution. The image presents the Wilburton Art to Science Inn, where my family works as a team delivering hospitality and education.

6. *The Compromise Role Assumption or simply Compromise is conveyed by the Short Story Test.* Here the author's Short Story presents the desired compromise necessary to achieve conflict resolution. "A Fiddler on the Roof of a Greek temple" reconciles the author's Judaic passion for justice and his Greek passion for logic. The union of justice and reason inspires harmony as the flags of all are nations waving in the same direction. (In another image, the flags are represented by the moral metaphor animals including the Lion of Judah, the Greek Sphinx, a Christian lamb, and a Biblical snake, a Chinese dragon, the American and German eagles, an Arabic camel, and the Russian bear. These animals are transformed into weightless, ideational figures encircling the temple in the same orbit. They are a cosmic tribute to order and a mathematical abstraction.

The fourth mural then serves as an illustration and as a validation of the Formal Theory's postulations of the integrative function of the Conflict Resolution Process. The first frame, The War of the Metaphors, is related to the sixth frame, the Dance of the Metaphors, as predicted by the theory. The first frame is formally related to the last as oppression, antagonism, and alienation in The War of the Metaphors to the state of compromise or resolution, as mastery cooperation and affiliation in the formal reconciliation of the metaphors. The mural demonstrates the six steps as adequate to advance the formal transformation defining the essence of the Conflict Resolution Process. The six-role process has integrated meaningfully the fragments of one person's experiences, validating the theory and the assessment, by accurately measuring the test taker's relational pattern: a dominant cooperative approach to life.

Indeed, here the individual escapes the threat of annihilation by rethinking the nature of fairness, by evolving an emotional education program, Power Management, toward effectively harmonizing the diversity of personal and cultural perspectives.

SUB-CHAPTER TWO

Mural 7 validates the foundation for the interpretation of CAB's metaphors in that emotions and the respective images are formally interrelated by the three formal operations.

Images are juxtaposed to impart awareness of the formal structure of the unconscious conflict resolution mechanism abiding by the principles of the equilibrial scale transforming conflict to resolutions. The metaphors of this mural demonstrate how the unconscious transforms passivity to activity, antagonism to cooperation, and alienation to mutual respect. The unconscious proceeds correcting the traumas as images of the formal transformations along the same symbolisms. The second tier shows images transformed along the three formal principles of mastery, cooperation, and mutual respect. The presentation demonstrates the unconscious following the three formal operations organizing emotional responses to the traumatic experiences transforming passivity to activity, antagonism to cooperation, and alienation to mutual respect.

Case Study:

"Cinderella," a 34-year-old survivor of child abuse, was as a mother afraid of not doing enough for her children. The mural illustrates the healing unconscious by contrasting a number of traumatic childhood experiences portrayed at the lower tier of the mural as formative traumatic experiences, corrected with formally related recovery responses on the upper tier of the mural. The significance of this case is in its images capturing the formal operations of the unconscious validating visually the theory's premise of the formal processing of emotions. The juxtaposition attests to the conflict resolution healing unconscious utilizing the equilibrial formal operations of the scale.

The testing may be easily differentiated into traumatizing developmental experiences, below and reactive, positive caring respectful role assumptions in the same symbolic language. Formal relational alternatives are clearly presented across all her metaphors.

Lower images portray her being physically and sexually abused as a child, as an adolescent, as a wife. In her metaphors of action she is reversing passivity, antagonism, alienation by asserting herself at the higher tier fighting the abuse, caring for her children, and animals and caring for people who are suffering. While overwhelmed by her caring she is setting limits to her children's needs.

Top row of the mural: Mastery conflict resolution phase • activity, cooperation, and mutual respect.		
THE MARITAL FAMILY BALLOONS Portrays the dramatic manifestation of closeness as balloons tightly held together. Their strings are long and tightly intertwined. Indeed, the infant is overlapping the maternal balloon.	MASK I Depicted as "Serenity", a cover up of feelings. "I hide my feelings to appear unaffected. I have done so for so long. I don't recognize my feelings anymore."	DREAM Slapping her ex-husband, a mother surrogate, while he was sitting on the toilet. "I pulled out a dress slipper made of emeralds. It tinkled. My boyfriend said "That's it. I'll get him with that".
PARENTAL FAMILY BALLOONS Portrays the abusive mother as a black and the abused client as a small blue balloon. Family members are far apart from each other and have short independent strings.	MASK II, hidden feelings Illustrates "anger, frustration, confusion, sorrow, hopelessness, and emptiness." The HEART is labeled 'Beauty With Mishaps.'	CHILDHOOD MEMORY OF ADOLESCENCE "My foster mother entered the bathroom and slapped my face while I was sitting on the toilet. I was embarrassed to be seen by my father, helpless, and exposed."

Bottom row: Childhood conflict-induction phase • states of passivity, antagonism, and alienation		
RECENT MEMORY Illustrates the patient escaping, hiding with her baby while her foster mother is directing her husband to go after her and the baby.	ANIMAL METAPHOR TEST The Shepard vs. Kitten is a metaphor that represents the depressed client resenting her demanding infant. "Would you stop licking me?" vs. "No, I won't." "Why not?" vs. "Because it feels good." "To whom?" vs. "To both of us." "I don't want you to bother me." vs. "Then I'll lay next to you." vs. "Okay."	SHORT STORY She is rescuing a kitten thrown in the garbage. "Oh look at the poor thing. It is a kitten. It is just real sick, I am going to take it home and make it better."
RECENT MEMORY OF CONFLICT Illustrates first husband abusing "Cinderella".	ANIMAL METAPHOR TEST- This Metaphor illustrates a passivity state her foster mother's abusive conduct. She is a 'vicious, manipulative, dominant Lion'. The patient is a 'timid, loyal, humble puppy'. Lion: "You rotten mutt, you do what I tell you or I'll eat you up. I'll crush your little bones, etc." Puppy: "No, no... please don't hurt me. I'll do anything you say. Please stop, you are hurting me."	CHILDHOOD MEMORY Portrays foster brother in his bed with patient underneath the covers. "I was two years old. He placed me between his knees and told me it was a baby's bottle. He didn't care about me, he used me as an object."

The Balloon Portraits of the parental family are in stark contrast to the marital family balloons. The arrangement of strings symbolizing dependency needs is short and separate in the parental system, while tightly interwoven in the marital system. In the parental balloons, her relationship with her mother is distant and tense. Her mother is a big black balloon. Hers is a blue small balloon. The benevolent foster father is yellow big but faraway placed balloon. In her marital family, the balloons are pleasantly colored, her infant baby is indenting her own balloon.

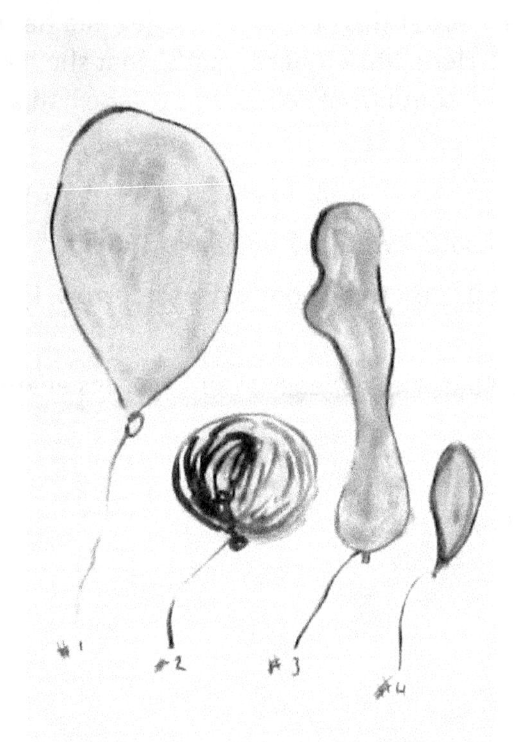

. PARENTAL FAMILY BALLOONS portray the abusive mother as a black and the abused client as a small blue balloon. Family members are far apart from each other and have short independent strings.

– MASTERY CON

2. THE MARITAL FAMILY BALLOONS portray the dramatic manifestation of closeness as balloons tightly held together their string are long and tightly interwined. Indeed the infant is overlapping the maternal balloon.

BALLOON PORTRAITS (Family of Origin)

#1: Dad, 60's A foster father, loving, wise, powerful

#2: (black) Foster mother, 50's. Mean, dominant selfish.

#3: S sister, quick, sensitive, responsible

#4: Myself, generous, understanding slow.

Dialogue:

#2 "What's this? is this what you did in school today?" #4 (eyes are large. Nods her head, yes.)

#2 "There's nothing on this paper but part of your name. What were you doing?"

#4 (shrugs shoulders).

#2 "Look at this one! (shoves it in her face) It's all wrong!" (Rips all the papers including the drawing she made of her father). You're so stupid. All my friends will laugh at me if they saw these papers. When are you going to do some good work in school? These are pitiful, you skinny, little blink (?). I'm sick of these papers. (Drags her by her hair over to the counter, and gets a wooden spoon from the drawer). "Here, maybe this will wake you up, so you can do your work in school." (Hits her on the legs, backside, back, arms, never letting go of her hair. The girl crumples on the floor and rolls into a ball. Still, she pulls her hair and hits her with the spoon and yelling until the spoon breaks. Then she begins to slap and twist - pinch the girl between the legs.

#4 "Stop. Stop it".

#2 (Slaps her and then grabs her throat with her thumb and finger) "shut-up. How dare you speak to me like that. If you talk to me like that, I'll cut your tongue out.'

#1 father, "Enough. Leave her alone."

#2 "You mind your business, you, other one. (to the girl) you, you filthy piece of dirt, (spits on her and then kicks her) get up, get in that chair. You sit there and wait till your sister comes home. (she lies on the couch opposite). Do you think she's going to like you when she hears about this? (She lifts one leg and her dress, she doesn't wear underwear, and makes an obscene gesture). Here. Stick it here, that's what she'll say. I don't know why I expect good work from you, considering where you come from. Why can't you be half as smart as your sister? Then I'd be happy."

Before:

#4 just come home from school. #3 was still at school. I do not know what # 1 and 2 were doing.

After: #3 comes home, listens to #2 and then says to #4 - "please, try to do your work tomorrow. If you do, we'll get you a pony, ok? Will you try?" #4 says "yes."

Title: Who's Child Is This? Conflicts: Everyone is afraid of #2. No one can speak to her. She runs everyone's life. Her heart is black and no one loves her.

Changes: What's to be resolved? There's no going back.

BALLOON PORTRAITS AND STORYMARITAL FAMILY November 6, 1986

Balloons:

#1. (yellow) B, husband, 43 yrs., male. Proud, strong, sweet.

#2. (blue) myself, 30, female. Sensitive, generous impulsive.

#3. (green) G, son, 7, male. Friendly, competitive.

#4. (red) W, son, 3, male. Aggressive, independent, spirited.

#5. (orange) P, son, 4 mos., male. Happy, strong willed, observant.

Dialogue:

#2 "B use your fork." (Feeding baby & eating same time).

#4 "No, I don't have to" (but he does)."Thank you, B."

#1 "Billy, stop sharing with the dog." # 4 (does it anyway).

#3 "Today, at school teacher read us a story about "Button Bear and ..etc."

#1 and #2 listen, ask questions, intermittently speaking to #4.

#3 "May I have more?"

#1 "It's up to your mom."

#2 "How about some peaches?"

Before:

#2 was cooking, dodging children, stepping over toys.

#1 was feeding animals, dodging children, stepping over toys,

#1 & #2 shooing children from kitchen.

#3 & #4 fighting, yelling, running. #5 crying.

After:

#2 puts #5 to bed. #1 gives #4 a bath. #3 looks at TV.

Title: "Mealtime at our home"

Conflicts:

#3 & #4 are unsupervised during meal preparation. #2 is unorganized. #1 priorities out of perspective. #5 schedule unsynchronized.

(There is an arrow next to #5 pointing up at #2.)

Changes: #3 & #4 given private time individually from #1.

#1 read story to #3 & #4 during mealtime preparation,

#2 care for #5 before mealtime preparation, feed animals simultaneously with meal preparation.

TRANSPARENT MASK TEST

The first mask portrays serenity, a pretty, smiling, content mask which has no eyesit has lips. Second Mask: scrambled brains, hurt, and tears. Third Mask (Heart): a landscape with mishaps
1st Mask: Title: "Serenity" No age given. Female. Emotions: Peaceful, content. Conflicts: None.

Resolution: Unaffected.

2nd Mask: Title: None given. No age given. Female. Emotions: anger, hopelessness, emptiness frustration, confusion, sorrow.

Conflicts: loss, defeat. Resolution: There is no light at the end of the tunnel.

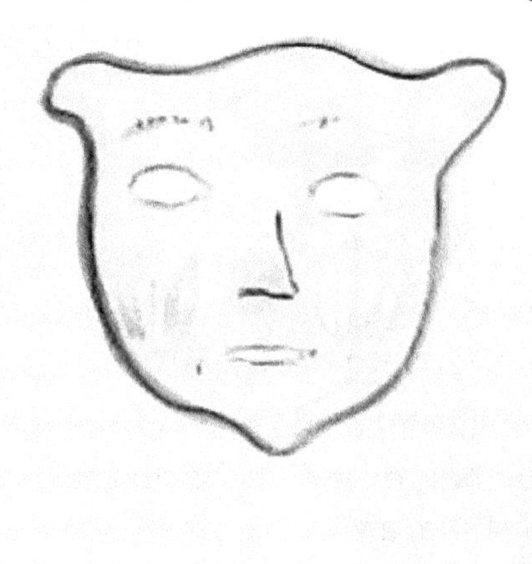

4. MASK I Depicted as "Serenity" is a cover up of feelings. "I hide my feelings to appear unaffected. I have done so for so long. I don't recognize my feelings anymore.

3. MASK II illustrates "anger, frustration, confusion, sorrow, hopelessness and emptiness." The HEART is labelled 'Beauty With Mishaps.

3rd Mask Heart: Title: Beauty with mishaps: Emotions: beauty, life and love thriving in spite of bumps and bruises. Flowers grow in spite of fire, moors are covered into rolling hills, a void filled with tears is a lovely pond. Conflicts: It's a nasty shame to try to ruin such beauty. But the earth is real and strong and can be more beautiful in spite of atrocities. A person's true nature can never be truly killed. Resolution: Most things that are broken are fixable, sometimes ever bettered, but weak points might always remain. Conclusions: Hide it to appear unaffected. Use it to become stronger. Search for relief. Keeps It a secret. Never really resolves it. Has not the capability to deal with it, so buries it.

Passivity is detected by what is found below the mask. Reactively, the first mask is her response to the stressors below it. Here, confusion and traumas but her responses are accepting hurts with a positive outlook.

4. A great deal about the mental operations and about overcoming trauma may be learned as we contrast traumatic with activities portrayed in dreams. Here, in the first image, a Conflictual Memories Test, passivity state has her invaded in the bathroom while sitting on the toilet, her mother slapping her across the face, her father sitting at the dining room table watching. She was loved and defended against the foster mother by the foster father figure, who came to her rescue. The memory of a dream years later depicts her as watching her second husband with a glowing glass slipper in his hand, attacking the first husband who intruded in their home; he was attacked while sitting on the toilet. Overcoming stigma is presented here as the triple reversal of passivities: of the embarrassing (third party witness), humiliation (being on the toilet and attacked, being slapped) which she experienced in her youth. Reactively she is witnessing (outside the bathroom) the evil mother figure impersonated by her first husband, (embarrassed caught in the toilet with pants down and attacked by her prince with Cinderella's glass slipper). Role reversal was needed for reducing the inner conflict with her evil mother.

CONFLICTUAL MEMORIES TEST—ADOLESCENCE,

Drawing: A young woman is sitting on the toilet. A big woman looks very angry and looks like she is slapping the young woman. A man is sitting at a table and is watching.

Characters: Myself, 18 yrs. old.

My foster mother, early 60's. My foster father, late 60's.

How person felt about you: She thought I was still her little ward of the state, that she could treat me like a slave of 1800's.

How you felt about person: Hate, pity, disgust, anger.

Incident: She asked me another question and I asked her if she could wait until I came out of the bathroom to have our conversation. She opened the door and came into the bathroom and slapped my face, while I was sitting on the toilet. My father, sitting at the kitchen table could see me, a young woman, his daughter, sitting on the toilet.

Before: I excused myself from the kitchen to go into the bathroom and closed the door. She stood on the other side of the door trying to have a conversation with me.

After: I stood up and slapped her back (a light tap on the arm) in full view of my father. (He smiled a secret smile, he was pleased that I hit her back). She carried on like she was having a heart attack and tried to get my father to avenge her.

Conflicts: It was a little turning point for me, that I wasn't going to let her hit me anymore.

Share: No answer given, Effect on life: No answer given. Repetition: No answer given.

Resolution in mind: maybe. Resolution in relationship: Yes. Changes: Cut-off all contact with her.

REPORT ON DREAM ANALYSIS DRAWINGS

November 11, 1986

Outstanding dream: Recent dream.

Content of dream: My husband and I, (unmarried at the time and in the dream) were asleep in my

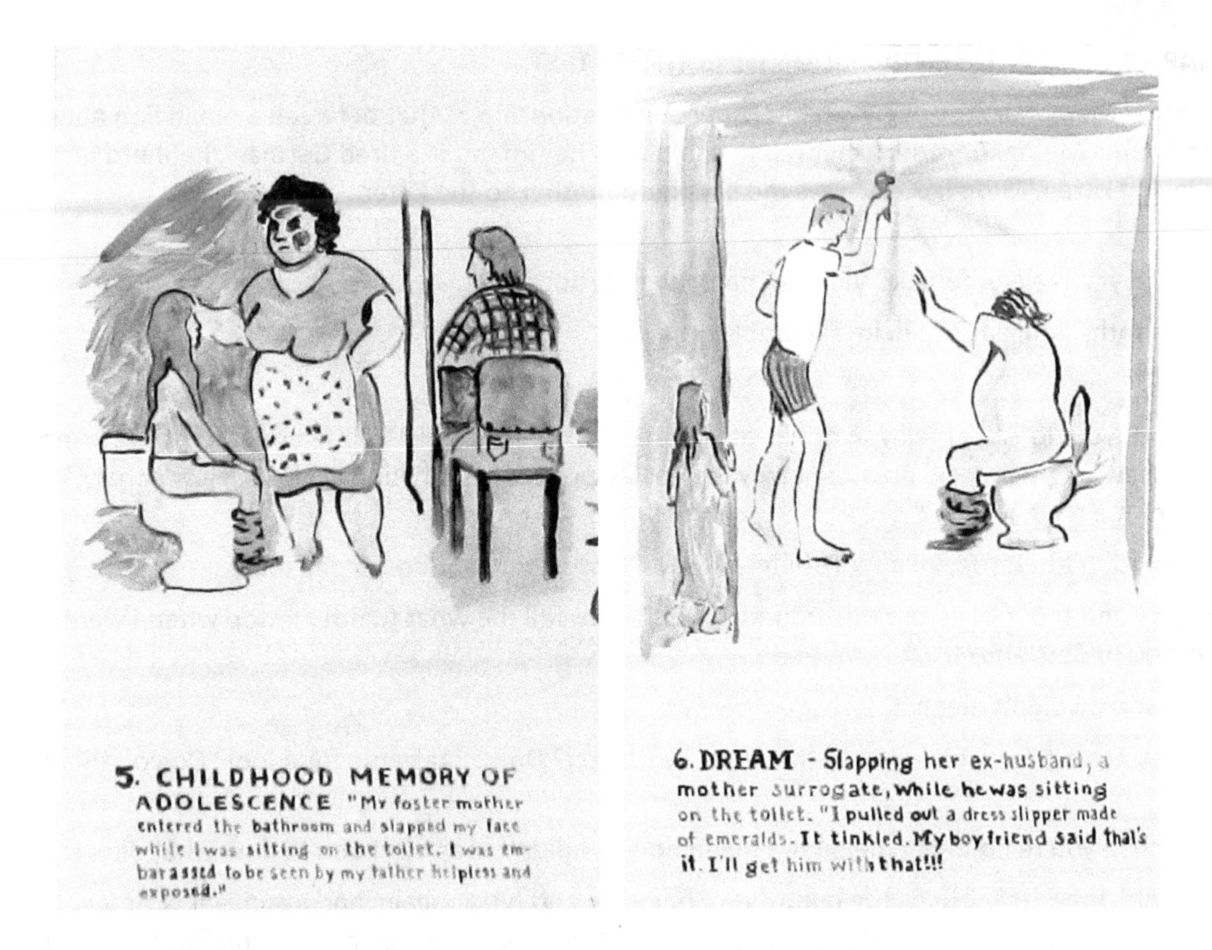

5. CHILDHOOD MEMORY OF ADOLESCENCE "My foster mother entered the bathroom and slapped my face while I was sitting on the toilet. I was embarassed to be seen by my father helpless and exposed."

6. DREAM - Slapping her ex-husband, a mother surrogate, while he was sitting on the toilet. "I pulled out a dress slipper made of emeralds. It tinkled. My boy friend said that's it. I'll get him with that!!!

bed, and were awakened by the radio, suddenly turned on blasting in the living room. I told B that a burglar came in to listen to the radio and (after seeing the bathroom light shining under the door) use our toilet. Bill began searching the room for something to use to defend us. I helped. We looked under the bed and sorted through my shoes. I found a rubber thong and Bill said he would use it. Then I showed him a sandal, he said that would be better, then he started to get up and go after the burglar.

I pulled out a beautiful dress slipper. It was made of emeralds and it sparkled and twinkled. It was not mine, I had never seen it before. Bill saw it and took it from my hand. He said, "that's it, I'll get him good with that." Then he went into the bathroom after the burglar. I hid in the hall and watched him attack the burglar, sitting on the toilet. As I watched from the hall, I recognized him. He was my ex-husband. I moved to the kitchen, so I could watch and not be seen. Bill dragged the resisting figure through the apartment to the door. Just before Bill was to heave him through the now open door, my ex-husband saw me. He suddenly got extra strength and escaped from Bill's grip. He said, "I told you you're never to be with anyone but me, and now you pay!" Then, from his hand came a sudden blinding light, I could see nothing but whiteness. End.

Three traits of participants: Myself, B, my ex-husband. No further answers given.

Conflicts: No answers given.

Before: We were actually awakened by the radio. It was an old radio with switches and timers to turn the radio on and off automatically. My son had played with it earlier that evening and left it to turn on at an odd hour. B got up and pulled the plug so it couldn't do that anymore.

Explanation of dream: I believed that B would protect me from the people of my past in lovely ways. There was guilt in me for sleeping with someone other than the man I had taken marriage vows with.

Dream a lot: yes.

ANIMAL METAPHOR TEST #2 INTENSIFICATION OF CONFLICT TEST

The intense Animal Metaphor Test depicts her mother-self relationship as that between a mean lion abusing a pup. The plain Animal Metaphor reflects her relationship with her infant as a tired German shepherd demanded upon by a loving kitten. "Stop licking." says the shepherd mother to the kitten.

Animals: #1 Lion, 8 yrs. male or female. Vicious, manipulative, dominant.

#2 Puppy, 3 - 4 months, female. Timid, loyal humble.

Dialogue:

#1 You rotten mutt, you do what I tell you or I'll eat you up. I'll crush your *!!!*, little bones. I can, you know. Like this. (places paw on puppy and presses slowly increasing pressure until puppy yelps). "How's that? Want me to do it? Want me to show you?"

#2 "No, no please, don't hurt me, I'll do anything you say. Please, stop, you're hurting me."

#1 (Hits the puppy and she rolls across the ground). "Don't ever tell me what to do! I'll stop when I want to and if I want to. Do you understand?"

#2 "Yes, yes, I'm sorry. I didn't mean it."

#1 (Hits the puppy again). "What the *!!!?'s the matter with you? Do you take me for a fool? Do you think I believe you?"

#2 "No, no, of course you're no fool. I meant it. I mean no, no, I didn't mean it. I don't know what did I say?"

#1 "Why you stupid, little !!**. (Holds the puppy with one paw and hits it again, and again, a few times). You're so stupid and ugly and I hate you. Why do I keep you around? You take up space and air and food. I think I'll throw you out in the trash.

#2 No, no please, don't throw me out. I'll do anything you say. I'll be better and I won't eat ok? Please, can I stay? Please."

#1 (Walks away).

Before: The lion was out napping or whatever with his friends. He was hungry and wanted the puppy to get his food.

The puppy was cleaning the lion's den and there wasn't any food there.

After: #1 "I'm so sorry I hurt you. Why do you make me hurt you? You know I love you, and don't want to hurt you, I won't do it anymore, ok? Do you love me?"

#2 "Yes, I love you. I'll be good so you won't have to hurt me. I promise."

Title: "The Lowly"

Conflicts: The lion is a nothing who needs to inflict his power over someone in order to be powerful. The puppy is easy prey. The puppy is naive and gullible and needs to survive.

Conflicts with world: No answer given.

Changes: No answer given.

Identification: The puppy. Counterpart: My ex-husband and my foster mother.

Pertinence: It could be a scene from either my childhood or my previous marriage.

Changes/resolution: No answer given.

Incident: No answer given.

Pattern: If someone seems to like me, I give my whole self over. I give them my love, trust, loyalty. I give them things, my personal things, gifts. I give too much, then I am hurt deeply when my friendship is treated lightly or rejected.

Willingness to change: No answer given.

ANIMAL METAPHOR TEST #1

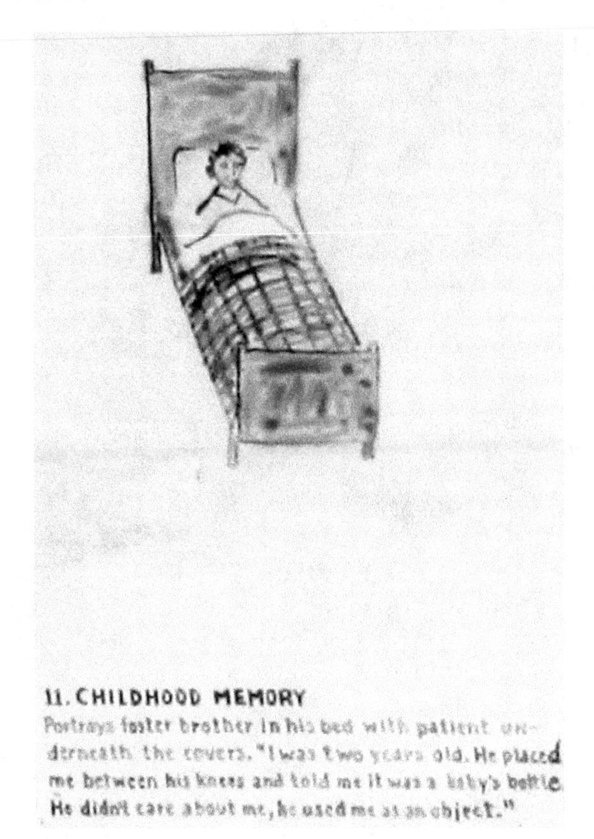

11. CHILDHOOD MEMORY
Portrays foster brother in his bed with patient underneath the covers. "I was two years old. He placed me between his knees and told me it was a baby's bottle. He didn't care about me, he used me as an object."

12. SHORT STORY – She is rescuing a kitten thrown in the garbage. "Oh look at the poor thing. It is a Kitten, it is just real sick. I am going to take it home and make it better."

10/24/86

Animals: "German shepherd, age 5, female; active, sensitive, rough. Cat, age 1, male; rough, affectionate, aggressive."

Dialogue:

#1: "Would you stop licking me?" #2: "No, I won't."

#1: "Why not?" #2: "Because it feels good."

#1: "To who? Me or you?" #2: "To both of us." #1: "I don't want you to bother me." #2: "Then I'll lay next to you." #1: "OK."

Before: "They just came in from outside after playing separately."

After: "They napped."

Title: "Evening Reunion"

Conflicts: "One wants to be alone to rest. The other wants to do some good soothing grooming."

Conflicts/world: "One wants some privacy and to not be bothered with anyone during this time. The other is looking for something that isn't there."

Changes: "One should get up and go in another room. The other should go find his sister or a human to pet him."

9. ANIMAL METAPHOR TEST-INTENSIFIED CONFLICT

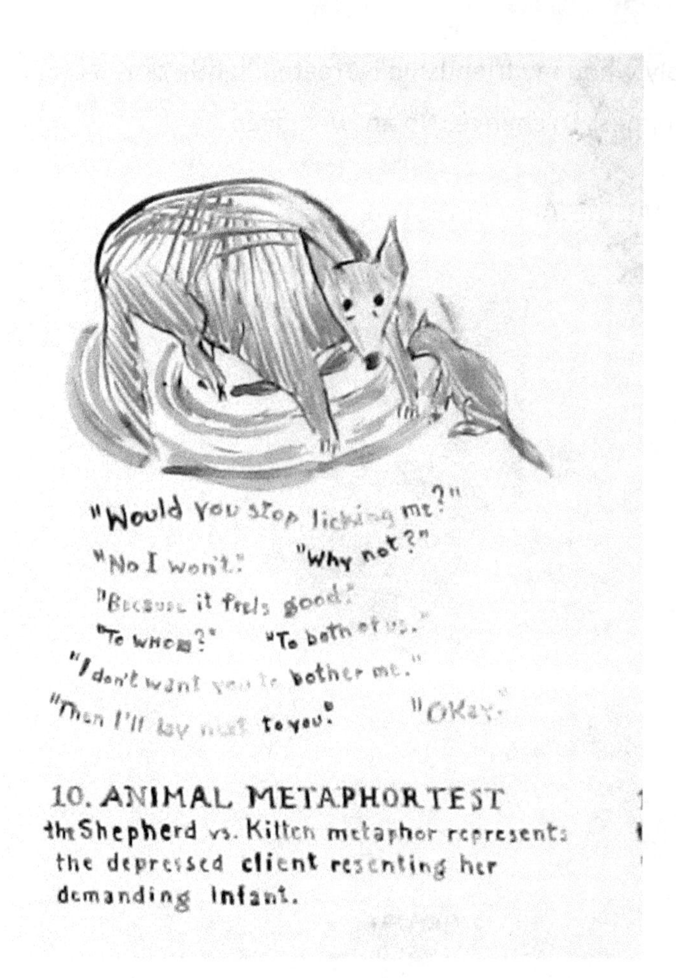

10. ANIMAL METAPHOR TEST
the Shepherd vs. Kitten metaphor represents the depressed client resenting her demanding infant.

Identification: “#1. Sometimes I want to be alone and not have to make someone else comfortable.” Counterpart: “My children. They’re always touching me or want me to do something for them.” [No further answers]

CONFLICTUAL MEMORIES TEST--RECENT CONFLICT

7. RECENT MEMORY OF CONFLICT
Illustrates first husband abusing "Cinderella".

8. RECENT MEMORY
Illustrates the patient escaping, hiding with baby while her foster mother is directing her husband to go after her and the baby.

Drawing: A very scary person in a costume is going after a young woman holding her baby. A heavy-set woman is pointing to where the young woman is.

Characters: G, my first husband, 29. My mother, early 70's. Myself, 24. My son, 1 yr.

How person felt about you: She did not believe me, she didn't care, she liked him because he treated me like she did. How you felt about person: Betrayed by her. I was angry and hated her.

Incident: She gave him my phone number and address. I was hiding my baby and myself from him.

Before: I took my baby and hid where he would never have found us. I filed for divorce and asked my mother never to tell him where we were. I was afraid for myself and my baby. I would never let him hurt my baby again.

After: He was there, everywhere, just like he said he would. Looking in my window, on the bus following, trying to touch my baby, yelling at me in public, threatening me and my baby, calling me on the phone, threatening me, frightening me.

Conflicts: I was trying to better my life with my baby and my mother kept holding me back.

Share: Trusting a woman who hurt me at every turn throughout my life.

Changes: Cut off all contact with her.

CONFLICTUAL MEMORIES TEST--CHILDHOOD

Drawing: A person sleeping. The drawing is covered in black very lightly, seeming to signify danger.

Characters: Myself - 2 or 3 yrs. , foster-brother, teenager.

How person felt about you: He didn't feel anything about me at all except maybe as an object or tool to be used to relieve his sexual urges.

How you felt about person: no answer given.

Incident: I was placed between his knees, under the blankets and told something to make me think of a baby's bottle.

Before: I was lifted from a crib after having been sleeping for a long while.

SHORT STORY METAPHOR

#1 N and #2 T a friend decided to go for a bike ride together. "Let's go to the park on M St." said N. "Okay," said T, "let's take the long way." "Yeah!" said N. And off they went. They stopped and bought soda, at the corner to drink on the way. When the cans were empty, Terry said "There's a trash can by the old grocery store up ahead. Let's get rid of the cans there." "Good idea," said N. The big parking lot was empty, and the store stood boarded up with some broken window, where some other kids got some crazy joy from crashing them. The girls were careful not to ride their bikes in the broken shards. [sic] T threw her can in the trash barrel, then N did. "Look!" said N pointing to a crumpled up bag lying on the ground. "It's just some trash, N, let's go." "No, look, it's moving" said N, getting off her bike. T stopped and watched the bag. "Be careful" she said as her friend went to investigate. "Oh, look at this poor thing. T, it's a kitten." "Is it alive?!" asked T looking at the thing lying limp in her friend's hand. "I think so, said N, I think it's just real sick. What a terrible, terrible person that was, whoever put it in a bag, and left it here to die. If we didn't come to throw our trash away here, it would have died for sure."

"What are you going to do with it?" asked T, "I'm going to take it home and make it better" said N while she wrapped her sweater around it and cradled it in her arm. "It's too late, N. That thing is going to be dead before you get it home" said T. "Well, I can't just leave it here. I've got to try. Aren't you going to help me?" asked N, as she got on her bike, with the tiny thing tucked under her arm. "I'm not touching it. It's probably got germs and stuff" said T. "Well, then I'll just have to do it by myself, come on" and she started toward home. "You're crazy N," said Terry as she followed behind her friend.

Characters: #1. N, age 12, female. Curious, soft hearted, strong willed. #2. T, age 12, female. Cautious, conscientious, pessimistic.

Before: The girls met after school as they usually do and chatted a while and then talked about what they were going to do.

After: T went home with N and watched her administrations and wondered if her friend could really help. N washed the kitten, wrapped it up, and force fed it some milk with an eye dropper.

Title: "Lucky"

Conflicts: N has come upon a helpless and doomed creature, and cannot bring herself to turn her back on it. She cannot understand why her friend doesn't feel as she does, or that someone could have been so thoughtless. T unwillingly gave up her outing because her friend has undertaken a silly, hopeless, and probably hazardous mission.

Changes: No answer given.

Identification: N. Other character: my sister, S.

Pertinence: I sometimes get myself involved in situations where I want to help the underdog no matter how hopeless or what people say. When I was 6, I begged my mother for a doll I saw at a store for weeks. A couple of days after I got the doll, I gave it to a playmate because she fell in love with it when I shared it with her and she cried when playtime was over and I was going inside with the doll. I felt sorry for her because I owned something she wanted. I got a beating for what I did, and then I had to take the doll back. After that I hated it and never played with it again.

When I was 8, my cousin and I went to the corner candy store. It was winter and the sidewalks were like sheets of ice. On our way home we found that a very old man had slipped and fallen on the ice. He was lying flat on his back and could not get up. I felt so sorry for him, that I almost cried. My heart hurt for him. It felt like there was a hand inside my chest squeezing it. I asked my cousin to help me get him up, but she refused saying that our mothers were waiting for us and that they would be mad if we took a long time. I started to help him by myself. I tried many different ways. It was impossible. He was so tall and heavy and he could not help because he was so old. The ice was slippery under my feet and he looked so fragile, I was trying not to hurt him in my efforts. All the while my cousin was telling me to forget it, and that we had to hurry or we'd get in trouble. Then she said she'd leave me because she didn't want to get in trouble. I kept trying. Then a car went by and I shouted at them to help.

The driver said he couldn't help but that he knew who the man was and he would go to his house and tell his people to come. After he drove away, I found my cousin had left me and I knew I was going to be in big trouble. Still, I could not leave the man lying on the icy sidewalk all alone. I knelt down and held his head on my lap until his people came. I talked to him even though he didn't speak any English.

His people were two men and a woman, they also spoke no English. After I saw them begin to help him, I ran all the way home. I got a beating for dilly - dallying and not staying with my cousin. I knew they wouldn't understand.

Changes/ resolution: Understand that there are times, when I won't make a difference. That other people do not have to feel the same as I do. That I cannot personally correct all the wrongs in the world. That it takes all kinds of people to make up the world.

Repetition: After discovering the creature in need, N felt it was her responsibility to correct a misdeed even though it meant forgoing the pleasure of an outing with her friend and without her friend's support and participation.

Pattern: I have a strong desire to make things right where I feel someone has been wronged. I rarely change my mind even after thinking things through and realizing any possible consequences.

Willingness to change: No answer given.

Pt: Sister asked me if I was the kitten. I like animals.

Dr: You have a great deal of compassion in spite of all the abuse you received.

Pt: Sister was saying about virtues my foster mother taught us. Not to be promiscuous. I said how could you learn from her? She was not very understanding or forgiving - she didn't talk to people for months on end - she didn't forget. She would drag up all old things. Promiscuous? She taught us sex is something you have to do. Why would you have to do it with somebody else?

Moral of sex stories: Father wasn't allowed to touch her neck. He'd have to bring her tea in bed and fluff up her pillows. She'd go out grumbling. She told me not to swear, but she swore at me and washed my mouth with soap. She used to accuse me of things I didn't do.

SUB-CHAPTER THREE

Mural 8 validates the foundation for the interpretation of CAB's metaphors in that emotions and the respective images have the natural science dimensions of three pendulum oscillations.

Theoretical significance of the mural

The metaphor profile of this 19-year-old applicant for the seminary is of great scientific significance because of the directionality of the images illustrating graphically the coincidence of the direction of images with the forces of emotions. The CAB sequence unfolds as emotions coinciding with the three oscillations of a pendulum. The evolving direction of metaphor figures of the "tempted seminarian" confirm the formal thesis that the self/ego is like a pendulum ball oscillating in a morally polarized magnetic/normative field in which the right pole coincides with power, and the left pole with powerlessness. The text associated with the images describes emotions confirming the directionality of the figures associated to power related emotions.

According to the associated texts profiles of figures oscillating to the right, the power pole, are associated with stories identifying sinful pleasure-seeking conduct, aggressive, impulsive, and conflict arousing limit testing behaviors.

The figures facing forward correspond to emotions of anxiety, conflict, self-consciousness and uncertainty corresponding to maximal action directed associations, kinetic energy.
When the figures are directed to the left, associations describe depression, regret, introspection, guilt, and repentance, pertaining to the seminarian's feelings as a sinner repenting for having transgressed. This association of directionality related to power dynamic-kinetic energy states has been confirmed examining multiple directional images as configurations associated with the alternative set of emotions as described in this case.

Interpreting the metaphors of the battery the syndromal sequence as three pendulum oscillations

The images reflect the battery's capacity to capture the emotional dialectic as a pendulum oscillating from a conflict to its resolution three times attesting to the process portraying energy being transformed along three oscillations from passivity to mastery, from antagonism to cooperation, from alienation to mutual respect.

'Bugs Bunny and Porky Pig' 'BB & PP is a 19-year-old candidate for the seminary, whose motivation to become a priest stemmed from a strong sense of guilt or sin that had tormented him with remorse for certain things that transpired in the past but which still unsettled his sense of self-control and self-esteem. These issues hindered his qualification and readiness for the seminary. The Conflict Analysis Battery tests revealed clearly the troubled nature of this candidate.

The Relational Modality Evaluation Scale identified both dominant and submissive qualities, he likes attention, is easily frustrated, is competitive, boisterous, and demonstrative. He does things to provoke and shock, has a tendency to be sarcastic; he identified submissive qualities such as avoiding to deal with angry people, keeping his anger under control, feeling worthless, being passive, brooding and vindictive. His psychic tension was elevated. He is anxious, dwells on certain thoughts incessantly. He is overwhelmed with guilt. He knows he is emotionally unstable.

The metaphor tests reveal his pattern of being highly conflicted between opposite ends of a moral continuum. He is torn between temptations, guilt and remorse, with high animosity for others and great damage to his own identity. We recognize how the testing assist the recognition of the emotional pattern as well as the motivation of conforming to the moral alternative. The study reveals both the science and the dialectic of emotions leading to identify the unconscious as a scientific conflict resolution or morality driven phenomenon and as an innate mechanism..

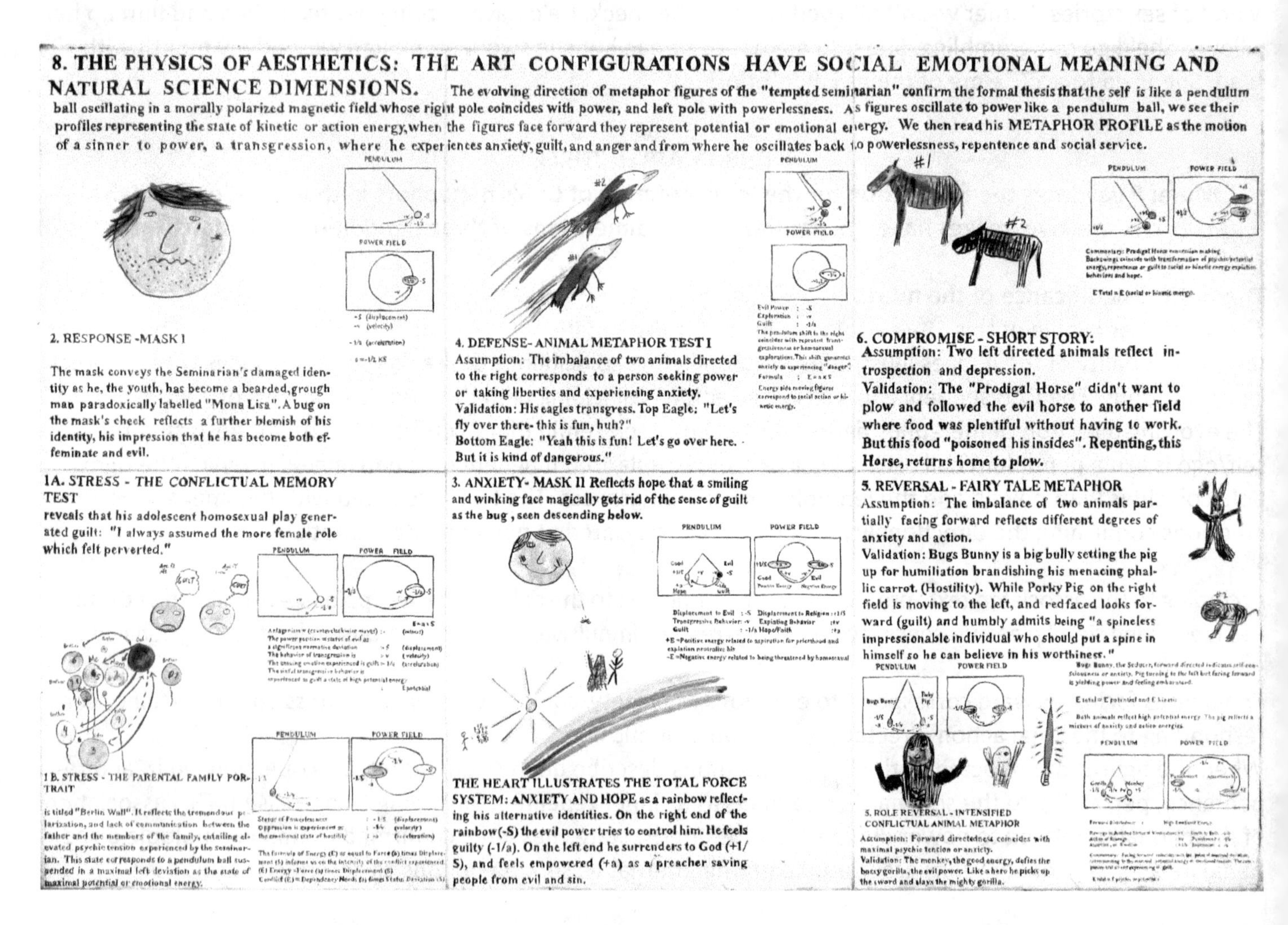

Examination of the emotional directionality of figures

2. RESPONSE MASK I The first oscillation is completed with a damaged identity. The mask conveys the Seminarian's, has become a bearded, gruff, male who is paradoxically labeled "Mona Lisa". A bug on the mask's cheek reflects the blemish of his identity, his impression that he has become both effeminate and evil.	4. DEFENSE, ANIMAL METAPHOR TEST Role Assumption: Two animals directed to the right correspond to a person seeking power, taking liberties and experiencing anxiety. Validation: His eagles transgress. Top Eagle: "Let's fly over there- this is fun, huh?" Bottom Eagle: "Yeah, this is fun! Let's go over here. But it is kind of dangerous."	6. SHORT STORY Compromise Role Assumption: Two left directed animals reflect introspection and depression. Validation: The "Prodigal Horse" didn't want to plow and followed the evil horse to another field, where food was plentiful without having to work. But this food "poisoned his insides." Repenting, this Horse returns home to plow. The third cycle is completed with closure as being reconciled by repenting.
1. STRESS – CONFLICTUAL MEMORY TEST reveals that his adolescent homosexual play generated guilt: "I always assumed the more female role which felt perverted." B. STRESS PARENTAL FAMILY PORTRAIT titled "Berlin Wall". It reflects the tremendous polarization, and lack of communication between the father and the members of the family, entailing elevated psychic tension experienced by the seminarian. This state corresponds to a pendulum ball suspended in a maximal left deviation as the state of maximal potential or emotional energy.	3. ANXIETY, MASK II Reflects hope that a smiling and winking face magically gets rid of the sense of guilt as the bug is seen descending below. THE HEART ILLUSTRATES THE TOTAL FORCE SYSTEM: ANXIETY AND HOPE as a rainbow reflecting his alternative identities. On the right end of the rainbow(-S), the evil power tries to control him. He feels guilty (-1/a). On the left end, he surrenders to God (+1/S) and feels empowered (+a) as a preacher saving people from evil and sin.	5. ROLE REVERSAL, FAIRY TALE METAPHOR The two animals partially facing forward reflects degrees of anxiety and action. Validation: Bugs Bunny is a big bully setting the pig up for humiliation brandishing his menacing phallic carrot. (Hostility). While Porky Pig on the right field is moving to the left, and red-faced looks forward (guilt) and humbly admits being "a spineless impressionable individual who should put a spine in himself so he can believe in his worthiness. INTENSIFIED CONFLICTUAL ANIMAL METAPHOR Assumption: Forward directedness coincides with maximal kinetic associations. The psychic tension or anxiety is converted to action. Validation: The monkey defies the bossy gorilla, the evil power. Like a hero, he picks up the sword and slays the mighty gorilla.

CONFLICTUAL MEMORIES TEST

Memory: Being upset, feeling guilty for a homosexual experience. Two faces with sadness associated with feelings of guilt portrayed with a pendulum maximal deviation experiencing guilt as a centripetal force.

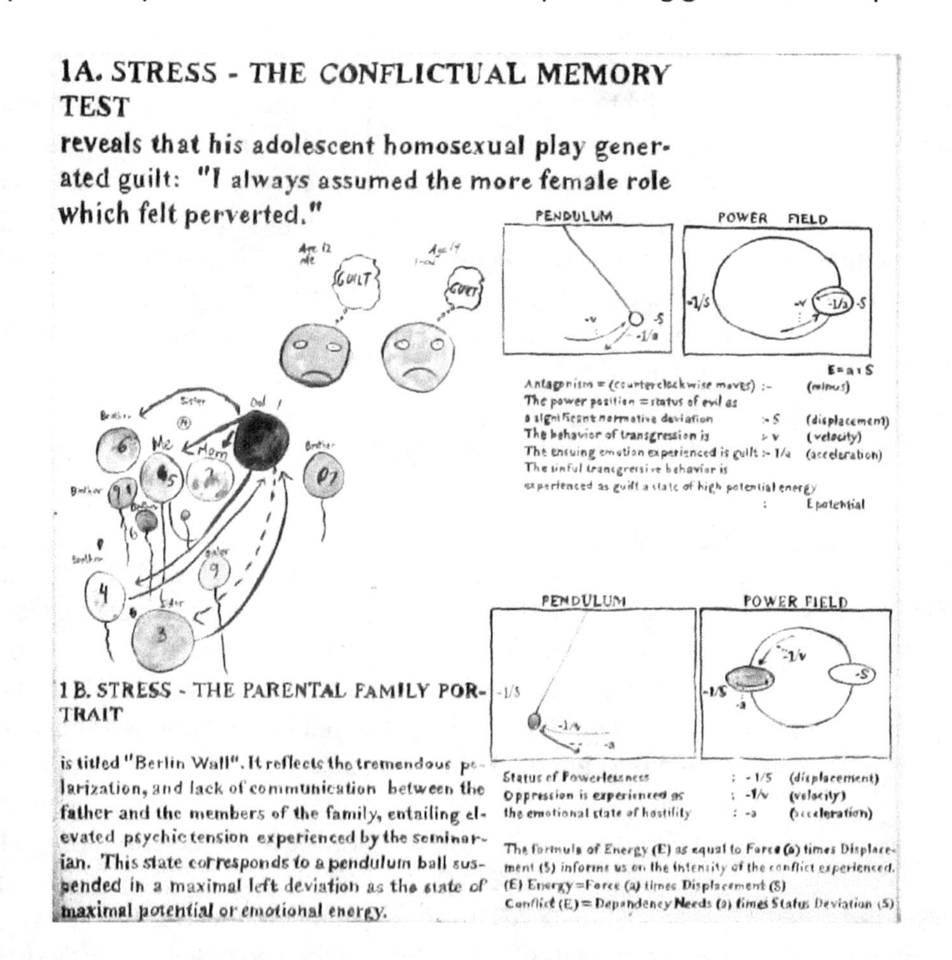

The Conflictual Memory focuses on feeling guilty. Guilt is written on the paper with big letters. The experience of preadolescent sexual involvement with his older brother (by one year) is described in detail: "The incident involved fondling between the legs and behind, no oral sex, no experience of orgasm. We even kissed sometimes, not passionately but almost jokingly."

He was curious, "looked at magazines but did not masturbate." His brother wanted to tell his father but 'BB & PP' did not let him. He explains a further complication of this experience which has consumed him with guilt and self-doubt ever since: "I always assumed the more female role which makes me feel like a perverted homosexual when I think back on it."

Balloon Family Portraits and Story: The Family Balloons reflect the tension in the family system. The test portrays his father in a very polarized interaction with the rest of the family balloons, who are close to each other yet individuated. He characterizes his father as domineering, bitter, and suspicious, his mother as selfless and smart. In the exchanges, father says "do it my way" and 'BB & PP' responds, "Dad, I am getting older. I'll do it my way."

To brother (one year older): "I love you but ever since we did that sexual thing together when we were 12-14, we built a wall between us. We can't tear it down." He calls the Balloon

Test the "Berlin Wall." The tension in the family brought him to reassure every member that he loves them: "They are crying and hugging and telling each other how much they loved each other."

8. THE PHYSICS OF AESTHETICS: TH NATURAL SCIENCE DIMENSIONS.

ball oscillating in a morally polarized magnetic field whose rigi profiles representing the state of kinetic or action energy, when of a sinner to power, a transgression, where he exper

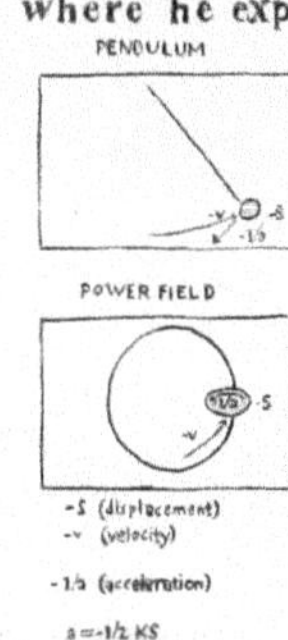

2. RESPONSE -MASK I

The mask conveys the Seminarian's damaged identity as he, the youth, has become a bearded, grough man paradoxically labelled "Mona Lisa". A bug on the mask's check reflects a further blemish of his identity, his impression that he has become both effeminate and evil.

3. ANXIETY- MASK II Reflects hope that a smiling and winking face magically gets rid of the sense of guilt as the bug, seen descending below.

PENDULUM

POWER FIELD

Good +1/S, Evil -S, Hope +a, Guilt -1/a

Good, Evil, Positive Energy, Negative Energy

Displacement to Evil : -S Displacement to Religion : +1/S
Transgressive Behavior: -v Expiating Behavior :+v
Guilt : -1/a Hope/Faith :+a

+E =Positive energy related to aspiration for priesthood and expiation neutralize his
-E =Negative energy related to being threatened by homosexua

THE HEART ILLUSTRATES THE TOTAL FORCE SYSTEM: ANXIETY AND HOPE as a rainbow reflecting his alternative identities. On the right end of the rainbow(-S) the evil power tries to control him. He feels guilty (-1/a). On the left end he surrenders to God (+1/S), and feels empowered (+a) as a preacher saving people from evil and sin.

Response: The Mask Test illustrates the stigma as a blemish on his face. He drew a disheveled, unshaven man's mask, which has a bug on it. He calls the face Mona Lisa, a woman's name. The mask conveys both confusion and hope. The bug is stuck on the face; the mouth is undulated as a wave reflecting a struggle, uncertainty of the evolving emotions.

Anxiety: The second mask is of a smiling face who has gotten rid of the bug. The mouth forms a smile of confidence as the bug is detached from the face. The face winking is getting rid of the bug, but the bug is not dead yet. The second mask reveals his defeated, blemished, stigmatized face and his fear of an effeminate identity. These role states complete the first oscillation.

In the heart mask we see the conflict played out across a rainbow and sun setting as the duel between forces of evil and good. He calls it 'optimism of assured victory'. The rainbow portrays the calm after the storm. His mouth from being turned down in the conflictual memory, undulations in the first mask, now has a smile associated with the resolution of conflict with the graphic representation of a rainbow and the inner struggle of seeking freedom from evil.

He has the strength of religion, the magic sword to protect him, on the one end of the rainbow but yet the past is still a concrete net that has a distinct hold on his hero who is portrayed smaller than the bug at the other end of the rainbow. He wants a following. Could he handle being a shepherd himself?

ANIMAL METAPHOR TEST #1

Defense: Animal Metaphor Test #1: The image shows two birds flying to the right pursuing a pleasurable behavior; it is about yielding to temptation.

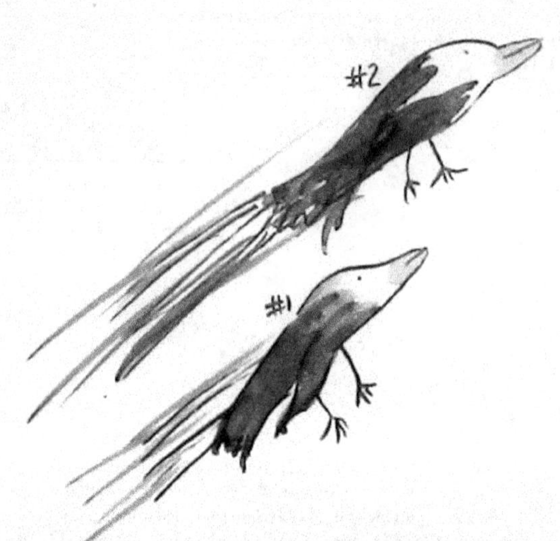

PENDULUM

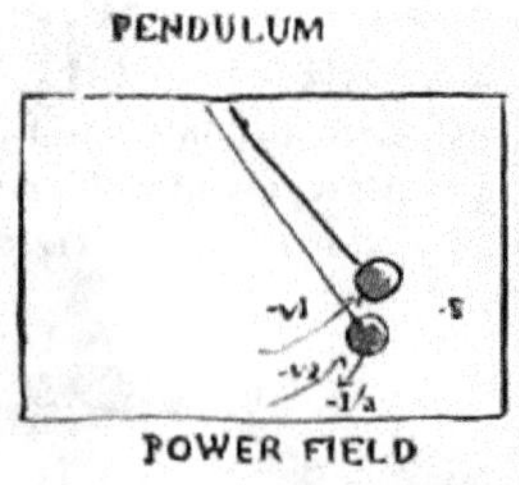

POWER FIELD

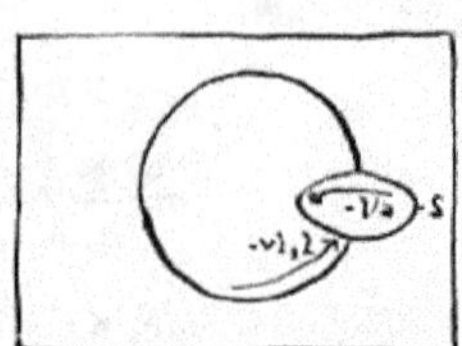

Evil Power : -S
Exploration : -v
Guilt : -1/a
The pendulum shift to the right coincides with repeated transgressiveness or homosexual explorations. This shift generates anxiety as experiencing "danger".
Formula : E = a x S
Energy side moving figures correspond to social action or kinetic energy.

4. DEFENSE- ANIMAL METAPHOR TEST I

Assumption: The imbalance of two animals directed to the right corresponds to a person seeking power or taking liberties and experiencing anxiety.

Validation: His eagles transgress. Top Eagle: "Let's fly over there- this is fun, huh?"

Bottom Eagle: "Yeah this is fun! Let's go over here. - But it is kind of dangerous."

In the Animal Metaphor #1, two eagles are seeking the limits of pleasurable exploration of their space. #1 is holding back for fear of straying beyond set limits. The outcome of this exploration was opposite of what he wanted. Instead of friendship he felt abandoned, rejected, and worthless.

Animals: "#1 Eagle, age 13, male; fast, impressionable, emotional. #2 Eagle, age 13, male; faster eagle (sleek), amiable, a leader."

Dialogue: "#2: Let's go fly over here. This is fun, huh? "#1: Yeah, this is fun! Let's go over here! "#2: Okay I guess so! "#1: That was fun, huh!

"#2: Yeah, it was. Hey, let's go over here!

"#1: I don't know, it looks like fun but it's kind of dangerous.

"#2: Oh come on, look how much fun it is over there.

"#1: Well okay but I have to be home pretty soon. I can only go for a 1/2 hour.

"#2: Okay. This place is fun huh? "#1: Yeah but I got to get home now.

#2: Okay but I'm going to stay here for a while. "#1: Okay, see you tomorrow.

"The next day: #1: Hey where were you today. I couldn't find you.

"#2: I was gone to that other place all day. "#1: But I was looking for you.

"#2: I know you were but I knew you couldn't really go where I was going.

"#1: But I'll go with you. Hey wait for me. Where are you going, are we still best friends??!! Please don't go, we were best buddies!!!!!! Aren't we friends, huh? Aren't we?"

Before the conversation: "They were having fun. Doing everything together. Playing, going on trips together. Always got along. Playing good wholesome games, tag, building things. Always competing but always in good fun."

After: "They didn't say much. Talked a little now and then. #1 was quite bitter after that. He didn't understand. He was hurt. Wounded."

Title: "The Greatest Pain"

Conflicts: "A conflict of interests. #2 wants to do more forbidden stuff and soar everywhere.

#1 is reluctant and #2 doesn't want to be slowed down so he flies away for good.

#1 tries for a short period to keep up with #2 but realizes it is impossible."

Conflicts with world: "Now #2 is unhappy. He realizes that there is more to life than always trying to fly faster. Now #1 after going against his nature has come back to his old wholesome ways."

Changes to be made: "2 should slow down and realize that faster isn't always better. He wants to but needs help. #1 has resolved the conflict and dealt with this pain. He now realizes that speed isn't everything."

Identification: " #1 represents me." Counterpart: "A former childhood buddy."

Pertinence: "When I was 10, we became best friends. He was 10 also. This grand relationship lasted until we were about 14 1/2, then he followed a more 'cool,' 'popular' group and just tried to forget we were ever friends. I was hurt and often tried to impress him with 'cool' things I had done, but after about a year or so he was no longer much of a factor in my life although I always wanted to know his true feelings and why he did this."

Changes to resolve conflict: "I would like to write to him and have him visit here."

Incident illustrating relational pattern: "Often times I get close to a friend, I begin to trust him. Then I am disappointed. I had a good friend from work. After I stopped working there he didn't call much."

Pattern: "I expect too much from other people. I put an unfounded trust in them and think they will never cross me. When they do I am disappointed."

Willingness to change: "I must rely most on Jesus Christ for companionship. Make him my closest friend. Rely on him for guidance.

Fairy Tale Metaphor

Fairy Tale: Two individuals facing forward associated with anxiety, being abandoned and concerned about morality.

The Fairy Tale is about Bugs Bunny and Porky Pig, his victim. Bugs, sly, sarcastic, with a carrot in hand, is setting up a stupid, relentless, born loser pig to experience humiliation. The story is labeled "Big Bully and a Spineless Pig." 'BB & PP' is the spineless Porky Pig always indulging his passion and desire. He has become weakened. "He is impressionable." The Fairy Tale story evoked more association of being dumped by his peers. He concludes: "I should put a spine in me." He wonders, "How could I stand up to someone when I didn't believe in myself or the immoral life I was leading at the time?"

ANIMAL METAPHOR TEST #2

Vindication, monkey killing gorilla, facing forward.

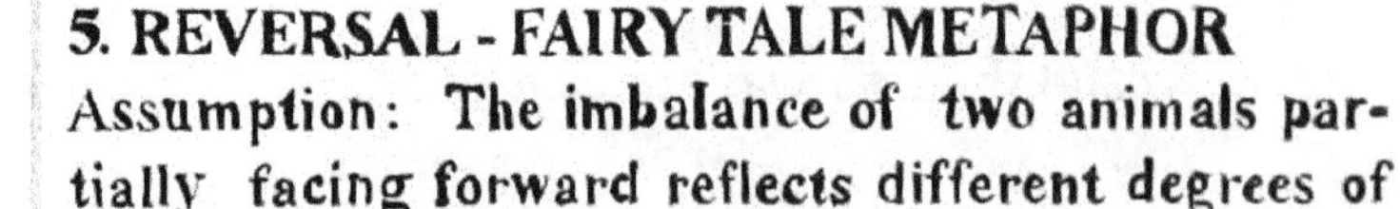

5. REVERSAL - FAIRY TALE METAPHOR

Assumption: The imbalance of two animals partially facing forward reflects different degrees of anxiety and action.

Validation: Bugs Bunny is a big bully setting the pig up for humiliation brandishing his menacing phallic carrot. (Hostility). While Porky Pig on the right field is moving to the left, and redfaced looks forward (guilt) and humbly admits being "a spineless impressionable individual who should put a spine in himself so he can believe in his worthiness."

Bugs Bunny, the Seducer, forward directed indicates self-consciousness or anxiety. Pig turning to the left but facing forward is yielding power and feeling embarassed.

E total = E potential and E kinetic

Both animals reflect high potential energy. The pig reflects a mixture of anxiety and action energies.

5. ROLE REVERSAL - INTENSIFIED CONFLICTUAL ANIMAL METAPHOR

Assumption: Forward directedness coincides with maximal psychic tension or anxiety.

Validation: The monkey, the good energy, defies the bossy gorilla, the evil power. Like a hero he picks up the sword and slays the mighty gorilla.

This AMT again presents the dramatic contrast of a hideous gorilla and an impressionable smaller monkey, who sports a magic sword. The gorilla, like his father in the Balloon Portraits and Story, says, "You best do what I say. You lied to your father, you are evil." The little monkey picked up the sword and slayed the gorilla who represents his father.

Animals: "Gorilla, age 7002, female; hideous, a great liar, evil, strong, very powerful. Gorilla [monkey), age 19, male; impressionable, weak (except for sword), frightened."

Dialogue:

"#1: You best do what I say. Don't you dare go over there. You're too weak. You've failed too many times in the past. Think of that time you lied to your father. That was when you had already decided to be a priest. Don't mess with me. You're too weak. Remember that lie, it was in front of your little brother. You're evil just like me.

"#2: You're right. God doesn't want me here, he wants me to make amends for my past life.

GET BACK SATAN.

"#1: Don't touch that sword. Nooo!!!

"#2: Disregards the big gorilla's threats, picks up the sword and slays the gorilla (This is a magic sword. If the gorilla even touches the sword, he is cut badly.) The big gorilla often tries to get the monkey to not use the sword. Then the gorilla knows he can have his way."

Before the conversation: "The animals were conversing. The big gorilla was telling him that the sword won't work on him and that nothing can stop him. But as soon as the monkey picks up the sword, the gorilla starts to scream in terror."

After: "They fought and the monkey slayed him."

Title: "The Little Monkey with the Magic Sword"

Conflicts: "The gorilla wants the monkey, to make monkey soup. The monkey wants to be less and less like the gorilla. His only hope is the sword.

Conflicts with world: "The gorilla has already lost his battle. Now he wants all the little monkeys to be like him."

Changes to resolve conflict: "The monkey should never fear in taking up the sword and realize that if he uses the sword he will always win."

A nightmare describes a torture act of his little sister, somebody is throwing razors at her face. In the discussion, he mentioned that Jim, his friend, drove the enemy away with a boomerang but he also stated that Jim was another bad experience. "I remember I kissed his butt when I was five. We used to rub tummies because it felt good. He also used to give me bloody noses. He was domineering."

SHORT STORY METAPHOR

Short Story: Two horses going to the left associated with being depressed and repenting as the Prodigal Horse.

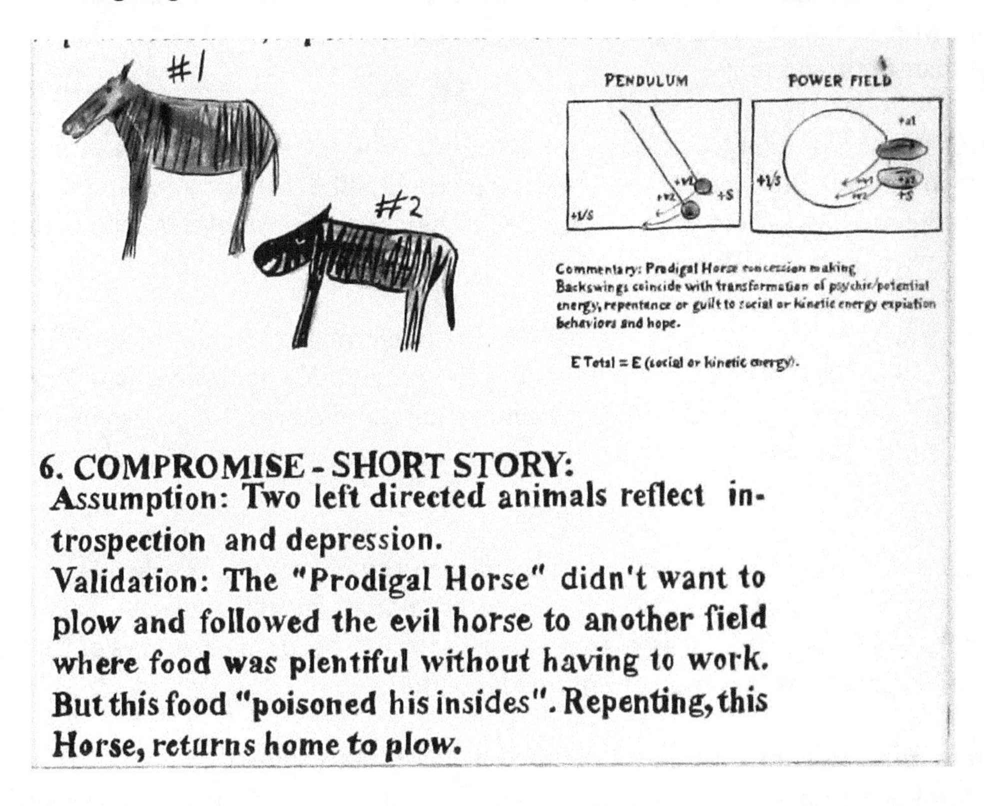

6. COMPROMISE - SHORT STORY:
Assumption: Two left directed animals reflect introspection and depression.
Validation: The "Prodigal Horse" didn't want to plow and followed the evil horse to another field where food was plentiful without having to work. But this food "poisoned his insides". Repenting, this Horse, returns home to plow.

His Short Story is again about sin and poor influence. It is the story of two horses. One horse strays in the prairie of the evil horse where he becomes the prodigal horse who eventually repents and returns home. Both pleasure seeking eagles were directed to the right. Here both depressed horses look to the left. They are the back swing of his exploration. The Bugs Bunny with a carrot and the eager pig show him in an intermediate phase of ambivalence. He continues: "I sat on Satan's knee. I wish to never return to his lap. I listened to what the black horse had to say, knowing that that was evil. I should never listen to him. I should pull that plow. I should pull it with tenacity and disregard the straying influence."

On the House-Tree-Person we see a modest house with a big attached garage representing his secret life, a phallic apple tree, and a face with a bewildered expression.

Conclusion: 'BB & PP' has been traumatized by early homosexual experiences. He fears being effeminate and feels worthless and guilt ridden. He used the testing process to reconcile himself with his brother. He has a readiness to confess and seek help from religion. He is still disturbed by temptation, feels being damaged, worthless and spineless. He has a tendency to try to prove himself instead of staying a humiliated subordinate. He needs to learn to feel good about himself and to be assertive.

His feedback was very positive. He gave the testing on the average 9/10 scores. He found out that he needs to be more self-confident and assertive: "That if I let a person walk on me then I become scared and do not fight back. I should stand up because I have nothing to fear."

Reviewing his testing, he recognized the powerlessness of the so-called homosexual experience with his brother: "I acted like a homosexual in the female role. I was submissive to my brother." He also realizes that he rebelled at his father when he turned 17: "I didn't care what he said."

Sub-chapter FOUR

Mural 9: The Metaphor Process as a Cost-Effective Methodology for Self-Discovery and Self-Healing.

The Workbook Guided Hannah, a 62-Year-Old Holocaust Survivor, to Recognize and Resolve her Conflicts. This case study demonstrates the effective utilization of the Conflict Analysis Battery (CAB), the self-guided therapeutic assessment, with "Hannah", a 62-year-old holocaust survivor, who sought a psychiatric evaluation as part of a holocaust restitution claim.

This mural integrates the intense emotions generated by completing the workbook as a dramatic, cathartic experience with great comforting outcome. The experience guided Hanna, to recognize and resolve deep seated conflicts in three sessions. She was able to make peace with herself to get rid of her 'inscrutable' mask and to accept feeling alive, vulnerable, and passionate again.

The premise of the Formal Theory of Behavior is that the creative process, the plot of stories, represents the unconscious as a conflict resolution mechanism abiding by two scientific phenomena, the Simple Harmonic Motion manifested as three pendulum oscillations, a syndromal six-role process, guided by the three equilibrial operations restoring balance to the trays of a scale leading to four alternative relational modalities, as wellness diagnoses.

The CAB guides test-takers to identify the syndromal six-part emotional conflict resolving energy transforming dialectic with a set of projective tests and identifying one's relational modality wellness diagnosis, personality type, with a personality inventory. The assessment helps a person to become conscious of this conflict resolving unconscious and to reduce pathology by optimizing resolutions.

This study illustrates a three-session CAB-based evaluation. The battery helped the patient to identify her relational modality, dominant cooperative, a wellness diagnosis and to understand how its syndromal unfolding integrated meaningfully her experiences as a wellness diagnosis. She identified unacceptable activities leading to her anxieties and associated defensiveness.

The assessment's diagnostic and therapeutic benefit was confirmed by the patient's observations and writings. Discussion examines Formal Theory's concepts, rethinking psychology as a science and the effectiveness of the assessment as a diagnostic and therapeutic intervention. The case study illustrates how the assessment transformed psychotherapy into a concise emotional education changing the role of a therapist to that of an educator.

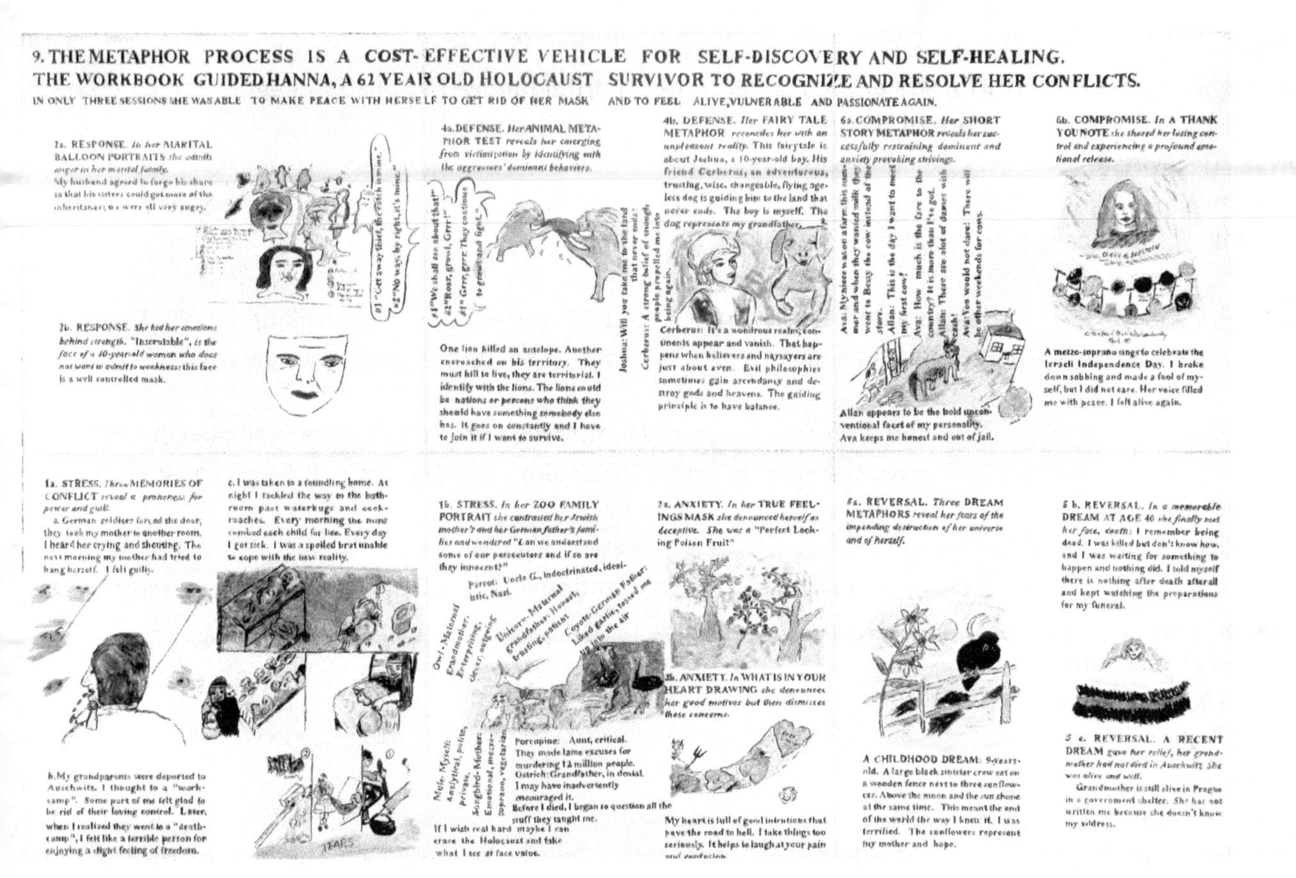

1a. STRESS

Three MEMORIES OF CONFLICT reveal a proneness for power and guilt.

German soldiers forced the door; they took my mother to another room. I heard her crying and shouting. The next morning my mother had tried to hang herself. I felt guilty. My grandparents were deported to Auschwitz, I thought, to a “work-camp.” Some part of me felt glad to be rid of their loving control. Later, when I realized they went to a “death-camp,” I felt like a terrible person for enjoying a slight feeling of freedom. I was taken to a foundling home. At night I tackled the way to the bathroom past water-bugs and cockroaches. Every morning the nuns combed each child for lice. Every day I got sick. I was a spoiled brat, unable to cope with the new reality.

1b. STRESS

ZOO FAMILY PORTRAIT

She contrasted her Jewish mother’s and her German father’s families and wondered, “Can we understand some of our persecutors, and if so, are they innocent?”

Unicorn- Maternal grandfather: Honest, trusting, patient
Owl - Maternal grandmother: Enterprising, clever, outgoing
Ostrich- Paternal grandpa: Strict, fair, strong work ethic.
Mule-Myself: Analytical, polite, private.
Songbird-Mother: Emotional, mezzo-soprano, vegetarian
Porcupine-Aunt: Critical, protective
Griffin -Uncle: Scientific, versatile, loving.
Coyote-German Father: Liked garlic, tossed me up into the air
Parrot-Uncle G.: Indoctrinated, idealistic, Nazi

1. Unicorn: Shouldn’t we have learned something since?
2. Owl: The wounds are emotional.
3. Mule: If I wish really hard, maybe I can erase the Holocaust and take what I see at face value.
4. Porcupine: They made lame excuses for murdering 12 million people.
5.Ostrich: I may have inadvertently encouraged it.
6. Parrot: Before I died, I began to question all the stuff they taught me.

2a. RESPONSE
In her MARITAL BALLOON PORTRAITS, she admits anger in her marital family. My husband agreed to forgo his share so that his sisters could get more of the inheritance; we were all very angry.
2b. RESPONSE, THE MASK
She hid her emotions behind strength. "Inscrutable" is the face of a 40-year-old woman who does not want to admit to weakness; this face is a well-controlled mask.
3a. ANXIETY
In her TRUE FEELINGS MASK, she denounced herself as deceptive. She was a "Perfect Looking Poison Fruit." This image reflected my being suspicious, alternatively gullible, that is taking things at face value.
3b. ANXIETY
In WHAT IS IN YOUR HEART DRAWING, she denounces her good motives but then dismisses these concerns. My heart is full of good intentions that pave the road to hell. I take things too seriously. It helps to laugh at your pain and confusion.
4a. DEFENSE
Her ANIMAL METAPHOR TEST reveals her emerging from victimization by identifying with the aggressors' dominant behaviors.
#1 "Get away, thief, the catch is mine."
#2 "No way, by right, it's mine."
#1 "We shall see about that!"
#2 "Roar, growl, Grrr!"
#1" Grrr, grrr. They continue to growl and fight."
One lion killed an antelope. Another encroached on his territory. They must kill to live. They are territorial. I identify with the lions. The lions could be nations or persons who think they should have something somebody else has. It goes on constantly, and I have to join it if I want to survive.
4b. DEFENSE
Her FAIRY TALE METAPHOR reconciles her with an unpleasant reality. This fairytale is about Joshua, a 10-year-old boy. His friend Cerberus, an adventurous, trusting, wise, changeable, flying ageless dog is guiding him to the land that never ends. The boy is me. The dog represents my grandfather.
Cerberus: A strong belief of enough people propelled me into being again.
Joshua: Will you take me to the land that never ends?
Cerberus: It's a wondrous realm, continents appear and vanish. That happens when believers and naysayers are just about even. Evil philosophies sometimes gain ascendancy and destroy gods and heavens. The guiding principle is to have balance.
5a. REVERSAL
Three DREAM METAPHORS reveal her fears of the impending destruction of her universe and of herself.
A CHILDHOOD DREAM: 9-years-old. A large black sinister crow sat on a wooden fence next to three sunflowers. Above, the moon and the sun shone at the same time. This meant the end of the world the way I knew it. I was terrified. The sunflowers represent my mother and hope.
5b. REVERSAL
In a memorable DREAM AT AGE 40, she finally met her fate, death: I remember being dead. I was killed but didn't know how, and I was waiting for something to happen, and nothing did. I told myself there is nothing after death after all and kept watching the preparations for my funeral.
5c. REVERSAL
A RECENT DREAM gave her relief. Her grandmother had not died in Auschwitz. She was alive and well. Grandmother is still alive in Prague in a government shelter. She has not written me because she doesn't know my address.
6a. COMPROMISE
Her SHORT STORY METAPHOR reveals her successfully restraining her dominant and anxiety-provoking strivings.
Ava: My niece was on a farm this summer, and when they wanted milk, they went to Bessy, the cow instead of the store.

Allan: This is the day I want to meet my first cow!
Ava: How much is the fare to the country? It is more than I've got.
Allan: There are a lot of dames with cash!
Ava: You would not dare! There will be other weekends for cows. Allan appears to be the bold, unconventional facet of my personality. Ava keeps me honest and out of jail.
6b. COMPROMISE.
In A THANK YOU NOTE, she shared her losing control and experiencing a profound emotional release. A mezzo-soprano sings to celebrate the Israeli Independence Day. I broke down sobbing and made a fool of myself, but I did not care. Her voice filled me with peace. I felt alive again.

The CAB metaphor tests have been selected to evoke the six role-states as interrelated emotions. The table below introduces the correspondence of the six roles syndromal process identified routinely with specific battery tests descriptively identified by Freud's defense mechanisms and Jung archetypes.

Stress, role oppression: parallel to Freud's repression, Jung's imago.	Conflictual childhood memories, witnessing her mother's rape and suicide
Response, role assumption: Jung's persona, Freud's denial	Dominant reactions: foundling home experiences as a brat, relief upon the deportation of grandparents, image of self as a mule, mask as inscrutable
Anxiety, anticipation of role reversal: parallel to Freud's projection and Jung's shadow	Feelings of guilt, regret : 'You are going to miss us following you', feelings unmasked as being damaged trees and a tree with poisoned fruits, and wishes as the path to hell.
Defense, counterphobic role assumption: as Freud's reaction formation, Jung's animus	Two lions fighting for spoils. Joshua's trip to the land that never ends Cerberus existing as long as you believe in him.
Role Reversal: as Freud's reversal and Jung's anima.	Dreams of the end of the world and of being dead
Compromise, role assumption: Freud's sublimation and Jung's alchemic transformation to the Self	Aspiring for a free meal coinciding with wishes for compensation from the German government and stealing from a lady to buy tickets averted by concession to moral insights averting her risking going to prison.
Evidence of Healing	Dream of reuniting with grand-parents leading her to relief and emotional vulnerability correcting defense of inscrutability
Feedback by the patient	Lengthy statement of gratitude for the approach to the healing experience

Diagnosis: Dominance Relational Modality
Her RMES dominance scores are consistently elevated while her submissiveness scores are consistently low. Psychic tension scores are elevated in the areas of anxiety and self-consciousness. Hannah's dominance contributes to her sense of anxiety and defensiveness and her deep-seated sense of guilt. Dominance generated anticipations of role reversal, as guilt, self-doubts, and her defensiveness to trusting her emotions. Her anxiety was not only due to the horrible childhood experiences, but to her own relational choices.

The clinical symptoms for dominance include a whole range of psychopathology (Source). Anxiety and paranoia are pervasive, manifested through a variety of clinical symptoms and social dysfunctional adjustments. Dominance is experienced as phobias, panic disorders, paralyzing emotions that can be disabling in many aspects of one's life, such as performance anxiety, sleep disturbance, interpersonal relations, but also discretely as insidious emotional resistance, a defense to vulnerability and a pervasive lack of trust reinforcing one's readiness to overreact and even proneness to think of suicide.

The syndrome

The images of the metaphor tasks reconstruct the syndrome of six-role states as formally interrelated emotions. The continuum reflects the unconscious along one's relational modality diagnosis. The metaphor tasks illustrate the conflict resolution syndromal sequence evolving along the six-role process departing from stress as the state defined as passivity, antagonism and alienation and leading to compromise, conflict resolution as mastery, cooperation and mutual respect. Indeed, examining the initial *stress tests, the Conflictual Memories,* we identify the relational attributes of conflict and examining the *Short Story* we identify the attributes of resolution.

Confirming the Formal Theory's premises, we note that Hannah's case affirms several key assumptions. Within her Metaphor Tasks, the six-role process presents reciprocally related states of passivity evolving to states of activity. The Animal and Fairy Tale Metaphor tasks are related as opposites, the antagonism from the Animal Metaphor evolves to cooperation in the Fairy Tale Metaphor. Finally, the correlative operation, the shift from alienation to mutual respect, occurs within the Short Story Metaphor. The aggressive act of robbing a lady, was intercepted, analyzed, and resolved with respect of others in relationships.

With the help of the CAB, Hannah shifted away from a defensive stance. Emotional catharsis and insights released her from feeling like a poison tree, like a dangerous lion, a woman seeking a free meal at somebody's expense. The outcome of the three sessions was the successful healing of a lifelong sense of alienation and self-doubt. Her statement: 'I was alive again' clarifies attaining the therapeutic goal.

Hannah's experience of the Holocaust was affected by her relational modality. Assertiveness/aggressiveness was bound with related guilt feelings. Her childhood responses of seeking independence from her grandparents had generated guilt about her defiant thoughts. Understanding her dominance personality pattern helped her with feelings about the past but also, in dealing with current troubling tendencies. This was observed in her metaphors as dominance, testing limits that still gets her in trouble. The evaluation helped her to understand her personality, her responses and guilt feelings. Understanding her conflicts released her from her guilt, from feeling that she was a terrible and cruel person, as portrayed in her Transparent Mask Test as the 'broken trees and one with poison fruits'. The release from guilt was manifested in her current transactions. The outcome of the consultation: she found that she was emotionally 'alive again'.

From Hannah's CAB, we learn that a central cause of her distress was guilt concerning the childlike sense of relief she had experienced when her Jewish grandparents were deported to an alleged labor camp. She later found out that they were killed. Evidence of this guilt and of her damaged sense of self was clearly illustrated in her Transparent Mask, in which she depicted herself as 'inscrutable' hiding underneath this mask her feelings of being two mutilated trees, her two parents?, and one in the middle bearing poison fruits, and her heart full of good intensions that 'pave the road to hell'.

A wellness diagnosis: the psychology and pathology of dominance

The relational wellness diagnosis of dominance entails recognizing the pathogenetic role of aggressiveness, anger, uninhibited expression of feelings as the normative deviation towards power positions. This may be graphically portrayed with vectors towards the power polarity in the concentric circles power field diagram. Antagonism is portrayed with counterclockwise vectors, while cooperation with clockwise ones. The response to the power positioning induces in the person psychic tension experienced as anticipations of role reversal; the person anticipates becoming the recipient of her/his aggressiveness. The state of anticipation of role reversal as 'projection' may be graphically portrayed in the peripherally positioned ellipse representing the psychic system of the individual as vectors, forces, countering the social system power displacements. These forces in the aggressive person induce the ensuing escalation of defensiveness, which leads to escalation of social conflicts and, which eventually leads to the social role reversal of the dominant individual. The sequence of states may be presented as a sine curve, reflecting the syndromal organization of her unconsciously experienced emotions.

Evaluation of the assessment experience
Hannah's CAB completion allowed her to shift away from a stance of defensive detachment and guilt and allowed her to remove her emotional guard. This release from guilt is documented in a dream that she had during the evaluation period in which she was reunited with her grandmother. Additionally, following completion of her evaluation, Hannah mailed me the record of a recent conflict, using the format of the battery tests. It included art and questions about this experience as organized in the CAB format. In it she described her losing her composure, breaking down, 'making a fool of myself in public', a very significant emotional experience for 'an inscrutable' person, upon listening to an Israeli singer during a celebration of the anniversary of the creation of Israel.

A HOLOCAUST SURVIVOR, evaluation of the experience
This case study, illustrated in mural #9, reflects the self-diagnostic, the self-healing therapeutic value of the completion of the metaphor testing, and the minimal need for professional services for the adequate generation and interpretation of the testing battery. Case study and comments in the section on assessment, third wall.

The following record presents Hannah's comments upon completion of consultation.
Hannah's comments: My '$5 Psychotherapy Sessions'
"The original purpose of my examination by Dr. Levis was the existence or non-existence of leftover psychological scars caused by my childhood experiences during the Nazi times. I was uncertain that any concrete proof of them could be established at all, and it appeared even more unlikely that it could be done within a short period of time. But that was before I knew of Dr. Levis' method of completing several creativity exercises. I was allowed to take the first part of the Conflict Analysis Battery with me as homework since I live some distance away.

Sitting at my kitchen table (a familiar non-threatening environment) I confronted a series of tests (in many ways similar in format to tests I had faced at school except that the only preparation I needed was having lived my life). The tests are about memories from my childhood, portraits of the family, dreams, animal and fairy tale metaphors. They started with a drawing and continued with a series of thought-provoking questions. The tests led me to painful memories, and to thinking of how to represent them. The questions about them (i.e. who was there? How did you feel about that person?) helped me to be analytical rather than to relive them alone. I had to keep my concentration within that experience quite clinically for a longer period of time than I think I ever had before. I was led through the series of questions to a solution of my own. I began to enjoy the unfolding stories and final answers. I found that I could not predict them; they wrote themselves, one reply leading to another. I began to understand what I had heard writers say, 'that characters behaved as they wished to, once they were conceived.'

Dreams had always been difficult to analyze on my own; I have tried. They reminded me of onions, one layer uncovered another, until I got quite confused. Suddenly a dream I had attempted to unravel for the past 53 years, whenever I thought of it, became a simple matter when subjected to Dr. Levis' method. Perhaps the act of creating a physical image gave it a more concrete reality in my mind. Whatever... it worked! Whenever I finished my assignment, the doctor received it asking additional questions or helping me see a missed clue. After three sessions he knew more about me than long-time friends and I had gained valuable insights, an unexpected bonus for me. I feel more secure now, because I know that my own mind can provide the answers to all my problems. I can follow the method of dealing with them.

As a member of an organization called Holocaust Child Survivors of Connecticut, Inc., I attend commemorative services for the slaughtered Jews during the reign of terror of the Third Reich. This is the first year I could look at it calmly as something like the honoring of veterans of wars or tortured prisoners and not as an invitation to relive a terrible time. (See the attached recent memory drawings and process). The healing fall-out of my therapy is not in yet.

Had the high school psychologist, who called me into his office after I became a student in America put a Conflict Analysis Battery of tests in front of me, I could not have gotten away with a simple "yes" to his question of "Are you happy?" when I was not at all.

My husband had abdominal pains, which doctors believed to be psychological during the early years of our marriage, which sent him to a psychiatrist. He was very uncommunicative in his sessions; he terminated therapy. His symptoms ceased altogether within two years. He probably would have completed Dr. Levis' tests (he told me when I showed him the ones I did) since they fitted into the pattern of testing he was used to from school rather than his image of a lunatic who is asked strange personal questions by a man he hardly knew.

I feel that the fact of having to reveal highly personal data in Dr. Levis' tests is masked by having to perform an introspective solitary task first with you alone as a witness. When the doctor reads back your material, he is telling you your story, and you make corrections or additions only, distracted from the realization that you have just confided in him.

As a person who recently completed a testing series with Dr. Levis, I am greatly impressed by the possibilities of his system. Judging from my experience it is a superior vehicle for screenings, such as for kids in a school and for conflicts in the workplace. The testing can be used for a fast, accurate psychological assessment or for a self-assessment at any point in time of a person's life. It reflects clearly one's state of mind. In psychotherapy or psychoanalysis, it can be taken to whatever detail is desired or necessary, greatly reducing the time required for the completion of therapy and the hours spent with a professional. This in turn reduces the cost providing a larger population with access to therapy.

In my last job as a budget analyst for the State, my boss had the belief that all problems presented could be reduced to asking what? why? and how? Dr. Levis's final process question is "how will I use this experience to change my behavior?" To my knowledge this question is absent from much of modern therapy. My New York City College roommate was still having weekly sessions, 15 years after I left the city, when our correspondence ended. Each test included in the battery I took, ended with the question "How will I change my behavior to avoid a conflict of this nature in the future?" The answer is that I have made peace with myself. One big burden, hate and guilt, have been lifted from my mind. I feel better about myself, resolved with my experiences. I am more spontaneous in my emotions and more open in my expressions.
In conclusion I can only say that I can glimpse a wide highway of uses for Dr. Levis' tests and that it travels a long way towards my generations' cry of "What the world needs now is a $5.00 psychoanalytic session."

I want to share an example of being spontaneous in my emotional expression.
"Chava Alberstein sang Israeli and Yiddish songs including the plaintive theme from Schindler's List which I know every note of but I only remember the often repeated "Kinderle" from the words. Her powerful responsive voice resounded through the Bethel Temple and I was aware of little else but that wonderful noise. I remember thinking how excellent her singing was, when I realized that I was crying and I didn't really know why. My emotions were rising and ebbing with the music that pervaded me and I stopped caring that I was making a spectacle of myself. Lest you think that I am always that emotional, let me hasten to say that I only did that once before, and that was at home listening to a record many years ago in my twenties. Though I don't know Yiddish, I knew the melodies of many of the songs. Did my mother or grandmother sing these songs when I was little? Or grandfather play them on his violin? The answer to this question will have to be added to the many mysteries of my early childhood. I am alive again."

Integrative therapeutic intervention: The assessment clarified the diagnosis of a relational modality, related pathology, it generated catharsis, reinforced with cognitive learning, and psychodynamic insights; it led to behavior modification, admitting feelings spontaneously.
The dominance diagnosis entails the realization of one's pathology as one's own transgressive display of power

as the origin of fears, anxieties, and disabilities. With this realization the patient becomes aware of the need of power management as reduction of his / her anger, or antagonistic tendencies. This case study reflects this consistent psychodynamic pattern: intense power positioning, be it cooperative or antagonistic, as responsible for the generation of paralyzing emotional and social, personal and interpersonal states of apprehension. The patient here realizes that the restraint of power was the secret in healing herself from disabling symptoms.

The significance of the study: measuring the unconscious as a syndrome related to a relational modality
The unconscious is shown as a syndromal entity integrating the metaphor tasks as interrelated in a continuum of six emotions, a sequence beginning with a conflict and ending with its resolution as a continuum of interrelated forms. In addition to being captured in the inventory, the RMES, Hannah's dominance is conveyed by a variety of relational attributes in her Metaphor Tasks: a mule, inscrutable, a lion, a social critic, a thief. All these emotions and behaviors are accounted by the wellness diagnosis, resolving conflicts along the relational modality of antagonistic dominance. This diagnostic impression is evident in her inventory and is confirmed by the content of the metaphor tests. Dominance generates anxieties as anticipations of role reversal, defenses, outcomes and resistance to compromises.

Conclusions
The case study validates Formal Theory's concepts of the unconscious as a syndrome and as a relational modality presented here as a study of dominance as a wellness diagnosis and the utilization of the battery assessment as diagnostic and therapeutic. The transcript of her tests explains the functions of the assessment: the battery was a cathartic narrative. The test taker became aware of her repressed emotions in her memories, the exercises released emotional blocks, like interpreting a dream that had preoccupied her for years. She identified unresolved conflicts; how her childhood attitude had generated bad feelings about herself, and emotional defensiveness. She was able to come to terms with guilt and self-blame. The related prompts generated insights that made the test taker self-aware guiding her to recognize patterns, to consider accepting responsibility of the developments, then identifying making changes.

Facing her own stories, her feelings changed from guilt and apprehension to relief, reconciliation, acceptance of her goodness as a scared girl facing the end of the world at 10. She was able to make peace with herself. She integrated the traumatic childhood memories, faced her feelings hidden behind the 'inscrutable' mask, equated with a tree with poison fruit and a person in whose heart she identified 'the path of good intensions leading to hell', her unforgivable feelings of relief upon the deportation of her grandparents. She also recognized a current pattern of testing limits: her transgresiveness across all her tests. She examined the continuity across her protocols. She was a little mule in the Family Zoo Portrait, 'inscrutable' in her Mask Test, as two lions fighting for the kill, in her Animal Metaphor Test. In her Short Story she was a girl looking for milking a cow in the country that required robbing a stranger. The review had led her to self-awareness and compromises.

Upon the third visit she had a dream of meeting her beloved grandmother. The brief evaluation led to her being vulnerable, free of the burden of self-blame. In the following social occasion, she broke down in public. She was now able to feel good about herself and join the world with spontaneous emotionality.

In the festivity that followed the evaluation a singer reminded her of her mother and of her loving culture, her childhood, the love that was lost but that now she was free to experience as a reunion with the past. The music had given her the opportunity to enjoy the occasion reminding her of her innocence and love experienced in her childhood. She melted down. She discovered that she was able to have good feelings again; she was vulnerable, not tough, and she was proud of being emotionally alive again. She thanked me both with the record of an additional metaphor exercise capturing the breakdown and with a warm endorsement of the intervention.

Therapy versus education

Hannah was very thankful to me personally but, she was conveying much about how appreciative she was for what the battery had done for her and how useful it could have been for her husband. In three sessions she had accomplished healing using the workbook on her kitchen table. Her recovery was not due to a great therapeutic relationship, transferential dynamics, dependency needs and interpretations. It offered her information on certain general principles; the testing that had helped her find out about herself. She thanked me but, the credit goes to the technology of creativity for self-discovery; indeed, she had duplicated the conflict analysis protocol in sharing the intense emotions upon the occasion of celebrating the anniversary of the creation of Israel.

Emotional education versus psychotherapy

In working with Hannah, my role was that of an educator; I explained simply how to organize the testing information meaningfully. Therapeutic achievement is shown to be enhanced by two factors: wellness relational modality diagnosis and the syndromal connection of life events through the utilization of the CAB self-assessment. The therapeutic transformation occurred without long-term therapy or effort by a therapist. Rather, Hannah, through completing the CAB, became conscious of her modality of power, without my instructing her about the theory. Completion of the CAB uniquely helped her identify her self-doubts and intense competitiveness and resealed her from her self-blame and guardedness. The metaphors conveyed her dominance as the key factor that generated her fears of being a bad person, her anxiety and cover up of feelings. The metaphors depicted the problem and the path to the problem's cure.

The role of the therapist as educator

Hannah's case study evidences the importance of the assessment instrument in psychotherapy over and above the importance of the role of the therapist. Within this case, the therapist is primarily an educator and facilitator, helping the client comprehend the assessment's role in identifying one's relational modality and its syndromal unfolding.

CAB is emotionally cathartic, but it offers more than that; it provided the meaningful integration of testing information along the path of the syndromal organization of emotions. What is also significant here is the shift of paradigms, from diagnoses as illnesses to diagnoses of wellness modalities. Psychology is neither aware of syndromal dynamics nor of a personality typology of wellness diagnoses. Modalities affect perceptions as distortions of reality and of related reactions to emotions.

In conclusion, the study indicates that therapy does not depend on the therapeutic relationship but on analysis of patterns along formal diagnostic criteria. This does not mean that the therapeutic relationship does not matter. On the contrary the therapist is needed as an educator and as the facilitator for furthering the identified need for changes. Learning about wellness diagnoses with syndromal unfolding can be imparted through the testing to a large number of people at the educational setting. The new diagnoses can enhance therapeutic outcome. The assessment, the diagnoses and the concepts of the Formal Theory have a place in education and in therapy. This type of learning is helpful as wellness emotional education, but it can enhance therapy.

Indeed, the CAB self-assessment is educational with a lengthy informative essay to be read prior to completing the assignments. The assessment is therapeutic learning without needing therapeutic professional services, but the assessment and the educational component can assist therapy work. The general public is in need for an emotional education. The assessment can enhance the conduct of therapy, but it can also be delivered as formalizing both personal and values education in the classroom.

Formal Analysis Profile (FAP)
The Formal Theory elaborates on understanding the particular aspects of organization of information, the symbolic universe of a conflict, as ex[plained in the chapter on epistemology. Below we identify the 10 levels of the profile, and then we are applying the levels in the analysis of Mural #7, 8, and 9.

Level 1: Universe of formative relational imprinting, includes that of positive and negative experiences.

Level 2: The constructs-variables of the particular formative conditioning: S, v, a, m.

Level 3: Formative pattern, as a process of a choice conflict energy and its components: E = F x S.

Level 4: Conservation of energy and its transformation into energetic modalities: E1, E2, E3.

Level 5: Types of conflict choices in relation of emotions reciprocal to deviation: a = -1/2 KS.

Level 6: The processing or overcoming oppression; conflict resolution, distinction of the six role process.

Level 7: Graphic presentation.

Level 8: Diagnosis of personality type.

Level 9: Quantification.

Level 10: Conversion of conflict into actionable insight as resolution.

The Formal Analysis Profile identifies ten scientific criteria in the analysis of metaphors of murals 7, 8, 9

Level 1, Formal distinctions between images illustrated in mural 7.

Level 2, Physical distinctions in images illustrated in mural 8.

Level 3, Formal characteristics of conflict identified as passivity, antagonism, alienation in personal self-assessment with the images of the Transparent Mask Test. Mural 9.

Level 5 Energetic conservation continuum evolving along five metaphors of Mural 8.

Level 6, Observing transformation as role continuity, a thematic integration of testing as a sequence of conflict resolution, stress to compromise, conflict to resolution, continuity as symbolic universes Mural 7, 8, and 9.

Level 8. Therapy by transforming illness diagnoses as traits to relational syndromes, and treating them as power management problems. Mural 7-9.

Levels 10. Therapeutic effectiveness of the assessment, mural 9, after three sessions the patient stated about her therapeutic relief: 'I am alive again'.

THE MEANINGFUL INTEGRATION OF KNOWLEDGE

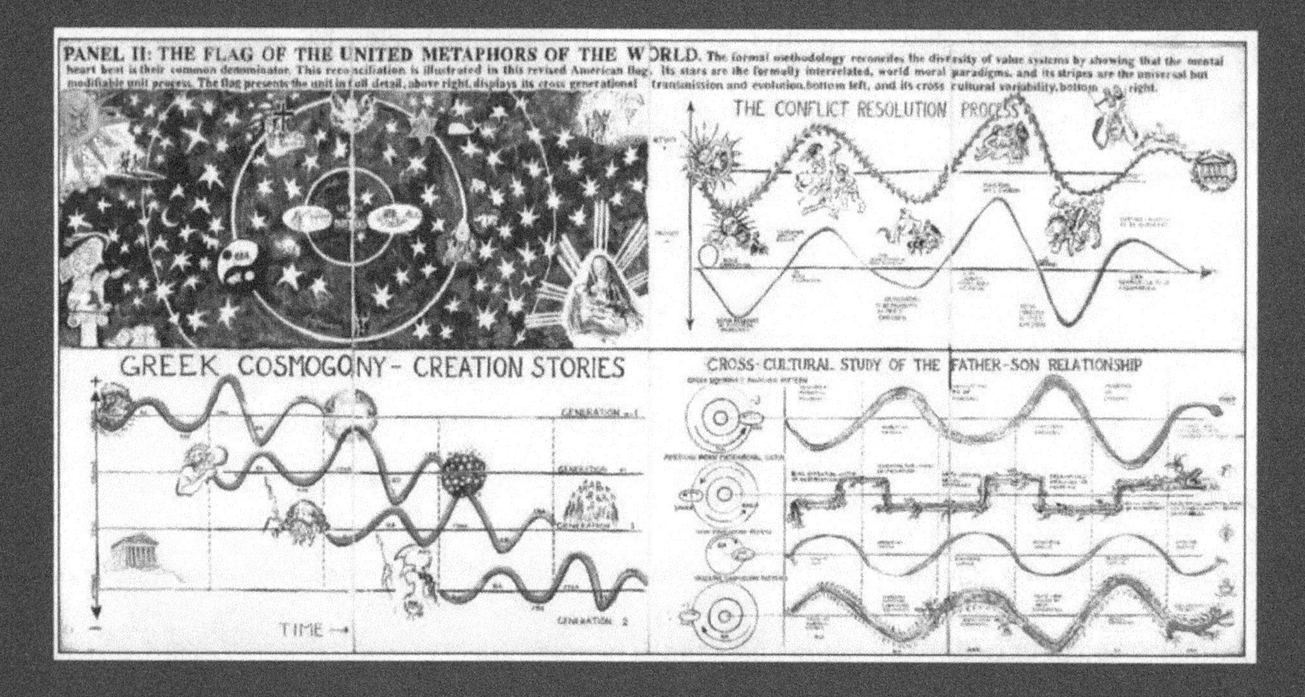

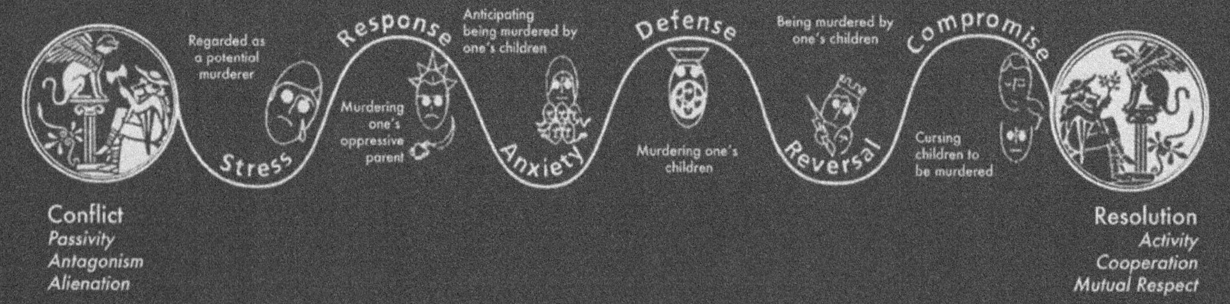

Volume Eight

Albert J. Levis M.D. & Maxwell Levis, Ph.D.

Normative Publications

<table>
<tr>
<td>

THE MORAL SCIENCE</td>
<td>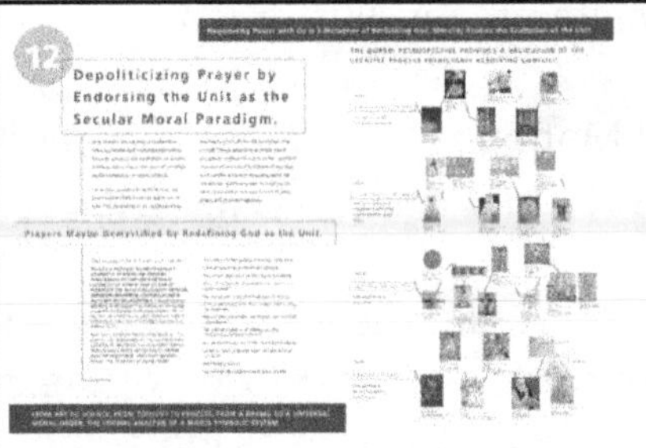

The unconscious is a universal measurable conflict resolution process, the atomistic unit of the social sciences</td>
<td>
Religions evolved as conflict resolutions improving the family institution and redefining the divine more abstractly</td>
</tr>
</table>

BOOK FOUR
WALL 4: 'THE MEANINGFUL INTEGRATION OF KNOWLEDGE'

CHAPTER ONE: ON MORALITY AS A SCIENTIFIC PHENOMENON

In every book we presented pertinent metaphors of the story of the Wizard and related clinical case studies illustrating Formal Theory's epistemology, diagnostic categories, assessment, and now the concept of morality. The challenge is in understanding morality by identifying the creative process as underlying all religions but also all creativity. The metaphor of the Wizard of Oz questioning the nature of religions as wizardry, as manipulation of the naïve heroes of the story, suddenly relieved of their problems by correcting their vision. Toto helped in that respect. This perception of religions dismisses the importance of religions but also of morality. What is morality then?

'The Meaningful Integration of Knowledge', introduces the unconscious, the atomistic unit, the scientific conflict resolution entity, entailing morality, as the essence of the unconscious motivation revamping the current conceptualization of the disciplines of psychology deprived of a moral component. The unconscious has been blamed of creating conflicts, as driven by libido and Thanatos. The formal premise introduces both science and morality into the core of the unconscious. The task of this chapter is understanding morality as a disciplines of psychology by demonstrating the scientific structure and the moral function of the creative process.

The Oz story is a turn of the century attempt at ghostbusting, demystifying gods and moral orders. The Oz figure is portrayed as a deceptive character, an imposter. This depiction shows how the twentieth century felt about religions. The public disparaged the notion of faith as naïve surrender to fabrications. The 20th century consensus was that religions were of historical significance but representing impediments to sociological progress as advanced by Darwin's findings on evolution. The Formal Theory introduces legitimacy to religions as forerunners of he Moral Science. The Formal Theory restores the legitimacy of morality placing its study on the creative process. It understands religions as metaphors that may be interpreted as discoveries of the alternative paths to conflict resolution.

The panels of the fourth wall rehabilitate the moral wisdom of religions by examining the Judaic theosophy as insights into the scientific nature of conflict resolution. The panels examine the principles of faith advanced by Maimonides, as insights on the creative process, Ten Commandments as discoveries of the three formal operations of the conflict resolution process, and prayers as conducive to the reduction of inner conflicts by accepting the divine as the mental state of rest. We thus establish morality as the conflict resolution nature of the unconscious and religions as discoveries of the process.

The three murals present the moral unconscious as a scientific phenomenon. Mural 4 integrates faith and reason. Mural 5 recognizes the evolution of religions as a syndromal sequence of relationally connected conflict resolution phases seeking the optimization of family relations. Mural #6 presents four religions as the complement of resolutions by introducing their graphic diagrammatic illustration.

The second chapter of this book, introduces Moral Monopoly, an educational card game, that integrates religions into the Moral Science as complementary discoveries of the alternative ways of resolving conflict.

The second chapter in this book, Moral Monopoly, addresses the integration of religions as complementary discoveries of the Moral Science; it uses the deck of cards as the template of the unconscious to retrace the evolution of religions as discoveries of the four relational modalities as moral monopolies, as representing complementary discoveries of the four types of resolving, the four modalities corresponding to the four suits of the deck. The religions follow the distinctions of the symbols of the suits of the card game spade to heart as the progression of religions to fairness in family relations and abstraction on the nature of the divine.

Religions are identified as measurable normative institutions sanctifying the four alternative types of conflict resolution. As such they are partial discoveries of the science representing partial truths, incomplete in their wisdom and unable to bring peace to the world. The Moral Science integrates the religions by establishing consensus on religions having measurable natural science dimensions. The Moral Science places religions on a scientific foundation and reconciles them as an evolutional continuum completing their mission for peace in the world. The moral values are reduced to the universal principles of conflict resolution governing the unconscious. Thus science fulfills their mission for peace in the world by establishing the scientific foundation of moral order.
The third chapter of this book addresses the creative process unconscious as the integrative paradigm of all disciplines of psychology.

CHAPTER TWO: THREE PANELS ESTABLISH THE MORAL FUNCTION OF THE CREATIVE PROCESS

Panels #10, 11, and 12
This study interprets religions as insights on the universal conflict resolving process representing humanity's quest for meaning and justice. Religions evolved by identifying over the ages how to improve the family institution, using explanations on the nature of the role model divine. The divine evolved by identifying modalities projected onto Gods as role models of the new conflict resolution inspiring the public with new values and norms.

Religions stem from the unconscious need for reduction of conflict. They have evolved through an ongoing need to reduce conflicts and advance justice and peace. Whereas each moral paradigm has finite dimensions, the evolutional sequence binds them dialectically together to the Science of Conflict Resolution. This observation shifts humanity from divisive partial truths to awareness of science underlying all moral orders and founded on the human unconscious. The Formal Theory defends the wisdom of religions as pioneers, and as poets of the Moral Science

- Multiple religions have identified the underlying order, the six-step syndromal sequence of conflict resolution as creation stories such as Genesis and the seven chakras.
- Religions discovered the principles of conflict resolution as moral injunctions like the Ten Commandments and the Egyptian Book of the Dead.
- They have identified the relational modalities like in the Passover story's four children responses to the question of 'What is special about this night?'
- God's attributes have been determined as anticipations of punishments and awards. They are determined by one's relational modality choices. Thus correcting one's relational modality can improve one's anticipations and the perception of God. Inversely, defining god as benevolent can inspire humans to improved their attitude.
- The Formal Theory reconciles religions as partial and complementary discoveries of science.
Moral Monopoly is an educational game, which integrates them into the Moral Science as a

progression of discoveries of the alternative ways of resolving conflict, improving the family institution and the abstract definition of the divine. Gods are qualified with the attributes of the unconscious.

- Religions have not resolved a key conflict in the family institution. They have not applied the principle of mutual respect in the gender relations. Women have been discriminated as lesser beings, or at least as evoking too much conflict and that they have to be highly regulated in their freedoms.

In the discussion of the Oz metaphor we show the scientific wisdom of religions by introducing the concepts of Judaism as accurate metaphors of the underlying moral order. Religions established insights into the psychology of conflict resolution. They represent metaphors leading to an effective emotional education. By praising God believers extoll the wisdom of conflict resolution.

Panel 10: Piety as Respect of the Universal Moral Order

Reconciling Faith and Reason through the Formal Analysis of Yigdal, Maimonides' Thirteen Articles of Faith.

Yigdal, Maimonides' Thirteen Articles of Faith On the Nature of God	Formal Theoretical Commentary On God As The Unit Of The Conflict Resolution Process
2. He is the One, unique.	Religions have evolved dialectically resolving conflicts of the family institution. They have progressed from Matriarchy to Patriarchy, from Daughter Power (Moon Goddess) to Son Power (Sun Gods), from Father and Son Monotheism to Mother and Child Messianism.

3. He has no body, no form.	Humankind has evolved from concrete toward abstract perceptions of moral order, e.g., from pagan worship to moral philosophies like Buddhism. Now it is possible to define moral order scientifically as a periodic, predictable, measurable, graphically portrayable Conflict Resolution Process coinciding with the human unconscious as a system of purely abstract formal connected energetic transformations.
4. He is eternal.	The moral truth, the Conflict Resolution Process is a scientific mechanism reflecting the formal and natural science properties of the unconscious process.
5. He alone is to be worshipped.	The moral authority to command our loyalty and respect are the abstract and universal scientific principles, the law of scientific phenomena.

On Prophets	**On Intuitive Thinkers**
6. The words of the prophets are true.	Prophets, artists and scientists alike are guided intuitively by their unconscious need for Conflict Resolution.
7. Moses was the greatest prophet.	Moses intuitively recognized the value of the universal Principles of Conflict Resolution as ones that people should deliberately adhere to as though identified by God.
8. The source of the Torah is Divine.	All moral scriptures, literature and creativity reflect the universal unconscious need for moral order.

On the Credibility of the Scriptures	**Scriptural Moral Discoveries Intuitively Perceived Science**
9. The Torah is immutable.	There are many sacred scriptures. They represent metaphorical, intuitive attempts to capture the nature of moral order and to present it as the divinely revealed absolute truth. Only science can capture the universal laws of order.
10. God knows the deeds and the thoughts of men.	Emotions, behaviors and biological states are organized as syndromal sequences which abide by the laws of science. Hence behaviors and emotions are predictable and measurable.
11. God rewards and punishes.	The four alternative syndromal ways of relating differ in their effectiveness in resolving conflicts. According to one's handling of power, one may experience happiness or unhappiness, sanity or madness.
12. The Messiah will come.	The scientific understanding of the Unit Process can free humanity from prejudice and divisiveness and unite all the cultures of the world to a universal moral order.
13. God forever praised will resurrect the dead.	Science reconciles all moral paradigms into an evolutional continuum of moral discoveries which have contributed to the dialectic development of awareness of the nature of moral order.

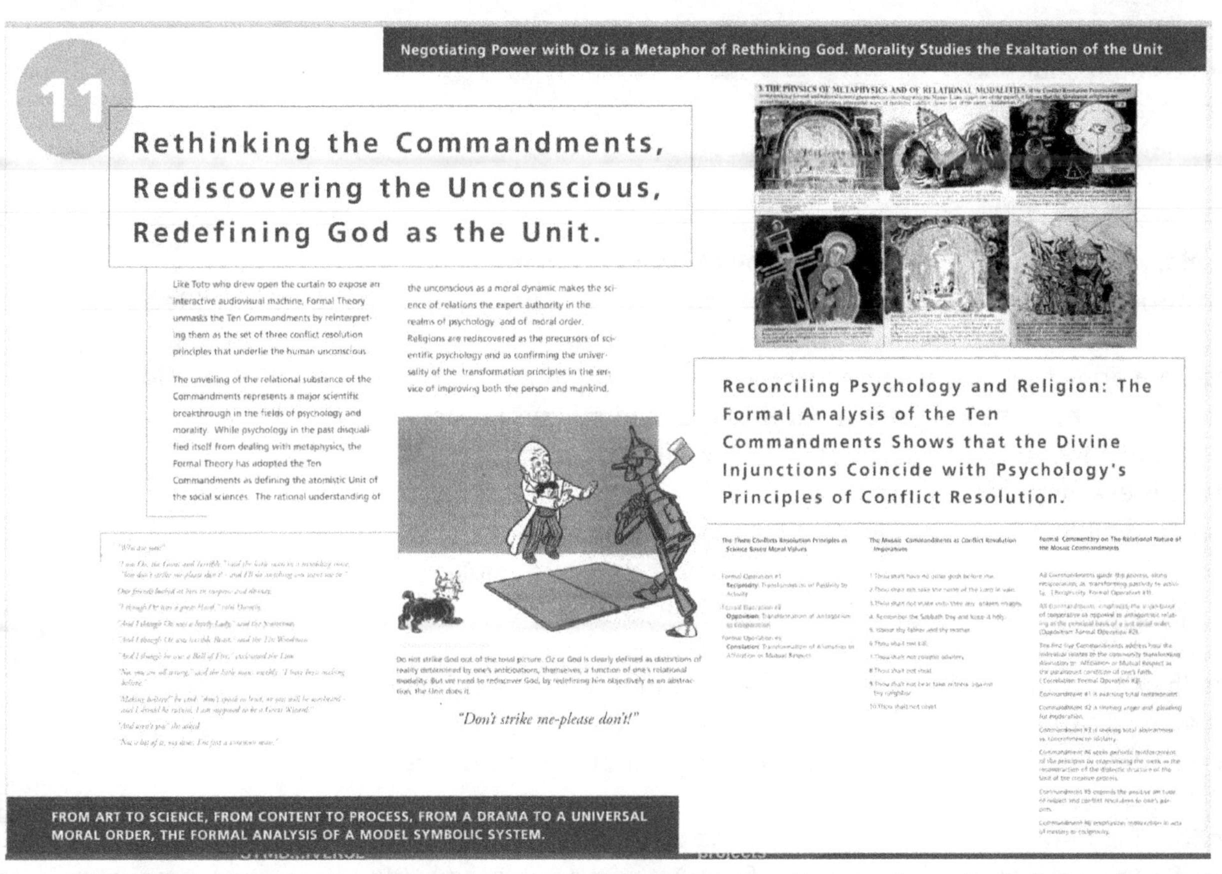

Panel 11: Rethinking the Commandments, Rediscovering the Unconscious, Redefining God as the Unit, Reconciling Psychology and Religion:

The ten laws discovered the injunctions averting the generation of conflict. While identifying norms of conduct they confirm the principles in the service of improving society. The Ten Commandments define the moral injunctions of mastery with moderation, cooperation instead of antagonism, and mutual respect. These are norms but also they have a scientific foundation. The Mosaic laws identified the unconscious moral dynamic, the science of relations, which current psychology has totally ignored. The Formal Theory unmasks incredulity of the non-believers by identifying the scientific wisdom of religions. We identify laws of science governing the human unconscious underlying the wisdom of Genesis and of the Ten Commandments.

The Judaic Commandments identified God as a caring human, defined by the mutuality of the Father-Son Covenant. The science clarifies the multiplicity of gods as reflections of alternative but evolving cultural relational choices. God has been redefined by the innate pursuit of conflict resolution. Though Oz as moral authority is a figment of imagination, the unconscious is a real moral authority that regulates all our behaviors.

The Formal Analysis of the Ten Commandments Shows that the Divine Injunctions Coincide with Psychology's Principles of Conflict Resolution.

The Three Conflicts Resolution Principles as Science Based Moral Values

Formal Operation #1 Reciprocity: Transformation of Passivity to Activity
Formal Operation #2 Opposition: Transformation of Antagonism to Cooperation
Formal Operation #3 Correlation: Transformation of Alienation to Affiliation or Mutual Respect

The Mosaic Commandments as Conflict Resolution Imperatives

1. Thou shalt have no other gods before me.
2. Thou shalt not take the name of the Lord in vain.
3. Thou shalt not make unto thee any graven images.
4. Remember the Sabbath Day, and keep it holy.
5. Honor thy father and thy mother.

6. Thou shalt not kill.
7. Thou shalt not commit adultery.
8. Thou shalt not steal.
9. Thou shalt not bear false witness against thy neighbor.
10. Thou shalt not covet.

Formal Commentary on The Relational Nature of the Mosaic Commandments
All Commandments guide the process, along reciprocation, as transforming passivity to activity (Reciprocity: Formal Operation #1). All Commandments emphasize the importance of cooperative as opposed to antagonistic relating as the principal basis of a just social order. (Opposition: Formal Operation #2). The first five Commandments address how the individual relates to the community transforming Alienation to Affiliation or Mutual Respect as the paramount condition of one's faith (Correlation: Formal Operation #3).
Commandment #1 is exacting total commitment.
Commandment #2 is limiting anger and pleading for moderation.
Commandment #3 is seeking total abstractness versus concreteness or idolatry.
Commandment #4 seeks periodic reinforcement of the principles by experiencing the week as the reconstruction of the Unit of the creative process.
Commandment #5 extends the positive attitude of respect and conflict resolution to one's parents.
Commandment #6 emphasizes moderation in acts of mastery or reciprocity.
The rest of the commandments instruct moderation, cooperation and mutual respect.

Panel 12: Depoliticizing Prayer by Endorsing the Unit as the Secular Moral Paradigm
Prayer, tainted with political bias, has been banned from American public education. This development has overlooked the healing function of this old institution. Humans are capable of deliberately reducing mental and interpersonal tension through prayer and meditation, as positive thinking, as the state of complete conflict resolution or peace of mind. The Formal Theory, advancing a secular moral paradigm suggests the rediscovering of prayer in the pursuit of inner conflict resolution. Education can reclaim the use of prayer to help the student to proceed to moderation, cooperation, and mutual respect as the path for inner peace and global harmony.

Demystifying Prayers by Redefining God as the Unit
"Hear my prayer, O Lord, and let my cry come unto thee". Prayer is a profound internal dialogue, a sequence of behaviors and emotions transpiring in the contemplative realm, leading to the ultimate state of conflict resolution. One has a sense of safety based on generating moderation, cooperation, and a self-other mutual acceptance. The individual, by admitting powerlessness, finds mastery, by advocating cooperation and respect, finds empowerment. By feeling loved, one feels enabled to become loving and forgiving. Deference to a benevolent god shapes one's positive attitude to all. Adon Olam, in Hebrew' Master of the Universe', is a prayer whose empowering value becomes universally acceptable by substituting the controversial, multi-defined concept of God by the scientifically redefined moral Unit phenomenon, the Conflict Resolution Process, also known as the Creative Process.

The Creative Process gives birth to every living thing.
When all was made as the Process ordained,
Then only It was known as the Creator and Master.
When all is ended, the Process will reign alone in awesome majesty.
The Process was, is, and will be glorious in eternity.
Peerless and unique is the Process, with none at all to be compared.
Beginningless and endless, the Process' vast dominion is not shared.
The Creative Process is our Master, our life's Redeemer, our Refuge in distress,
Our shelter sure, our cup of life, its limitless goodness.
I place our spirit in its care when we wake as when we sleep.
The Process is with us. We shall not fear, body and spirit are in its keep.

Panel 12: The Gorski retrospective as a validation of the creative process predictably resolving conflict.

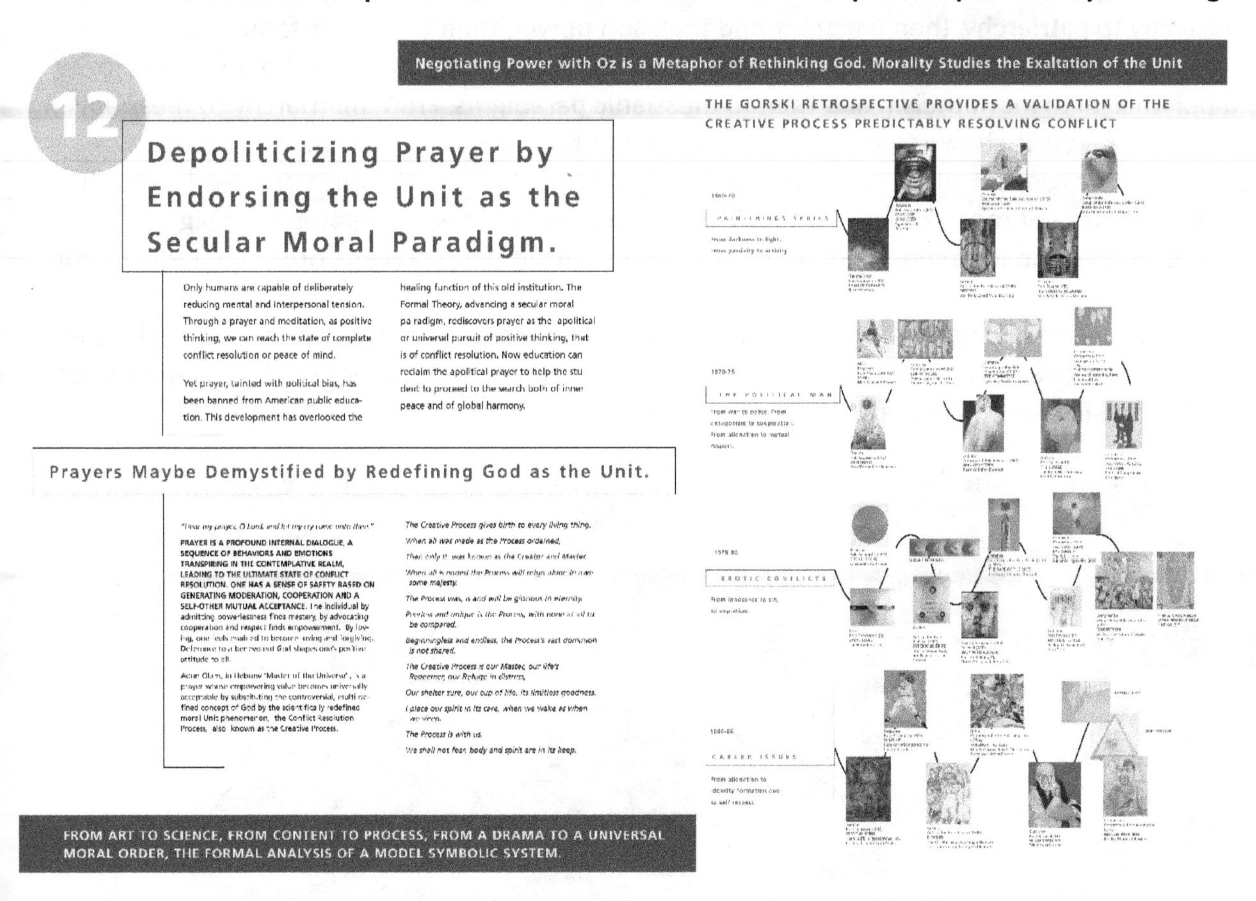

CHAPTER THREE: MURALS 4, 5, AND 6 OF THE FOURTH WALL ARE ABOUT UNDERSTANDING RELIGIONS AS MEASURABLE CONFLICT RESOLUTIONS THAT HAVE SPONTANEOUSLY EVOLVED TOWARD THE MORAL SCIENCE.

Three murals address the validation of the Formal Theory by examining religions, morality in general, as a scientific conflict resolution phenomenon. The first, M4, presents my metaphors validated as a six-role process seeking conflict resolution through the use of the CAB. The sequence begins with the conflict of metaphors, religions and ideologies of the WWII, leading to the reconciliation of metaphors through the discovery of the CRP, the scientific process integrating faith and reason. The process integrates the creativity tasks of the Conflict Analysis Battery's metaphors into reconstructing the personal syndromal way of resolving conflicts. This mural is presented in detail in the section on the use of the Conflict Analysis Battery. It is relevant here merely in the context of my quest for meaning in resolving my personal conflicts illustrating the universal quest for conflict resolution integrating art and science, psychology and morality.

Mural 5: Our Cultural Metaphors as a Continuum of Evolving Moral Order

Mural five depicts the interrelation of the pagan religions as the epics of the goddess ushering in Judaic monotheism. This harmonic integrates cultural resolutions of domestic gender conflicts, which improve the formation of the stable family institution. The mural retraces the formal interrelation of religions as a six role-state sequence as discoveries of conflict resolution integrating them into the Moral Science. The discoveries of the conflict resolution process are presented as restructuring family role relations as normative institutions founded on redefined role model divinities. The six-role states present how moral thinking evolved from conflictual interpretations of reality to the fairer structuring of relations and the more abstract understanding the divine. The Moral Science integrates the religions ushering in an era of clarity and consensus on moral reason. Science represents the definitive definition of enlightened thinking.

Mural # 5 presents the evolution of moral paradigms along the six-role unit process showing the resolution of family conflicts through the restructuring gender role relations. The progression shifts genders in control of the family from matriarchy to patriarchy, then daughter and then son power, then the Judaic father-son covenant and finally the messianic mother child alliance. The progression evolves the attributes of the moral authority, the divine from polytheism to monotheism and then to messianic paradigms. From matriarchy to messianism, the conflict resolution process is shown to integrate the religions of the world into a continuum of ever-improving family relations. Religions evolved increasing restraints on female sexuality while also leading to the abstract and universal nature of moral order. The mural shows how the process integrates the religions of the world as partial intergender and intergenerational conflict resolutions into a civil rights order upgrading entity.

This mural shifts paradigms from dogma to science-based moral principles. Science redefines god as the Unit of the conflict resolution process. The three formal operations, the relational principles leading to Moderation, Cooperation, and Mutual Respect are equated with moral values.

RESPONSE:	DEFENSE:	COMPROMISE:
Greece's Oedipus, outwitting and dominating the Sphinx monster and marrying his mother, represents Patriarchy's Greek snake man. He is rising to power over women but then as the son upstaging the father then fighting inner dependency needs with rules for competitive behaviors, political, athletic, cultural.	The moral ascendance of men over women is reflected in the sacredness of snakes, flying dragons, and feathered serpents, gradually identified with the worship of the sun and the single male god.	Christianity's Virgin Mother and self-sacrificial child, Islam's crescent and star reflect the shift of power balance from Judaism's father-son Covenant to Messianism's mother-child alliance as the commanding moral order.

STRESS: The Mexican eagle immobilizing and devouring a snake is the metaphor representing Matriarchy's omnipotent mother. intimidating her weak partners and children	ANXIETY: Women return to power through Hinduism's moral discovery of cooperation. Six-armed Kali is dominating and nurturing her partner Siva. Siva is the cooperative partner in his turn, stepping on his inner child-like self, corresponding to canceling his sexual desires.	REVERSAL: The comeback of women as seductive Eve reducing Adam to a charmed snake backfired on women. It evoked the father-son covenant alliance, the monotheistic male-dominated moral order.

The fifth mural validates the formal thesis by showing that the religions of the world are formally interrelated partial conflict resolutions within the Conflict Resolution Process totality. God is redefined by each religion as a distinct relational modality structuring of family relations. The mural integrates the family restructurings into a global or ecumenical Conflict Resolution Process.

The matriarchy of Mexico is the Role Oppression characterized as submissive antagonism. Patriarchy in Greece is the Role Assumption reciprocal to matriarchy as dominant antagonism. The Moon Goddess daughter power of India corresponds to the Anticipated Role Reversal state and is opposite to patriarchy. It represents the submissive cooperative mode of relating. The Sun God power of Egypt, China and Japan is the Counterphobic Role Assumption. It is reciprocal to the moon goddess religions. The father-son alliance of Judaism, the Role Reversal state, is correlative to the prior religions. It represents the dominant cooperative mutual respect modality. Finally, the messianic mother and child alliance of Christianity and Islam, the Compromise Role Assumption, is a correlative form of the father-son covenant.

We may follow the formal transformations on this mural as the continuum of the eagle-snake animal metaphors symbolic system modified in the consecutive religions. This animal metaphor evolves in the symbolism of the six key cultural, moral paradigms, retracing the anthropological, historical transformation of domestic relations. This evolution dramatizes the continuity among these paradigms as the ongoing restructuring of domestic interpersonal relations to achieve eventually greater family relations effectiveness. Mural #6 illustrates the evolution of the metaphor figures and the corresponding family members with vectorial changes within the formal circle, reflecting the restructuring of the cultural paradigms.

Thus, the innate Conflict Resolution Process has been responsible for the moral developments and now it may be used to integrate the religions of the world into the unconsciously driven upgrading of order. The science connects the isolated religions of the world into the single abstract totality of the unit conflict resolution order. The evolving domestic intergenerational and intergender relations lead to awareness of the need for reduction of domestic conflicts by improving fairness for all members of the family system. The mural conveys the history of civilization as the restructuring of the family role relations evolved from ineffective cruel resolutions of conflict to provide fairness, goodness and societal effectiveness for all members. Yet the current family configuration based on the Abrahamic religions is based on inequity between the genders.

1.The first frame corresponds to the Role Oppression state of the process. The matriarchy of Mexico dramatizes the conflict between an eagle and a snake. The eagle symbolically represents both the powerful mother earth goddess, Coatlique, and her son, the Sun, Huitzilopochtli. The snake symbolizes Earth's daughter, the moon goddess Coyoxauhqli and Earth's children, the stars, punishable as rebellious. The eagle and the snake are framed by a big counterclockwise or antagonistic circle. The vectors symbolize the culture's dominant, antagonistic polarized structuring of the mother-daughter conflictual relationship.

2. The second role state, Response, corresponds to the Role Assumption state of the six-role process. We see the male gods of patriarchy in Greece triumph over the mother Earth goddess. Symbolically the mother earth goddess from an Eagle is weakened to a Sphinx, a hybrid eagle, lion, and woman who is outwitted by men and is toppled off her pedestal. The Greek mother, Jocasta, tried to prevail over a young person who turned out to be her own son. The Sphinx-like woman who killed men was outwitted. Jocasta as a wife, recognizing her self-righteousness and killed herself. Oedipus, represents the Greek man's consistent effort to assume power over the powerful, angry or seductive, Sphinx-like Greek women. The Greek culture favored men. The reversal of matriarchy is a step toward resolving intergenerational conflicts, but it also reveals the Greek norm of male domination, reversing the maternal and filial alliance antagonistic to the father. The Homeric Epics attest to the punishment of Helen, the antagonistic spouse, and the promotion of Penelope as the cooperative role model for Greek women but also the new alliance of mother Penelope and son Telemachus, as respectful of the father, Odysseus.

3. The third frame corresponds to the Anticipated Role Reversal state of the six-role process. It is established by young women violated by patriarchy, escaping the power of Greek men and women rivalries. A concubine of Zeus was transformed to a cow, who escaped the confines of her husband Argos Panoptes, to find freedom in India, where cows are sacred. Kali symbolizes the moon goddess empowerment of women in India. The six-armed Hindu goddess can nurture, but also destroy. She is portrayed in a characteristic sitting position, her feet planted on her spouse Siva. She is keeping him underfoot but caring for him. Siva, in his turn is presented as a male dancer standing with one foot on a diminutive figure, a child respectful of his master. He, an asexual male, is stepping on a child. He is in control of his inner child as desires. Desires are strongly repressed in Hinduism and Buddhism, both aggression and sexuality. The image represents the Hindu man's cooperative submission to the power of the exalted maternal authority, the beloved and dreaded moon goddess Kalli. The accomplishment of this culture is that it discovered cooperation and submission. The vectors of the power grid evolve in a cooperative clockwise fashion. Greek man's aggression and anxiety is evolving into Indian man's peacefulness as submission to a pacifist world outlook. The Indian man is willing to be stepped on.

4. The fourth frame corresponds to the Counter-Phobic Role Assumption state of the six-role process. It presents men capturing power and control as powerful dragons, sun gods commanding the respect of the family. All cultures have celebrated sun gods as dragons and snake gods; sons and fathers emerging to control the domestic system. Chinese dragons, like the respective benevolent patriarchs, fly on top of the earth, omnipotent like the fiery sun. The Mexico has a dragon too, Quetzalcoatl, the Feathered Serpent; he is also moving in a dominant cooperative way into the sky. Snakes have a sacred reference in Greece. The healing rod of Aesculapius and Hermes are intertwined snakes reflecting power and cooperation. The crown jewel of Egyptian crowns is an asp. The Hindu charmed cobra represents the Hindu man's mastery of instincts. Their snake charmer rituals represent maximum self-restraint, that is, submission and cooperation.

5. However, the snake in Judea represents the impersonation of evil, antagonizing God's will associated with the perception of unresolved gender conflicts, seductive women as Eve, inspired by the seductress – Ishtar of the Gilgamesh epic. This re-emergence of women to power through seduction generated the Biblical man's role reversal and reactive moralism of the father-son alliance to neutralize the seductive power of women. This eventually led to a restructuring of domestic relations. The alliance of father and son fostering the new moral paradigm of monotheism reduced women's power promoting chastity, and spirituality.

We must note the coincidence of Abraham's wanderings and the war of Troy: both moral paradigms emphasize the alliance of men to contain the power of seductresses, Helen, Eve, and Ishtar. The seduction of men by women corresponds to the Role Reversal state of the evolutionary sequence portrayed in the fifth tile. Here monotheism represents the next evolution in the conflict resolution between genders, the alliance between men across generations. Monotheism fostered an alliance between men of two generations as alluded by the two lions of Judah guarding the tablets. The seductress Eve is portrayed in her attempt to reach the forbidden fruit. She is also the scapegoat.

Women were transformed from eagles into Sphinxes. Then they were perceived as dangerous and oppressed for any sexual liberties. They came to be protected by Christ. And defended by Mohammad identifying Ismael as the heir of the moral authority of Abraham. The oppression of women, a political reality eventually would haunt Judaism since it eventually led the two messianic religions, the alliance of the mothers and their sons in Christianity and Islam.

6. The sixth frame of the sequence is the Compromise Role Assumption. In the anthropology of religions, this corresponds to the messianic movement and religions. Christianity professed humility but Islam professed militancy. Formally Messianic gods represent conflict resolution across the generations and the genders. In both Christianity and Islam, sons enter in alliances with their mothers, a choice reciprocal to Judaism's father-son covenant. Christianity and Islam may be conceived as reciprocal to Judaism and as opposite to each other in the subsystem of two reactions to Judaism.

We can portray them as ellipses. Christianity is presented as the crucifix choosing cooperation and powerlessness. The Islamic model is represented with Mohammed riding its colorful woman-horse, Barak, to heaven; he chooses might to prevail on the infidels. The Islamic crescent and star represent the alliance of a reduced moon goddess-mother with a child thought of as a bright star—the sacred relationship of triumphant Ishmael, who is unlike self-sacrificial Jesus.

Mohammed is a warrior, a powerful fighter. He was active sexually; he had several wives. Unlike Christian symbolism of humans as sheep and fish, the Islamic flock identifies with warriors proceeding to power in battle and promised sexuality in heaven as modeled by their powerful, aggressive leaders on earth. The end, a moral objective, justifies violence. "Islam" means submission to God. Polygamy instead of providing security to scapegoated women, fosters rivalries and intrigues that parallel and extrapolate the unresolved conflicts of Abraham's two wives. Women compensate for their self-effacedness through competitive tendencies fostered in their sons reflecting intrafamily conflicts.

The first frame of the matriarchal mother-child conflictual relationship, is transformed in the sixth frame to the resolution of the empowered mother-child relationship. While the initial eagle-snake metaphor illustrates the oppression, antagonism, and alienation of the child, especially clear in the mother-daughter rivalry, Mother Earth Coatlique vs. Moon Daughter-Coyoxauhqli, the final frame of the mural, that of the two messianic religions, presents the mother-son/child alliance promoting love, cooperation, moderation and respect or affiliation. All the same, the resolution of the Abrahamic family's conflicts has not yet been reached, and we are experiencing them in our days as the unresolved conflicts of the Abrahamic siblings.

Mural 6: From Art to Science in the Search for a Better Paradigm

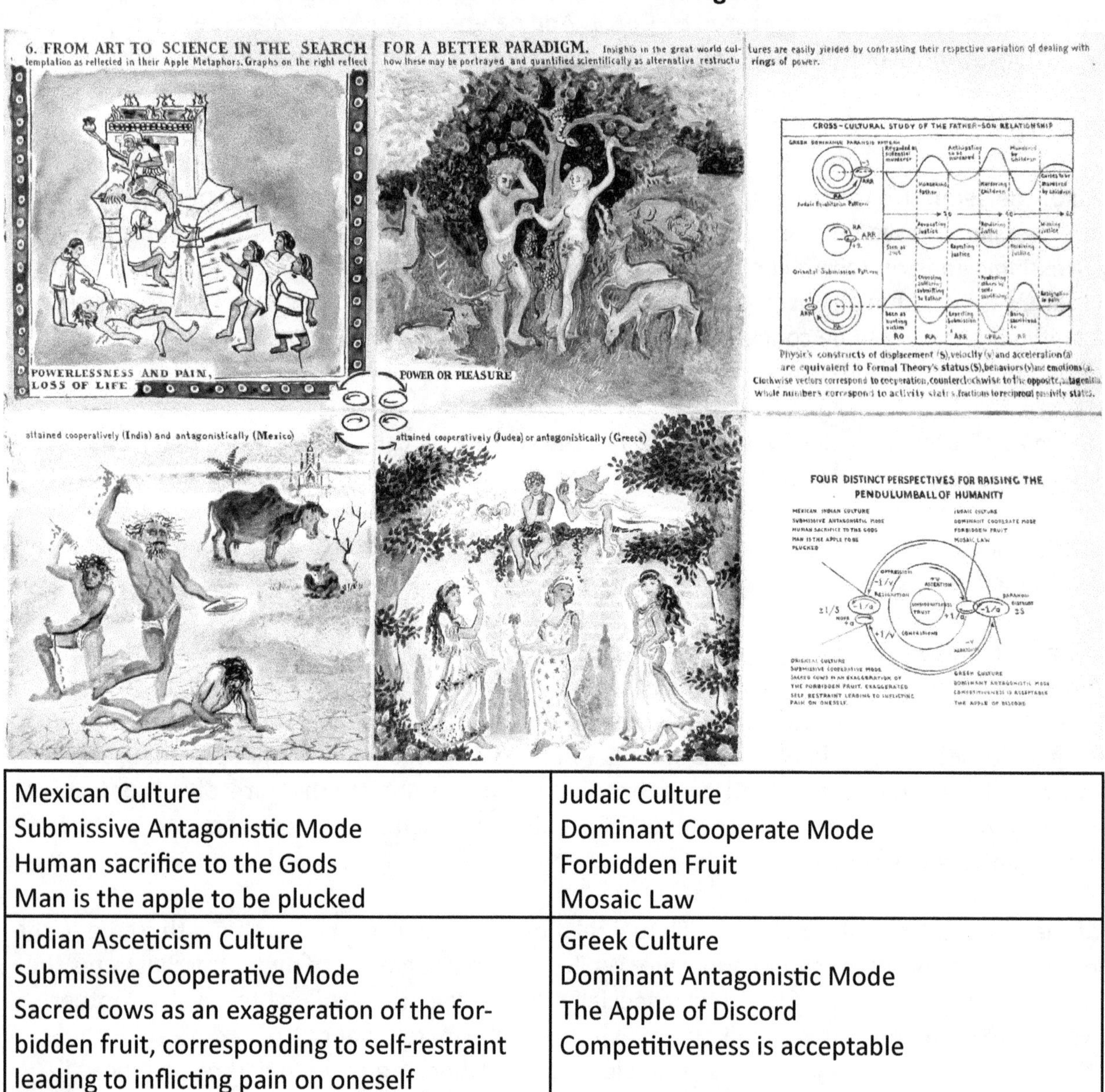

Mexican Culture Submissive Antagonistic Mode Human sacrifice to the Gods Man is the apple to be plucked	Judaic Culture Dominant Cooperate Mode Forbidden Fruit Mosaic Law
Indian Asceticism Culture Submissive Cooperative Mode Sacred cows as an exaggeration of the forbidden fruit, corresponding to self-restraint leading to inflicting pain on oneself	Greek Culture Dominant Antagonistic Mode The Apple of Discord Competitiveness is acceptable

Mural # 6 contrasts four cultural paradigms in their handling temptation; these correspond to the four relational modalities. The four cultures illustrate the four modalities and the evolution of moral paradigms in the direction of fairness and abstraction redefining morality, the divine, and restructuring family role relations. In the same mural the cultural resolutions are portrayed graphically with constructs of physics. This Mural juxtaposes four cultural ways of dealing with temptation as relations between people contrasted to their formal diagrammatic representations. The graphic portrayal validates the relevance of the formal and natural science method in analyzing moral order systems as normative institutions with natural science dimensions.

In parallel, the art is reduced to science as the four interrelated cultural ethical paradigms considered are formally abstracted as the reciprocal and opposite forms of relating, as dominant vs. submissive and as cooperative vs. antagonistic. Along the dominant modes, the Judaic is the dominant cooperative (forbidden fruit), and the Greek is the dominant antagonistic (apple of discord). Along the submissive modes, the Indian is the submissive cooperative (sacred cow), and the Mexican is the submissive antagonistic alternative (the mother goddesses demands the beating hearts of the humans in order to be appeased and to not destroy the world).

The evolution of resolutions reflects the evolution of relational modalities, as a progression of effectiveness in resolving conflict. It also reflects the gradual increase in fairness leading to happiness for all members of the family system. The conclusion is that the syndrome of cooperative dominance has prevailed as the most effective relational modality, and the syndrome of submissive antagonistic relating has been abandoned as the least effective way of relating. This conclusion parallels the four relational modalities of psychology to the four groups of religions and clarifies why religions evolved in popularity on the basis of reducing conflicts and promoting peace.

The Apple symbolism of desire and conflicts

The mural portrays four cultural relational responses to the same stressor: the apple as the symbol of temptation. The second part of the mural illustrates how the art of these metaphors is interpreted with the abstractions of science: graphs capture the relational differences of the four cultural alternatives. The four relational alternatives reflect the cultural dimensions as diametrically opposite and as reciprocal to each other.

The four cultural perspectives are compared by contrasting their apple metaphors, that is, equivalent metaphors regarding dealing with temptation. The differences are key distinctions of the four cultures as the ethical or normative regulation of man's relationship with his fellow man or woman as reflected in sacred texts prescribing injunctions on how to deal with desires and power. These normative injunctions for power conveyed metaphorically are presented here as the formal spectrum of relational modalities as the moral alternatives.

Insights in the great world cultures are easily yielded by contrasting their respective variation of dealing with temptation, as reflected in their Apple Metaphors. The graphs reflect how these may be portrayed and quantified scientifically as alternative restructurings of power.

In both dominant cultures, Judea and Greece, men saw the world as a place of empowerment and pleasures, as one in which they could find love and understanding and have their needs satisfied. Man could prosper, master uncertainty, and pursue immortality. In Judea, the condition for permanent happiness, that is, immortality or paradise, was that the apple, the symbol of temptation, be treated as forbidden. In order for a human to enjoy peace of mind, he had to respect limits. Injunctions equivalent to the apple being forbidden, indeed, the Mosaic laws, confirmed the importance of cooperative behaviors by specifying respect for God, one's parents, and another man's property, authority, wife, and rights.

By contrast, in Greece, the apple was defined as an enviable and desirable trophy. It was a glittering golden object inscribed by Ares, the god of war, "To the fairest." The legendary apple of discord was instrumental in the proliferation of strife, which led to the Trojan War, the inspiration of the great Homeric epics, and of a great number of competitive athletic and political activities but also tragedies. It metaphorically characterized the ubiquitous competitive Greek pattern of pursuing power, women, adventure, political and athletic trophies and paying the consequences, domestic conflicts and never-ending political strife.

Inversely in both submissive cultures, Mexico and the Orient, existence was perceived as painful and to be endured; man was threatened with pain from birth and was doomed to pain after life, conceived as reincarnation, as potentially painful rebirths. Hence, man did not strive for immortality; on the contrary, he sought enlightenment to achieve Nirvana, death as freedom from pain.

In Mexico, humans were systematically captured and offered as live sacrifice to the bloodthirsty, unforgiving gods to avert the total and definitive destruction of the universe. Man's beating heart was wrenched from his chest like an apple plucked from a tree and placed on Chacmool's open palm on top of the pyramids. Mexican poetry defined man as "an ephemeral flower, here today and gone tomorrow." The Mexican mortal had little control over his world or personal life unless he could trap his fellow man before he was entrapped. Predictably, in their role reversal, entire civilizations perished through intense mutual warfare.

In the Orient, the third noble truth of Buddhism suggested that man should exercise total control over his cravings in order to protect himself from pain and to attain enlightenment. Self-containment made the apple so forbidden that it was transformed into the sacred cow. The social correlate of the sacredness of the cow was total self-restraint, acceptance of the status quo. In India, this mentality led to the creation and perpetuation of the social inequities of the caste system. The absence of social strife deprived the society of social evolution, but it fostered the evolution of the psychic space and the victory of mind over body.

Each of the four cultures succinctly presented above has generated through the dynamics of self-fulfilling prophecy its own total cultural environment with psychological and sociological implications. All citizens of each system are immersed in its moral imperatives as absolute, unquestioned truths.

The mural features side by side the formal and natural science graphic portrayal of the four cultures in two modes: (a) The sine curves contrast the process as function of time while (b) the power field contrasts the four cultures at any one time. The formal theoretical interpretation of cultural, religious, political, and psychological paradigms addresses the fact that we have all existed in a world of uninterpreted metaphors, a world of popularly endorsed cultural standards.

The formal scientific breakthrough allows us now to have a conceptual language that can let us explore our moral choices scientifically so that we can assume personal responsibility in our ways of managing power, not dominated by our sacrosanct traditions and value systems, but pursuing deliberately the innate relational principles.

CHAPTER FOUR: THE INTEGRATIVE POTENTIAL OF THE CONFLICT RESOLUTION PROCESS AS THE ATOMISTIC UNIT OF BEHAVIOR

A. Abstract

B. Introduction: The Phenomenological Fragmentation vs. The Reductionist Reintegration of The Social Science Continuum.

Phenomenology versus Formal Reductionism as the Epistemology of the Unconscious

C. Method: The Epistemology of The Conflict Resolution Process as The Atomistic Unit of Behavior

D. Findings: The Six Comparative Tables Attest to the Advantages of Reductionism

E. Discussion: The Moral Significance of a Science Based Unconscious Process

This is an article composed in 1990, introducing the formal theoretical conceptual position as the integrative paradigm reconciling the disciplines of psychology into the Moral Science. It is dated in terms of addressing the DSM4 version of diagnostic categories and seeking to find parallels in the formal analysis profile analysis of diagnoses. But this article is valuable as reviewing each of the disciplines as fragmented knowledge and introducing a unifying conceptual entity in the social sciences.

Abstract

Objective: The lack of a clear conceptual-methodological language in psychology has led to the absence of a central unifying paradigm and the fragmentation of the field into a number of empirically established specialty domains. This study introduces Formal Theory's redefined unconscious as a methodologically clear, conceptual construction identified as a unit periodic phenomenon: the Conflict Resolution Process.

The study focuses on the integrative function of the process as the atomistic unit of the disciplines of psychology: Epistemology, Diagnosis/Nosology, Assessment, Morality, Therapy and Education.

Method: The Creative Process as a Conflict Resolution Phenomenon is introduced as a predictable, qualifiable, quantifiable, graphically portrayable moral order upgrading entity, the atomistic unit of the social sciences. This reductionist unit of behavior is contrasted with the equivalent phenomenological constructs of six disciplines of psychology: The Psychoanalytic Unconscious, DSM 5 Diagnostic Categories, Psycho-assessment's testing, Religions' Moral Paradigms, Psychotherapeutic Treatment Modalities, Education's traditional Literacy.

Findings: The format of the six comparative tables helps to identify the parallels between the phenomenological and the formally redefined concepts and the ensuing advantages of the formal conceptualization: The Conflict Resolution Process integrates information in each discipline of psychology and also leads to the disciplines' integration into a rigorous scientific continuum, the Science of Conflict Resolution or the Moral Science.

Conclusion: This study shows that the Creative Process is a scientific Conflict Resolution Phenomenon establishing continuity to the disciplines of psychology, transforming psychology into a cohesive rigorous field. The scientific moral paradigm represents the common denominator of a new epistemology, a personality and psychopathology dynamic taxonomy, a psychoeducational diagnostic and therapeutic testing battery, a science-based morality as a comprehensive psychotherapeutic and psycho-educational program.

Introduction

'Conflict Analysis, The Formal Theory of Behavior' identifies the creative process, the plot of stories as a scientific conflict resolving phenomenon, where conflict resolution is synonymous to moral order, as the object for the study of behavior. Formal Theory's thesis that the unconscious is a scientific conflict resolving homeostatic mechanism, the atomistic unit of the social sciences, is founded on the formal and energetic analysis of the creative process. The introduction of the unconscious as a scientific conflict resolving mechanism allows understanding motivation as the need to transform psychic tension to moral order, moral growth, negative entropy, attitude change, leading to a person's social adjustment.

The unconscious is viewed as a mechanism that automatically resolves conflict as unpleasant energy by transforming psychic tension, to the pleasure of sociological adjustment. Energy is transformed following the laws of the Simple Harmonic Motion along a six-part psychodynamic sequence. Resolutions vary following three attitude-modifying formal operations identified in Felix Klein's formula of equilibrial principles. Accordingly, resolutions lead to four alternative relational modalities, identified as wellness diagnoses.

Thus, the unconscious is examined as the integrative natural science moral paradigm reconciling the separate disciplines of psychology and their subdivisions into the cohesive and integrative natural Science of Conflict Resolution, the Moral Science. This concept revamps psychology by integrating the separate social science disciplines into a single cohesive science.

The study reviews each one of eight disciplines introducing conceptual cohesiveness. It reconciles the disciplines introducing the process as the unconscious, qualified as in the diagnostic alternatives, as measurable with an assessment instrument, and as modifiable with proper interventions guiding to wellness.
The first section introduces the unconscious as a scientific phenomenon consisting of six-role state sequences resolving conflicts abiding by two scientific phenomena: The SHMs as energetic transformation and with the equilibrial principles restoring balance in the trays of a scale. It contrasts the formal unconscious with the psychoanalytically defined unconscious.

The second section is about the new diagnostic categories, four syndromal relational modalities as wellness diagnoses and contrasts them to the DSM 4 illness diagnoses.
The third section is about the Conflict Analysis Battery, a self-assessment that measures the relational modalities and their syndromal unfolding and contrasts the battery with current atheoretical assessments.
The fourth section is about the use of the assessment as a psychoeducational concise program of emotional education deliverable as a workbook and online shown to be therapeutically effective contrasted to CBT.
The fifth chapter is about religions as of psychological origination integrated as partial and complementary discoveries into the Moral Science. We present Moral Monopoly, an educational card game, based on the analysis of cultural stories, religions, evolving as discoveries of the relational modalities and integrated as a continuum improving the family institution completed by the Moral Science.

The sixth section is about emotional and moral literacy revamping education to deliver the integration of knowledge, self-knowledge and clarity of moral values.

Section one on the unit process, epistemology and method: The Phenomenological Fragmentation vs. The Scientific Integration of The Social Science Continuum

Since the time of Aristotle, the quest for an integrative paradigm has preoccupied philosophers and theoreticians of behavior. According to Millon to qualify for this task, paradigms must organize information at four levels: the epistemological, the psychodiagnostic, the psychoassessment, and the psychotherapeutic, accordingly:

"Integrative therapy is considered as a logical derivative of a mature clinical science that must (1) embody conceptual theories from which propositional deductions may be derived. (2) Lead to the construction of a coherent taxonomy for the subject domain (here personality disorders), (3) Possess a variety of empirically oriented instruments that can identify and quantify taxonomic constructs and (4) Produce change-oriented intervention techniques consonant with both given theory and the integrative root metaphor of the personality itself." [1]

Formal Theory introduces the Conflict Resolution Process, a process integrating conceptually the disciplines of Behavior into a cohesive science. [2] This paradigm presents the unconscious as a periodic phenomenon organizing emotions as energies, as mental associations into conflict resolution energy transformation units. It is the Aristotelian Dramatic Process rediscovered, qualified, quantified as applicable to all samples of creativity.

The Formal Paradigm accounts for Millan's four prerequisites for a sound theory of behavior: 1) it addresses the conceptual issues with the rigorous epistemology of an operationally redefined unit unconscious phenomenon, 2) The conflict resolution process constitutes a set of relational modalities unfolding as syndromes as wellness diagnoses, accounting for both wellness and illness, 3) The process has a distinct qualifiable and quantifiable structure that may be rediscovered by a psycho-assessment battery and finally 4) The conflict resolution process is a moral paradigm and the principles of conflict resolution coincide with moral values. Religions have evolved as alternative ways of resolving conflicts. Hence conflict resolution is the common denominator of the social sciences.

The formal paradigm is a holistic unit. Unlike Millon's evolutionist phenomenological paradigm, the Conflict Resolution Process is an abstract formal and natural science entity; accordingly, the ensuing taxonomy of personality syndromes, as alternative type of resolutions, the psycho-assessment, as a psychotherapeutic instrument and intervention techniques conceptualized along a rigorous that is as a scientific language.
"Integration insists on the primacy of an overarching gestalt that gives coherence, provides an interactive framework and creates an organic order among otherwise discreet units or elements. It is eclectic of course, but more. It is a synthesized and substantive system whose distinctive meaning derives from the old chestnut: The whole is greater than the sum of its parts." [3]

In this study the Conflict Resolution Process is introduced as the universal paradigm, as the common denominator of all the disciplines thus integrating them into one cohesive field. As a formal and a natural science entity this paradigm not only integrates the disciplines of psychology, it also bridges the social sciences with the rigorous sciences. Thus, this unit transforms behavior into the cohesive field of a single measurable and predictable overarching conceptual entity. Furthermore, since the formal paradigm has been validated experimentally,[4,5,6] the Formal Theory represents the breakthrough of achieving the scientific conceptualization of psychology. The clinical sciences therefore can enjoy the scientific clarity of the rigorous sciences and mental events may be seen to abide by the rules that govern all nature.

Kurt Lewin stated: "There is nothing so practical as a good theory. Theory when properly fashioned, ultimately provides more simplicity and clarity than unintegrated and scattered information. Unrelated knowledge and techniques, especially those based on surface similarities, are a sign of a primitive science." [7] The Formal Theory goes beyond primitive science, and beyond providing just a heuristic metaphor. The Conflict Resolution Process is a periodic phenomenon that abides by the laws of the logic of relations, the laws of mathematical groups, and finally the laws of the Simple Harmonic Motion. [8] It thus targets nothing less than delivering the ultimate deductive theory of behavior ready for extensive practical applications and for further duplication of its findings. The Formal Theory is reductionism at its best.

Behavioral scientists frown upon reductionism considering it as synonymous to oversimplification. Yet it is only the clarity and abstractness of scientific concepts that can allow both deductive insights and then simultaneously the needed integration of the disciplines of psychology. While reductionist language has been frowned upon, the concept 'science' has been used loosely in psychological literature. Experimental methodology and quantification in the behavioral field have been identified with science. We must distinguish formal reductionism as conceptual purity and as the minimum of assumptions, from correct experimental methodology referring to the validation of hypotheses on narrow conceptual theses. Even correctly administered and monitored experimental work does not amount to "pure science".

Formal reductionism introduces science as the valid concepts of a rigorous epistemology as opposed to the invalid-impure concepts of the prevailing epistemology of phenomenology.

Phenomenology has been the prevailing epistemology of psychology. Phenomenology unlike formal reductionism uses descriptive categories, surface criteria, shallow concrete constructs and multiple contradictory assumptions for the formulation of order in its fields of inquiry. For instance, phenomenology espouses the medical model and invalidates the psychodynamic or reductionistic perspective of knowledge. Proponents of the medical model summarily dismiss dynamic psychological postulations as too speculative.

The phenomenological method is the scientific basis of the current psycho-diagnostic categories, DSM IV. [9] Accordingly, diagnostic categories consist of clearly observable symptom clusters rather than any underlying psychodynamic correlations of interrelated abstract variables.

Phenomenology is also the methodology of the discipline of psycho-assessment. Psychological tests have always relied on purely empirical distinctions. Clinical psycho-assessment instruments, both inventories and projective techniques, lead to atheoretical tabulations of statistically significant clusters and distinctions of unrelated trait groupings and symptoms.

Phenomenology has also dominated the field of morality. Indeed, our religions are based on diverse axiomatically or dogmatically postulated definitions of moral order.

Phenomenology is the epistemological basis of the discipline of psychotherapy. Therapies are geared to the treatment of mental illness as symptoms of medical disorders and as singular behavior problems. Verbal psychotherapies and pharmacotherapies are the well-established treatments of choice. The trend is to abandon psychodynamic therapeutic models favoring standardized versions of manual driven psychotherapies. [10]

Phenomenology is the epistemological basis of education. Phenomenology arbitrarily fragments knowledge into the sciences on the one side and the humanities on the other. Indeed, literacy is defined as the technological knowledge of writing, reading and computation, and by definition it excludes its pertinence to self-knowledge and moral values as pertaining to controversial information beyond the educational mission. Yet because of its phenomenological foundation, traditional literacy distances itself from psychological and religious moral paradigms and is personally and morally irrelevant, providing concrete unintegrated information alienating the student from wisdom.

No wonder the phenomenologically conceptualized disciplines of psychology: epistemology, psychodiagnosis, psycho-assessment, morality, psychotherapy, and psycho-education amount to an unsolvable puzzle consisting of ill defined, loosely connected aspects of a poorly understood continuum. These disciplines have been established empirically and differentiated by extensive scholarships, which have alienated the experts from each other reinforcing the fragmentation of the underlying continuity. The phenomenological conceptualization of the field of Behavior has fragmented the social sciences into a number of separate operational territories unrelated to each other, hence the non-cohesive, non-meaningful, not orderly and non-predictable universe of Behavior. This bleak phenomenological landscape must be kept in mind to appreciate the contribution of Formal Theory's integrative reductionist epistemology.

The Formal Theory introduces a unit process, which abides by the laws of the rigorous disciplines. It utilizes a minimum of assumptions necessitating a minimum of variables, which revert to the pure constructs from the realms of logic, mathematics and physics. This conceptualization broadens insights in each one of the disciplines and simultaneously integrates them into one universal conceptual continuum, which is compatible with that of the rigorous sciences. This abstract rigorous conceptualization eliminates the subjectivity and divisiveness incurred by the phenomenological perspective and leads to bridging the gap between the humanities and the rigorous sciences. Behavior then becomes the continuum of the interrelated aspects of a periodic, predictable, graphically portrayable, measurable, universal, science-based unit entity, the conflict resolving process as the unconscious.

Method: The Epistemology of The Conflict Resolution Process as The Atomistic Unit of Behavior.
The Conflict Resolution Process is a 6-role state sequence of formal and energetic transformations contained in the structure of any story as a circumscribed sample of creativity. This process was originally identified in

the Greek Cosmogony stories as a reoccurring cross-generational pattern consisting of six episodes. The Greek gods' lifetime sequence was observed to be interlocked with the end three role states of the preceding and with the initial three role states of the following generations. The roles were identified as Role Oppression (RO), Role Assumption (RA), Anticipation of Role Reversal (ARR), Counterphobic Role Assumption (CPRA), Role Reversal (RR) and Compromise Role Assumption (CRA). The labels were simplified as: Stress, Response, Anxiety, Defense, Reversal and Compromise. Each role state was observed to be in a formal relationship to the others within the unit totality. The Formal Analysis of the process clarified that resolution is accomplished automatically by the "unconscious" redefined operationally as a series of three formal equilibrial transformations identified in the Kleinian formula describing the responses to an equilibrial disturbance of a scale, seeking to restore its balance: Identity is equal to the product of Reciprocity, Opposition or Negation and Correlation. I=R.N.C, accordingly, conflict resolution is defined as the unconscious transformation of a role state of passivity to its reciprocal one of activity, of a role state of antagonism to its opposite, a state of cooperation and finally, of a role state of alienation to its correlative one of affiliation or mutual respect.

This six-role states syndromal sequence of formal transformations became the unit entity of the unconscious and was observed to manifest spontaneously as a sequence of associations in samples of creativity as completed stories. This phenomenon was described by Aristotle in the Poetics as the dramatic process uniting the acts of Greek tragedies. The observation of this predictable periodic phenomenon led me to formulate the hypothesis of the unit conflict resolution process as a six-role-state entity coinciding with periodic phenomena from the realms of logic and physics. I hypothesized that the unit could be conceptualized in logical terms as an equilibrial totality of formal transformations and in physics terms as a conserved energetic quantity of oscillating intertransformable energetic modalities completed by the upgrading of order, the creation of negative entropy.

The process then was conceived of as both formally related states and of energy, transformed from psychic or emotions to social energy or actions and biological chemical energy as thoughts and impulses leading to Conflict Resolution as the moral or normative end. The teleological or moral directedness coinciding with normative conciliation, the reduction of chaos, and increase order entailed directionality to the reversible process. This irreversibility in the realm of the mental operations is the key to the pursuit of moral order characteristic of the human unconscious. This hypothesis has been validated as reported elsewhere examining samples of creativity.

This structure of associations was identified using the metaphor testing of the Conflict Analysis Battery, the formal theoretical self-assessment[17]. Thus, research on the formal unit has validated the formal hypothesis and confirmed that the unconscious Conflict Resolution Process is an order-upgrading unit consisting of formal and energetic transformations. The unit order was observed to abide by the natural science laws: the equilibrial trays of a scale, obeying the laws of logic, and obeying the law of conservation of energy as manifested in the pendulum's oscillation, the Simple Harmonic Motion.

The deterministic moral result of the formal process may be explained adequately in physics terms as a state of increased internal order or heightened negative entropy. Aristotle's entelechy is the end state of dramatic plays entailing conflict resolution as normative compliance, reinforcing the prevailing established moral order. Therefore, Formal Theory's basic assumption suggests that the unconscious is a natural science equilibrial phenomenon, the unit of the social sciences, both a scientific formal energetic entity and a moral process. The assumption identifies a deterministic outcome built into the unit order's formal and energetic fabric since the process shifts transactions predictably in the direction of converting chaos or conflict to order, moral consensus that is resolutions.

Thus, Formal Theory's basic assumption is equating the unconscious Conflict Resolution Process with both a system of three formal and six energetic transformations; this equation confers to a moral social science phenomenon the constructs and formulas of the equilibrial scale, Kleinian set theory, as the formal and of the pendulum's oscillations as an energetic phenomenon. The validation of this hypothesis has allowed the introduction of the set of constructs and formulas from the disciplines of relational logic and of physics Simple Harmonic Motion into the realm of mental associations. It has been possible to introduce the conceptual clarity of the two rigorous phenomena into behavior as psychology's very own scientific language. We have shown elsewhere the correspondence of ten levels of formal analysis to the social science phenomenon. We show how behavior appropriates the rigorous constructs and the formulas of the pure sciences as equivalent to the social science variables and laws.

Volumes of art exhibits and case studies, volumes 4, 5, and 6 of Normative Publications, validate this key assumption of the Formal Theory demonstrating the presence of formal order in all samples of creativity examined. The current study departs from the premise that the six-role process is a unit entity, which we like to introduce as the integrative paradigm of the social sciences. Studying six domains of social science phenomena we explore the unit's application as the universal conceptual paradigm. The implication is that the disciplines of psychology may be integrated into a new domain unifying psychology with morality based on the scientific analysis of the creative process. We identify this new realm as the Moral Science.

To accomplish this integrationist task six tables, contrast current phenomenological with formal reductionist conceptualizations. The reductionist conceptualization of the unit is sequentially contrasted to the prevailing equivalent constructs of each one of the 6 disciplines of psychology. In this study it is suggested that the unit of the Conflict Resolution Process upgrades order in each discipline and unifies them into the single domain of the Moral Science. The six tables attest to the advantages of the formal conceptualization yielding insights and cohesion in each discipline and integrating them all into a unified science.

Findings

This study implementing the application of the Conflict Resolution Process unit in several disciplines seeks to show the possibility of the integration of these disciplines into the Moral Science, the Science of Conflict Resolution. The fragmented knowledge of the above six disciplines of psychology is integrated by using the Conflict Resolution Process as the atomistic unit of all of them yet manifesting itself under a different name in each discipline.

Table #1, the unconscious

In the field of Epistemology, the unit process is contrasted with the psychoanalytic, psychodynamic unconscious. The unconscious is redefined as a purely formal and quantifiable predictable dynamic unit entity. The unit of the conflict resolution process integrates psychic, social and moral events with the rigorous sciences using reductionist constructs. Because Conflict Resolution is conceived of with formal and natural science energetic constructs, science recognizes conflict resolutions as the upgrading of order, the increase of negative entropy. Morality and Teleology or Determinism then are redefined with natural science concepts.

The recognition of this unit and its order enhancing quality was described by Aristotle as the "perfect totality" "the Teleion Holon" of the structure of dramatic plays. Aristotle described drama as "the perfect universe or totality" as a role system with a beginning, a middle and an end, with a proper internal balance, which provides the continuity of action across the dramatic totality. The dramatic role system leads to catharsis that is, the upgrading of inner order, inner meaning or Endelechy[12]. The Formal Theory expands this Aristotelian entity, first, by considering it as the universal atomistic unit of mental phenomena not merely present in dramatic plays alone and second, the Formal Theory redefines the Aristotelian unit as a formal periodic phenomenon, consisting of a sequence of formal transformations abiding by the laws of logic and as a conserved natural science energetic phenomenon abiding by the laws of physics. Thus, the Formal Theory describes behaviors, social deviations and emotions in terms of interrelated and graphically portrayable constructs from logic, mathematics and physics [13].

Rethinking the Epistemology of the Unconscious

The first table contrasts the psychoanalytic "unconscious", with Formal Theory's unconscious as a periodic unit phenomenon. Psychoanalysis centered its theoretical position on a vague amoral and genetically determined unconscious with several dynamic references, the topographic model, the structural model, the energetic model and the transference relational system. By contrast the formal unconscious is a scientifically conceptualized relational and energetic, periodic, predictable and quantifiable entity with precise clinical, developmental, psychometric and moral values parameters. It is a physiological, homeostatic phenomenon.

The Formal Theory is refining and completing the task of psychodynamic analysis of the unconscious by defining the unconscious as a perfect process with a beginning, a middle and a moral end, as a periodic unit phenomenon and hence studied, analyzed and recognized as abiding by the rigorous scientific principles. The unit may be observed, captured, categorized and facilitated in its evolution.

Psychoanalysis attributed the source of behavior and emotions to unconscious motivation. Freud ("The Id & The Ego...") offered the structural model of the psyche to describe its three components as the id, ego and superego. He used the flow of free associations as the methodological tool to access the unconscious and to grasp its content as the means to healing. Psychoanalysis did not evolve clear scientific methodological insights into the orderly nature of the unconscious (Dennett, 1991, Consciousness Explained)). It did not lead to the development of a comprehensive nosology. It failed in the development of standardized assessment tests to measure the unconscious. It failed in integrating religion, morality and spirituality into a continuous body of knowledge (Psychotherapy integration). It failed to evolve effective procedures to treat illnesses and psychopathology, psychotherapy, morality and psychoeducation.

TABLE #1: RETHINKING THE UNCONSCIOUS

A. Epistemological Issues:	Unconscious--Psychoanalysis Basic Assumption	The Unconscious as the Formal Theory's Unit Process
a) The epistemological definitions of the unconscious as psychology's essential phenomenon: a vague psychoanalytic construct vs. Formal Theory's unit Conflict Resolution Process, a scientific moral order phenomenon.	Psychoanalysis defines the unconscious as a hybrid domain of dynamic, biological, psychosocial, intrapsychic unpredictable forces, which determine a person's conflict arousing emotions and actions.	The Formal Theory defines the unconscious as the atomistic unit of behavior, a perfect totality of formal transformations and a predictable and quantifiable natural science entity whose function is homeostatic that is reducing psychic tension by resolving conflicts, upgrading order, reconciling the individual with his/her environment, transforming normative deviation to normative conciliation in six steps: stress, response, anxiety, defense, reversal and compromise guided spontaneously by three attitude modifying formal operations resolving conflicts along four alternative relational modalities.
b) The paradigms, two Greek myths the story of Oedipus vs. the Greek Cosmogony represent two methodologically different definitions of the unconscious.	The Oedipus Story as a metaphor was interpreted by Freud as a concrete universal paradigm of a biologically determined set of emotions and behaviors affecting a young child's relationship to his parents. Accordingly, the six-year-old child innately wishes to kill the same sex parent and to possess the opposite sex parent. Methodologically, epistemologically, Freud's interpretation abides by the phenomenological method; it is an arbitrary axiomatic determination.	The Formal Theory uses the Greek creation story as a paradigm of formal analysis. It is viewed as a pattern transmitted across the five Cosmogony generations abstracted into a formal, periodic, six-role-state sequence with the inherent function to resolve conflicts. This unit pattern is a Conflict Resolution Process. It is reduced to a natural science periodic phenomenon abiding by the laws of relational logic, of mathematics' group of transformations and by the laws of the physics of the Simple Harmonic Motion. Thus, the Greek Cosmogony is a comprehensive and abstract paradigm of the manifestation of the unconscious as a dialectic unit process. It is used to interrelate associations as well as developmental experiences as the six- role states of a holistic entity of formal transformations. The Oedipal drama corroborates the formal analytic principles resolving conflicts along the Greek culture's dominant and antagonistic version of resolving conflicts.

c) The structure and the function of the unconscious: instincts, reality and inhibitions vs. an ongoing equilibrial tension reducing process.	The Freudian unconscious is thought of as a psychodynamic process, yet the multiple assumptions are concrete, or phenomenological. The structural model describes the unconscious as consisting of three entities and functions. These three components are: (a) the id, one's biological drives: the libido and thanatos, sex and death; (b) the ego which conveys one's inner representations of reality determining one's choice of defense mechanisms, and (c) the superego, which contributes one's moral injunctions stemming from the acculturation of the individual.	The process is a dialectic of interrelated parts and the Freudian structural model may be integrated into the three cycles of the unit six role formal process as a syndrome of formally interrelated emotions. The Conflict Resolution Process is an oscillation of an energetic quantity transformed from emotions to actions, and biological states. It is driven by an innate need to preserve a state of well-being identified with low psychic tension, coinciding with normative compliance. Resolution coincides with a higher order or negative entropy mental state coinciding with the necessary moral outcome as an attitude change.
d) Two conceptualizations of the unconscious: a hybrid entity vs. a pure formal and energetic unit process.	Psychoanalysis' structural model the id, ego, and superego system is methodologically an assumption. The three dynamically interrelated components are contaminated by three unrelated systemic references. The id reflects biological referents; the ego, sociological ones and the superego, developmental experiences and moral injunctions. Similarly, Freud's two types of process thinking primary vs. secondary methodologically follow two types of logical reasoning. Thus, the psychoanalytic unconscious is an ill-defined dynamic, scientifically impure, unpredictable, and non-quantifiable, not measurable entity.	Formal Theory's unit conceptually is a pure formal relational and a natural science energetic entity. The Conflict Resolution Process constitutes a perfect symbolic or ideational totality, a unit entity, manifesting itself at all levels of reference. By definition the formal equilibrial process transforms conflict to resolution along a predictable formal sequence. Passivity is transformed to its reciprocal: activity; antagonism to its opposite: cooperation, and alienation to its correlative: mutual respect. Also, by definition the process is a natural science oscillation, an intertransformation of energies evolving from labile energies to stable ones. As such the unit unconscious process abides by the laws of logic (paradigm: scale) and by the laws of physics' energetic conservation (paradigm: the pendulum oscillation). Accordingly, it may be quantified and graphically portrayed. Thus, the unconscious process is both a pure formal and a natural science phenomenon.
e) Implications of the paradigms in defining order in the realm of behavioral phenomena: relational defense mechanisms are integrated into the six role syndromal sequence.	The Oedipal paradigm attempts to account for order in several fields of behavior without introducing scientific constructs and correlations: The structural model attempts to integrate the biological aspects of behavior with the psychological and sociological aspects into a continuous field of knowledge. •The economic model attempts to connect ideas with an energetic substance. Cathexes have biological origin and ideational and behavioral manifestations. •The topographic model recognizes boundaries between the unconscious and the conscious realms and addresses the primary and the secondary processes as following different logical rules. •The dynamic model addresses the paradigm's clinical manifestations as relational a number of defense mechanisms observed in the analysis of transference and ego development.	The Conflict Resolution Process accounts for order across all fields as a unit abiding by rigorous constructs and formulas. The rigorous unit is present in all samples of creativity: myths, art, religions, psychopathology, civilizations and law. The universality of the oscillatory process across all the fields of the humanities, and the sciences integrates the social science disciplines with the pure sciences into a universal orderly domain. The formal paradigm interfaces the humanities and the sciences along the ten-levels of the Formal Analysis Profile defining respectively constructs and covariations: Level 1: formal, symbolic correlations; Levels 2, 3 and 4: energetic; Levels 5 and 6: clinical syndromal; Level 7: graphic; Level 8: relational modalities Levels 9: quantitative, and Level 10: qualitative or effectiveness variations of the personal Conflict Resolution unit. (FAP Reference). The six role process is a relational continuum unifying the defense mechanisms as formal operations. I.e.: Denial and repression correspond to Role Oppression and Role Assumption, projection corresponds to Anticipation of Role Reversal, reaction formation corresponds to Counterphobic Role Assumption, role reversal is a role state in the sequence of the six roles. Sublimation is equated to Compromise Role Assumption. Defense mechanisms are bound as the six-role process.

f) Implications of the paradigms for the definition of human nature: homo sapiens as a destroyer vs. as a creator.	Analysis defines humans as dangerous, amoral, impulse ridden biological time bombs. Predictably they are driven to sexuality and violence by unconscious forces: Oppression, Hostility, Aggression, barely restrained by the repressive forces of their moral injunctions.	The Formal Theory defines humans as homeostatically monitored biological entities creating moral order. Morality is a dialectically compounded order guaranteed by an unconscious need for stability of the individual in the social system's normative boundaries. Conflict resolutions are both internalized and societally reinforced compromises such as religions and political constitutions.
B. Psycho-assessment for the quantification of the unconscious. Psychoanalysis' failure in evolving measurement of its constructs vs. Formal Theory's success in assessing the syndrome and the modalities as the unit and in validating the theoretical premises.	Psychoanalysis provides no experimental measurement of the unconscious or its components. No psychological tests have been devised for the quantitative determination of the psychoanalytic unconscious. According to Eysenck (1959), * projective tests: HTP, Rorschach and TAT, and object relations tests utilizing psychodynamic assumptions are highly unreliable and show little evidence of validity. *Eysenck, H.J., 1959. "The Rorschach Test." In O.K. Buros, ed., Mental Measurements Yearbook, Vol. 5, Gryphon, New York.	Formal Theory's Conflict Analysis Battery qualitative of tests compliment and cross validate each other by identifying the relational modality and its unfolding. The test-derived information validates the assumptions of the Formal Theory, the theory's constructs and their formal interrelatedness. The insights are of educational and of clinical relevance. The testing leads to identify the process at the level of the unit metaphor and at the level of the integration of metaphors. The interpretation of the tests is organized along the ten levels of the Formal Analysis Profile.
C. Psychodiagnostic Issues a) Personality categories: Relevance of the paradigm of the unconscious for the conceptualization of wellness and illness, normalcy and psychopathology.	Psychoanalysis is the psychology of drives which, when interfered with, lead to symptoms. It regards normal psychological development as proceeding along maturational age-related objectives (Erikson). Preoccupations evolve progressively toward moral growth. Personality categories are identified as phases along the genetic model's developmental progression as oral, anal and phallic. Neuroses pertain to fixations along the developmental sequence. Ego psychology has shifted focus to the interpersonal realm, yet focus is on transference rather than on innate relational modalities.	Formal Theory is the psychology of Power Management. The Conflict Resolution Process underlies the syndromal nature of behavior as a sequence of formally interrelated reactions: Stress elicits responses, and these evoke related anxiety, as anticipations of role reversal, they evoke defenses, which precipitate reversals and finally lead to compromises. The formal variations determine personality types differing in terms of the degree of interpersonal effectiveness they entail. The process's formal variations determine the four principal relational modalities: Submissive, and Dominant Cooperative, Submissive and Dominant Antagonistic. The Process's quantitative variation of conflict determines one's psychic tension and related psychopathology.
b. Transference vs. four syndromal genetically and developmentally determined relational modalities	Transference refers to reenactment of developmental emotional-behavioral patterns. The dynamic model of illness defines neuroses like personality disorders, as related to developmental disturbances generated by impulse flow and related excessive repressive defense operations as categories of fixation or regression at the oral, anal and phallic phases.	Relational modalities are genetically determined and developmentally modified power making choices determining the syndromal nature of wellness and of psychopathology. Health entails the most effective way of resolving conflicts or managing power. To seek relief from conflicts, from adverse experiences and from psychopathology, one merely needs to monitor one's pattern of relating and manage one's power and attitude. The relational modalities influence the development of psychopathology and entail appropriate psychotherapeutic interventions. Civilizations and religions are also characterized by the same relational dynamics as individuals; they thrive on relational modalities and suffer of the related relational pathologies.

D. Psychotherapy Issues a) The paradigm's relevance for pathogenesis	Psychopathology is determined by developmental conflicts as fixation-regression to a biopsychosexual maturation phase: oral, anal and phallic, further maturational ego phases.	Syndromal relational modalities are genetically determined but their intensity is environmentally affected. There are four basic relational modalities: dominant vs. submissive, cooperative vs. antagonistic. They are affected by developmental experiences, which may evoke fixations and pathology.
b) Psychotherapy in both schools of thought starts by making the unconscious conscious. But whereas psychoanalysis promotes interpretations of transference, the formal model fosters identifying relational modalities and syndromes as diagnostic categories and pursuing power and attitude management.	1. The focus in psychoanalysis is on making a person conscious of one's unconscious by identifying one's transference. The patient therapist relationship is manipulated toward creating an interactional vacuum, which will elicit the manifestation of the patient's transference as anxieties and defenses revealing the person's underlying relational distortions. 2. Psychoanalysis, by the nature of its intensity, encourages the client to become highly dependent on the therapist's interpretations and judgments. 3. The analysant is expected to endorse the psychoanalytic interpretations	1. The focus in Conflict Analysis Training is on making the person aware of her unconscious by identifying one's relational modality and its syndromal unfolding. The cognitive study of the mental unit facilitates grasping one's pattern through the self-assessment. 2. Trainees pursue creativity for self-discovery In Conflict Analysis the client is active and pursues the identification of one's own relational modality as a syndrome. 3. The self-assessment is educational-cognitive, diagnostic and therapeutic. It also seeks spirituality as the ultimate morality. One seeks to identify one's power deviation and to consider its correction through effective power management. Thus, the client arrives at insights about patterns, personal deviations, learns how to optimize one's relating and find appreciation of sacrifices entailed in resolving conflicts.
E. Cost Effectiveness Issues: a) The paradigms' relevance for cost effectiveness of professional services.	Psychoanalysis is very costly. The therapeutic techniques require a long term and intense therapy program delivered only by skilled professionals.	Formal Theory programs are cost effective. The Training promotes knowledge, self-knowledge and moral values. The standardization of the program shifts the work to self-reliance and self-awareness. The therapist is a facilitator educator with special training. Skills include awareness of the constructs, and the use of techniques, personal analysis, and self-discipline to abide by the moral values of conflict resolution. The moral values promoted are intrinsic in the nature of the unit paradigm. They are the science-based principles of mastery, cooperation and mutual respect. The therapeutic model promotes creativity, good communications and responsibility.
b) The impact of the analysis on therapeutic modalities is proliferation vs. Formal Theory's integration of psychotherapies	Offshoots of classical psychoanalysis have evolved around several directions. Practitioners of analytic modalities apply their perspectives: i.e., In group therapies, psychodrama, group analysis and analytic psychotherapies, art therapy, play therapy, etc.	Conflict Analysis Training integrates a number of psychotherapeutic modalities and fosters universal conceptualization, professional development and therapy skills. The program is intrinsically cognitive and educational. It promotes creativity for self-discovery and insights. It fosters behavior modification and skills development. Finally, it encourages the acceptance of a set of science-based conflict resolving relational guidelines or values/insights, which foster behavior modification and skills development.

Table #2, Diagnosis

In the field of diagnosis, the unit becomes the syndromal personality type organization of associations, emotions and behaviors. We detect conflict resolution as the unit's six role process and also the range of formally interrelated manifestations of a personality typology. The formal psychodiagnosis studies the compliment of alternative ways of resolving conflict as a wellness personality typology. [14] The new way of conceptualizing diagnoses identifies wellness typology also accounting for particular pathologies.

Rethinking Psychodiagnosis

The second table compares the phenomenological method of DSM 4 to the purely psychodynamic formal syndromal diagnoses of a wellness personality typology. The psychic tension dimensions reflect the areas of pathology. The table contrasts the phenomenological diagnostic categories to the clinical manifestation of the unit as a syndromal entity with four formal variations, the relational modalities, wellness diagnoses, with quantitative variations referring to psychic conflict tension.

The unit yields a personality typology of four psychodynamic syndromes accounting for wellness and illness along the formal and quantitative variations. Unlike DSM 4 empirical cluster of symptoms categories, the formal distinctions identify four ways of resolving conflict as formally interrelated relational modalities. DSM is a nosology. Formal diagnoses are wellness categories. DSM diagnoses consist of phenomenological or descriptive symptom clusters correlating mental states to medical model dysfunctions and to biologically determined imbalances. Formal Theory's categories are wellness relational modalities differing with each other in the degree of effectiveness of attitudes in the completeness of conflict resolution. The formal categories are syndromal, predictable, quantifiable and graphically portrayable entities, which under stress may decompensate into predictable psychopathology and symptoms. These categories entail qualitative and quantitative formal measuring and corrective restructuring that restores wellness through the optimal management of power. The modalities are genetically determined but developmentally and culturally modified. The DSM diagnoses are symptom based, symbolic fixations.

TABLE #2: RETHINKING THE NATURE OF WELLNESS AND ILLNESS IN TERMS OF RELATIONAL MODALITIES AND SYNDROMAL CATEGORIES

	Medical Model's Phenomenological Method	Formal Theory's Reductionism
A. Epistemological Issues: a) The methodology of category formation	The DSM diagnostic categories are purely descriptive phenomenologically distinct entities identifying categories of illness; diagnostic categories are Identifying psychopathology; they are not Identifying wellness or normal personality variations. The diagnostic entities do not consider psychodynamic correlation of experiences, defenses and symptoms accounting for the phenomena observed; they constitute phenomenological descriptively identified symptom clusters. The individual conditions are further qualified along five axes of a biopsychosocial continuum. But again, Axis I-Psychic, and Axis II-Social, Axis-III-Biological Pathologies, Axis-IV Stress and Axis V-Global Functioning are factors dynamically unrelated to each other.	The formal relational and natural scientific method regards the personal Conflict Resolution Process as a syndromal sequence with qualitative symbolic, formal and quantitative energetic, measurable dimensions. Relational modalities are categories of wellness. Relational diagnoses accurately predict normal and disturbed behavior. The syndromal categories describe wellness and illness along a continuum of qualitative and quantitative distinctions. The syndromal entity is examined along Formal Analysis Profile's ten levels of formal correlations of variables: Level 8 of the Profile makes qualitative distinctions along four relational modality alternatives, which constitute the normal syndromal personality typology. Level 8 corresponds to Axis II personality category distinctions. Level 9 pertains to the quantitative distinctions, which may occur across all relational modalities, which is referred to as relational intensity and psychic tension. This variable indicates the intensity and type of socio-psychopathology and coincides with DSM's Axis I.

b) Pathogenesis: chemical vs. power imbalance or formal disturbance.	According to DSM 4, mental illness is determined by chemical-biological-neurological and genetic factors. Therefore, the person is not considered responsible for the mental condition and is not expected to control the process of wellness and illness. Biopsychosocial factors are independent of each other. Therapeutically the emphasis is on the cognitive and chemotherapeutic management of illnesses regarded as chemical imbalances. Cognitive behavioral and emotion-focused therapies address alternative aspects of the dynamic continuum but not as a syndromal totality.	The formal method explores wellness and illness as a continuum of relational syndromal power and attitude management alternatives. All wellness and many mental illnesses are viewed psychodynamically and accounted for by the simple power and attitude management process. The four formal alternative ways of resolving conflict differ in the degree of relational effectiveness. Proper power management improves one's state of wellness. Relational disturbances affect the body chemistry, a state that can be reversed utilizing medications.
c) Graphic presentation of diagnostic entities. Descriptive graphic representations of pathology vs. systemic abstract constructs and their graphic representation. Graphs clearly describe the relational syndromal entity.	Freud used a linear graphic representation separating the conscious from the unconscious. Analysis does not have a systemic or abstract conceptualization of the unconscious as a natural science phenomenon.	The unit process consists of two natural science phenomena that may be graphically presented as a trigonometric sine curve unfolding along a system of three revolutions, corresponding to the sequences of stress-response, anxiety-defense, and reversal-compromise. The cross section of this process graphically portrays the person's position within the power field at any given moment following the graphically indicated formal operations. Vectorial sets describe attitude, intensity, normative deviation, and intensity as deviations in the concentric circles.
B. Psychodiagnostic Issues:	DSM Phenomenology	Formal Reductionism
a) Biopsychosocial aspects of the illness continuum.	In its earlier version DSM 4 diagnoses were examined along five axes as a biopsychosocial continuum fragmented into independent and unrelated phenomenologies scored along the Five Axes.	The Formal Analysis Profile consists of 10-levels of distinctions pertaining to energetic and formal correlations affecting the individual's biopsychosocial functioning, along the continuum of relational or power choices.
Axis I. Psychopathology	Axis I. Pertains to Psychopathology as identified by symptom clusters unrelated to each other and unrelated to Axis II, personality disorders.	Level 9 corresponding to elevated Psychic and social tension. Pathology symptoms are secondary to relational Power Management deviations determined by one's relational modality.
Axis II. Sociopathology	Axis II. Pertains to concurring personality disorders which are unrelated to Axis I, the type of pathological experiences and symptomatology.	Level 8 relational modality diagnoses differs from Axis II, personality pathology categories of DSM. Relational diagnoses pertain to the social systemic power positioning along the range of four formally interrelated syndromal relational modalities. Social systemic deviations may decompensate but they do not lead to personality disorders diagnosed by DSM axis 2. They are based on relational modalities. Intensity of psychic tension leads to general psychopathology.
Axis III. Medical Pathology	Axis III, pertains to coinciding biological-medical disorders, which might be totally unrelated to the Axis I and II psychological sociological diagnoses.	DSM Axis III or Incidental Medical Pathology in the Formal Evaluation is not pertinent to syndromal power states except as a stressor. But we are interested in bodily functioning as symbolic somatized manifestation of psychic conflict.
Axis IV. Recent social Adjustment	Axis IV, pertains to external stressors affecting the individual. It does not consider self-induced stressors generated by the person's relational disposition.	Social adjustment is considered under levels levels 3-4-5 pertaining to the psychic tension as a conserved entity. The three correlations determine how the individual's emotional behavior is a quantity of energy affected by external and internal factors. It is comparable to Axis IV.

Axis V. Global Assessment	Axis V, The GAF, global adjustment describes the quality of one's adjustment as a percentage of the state of wellness of the individual.	Level 10 is comparable to Axis V. The normal person's effectiveness as adjustment and performance is considered in the context of one's relational choices, one's relational modality. Intense conflict leads to intense dysfunctional relating.
b) Evaluating the interpersonal system	DSM, Axes I-V diagnostic categories explore fragments but overlook the total picture. They examine the medical model checklist but overlook the inner bio-psychosocial interplay. The relational and quantitative power structure of the social initiative and personal psychological component is not considered in the diagnostic evaluation and the ensuing therapies.	The Formal Evaluation addresses the biopsychosocial-cultural relational continuum as a simple problem of engineering of power. Evaluating one's interplay in the social system is pertinent for diagnostic and therapeutic purposes. Included in the individual's evaluation are the key partners of the social system and the client's developmental cultural value system.
c) Evaluating the biopsychosocial continuum as factor covariation.	DSM IV's Five Axes phenomenology, fragments the continuum into the psychic, social, biological, sociological stress and social adaptation areas practically unrelated to each other and deprived of formal covariation. I.E. An anxiety disorder (Axis I) may be disabling but it does not entail that the condition is personally induced, i.e. through a person's transgressive relational tendencies (Axis II) generating stress. It does not entail that personal power management leads to conflict resolution (Axis II) and that this can diminish the anxiety (Axis I) thus instantly providing relief from the symptoms.	The Formal diagnosis addresses the correlation of the social-psychic biological developments as interrelated sequences of behaviors and emotions, e.g.: dominance disorders (Axis II) generate anxiety and paranoia symptoms (Axis I) leading to social defensiveness and a high incidence of panic disorders, and finally social withdrawal (Axis V). Submissive disorders (Axis II) lead to hostility and depressive symptomatology (Axis I). Submissive individuals handle stress well, are persistent, and function in supportive roles but predictably may rebel against the respected authorities (Axis V).
C. Psychotherapeutic Implications: a) Therapeutic effect of the diagnostic process. The medical model intake is about fact-finding vs. the formal intake constituting a relational self-assessment with cognitive and therapeutic implications.	DSM diagnoses identify symptoms and circumstances. The intake ignores the relational and interpersonal power disposition and misses the implications of the diagnosis for pathogenesis and for therapeutic choices. Chemotherapy is effective in dealing with symptoms. It fosters substance dependence rather than the development of self-sufficiency in developing insights and responsibility for proper power management and behavior modification. The DSM does not have diagnostic distinctions for the so called well public. The diagnostic categories represent stigmatization. DSM diagnostic labels entail the choice of the appropriate chemotherapeutic interventions, which are effective in alleviating symptoms. DSM diagnoses ignore the dynamic relation between one's choices of conduct and psychic and biological experiences as medical psychotherapies do not address relational issues. DSM diagnoses may alienate the person and reduce him/her to a passive role, to the primacy of his/her chemically determined illness.	The diagnostic process of the Conflict Analysis Battery standardized self-assessment evaluation represents an emotional growth experience proceeding from creativity to self-discovery and articulating one's wishes for changes toward more effective interpersonal relating. The introductory training educates the client along clear concepts, which are illustrated by one's personal symbolic language and the subsequent analyses of insights, cognitive reinforcement of insights and the urge to change. The program leads to knowledge and self-knowledge and to accepting responsibility for one's symptoms as consequences of one's way of relating. The values of conflict resolution are moderation, cooperation and mutual respect. They entail clear directives for attitude change and the pursuit of wellness. The Conflict Analysis Training represents a psychoeducation. This approach fosters exploration of creativity for self-discovery that is introspection and the development of insight and acceptance of responsibility in making changes identified by the person. Diagnostic categories are not stigmatizing, they pertain to the well person. Formal self-assessment and the subsequent psycho-educational training are relevant for the well and the ill person alike; the testing may be delivered and processed without professional help. It can be helpful in therapeutic work and can contribute dramatic and lasting results. For example, educators may deliver this training in the classroom. This training reinforces the relevance of science of interpersonal effectiveness as it enhances creativity and communications and the appreciation of moral, relational values. This psychoeducational program provides information, insights, values and life skills to the well and ill public alike. The outcome is lasting long-term power management leading to wellness.

b) Delivery of psychodiagnostic and psychotherapeutic services cost-effectively	Medical therapies require a physician/ nurse for medication management and a number of mental health counselors. Specialists: e.g., social workers, art therapists, vocational therapists, etc. frequently deliver special services unrelated to each other.	The Conflict Analysis Training is an assessment integrating many modalities of psychotherapy. These may be delivered as a complete training program without the high cost of multiple professional experts. It may be delivered cost-effectively by any professional appropriately trained therapist or educator.

Table #3, Psycho-assessment

The unit of the creative process becomes the stream of associations manifested in the natural development of a story. Thus, the unit is identified by examining the formal structure of associations in samples of personal creativity. The sample creativity is formally analyzed that is qualified, it is examined for its energetic intensity, that is quantified, and it is graphically portrayed as the sine wave of the personal way of resolving conflict. The experimental measurement of the unit leads to the validation of the theory's assumptions. [15]

Rethinking Psycho-assessment

The third table contrasts the Conflict Resolution Process, as the unit syndromal and relational structuring of associations, with the statistical trait analysis of current psycho-assessment instruments. The Conflict Analysis Battery combines an inventory with a set of projective tests. The findings of the projective techniques, the metaphor construction exercises, confirm the inventory test findings about the personal way of resolving conflict. Another unique feature of the formal testing is the fact that the Battery identifies categories of wellness but also of psychopathology.

The Conflict Analysis Battery is the Formal Theory based psycho-assessment instrument. This battery identifies the personal pattern utilizing the systematic analysis of samples of creativity. The metaphor tests of the Conflict Analysis Battery reconstruct the six-role process and determine the unit process as a syndromal entity. The RMES, the Relational Modality Evaluation Scale, the Formal relational inventory personality test, leads to identify the four relational modalities and the intensity of psychic tension as five scales. There is overlap of findings between the inventory diagnosis and that of the metaphor analysis. Formal testing evaluates the relational and psychodynamic way of resolving conflicts compared to the focus on unrelated traits of the empirical atheoretical phenomenological assessment technologies.

There is overlap between the modalities and the five-factor primary or independent variables as shown in the statistical analysis of traditional personality psychological testing. [19] There is also overlap of these categories with Timothy Leary's personality checklist [20]

The Formal Theory's Conflict Analysis Battery identifies types of formal transformations of the unit process along a taxonomy of behavior. It encompasses wellness and illness alike. The unconscious is the person's way of resolving conflict. One single personal metaphor and a sequence of juxtaposed metaphors reveal the unconscious process, its characteristics, its categorical attributes and its need for remediation, correction or adjustment.

TABLE #3: RETHINKING PERSONALITY ASSESSMENT

	Empirical Atheoretical Psycho-assessments	Formal Theory's Conflict Analysis Battery
Phenomenology is the philosophy of testing that leads to separate inventories and projectives versus reductionism, a theory-based integrated battery of psychometric procedures inventory and projectives.	Traditional testing is atheoretical. It is based on purely empirical standardized, statistically validated means of gathering and sorting information about several arbitrarily labeled personality variables considered as statistically significant trait clusters Psycho-assessment instruments are fragmented into unrelated projective testing: HTP, TAT, Rorschach, etc. and inventory tests e.g.: Five Factors, MMPI, CPI, DiSC, 16PF, etc. The individual personality is determined by traits reflected in scales and subscales in the inventory tests, and the prevalence of mental preoccupations in the projective techniques. Projective and inventory reports are not complimentary to each other; they do not address measuring a set of variables.	Conflict Analysis Battery, (CAB) the Formal Theory based testing measures the qualitative and quantitative parameters of the personal way of relating one's Conflict Resolution Process unit. The Battery integrates both a personality inventory, the Relational Modality Evaluation Scale (RMES), with a set of projective instruments, the metaphor construction techniques. Both the inventory and projective techniques contribute to the measurement of the syndromal mental unit, the Conflict Resolution Process. The inventory identifies one's social interpersonal relating, one's personality as one of four principal syndromal relational modalities reflected by four scales unlike (Axis II) personality disorders this inventory contributes information for normal personality types. Psychopathology is a question of degree of elevated intensity in the relational attributes revealing relational pathology. A fifth scale of the inventory identifies one's psychic tension independently of one's relational modality. It addresses quantitative issues in the area of symptomatic dysfunctional manifestations. This section of the inventory corresponds to Axis I psychopathology.
B. Scales as factors: psychology's five unrelated factors vs. formal battery's interrelated four interpersonal and one intrapsychic scale.	Statistical analysis of testing has empirically led to identifying five unrelated universal factors. These seem to describe unrelated types of behavior and emotions: (Costa-McReedy) Testing identifies psychopathology but does not identify wellness as relational categories. Neuroticism or negative emotionality Extraversion or positive emotionality Openness, imagination or intellect Conscientiousness or constraint Agreeableness Traditional testing does not provide continuity between states of normalcy and states of illness or pathology	Conflict Analysis Battery's five scales coincide with the five factors: but pertain to interrelated formal relational qualifications and the quantification of the unit process. Formal testing identifies clearly normal relational distinctions as well as pathology. -Neuroticism corresponds to the intrapsychic variable of Psychic Tension quantifying of the integration of the Conflict Resolution Process (Axis I). -Extraversion corresponds to Dominant Antagonistic syndromal relational tendencies -Openness corresponds to Dominant Cooperative syndromal relational tendencies -Conscientiousness corresponds to Submissive Antagonistic syndromal relational tendencies -Agreeableness corresponds to Submissive Cooperative syndromal relational tendencies. Formal testing correlates normalcy and psychopathology along a continuum of quantitative distinctions spanning all 5 scales.
C. Traditional testing identifying types of pathology vs. formal testing identifying types of wellness and relational psychopathology	Traditional testing does not provide continuity between states of normalcy and states of illness or pathology	Formal testing correlates normalcy and psychopathology along a continuum of quantitative distinctions spanning all 5 scales.
D. The role of the client: information is made available to the therapist versus the client and the therapist.	Testing findings are generated by a professional and communicated to professionals. They are not generated by the client; they are not available and are not meaningful to the client. Self-assessment tests are used in clinical medication monitoring programs and in psychoeducational settings.	The findings are available both to the client and to the therapist/evaluator. They are used extensively in the clinical and the educational setting and constitute an integral part of the Conflict Analysis Training a diagnostic, educational and therapeutic package of services. It also clarifies the syndromal manifestation of the relational modality.

Instruments	Traditional Porjective Testing: TAT, Rorschach, House-Tree-Person	Formal Theory Projective Testing- The Metaphor Tests reconstruct the syndromal six-role process confirming the relational modality.
The role of the professional: projective techniques, require a trained person vs.CAB not requiring a psychologist in the delivery and the interpretation of findings.	Except for the House-Tree-Person Test and the Bender Gestalt Test, the stimuli art is standardized images and does not reflect personal choices. TAT pictures and Rorschach ink blots provide a set of standardized images to evoke a pattern of personal distortions. The test responses can be interpreted only by well- trained professionals.	The findings are available both to the client and to the therapist/evaluator. They are used extensively in the clinical and the educational setting and constitute an integral part of the Conflict Analysis Training The assessment is delivered online without the need for professional services, yet it is effective along three functions: it is educational, diagnostic and therapeutic.
F. Cost effectiveness: the benefit generated to the client and the cost of professional services necessary to generate the report versus the CAB delivery benefit and cost of services.	The benefit to the patient is indirect as the information generated is communicated to the client's therapist and to pertinent authorities rather than to the client. Findings are usually accurate and reliable but limited in their relevance to the patient toward evolving insights, making changes and in monitoring progress. The generation of the report is time consuming and expensive. The work effort requires highly trained professionals. Hence while the personal benefit is low, the cost of the professional services is high, hence testing is cost ineffective.	The battery is a self-assessment. The benefit of the information is delivered directly to the client. The delivery process is diagnostic, educational and therapeutic. The testee creates the art, the commentary and the interpretations. Hence the insights are accurate, helpful meaningful and reliable. They reach both client and therapist. The production of the testing battery's metaphor profile increases self-esteem, deepens insights and consolidates growth. But it is also the point of departure for further learning on the nature of the mind and morality. There is minimal need for professional expertise in the generation and in the interpretation of protocols. Hence testing is user-friendly and cost effective.
Value/Relevance of Information Derived from the Inventory Test	MMPI, California PI, Timothy Leary Checklist, five factors, constitute for the patient meaningful reports but without providing diagnostic distinctions.	The Relational Modality Evaluation Scale (RMES) constitutes a self-assessment inventory, leading to identify the relational modality within holistic relational alternatives. The inventory results confirm the projective findings. Relational patterns determine the psychosocial adjustment.
Predictive, Therapeutic, and Diagnostic Value	None to client, but helpful to clinician or employer.	Maximal value to the testee, by identifying his/her pattern, its developmental origin, its impact on interpersonal relations and on one's own distorted perceptions of reality.
Projective tests	Traditional Projective Testing: TAT, Rorschach, House-Tree-Person	Formal Theory Projective Testing- The Metaphor Construction Tests

Empirical vs. Formal ten point formal analysis of Information	The information is processed according to statistical incidence along the range of test scales-subscales. These have a certain empirical correlation with clinical symptomatology and pathology.	The information of the Formal Theoretical Testing is analyzed along the ten levels of the Formal Analysis Profile determining the qualitative and quantitative parameters of the personal Conflict Resolution Process syndromal entity: 1. Symbolic universe and formal dichotomies. 2. Aesthetic balance, natural science criteria and constructs. 3. Intensity of conflict energy as judged from the Family Balloons, Conflictual Memory tests and the psychic tension scale. 4. Inter-transformation of energetic modalities judged by the overall flow of communications. 5. Symbolic conflictual issue reflected in the Conflictual Memory Test. 6. The six-role process syndromal sequence reflected in all metaphor tests. 7. The graphic presentation of the personal pattern. 8. Relational modality choice identified by the RMES and confirmed by the projective testing. 9. Quantification of psychic tension and identification of symptoms. 10. Therapeutic effectiveness judged from one's capacity to generate insights and formulate need for changes.
Validity and Reliability,	Empirical Testing is Marked by Low Validity and Reliability.	Formal Theory Testing Very high reliability and validity.
Tabulation of Findings	Findings are tabulated along a Matrix with linear presentation of personal scores. The scales and subscales provide fragmented information, not cause-effect facts. The meaning of these findings to the client is minimal, hence non-therapeutic. They are mostly valuable to the psychologist and therapist. The client does not contribute to the interpretation of the information, feels passive, antagonistic, defensive, judged arbitrarily, criticized and misunderstood, hence is alienated by the procedure.	Findings are summarized along the ten levels of the Formal Analysis Profile. The systemic organization is presented in diagrammatic longitudinal and cross-section graphics presenting the individual's social deviation and psychic tension experienced. The metaphor profile visually sums up the artwork as symbolically interrelated information integrated in a meaningful pattern. The integration of information provides both to the person and to the therapist meaningful insights of profound significance. The generation process of this testing imagery and insights generates in the client catharsis, self-esteem, pride and enlightenment. The usefulness and relevance of the personal ubiquitous and universal pattern is of cognitive and moral significance. The impact of this learning process has educational and therapeutic value.

Table #4, Rethinking Morality

In the field of morality, the conflict resolution process becomes a formula with an optimal solution; it corresponds to the formal operations, laws structuring relations towards increasing personal effectiveness. Optimal Conflict Resolution represents morality abiding by the formal principles of Conflict Resolution: moderation, cooperation and mutual respect; the operations coincide with three key moral values.

The anthropology of religions becomes the search for peace, reduction of conflicts, in the family. The family institution has been constantly restructured by religions. The Formal Theory has evolved awareness of the unconscious need to resolve conflict and the conscious deliberate adoption of formal principles marking the evolution of civilizations. The gradual evolution of moral orders leads to our finally becoming aware of morality in terms of the three pure principles of conflict resolution. [16]

The fourth table addresses the unit as a moral paradigm and contrasts dogma-based moralities to the science based moral order. Dogma based moral orders present moralities as normative systems. They have evolved defined for humans by revelation, superhuman transcendence of knowledge - moral orders predicated on the existence of an external, omniscient and omnipotent authority. By contrast the formal paradigm presents morality as stemming from the unconscious, as an inner dynamic mechanism spontaneously seeking the reconciliation of opposites as in conflict resolution or moral order. The formal position states that the unconscious need for conflict resolution is universal and that it underlies all moral thinking. Indeed, the formal methodology applied to the religions of the world, integrates them as a dialectic evolution of moral paradigms targeting increased effectiveness and stability in the area of domestic relations.

The formal position suggests that civilizations have evolved in the course of history towards increased fairness in the distribution of power to all members of the family. In the course of history accordingly, civilizations have evolved from primitive cultures espousing incomplete conflict resolution to more advanced and effective cultures introducing covenants. This evolution has occurred based on a sequence of moral discoveries corresponding to identifying and institutionalizing each one of the abstract principles of conflict resolution.

The formal moral paradigm provides clear awareness of the purely abstract nature of the unconscious need for Conflict Resolution. It places morality on scientific principles and frees it from its association to dogma shaping norms. While civilizations and religions have promoted paradigms of conflict resolution, the formal morality suggests deliberately espousing the principles of Conflict Resolution as the totality of moral guidelines. While religious moral paradigms have advocated partial moral solutions of conflict, the Formal Theory makes us aware of how to consciously pursue moral order beyond the dogmatically dictated partial moral solutions. The Formal Theory demystifies morality by targeting relational effectiveness through the proper management of power.

The Table

Formal interpretation of metaphors leads to identify a person's syndrome and relational modality. The metaphors are integrated as a system of formally interrelated states. The totality illustrates conflict resolution. The tests are formally interrelated, evolving awareness of a process: the methodology accounts for individual relational modality choices.

Phenomenology like the diversity of moral paradigms has divided humanity by construing contradictory sacred metaphors and holy causes and partial conceptions of Conflict Resolution both in psychological theory and in versions of metaphysics. By contrast, the formal interpretation of metaphors is the methodology that leads to scientific moral principles, which reconcile metaphors and the disciplines of the sciences as formally interrelated conflict resolutions that evolve to awareness of the process beyond content: the methodology accounts for individual perceptions and differences and for theoretical perspectives. The distinctions between phenomenology and relational formal reductionism is that between a puzzle with many solutions and one that has scientific clarity. Becoming conscious of the personal scenario of power management as a structured ideational system helps to realize that science is present even in simple samples of creativity.

We are living in divisive normative realities. They highlight dramas that we all take seriously as determining our moral choices. Only with a science of behavior can we measure the ethical dimensions, and extricate ourselves from living in metaphorically determined moral orders. Science ethics aspire for an equitable, orderly structured universe. The world has a clear choice between tradition as partial truths versus evolving a new orderly and friendly, controllable and manageable normative ethical reality.

TABLE #4: RETHINKING SPIRITUALITY AND MORALITY		
	Dogma Based Phenomenological Religious Moral Orders	**The Conflict Resolution Process as A Moral Paradigm**
1. Rethinking Morality: Phenomenological vs. reductionist perspectives	Religions are dogmatically defined as knowledge transcending rational explanations. Morality is defined as a system of values explained by the norms of a religion or a culture. Religions are normative institutions, ethical orders seen as particular types of conflict resolutions.	The unconscious mental process needs rest, defined as adjustment to norms; this is clarified as the moral motivation, the origin of all conflict resolutions as moral order; Reconciliation with the rest state has found alternative resolutions. Moral order is the sequence of emotional formal transformations necessary to evolve from a conflict to a resolution. Gods are the attribution of this internal need to resolve conflicts to external optimal authority figures. Religions are metaphors of conflict resolution Religions, gods, evolved discovering the principles of conflict resolution proceeding unconsciously from passivity to activity, from antagonism to cooperation and from alienation to mutual respect. Religious metaphors have evolved across the history of civilization like an ongoing conflict resolution process. Religions evolved from concrete to abstract, from the very oppressive, cruel, antagonistic, alienating ones to the masterful deferential-cooperative, spiritual ones. Formal Analysis integrates religions and interrelates them into a continuum of dialectically interrelated domestic relations evolving towards fairness.
2. Redefining the divine authority as an external reality vs. an internal process.	The Concept of God Classical religions are concrete not abstract or philosophical. They hence define God as an external authority, an omnipotent, sometimes forgiving and loving God, as the principal authority to prostrate oneself in front of and to be inspired by. God is identified by each religion as a different omnipotent entity, yet with varying attributes. Religions empower the faithful but divide the globe. They generate hope and confidence but also prejudice and fanaticism. The divisiveness of religions has led to the banning of prayer in the American public school and the loss to education of the formative importance of spirituality as respect for universal moral principles.	The scientific redefinition the Divine Authority stems from improved understanding of the unconscious need for rest, or peace. The scientific recognition of the unconscious as a conflict resolution process clarifies the common origin of all religions. The unconscious organizing principles may be identified as the Unit phenomenon as the ultimate definition of morality. The difference between God and the Conflict Resolution Process is that the process is abstract like Genesis, while gods are role model resolutions. Creativity is a formula that transforms conflict gradually to resolution Gods represent the particular resolutions to the formulas of conflict resolution. Creativity leads to resolutions as the plot of all drama, art, prose, lyrics and music. The creative process expands the ritual of prayer as emotional communication, to the diversity of resolutions. Emotional Education fosters the study of the universal principles of moral order and improves the personal way of resolving conflict or managing power.

3. **"Hear my prayer, O Lord, and let my cry come unto thee."**	The traditional Definition Of Prayer is a profound internal dialogue with God.	Formal Redefinition of prayer defines it as a sequence of behaviors and emotions transpiring in the contemplative realm. The ritual of prayer reinforces the spontaneous conflict resolution values and has a profound formative and self-healing effect. The dialogue of prayers has the structure of the Conflict Resolution Process. It starts from admitting powerlessness in one's address and seeking empowerment through divine grace. Receiving grace follows the six-role sequence in the cooperative mode. The desirable attitude of feeling loved enables one to be loving and feel freed of conflict. Deference to God reinforces positive attitudes to others. Reciprocating to God one becomes loving by assuming His relational attributes.
4. **Redefining Spirituality as Respect for the Creative Process and the Pursuit of Ever Broadening Identities.**	In the classical religions spirituality coincides with identifying with the spirit of a particular religion. The sense of security emanating from identifying a union of the parishioners and the Divinity inspires the experience and the development of a community.	Formal spirituality coincides with addressing the personal and interpersonal conflicts by evolving resolutions, by following progressively broader affiliations, and freeing oneself from old categories and stereotypes (adults vs. children, whites vs. blacks, etc.) Spirituality then amounts to feeling reconciled with opposites in more encompassing categories. Prayer Is the active pursuit of conflict resolution or moral order. Indeed, prayer frees the person from conflicts, experiencing healing and discovering a language of self-reassurance.

Table #5, Psychotherapy

In the fields of psychotherapy and psycho-education the unit becomes the scientific principles governing the unconscious and their relevance in the reduction of emotional distress. Psychotherapy addresses the systematic study of the personal emotional adjustment and of its optimal restructuring. Indeed, the fields of education and therapy differ in that they deliver the same knowledge with different degrees of emphasis to two client populations: psycho-education is needed by the general "well' public, while psychotherapy is needed by the public experiencing intense conflicts.

Rethinking Psychotherapy

The fifth table contrasts traditional psychotherapies with Formal Theory's Conflict Analysis Training, a standardized program of emotional education focused on managing one's power and attitude. The program of emotional education is available both for the classroom and for the therapeutic setting.
a) The formal training targets clear cognitive understanding of the nature of the unconscious or creative process and of power management by identifying the scientific nature and properties of the Conflict Resolution Process Unit.
b) The therapy targets self-discovery and change by tapping one's creativity to identify the personal way of resolving conflict, and
c) It finally targets consciously capturing the optimal way of resolving conflict, and deliberately improving one's way of communicating following the three science-based moral guidelines, the conflict resolution principles of moderation, cooperation and mutual respect. This approach is contrasted to the unintegrated plethora of non-science and non-moral order inspiring psychotherapeutic modalities.

The objectives of correct and healthy behavior are defined as the moral values of the Conflict Resolution Process, which accommodate the moral prescription of religions strengths and shortcomings and needs for fixing it. The individual recognizes the syndromal nature-category and the impact it has on perceptions, distortions and potential conflicts in interpersonal relations and in personal functioning. The trainee is able to put the fragmented pieces of reality together into the continuum of his/her pattern. The person also understands that patterns are styles of power management and identifies his/her own need for improved power management in his/her own power in behavior. Power Management becomes clear messages about structure, rules, definition of authority and the value implicit in creativity, spirituality, dream analysis, communicational and conflict resolution negotiation skills. The values are guiding relational principles of conflict resolution: moderation, cooperation, mutual respect. The objectives of correct and healthy behavior are defined as the moral values of the Conflict Resolution Process, which accommodate the moral prescription of religions intuitively capturing the Conflict Resolution Process. The training is perfecting the means of understanding values and resolving conflict. The unconscious moral values are also recognized in their political, ethical and judicial process manifestations. They are recognized in their spiritual function of resolving conflicts and promoting the same values and appreciated in their manifestation in the arts.

TABLE #5: RETHINKING THERAPY

	Current Medical Model Emphasizes Medical Psychotherapies	**Power Management as the Relational Model of Therapy**
A. Epistemological Issues a) Phenomenological vs. Reductionist Conceptualization of Illness and Wellness	Traditional Psychotherapy addresses mental illnesses as chemical imbalances that is biological or medical disorders, phenomenologically distinguishable by their sets of symptoms. Hence therapy relies on symptom control, chemotherapies and other medical management of symptoms.	Formal Psychotherapies address wellness as power and attitude problems manifested as relational syndromes. Relational syndromal power imbalances impact the whole person, body-mind-and sociations. Hence, therapy reverts to the improved management of power and attitude deviations addressing their correction as purely relational pathology.
b) Function of Psychotherapy - Symptoms versus Relational alternatives	Psychotherapies address disorders. Therapies include cognitive, behavior and emotional modification as therapeutic modalities. Interpersonal therapies are being standardized in their delivery, but unlike the Conflict Analysis Training, they do not integrate several therapeutic modalities.	The Conflict Analysis Power Management approach is used for the well and the ill persons as a comprehensive emotional education program. The emphasis of the diagnosis and therapy is on power/attitude management targeting relational changes to achieve interpersonal effectiveness and the lowering of the personal/interpersonal conflicts. The Conflict Analysis Battery is a manual driven standardized program of emotional education. It integrates several therapeutic modalities, such as creativity, cognitive, insight, behavior modification, value clarification and skills development. The training is based on the cognitive study of the Conflict Resolution Process as the universal harmonic and on the Conflict Analysis Battery, a self-assessment and self-healing process. The assessment identifies both the syndromal relational deviations and the psychic-tension-symptomatic components. This therapy may be used in conjunction with chemotherapy for the reduction of symptoms.
B. Psychodiagnosis	The Biological Model	Power Management, the Relational Model
a) Medical Assessment vs. Psycho-assessment.	The medical model therapies address assessing the body rather than the person using multiple assessment techniques. Psychological testing consists of scales measuring specific groups of symptoms, i.e., depression, obsessive/compulsive, psychoticism etc. Medical techniques include brain imaging and blood level monitoring of chemicals.	The Formal theoretical model addresses primarily the person. Power Management utilizes the Conflict Analysis Battery Inventory and Projective tests. The self-assessment determines one's way of relating or managing power. The Conflict Analysis Battery leads to a cost effective, personal psycho-social self-assessment yielding a meaningful diagnostic and therapeutic clinical record with minimal need for professional services. The psycho-assessment is educational, diagnostic, and therapeutic.

b) The Impact of the Assessment on the Patient-Client	The medical model assessment reduces the client's share of responsibility in the process of creating wellness. The person feels the body is the object treated while the mind or psyche is ignored, hence the patient feels alienated and dehumanized. Indeed, the therapist avoids transferential distortions treating the mental illness as a physical ailment. Behavioral therapies target behaviors, cognitive therapies target distorted perceptions. Occasional psychological assessment findings are not communicated to the patient but to the psychotherapist.	The formal therapy engages the client to resolve conflicts through a joint role model working relationship. The patient is encouraged to evolve from passive to active, from antagonistic to cooperative, from feeling alienated to experiencing respect. The self-assessment is generated by the client as a trainee; information is automatically generated and delivered to the test-taker. The training-therapeutic experience is of emotional significance and of great educational-cognitive moral and therapeutic value. It is meaningful and corrective. It empowers the client, rewards creativity, it is intellectually satisfying, it is socially corrective and spiritually enlightening. It leads to the release of emotions, to the generation of actionable insights and to the identification of corrective changes. It leads to the affirmation of relational options of conflict resolution and to improved interpersonal skills.
C. The Passive vs. Active Role of the Client in Psychotherapy	The Biological Model	Power Management
a) Passive fragmentation vs. active integration of the self, accountability, responsibility and control.	Traditional psychotherapy fragments the therapy into a plurality of unrelated approaches addressing symptoms. The assessment does not give the patient insights in the continuum of behavior, emotions, biology, and social experiences; hence it deprives the person of a sense of accountability and responsibility for the dysfunctional experiences. Thus, the patient is deprived of having a handle on his state of wellness and illness.	Conflict Analysis is a comprehensive psychotherapy; it addresses integration of the psychosocial continuum of wellness/ illness as a relational composition. It addresses the patient as responsible for the pathology but also as able to control the relational process through optimizing power and attitude management. The pattern explores pathology in the context of one's formative experiences, family relations and cultural norms. Diagnosis integrates the person's symbolic choices as a system of interrelated emotions. The diagnosis entails clear relational choices increasing effectiveness in reaching one's objectives.
b) Medicalization vs. formalization of illness, medical management vs. insight and Power Management.	The medicalization of mental illness increases dependency on medical management rather than on self-management. Cognitive and behavior modification therapies address the social polarity of problem manifestations independently of the related psychic emotional state. They address the psychic tension state symptomatically, using relaxation, awareness, other therapies (AA and behavioral counseling) use theistic or purely spiritual approaches without analysis of either the social interpersonal or personal emotional implications of these value systems.	The patient evolves insights on the effective management of power, thus he/she applies the relational power process across the range of his/her experiences.

D. Psychotherapeutic Modalities	The Biological Model	Power Management
Traditional Fragmentation of Services Into separate Therapeutic Modalities vs. Formal Standardized Integrated Delivery of Several Therapeutic Modalities.	Traditional psychotherapy is delivered along a number of unintegrated therapeutic modalities.	Formal psychoeducation integrates a number of therapeutic modalities into one comprehensive, standardized, easy to deliver package available at the individual and or group therapy settings.
a. Art Therapy vs. Creativity for Self-discovery and Self-healing.	Creativity is not routinely explored. Art therapy as a specialty is parenthetical to treatment and is provided only by skilled art therapists. Procedures and interpretations are not standardized and they depend on the therapist, rather than the client.	Creativity is used for self-discovery, self-disclosure and self-healing. Art exercises identify patterns. Unconscious choices are identified through the use of projective testing protocols, which elicit and structure personality determined relational choices. Structured dialectic questionnaires guide the test taker to amplify relational choices. Insights inspire contracting for changes. Evaluation and processing of information require minimal intervention by professional specialists, psychologist and art therapists. Interpretation by the client is usually accurate, and facilitates the interpretive effort of the therapist.
	Information is not integrated into lifelong relational patterns.	Standardized integration of art and insight information reconstructs the personal conflict resolution process, which reflects a lifelong relational pattern. This information may be graphically illustrated and conceptually integrated into a formal syndromal continuum, which validates the Formal Theoretical postulations.
	The Biological Model	Power Management
b. Cognitive Therapies	Cognitive therapies emphasize understanding the nature of cognitive emotional responses and how to manage them. Reasoning makes irrational anxiety eliciting situations become manageable, as the individual evolves practical solutions to control reality as opposed to feeling helpless and overwhelmed by emotional reactions. The patient is shown how to deal effectively with situations rather than be paralyzed.	The cognitive component of the Formal Theory emphasizes awareness of how the conflict resolution process organizes information and how it reconciles the fragments of one's experience into the syndromal cause effect continuum. The individual understanding the syndromal psychodynamics becomes able to understand symptoms as related to power choices. Cognitive mastery continues to occur as the person monitors the relational progress through the use of creativity exercises.
c. Spiritual Therapies	Alcoholics Anonymous and pastoral counseling use the theistic/higher power paradigm to inspire moderation and elicit cooperation and respect, all positive behavior modifications. God is perceived as the benevolent role model authority inspiring rest and the modification of aberrant relational patterns.	The cognitive formal therapy component addresses the integration of theistic paradigms into affirming the conflict resolution process values as a universal moral order paradigm. This integration enhances appreciation of the formal values of moderation, cooperation and mutual respect as the universal moral values effectively relieving one from interpersonal and psychic conflicts.

d. Insight-oriented therapies	Several therapeutic approaches pursue insights, that is, making the unconscious conscious. Psychoanalysis, foremost among them, placed emphasis on a wild unconscious driven by sexual and aggressive urges, a weak vs. strong ego and its related defense mechanisms and finally a rigid or benevolent superego. The biological drives, the developmental fixations and cultural injunctions have been seen to manifest in complex transferential patterns that are made conscious through interpretation, hence made to disappear.	Formal Psychotherapy pursues insights on the syndromal organization of the personal experience in terms of the Conflict Resolution lifelong relational modality choices. Relational modalities determine the systemic organization of social preferences and emotional consequences along a range of formal alternatives. This unit shapes one's syndromal, personal and social experiences. The formal psychotherapy has three targets: 1. Cognitive-conscious awareness of the unit, how the mind functions resolving conflict and this unit has universal manifestation. 2. The identification of one's syndromal unit through the use of metaphor testing. Insights are profound, accurate, valid and reliable. The testing yields cognitive information reinforcing the nature of the unconscious Conflict Resolution Process. 3. Clearly understanding relational choices toward restructuring relationships and increasing effectiveness.
e. Effectiveness of insight therapies	The failure of psychodynamic psychotherapies of slow, questionable progress, difficulty in demonstrating effectiveness, has undermined the influence of psychoanalysis and has generated resistance to psychodynamic therapies.	The formal psychotherapy is integrative and self-validating. The insights are reinforced with cognitive education on the nature of the unconscious Conflict Resolution Process, and by the effective control of symptoms accomplished through the deliberate restructuring of relationships.

Table #6, Psycho-education

The practical alternative to psychoanalysis costly process of therapy is in the classroom delivery of the creativity for self-discovery training for the student population to evolve insights on their personal way of resolving conflict examining their metaphors identifying their relational modality pattern and examining how this manifests in their relationships with fellow students and in dealing with authorities. In the classroom this can be transformed, monitored and modeled as effective communications optimally manageable at peer level. Therapy then is transformed to social skills preparation of the individual for excellence in the realm of interpersonal relations, marital, parental and vocational roles. Self-awareness as a relational diagnosis and relational training coincide with the goals of education and morality.

This educational process then claims effective moral education equivalent to religious-based moral indoctrination but free of dogma. It claims respectability and authority for the management of most emotional and behavioral matters over dependence on dogma and on therapists. Thus, education is integrative, personally relevant and culturally meaningful. Formal Theory empowers education with science to provide emotional literacy.

The sixth and final table contrasts traditional literacy with emotional literacy. Traditional Literacy consists of technological, agnostic personally irrelevant information. Emotional Literacy,
1) integrates the humanities and the sciences,
2) leads to personal insights and
3) to the appreciation of clear relational conflict resolution values.
The above three items are the distinct objectives of formalist education. Emotional Literacy thus targets integration of knowledge and its personal relevance for the development of self-knowledge, that is insights, values and skills for proper power management. It is an education that should be delivered in the modern classroom by retraining the faculty.

This comparative analysis leads to the conclusion that the Formal Theory's scientific moral paradigm representing new epistemology, rigorous diagnostic taxonomy, a comprehensive testing battery, a science-based morality and a comprehensive psychotherapeutic and psycho-educational program. The conclusion of this comprehensive study is that all the disciplines may flow one from the other, based on the formal cohesion binding fragments into a totality, which manifests at all levels of observing reality.

The self-assessment is an integral part of therapy and education. It focuses on one's creativity and associations by observing samples of the unit process. Thus, the self-assessment is an educational instrument of healing and growth and a way of resolving conflicts as revealed through the orderly construction of metaphors. The testing instruments lead therefore to the non-resisted capturing of the personal process with several significant applications: educational, therapeutic, research for validation issues abiding by stringent cost effectiveness. The testing is integrative and multipurpose.

The Formal Theory's Conflict Resolution Process redefines the unconscious as consisting of a formal and energetic entity, the atomistic unit of behavioral phenomena. What concerns its measurement techniques: The Formal Theory's testing, the Conflict Analysis Battery identifies accurately, reliably and validly this personal unit unconscious process as one's syndromal relational modality. The Formal Theory introduces a standardized battery of testing for the determination and measurement of the structure of the personal way of resolving conflict introduced a scientific method in understanding religion and morality.

The Formal Theory introduces a comprehensive program of psychoeducation and power management as the chief means to interpret education and therapy as the didactic and the experimental aspects of one continuous and standardized emotional education. Conflict Analysis integrates scientific knowledge on the process with its validation through identifying the personal unit process and recognition of the optimal ways of resolving conflict. Hence it integrates knowledge, self-knowledge and the study of values towards facilitating optimum attitude changes. Thus, the study of the unconscious is the key to evolving a standardized power management psychoeducational program that may be delivered cost effectively within education and therapy alike without engaging the person in the complexities of transference and counter-transference.

Beyond the clinical implications of the Formal Theory, the formalist student learns to utilize the technology for analysis of all realms of creativity. The unit category has impact on perceptions, distortions and in generating conflicts in personal functioning and in interpersonal relations. The trainee can put the fragmented pieces of reality together into the continuum of his/her pattern. The person also understands that patterns are styles of power management and identifies his/her own personal need for improved power management in his/her power in behavior.

Power Management becomes clear messages about structure, rules, definition of authority and the value implicit in creativity, spirituality, dream analysis, communicational and conflict resolution negotiation skills. The guiding relational principles of conflict resolution are moral values: moderation, cooperation, mutual respect. The objectives of correct and healthy behavior are defined as the moral values of the Conflict Resolution Process. They accommodate the moral directives of religions intuitively capturing the Conflict Resolution Process.

TABLE #6: RETHINKING EDUCATION		
	Traditional Literacy	**Power Management as Emotional Literacy**
A. Epistemological Issues a) Comparing Paradigms, The Phenomenological vs. Reductionistic Conceptualization of Reality.	TL methodologically is phenomenological and pluralistic in the fact that it acknowledges many coexisting paradigms and it lacks a common denominator or a universal integrative paradigm. Hence the field of knowledge is fragmented into (a) the humanities, (b) the sciences, (c) moral paradigms and (d) the several social sciences including psychology and sociology. Encyclopedic knowledge of these unrelated disciplines is cumbersome, riddled with contradictions and is personally irrelevant to the individual; it does not clarify moral values and does not contribute self-knowledge.	EL methodologically is founded on a science based universal process paradigm, which integrates knowledge. This process provides a design for analysis of problems leading to self-knowledge and to the establishment of clear relational conflict resolving values. Education is enhanced by the universality of this paradigm as the periodic phenomenon of the humanities and the sciences as well as in all creativity and all moral paradigms. EL education is meaningful and personally relevant. It connects the disciplines of knowledge with understanding and improving one's self-knowledge by managing power. Morality amounts to respect of the universality of a scientific moral paradigm and its effectiveness for the resolution of conflicts.
b) The Message, its Delivery and its Psychological and Sociological impact.	The message of traditional education is fragmented and so are the messengers. Specialization of teachers compounds the encyclopedic nature of knowledge as that of many messages, many contradictory paradigms and perspectives, which entail unresolved conflict and sustained power play. Personally and morally, this information fragments knowledge. This education leads to divisiveness and alienation, the loss of clarity of values. It promotes unthinking compliance or inversely, opportunism, anarchy and escapism. It reinforces the uncritical disposition of "political correctness" which implicitly denies the possibility of critical evaluation of any one set of moral systems.	Syndromal thinking along relational modalities allows analysis of all creativity. The message is a singular universal multifaceted methodological paradigm. It is at the same time a formula, a cosmogony story, the plot of a play, one's metaphors, and a moral paradigm. ELs program may be delivered by teachers to students and therapists to patients. All studies reinforce the same message in the variety of its manifestations thus integrating knowledge by reestablishing continuity and inspiring personal meaning and insights. This education promotes cohesion and unity with consensus on the universal moral principles of the conflict resolution process: moderation, cooperation and mutual respect. This methodology integrates the history of civilization as discoveries of the orderly conflict resolving process.
B. The Integrated Humanities and Sciences Curriculum a) Fragmentation of knowledge and loss of its personal relevance vs. integration of knowledge and recognition of its personal and moral relevance	Phenomenological education leads to several unrelated aspects of a fragmented universe.	The formal methodology leads to the integration of knowledge. First, the Conflict Resolution Process is the common denominator across the humanities and the sciences as it is transformed into the unit of each field. Second, the unit integrates personal knowledge, it makes knowledge personally relevant.
a. Science Education	(a) The principles of science are irrelevant for the humanities.	(a) The principles, constructs and formulas of the rigorous sciences: logic, mathematics and physics are applicable to the understanding of the unit structure and to all social sciences.
b. Humanistic Education	(b) TL regards the mind as separate from science and from biology. The Humanities are irrelevant for the sciences. Phenomenological thinking, dogma, determinism and transcendence axiomatically suggest a diversity of moral paradigms.	(b) The formal role process accounts for the order in the various fields of the humanities, e.g., drama, myths, creativity, religions, psychology. The mental process also as an energetic state affects biology. EL fosters a conceptual continuity between ideas, physiology and emotions.

c. Moral Education	(c) The controversy of the arbitrariness of moral systems has led to the separation of church and state leading to a public education sponsoring atheistic morality, agnosticism and conducive to alienation. Alternatively, multiculturalism has engendered uncritical "political correctness "which views all moral paradigms archaic and evolved as equivalent and as equally acceptable.	(c) The process is the diagnostic unit, the syndromal sequence, it is also the moral paradigm integrating the cultures of the world as discoveries of the process. It integrates personal emotions and behaviors into patterns and identifies these as individual and cultural distinctions. It allows for classification of relational categories offering predictive accuracy. The diagnoses entail moral values as they differ in the degree of conflict resolution they impart and the degree of interpersonal effectiveness they confer.
d. Psychological Education	(d) TL lacks a generally acceptable psychological and moral paradigm: Hence TL cannot integrate cultural diversity and identify personal patterns as wellness diagnoses.	d) Clarity of the psychology of conflict resolution leads to promoting clear scientific principles. Formal analysis integrates values and moral paradigms into one ongoing conflict resolution continuum driven by the need for fairness in relations entailing relational correctness and uniform protection of the rights of all individuals. The history of civilization integrates cultures as discoveries of science.
C. Moral Values a. Agnosticism; partisanship vs. the universality of conflict resolution principles.	Traditional literacy is agnostic or pluralistic and alternatively sectarian, isolationist and exclusivist. It either follows a political correctness based on the respect of all traditions lacking dialectic integration or alternatively it follows a narrow focus on one religion-based paradigm at the expense of all other paradigms.	Emotional literacy provides insights as well as values. The focus is on the universal unconscious conflict resolution process and on its manifestation at the personal and the sociological levels. The paradigm integrates knowledge and makes it relevant as personal creativity informs the person on his/her unconscious way of resolving conflict, integrating one's emotions and behaviors.
b. Focus on content vs. Process; relational versus methodological correctness	Traditional Literacy (TL) as unintegrated knowledge focuses on the study of either amoral, atheoretical empirical knowledge and on personally irrelevant science and technologies or alternatively it focuses on a single moral paradigm, a partial truth entailing prejudice toward other truths as alien. TL's content has remained unintegrated encyclopedic information. It is not providing universality of moral values and personal insights. It is not personally relevant.	Emphasis on a universal process reduces the burden of encyclopedic knowledge. The truth is in the process integrating all information rather than in the diverse contents or partial truths. The universal laws of science are reencountered in all realms, a finding which reduces the sense of informational overload and personal alienation. At the moral values level, definition of the formal process leads to the redefinition of moral order and the nature of God. It clarifies human destiny inspired by morality, the conflict resolution principles of science.
c. Political correctness versus formal analysis	Political Correctness has allowed the uncritical coexistence of contradictory value systems. Many moral paradigms are given equal respectability at the expense of the set of superior universal relational values. Methodologically political correctness values, the righteousness of all moral paradigms without considerations of how such affect each other and their impact on internal systemic structuring of relations.	Power Management focuses on the process and the universal principles of moral order. Understanding of the process allows addressing interpersonal as well as cultural issues as evolutionarily interrelated systems of relational modality alternatives. The program explores effectiveness along the criteria of conflict resolution and of evolving insights and awareness of the process. Cultural values are respected according to their capacity to lead to personal and interpersonal international levels. Political correctness is abandoned for methodological correctness that values the universality of the conflict resolution process.

D. Interpersonal Education vs. Personalized Growth a. Assessment of intellectual Functioning vs. Self-Assessment for the integration of the whole person.	Standardized educational testing measures only the individual's intellectual development. Judging the individual along their conceptual competence skills in a few literacy areas e.g., Math and English, but it overlooks the areas of personal maturity, capacity for comfort, as moral values and competence with interpersonal skills.	Formal Theory's Conflict Analysis Battery is a self-assessment instrument that permits to accurately measure the personal way of resolving conflict. The Battery protocols consist of art exercises generating personal insights. The client creates the art and interprets the symbolic metaphorical language. The protocols may also be interpreted by an educator or a specialist. The Formal Theoretical testing is comprehensive, valid, reliable, cost-effective and easy to assess. The Battery may be repeated periodically to monitor education and emotional progress. Testing reflects both the intellectual and psychological or moral development of the student and it also addresses correcting it. The program may be delivered within a therapeutic setting or within a classroom.
b. The social acceptability of personal psychological issues.	For the purpose of personal education, the DSM diagnostic test and categories are inadequate and irrelevant. Diagnostically they confer stigmatizing labels, pigeon-holing the person as dysfunctional or genetically impaired, mentally handicapped and needing medications rather than identifying our attitude problems and indicating the need for help. Hence, testing is of limited use for self-assessment and self-improvement. Testing addresses exclusively the intellectual proficiency of the student.	The formal diagnostic labels measure relational modalities and emotional pathology. They do not stigmatize. They yield the information to the testee as useful insights, which integrate personal experiences and account for symptoms. The relational diagnosis explains communicational patterns, their pathogenesis and entails the direction for changes. Insights help the well person to understand oneself and to recognize the importance of conflict resolution values towards increasing one's effectiveness through attitude change.

Discussion: The Six Comparative Tables Attest to the Advantages of scientific Abstraction
The Significance of a Science Based Unconscious Process

The universality of the unit process allows integrating the disciplines into the cohesive field of the new Moral Science. With these tables we seek to show that the unit of Conflict Resolution manifesting itself in a variety of identities is the common denominator unifying the disciplines. The unit integrates the disciplines while it increases meaning in each one of them. The scope of this study is to contrast the phenomenological and formal perceptions of the psychological observations side-by-side in each of the six disciplines. Contrasting the concepts in each field item-by-item along parallel columns clarifies the efficacy of the formal theoretical unit in increasing insights at each discipline and confirms its overall efficacy as the universal methodology equally meaningful for the six disciplines.

The efficacy of the unit as a conceptual tool proves the effectiveness of the rational rethinking of abstraction along formulas of science. The paradigm shift introduces science to the disciplines. It changes them from their status of empirical sciences to the enviable status of one pure formal and moral science of behavior.

Parenthetically, here let us clarify that we must distinguish pure abstraction, as reductionism from the impure reductionism of rationalism. Rationalism inspired the ideologies of the 20th Century, the Marxist materialistic social dialectic, communism, and Freud's intrapsychic dialectic of psychoanalysis. The collapse of both theoretical positions at the end of the 20th Century has led to mankind's disillusionment with rational systems and to reverting to the default phenomenological alternatives of traditional paradigms: medicalization of psychology, revival of religiocity, ethnocentrism, prejudice, and intolerance. In the area of psychology, the collapse of the psychoanalytic paradigm has facilitated the acceptance of the concrete DSM distinctions of the medical model.

Thus, the failure of rational thinking has precipitated the reemergence of phenomenology and the related fragmentation of the disciplines and the ensuing discord and ineffectiveness in the fields of politics, psychology, morality and education. National and international security as well as personal mental health and relational effectiveness are threatened by the return to the divisive, alienating and concrete phenomenology of the diversity of concrete axiomatic paradigms. The new options are equally deplorable, polarized alternative value systems dividing the public into fundamentalists or moralists on the one side and atheists, anarchists, exponents of political correctness, nihilists and opportunists on the other.

It is the ineffectiveness of phenomenology across the disciplines of behavior, that dictates the pursuit of science in order to evolve the needed reintegration of reality, the discovery of an objectifiable continuum, the building of a rational consensus in the social sciences as the means to address the needs of our evolving societies. Integration of the behavioral sciences is pivotal in a geopolitical context toward implementing a global revision in the way we think about behavior, education and moral values. This study then addresses the conceptual limitations of our times, which are squarely responsible for the tremendous ineffectiveness and suffering experienced by humankind, disunited because of the absence of a universally acceptable that is a science-based psychology and moral order. The Formal Theory seriously and scholarly addresses this need by reconceptualizing behavior and moral order reconciling the disciplines of psychology and bringing meaning to the alienated public, scholars, believers and disbelievers.

The precise scientific structure of this unit is described in the volume of *Conflict Analysis--The Formal Theory of Behavior* [18]. Here, the unit is presented as the common denominator, as the universal atomistic unit of six empirical fields of psychosocial knowledge with two implications.

- First, the formalization of the fields of Epistemology, Psychodiagnosis, Psycho-assessment, Morality, Psychotherapy and Psychoeducation immediately leads to increasing the organization of ideas and of insights in the respective disciplines.
- Second, by reducing the six disciplines to one formal unit process, the new method reconciles the six disciplines into a single cohesive scientific continuum. Thus, the traditional phenomenological approximations may be replaced by the formal scientific equivalents. We may conclude that the comparative study confirms the possibility of the integration of all the social sciences as complimentary to each other within one rigorous continuum.

The six tables contrast traditional phenomenological views with those of the Formal Theory's reductionist integration of information in six disciplines of psychology. This comparative format helps to identify Formal Theory's conceptual advantages for each field and for the integration of all six social science disciplines into a cohesive continuum.

The six tables establish the integrative potential of the Conflict Resolution Process as the atomistic unit of behavior. This unit's comprehensive formal and natural science methodological revamping of the social sciences undoes the fragmentation of the behavioral continuum by reducing the complex field into clearly defined concepts and the respective formal relational and natural science energetic laws. The Formal Method effectively revamps the fields of epistemology, diagnosis, testing, morality, psychotherapy and psychoeducation, addressing simultaneously the creation of new categories of mental wellness and illness, a new psycho-assessment, a new moral paradigm, and a new training and therapeutic program. The science-based training, a standardized cost-effective emotional education integrates general knowledge, personal insights with implicit behavior modification relevance, and clear relational conflict resolving values. This program may be delivered to emotionally upset individuals as therapy and to the well population in the classroom as emotional education. Thus, the theory and its practice have far reaching implications for the future of education, health care and moral development.

It seems appropriate here to address the integrative significance of the Conflict Resolution Process Unit as a moral process towards establishing a Moral Science of behavior, as the foremost feature of this integrative study. This integrative breakthrough has been accomplished through recognizing the link between science and morality by establishing that the unconscious upgrades moral order. The foremost contribution of this study is in demonstrating that the formal methodology accomplishes the scrutiny of moral orders reducing them to metaphors, which have distinct structural features. This represents a radical progression evolving moral consensus and the legitimacy of a moral education where it is most needed, in psychotherapy and education. The Formal Theory introduces integration to the cultural and moral pluralism by advancing a universal science-based paradigm of moral order, which integrates the cultural and moral orders as complimentary, formally interrelated partial truths bound together in a global Conflict Resolution Process.[22] The formal reconciliation of religions confirms the advantage of the abstraction and universality of the moral unconscious process.

The significance of the unit process therefore goes beyond introducing a purely abstract universal, predictable and quantifiable order into the social sciences; it goes beyond placing behavior within the boundaries of science. It addresses the unresolved grand issue of what is the nature of moral orders. The formal methodology leads to the scientific understanding of moral values and establishes credibility in the rational construction of moral reality. This is the point that needs to be elaborated in this discussion because we are not only in need of a behavioral science but of showing that the science of behavior inherently entails upgrading moral order and identifying moral values.

At the outset we must start by recognizing the experimental validation of the Conflict Resolution Process as abiding by the universal principles of science. This finding is confirmed by the several testable correlations specified by the formulas of the Formal Analysis Profile's ten levels of formal analysis grounded on formulas from the fields of Logic, Mathematics and Physics. The experiments validate these correlations and confirm the formal and scientific structure of the unconscious. The Conflict Resolution Process then may be regarded as validated to represent the universal unconscious mental mechanism automatically striving for social adjustment. Creativity is guided by this conflict resolving dynamic to pursue conflict resolution as a paramount psychic necessity.

Formal reductionism shifts our conceptual perspective from moral fragmentation caused by the arbitrariness of the current phenomenological moral perspective to the acknowledgment of a universal moral unconscious seeking reduction of psychic tension. Aristotle's "Perfect Totality" is ubiquitous, rediscovered as the universal mental operation automatically striving for moral justice manifested in all creativity, from artwork to musical compositions as well as in the religions of the world. The Formal Theory redefines this unit as the science-based moral order underlying all thought, and all symbolic systems. The experimental validation of the process confirms the formal methodology as the proper way to analyze statements of creativity and exacts respect of the intrinsic mental need for moral order as the paramount human instinctual drive. The need may be equated with Aristotle's "ananke" as the innate quest for reduction of psychic tension corresponding to social adjustment.

The morality inspiring formal unconscious differs from the sexually driven and violent conflict generating psychoanalytic definition of the unconscious. The Formal method shifts our attention from the phenomenological focus on content and dogma of moral metaphors to the universal formal structure of all thought process. This shift leads us to address the structure of the creative process as the core challenge for the scientific and moral study of the humanities. Accordingly, we may identify the formal as coinciding with the moral construction of reality and we may detect this order in the ongoing upgrading of religious moral orders as the dialectic restructuring of role relations in the pursuit of equitable Conflict Resolution.

Thus, the formal method rediscovers moral order as inherent in the mental process but it also clarifies that moral orders are formally interrelated samples of power and attitude. Cultural systems predictably and dialectically evolve towards the totally abstract paradigm of a science-based morality or justice. The dialectic integration of moralities yields the unit as the abstract reconceptualization of god and of morality and as the definitive definition of moral order.

We now therefore may admit that moral order originates in the human unconscious and the moral order upgrading function of plays is the projection of an internal process rather than of an external moral order stemming from an omnipotent cosmic authority. At the end of classic tragedies, regularly the emissary of the gods is descended on the stage suspended by a pulley to pronounce the divine verdict, communicating a moral resolution dictated by the gods to the conflicted parties. This apparition of the emissary of the gods combined with the mini apocalypse of moral decisions was designated by Roman thinkers as the "deus ex machina". The Formal Theory attributes this apocalyptic process as emerging from the intrapsychic ideational mental mechanism.

God is not emerging from the external realm but from the mental process. God is not descending from the pulley as an actor delivering a judgment but emerges from every play of ideas as the innate need for conflict resolution predictably fabricating justice. Thus, God is a concrete manifestation of the universal unconscious need for conflict resolution. God is reencountered in all mental plays as the natural outcome underlying the conflict resolution process. It is this unconscious pursuit for meaning or moral order that is manifesting in the metaphor creation stories elicited by the Conflict Analysis Battery. It is this same unconscious process spontaneously shaping the verses of poets, thoughts of philosophers and inspired pronouncements of prophets. It is the unconscious that predictably dictates the systematic organization of ideas. It is the unconscious process that predictably leads to the creation of moral order as justice for all. Morality and Gods are manifestations of the unconscious process. It is this mental process that transforms chaos or conflicts to order or resolutions. The divine wisdom emanates from the dialectic of ideas progressing predictably through the dramatic interplay of roles to yield the needed compromise, the resolution of conflict, the 'lysis' or resolution of tragic plays.

Unlike other machines, the psyche instead of entropically deteriorating the energy propelling it, it transforms this energy by increasing its negative entropy, by creating order. The Psyche equated with the Muses, who transform conflict into verses, music, is now accounted for by science changing a person's attitude upgrading order. Moral order then emerges from the human mental process rather than artfully descending from Olympus or the Heavens. The Greek stage, Olympus, the Judaic Mt. Sinai, the Biblical Ararat are props for the same internal dramatic function projected on the mythic cosmic horizon. Theatrical stages, television screens, and religious temples alike, are pedestals for the celebration of the inner need for moral justice, for the authentication of human insights as external revelations of moral order. Miracles and dramas represent equivalent manifestations of the conflict resolution process. They constitute metaphors defining Gods as the architects of the optimal structuring of power in domestic and in societal relationships.

Finally, science is aware of the formal structure of our unconscious and can retrace mankind's odyssey through conceptualizations of morality, tracking its evolution as significant cultural moral discoveries. The reason psychology has not progressed to science has been its difficulty in understanding the underlying individual and universal need for moral order. The Formal Theory recognizes the universality of this moral structure, equates it to formal and natural science quantifiable equivalent processes, rediscovers the moral significance of the process in the context of psychology and religion and finally integrates these disciplines as the components of the comprehensive Moral Science.

While the human mind has reinvented god and worship in the most isolated primitive cultures, a fact that reflects the universal need of the psyche to bring order in the mental and then in the societal community, it has taken science a long time to understand the psychology of this moral process. Gods have represented the universal need of looking outwardly, projectively, for the anticipated answer be that punishment or grace- one's undoing or blessing by divine grace. It has taken time to understand that gods are figments of our morality inspired imagination. It has been hard to raise our awareness by regarding religions as of time-limited value, and as mere evolving manifestations of our pursuit for moral order. Yet now we can see how gradually religions evolved as humanity has been learning to resolve conflicts more effectively. Mankind devised new religions that resolve conflicts more fairly, less arbitrarily.

Humanity discovered gods of self-restraint and hope instead of aggression and destruction. It discovered gods of cooperation as preferable to gods of antagonism, gods of mutual respect in the East and in the West over primitive gods alienating humans. Mankind has invented self-sacrificing gods inspiring respect and identity formation instead of fostering alienation and resignation. Now finally mankind can circumvent Metaphysics following the physics of the intrapsychic structuring of relations. Mankind can also credit itself for the scientific understanding of the evolving presentations of moral order and spare itself from prostrating itself to authority abusing religious potentates who perpetuate distorted perspectives of justice as god sent and as everlasting. God loving people now can see through the inspirational paradigms of religious metaphors particular power structurings in authority relations. The public must learn to distinguish between dated concrete power structurings and the cherished human right to think correctly and to evolve freely beyond submission to unfair authority models.

The Formal Theory shows how the secret formal nature of the unconscious pursues morality by facilitating the process, by pursuing deliberately conflict resolution in interactions and in dreams, religious metaphors, and in dramatic theatrical performances. The mental process is an emotional experience of energetically loaded ideas; it is forces that motivate us; it is interrelated ideas progressing from conflicts to resolutions. It is a mental roller-coaster that seeks a moral uplifting, relief from suffering through fair power management.

In today's medical model centered psychology, we must acknowledge that this conflict resolution process is also a biological process compelling us to cyclic chemically-driven actions. We must acknowledge that ideas are energy reflecting the chemical substrate of our bloodstreams and of our neural synapses. It is true that when we watch a show and we respond to the energy of a conflict: our hearts accelerate, the adrenaline pours into our system, our breathing is halted, our hands sweat and clutch for support. This state is relieved upon the conclusion of a drama, as a resolution emerges. This happy ending or moral empowerment yields a general sense of tranquility and physical rest. There is something very mechanical and chemical about these mental and physiological transformations that animate T.V. audiences, motivate shoppers, gamblers, stock market investors, religious zealots and sports fans alike. We can explore the chemistry of these systemic ideas, but we may also deal with them as ideational symbolic systems. These systemic ideas are the secret of deviations, of retributions and of resolutions. They are the manifestation of the inner process leading from conflict to resolution.

We must acknowledge that moral order emanates from the unconscious as a pure powerful mental and biological reality. This assumption can free us from both moral dogmatic imperatives and from agnostic chemical reductionism. It is the moral unconscious that has driven humanity and the individual towards improvement of our world. Thus, it is also important to alert humankind that the secret of happiness is not in chemistry controlling our destiny, but in our capacity to interpret metaphors, to facilitate our pursuit of goodness. This capacity is the freedom and the ability to think correctly and to evolve along the optimal management of power.

Phenomenology like the diversity of moral paradigms has divided humanity by constructing a multiplicity of contradictory sacred metaphors and holy causes and partial conceptions of Conflict Resolution both in psychological theory and in versions of metaphysics. By contrast the reductionism of the formal interpretation of metaphors is a methodology that leads to science based moral principles, which reconcile personal and cultural metaphors as formally interrelated conflict resolutions that evolve towards the awareness of the process as more significant than their contents. The formal methodology thus accounts both for the individual moral perceptions and differences and for a universal moral perspective.

The methodological distinction between phenomenology and formal reductionism coincides with the one between adhering to illusions versus opting for science-based reality. Becoming conscious of the partial realities as personal and cultural scenarios of power management particularly as structured ideational systems, as illusions, helps us to realize that reality is beyond the world of illusions. Cultural realities are dramas that we all take too seriously out of fear of venturing forth. Only with a science of behavior can we extricate ourselves from inhabiting metaphorical worlds. We can now grasp the unadulterated truth of the universal sciencebased moral principles that have always inspired creativity. Science respects cultural metaphors. Cultural metaphors will be respected as moral institutions provided, they respect the wider reality of a science based moral and political order.

The public now has a clear choice between staying entranced with dogma inspired drama or exiting the drama like rebellious puppets breaking the strings holding them captive to pursue a more orderly, friendly, and manageable reality. An equivalent process of liberation must be initiated by scientists who themselves are hostages to phenomenological theoretical paradigms that confuse them and render them ineffective by dividing them into contradictory positions.

Bibliography

1. Millon, Theodore, and Everly, G. and Davis, R., How Can Knowledge of Psychopathology Facilitate Psychotherapy Integration? A View from the Personality Disorders. Journal of Psychotherapy Integration, Vol. 3, No. 4, p. 331, (1993).

2. Levis, Albert J., M.D. Conflict Analysis -The Formal Theory of Behavior, A Theory and Its Experimental Validation. Normative Publications Manchester, Vermont (1988).

3. Millon, Theodore, and Everly, G. and Davis, R., How Can Knowledge of Psychopathology Facilitate Psychotherapy Integration? A View from the Personality Disorders. Journal of Psychotherapy Integration, Vol. 3, No. 4, p. 334, (1993).

4. Levis, Albert J., M.D. Conflict Analysis -The Formal Theory of Behavior, A Theory and Its Experimental Validation. Normative Publications Manchester, Vermont, (1988).

5. Levis, Albert J., M.D. Conflict Analysis -The Formal Theory of Behavior, A Theory and Its Experimental Validation. Normative Publications Manchester, Pp. 363-422, Vermont, (1988).

6. Levis, Albert J., M.D. The Clinical Effectiveness of Creativity and Power Management - A Time-limited, Well-structured, Comprehensive Integrated Psychotherapy. Articles, (1996).

7. Lewin, Kurt. Principles of Topological Psychology. New York: McGraw-Hill. (1936).

8. Levis, Albert J., M.D. Conflict Analysis -The Formal Theory of Behavior, A Theory and Its Experimental Validation. Normative Publications Manchester, Pp. 32-35, Vermont, (1988).

9. Spitzer, Robert, M.D. and Michael Sheehy, M.D. "DSM Guiding Principles". Psychiatric Diagnoses, ed. New York: Brunner/Mazel. (1977).

10. Weissman, Myra M., PhD. and John C. Markowitz, M.D. Interpersonal Psychotherapy. Archives of General Psychiatry, Vol. 51, August, (1994).

11. Levis, Albert J., M.D. Conflict Analysis Training. Pp. 11-12, Normative Publications Manchester, Vermont, (1988).

12. Aristotle. The Poetics.

13. Levis, Albert J., M.D. Conflict Analysis -The Formal Theory of Behavior, A Theory and Its Experimental Validation. Normative Publications Manchester, Pp. 19-119. Vermont, (1988).

14. Levis, Albert J., M.D. Conflict Analysis -The Formal Theory of Behavior, A Theory and Its Experimental Validation. Normative Publications Manchester, Pp. 32-38. Vermont, (1988).

15. Levis, Albert J., M.D. Conflict Analysis -The Formal Theory of Behavior, A Theory and Its Experimental Validation. Normative Publications Manchester, Pp. 239-265. Vermont, (1988).

16. Levis, Albert J., M.D. Three Art as Evidence of Science Exhibits. Articles, (1996).

17. Levis, Albert J., M.D. Conflict Analysis Training and Metaphoria Studies Normative Publications Manchester, Vermont, (1988).

18. Levis, Albert J., M.D. Conflict Analysis -The Formal Theory of Behavior, A Theory and Its Experimental Validation. Normative Publications Manchester, Vermont, (1988).

19. Costa, P.T. and McCrae R.R., Personality in Adulthood: A Six Longitudinal Study of Self-reports of Spouse Ratings on the NEO Personality Inventory. Journal of Personality and Social Psychology, 54, 853-863. (1988)

20. Leary, T. Interpersonal Diagnosis of Personality: A Functional Theory and Methodology for Personality Evaluation. New York: Ronald Press, (1957).

21. Levis, Albert J., M.D. The Art To Science Exhibits at The Wilburton Inn. Manchester, Vermont (1996).

22. Levis, Albert J., M.D. The Panels of The Metaphoria Gazebo at The Art To Science Exhibits at The Wilburton Inn. Manchester, Vermont (1996).

23-6 More volumes on the Formal Theory that need to be inserted in bibliography:
Science Stealing the Fire of the Gods, and Healing the World
Creativity and Power Management, two volumes of case studies.

CHAPTER FIVE
MORAL MONOPOLY AN EDUCATIONAL GAME
COMPLETING THE PROGRESSION OF RELIGIONS INTO THE MORAL SCIENCE

Moral Monopoly's game board bridging the humanities and the sciences

<table>
<tr>
<td>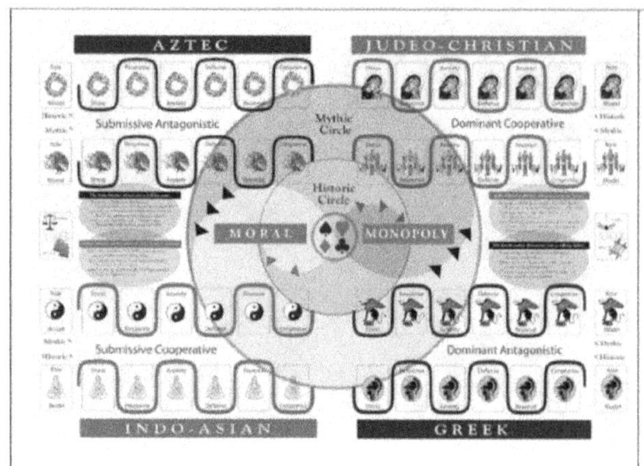
</td>
<td>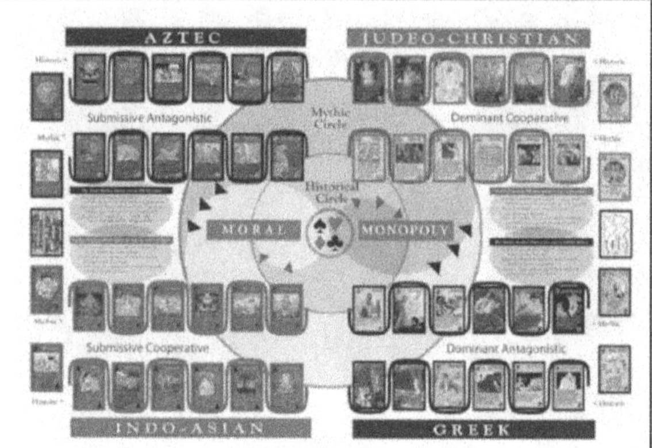
</td>
</tr>
<tr>
<td>THE MORAL SCIENCE INTERPRETES STORIES IDENTIFYING THEM AS HAVING NATURAL SCIENCE DIMENSIONS PARALLEL TO THE DECK OF CARDS: 1. EACH SUIT AS TWO STORIES TRANSFORM CONFLICT ALONG THE SIX ROLE PROCESS 2. CULTURES DISCOVERING THE FOUR RELATIONAL MODALITIES AND 3. FOUR CULTURES EVOLVING ALONG THE FOUR SIGNS SYMBOLIZING IMPROVEMENT IN THE CULTURES' CONFLICT RESOLUTIONS.</td>
<td>MORAL MONOPOLY RETRACES THE HISTORY OF CIVILIZATION AS RELIGIONS PROGRESSING AS DISCOVERIES OF SCIENCE EVOLVING AS MONOPOLIES OF VIRTUE. THE GAME INTEGRATES THEM INTO THE CONTINUUM OF THE TEMPLATE OF THE DECK, CULTURAL STORIES PRESENTING THE ALTERNATIVE WAYS OF RESOLVING CONFLICT IMPROVING THE FAMILY INSTITUTION.</td>
</tr>
</table>

SUB-CHAPTER ONE:
MORALITY GENERATED BY FORMAL THEORY'S UNCONSCIOUS

Religions as complementary discoveries of science

The Formal Theory interprets religions as stories having scientific conflict resolution dimensions: dialectic sequencing of emotions as energetic transformations following the three formal operations to four alternative conflict resolutions. As energy transformations they abide by the two natural science phenomena: syndromal sequences of conflict resolution and the four alternative relational types of conflict resolution.

Religions are psychological phenomena utilizing metaphors in identifying the key concepts of the unit process: They identified the unconscious as divine moral authorities, the syndromal structure of the unconscious as cosmogonies, and the favored sanctified resolution of conflicts as the alternative relational modalities. The Bible celebrated the unconscious creative process as the one God, the syndromal process as Genesis and the optimal conflict resolving relational operations descriptively with the Ten Commandments.

Religions evolved reducing the conflicts of the family identifying the alternative conflict resolutions, as Moral Monopolies. The players of the game examine their progression as discoveries of the types of resolution required in improving the family institution as a continuum of partial and complementary discoveries of the Science of Conflict Resolution. They are seen as monopolies, each identifying very different resolutions in the structure of the family institution and the definition of the divine. The game integrates them into the Moral Science by recognizing them as discoveries of the modalities guided by the innate principles of the unconscious. Science completes the mission of religions for peace in the world.

Formal Theory's methodology: the thought process as syndromes and relational modalities

The problematic issue in understanding religions has been the lack of a distinct object of study and of a methodology for this object's correct conceptual analysis. How can we analyze religions as intelligible measurable entities? The Formal Theory identified the creative process as the object for scientific analysis and introduced physics and relational logic as the method for its analysis. It clarified the thought process as manifested in a story as a totality that can be analyzed both as an energetic, scientific and as a behavioral, moral, emotional conflict resolution mechanism. The Formal Theory recognized the creative process, reflecting the unconscious resolving conflicts as a scientific entity and also as the origin of moral thought. From this analytical perspective, religions, stories of conflict resolution, are examined as scientific moral order phenomena totally devoid of the need for metaphysical revelation and hence not requiring a special type of reasoning for their analysis. The Formal Theory canceled the need for dualism reducing metaphysics to the simplicity of physics, of scientific well tested formulas.

The unconscious as a scientific conflict resolution process, the new moral paradigm

The Formal Theory identifies the unconscious as a natural science process abiding by the laws of two scientific phenomena:

The first phenomenon is the Simple Harmonic Motion.

The unconscious creative process transforms energy, chaos to order as a six-part totality, the mental heartbeat. This physiologic homeostatic phenomenon transforms unpleasant psychic energy of conflict to comforting social adjustment resolution by spontaneously, unconsciously, changing a person's attitude. The unconscious process is an energy transforming mechanism; it is a natural science orderly phenomenon, an energetic quantity generated upon an individual's normative deviation, as this occurs to a pendulum displaced from its rest position. The energy generated through a normative deviation is transformed to social adjustment through an automatic attitude modification. This transformation occurs following three formal attitude changing operations guiding the pendulum oscillations three times to transform conflict's psychic energy to inner meaning and to normative compliance.

The six-role process identified as Stress, Response, Anxiety, Defense, Reversal, and Compromise as three energetic cycles of emotions end with an energetic upgrading experienced as attitude change. The syndrome of emotions leads to a resolution as energy transformed to a higher order, experienced as attitude change in the service of social adjustment. The mind oscillates like the pendulum ball from kinetic energy, behaviors, to dynamic energy, emotions, back and forth three times. Then upon the third oscillation, the energy is upgraded to meaning, attitude change, and the mental oscillations as associations stop upon the individual's resolution of a conflict. Stories end with a moral conclusion. Resolutions occur upon achieving mutual respect as the individual makes peace with the normative reality, the wisdom of the prevailing order, i.e. a religion.

The six-role chain reaction transforms conflict energy to resolution energy:

E conflict to E resolution:

(E= S. F: conflict energy E consists of the product of the individual's normative deviation, S, times her emotional needs, F. Resolution occurs upon the individual attaining the normative adjustment experienced as reduction of the S, the normative deviation.)

We observe this energetic transformation in the fact that stories consist of a six-role state structure that begins with conflict energy and that ends with a moral conclusion, its resolution, upgrading the energy of conflict to the pleasant feeling of the state of rest, moral order as happily ever after, and wisdom upon a satisfactory conclusion. The 'deus ex machina' reflects this mental moral experience occurring upon the conclusion of Greek tragedies.

The second phenomenon is the equilibrial scale.

Moral resolutions vary as a range of choices provided by the science of the equilibrial alternatives illustrated by the three principles involved in the maintenance of balance in the trays of a scale. The mind automatically transforms associations along three alternative pathways in restoring the equilibrium disturbed by a weight on

a tray of the scale; these operations reduce the imbalance as the sense of emotional discomfort. Change as a weight placed on one tray, as conflict, may be offset with three different operations:
The three formal operations restoring the balance of an equilibrial scale are portrayed graphically with vectors within concentric circles.

1. Reciprocity corresponds to adding a weight on the other tray, as reacting to a state of passivity with activities—power or mastery choices on the right field of the circles versus powerlessness or passivity on the left.
2. The opposite relation Negation is portrayed as clockwise vectors corresponding to cooperative versus counterclockwise vectors corresponding to antagonistic behaviors.
   The two formal dichotomies: power and attitude, divide the concentric circles into four quadrants pertaining to the four relational modalities.
3. The third dichotomy: Correlation restores the balance merely by shifting the small weight on the fulcrum corresponding in behavioral terms to transforming alienation to mutual respect. The later operation, correlating, pertains to abstract thinking; it is illustrated by the difference in the size of the concentric circles and ellipses. Mutual respect leads to the reduction of alienation as a reduction of polarization; it corresponds to shifting from an outer tense circle to the inner circle of adjustment to norms.

These operations correspond to alternative ways of resolving conflict along the three relational principles: passivity is balanced by activity, antagonism by cooperation, and alienation by mutual respect.

The formal analysis of diagnostic categories as four relational modalities
The complement of two dichotomies: Reciprocity's passive-active states and Negation's cooperation antagonism lead to four alternative equilibrial paths, the relational modalities, four types of conflict resolution: Dominance and Subordinancy modulated by cooperation and antagonism. The third formal operation pertains to intensity in resolving conflicts, as reflected in the dichotomy of alienation versus mutual respect pertaining to differentiating illness from wellness.

Relational criteria of the four relational modalities

Relational criteria	Subordinancy	Dominance
Cooperation	Submissive cooperation	Dominant cooperation
Antagonism	Submissive antagonism	Dominant antagonism

The Formal Theory interprets religious stories, dogma, by examining them with the traditional approach of interpretation of the creative process as a measurable conflict resolving system with two components: first, a syndromal, energy transforming structure, manifested in the plot of stories structured as a six-role state conflict resolution continuum and second, as attitude modifying formal operations leading to one or a spectrum of the four relational modalities. All religions feature a creation story as the syndrome of conflict resolution. Bible's Genesis, the Greek Cosmogony, the Yin Yang of oriental cultures, the six chakras along one's spine and the seventh on top of one's head are metaphors of the six-part syndromal conflict resolution dialectic of emotions; the science reduces the creative process into a six-part dialectic mechanism leading to resolutions; it reduces the emotional mechanism to a formal energetic transformation.

Religions using dogma identified the alternative modalities of conflict resolution attributing them to a role-model divine authority. The modality is spelled clearly as in the Ten Commandments, a typical set of moral injunctions advocating moderation, cooperation and mutual respect between father and son, God and his faithful. The commandments were identified descriptively in Egypt's Book of the Dead; one qualifies for immortality if the dead man's heart is lighter than a feather. The Buddhist conflict resolution injunctions are identified as four noble truths in dealing with attitudes. The four noble truths identify life as painful; they explain desires as the cause of pain, and the cessation of desires as the means of reduction of conflict, the fourth truth identifies the eightfold path of moderation as enlightenment. Religions' values differ as the spectrum of relational modalities: Judaism promotes power as the Promised Land, identifying the believers as the Chosen people, while Buddhism inspires self-control, suppression of desires, restrain of power along the eightfold path.

Moral Monopoly is a game that retraces the evolution of religions as a progression in clarity on the process as a syndrome, and as a continuum of discoveries of the alternative conflict resolution injunctions. Religions evolved becoming progressively more fair and more abstract. The game shows how religions evolved identifying sequentially the conflict resolution principles of identity, reciprocity, negation and correlation. The matriarchal cultures, the Aztecs and Greece, identified the beginning of the family institution as cruel, blood thirsty, power hungry matriarchal mother earth goddesses. In Greece matriarchy evolved to patriarchy by discovering the principle of reciprocity as mastery, men reversing power with women. Patriarchy evolved to asceticism in India by the culture discovering the principle of negation transforming antagonism to cooperation turning Grecian antagonism to asceticism's cooperation. A new balance of gender power evolved in Judea with monotheism discovering the principle of mutual respect in the father-son relationship transforming Grecian alienation between father and son to mutual respect between man and the father, God, the father-son covenant. The Messianic religions discovered mutual respect between mother and child.

The evolution of religions as discoveries of the formal operations: mastery, cooperation, and mutual respect
Religions evolved from polytheism to monotheism as abstractions of the rational organization of human thinking. All cultures sequentially introduced broader and more abstract conceptualizations improving the family and redefining the divine as increasingly benevolent and universal abstract role model. The divine was ascribed the formal relational attributes of the unconscious process. Theistic moral injunctions identify the optimal approach of relating in the family institution. Religions evolved as normative institutions regulating the gender role relations.

Religions use metaphors, parables, to identify models of conflict resolution. Gods were identified as the creators, like in Genesis. In reality it was the unconscious that wrote the multiple creation stories. The Moral Science understands the origin of morality as the unconscious automatic need to deal with conflicts. So the players of the game analyze cultural stories as syndromes and as modalities that have evolved intuitively as discoveries of the underlying scientific principles. The players analyze the religions to become aware that they are measurable resolutions of conflict with the mission for justice for all as peace on earth.

The game examines the normative institutions evolving progressively as discoveries of the abstract ways of conceptualizing creation by restructuring family relations. The injunctions evolved as the increasingly effective approaches to conflict resolutions in domestic relations. The original cruel cosmogonies evolved to kindness in relations. The progress of faiths reflects the human motivation of making life more manageable by reducing the family institution's conflicts. The problem of religions is that they evolved ascribing qualities of conflict resolution to gods instead of attributing these qualities to the human unconscious. Science reclaims the attributes of the divine for the unconscious and examines religions as normative institutions that promise peace or conflict resolution, but that have been unable to complete their mission.

They discovered the order of emotions intuitively. Wise thinkers as storytellers sensed the conflict resolution structure of creations and attributed it to external moral authorities. Creation stories evolved discovering the syndromal structure of the process and the formal alternative conflict resolutions. Creation stories evolved from the cruel Cosmogony of the Greek gods, to the simplicity of Genesis' six days of creation very close to the dialectic of the six-part conflict resolution process as the formal dialectic of emotions. Story tellers also sensed the moral alternatives in the conduct of life, and chose sets of commandments specifying the optimal ways of relating. Humans discovered metaphorically the abstract principles of conflict resolution: reciprocating with moderation, promoting cooperation, and reducing antagonism; they expressed restrain in dealing with temptations and respect for moral authorities. They evolved the relational alternatives of the emotional language: passivity was turned to activity, negative thinking to positive. Thus, religions identified the principal alternatives in resolving conflicts, the formal operations but as theistically determined.

Religions evolved by charismatic leaders, philosophers advocating the alternative role model types of relating modifying inequities by promoting cooperation instead of antagonism, moderation as passivity rather than activity, etc. The Formal Theory goes a step further, reducing the complexity of dogma as attribution of moral order to the divine authorities by promoting the simplicity of the underlying relational phenomena as scientific formulas pertaining to energy transformation along formally related alternative solutions. The Formal Theory explains the evolution of religions as the public spontaneously gravitating to justice, modifying traditional norms.

The two formulas present the four alternative ways of resolving conflicts as founded on energy transformation along with the principles of power and attitude change. The models of the pendulum and the scale clarify how the mind resolves conflicts as a six-step syndromal process, transforming passivity to activity, antagonism to cooperation, and alienation to mutual respect thus leading to the alternative modalities. The formal analysis of metaphors introduces scientific reductionism that integrates the many world religions as modifications of the belief systems based on the two formulas of the conflict-resolving unconscious shaping human thought and behavior.

- The formulas explain how religions evolved gradually discovering the three formal operations: Matriarchy discovered the concept of a family. Matriarchy began with the conflict of a powerful mother, who feeling threatened by her daughter, to be appeased, required live human sacrifice. This problematic state is exemplified in the Aztec cultures in which the mother kills her daughter as her rival. Protecting his mother, her son, the luminous sun, dismembers his sister, the moon, upon sunrise. Matriarchy discovered the identity operation, the concept of a weight placed on the tray of the scale; this moral tradition structured antagonistic relations between people symbolized in the Mexican national flag as the image of the eagle holding in its talons a dangerous but helpless snake.
- Patriarchy in Greece began with matriarchy as presented in the cosmogony stories. A mother manipulated her son to kill his father, women killing their husbands, men responded to women, reciprocating their cruel behavior by assuming power, mastery, decapitating the menacing Medusa seeking to domesticate Helen of Troy and dramatic heroines as reported in the Homeric Epics, the Iliad and the Odyssey and many Greek tragedies bearing the names of women. The Greek hero Oedipus is portrayed in a life-threatening encounter dealing with the matriarchal Sphinx: Solving the riddle led to the tragic failure of matriarchy, justifying the evolution to patriarchy.
- India responded to men's antagonistic dominance discovering submissive cooperation as the way of dealing with women reflected symbolically with the public revering cows as sacred, with asceticism, the practice of men controlling desire, while women are depicted both as powerful and as loving. Kali, the six-armed woman, goddess of creation and destruction guided her consort Shiva who decapitated her son, Ganesha into restoring life to him. Shiva gave her son the head of an elephant. Shiva is portrayed standing with one foot on top of a child. This might be interpreted as a father figure commanding total power from a cooperating son, but it can also be interpreted as Hinduism's asceticism seeking inner balance, the good person defined as stepping on his inner child. Hinduism evolved to Buddhism as the philosophy of detachment from desires as enlightenment. While women advanced in power through sanctifying sexual freedom, in tantric Thailand, China and Japan reversed the gender role order, evolving norms reducing the power of women by having their feet bound and by defining their role as that of geishas.
- Judea discovered love in the divine, establishing mutual respect between fathers and sons. Men avoided conflicts with women perceived as dangerous temptresses. This religion found love stemming from the One God, identified in alliance with men in the father-son covenant. Thus, the Bible neutralized the power of women. Women accepted social restrains as they perceived fathers loving their sons. Indeed, fathers empowered their sons welcoming them to the temple upon their adolescence as students of the biblical wisdom worshiping the loving divine.
- The Messianic religions identified the counterpart resolution in the family: the mother-son alliance.
- The problem of all the Abrahamic religions today is in the lack of mutual respect between men and women as the cultural norm. These religions progressed in discovering mutual respect between father and son, mother and child but not between mother and father. Intuitively, they discovered the scientific principles, but have not completed the discovery of mutual respect between the genders.

Biblical metaphors as discoveries of science

Religions progressed as psychological theories evolving insightful metaphors underlying theistic moral order. The biblical dogma came very close to identifying the abstract aspects of the thought process:

- The oneness of a divine accounts for causality. The concept of *monotheism* reduced the many explanations represented by alternative divinities, like the 12 gods of Olympus fragmenting the universe into domains of influence. Poseidon ruled the sea, Hades the underworld, and Zeus the earth. The Bible attributed all domains as creations of one god, cause effect simplicity, by corresponding to the discovery of universal scientific causality equivalent to identifying the uniqueness of the principle of the conservation of energy.
- *Genesis* identified the dialectic of the six-role process and the importance of resolutions as the *day of rest*, celebrating the conflict resolution process and its moral outcome respecting the moral value of the seventh day as Sabbath.
- The voice of God was captured by Moses and inscribed on the tablets. *The Ten Commandments* correspond to the principles of conflict resolution: moderation, cooperation, and mutual respect.
- Bible's dogma as Genesis and the Ten Commandments represent metaphors of the underlying scientific unconscious process, but they attribute the features of the creative process to the divine authority instead of ascribing them to the unconscious.
- *The four children of the Haggadah* identified the relational modalities as diagnoses of wellness. The traditional question, 'what is special about this night?' represents the first psychological assessment technique advanced to identify the four types of relating, wellness diagnoses, and introducing the therapeutic interventions as directions on how to respond to each child.
- The Bible introduced the *celebration of the unit of 7* and its multiples as a continuum of formative celebrations. The weekly moral significance was compounded by holy days timed on multiples of seven. Seven weeks after Passover, the exodus from Egypt, the Bible celebrates the delivery of the Ten Commandments. The New Year is celebrated upon the 7th month. Ten days later the new year festivities culminate to Yom Kippur, the day of atonement or introspection as a self-examination on how we manage power and attitude. The faithful confront themselves and make sacrifices, thus assuming responsibility in resolving conflict along the set of divinely determined norms.

Biblical dogma by sanctifying metaphors identified the underlying science of psychology and sociology. Using the authority of a heavenly master amplified the significance of the conflict resolution process introducing to religions the energy of emotional experiences, implicitly transforming energy of personal emotions empowering the moral values of this tradition. Judaic wisdom evolved by Jewish people wandering from culture to culture, from Mesopotamia to Egypt, on the way to the elusive Promised Land, and by returning to Jerusalem next year, empowering people to be united throughout history, wandering around the world yet inspired by the communal elusive spiritual end, the sacredness of justice identified with one God.

Upon encountering Greek reason, and the Olympian pantheon Judaism was modified to Christianity with an anthropomorphic God. The set of new metaphors, the new parables of conflict resolution upgraded Bible's resolving family conflicts with the New Testament. The new version of moral order became the most successful response to the riddles of life as its normative injunctions resolved many of the problematic family role relations issues. Dogma in its variations united people in worshiping the benevolent divine as their role model. The Bible has been the manual of conflict resolving paradigms based on the believability of its metaphors.

Can the Moral Science simply as rational cognitive laws introducing formulas without a core drama inspire the public? The answer is in respecting emotional charges by interpreting creativity as equivalent to the inspirational biblical stories. Thus, reviewing personal and cultural metaphors could be as intense an emotional experience as attending a ritual religious ceremony, as paradigmatic parables.

SUB-CHAPTER TWO: FORMAL ANALYSIS OF THE DECK OF CARDS

In parallel to evolving creation stories revamping norms in family relations, the public explored conflict resolution playing table games about family feuds. Chess is a game of family conflicts with clearly assigned roles for the members of the family as chess pieces. The deck of cards is about conflicts between four families. The system examines family role-relations along formal distinctions between the four suits of the deck. The differences between them are symbolized only in the signs of the suits; the suits may be analyzed as in formal relation to each other reflected by the formal interrelation of the four signs: the spade, the club, the diamond and the heart.

Formal analysis of the signs of the card game

The four suits coexist in a system with the sole difference of signs and colors. The Formal Theory interprets the colors as symbolizing cooperation in red and antagonism in black as pointing to an opposite relationship. Spade and club in black, diamond and heart in red may be viewed as symbolizing the opposites of antagonism and cooperation. We may infer a hierarchical interrelation between the same-colored signs: The spade is an upside-down heart in black, needled by an arrow portraying passivity and antagonism. The club represents the reciprocal state to the needle of the spade: explosion. The subdued spade is passivity versus the club card exploding as an activity state.

Similarly, the diamond as straight lines, symbolizing containment, passivity, while the heart is a symbol of bliss or activity in a reciprocal position to the diamond. Both the diamond and the heart as red denote cooperation. Both spade and diamond reflecting passivity and as opposite in color, reflect antagonism and cooperation. Similarly, the club and the heart both in mastery positions differ in color as the opposites of cooperation and antagonism. While the spade symbolizes conflict as passivity, antagonism, and alienation the heart symbolizes conflict resolution: mastery, cooperation and mutual respect.

We may infer in the symbolism of the signs the continuity of emotional power and attitudinal formally connected states. We may examine these distinctions as corresponding to the formal alternatives of opposites, red and black, and reciprocals, as spade versus club, and diamond versus heart. Thus, the deck of cards brings together in one symbolic system the microcosm of the unconscious relational structurings.

Formal Analysis of the structure of the deck of cards

The card game presents metaphorically the features of the human unconscious as a six-role process, as four relational modalities, and as a system of evolving self-improvements all based on scientific principles:

1. The four suits beginning with family dynamics: king, queen, Jack are followed by the numbered cards. Each suit represents the syndromal unfolding of the six-role conflict resolution process. We divide the numbered cards into two stories, a mythic and a historic one. The mythic is about the culture's conflict and the historic about the conflict's resolution.
2. Each suit leads to a different type of conflict resolution. The deck's four suits correspond to the four relational modalities.
3. The four signs of the card game, spade, club, diamond, and heart are shown to be formally interrelated as the four types of conflictual resolution. The symbols are formally related beginning from the spade as a black, upside down heart that is poked, evolving to the upright red heart. The signs connect the four modalities into a cyclic evolutional dynamic.
4. The two jokers represent the two phenomena of science underlying the orderly game of morality.

The game board as the map of the unconscious

The template of the deck presents the features of the game graphically with eight sine curves providing spaces for the six episodes of eight stories, two concentric circumferences with vectors clarifying the power and attitude dimensions of four conflict resolution modalities. The figures of the signs as modalities are inserted as the symbols of the hours of a clock. They evolve like the hours but diagonally on the template. The evolutional dynamic is like the four seasons of the year rotating sequentially toward optimizing conflict resolution in any relational system. They illustrate the references of periodicity in the cyclic improvement of conflict resolution. The power, attitude and intensity are graphically portrayable variables of the measurable relational operations. The six-role process is an emotional dialectic, the mental heartbeat, driven by the three formal operations as the steering mechanism, the moral compass. The game board is the map of the unconscious creative process determining the individual's relational totality.

The natural science dimensions of the game board

The above features of the game board form a field that has measurable dimensions determined by the two scientific phenomena pertaining to the analysis of the thought process:

- The Simple Harmonic Motion as a six-part pendulum oscillation as a sine curve is the structure of every one of the eight stories. The oscillations represent the emotional heartbeat as the six episodes resolving conflict transforming energy from chaos to order. The process corresponds to motivation as the driving force to reduce psychic tension, conflict energy, displeasure as psychic tension and to increase pleasure as social adjustment.
- The laws of the equilibrial scale as a set of four formal attitude-changing equlibrial operations: I=RNC. divide the board into four quadrants corresponding to the four relational modalities.
- The four relational modality dichotomies are presented graphically as a system of vectors within the concentric circles. The circles' diameter corresponds to power differential as dominance versus subordinancy. Vectors within the circles present the opposites of cooperation as clockwise and antagonism as counterclockwise directions.
- The concentricity of the circles and ellipses allows to indicate the level of intensity reflecting alienation versus mutual respect within a system.

The relational modality distinctions of the normative totality make the game-board into the map of the unconscious: each quadrant corresponds to a culturally distinct relational modality. In the Moral Monopoly game board, the suits placed on the quadrants represent the four religions as discoveries of the four relational modalities.

The game board portrays syndromes and relational modalities

The four syndromal relational alternatives combined with the eight harmonics of the process provide the graphic dimensions of the unconscious. The map helps to retrace the evolution of the religions of the world as a complement of the alternative ways of resolving conflicts. Thus, the game board template introduces three key constructs of the scientific variables of the unconscious thought process:

Table showing continuity in cultural paradigms as relational modalities.

Matriarchy Submissive antagonism	**Judaic Monotheism** Dominant cooperation
Asceticism, Buddhism Submissive cooperation	**Patriarchy** Dominant antagonism

1. **Suits as energy transformation sequences**:

We identify in the composition of each of the eight stories the representation of a family conflict resolution. Each suit as a conflict resolution pattern begins illustrating the family with a face card illustrating the image of the family. The story cards present the episodes of the stories as a process.

In the Moral Monopoly we took the initiative of modifying the suit of 13 cards structure by splitting it into two stories, one from mythic times, the other from historic periods. The two stories have different face cards: The mythic story presents a conflict from culture's mythology; the role model card portrays the image of family relations. The historical story is from the culture's epic, the role model image illustrating the culture's dealing with temptation as in the apple of temptation story. Thus, the new suit has two face cards representing the role models of the suit, followed by two sets of six-role states in the place of the deck's numbered cards. The relation between the two stories mythic and historic represents the culture's own conflict resolution accomplishment.

2. **Four suits as attitude transformation order**

The deck using the distinctions of the equilibrial scale introduces the four signs symbolizing the four alternative ways of resolving conflicts, the relational modalities. The four signs: the spade, club, diamond and heart occupy the four quadrants of the circles of the game board representing the four alternative types of conflict resolution, the relational modalities spelled out in the quadrants.

3. **Periodicity of modalities**

The signs introduce the periodic transformation of relational modalities of conflict resolution choices. The signs represent the predictable evolution, like the seasons of the year, of the unconscious optimization of the conflict resolution process. The signs are indicators of the unconscious cyclic periodicity. The red heart conclusion of one cycle becomes the spade departure for a new cycle of transformations. The sequencing of the four signs, modalities, is itself a periodic phenomenon. The game thus becomes a metaphor of the structure of the syndromal process, and of its four relational modalities, also of the evolution of the modalities of conflict resolution as a system that automatically progresses to self-improvement.

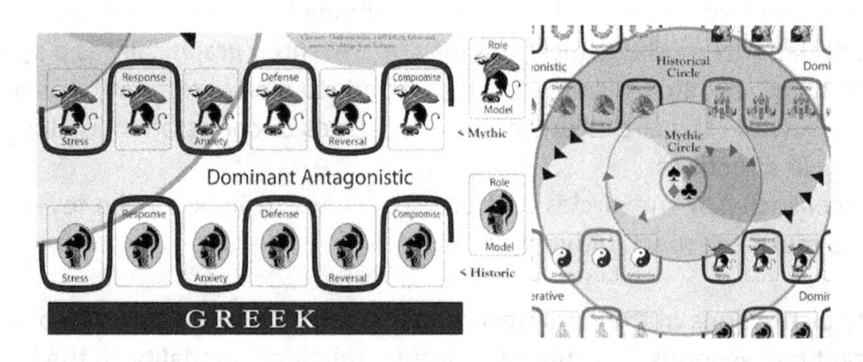

Figure Representation of the three scientific phenomena of the unconscious converge to map the unit conflict resolution process. The image illustrates the six-role state syndrome, the set of the four types of resolutions as the four signs, and the sequencing of the four modalities as the periodicity of self-improvement cycle.

The card game presents the self-improving, self-adjusting unconscious

The story cards on the orderly template of the game board, establish the formal structure of the deck along the three components of the unconscious; they establish the psychological correspondence of stories to the scientific variables of the template and reflect the order provided by the science to the humanities.

Each culture is exemplified by two stories, mythic and historical, as the syndromal six-role structure of stories. Eight stories reflect how religions evolved, improving the family institution from matriarchy to patriarchy, to asceticism and monotheism. The players examine the formal attributes of each cultural story beginning from the Aztec culture, then the Greek, Indian, and Judaic.

The six-role process is inscribed on the board with the names of the six roles to accommodate the cards of eight stories, two from each of the four cultures. Eight sine curves present the cards of each suit as six-role state episodes of stories as conflict resolution sequences. The cards of each suit, the six-role process represent episodes of conflict resolution stories.

Each quadrant represents a different relational modality. The four suits correspond to the designated relational modalities. The suits resolve conflicts along the ascribed relational modality-diagnosis. The four signs with circles and vectors are in the center. The signage of the suits, spade to heart, reflect symbolically incremental effectiveness. The modalities evolve, improving relations in the family along the signage from the black upside-down heart of the spade, to the black explosive club, through the red diamond to the upright red heart.

The compounded image features the four suits dividing the field into four quadrants for each of the four relational modalities, populated now by the stories of the four cultures. These stories are presented as harmonics for each of the cultural stories. The game-board is the self-improving moral unconscious encompassing all religions as an orderly progression improving family relations and redefining the divine. This evolution of modalities is like the periodic seasons of the year evolving from stressful winter to the pleasant harvest time. According to the Formal Theory, religions are integrated as complementary discoveries of the Moral Science, which clarifies the six-role process evolving along the three attitude-changing principles of conflict resolution seeking mastery, cooperation, and mutual respect. The board then, as the map of the unconscious bridges science and psychology into the Moral Science. The game allows the scientific interpretation of religions as metaphors of an organic system of interrelated self-improving conflict resolutions.

SUB-CHAPTER THREE: THE RULES OF THE GAME

The game retraces the history of religions on the scientifically constructed template of the unconscious. It thus integrates the humanities and the sciences.

The players insert each story sequentially following the signs of the card-game, as the conflict resolution progression, almost as a historical path, inserting religions' stories on the four quadrants of the template of the game board of scientific distinctions. The cards for each story are arranged to comply to the two phenomena of the unconscious, the six-role syndromal process and a relational modality in each quadrant. Players then ask a set of questions on the evolution of religions as discoveries of science and as improvements in family relations. They examine cultural stories as a continuum of evolving resolutions along the two phenomena of science: energy and forms.

Examining the cultural stories questioning the premise of the Formal Theory

The game-board is inscribed with labels on the type of conflict resolution as one of four relational modalities; the players read the story cards as a continuum and reflect sequentially the questions on the following distinctions advanced by the game-board:

Are cultural stories resolving conflicts in syndromal sequences of six emotions?

Do the religions resolve conflicts along the four relational modalities ascribed to them inscribed on the template?

Is the conflicts of the mythic story of each culture resolved in the historic story?

Are religions evolving as discoveries of the three principles of conflict resolution, as mastery, cooperation and mutual respect?

Do religions evolving along the discoveries of the modalities of conflict resolution, along the four alternative resolutions improve the family institution?

Do the attributes of the divine figures pertain to the unconscious conflict resolution process?

Can science integrate religions, and complete their mission for peace on earth?

First, players examine the stories as the alternative ways of resolving conflict evolving predictably by improving the family institution. The card game serves as the scientific method allowing the formal integration of religions with each other within the continuum of global developments. The template presents the natural science dimensions integrating the religions as formally interrelated modalities into the Moral Science power field.

Second, the players examine the four key civilizations, placed as stories onto the board game as having the characteristics of the six-role process and of the four modalities of conflict resolution ascribed to them; They identify the suits' relational modality and examine if it complies with the modality assigned to it inscribed on the board. They question the scientific qualities of religions as conflict resolutions as moral monopolies, professing exclusivity of virtue in their normative domains.

Third, players examine the evolution of religions along the four modalities and explore the relational continuity between them as a pattern of transformation. They seek to integrate the cultures displayed into a continuum. They examine the evolution of matriarchy of the Aztec culture, into the patriarchy in Greece, into asceticism in India, then monotheism in the Middle East, itself evolving to Christianity representing the messianic religions.

Players retrace the evolution of religions by examining their scientific and moral parameters and explore the condition necessary for their integration into the scientific and moral psychology, the Moral Science. Are religions evolving improving the family institution and progressing to more abstract understanding of the divine by identifying the operations of the unconscious mechanism?

Finally they examine which is the outstanding formal operation that can integrate religions as moral monopolies into the Moral Science? Is it mutual respect between the embattled genders?

The search is facilitated by identifying the deck of cards as a perfect symbolic system, the calculus of the conflict resolution process, presenting metaphorically and diagrammatically the formal characteristics of the conflict resolution mechanism:

- Each suit of the deck presents the conflict resolution process of one culture as consisting of two stories, one from mythology, the other from the historic times of the religion. Each story has six episodes depicted pictorially and with a statement in the cards.
- Each culture of the game has two role model cards. One depicts the family in a phase of conflict resolution, another card depicts the cultural way of resolving conflict as a choice in the metaphor of dealing with the apple of temptation.
- The four suits of the deck present the four modalities: matriarchy illustrates the submissive antagonistic way of resolving, patriarchy the dominant antagonistic, asceticism the submissive cooperative and monotheism the dominant cooperative modality.
- The signs in formal relation to each other have paradigmatic resolution value, (spade as an upside-down black heart poked by an arrow symbolizing conflict and the red upright heart, its resolution), implying the evolution of religions along the cultural resolution choices as improvements of the family institution. The players identify the cultures, their modalities, their progression to happiness and they also seek to assist them to perfect conflict resolution by identifying the condition integrating them into the Moral Science.

Conclusions from playing the game

Players conclude that religions are normative institutions espousing alternative modalities of conflict resolution. They identify them as moral monopolies, whose norms are defined by the principles of conflict resolution. This rational finding can inspire the public to adopt reason instead of clinging to the traditional divisive formulations based on dogma as incomplete understanding of moral psychology. We need to remember that religions have paved the road to science wisely yet intuitively without founding their beliefs on reason. Because of this lapse they have not been able to complete their mission in delivering peace to the world.

The formal analysis of religions

The distinctions of the game identify the equivalences between the card game and the psychological concepts defining the unconscious. Each suit is the syndromal process, each sign corresponds to a relational modality, and the cyclic sequencing of the four signs represents periodicity in self-improvement. The card game then is validated summing up the mental calculus as the metaphors integrated as a continuum on the formal symbolic system. The integration reflects the unconscious as representing the maturation of the problem solving faculty along the distinctions suggested by the Formal Theory.

The structural analysis of the card game as four modalities is a metaphor reflecting the unconscious in a parallel way of using the story of the Wizard of Oz. The Oz characters as metaphors identify the relational modalities as wellness diagnoses. Each of the four suits corresponds to one relational modality syndrome. The four cultural stories thus represent the scenarios of four respective conflict resolution modalities as the formal alternative ways of resolving conflict. They correspond to the four formal operations of the unconscious presented by the formula of the scale: I=RNC. The modalities adopt the symbolism of the four signs of the card game. Each sign corresponds to one formal operation: identity, reciprocity, etc. and the respective relational modality.

Identity, spade, is an upside-down black heart represents anger held in as resignation: it represents the experience of unresolved conflict. The Aztec matriarchal culture represents the submissive antagonistic modality of relating.	**Mutual Respect:** the red heart represents resolving conflict through the operation of correlation that is mutual respect between partners, here the fathers and sons, the modality of dominant cooperation.
Negation, diamond, a red sign, is experienced as conflict resolved through the operation of Negation of antagonism, the choice of cooperation. The ascetic culture is the submissive cooperative modality.	**Reciprocity** as club, a black inflated upside-down heart, corresponds to conflict resolved by power, mastery, expressing anger. The modality is manifested in the Greek dominant antagonistic culture.

The compatibility of psychology and science is highlighted with the two joker cards, each pertaining to a phenomenon of science. The first joker identifies the pendulum oscillation as a six-role process. The second joker card identifies three operations of the equilibrial scale defined as moderation, cooperation, and mutual respect.

The process of conflict resolution organizes personal and cultural symbolic systems.
It is desirable to validate religions as scientific phenomena so that we can release the public from dogma, while honoring religions as discoveries of natural science laws, the moral values as the principles of the Moral Science. We wish to demystify religions as monopolies but rehabilitate them as the forerunners of psychology as the Moral Science.

The key objective of the Moral Monopoly game is exploring the interpretation of cultural stories and recognizing the evolution of family role relations restructuring gender roles, parental children alliances, sibling rivalries and finally gender relations. The game highlights religions representing metaphors of relational developments as a progression of scientific and moral or conflict resolution discoveries, whose mission for peace in the world may be achieved by them becoming merged into the Moral Science.

With the objectives of validating these premises in mind, the game demystifies religions and demonstrates the moral and scientific nature of the unconscious. We come to realize that the attributes of the divine describe the human psyche, commanding resolutions for the reduction of psychic tension through the social adjustment of the individual.

Playing the game leads to conclusions on the nature of religions.

- The creative process is a scientific conflict resolution phenomenon. The unconscious seeks inner balance.
- Religions as stories are measurable natural science phenomena. The stories' scientific context integrates psychology and morality.
- The game demystifies religions as discoveries of science. The process leads to understanding psychology as the Science of Conflict Resolution and recognizing religions as discoveries of the relational modalities, which can be integrated into the Moral Science.
- The dialectic connection of the episodes of cultural stories reconstructs the six-role process for each of the four suits of the deck of cards.
- Each set of cultural stories is shown to lead to a relational modality diagnosis characteristic of the culture. The game confirms the organization of four cultural resolutions along the four diagnostic categories.
- Eight stories in succession as a continuum are presented in the game as illustrating the historical progression of cultural conflict resolutions improving the family institution.
- The game of cards is a good model of the thesis that stories have dimensions, and that individuals and cultures have evolved as a continuum of discoveries of the alternative ways of resolving conflict. The game deals with religions integrated as partial and complementary discoveries leading progressively to the Science of Conflict Resolution, the Moral Science. The outstanding ethic of power management

advanced by religions is the operation of mutual respect between the genders. The game helps to understand the importance of mutual respect as the necessary requirement for achieving healthy relations experienced as justice and therein as happiness.

- The players learn about the psychology of conflict resolution and religions as complementary discoveries of the science. Religions have evolved empirically, improving family relations. The content of each story displays social strife, conflicts between members of the family. The succession of religions shows cultures ascending a ladder of resolutions to happiness, meaning, and science.
- Evolution is the calculus of self-improving structures. The game provides a template, grid, map of the evolution of emotional competence, a structure of the human unconscious on the nature of the moral equilibrial laws of the unconscious order. The game is a metaphor for an ever-evolving systemic balance. In the template of the unconscious, we detect a built-in dynamic of cyclic transformations upgrading order.

We see the parallels of art and science. The game leads to the reconciliation of psychology and religions based on the scientific interpretation of the metaphors of dogma. The Moral Monopoly game is a directional evolution process retracing cultural determinism as the direction to the redefinable goal to happiness, in the game it is symbolized as the red heart. The heart is a sign portraying an evolving target, the gradient to happiness as the effectiveness of the redefinable conflict resolution.

The game's role in establishing equivalences between biblical dogma and Formal Theory concepts

The modified deck of cards as an equilibrial system	Biblical metaphors or dogma	The Formal Theory's interpretation of metaphors
Suits as two face-colored cards and two six role state episodes of two stories, myths, and history	Genesis as six days and Sabbath	Conflict resolution six-parts process leading to a resolution
Four signs corresponding to the four formal operations	Ten Commandments as principles of moral order	The formal operations as relational modalities
Qualifying the signs as a progression along the four modalities differing in effectiveness of resolutions	The four children of the Haggadah recognizing optimal conflict resolution wise, wicked, dumb, and quiet.	Four relational modalities as syndromes of alternative effectiveness in resolving conflicts
Two jokers	The single divine as predictability of universal justice, order	Two phenomena of science
Winning and losing in the game black to red, spade to heart	Universal order entails rewards and punishments	The map of the unconscious
Pleasure of playing the game	Prayer spiritual gratitude	Motivation through reduction of conflict

SUB-CHAPTER FOUR: FORMAL ANALYSIS OF MORAL MONOPOLY'S CULTURAL STORIES

Eight stories as psychological and sociological measurable phenomena

The game seeks to reconcile cultural stories with the template's two scientific phenomena. The importance of this reconciliation is that it demonstrates the bridging the humanities that is of psychology and religion with the pure sciences, the two scientific phenomena displayed schematically by the distinctions on the board. The game therefore serves to validate the human unconscious conflict resolution process as a scientific mechanism.

This objective is reached by establishing equivalences between the cultural stories and the game board's symbolisms as a system having natural science dimensions. The scientific distinctions of the Formal Theory are new and might seem vague, but they become clear as we illustrate them with the familiar constructs from the game of cards. The first step in the game is studying the game board's scientific distinctions and second, examining the cultural cards as representing scientific phenomena. The equivalences bridge the humanities and the sciences by identifying the features of the deck of cards human dramatic developments as corresponding to the abstract formal distinctions underlying the game board.

The numbered cards correspond to the six syndromal episodes of cultural stories.

The traditional deck's ten numbered cards are revised to 12 cards representing two stories, each with six interrelated episodes. Each card illustrates with an image and text one of the six-roles as an episode of the particular cultural story. The two stories, one from mythology, the other from history of the culture, are deployed as the six episodes of the process; they are accordingly identified with the names of the six role states of the conflict resolution process. Each card accordingly is marked respectively as stress, response, anxiety, defense, reversal, and compromise. Each card features an image and a description of the episode of a story corresponding to the appropriate role state of the six-role process.

Description of the face cards of the cultural suits

The new family cards replacing the King, Queen and Jack with two role model cards: The creation family of each culture and the cultural choices in dealing with temptation.
Instead of three family face cards we distinguish two role model cards: 1. The mythic cycle card illustrates the creation story of each culture juxtaposing the members of the core family role configuration identifying the culture's way of resolving conflicts.
2. The historic cycle introduces the cultural metaphor of an individual dealing with temptation identifying the culture's dealing with temptation, symbolized as the proverbial apple metaphor, as a choice in managing power along the four alternative conflict resolution modalities.

The two role model cards symbolize role model changes from a mythic phase story to a historically recorded phase representing a type of conflict resolution within each culture:
The role model cards are placed on the game board ahead of each of the cultural stories.

The face cards reflecting the relational modalities

The board's relational distinctions of the four card game symbolisms: spade and club, diamond and heart are metaphors of the four formally determined ways of resolving conflict, the four relational modalities indicating the respective diagnoses of the cultural stories. The four symbols of the cards are determined by two relational distinctions: Attitude as cooperation and antagonism, and power as dominance and subordinancy. Two suits marked in red, referring to the heart and diamond, correspond to cooperation; two suits marked in black symbolized as the spade and club refer to the antagonistic cultures. The heart and the club correspond to another distinction: they are the dominant cultures; the diamond and the spade correspond to the submissive cultures. The players identify the correctness of the diagnostic determinations by evaluating the cultural stories.

Formal transformation from the mythic to the historical story

The conflict resolution in each story is illustrated subtly with symbolism corresponding to the insignia of the four traditional suits. The new insignia portray the transformative process into the design of the four cultural stories. The two insignia on each cultural modality differ as pertaining to the mythic and the historical resolutions alluding to a transformation occurring from the mythic to the historical stories of each culture.

- The insignia of the Aztecs, the eagle and the snake in the mythic story cards changes to convey resolution as their merger into the feathered serpent in the historic series.
- Similarly the matriarchal polygamous Sphinx of the mythic Greek stories is transformed to the wise virginal Athena, goddess of the historic era of the Greek culture.
- Hinduism's asceticism is reconciled with the historical Buddhist enlightenment. Yin yang is borrowed from Taoism and introduced as Hinduism's symbolism.
- And the almost mythic Judaic Father-Son Covenant progresses to the historical Virgin and Child alliance.

The first set as mythic role model cards

Four cultures role models as alternative ways of dealing with temptation

Dominant cultures on the right, submissive cultures on the left. Cooperative cultures on the top and antagonistic cultures on the bottom ranks.

The second set as historic role model cards

Cooperative cultures on the bottom and antagonistic cultures on the top ranks.

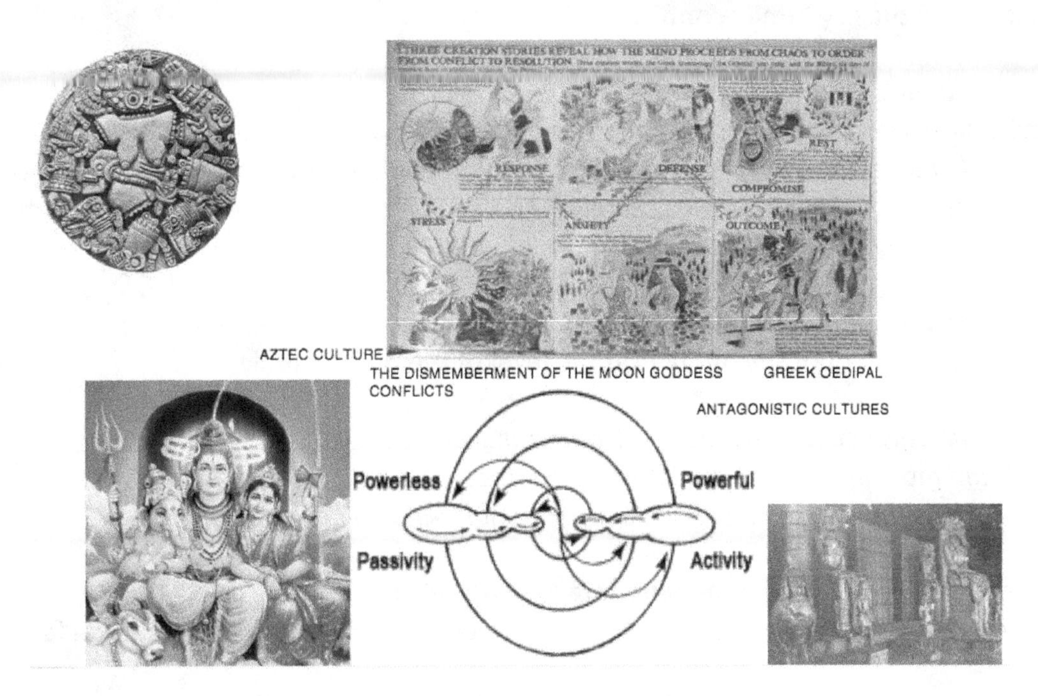

The four cultures are connected dialectically as discoveries of relational operations.

- The family began with matriarchy as the most conflictual state of relationships.
- Greece discovered mastery transforming passivity to activity but remained antagonistic as in matriarchy.
- India discovered passivity, subordinancy, and cooperation as the alternative to dominance and antagonism.
- And Judea discovered transforming alienation to mutual respect pertaining to the father-son covenant. The Judaic religion did not advance mutual respect between the genders.

Evolution of religions by establishing relational continuity

The new card game, unlike the traditional deck of cards, introduces continuity between the four suits as representing a sequence of formally related distinctions. The principles of conflict resolution are demonstrated in uniting the cultures/suits into an evolutionary continuum of moral discoveries manifested in the ongoing increase of trust between partners in the family system. We see this formal relational evolution in the continuity between the Oedipal Greek family of distrusting partners and the Judaic father-son covenant of mothers trusting their husbands and children trusting their fathers.

The four cultures, as the four suits are evaluated as the four modalities of resolving conflict. Cards of the four civilizations placed on the board in the designated positions of power versus powerlessness and cooperative versus antagonistic relating are examined as corresponding to the four formally interrelated signs as a progression to improvements of family relations.

Though cultures might have evolved independently of each other, the game implies continuity as stemming from inner and social forces pressing the mind to complete the continuum of complementary discoveries of science, in order to diminish the pain of psychic and social conflicts. The progression of discoveries has occurred because the human mind needs peace as increments of resolutions both in implementing justice and by increasing meaningfulness. This finding confirms the secrets of morality: mastery, cooperation and mutual respect, the mental dynamic, as coinciding with principles of science.

The four cultures are connected dialectically as discoveries of relational operations.
The evolution of religions establishes relational continuity. Below are sample exchanges between partners in each culture identifying the key family conflict.

1. **Matriarchy's Coatlicue**

Aztecs' Matriarchy illustrates the intense submissive antagonistic pattern in the definition of being a member of that culture. The Aztec calendar warns the public of the impending fifth cycle of destruction of the universe that can only be averted through human live sacrifice. The person must submit to the knife cutting one's heart out to be offered to the bloodthirsty mother Earth.

Coatlicue asks her son Huitzilopochtli, the Sun, to kill his sister, Coyolxauhqui, the Moon, and his siblings, the stars. This was the predicament of the humans at the level of the divine family.

Matriarchy's Coatlicue tells her son: Protect me from your sister, the Moon, Coyolxauhqui.
Coyolxauhqui: I found mom in bed with my husband. Mother is a whore; she only cares about herself.
Son, the sun, Huitzilopochtli: I am the eagle. You are the snake and you are going to die.

2. **Greece illustrates the dominant antagonistic pattern.**

Matriarchy in Greece: Mother Earth asks her son Kronos to use a scythe to kill his tyrannical father, the Sky, Uranus.
Uranus: Another Titan to be thrown into Tartarus, "to Hell with you".
Mother Earth to her son Kronos: Here is a scythe, Go kill your father.
Kronos: I love you mom. I will kill my father and rescue my siblings from Tartarus.

In the Homeric epics Greek men reduced the power of women /matriarchy. The Trojan War ended the reign of Helen, the seductress, and of Clytemnestra her sister, who killed her victorious husband upon his homecoming from the War of Troy. Unfaithful Clytemnestra was murdered by her own children: Orestes and Electra. They killed their mother and thus put an end to matriarchy by restructuring the gender role-relations. Greek men emulating Zeus dominated the family system.

3. **India discovered cooperation of men with women.**

The family relations were restructured in India. Kali asks her son Ganesha to protect her standing on the threshold of her chambers. Siva, her consort, infuriated, beheaded him but then, as Kali pleaded with him, he gave the child the powerful but benevolent head of an elephant. Ganesha as a kid enjoyed playing with a mouse. Siva is depicted stepping on a child. I identify this as the inner child.

Kali: I am the sacred Cow. You will have to respect me and my children, the sacred monkeys.
Siva: I delight dancing on my inner child and feel in harmony with the universe.
Ganesha: I am the loved elephant child. I delight playing with mice.

4. **Judea discovered mutual respect between fathers and sons**

Sarah allowed her husband Abraham to sacrifice their son Isaac to God, the Akedah.

Abraham: God tells me to sacrifice one of my children. Which one of my two wives is willing to offer her child for sacrifice to the almighty?
Sarah: Isaac listen to your father. If he wants you sacrificed, carry the wood.
Isaac: My life is in his mercy. The almighty loves me. I am happy to respond to his calling. I love him with all my heart and soul.

The cultural stories inscribed on the game board as a continuum of discoveries of science
The game-players examine sample vignettes inscribed on the game-board and explore the implication of the statements as representing the evolution of family relations. While the unconscious resolves personal adjustment conflicts complying to the normative standards, religions new moral authorities advanced contradicting normative traditions by restructuring family relations. Cultural leaders pioneered normative changes. Greek Epics advanced mastery of men, patriarchy over matriarchy. India discovered cooperation of men with women promoting asceticism; Buddhism modified it into a philosophy of detachment and enlightenment; Judea modified it by introducing mutual respect between father and son. The Messianic religions promoted mutual respect in the mother-child alliance.

The 'morality game' retraces the religions of the world as discoveries of science corresponding to improvements in family relations, by extension becoming the role models not only of the family relations system, but of all relationships, i.e., the political system. The competitive Greek moral code identified democratic political relations; the cooperative Indian philosophy inspired passive resistance; the authoritarian Islamic values inspired the dictatorial regimes of many Islamic governments.

The science identifies the formal operations of the unconscious completing humanity's Odyssey to social justice. The gender conflicts in the family decreased as the religions of the world discovered civil rights as the alternative equilibrial principles of conflict resolution.

IN DEPTH STUDY OF CULTURES: THE MATRIARCHAL CULTURE

The journey to happiness started with matriarchy, illustrated in the Aztec civilization. The family institution introduces a relational problem, the identity formal operations, marked with the conflicts between mother and daughter. These are dealt with a son protecting his mother by killing his sister and his siblings leading to the submissive antagonistic cultural pattern. Although there was great cruelty manifested in the live sacrifice of opponents or defeated athletes and innocent virgins, this was a great civilization that left behind ruins of magnificent palaces, temples and pyramids on top of which the culture committed live sacrifices to appease the ferocious Coatlicue mother earth, who threatened to deliver the fifth destruction of the universe as inscribed in the Aztec Calendar.

The mythic cycle

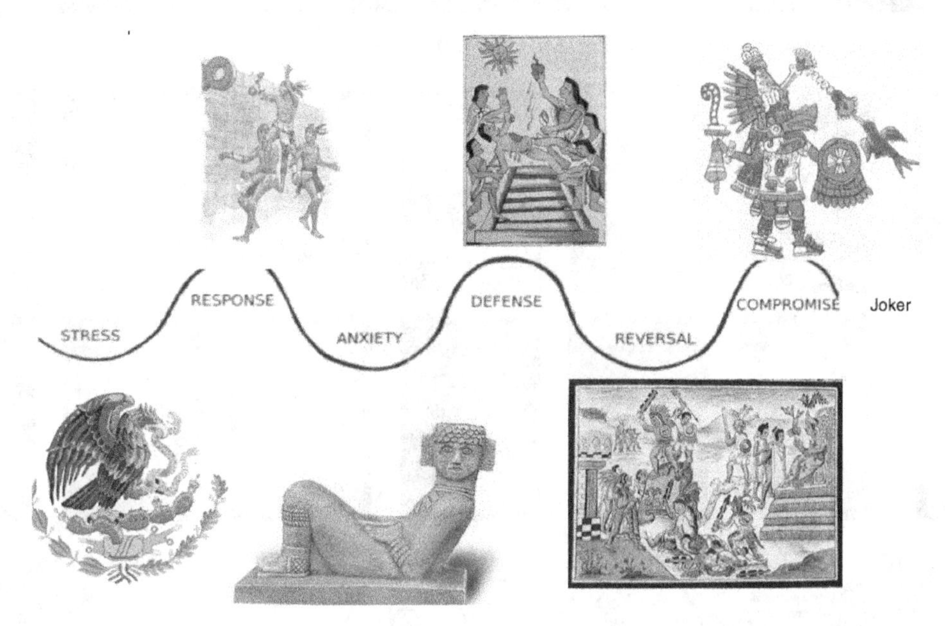

In the second, the historical story of the culture, we follow a resolution: the conversion of the cruel Aztec rituals to the altruism and kindness of Christianity. The virgin mother of Christianity, the forgiving Virgin of Guadeloupe, replaced the cruel goddess.

The cruelty, of the submissive antagonism, was metaphorically captured in the culture's emblematic metaphor of an eagle destroying a helpless snake as the symbolism of the eagle and the snake featured in the Mexican flag. This cultural power structure still manifests in the present times as the reemergence of cruelty in killings occurring in the war of the drug cartels exterminating rivals.

The historic cycle

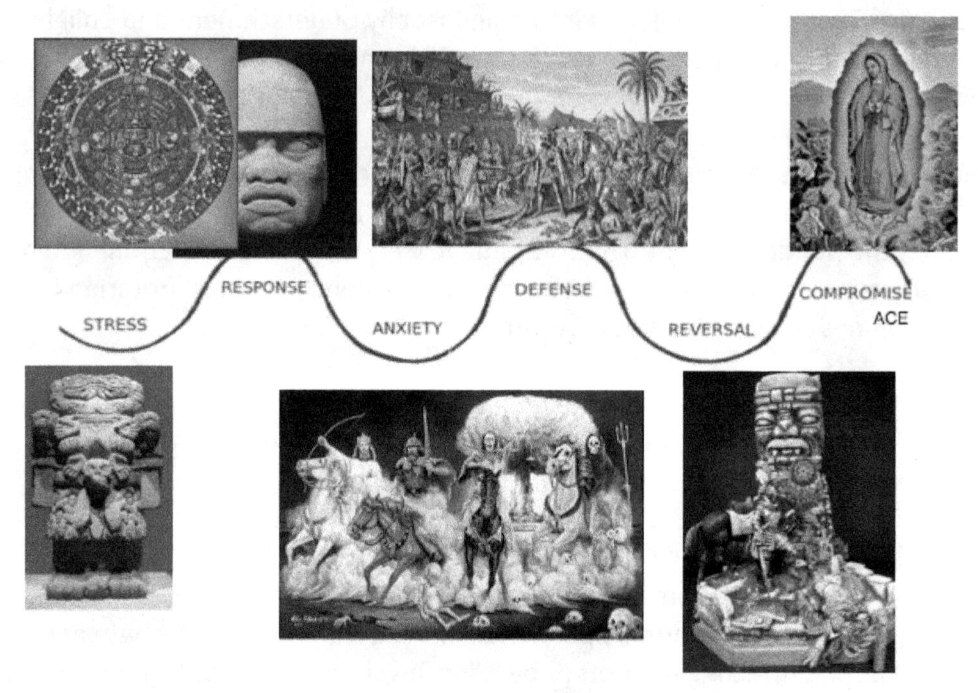

The set of cards of the matriarchal phase

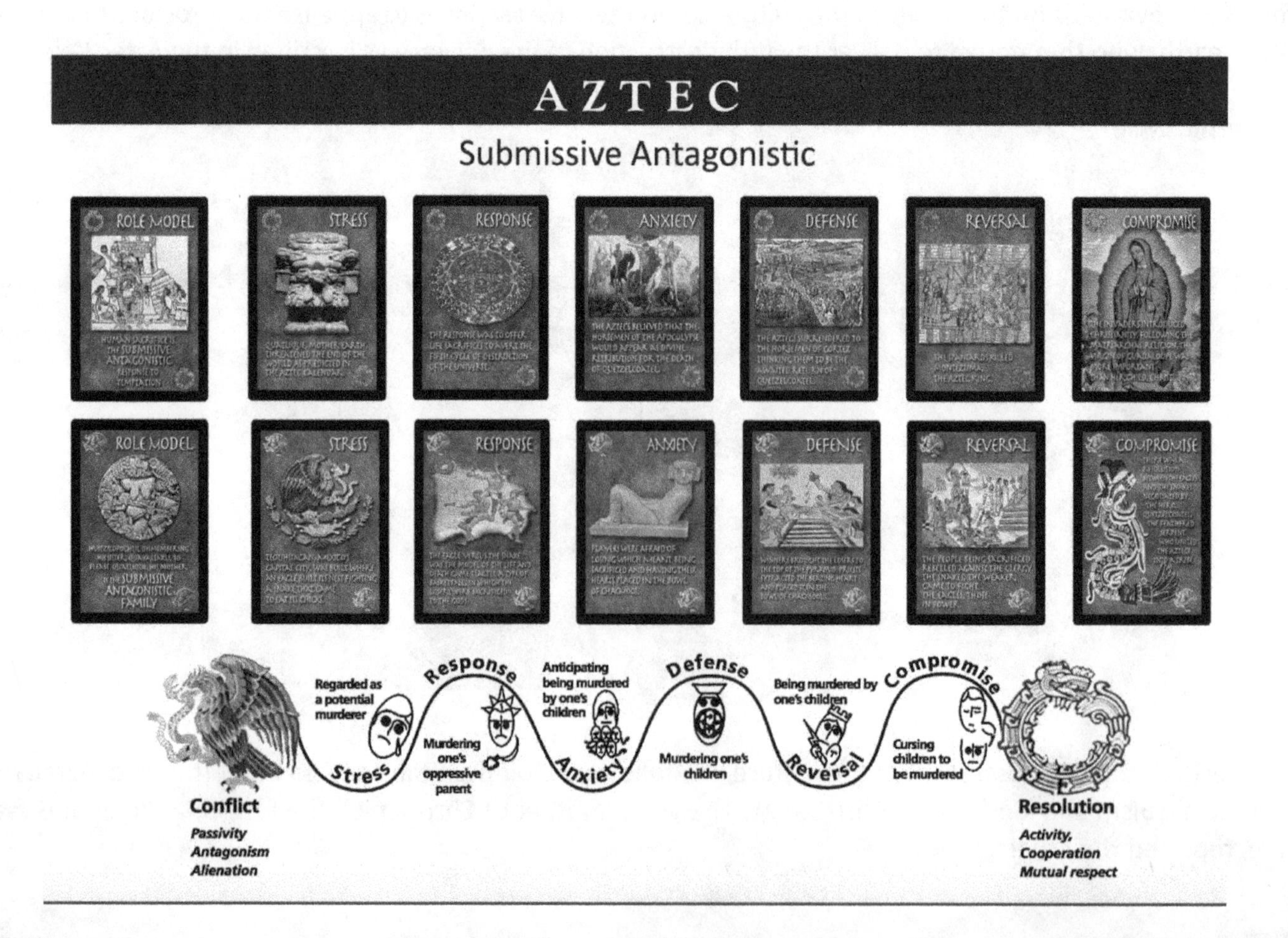

The emotional dialectic of the two cycles of the Aztec cards

Two sets of six cards, retrace the cultural pattern of the oppressive violence between opposing parties as identified in family relations in mythology and explaining the actual historic events that followed Columbus and Cortez invasion of this culture.

Bottom row, mythic story

1. STRESS: The establishment of Tenochtitlan, Mexico's City state, where an eagle built its nest fighting a snake that came to eat its chicks.
2. RESPONSE: The eagle versus the snake became the life and death game of Tlachtli, in which the looser is sacrificed to the gods.
3. ANXIETY: Players were afraid of losing and being sacrificed having their hearts placed on the dish of Chukmool.
4. DEFENSE: The winners were heroes who brought the spoils on top of the pyramid. Priests extracted the beating heart of the sacrificial human and placed it on the dish of Chukmool.
5. REVERSAL: The sacrificial people rebelled like snakes that came to fight the eagles.
6. COMPROMISE: There was a resolution between the eagles and the snakes, the man named Quetzelcoatl, reconciled the opposite factions into feathered serpents.

Top row, historic cycle

1. STRESS: The city state civilizations were established with the fundamental philosophy of the upcoming end of the world as predicted in the Aztec Calendar. The divinity was Coatlicue, mother Earth.
2. RESPONSE: The response to the predicament was to exalt the gods and build monumental cultures symbolized as the Olmec heads and temples on pyramids.
3. ANXIETY: The anticipation was that horsemen, knights of the Aztec Apocalypse, would appear as the divine revelation.
4. DEFENSE: Aztec public welcomed the horsemen of Cortez.
5. REVERSAL: The Spaniards killed the Aztec king, Montezuma, and introduced Christianity, a new religion.
6. COMPROMISE: The Indians modified the Christian religion into one of the Virgin of Guadeloupe, the philosophy of Christianity restructuring the mother child relationship. Christianity offered better resolution in the matriarchal family and made social relations peaceful. The mother figure prevailed over Jesus as a god.

CONTEMPORARY CYCLE

This cultural power structure of submissive antagonism still manifests in the present times as the symbolism of the eagle and the snake featured in the Mexican flag and the reemergence of cruelty in killings occurring in the war of the drug cartels exterminating rivals.

Match the emotions into a pattern:

1. Life is dangerous, kids abused, recruited as cartel agents
2. Be ready to attack, join cartels of violence
3. Anticipate being attacked
4. Kill or escape north.
5. Being caught in the cross fire of the feuding parties versus escaping north of the border.
6. Celebrating death as being reconciled with the culture of violence.

GREECE DEALT WITH MATRIARCHY BY DISCOVERING THE PRINCIPLE OF RECIPROCITY, TURNING PASSIVITY TO ACTIVITY, MEN DOMESTICATING THE FIGHT AND FLIGHT SPHINX-LIKE IDENTITY OF WOMEN.

Greece discovered how to use the principle of mastery in domesticating women. Patriarchy in Greece reversed the matriarchy's cruelty as Perseus decapitated Medusa. The Trojan War was about thousand ships of men retrieving Helen, a run-away wife, and punishing Clytemnestra, a murderous unfaithful wife, as her children, Orestes and Electra, united in killing her and thus putting an end to the reign of mothers. The Odyssey completed the reversal of roles of power in the family as it celebrated a man struggling single-handedly with the dangers of seduction. He was able to resist the power of destructive Sirens, enchanting witches like Circe and Calypso and even a young princess Nausicaa, as he was able to find his way back home to faithful wife Penelope.

Greece, patriarchy responding to matriarchy along the principle of reciprocity

Greece dealt with matriarchy by discovering the principle of reciprocity, turning passivity to activity, men domesticating the fight and flight Sphinx identity of women. Patriarchy in Greece reversed matriarchy's cruelty as Perseus decapitated Medusa. Greece discovered how to use the principle of mastery in domesticating women. The Greek epics of Homer, were about the Trojan War as thousand ships of men retrieving Helen, a run-away wife, and punishing Clytemnestra, a murderous unfaithful wife, as her children, Orestes and Electra, united in killing her and thus putting an end to the reign of mothers.

The Odyssey completed the reversal of roles of power in the family as it celebrated a man struggling single handedly with the dangers of seduction. He was able to resist the power of the destructive Sirens, enchanting witches like Circe and Calypso and even a young princess Nausicaa, as he was able to find his way back home to faithful wife Penelope.

While Greece decapitated the Medusa of matriarchy, men became abusive of power and a woman victim of this antagonistic divided family, transformed into a cow, found shelter in India, where cows are sacred.

Mythic cycle

1. STRESS: Prometheus creator of humans sees them suffering.
2. RESPONSE: He steals the fire of the gods and gives it to the mortals.
3. ANXIETY: He was punished by Zeus tied on a rock and attacked by the eagle nightly.
4. DEFENSE: As a foreteller he informs Zeus' of his predicament; Zeus swallows Metis, like Kronos had eaten the Olympian children.
5. REVERSAL: Zeus thanks Prometheus; he freed him from the rock, and gave him Pandora as a present.
6. COMPROMISE: How do Greeks deal with the woman with the box, the womb and its surprising jewels? They seek to solve the riddle of the Sphinx, dealing with the angry seductresses.

The historic cycle: The Iliad and the Odyssey

1. Stress: Odysseus tempted by the sirens.
2. Response: He restrained himself on the mast of his boat
3. Anxiety: He is afraid of the power of women, sorceresses able to transform men into pigs.
4. Defense: He set limits to the women of the isles distancing himself from them as sorceresses.
5. Reversal: Shipwrecked he found his way home to Ithaca and killed the suitors
6. Compromise: Odysseus was recognized by his loyal wife Penelope resolving the marital conflicts between husbands and wives, aggressive men and unfaithful dangerous women.

GREEK

Dominant Antagonistic

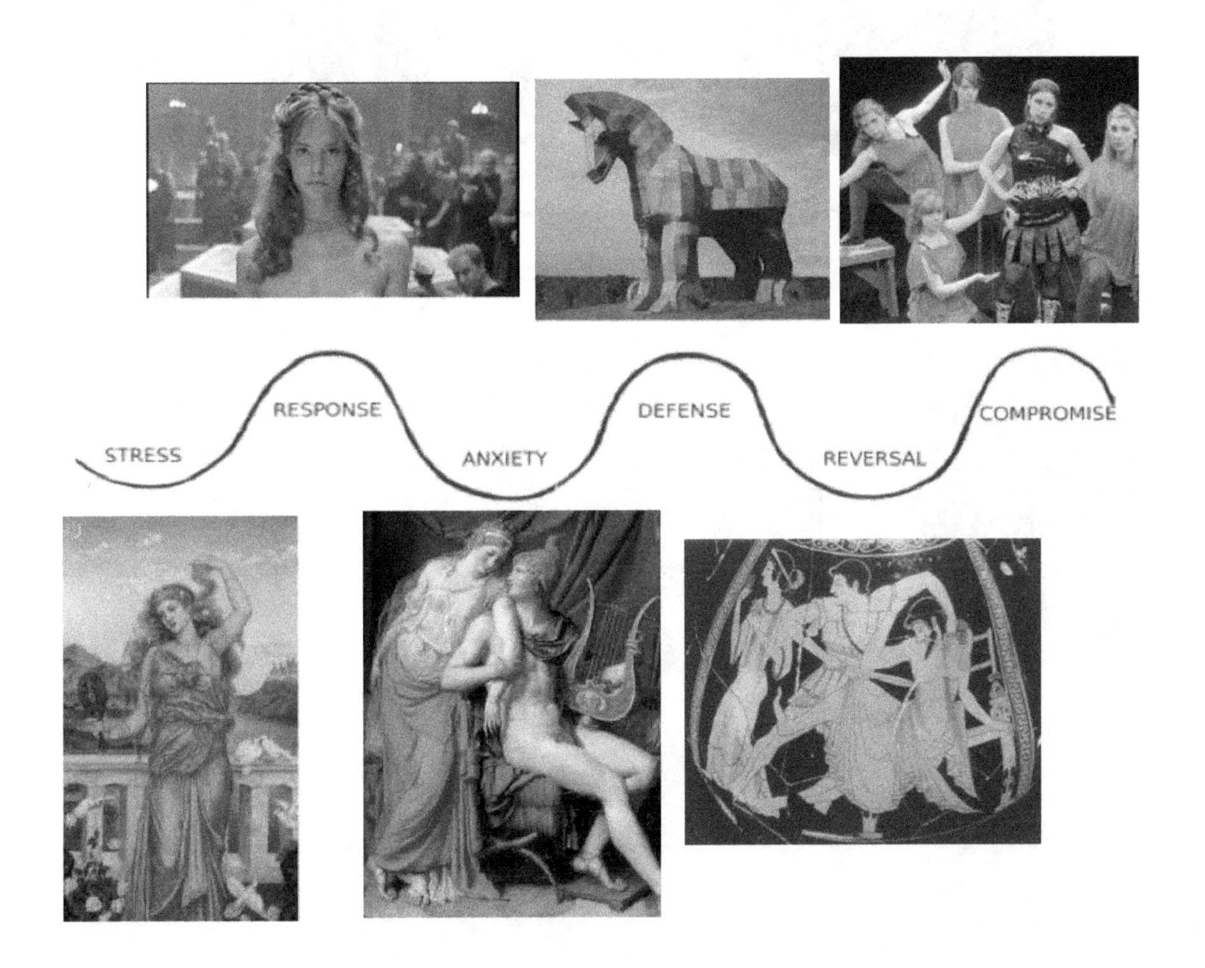

STRESS
RESPONSE
ANXIETY
DEFENSE
REVERSAL
COMPROMISE
www.theoi.com
STRESS
RESPONSE
ANXIETY
DEFENSE
REVERSAL
COMPROMISE

INDIA DISCOVERS COOPERATION AS THE MODE OF RESOLVING CONFLICTS

While Greece decapitated the Medusa of matriarchy, men became abusive of power, Zeus had fifty extramarital relations, antagonizing Hera, his wife on Olympus. Hera transformed Ios, one of his mistresses into a cow. This woman escaped her husband, Argos Panoptes, the man with one hundred eyes, pinned down by Hermes; she run away to found shelter in India, where cows are sacred. Hera placed the eyes of failed Argos on a peacock's tail.

Asceticism in India discovered the importance of cooperation and self-restraint, submissiveness, complemented with respect for women. Siva found this delicate balance standing with one foot on a child, the inner demon of self-ishness. Buddha in the historical phase of the culture furthered the discovery of cooperation and self-restraint with the introduction of mindfulness, meditation, and detachment from worldly hedonistic and materialistic pursuits.

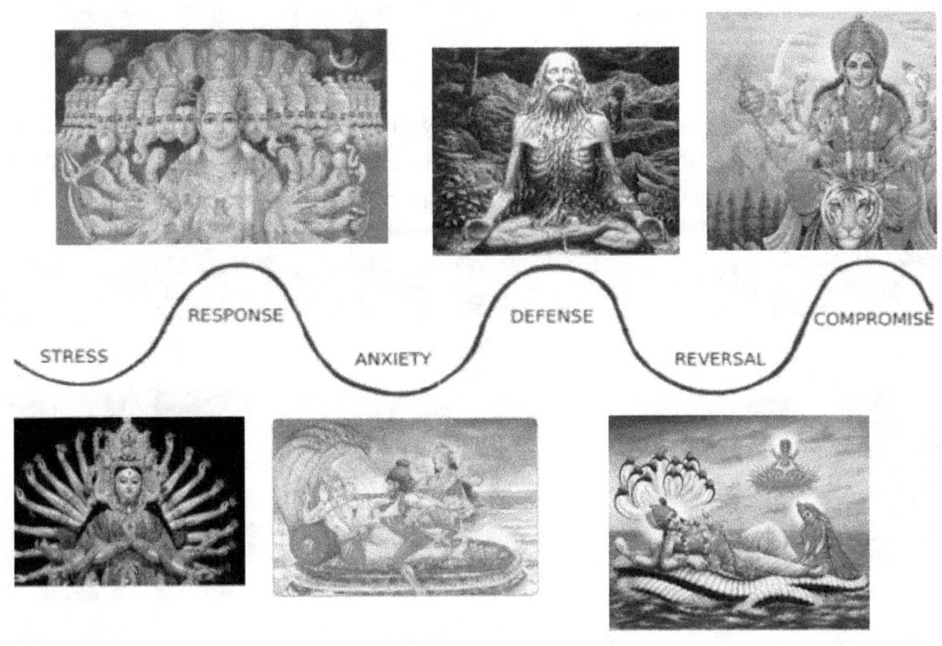

Hinduism's mythic family:

1. Respect for powerful Kali, Lakshmi and Durga.
2. Vishnu is a happy king, with many avatars.
3. He is tested by a demon, who kicks him on the chest.
4. He responds ascetically, with more concern of others than himself: Did you hurt your foot?
5. Wife strokes his feet allowing him to experience release of anger and hurt.
6. Vishnu is in peace with many gifts as emotional skills; he is empowered like riding on a ti

Buddhism, historical phase

1. Gautama's mother died upon his birth; he was loved as a child perceived as a prince. He was sheltered from pain and exalted at a young age.
2. Eventually he was married and had a child of his own.
3. He recognized suffering and was anxious about life's meaning. He left home, cut his hair and changed his royal attire.
4. He pursued asceticism choosing detachment, deprivation and starvation.
5. He almost died from starvation but before collapsing he found enlightenment under the Bodhi tree. He discovered moderation as the alternative to asceticism.
6. Buddha delivered a sermon to other yogis about enlightenment as moderation in the place of ascetic traditions. Offering this new type of resolution he became the philosopher of compassion and moderation.

Exporting Buddhism to China and Japan

Women empowered sought sexual liberation as tantric spirituality. Men in China were afraid of women's power as exquisite desirable, irresistible creatures. They responded to this extreme behavior by restraining women's mobility by handicapping the growth of their feet. Men reclaimed supreme authority identifying with dragons.

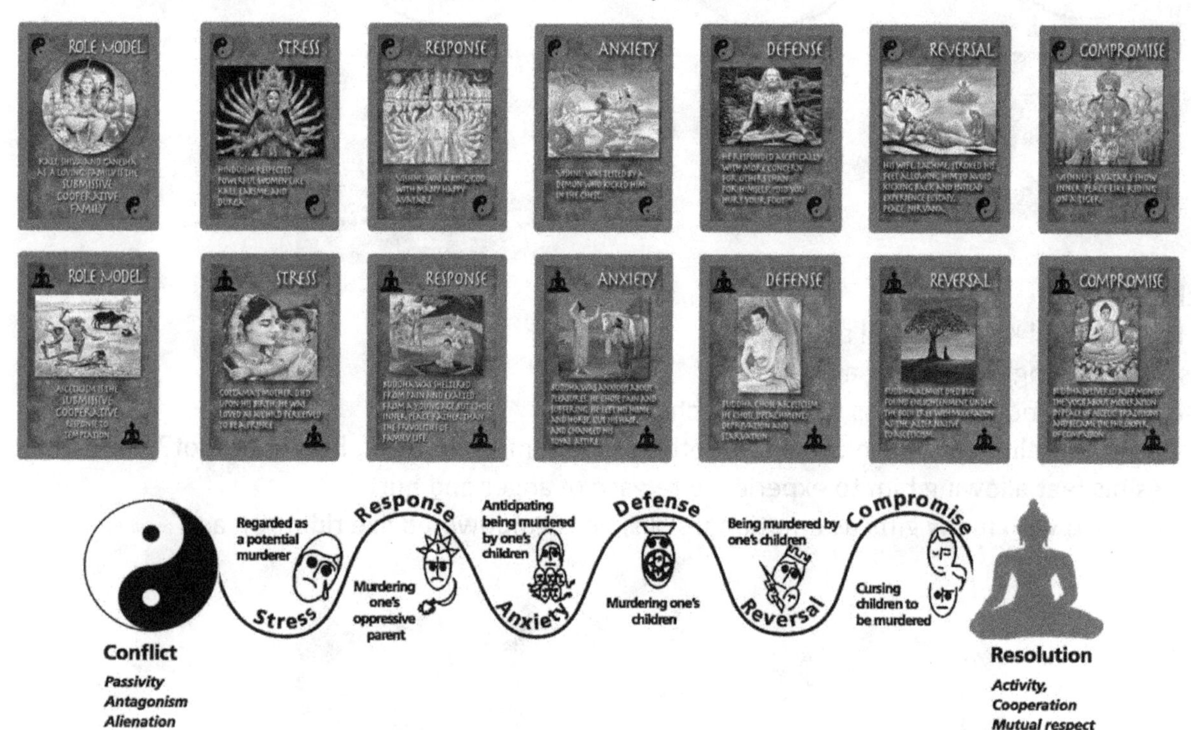

Judaism discovered the operation of mutual respect between father and son

Women, emboldened like Ishtar in Mesopotamia sought power over men. Gilgamesh wanted mutual respect, the assurance of lifetime commitment and entered into a war with women. Judaism moved a step further from the polarization of the genders by identifying God as the loving partner in dealing with women. They conceived of God as the creator of the universe. With doubt on women and trust in an immortal spirit Judea discovered mutual respect in the father-son covenant relationship. The god's love neutralized the power of women. Love came from the benevolent father. Women were inspired by the love of God reconciling fathers and sons. They were give different roles. They were not allowed to pray with men. They were proud to sacrifice their own needs serving a unified loving family.

THE MESSIANIC RELIGIONS DISCOVERED MUTUAL RESPECT BETWEEN MOTHER AND CHILD

The messianic religions identified the counterpoint resolution to the father-son covenant. They applied mutual respect to the mother-child alliances. Islam pursued the alternative to Christian self-denial, by evolving the cult of domination seeking total submission of the faithful. Mohammad modeled the authoritarian leadership as militancy of faith saving the world.

JUDEO - CHRISTIAN

Dominant Cooperative

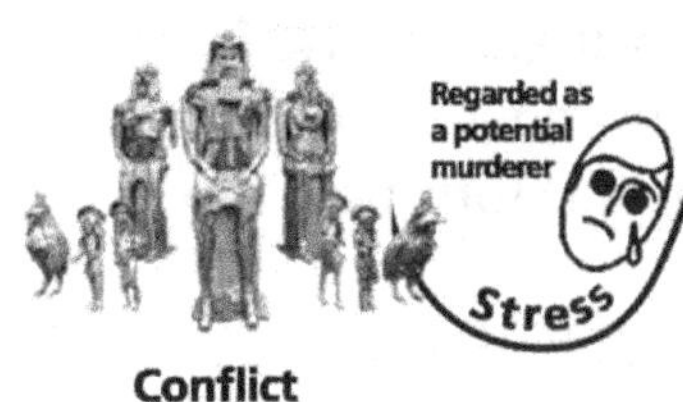

Response
Anticipating being murdered by one's children
Murdering one's oppressive parent
Anxiety

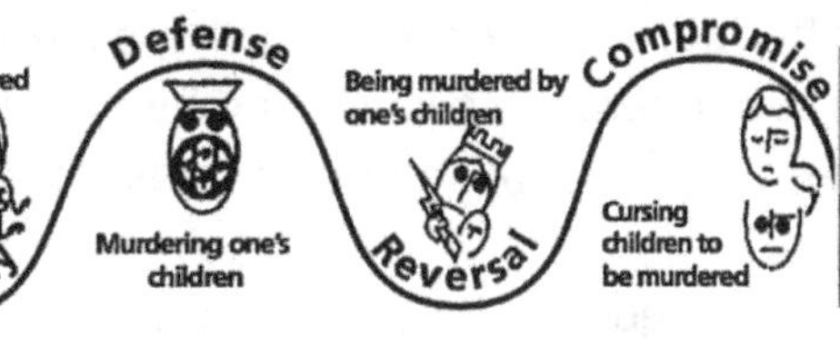

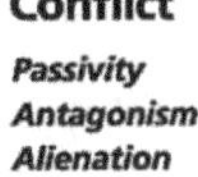

Conflict

Passivity
Antagonism
Alienation

Resolution

Activity,
Cooperation
Mutual respect

Judea discovers correlative relating, mutual respect between father and son, as the condition of conflict resolution

Judaism moved a step further from the ascetic polarization of the genders and of the caste social order, by identifying God as the loving creator of the universe. Judaism discovered the operation of correlation as shifting from alienation to mutual respect. This relating between father and son was the optimal mode of resolving conflicts. This choice neutralized the power of women. Love came from the benevolent father. Women were sequestered from men; not allowed to pray with men. They were proud to sacrifice their own needs serving a unified family.

STRESS: The Gilgamesh epic is about a prince perceiving a princess as unfaithful. Ishtar offered love to Gilgamesh. He rejected her advances wanting loyalty, a lifetime commitment. A war ensued. He fought women assisted by Enkidu, a super hero, who was killed by the women. Gilgamesh pursued immortality of his companion. This story inspired Bible's Adam and Eve distrust of women, while the Enkidu story inspired the father son bonding.
RESPONSE Abraham identified this bond in the father son covenant. Moses recorded this love in the 10 Commandments and the five books of the Bible. During Passover, reenacting the
Exodus, the prayers celebrate the flight from Egypt with unleavened bread. Jews were assisted by God with the 10 calamities inflicted on the Egyptians and the miracle of their crossing the sea.
ANXIETY Jews felt love as the chosen people and those to be given the promised land. This love of God reduced the need for love from women and improved family relations.
DEFENSE Abraham tested his wife's love with the sacrifice of Isaac. This test established for boys the love for God as more important than love from women, mothers and wives.
REVERSAL Upon the day of atonement the faithful examine their personal relationship with God. The day generates introspection, humility and compassion.
COMPROMISE Jews having departed from Egypt celebrate God's love every seven days, every seven weeks, every several months, always expecting the Messiah to heal the world. The end of the reading of the Bible is celebrated as the highlight of enlightenment confirming the loving bond between people and the divine.

The messianic religions discovered mutual respect between mother and child. They identified the counterpoint resolution to the father son-covenant. They applied sacredness as mutual respect to the mother-child alliance. Islam pursued the alternative to Christian self-denial; it established the cult of submission allowing domination by men in spiritual authority. The pursuit of power by leaders and total submission of the faithful, represented authoritarian rule as the societal norm. Clergy pursued militancy of faith in the name of the prophet, justified in saving the world on the name of God.

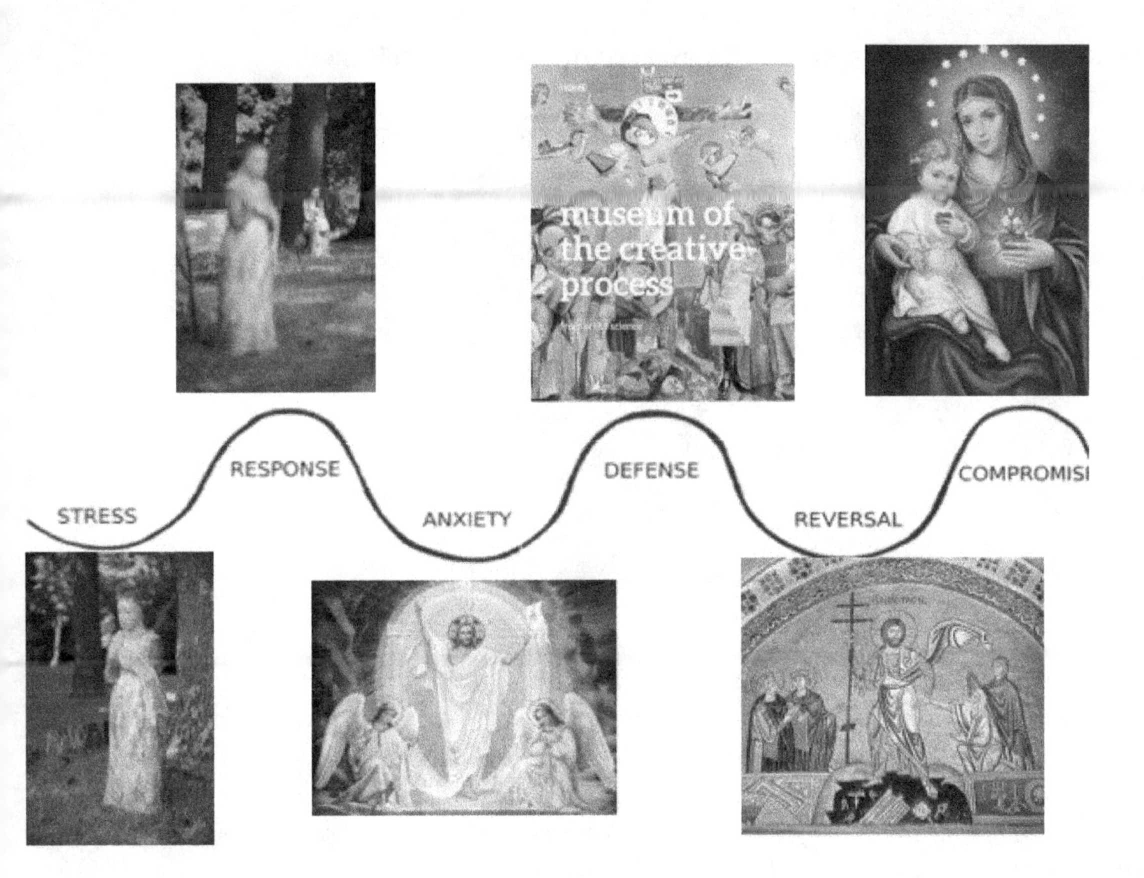

Historic Times

1.STRESS: Women become brave under Hellenistic influence, fact that inspired antagonism. Women claimed that 'Girls are as good as boys'.
2. RESPONSE: Some women got sexually active and became pregnant. The Laws prescribed punishment for such behavior. Women claimed 'God is not with the father and the son but with the mother and the child'.
3. ANXIETY: Jesus offered support to the transgressive women advancing moral justice as respectful of women.
4. DEFENSE: Jesus exemplified love as compassionate self-sacrifice, which became the new moral norm. His crucifixion empowered his philosophy, which spread posthumously.
5. REVERSAL: Resurrection represented the vindication of Jesus sacrifice. Jesus was celebrated as the God of the New Testament.
6. COMPROMISE: Judaism was modified by the two messianic religions exulting the mother child relationship celebrating the empowerment of women as the mother-child, crescent star, alliances.

Formal variations of the Abrahamic ways of resolving

1. THE prophet's beginning as a hero, partner of a widow
2. Leading a revolution, multiple wars
3. Resistance to conversion infidels need help to see the truth
4. Converting others with a war, strict codes for behaviors no alcohol allowed.
5. Criticism and setbacks;
6. A jihad, militarily action to overcome criticism and establish a great culture with an authoritarian mentality. Men may marry several wives

The definition of the inequities in the Abrahamic Family, as a sculpture by Judith Brown.

The sculpture is identified as the Abrahamic family consisting of three Patriarchs, four diminutive Matriarchs, and two Horus birds, the concubines. The sculpture by Judith Brown stands in front of the altar for the sacrifice of Isaac, as Abraham's test of the loyalty of his wives and sons. This image illustrates the best family power distribution improving the family system for the times of Abraham, but this constellation also presents the troubling inequity between the genders and the need for the reconciliation of religions and science by resolving the current problem by introducing mutual respect into the gender relations.

Formal variations of the Abrahamic ways of resolving

It is the Abrahamic religions that today remind us that religions are dangerous in their self-righteousness as beliefs that arbitrarily sanctify norms on the name of god rather on the name of reason. Norms of the Abrahamic religions differ. The Christian and Islamic religions are diametrically opposite. Just consider the different values and lifestyles of the Pope and the Sultan/Caliph: the Pope is celibate, asexual, with multiple self-restrains, modesty, care-giving, self-sacrifice, advocating respect for life and use of sexuality only for procreation.

The Sultan enjoyed sexuality for sheer pleasure, had a harem of sex slaves managed by his own mother, sterilizing his male servants into eunuchs. The Sultan was super powerful. He was at the same time the political ruler, the spiritual leader and a militant jihadist promoting expansiveness of the faith as a virtuous endeavor. This dominant model does not allow any criticism; it suppresses freedom of speech and free press. Beliefs in the core values is reinforced with prayers five times a day.

Many Islamic regimes do not separate the rule of church and state, laws suppress women's rights, they enforce the Sharia type of justice. Infidels questioning the authority of the prophet may be killed. This happened with the author of Satanic Verses, Salman Rushdie, and it was the end of the French humorists. The role model of the caliphate is assumed by the Ayatollahs of Iran, committed in destroying their enemies with nuclear devices. Mohammad said there will not be another prophet after me. The problem is that there were two prophets before him.

The current conflict for political moral domination has resulted to the contemporary wars between the United States and Islamic orthodoxy movements. This war is targeting authoritarian power structure in politics and in religions. It has led to activate Islam's internal conflicts and external restlessness. The image of the Abrahamic family in front of the burning twin towers highlights the intensity of the conflicts between the monotheistic religions founded on their alternative ways of resolving conflicts.

The Abrahamic prophets' relational modalities

	Christ	Moses	Mohammad
Power key words	Turn the other cheek	Tolerance Justice merciful	Sharia
Choice role model behavior	Crucified	Exodus, diaspora	Jihad
Temples	Churches with belfries	Synagogues	Mosques with minarets and muezzins
Political structure	Pope, cardinals	Synod	Caliphates
Frequency of prayers	1/week	Daily	5x daily
Sexual behaviors	Asexuality	Monogamy	Polygamy
Prayer	Don't lead us to temptation	Adonai Olam Love of the creator	

SUB-CHAPTER FIVE: PREPARATION TO PLAY THE GAME, LEARNING ABOUT THE PREVALENCE OF A RELATIONAL PATTERN IN THE GREEK CULTURE

The preparation of the players consists in educating them on the concepts of the Formal Theory of Behavior. They are briefed about the concept of the creative process reflecting the unconscious manifested in the six-role process structure of stories and their conflict resolution function: four relational modality wellness diagnoses. They are instructed on the two phenomena of science underlying the process and making it measurable. The first is the Simple Harmonic Motion, SHM, an energetic transformation upgrading order. The second is the three equilibrial operations of the scale restoring the balance of the trays after a weight has been placed on one of them. This knowledge is exemplified as a laboratory exercise by dealing with a card arrangement challenge. The players as a group are given the task of identifying the key concepts of the Formal Theory in studying stories from the Greek mythology.

The challenge consists in players organizing the set of cards that pertain to four stories from the Greek culture. These cards do not have the six-role indicators of the conflict resolution process. The players identify the six-role sequencing of the cards organizing the stories meaningfully to conflict resolutions along alternative modalities. The key conflict throughout the stories highlights the ongoing problem of Greek culture's gender relations, conflicts and resolutions.

They detect the six-role pattern across in each story and how it evolves along alternative relational modality across the chronological succession of the stories. The players are requested to study the concepts of the game by 1. Identifying in each story the six-role states as a conflict resolution sequence and 2, Identifying relational modality changes.

Below we list the stories from the Greek culture and the respective conflict resolutions as a continuum of resolutions with normative changes.

The Greek Cosmogony reflects a dominant antagonistic modality pattern repeated in several generations of the Greek cosmogony. It began with Mother Earth asking her son Kronos to use a scythe to kill his tyrannical father, Uranus, the Sky. The antagonistic pattern was repeated in many stories but we see its transformation into resolutions, such as the confirmation of the marital vows, the reconciliation of the feuding Greek city states unified by the Aristotelian concepts promoted by Alexander the Great, and how these concepts unified the cultures of the world.

The first story: Zeus versus Hera

1. Stress: Hera and Zeus relationship beginning with the conflict between the Argive fifty brides killing forty-nine grooms, the initial story of the Mycenaean culture.
2. Response: Afraid of women, afraid of his angry wife, Hera, Zeus seeks pleasures seducing loving women. He is unfaithful to Hera with pretty Ios.
3. Anxiety: Hera punishes Zeus by transforming Ios into a cow and giving her husband Argos, 100 eyes to watch over her. He became Argos Panoptes.
4. Defense: Hermes with his music puts Argos' eyes to sleep and his wife, Ios, escapes.
5. Reversal: Ios the cow escapes over Bosporus, means Jump of the Cow, to India, where cows are sacred.
6. Compromise: Hera angered at Argos transformed him into a peacock, and placed his hundred eyes onto his tail. The man is proud of his beauty, while being paranoid about unfaithful women. Greek stereotype: aggressive lovers become possessive jealous husbands, guardians of potentially unfaithful wives.

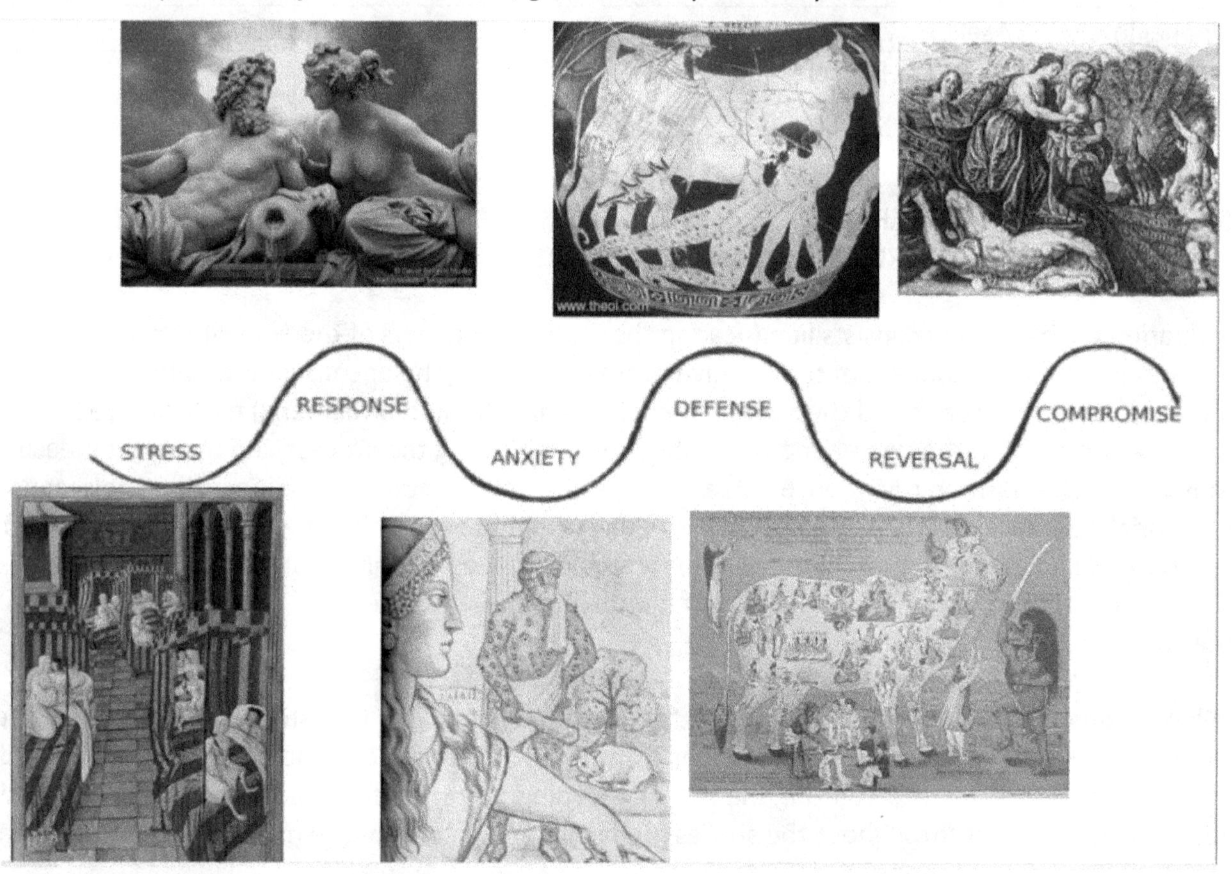

The second story: The Iliad, Helen versus Menelaus

The Iliad is about the War of Troy illustrating the fundamental conflict between spouses: Helen espoused the vows, but then broke them escaping with Paris, a young lover. Her sister Clytemnestra killed her husband, Agamemnon, the victorious leader of the Trojan War upon his homecoming. Orestes and Electra killed their mother.
Stress: Helen of Troy is a woman with many lovers.
Response: So Greek men gave her a choice to marry one of them; Helen married Menelaus taking the vows.
Anxiety: She broke her vows, she was unfaithful with Paris. She behaved like the matriarchal Sphinx, the fight and flight woman.
Defense: Greeks captured Helen upon the War of Troy by misleading the Trojans with the Trojan Horse.
Reversal:Agamemnon is punished by his wife, who killed him upon his homecoming assisted by her lover, Aegisthus.
Compromise: Clytemnestra was killed by her children, Electra and Orestes, a development, which ended Matriarchy, but celebrated the respect of the marital vows.

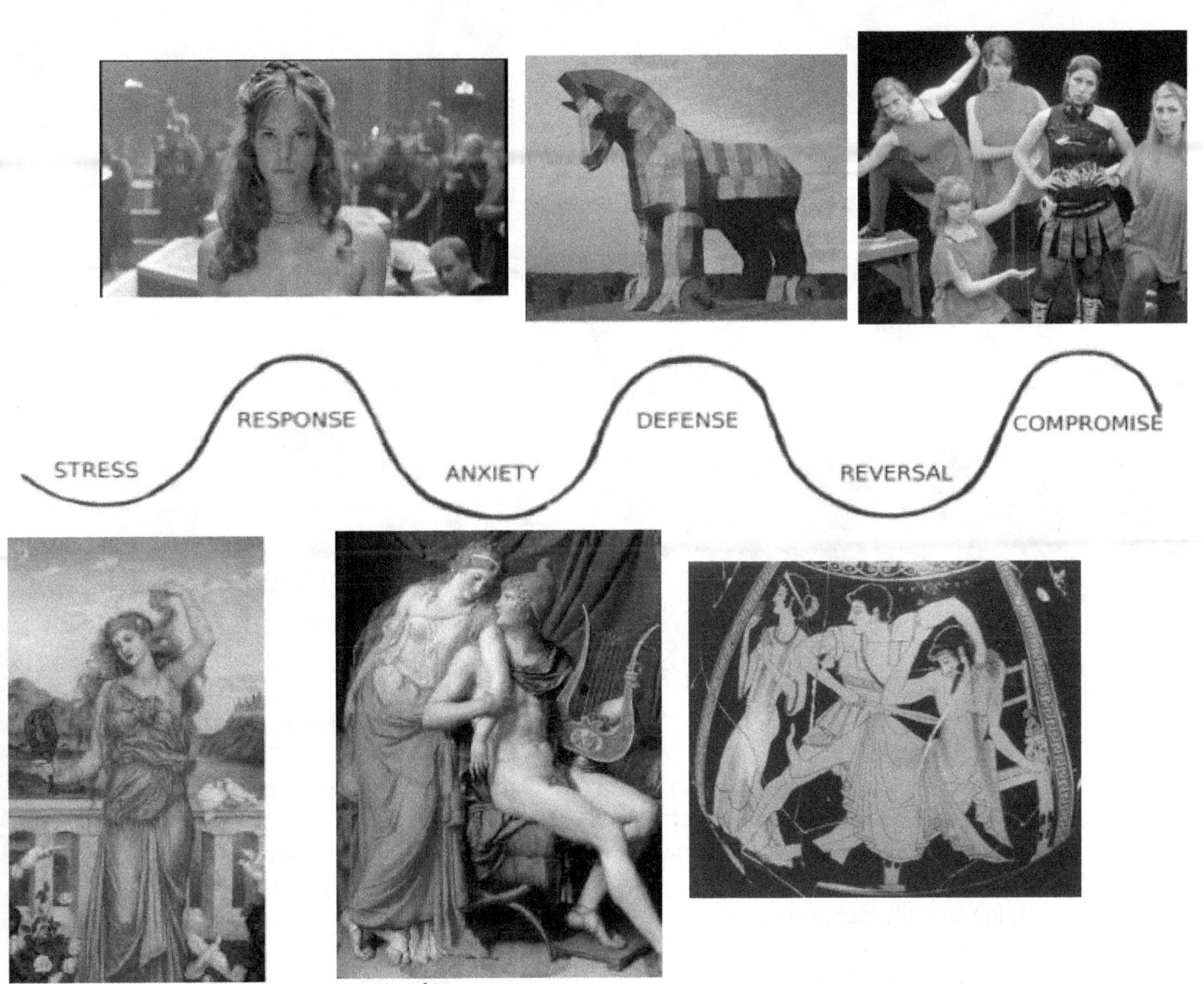

The third story: Odysseus versus Penelope

The Odyssey, Odysseus dealing with the Sirens of the Greek islands, and Penelope fending off the suitors, leads to a happy ending the celebration of the vows.

The fourth story: The Peloponnesian War, Aristotle versus Lysistrata

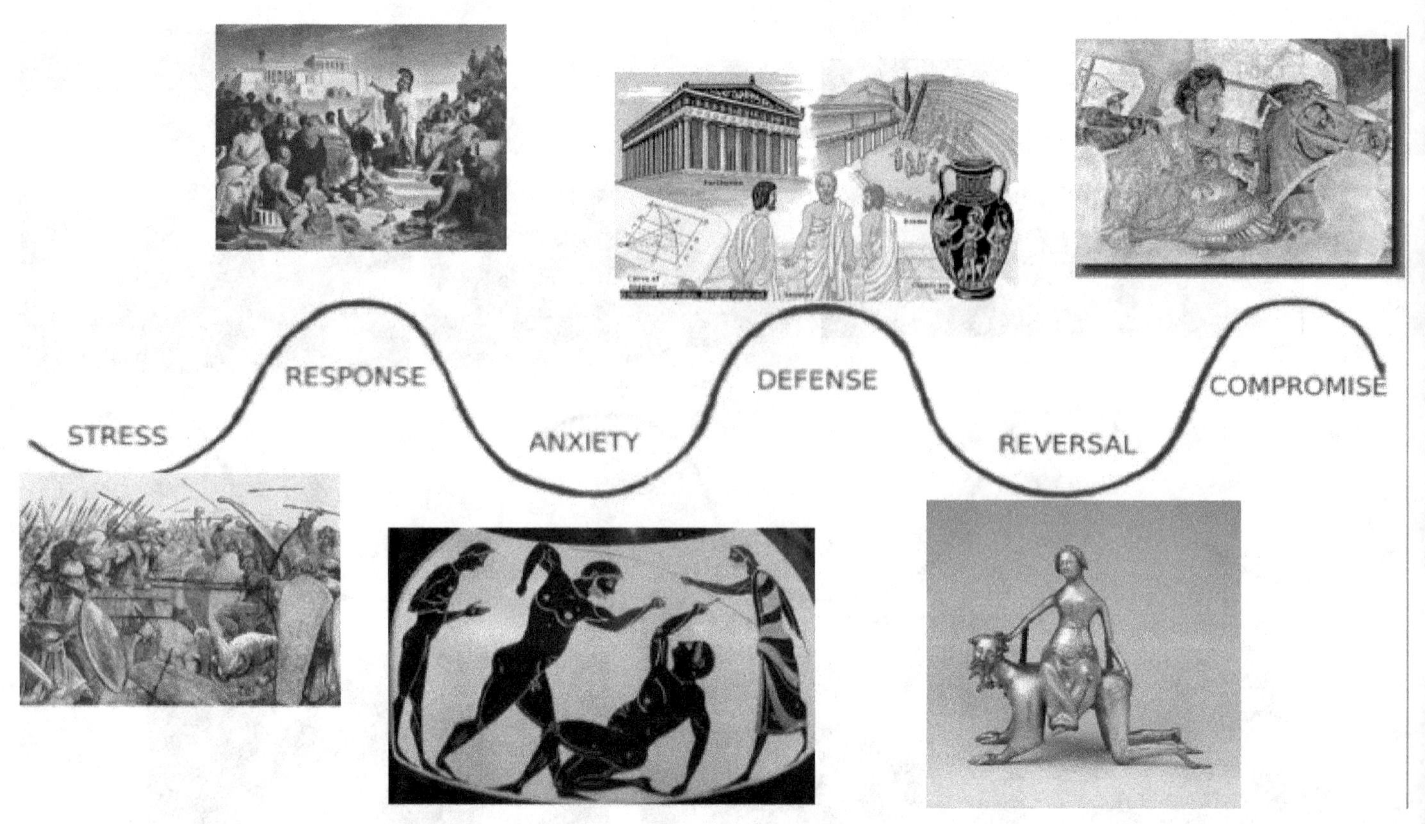

Alexander promoting conflict resolution, first uniting the Greek City states and then spreading the Aristotelian Hellenistic culture unifying the world.

1. Stress: Civil rivalries among Greek City States culminated into the destructive Peloponnesian War.
2. Response: The Athenians were very proud of their civilization.
3. Anxiety: Competitiveness was allowed in the Olympic games, democracy and dramatic theatrical productions.
4. Defense: Philosophies prevailed as the institutions of democracy, oligarchy, philosophy and science.
5. Reversal: Lysistrata resisting warfare, civil war. Aristotle reconciled with women philosophically. He is saddled by the concept of justice and compassion for women.
6. Compromise: His disciple, Alexander, the Great, unified the Greek cities and spread the Hellenistic value system uniting the world.

Players are requested to identify continuity in the cultural conflict resolution dynamics: The six role process and the shift from antagonism to cooperation in family and cultural relations. What is the dynamic progression in the evolution of conflicts to their resolution? The question is targeting the underlying common theme of all stories as the six-role process, pertinent in resolving gender relations in the Greek culture and identifying the resolutions in dealing more effectively with both family and cultural role relations. The pattern is evolving across the generations from deadly family conflicts, Uranus versus Kronos, Zeus versus Hera, to Prometheus versus Zeus, Agamemnon versus Clytemnestra, Odysseus versus Penelope, to Athens versus Sparta resolved by Lysistrata and Aristotle, wars of city states, tragedies played out symbolically, the understanding the dramatic process with Aristotle, and seeking to educate the world with his concepts by Alexander representing the Greek philosophers.

The theme of gender conflicts is very clear in all Greek heroic battles from the Cosmogony, the Trojan war, Prometheus stealing the fire, identifying Zeus' wife being dangerous, leading Zeus to swallow her, and to give birth out of his head to Athena, to Oedipus killing his father and marrying his mother, the Iliad as Greek men seeking to restrain the runaway wife, diminishing the autonomy of women, through the Odyssey as overcoming the power of temptation and thus reducing antagonism. Then Aristotle evolving insights into the nature of the dramatic process and Lysistrata seeking conflict resolution as a gender empowering women play, the world evolved better understanding of the powerplay and the need to reduce conflicts. Two hundred tragedies about gender conflicts reconciled men with women by becoming philosophical about the process of conflicts and resolutions. This moral insight as the many philosophies of Athens was the message that Alexander brought out of Greece to unite the cultures of his times.

In contrast to the conflicted Grecian family we detect in other cultures alternative conflict resolutions. The Judaic family introduced relating of a mother inspiring trust in the father, rather than Greek mother's undermining him. The key to the culture's resolving conflicts between genders is shifting dependence from women's love to the loving creator, God. This shift led to the adoration of theistic resolutions promoting broadening the understanding of moral justice. The preoccupation of approval of the divine diminished the importance of women, through definition of love as piety towards god, rather than dependence on capricious and divisive fickle women. The Biblical passages of the holy days of New Year and of Yom Kippur refer to mothers' willingness to sacrifice their sons, and to grant sons to the worship of the divine.

The players are challenged to utilize the game-board to learn about the principles of psychology in the evolution of religions. So the card-players can use science to detect both personal and cultural solutions as scientific laws underlying the evolution of personal and moral paradigms.

SUB-CHAPTER SIX: THE GAME SPIRITUALIZES PSYCHOLOGY AND DEMYSTIFIES MORALITY

Morality is a science. In order for the world to become free of cross-cultural strife it must become aware of the nature of religions as natural science measurable phenomena representing partial truths that are reconciled into the Moral Science. The game is a laboratory experiment where the players are researching the validity of a theoretical position that can unite the world and free it from cross-cultural conflict currently dividing the public into rivals as believers and infidels. The conclusion of the game is that religions are natural science measurable phenomena of psychological not metaphysical origination, that have introduced principles of science in the structuring of family relations. The game's function is to educate the public on psychology as the Science of Conflict Resolution, thus spiritualizing psychology and demystifying religions.

Establishing continuity among the cultures

The scientific distinctions of the process and modalities become clear illustrated by the familiar constructs of the game of cards. The deck presents metaphors that help to understand the scientific structure of the unconscious by establishing equivalences between the deck of cards abstract physical and formal distinctions and the key concepts of psychology, the unconscious and the relational diagnoses. Humanity's stories are placed on the game-board's two phenomena of science: the six-role energy transformational phenomenon uniting the numbered cards and the four alternative resolutions as the four suits of the deck of cards. The suits become metaphors of the process of the unconscious resolving conflict. The symbols heart, diamond, spade and club are metaphors of four syndromal relational modalities: The players examine the cultural stories, and learn about the cultural differences interrelated into a continuum. The four suits represent the sequence of the four scientific alternatives as formally related distinctions. The three principles of conflict resolution unite the cultures into an evolutionary continuum of discoveries of the moral principles of conflict resolution reflected in the ongoing increase of trust between partners in the family system as reflected in the relational continuity between the polarized Aztec, the Oedipal Greek distrusting partners, the peaceful ascetic family of India, and the inspired, mystified Judaic father-son covenant institution in which mothers trust their husbands with sacrificing their sons.

Though cultures might have evolved independently of each other, the game implies continuity as stemming from inner and social forces pressing the mind to complete the continuum of complementary discoveries of science in order to diminish the pain of psychic and social conflicts. The progression of discoveries has occurred because the human mind needs peace as increments of resolutions both in implementing justice and by increasing meaningfulness. This quest leads finally to identify the secrets of the mental dynamic as principles of science introducing formal continuity into the traditional moral paradigms. Religions are reconciled as partial but complementary discoveries of science.

The traditional card game insignia corresponding to the evolution of relational effectiveness
Cards are identified with their cultural characteristics and placed on the board in the designated positions of power versus powerlessness and cooperative versus antagonistic relating. The four suits correspond to four civilizations formally interrelated as a progression to improvements of family relations. Four cultures as the four suits become the four modalities of resolving. The four symbols of cards are interpreted as two relational distinctions: Cooperation and antagonism, dominance and subordinancy. Two suits marked in red: the heart and diamond correspond to cooperation; two suits marked in black symbolized as the spade and club refer to the antagonistic cultures. The heart and the club correspond to another distinction: they are the dominant cultures; the diamond and the spade correspond to the submissive cultures.

The evolution of cultural conflict resolutions
Following the cultural deck of cards life begins from the painful submissive antagonistic modality of matriarchy, illustrated with the Aztec civilization. Matriarchy is reversed in Greece by the discovery of mastery by the dominant antagonistic patriarchy. Patriarchy is then offset by the discovery of cooperation through the Hindu and Buddhist submissive cooperative moon goddess religions. The gender dominance is reversed by the Oriental, Chinese and Japanese, male authority traditions. The final discovery is of the need for mutual respect contributed by the dominant cooperative structure of the monotheistic father-son covenant of Judaism balanced off by the Messianic mother-child alliances. The outstanding problem of the Abrahamic religions may now be addressed by the Science of Conflict Resolution: Perfecting happiness is predicated on implementing mutual respect between all partners in the family, especially between the marital partners.

The Formal Theory identifying the science of the process revamps psychology's concepts of the unconscious, of diagnostic categories, and of the object and methods to be used in assessing behavior. The theory demystifies morality as conflict resolution abiding by laws of science. It thus places psychology and morality on the same foundation: the scientific analysis of the creative process correcting agnostic psychology and theistic faiths by understanding the process as an orderly emotional dynamic reducing conflicts and promoting resolutions as normative adjustments.

We may enjoy discovering the card game as the metaphor of psychology as a conflict resolution experience. The card-game retraces the evolution of alternative resolutions as the succession of discoveries of science in the quest for meaning. The insight is about finding meaning in conflict resolution. Science completes the universal quest for peace as the dynamic of the card-game symbolizing resolving properly the power play puzzles of life. The insignia reflect on the evolution of conflict resolutions in the power structures of the family role relations. The conflicts portrayed in the mythic cycle are resolved in the historical one. The historic cycle's partners are less polarized; they evolve trust in each other. But this trust has not been attained yet in the gender relations of the three Abrahamic religions.

The players consider the completion of the evolution of family relations by recognizing the importance of mutual respect between the genders for the effective resolution of the Abrahamic religions' cultural conflicts. They address the last scientific operation mutual respect as necessary for the final restructuring of family relations.

The public may adopt the principles of science as the guides to happiness in personal and in family relations as the ethical model of managing power. The public may also enjoy traditional religions but knowing that their values are based on reason rather than dogma. The universal divine then is manifested in all creativity as the formulas of inner order searching justice, rather than the values of the isolated theistic perspectives. The new science reconciles religions as partial and complementary discoveries of conflict resolution. According to the theory religions are integrated into the map of the unconscious as the range of relational modalities.

The scientific morality makes religions accountable to science
The Moral Science demystifies religions by placing them and behavior on a scientific foundation; we can analyze behavior as an exact science that respects conflict resolution as optimal power management and alerts all cultures about their value-systems as alternative relational modalities, each having strengths and weaknesses as well established in their cultural heritage. The science entails that religions need to be demystified to be respected but also to become accountable to the principles of moral justice ending the interfaith wars and allowing the management of pathology generated by each modality. The science provides insights to all religions to become self-aware and motivated to improve their adjustments to the current global realities, ecology and economy. All religions, like the respective individuals, suffer of certain kinds of psychopathology.

The card game completes the progression to healing the world by identifying the three formal operations that resolve conflicts. The players recognize the problems and ponder on resolutions reconciling the religions as partial discoveries of the Moral Science.

Through the ages the world has evolved resolving conflicts between religious factions with military confrontations. The record is that wars have led to reforms and most of the time improvement of moral paradigms. The current world is again fighting a religious conflict. Can science help to resolve the battle between moral alternatives? Can the Moral Science reconcile the rival moral traditions? The answer rests in validating the Moral Science, whose premise is that morality is a science and that religions are simply partial and complementary discoveries of the Moral Science. As partial knowledge they mislead the public as revealed truths. To prevail over religious dogma the players must validate the theoretical premise. They must agree on the premise that morality is a psychological natural science homeostatic phenomenon and that it is not hinging on dogma. The students should debate the issue of morality being a scientific phenomenon independent of metaphysical revelation. The game may assist reduction of fanaticism by demonstrating the psychological, sociological, and scientific nature of morality.

VALIDATING THE PREMISES OF THE MORAL SCIENCE
1. The unconscious is a natural science conflict resolution phenomenon reflected in all samples of creativity
2. We recognize four alternative ways of resolving conflict as the correct diagnoses of personality: four relational modalities
3. The conflict analysis battery is a self-assessment that uses creativity for self-discovery; it is didactic, diagnostic, and therapeutic
4. Religions are normative institutions partial and complementary discoveries of the science. They represent particular relational alternatives, narrow perceptions of causality, leading to alternative structuring of roles in the family and in social systems

The challenges for the players: evolving scientific moral consensus
The validation game of cards engages the players to an interactive study of four questions on the nature of stories:

- *Does each one of the cultural stories demonstrate the conflict resolution process?*
- *Are the relational dimensions for each culture correct?*
- *Are the postulations of the integration of religions into a scientific continuum correct?*
- *Is the divine a projection of the unconscious compelling the reduction of psychic and social tension?*

Players of the card game recognize the science underlying the cultural differences. The conclusion is becoming conscious of the creative process as a scientific conflict resolution innate phenomenon integrating the religions of the world into the Moral Science. They learn about a series of orderly phenomena:

1. **The Process:** The game provides information on the nature of conflict resolution. The formal interpretation of metaphors identifies the six-role state structure of stories as a psychological energy-transforming

phenomenon; the unconscious conflict resolution mechanism is a psychodynamic entity resolving conflicts to reduce psychic tension. It is identified as the innate emotional process automatically leading to change of attitude and social adjustment. This entity is the unit of the social sciences. It converts conflicts to resolutions and moral growth.

2. **The distinctions of alternative ways of resolving conflict:** The six-role process leads to alternative resolutions as relational modalities. Players recognize the alternatives but also the progression of religions' as partial and complementary restructurings of family relations pursuing optimal conflict resolution.

3. **The evolution of religions and of the divine:** The game integrates the religions of the four quadrants as a continuum of improvements in resolutions in the realm of family relations propelled by the need for changes to reduce conflicts by improving social justice. This compelling sociological dynamic for change underlies the progression of religions. It clarifies the divine as the deification of the individual responsible with the normative change. The current progression in resolutions is based on the need to resolve conflicts in the Abrahamic religions. The challenge is to reconcile religions and science.

4. **Prophets upsetting norms to resolve social conflicts:** The ordinary person resolves her conflicts by changing her attitude and fitting into the social normative environment. Alternatively the prophetic heroes have challenged the norms and succeeded in changing them to improve social justice. The cultural heroes of the game: Quetzalcoatl, Prometheus, Buddha, Moses and Jesus, at great personal sacrifice challenged dated moral paradigms to introduce justice by changing the norms of their societies. By recognizing all leaders, all prophets, as normative change agents improving social justice, the game establishes the psychological and ends the metaphysical origination of religions.

Confirming the scientific and moral unconscious

Through the process of debate the players evolve consensus on the issues considered above. They agree on the assigned distinctions of the six-part structure of the stories; they also agree on the range of four modalities qualifying the alternative approaches to conflict resolution. They agree on the dialectic evolution of religions and of the concepts of the divine. Thus at the end of the game the players may conclude that religions represent discoveries of alternative ways of resolving conflict, validating the premise of the Formal Theory of Behavior on the nature of the unconscious motivated by the need to reduce conflict as personal and domestic relations problems and thus improve family relations. The players may recognize that identifying the unconscious as a scientific conflict resolution phenomenon reconciles the humanities and the sciences, and integrates the religions into the Moral Science.

The players thus gain knowledge about the unconscious as a conflict resolution mechanism the unit of the social sciences and the basis of recognizing alternative diagnostic categories. They learn about the four wellness personality types as diagnostic categories. These pertain to the four cultures of the card game, as the alternative ways of resolving conflict. The game also educates the players on the scientific nature of moral values as the three principles of conflict resolution: mastery, cooperation and mutual respect.

The game is didactic, teaching both science and the application of science in the realm of the humanities. It helps to become conscious of the unconscious corresponding to a set of formulas, the software of the mind, rethinking traditional psychology and religious beliefs. It confirms a paradigm shift: Instead of believing dogma-based stories the players learn to respect the science of the process explaining morality and understanding history by completing the evolution of religions into pure science conferring the optimal way of resolving conflicts.

The game is reaffirming morality. The players recognize the nature of the divine as founded on the scientific nature of the process. At the end we see the divine and morality as defined by science. God or morality is in the scientific nature of the human unconscious striving for peace of mind, reduction of conflict.

The unconscious process has led the savages of the world in all parts of the globe to evolve religions independently of each other. The humans emerged from the jungle to establish great civilizations but in conflict with each other. The missing element from religions to be reconciled is understanding the importance of mutual respect between the parties in a system, here between the genders in the Abrahamic family. Men still after thousands of years do not trust women and do not allow them the status of parity; religions perpetuate the status quo. Science completes their mission for peace in the world by clarifying the outstanding conflict resolution principle in their ways of resolving conflict.

This game presenting the religions of the world as a progression to fairness in family relations and to abstraction on the nature of the divine introduces moral consensus founded on the abstract concepts of science. The religions are scientific psychological, not arbitrary metaphysical phenomena. They have offered us intuitively awareness of the alternative paths to happiness. Learning about science the world can be deliberate in resolving conflicts but also still respect religions as the emotional language, the dramatic treatment of the dry principles of science. Without the excitement of worship the science would be encyclopedic knowledge rather than emotionally engaging wisdom. There is ample room to pursue traditions while understanding their limitations. What would life be without Christmas, Easter, Passover and Hanukkah?

The Moral Science, the scientific and moral psychology

The end result of the game is reconciling the humanities and the sciences leading to the scientific understanding of psychology and morality. Though solving the problems of our world-religions is a theoretical exercise, the game accomplishes a real significant educational objective for the players. They experience the integration of the humanities and the sciences predicated on a scientific and moral unconscious. They learn about the integration of the sciences and the humanities as based on the unconscious, as the unit of psychology transcending religions by identifying morality as inherent in the dialectic of the six-role state conflict resolution process.

The players learn about the Moral Science, rethinking the traditional concepts of psychology.

1. Motivation is not driven by sex and power, libido and thanatos, but by the need to resolve conflicts. Psychology is transformed from irrational, unpredictable, neurobiologically directed and agnostic to the exact Moral Science abiding by the laws of nature, spelled with constructs, formulas and graphs of logic and physics.

2. The unconscious is no longer agnostic and amorphous. It becomes the scientific moral order unit entity, a six role state process identifying four alternative paths to resolution. It becomes the unit entity of conflict resolution, the mental heartbeat, the measuring rod, a finite entity leading to identify a circumscribed entity having a beginning, middle and end, closure, hence also periodicity, and measurability. This unit entity gives form and function to the creative process as the object for the study of behavior and revamps contemporary psychology by integrating it with morality and science.

3. Psychological diagnoses are no longer illnesses, clusters of symptoms, but wellness diagnoses, the four alternative relational modalities syndromes also determining psychopathology and psychotherapeutic changes.

4. Assessment is no longer identifying unrelated traits as conferred by personality inventories like DiSC, Five factors OCEAN, or Myers Briggs. The Conflict Analysis Battery, a self- assessment, is based on creativity for self-discovery and self-improvement; it identifies the unconscious as measurable alternative syndromal types of resolving conflict. Assessment information recognizes the personal relational modality as a syndrome, a six role state conflict resolving entity, a chain reaction transforming a conflict to its resolution.

5. Morality is clarified and demystified; it is no longer determined by dogma but by reason, by the set of scientific formal operations of conflict resolution: mastery, cooperation and mutual respect, determining social justice and cultural norms more clearly than religions. Religions merely deify the role models of particular ways of relating. Historically regarded, religions have progressed improving conflict resolution in family relations and clarity on the nature of the divine. The Moral Science completes their mission for peace in the world. Moral

values are no longer based on dogma. They are the scientific principles of balance.

6. Education is no longer unintegrated and personally irrelevant encyclopedic information. It can deliver meaning as a universal harmonic integrating the humanities and the sciences that can provide self-knowledge utilizing creativity for self-discovery, and that clarifies moral values as principles of science. Psychology and morality merge into one scientific domain allowing self-knowledge and clarity of moral values. The game and the Conflict Analysis Battery complement each other in a concise program of emotional educational. Creativity and Power Management is a program of emotional and moral education that is didactic, diagnostic, therapeutic and with the help of the game it becomes spiritual.

A methodological Paradigm Shift: the end of idolatry

Moral Monopoly can 'Heal the world' allowing the development of moral consensus by integrating art and science, religions and psychology with science, thus methodologically shifting paradigms from trusting the content of stories to understanding the plot of stories as the integrative measurable essence of the humanities. The unconscious process is the universal harmonic as the vital force for conflict resolution inspiring spirituality and manifested in all samples of creativity. The end of idolatry is in the end of believing stories as true by recognizing the science underlying all of them, the universal harmonic as the integrative paradigm. This is the unit order of the social sciences and it makes everything meaningful as bound by the universality of a positive development.

Insights based on the discovery: normative relativity

The key concept of the new science is that the unconscious mind is propelled by a need to adjust to social norms, but that social norms also evolve into alternative normative institutions with different values inspired by the ultimate awareness of improving social justice. The game thus shows religions as normative institutions determined by three relational equilibrial principles meant to decrease social strife. While morality as a set of rules or norms traditionally has been determined by religions now it is reduced to formal relational choices inspired by respect for one of the three scientific principles of the conflict resolution process. While morality guides the person to conform to rules or norms, religions stem from individuals who change norms seeking to improve social justice by restructuring roles in the family system, and by redefining the nature of the divine more abstractly, more inclusively, as the role model of the reforms.

The new divine is equated with the unit process. Science rediscovers the moral values of religions as the worship of the process as respect of the unit of conflict resolution. The unit reconciling science and religions is already the object of adoration as spelled in the Greek words of the divine as oneness, monas or a unit. The end definition of the divine as mono-theism, coincides with the scientific understanding of the unconscious conflict resolution process as the unit, a scientific periodic conflict resolution order bridging religions into the Moral Science. The Moral Science rediscovers both Genesis and the Ten Commandments.

The moral of the game: The experiential validation of Formal Theory's claims

One learns by listening to a lecture or reading a book about concepts but one learns even better by being actively engaged in an experiential process; this is the idea of learning about behavior being engaged into playing a game of cards. A group is engaged in the exploration of dealing with evolving moral consensus on an abstraction becoming tangible knowledge. The players collaborate to win a battle with the mystified unknown.

In our times of cultural conflicts this game addresses ideas of morality following principles of natural law, science. Can science integrate the diversity of religions into the simple principles of science as complementary alternatives of conflict resolution? The game validates this premise by identifying the physical structure of moral thinking in all cultural stories that is in all religions. The players recognize moral thinking as a scientific phenomenon integrating all religions into the Moral Science. Since the creative process is a scientific moral order phenomenon, morality becomes the Science of Conflict Resolution and religions become reconciled into the Moral Science.

The Moral Monopoly card game teaches the scientific understanding of moral order by identifying the conflict-resolving nature of stories reflecting the unconscious as a scientific moral order phenomenon manifested in the universality of stories. The game demonstrates how this process of conflict resolution as a scientific and moral order entity reconciles all religions as partial and complementary discoveries of the Science of Conflict Resolution, the Moral Science.

The game reconciles the religions as compromises in the battle of the genders leading to improvements in family relations and clarity on the mystery of the creator. The unifying theme of the cultural stories is the evolution of the family institutions as resolutions of domestic conflicts, the battle of the genders for power and control of authority and control of the family. The religions evolved redefining the role of women and men, parents and children, restructuring the family role relations seeking to diminish strife. Have they succeeded in doing so?

The players ponder on the properties of the stories as conflict resolutions and navigate the history of religions as evolving from one culture to another recognizing this conflict resolution order modified along four alternative types of resolutions. They recognize that each culture discovered an alternative way of resolving conflict improving family relations. The game thus integrates religions as a continuum of partial and complementary discoveries of the underlying science, which is now identified as the Moral Science.

The players realize retracing the history of religions their evolution in fairness in the structure of family role relations and the progression in the abstraction on the nature of the divine leading from stories to the universality of the plot of stories as formulas with many solutions. They realize that the plot is an innate unconscious conflict resolution phenomenon that has a scientific structure, and that becomes the unit of the social sciences integrating them into the Moral Science. At the end they realize that it unifies all cultural stories as alternative ways of resolving conflict and thus advancing morality from faith to reason, from art to science, from religions to a scientific and moral psychology.

SUB-CHAPTER SEVEN:
THE BENEFITS OF THE EDUCATIONAL GAME

Healing the world by demonstrating that morality is an exact science putting an end to the cross-cultural conflicts
Science does not cancel morality; it simply perfects it. It does so not by canceling religions but instead validating them as brilliant partial discoveries of science and shifting the worship of the divine to celebrating the universal harmonic as it manifests in all samples of creativity, all metaphors, as the great arbiter. This discovery needs celebration but we can still benefit from the inspirational religious traditions.

The game confirms the conceptual revolution of the Moral Science identifying the unconscious reflected in the creative process as having a scientific structure and a moral function. The scientific structure is that the mind follows two equilibrial phenomena: the pendulum's oscillation, and the formal operations of the trays of a scale. The moral function is in that the mind automatically transforms a conflict, as a normative deviation, to its resolution, a normative conciliation or also normative improvement.

The game confirming science validates the study of creativity for self-discovery. The Conflict Analysis Battery is about generating stories to identify the personal relational dimensions. While the players begin with the stories as having preset scientific structure and moral direction they identify the correctness of these scientific assumptions. The opposite of what happens in the game where we puzzle already existing stories, in the battery the test taker creates stories to find out about one's approach of resolving.

Why is the scientific and moral unconscious a significant discovery?

It is because the world is at an impasse in reaching consensus on moral values, and suffers of ineffective psychology as well. Without understanding the moral process psychology and education misunderstand humans. The game by studying the creative process as the unconscious conflict resolution process contributes a methodological paradigm shift introducing the process as the integrative paradigm. Instead of being divided by the content of multiple stories the process introduces what is universal in all stories, their plot examining their structure as a scientific morality bound, conflict resolution natural science phenomenon.

By understanding the science of conflict resolution the world can evolve moral consensus by examining its cultural stories as reflecting the six-role conflict resolution process. In their continuity thinkers will have to agree on the evolution of faiths toward science's abstract type of justice.

Values and norms

The card game is a study of the sociology of norms as discoveries of the underlying psychology of the unconscious need for conflict resolution. Religions have evolved toward abstraction and the Moral Science reconciles them as partial and complementary discoveries of the Moral Science and completes their mission.

One of the conclusions from this research is that psychology is about experiencing conflict as a normative deviation. Norms though are not a stable reference as they change according to cultural standards. In our times norms change by decisions spelled out by the Supreme Court, which establishes new laws altering what conducts are acceptable by the culture and which are not acceptable. In the history of civilization it has been religions that have been the normative institutions. They have consistently evolved norms restructuring family relations, most of the time promoting increased fairness in the family relations but frequently setting norms that are less adaptive.

Religions' progression in redefining the divine is completed by identifying morality stemming from the scientific unconscious. The game retraces the evolution of religions as discoveries of science and continues their evolution toward science by seeking the answers in the two jokers representing the wisdom of the two scientific phenomena. The game's challenge is not to unmask the Wizard playing the role of Toto in the story of the Wizard of Oz but to identify morality as the mechanism of conflict resolution and thus respecting the contributions of all Wizards, all religions, all storytellers.

The game demystifies religions but respects them as the deifications of the individual principles of the Science of Conflict Resolution demonstrating their progression to fairness in dealing with conflicts of the family institution and furthering the abstraction of the divine from totemism to the universal process. The game does not dismiss morality; it simply redefines it as a scientific phenomenon.

The players learn about psychology as the science of conflict resolution

Concluding, the card game introduces the Science of Conflict Resolution integrating psychology and morality by understanding the unconscious quest for peace as manifested in all creativity; they learn about the plot of stories as measurable with the constructs of the two phenomena of science as a sequence of six emotions guided by three formal operations.

They learn about how religions evolved as discoveries of science, by identifying the four relational alternatives sequentially as the game retraces the history of love leading to improved family relations by introducing resolutions as new norms. They identify the religions/cultures with a respective discovery of one of the principles of conflict resolution:

- They identified the formal operation of identity as the creation of a conflict. The matriarchal society exemplified with the Aztec culture represents the beginning of the family institution leading to intense polarization between partners, antagonism and alienation between mother and daughter, metaphorically portrayed in the conflict between an eagle and a snake. This conflict was resolved by their merger into the feather serpent.
- Greece discovered the principles of reciprocity as mastery of patriarchy defeating matriarchy, men from a passive position claim submission of women through the covenant of marital vows. The family institu-

tion is celebrated in the Homeric Epics as the punishment of unfaithful women, Helen and Clytemnestra, and the honoring of a loyal wife, Penelope.

- India discovered the principle of negation, transforming antagonism to cooperation manifested in asceticism and the respect of cows and monkeys as sacred animals, and a Kali's child Ganesha featuring the head of an elephant.
- Judea discovered the principle of correlation transforming alienation to mutual respect in the father-son relationship symbolized as the two lions of Judah as the guardians of the Bible. The two messianic religions discovered mutual respect in the mother child alliances, but Abrahamic religions have not discovered mutual respect between the genders. Christianity adopted the concepts of humans as sheep and their guardian as a shepherd, while Christ has been portrayed as a fish and a fisherman. Islam presented the alliance as a crescent and a star.

The problem of religions has been identifying partial resolutions proclaiming them as the universal moral paradigms thus leading the world into conflicts based on metaphors.

Players discuss the cultural stories as a progression that leads to our times examining the impasse of cross-cultural versions of the truth. They examine the problems of the Abrahamic religions in defining the role of women. They recognize the unsolved problem of gender conflicts. The players understanding the mental mechanism as a software determined by the two equilibrial phenomena endorse the mental quest for the reduction of inner and social conflicts as correctable by introducing mutual respect into the realm of gender relations. This educational game is relevant for our times of dangerous religious conflicts originating on the unacceptable conduct in the name of God. The world needs healing and science offers the solution on the scientific nature of morality.

The game is part of a concise program of emotional education that respects morality as the function of the unconscious, leading to demystifying religions and spiritualizing psychology as the exact science of morality. This program delivers education's three elusive objectives:

1. The integration of the humanities and the sciences studying the creative process as the scientific moral paradigm.
2. Utilizing creativity for self-discovery, self-knowledge.
3. Respecting religions as having deified the values as discoveries and celebrations of the alternative principles of conflict resolution.

The relevance of the formal interpretation of metaphors is in the integration of psychology and religions into the Moral Science

The players examine the cultural stories as displayed on the game board. The stories of the world displayed on the board along the scientific template of the unconscious present their evolution from art to science, from conflicts to resolutions, propelled by the inner need of reducing discomfort in one's mind and in our family relations. The game leads to the integration of psychology and religions into the Moral Science, a development of extraordinary relevance in our times of an agnostic medicalized psychology and dogma-based fundamentalisms. The game ends by generating awareness of the formal principles and in identifying mutual respect between the genders as the key to perfect conflict resolution in family relations.

The players evolve moral consensus

Players of the card game recognize the science underlying the cultural moral diversity; they comprehend the thesis of the Formal Theory on the nature of the creative process as a scientific conflict resolution innate phenomenon. With processing of information players can approach the topic of psychology and religions as scientific conflict resolution phenomena reconciling the humanities and the sciences and integrating religion and psychology into the domain of an exact science. The players have evidence to reconcile psychology and morality and to conclude that the world has become progressively more resolved. Deities as conflict resolution have advanced moral paradigms. We are able to understand the religions as advancing more effective relational modalities promoting the principles of mastery, cooperation, and mutual respect.

Through the process of observation and debate, the players evolve consensus on the scientific principles governing the unconscious applied to the analysis of religions. The assigned distinctions of the six-part structure of the stories, the syndromal entity, and of the four modalities qualifying the alternative approaches to conflict resolution are confirmed by the players as the departure on the scientific nature of religions and of their dialectic evolution as discoveries of the Moral Science.

The conclusions are listed below:
First, each culture evolves resolving a conflict along two stories: the mythic phase using symbols of animal metaphors and the historic resolves the conflicts with human heroes. Both stories demonstrate the conflict resolution process according to the two scientific phenomena.
Second, the inscribed relational dimensions for each culture are correct; religions differ as discoveries of the three principles of conflict resolution.
Third, religions on the template evolved sequentially, historically, optimizing the family system. They evolved into a formal relational continuum of the four ways of resolving conflicts.
Fourth, the cultural heroes as divine role models are defined with the evolving attributes of the unconscious conflict resolution mechanism. The missing condition for the completion of the evolution of the Abrahamic religions into the Moral Science is introducing mutual respect between the genders.

The players reach a consensus on the scientific nature of morality, as the moral psychology.
1. The Process: Indeed stories unfold along the six-role state structure. Stories evolve resolving conflicts reducing psychic tension and increasing social order. The process changes one's attitude enhancing social adjustment. The unconscious spontaneously converts conflicts to resolutions leading to moral growth.
2. We recognize four alternative ways of resolving conflict: We recognize four alternative resolutions the relational modalities as affected by different formal operations. We recognize the alternatives as complementary restructuring optimizing domestic relations.
3. **The evolution of religions**: We can integrate religions as a continuum of improvements in family relations propelled by the need for social justice. The Moral Science challenges the Abrahamic norms. Religious norms are evolving responding to the public's needs for civil rights.
4. **The premise of challenging normative systems.** The heroes of all religions have challenged established norms and succeeded in modifying them to alternative types of social justice. The cultural heroes of the game: Quetzalcoatl, Prometheus, Buddha, Moses, Jesus, and Mohammad at great personal sacrifice, challenged the moral paradigms of their times changing the norms of their societies. Yet the question remains, can the scientific principles challenge the religions' intuitively established norms thus ending the need for divine imperatives, revelations, metaphysical explanations toward achieving moral consensus and peace in the world? Can the Moral Science heal the world?

The game entails insights and changes
The game introduces science in the realm of the humanities. It helps to become conscious of the unconscious corresponding to a set of formulas, the software of the mind, rethinking traditional psychology and religious beliefs as scientific measurable phenomena. It confirms a paradigm shift: Instead of believing dogma-based stories, the players learn to respect the process explaining morality as a science and understanding history as the evolution of religions into pure science. Doing so should not be objectionable to religions. Science is completing their mission by identifying mutual respect between the genders as the optimal way of resolving conflicts.

The game is affirming morality as a scientific order consistent with religious traditions. It presents religions as discoveries of science with sociological impact. Players recognize the nature of morality as founded on the

scientific nature of the process and that science is relevant in the world, where religions have fallen short of advancing justice and peace. The implication of religions' suffering from unresolved conflicts is in their need for more abstract understanding of moral order. Science can help them resolve their conflicts. This realization allows the players to consider respectfully addressing the outstanding conflicts of our cultures in terms of the history of religions as having improved the family institution by regulating gender relations.
The unconscious process has led the savages of the world in all parts of the globe to evolve religions and cultures independently of each other. The humans emerged from the jungle to establish great civilizations based on covenants on family relations. The problem has been reconciling the alternative religions in conflict with each other. The suggested resolution is in improving humanity's understanding of the multiple divines integrated as aspects of the innate problem solving unconscious mechanism.

The religions have accomplished progress. The missing element from religions to be reconciled is in the scientific understanding the origin of all moral thinking as stemming from the unconscious by comprehending the principles of conflict resolution. The principles have been applied to regulating gender relations. Men, still after thousands of years, do not trust women and do not allow them the status of parity; religions perpetuate inequity in gender relations. Science completes their mission for peace in the world by clarifying the condition for peace as the optimal way of resolving conflicts of the world.

The game presents the religions of the world as a progression to fairness in family relations and to abstraction on the nature of the divine; it introduces moral consensus founded on the abstract concepts of science. The religions are scientific psychological, sociological not metaphysical phenomena. Intuitively, they have offered us awareness of the alternative paths to happiness. In learning about the Moral Science, the world can be deliberate in resolving conflicts but also still respect religions as the emotional language, the musical and dramatic treatment of the principles of science. Without the excitement of worship, the science would be encyclopedic dry knowledge rather than emotionally engaging wisdom. There is ample room to pursue traditions while understanding their limitations.

Religions demystified and humanized

The Moral Science demystifies religions by placing behavior on the scientific foundation of the formal analysis of the creative process; we analyze conflict resolution as an exact science that identifies optimal power management and alerts all cultures about their value-systems as alternative relational modalities, each having strengths and weaknesses as established in their cultural heritage. Science invites faiths to become accountable to reason. They must identify their shortcomings and accept their moral obligation to evolve from arbitrary positions to conforming to the norm of morality abiding by universal laws, the principles of equilibrial systems.

All religions, like the respective individuals, suffer of certain kinds of power management psychopathology. The Moral Science demystifies personality and religious pathologies by making them aware of the principles of moral justice. The science makes the person and the cultures aware of their distortions of reality and the adverse impact of distortions on the individual and on the group of faithful; relational modalities intensified create pathologies; religions generate fanaticisms, individuals and religions become leaders in advocating conflicts leading to sectarian and interfaith violence. The science provides insights to the person and to the religions to become self-aware and motivated to improve their adjustments to the global realities, ecology, and economy.

The card game completes the progression to healing the individual and the world by identifying the three formal operations that resolve conflicts. The players recognize the inherent conflicts and ponder on resolutions reconciling the traditions focusing on general motivation for sociological progress. The conclusion is that religions are natural science measurable phenomena of psychological origination, totally free of metaphysical connections, and that the civilizations have intuitively introduced principles of science in their respective religions. Religions have limited capacity to reconcile differences and to optimize resolutions. Science is the new normative development that may make the world aware of the nature of religions as unable to make changes and that it is the public that has an interest to modify the theistic definitions of morality through the secularization of faiths.

Religions misunderstand the nature of morality

The game is a laboratory experiment, where the players are researchers examining the validity of a theoretical position on the scientific nature of morality by charting the evolution of the religions of the world as ever evolving normative systems. Once in power each religion has tried to arrest the world's moral evolution, contributing in the escalation of conflicts caused by cross-cultural differences between believers and non-believers stigmatized as infidels.

Through the ages, the world has evolved resolving conflicts between religious factions with military confrontations. The record is that wars have led to reforms and, most of the time, improving moral paradigms. The current world is again fighting religious conflicts. America in our times is torn between conservative and liberal factions. It is at war with conservative Islam and its social values. Can science help to resolve the battle between moral alternatives in this country as well as in international relations? Can the Moral Science reconcile the rival moral traditions in the era of the enlightened psychology?

The answer rests in validating Moral Science's premise that morality is a science through the scientific analysis of metaphors, and that religions are metaphors with natural science dimensions. Thus we show that they simply are partial and complementary discoveries of science. As partial knowledge, they have inspired the world great civilizations each making great contributions. The world has benefited from each moral system. The problem in the era of globalization is the manifestation of their differences as problematic. To prevail over religious dogma, academia must discover the correctness of the new theoretical premise.

Eventually leaders must agree on the premise that morality is a science, founded on recognizing the unconscious as a psychological natural science homeostatic measurable function. The awareness of morality as a science is reassuring. The public needs moral order. Only assurance of a better moral order will free the public from surrendering to the arbitrariness and divisiveness of dogmata. Scientists should debate the issue of morality being a scientific phenomenon independent of metaphysical revelation and associated moral codes and normative restrictions in civil rights. The game assists in demonstrating the psychological scientific nature of morality.

Clarifying the concepts of the Moral Science

The benefit of playing the game is reconciling the humanities and the sciences, leading to the scientific understanding of psychology and morality and solving the current problems of the pre-paradigmatic psychology and morality based on dogma rather than reason. The game is a conceptual exercise that accomplishes a real significant educational objective for the players and for our cultures in moral crisis. The players experience the integration of the humanities and the sciences predicated on the scientific and moral unconscious. They learn about the integration of the sciences and the humanities as based on the unconscious as the unit of psychology, transcending religions by identifying morality as inherent in the dialectic of the conflict resolution process. Science's three attitude modifying formal operations are the ultimate definition of moral values.
The players may conclude the validation of Formal Theory's premise:

1. The unconscious is a natural science conflict resolution phenomenon manifested in all samples of creativity
2. We recognize four alternative ways of resolving conflict as the wellness diagnoses of personality: four relational modalities
3 The Conflict Analysis Battery is a self-assessment that uses creativity for self-discovery; it is didactic, diagnostic, and therapeutic
4 Religions are normative institutions, partial and complementary discoveries of the science. They represent relational narrow perceptions of causality, leading to alternative structuring of roles in the family and in social systems. They evolved as metaphorical partial discoveries of the science and as partial truths, that need

to complete their mission for peace in the world by making concessions, sacrifices, in order to be reconciled into the truths of a science.

Overcoming traditions, refuting dated paradigms

The players learn about the Moral Science, rethinking the traditional concepts of psychology.

1. Motivation is not driven by sex and power, libido, and Thanatos, but by the need to resolve conflicts. Psychology is transformed from irrational, unpredictable, neurobiologically directed, and agnostic to the exact Moral Science abiding by the laws of nature, spelled with constructs, formulas, and graphs of logic and physics.

2. The unconscious is no longer agnostic and amorphous. It becomes the scientific moral order unit entity, a six-role state process identifying four alternative paths to resolution. It becomes the unit entity of conflict resolution, the mental heartbeat, and the moral compass, the measuring rod, a finite entity, a circumscribed phenomenon having a beginning, middle and end, closure, hence also periodicity, and measurability. This unit entity gives form and function to the creative process as the object for the study of behavior and revamps contemporary psychology by integrating it with morality and science.

3. Psychological diagnoses are no longer illnesses and clusters of symptoms, but wellness diagnoses. The four alternative relational modality syndromes determine psychopathology and the pivotal approach for effective psychotherapeutic changes.

4. Assessment is no longer identifying unrelated traits as conferred by personality inventories like DiSC, Five factors, OCEAN, or Myers Briggs, MBTI. The Conflict Analysis Battery, a self-assessment, based on creativity for self-discovery and self-improvement identifies the unconscious as measurable alternative syndromal types of relational modalities. Assessment information recognizes the personal relational modality as a syndrome, a six-role state conflict resolving entity, a chain reaction transforming a conflict to its resolution that can be managed to optimize one's power and attitude in resolving conflicts and thus eliminate medical symptoms.

5. Morality is clarified and demystified; it is no longer determined by dogma but by reason, by the set of scientific formal operations of conflict resolution: mastery, cooperation, and mutual respect, determining social justice and cultural norms. Religions have evolved deifying the range of role models of relating. Historically regarded, religions have progressed, improving conflict resolution in family relations and clarity on the nature of the divine. The Moral Science completes religions' mission for peace in the world. Moral values are no longer based on dogma. They are the equilibrial principles of the scale.

6. Education is no longer unintegrated and personally irrelevant encyclopedic information. It can deliver meaning as a universal harmonic integrating the humanities and the sciences that can provide self-knowledge utilizing creativity for self-discovery, and that clarifies moral values as principles of science. Psychology and morality merge into one scientific domain allowing self-knowledge and clarity of moral values. The Moral Monopoly game and the Conflict Analysis Battery complement each other in a concise program of emotional and moral education. Creativity and Power Management is didactic, diagnostic, therapeutic, and spiritual.

End of idolatry as the shift of paradigms from the content to the process of stories

'Healing the world' hinges on integrating religions and psychology with the sciences, thus methodologically shifting paradigms from trusting the content of stories to understanding the plot of stories as the integrative measurable essence of the humanities. The unconscious process is the universal harmonic as the vital force for conflict resolution, inspiring spirituality, and manifested in all creativity. The end of idolatry is in the end of believing stories as true by recognizing the science underlying all of them, the universal harmonic as the integrative paradigm. Conflict resolution as the unit order, is the atomistic core of the social sciences. It makes everything meaningful as bound by the universality of laws of science. God is not another story. God is the plot of all stories.

Normative relativity

While morality guides the person to conform to rules or norms, religions stem from individuals who have changed norms seeking to improve social justice by restructuring roles in the family system. Innovators have interrupted norms by redefining the nature of the divine more abstractly, more inclusively, as the role model of the reforms. This is the role now of the Moral Science.

The key concept of the new science is that the unconscious mind is propelled by the need to adjust to social norms, but that social norms evolve into alternative institutions with different values inspired by the evolving awareness of social justice. The game thus shows religions have evolved as normative institutions determined by the times identifying the three relational equilibrial principles needed to decrease social strife. While morality as a set of rules or norms traditionally has been determined by religions, now it is reduced to formal relational choices, the three scientific principles of the conflict resolution process. The Supreme Court recognizes changes on the basis of the formal principles in making morally correct social judgments.

The new divine is equated with the unit process deliberately guided by the moral values of scientific principles, laws of science, the unit of conflict resolution. The unit reconciling science and religions is already the object of adoration as spelled in the concept of the divine as oneness, monas, or a unit. The end definition of the divine as monotheism coincides with the scientific understanding of the unconscious as the unit, the scientific periodic conflict resolution order bridging morality and psychology into the Moral Science.

The game as the experiential validation of Formal Theory's claims

One learns by listening to a lecture or reading a book about concepts, but one learns even better by being actively engaged in an experiential process; this is the idea of learning about behavior by playing the Moral Monopoly game of cards. A group is engaged in the exploration of dealing with evolving consensus on an abstraction becoming tangible knowledge. The players collaborate to win a battle over demystifying metaphors to discover pure science.

In our times of cultural conflicts, this game addresses morality as following principles of natural law, science. Science integrates the diversity of religions into the simple principles of science. The game validates this premise by identifying the physical structure of moral thinking in cultural stories. The players recognize moral thinking as a scientific phenomenon. Since the creative process is a scientific moral order phenomenon, morality becomes the Science of Conflict Resolution, and religions become reconciled into this science.

Moral Monopoly was originally identified as Tikkun Olam meaning in Hebrew, 'Healing the World'. The card game teaches the scientific understanding of moral order by identifying the conflict-resolving nature of the unconscious as a universal scientific moral order phenomenon. The game reconciles the religions as episodes in the ongoing battle of the genders for power and control of the family leading to improvements in family relations based on redefining the divine and restructuring family role relations ending with clarity on the mystery of the human unconscious. The unifying theme of the cultural stories is the evolution of the family institution, reconciling the many resolutions of domestic relations. The religions evolved redefining the role of women and men, parents, and children, restructuring the family role relations seeking to diminish strife. Science has succeeded in enlightening players about wisdom, pondering on religions as evolving from one culture to another, recognizing this underlying conflict resolution order modified along four alternative types of resolutions. They recognize that each culture discovered an alternative way of improving family relations as a continuum of partial and complementary discoveries of science.

The players realize retracing the history of religions their evolution in fairness in the structure of family role relations and the progression in the abstraction on the nature of the divine leading from stories to the universality of the plot of stories as formulas with many solutions. They realize that the plot is an innate conflict resolution phenomenon that has a scientific structure, and that becomes the unit of the social sciences integrated into the Moral Science. At the end, they realize that the science unifies all cultural stories as alternative ways of resolving conflict advancing morality from faith to reason, from art to science, from religions to a scientific moral psychology.

Science does not cancel morality; it simply perfects it. Science does so, not by canceling religions, but instead by validating them as partial discoveries of science and by shifting the worship of the divine to celebrating the universal harmonic as it manifests in all samples of creativity, all metaphors, as the great magician, rediscovering Oz as the metaphor of the internal moral authority manifested in our own creativity. This discovery needs celebration for the universal creative process as the ultimate moral authority present in all religious traditions. The game confirms the conceptual position of the Moral Science identifying the unconscious reflected in the creative process as having a scientific structure and a moral function. The scientific structure is that the mind follows two equilibrial phenomena: the pendulum's oscillation, and the formal operations of the trays of a scale. The moral function is in that the mind automatically transforms a conflict, as a normative deviation, to its resolution, a normative conciliation, and alternatively a normative improvement.

Why is the scientific and moral unconscious a significant discovery?

It is because the world is at an impasse in reaching consensus on moral values and suffers from ineffective psychology and misleading moral paradigms confusing partial truths with the scientific truth. Without understanding the moral process, psychology and education misunderstand humans and humanity. By studying the creative process as the unconscious conflict resolution process, the game contributes a methodological paradigm shift introducing the process as the integrative paradigm of both psychology and religions. Instead of being divided by people's modalities, and the content of multiple cultural stories, the process introduces what is universal in all personal and cultural stories, their structure as a scientific morality bound, conflict resolution, natural-science measurable phenomenon. By understanding the science of conflict resolution, the world can evolve moral consensus on behavior and on society by examining stories following science's abstract laws. Scientific language can help to develop consensus on moral issues.

Values and norms, science as the normative moral authority

One of the conclusions from this research is that conflict is about experiencing energy upon a normative deviation. Norms though, are not a stable reference as they change according to cultural standards. In our times, norms change by decisions spelled out by the Supreme Court, which alters norms on conducts' acceptability. In the history of civilization, it has been prophets seeking reforms and religions that have been the normative institutions. Religions have consistently evolved norms restructuring family relations, most of the time promoting increased fairness in the family relations, but frequently setting norms that are unfair. The card game is a study of the sociology of norms as discoveries of the underlying psychology of the unconscious need for conflict resolution. Religions have evolved toward abstraction and the Moral Science reconciles them and completes their mission changing science as the moral authority.

Religions' progression in redefining the divine is completed by identifying the unconscious as the scientific conflict resolution process.

The game retraces the evolution of religions as discoveries of science and continues their evolution toward science by seeking the answers in the two scientific phenomena. The game's challenge is not to unmask the Wizard playing the role of Toto in the story of The Wizard of Oz but to identify morality as the scientific mechanism of conflict resolution, thus respecting the contributions of all Wizards, all religions. The game demystifies religions but respects them as the deifications of the principles of the Science of Conflict Resolution, demonstrating their progression to fairness in dealing with conflicts of the family institution and furthering the abstraction of the divine from totemism to the universal process. The game does not dismiss morality; it simply redefines it as a scientific phenomenon, a formula true for all values of its variables.

Reviewing the benefits of the educational game

The players learn about the psychology of conflict resolution the history of religions, as how they evolved as discoveries of science by identifying the four alternatives modalities sequentially as the game retraces the history of love leading to improved family relations by introducing new norms of resolution. They identify the religions/cultures with a respective discovery of one of the principles of conflict resolution:

- The Aztecs are a matriarchal society leading to intense polarization between partners, antagonism between mother and daughter, eagle and snake, resolved by the feathered serpent. They identified the power differential in establishing a dyadic relation.
- Greece discovered patriarchy defeating matriarchy, introducing the principles of mastery and antagonism.
- India discovered mastery as asceticism corresponding to the second principle of balance: cooperation.
- Judea discovered mutual respect between father and son, the two messianic religions discovered the mother-son alliances, but none has yet discovered mutual respect between the genders.
- So, all religions identified partial resolutions misleading the world by proclaiming them as the universal moral paradigms.

Concluding, the card game introduces the Science of Conflict Resolution integrating psychology and morality by understanding the unconscious quest for peace manifested in all creativity; we learn about the plot of stories as measurable with the constructs of two phenomena of science: a sequence of six emotions guided by three formal operations.

The players discuss the cultural stories as a progression that leads to our times examining the impasse of alternative cultural solutions. They examine the problems of the Abrahamic religions in defining the role of women. They come to realize that the outstanding resolution of moral conflicts may be corrected by introducing science into the realm of psychology and religion by understanding the mental mechanism as a software determined by the two equilibrial phenomena. The players realize the mental human quest for justice resulting from the need for the reduction of inner and social conflicts as the origin of all moral thought and all religions. This educational game is relevant for our times of dangerous religious fanatics and renewed cultural conflicts justifying unacceptable conduct in the name of God. The world needs healing, and science offers the solution to the nature of our current search for meaning and justice.

The game is part of a concise program of emotional education that respects morality as the function of the unconscious, leading to demystifying psychology as an exact science identifying religions as celebrations of the alternative principles of resolution as moral values.

This game as part of an emotional education program delivers education's three elusive objectives:

1. The integration of the humanities and the sciences
2. Self-knowledge The game confirming science validates the study of creativity. The Conflict Analysis Battery is another approach to validating the theory. The battery is about generating stories for self-discovery, to identify the personal relational dimensions. While the players begin with the stories as having preset scientific structure and moral direction to identify them as relational modalities, the opposite happens in the battery. The test taker creates stories to find out about one's approach of resolving.
3. Clarity of values by respecting religions as having deified the values.

CONCLUSION
INTEGRATING PSYCHOLOGY AND MORALITY INTO THE MORAL SCIENCE

CHAPTER ONE:
THE SCIENTIFIC AND MORAL NATURE OF THE UNCONSCIOUS AS THE UNIT ORDER OF PSYCHOLOGY

The Formal Theory was inspired by observing a periodic phenomenon transmitted across the five generations of the Greek Cosmogony. This periodic phenomenon was conceptualized as reflecting the unconscious having a distinct structure: six role states and a distinct moral function: conflict resolution. Creativity as the conflict resolving unconscious was studied as a natural science emotional dialectic abiding by the constructs and formulas of two equilibrial models: the pendulum's Simple Harmonic Motion and the three formal operations of balancing of the trays of a scale. This entity became the unit of the social sciences, the common denominator of psychology, creativity, morality and the sciences. The concept was validated by art exhibits and with its application in delivering a program of psychoeducation to well people and to patients.

The key assumption of the Formal Theory thus introduced the unconscious as the integrative unit order. It identified the creative process, the plot of stories, as the circumscribed object for the study of behavior as consisting of the interrelation of six emotions in formal relation to each other united in the moral process of four types of conflict resolution, the relational modalities. These represented a personality typology, wellness diagnoses that also corresponded to alternative pathologies.

This unit was shown to be measurable with the self-assessment. The case studies presented the measurement of the unconscious and its diagnostic and therapeutic impact. The assessment program was transformative. It validated the traditional therapeutic principle of becoming conscious of the unconscious as finding wellness by knowing oneself. The assessment's clinical effectiveness was confirmed by the statistical findings of the online delivery of the assessment. The evidence validated Formal Theory's assumption that the creative process, the projection of the unconscious, is a measurable scientific conflict resolution mechanism.

The significance of this concept is that it bridges behavior's opposite positions: agnostic psychology and dogma-based moralities by delivering clarity to the unconscious as seeking a moral end through an orderly psychological and physiological mental automatism. Thus the conflict resolution concept ushers in the scientific era in thinking about psychology and morality.

Conflict is experienced as psychological discomfort upon a normative deviation. Conflict is energy occurring as a person distances oneself from the position of 'acceptable behaviors', the social gravitational force, one's state of rest. This distancing from the point of moral gravity induces a centripetal force, a motivational force, in the unconscious. This force opposite and reciprocal to the displacement represents the force driving the person to conflict resolution targeting normative compliance and also normative change.

In the case studies we observed the process manifested along the four alternative relational modalities unfolding along the six role-states. The case studies testing-imagery demonstrated first the clarity of relational modality diagnoses and showed the unfolding of the process as a harmonic, a triple dialectic emotional oscillation, progressing from a conflict to its dramatic resolution. The motivation driving this unconscious is attributed to the need to reduce psychic tension by reconciling the person with the personal normative structure of her/his symbolic universe. This explanation defines the driving motivational force to morality as originating in the psychic need to comply to societal rules/norms. Morality is in the spirit of normative compliance originating in the unconscious.

The restoration of inner balance unfolds as a pendulum oscillation manifested in all samples of creativity as a triple cycle harmonic. Returning to the point of rest the mind is released from the discomfort of conflict. But something changes in the process. The energy of conflict is captured into the affirmation of the normative moral order intensifying the normative reference. If the gravitation is religious norms, the impact of the resolution is intensification of the investment in the faith. In this fashion instead of the person learning about psychology s/he becomes more religious.

Knowledge of this unit entity greatly improves psychological services: diagnosis and therapy. The case studies reported in this volume utilizing the Conflict Analysis Battery demonstrate the manifestation of this measurable unconscious. Objectivity of the orderly findings cancel the subjectivity of most theoretical systems. Evidence conferred by the science, by the test takers' protocols, concurs on the correctness of the measurable unconscious, the meaningfulness of the relational diagnoses, of the therapeutic effectiveness of the assessment, and of the moral value of the Power Management conceptual approach. These findings validate Formal Theory's assumptions on the scientific and moral unconscious. What is also discovered by observing this mechanism is learning about the self-empowerment of normative institutions. This finding places morality on scientific foundation originating in the unconscious thinking but also raises the importance of the normative institutions determining what is ethical behavior.

CHAPTER TWO: MORALITY DEFINED THROUGH NORMATIVE CRITERIA

In the course of the history of civilization religions advanced norms as covenants like the marital vows, the father-son covenant, and the Ten Commandments regulating individual behavior in seeking to reduce interpersonal conflicts. Covenants specify the acceptable structuring of family relations. Religions evolved historically changing domestic norms by restructuring gender and generations role relations. They evolved from matriarchy's covenant of life sacrifice, to patriarchy's covenant of the marital vows, women being loyal to their spouses. India espoused the vow of asceticism, and Buddhism of the four noble truths. Monotheism was established on the father-son covenant and the messianic religions on the mother-child alliance. So, religions evolved from alienation in Mexico to mutual respect in Judea and from Greek antagonism between the genders to Indian cooperation of men and women. Religions discovered aspects of the scientific conflict resolution process attributing the qualities of the unconscious to the divine, as the moral authorities modeling behaviors and attitudes regulating the roles of domestic partners.

Religions' conflict resolution models are parallel to the personality types of their advocates. They are offering to their constituencies alternative normative injunctions in conflict resolution by identifying different formal operations in resolving conflict. The following cultures advanced the three alternative operations and corresponding resolutions: mastery, cooperation and mutual respect.

- Greece in the Homeric Epics discovered the principle of mastery as patriarchy domesticating the wild aggressive and paranoid women of matriarchy instituting dramatically the covenant of the vows. Zeus is a role model of male chauvinism in being both powerful as a lover and as a transformer of women. His weapon was the lightning bolt and his prowess claiming fifty recorded extramarital relations, which of course antagonized his wife Hera, who constantly undermined his escapades. Patriarchy's men in the Iliad overpowered the matriarchal woman: Helen of Troy but were defeated by Clytemnestra her sister, who killed her husband, Agamemnon upon his homecoming. The role of women changed in the Odyssey as Odysseus overcame the challenges of the Sirens, Circe and Calypso, and pretty innocent Nausicaa. Odysseus enjoyed a welcome upon his homecoming by his loyal wife, respectful son Telemachus and his dog. The Homeric Epics defended men's right for exclusivity in partnership with a woman established by the concept of the marital vows, fidelity to one man, as negotiated between Helen of Troy and her ten suitors. Aphrodite undermined the vows covenant by creating the challenge of the apple to the fairest. She bribed Paris, the judge, by offering him Helen, a married woman. Aphrodite was defending sexual freedom for women. She was defeated by the outcome of the Trojan War. The claim of ownership of a woman was a major conflict during the Trojan War as Agamemnon usurped a trophy woman from Achilles and was punished by Achille's withdrawal from the fight against the Trojans. Agamemnon motivated to reclaim Helen, a married woman, had to learn to respect other men's marital claims. Penelope, the loyal wife, who kept the suitors at a distance for many years became the role model for the virtuous Greek women.

- India discovered in Hinduism and later Buddhism the formal operation of cooperation. Men cooperate with women, and respect them as in the relation between Vishnu and his wife Lachsmi. Shiva had to restore Ganesha's severed head, complying to his consort's, Kallie's request. He restored Ganesha's severed head with an elephant head empowering the child, redefining the child's identity as a powerful but pleasant, cooperative elephant, a friendly hard working giant. India still reveres Sacred Cows and Monkeys symbolic of the societal role of women and children. Hinduism promoted asceticism, men suppressing desires. Lord Siva steps on the demon of his inner child. Buddhism is the philosophy of moderation through the eightfold path to enlightenment. Self-discipline and detachment from desires to reduce pain or conflict. This lack of antagonism explains the sociological institution of the cast system in India. Nobody challenges sociological inequities. India never came close to communism.

- Judea discovered mutual respect in the Father-Son covenant. The Judaic premise was that Eve yielding to temptation punished humans with the exile from Paradise. Noam's first wife, Lilith was viewed as a witch. Abraham destroyed his father's pagan idols, sculptures of women. Polygamous Ishtar of the Gilgamesh Epic was viewed as the enemy of the noble prince. The Judaic religion exacted a concession from mothers, with the utmost sacrifice of their power, as in Sara's willingness to see her only son sacrificed. Mothers' concession of power established the father-son covenant. Women as mothers trusted their husbands with their sons. Women became respectful of their husbands surrendering their offspring to them and their social power. Women were discriminated. Rules were introduced for them to conceal their beauty, their power of attractiveness. The concept of divinity evolved from Grecian polytheism to male Monotheism based on a loving and just male authority.

The integration of knowledge prepares the thinking public to examine critically our religions and accept their contributions but also to recognize their limitations and biases, leading to pathologies that need to be addressed for the health of the public. The MS shows that religions represent human personality types with the respective characteristics and the corresponding pathologies. Christianity, Christos means being good, pursues the submissive relational option, while Islam, means Submit, pursues the dominant alternative value system. Both religions inspired civilizations but they have different values and different pathologies.

Dogma based assumptions complicate the fair resolution of societal conflicts. Religions are important spiritual traditions but they suffer of multiple problems. An example is the lack of mutual respect is the case of the Abrahamic religions. They discriminate in judging genders, placing men as superior to women, hence they do not evolve to mutual respect between the genders. Such discriminations are unacceptable from the perspective of contemporary normative civil rights standards, which advocate equality hence mutual respect among all people. While social norms have evolved from the times of Abraham, the Abrahamic religions are frozen, abiding to the dated norms, the ones introduced as normative improvements at the time of their inception.

This formal analysis introduces religions as normative institutions determining diverse acceptable ways in resolving conflicts. These evolved by cultures espousing the alternative conflict resolution modalities. Religions evolved endorsing relational modalities as normative philosophies regulating the lives of the faithful attributing their choices to their respective prophets. We may then say that religions are sanctifications of relational modalities as cultural philosophies or belief systems. Religions as self-differentiating normative institutions evolved their respective value preferences with multiple stories of their respective role model heroes exemplifying virtuous conduct. Thus religions evolved in the history of civilization improving the family institution by regulating female sexuality and moderating men's attitude toward their sons.

The Moral Science retraces the evolution of normative systems

We may conclude that morality, a sociological order, originates in the physiology of the unconscious as the motivational force propelling conflict resolution by the innate need to reduce the painful experience of psychic tension. Religions established normative systems identifying patterns of relating in domestic relations determined as a progression of alternative types of conflict resolution. Cultural systems as normative institutions represent diversity of conflict resolutions. We detect continuity in the moral or conflict resolving evolution of religions progressing toward fairness in regulating family relations and in the trend of redefining the divine more abstractly. One of the descriptions of the Judaic divinity coincides with the conflict resolution process as 'God is he who was, is and will be' reconciling the diversity of gods redefinitions. Religions may be reconciled into the Moral Science as partial and complementary discoveries of the innate conflict resolution process.

Moral Monopoly, the educational game, retraces the evolution of religions in succession to each other in the course of the history of civilization restructuring family role relations improving the family institution through the ongoing revamping of norms. This game reflects the evolution as improving fairness in the structure of family relations and increasing the abstraction on the nature of the divine. Religions, observed in an evolutional perspective, represent phases in the history of civilization. Gods have become less anthropomorphic and more conceptual.

Society's ongoing normative evolution represents humanity's pursuit of rectifying social injustices seeking peace as the ultimate or global determination of moral order. In the process of this evolution each religion is a discovery and also a hurdle to progress. Each religion has innovated and also resisted progress: stronger the convictions, more resistant the faith in yielding power to a new belief system. So religions resist change to improving relations beyond their sanctified normative sociological discoveries.

Studying the evolution of religions we observe that norms, as social covenants, are time limited. Religions evolve by upstaging older religions. Religions freezing progress as bound to their sanctified normative beliefs are replaced by new religions and ideologies with more liberal normative solutions. The Messianic religions, the Mother-Child Alliances, were an adjustment response to Judaism's Father-Son Covenant. Generated to rectify social injustices, messianic religions too became institutions that have frozen evolution at a set of norms resisting civil rights legislations, which are constantly revised. So religions defend dated paradigms. They cannot evolve to the ultimate science-based definition of moral order.

This normative battle pertains to the contemporary conflicts between the Abrahamic religions' gender discrimination. All Abrahamic religions are entrenched in the predicament of resisting criticism and modification. They defend their norms as sanctified by the moral authorities of the respective prophets blocking criticism and not allowing societal progress. These religions, while having dramatic inspirational value, generate normative conflicts with modern civil liberties. As usual the originally innovative revolutionary norms gradually become reactionary and unjust normative institutions sponsoring inequities in view of societal civil rights progress.

Religions have been ahead of psychology in deliberately guiding behavior morally, focusing on the one or the other of three conflict resolution principles or formal operations in their respective catechisms, their programs of emotional education. But now we have a new reality. The Moral Science modifies psychology and morality by understanding the unconscious as the origin of moral thinking. Psychology catches up with religions by clarifying the origin of morality in the nature of the unconscious conflict resolving process thus demystifying religions. The new challenge is in the respectful integration of psychology and morality with science.

CHAPTER THREE: RELIGIONS ARE MEASURABLE NATURAL SCIENCE MORAL ORDER PHENOMENA

The Moral Science addresses normative conflicts as originating in the relational modality choices of individuals and religions

Science respects but demystifies religions. Science recognizes the three principles of conflict resolution as the abstract equilibrial principles guiding moral thinking and moral motivation. It is the unconscious that now is the origin of morality founded on an innate scientific mechanism. The mechanism's formal operations account for the qualities of the divine: mastery with moderation, cooperation, and mutual respect; these are the physiologically determined moral values that we must deliberately adopt to effectively resolve conflicts. Morality becomes the essence of the study of psychology. Science integrates psychology and religions placing them both on the scientific foundation of the study of the creative process.

The 9/11 experience demonstrates relational psycho- and socio-pathology and the need for conceptual changes in religions and psychology. In the twentieth century, the public shifted from trusting religions to supporting ideologies: communism and psychoanalysis. A century later both ideologies failed. Freud's unconscious was not resolving conflict but creating it and justifying it. Communism was based on economic parity as resolving the discrepancy between classes encouraging people to inflict radical societal changes. Upon the end of the century and the failure of these ideologies, the world has returned to religions as the default moral paradigms. Today's world is fragmented by believing theistic paradigms normative standards as the trusted moral imperatives. Iran's clergy are obsessed with developing destructive weapons to be used in the name of God. North Korea's communist leaders similarly seek weaponry, in a world which has abandoned the communist ideology. Representatives of religion and ideologies inspire their followers to die for their belief systems. This is where religions and ideologies mislead the public, recklessly endorsing norms that endanger the planet's ecological survival.

Here is the role of the Moral Science interpreting metaphors and unifying psychology and morality as the path to personal and political healing. The Moral Science demystifies religions as sociological natural science normative institutions and formalizes psychology by showing the scientific nature of personality types.

Applying formal analysis to the conflict between Trump and Islam

The Formal Theory understands the nature of the unconscious as a scientific phenomenon providing diagnostic categories applied to people and to religions. To understand the current conflict between Islam and the USA, we need to go back in history, examining the developments of the 20th century. Darwin's findings in evolution further undermined the credibility of religion, and the century gravitated to two alternative moral directions as ideologies. It was two Jewish contemporary prophets, who revolutionized the world with alternative moral paradigms addressing solutions for sociological and psychological problems. Marx addressed the economic inequalities promoting the socialist, communist revolution. Freud addressed psychological suffering promoting freedom from oppressive sexuality norms. Hitler a dominant paranoid personality threatened by Judaic political power responded to the two Jewish ideologies offering his racial superiority theory entitling him to destroy Judaic leadership by establishing Arian dominance. His war led to the destruction of Europe and the Holocaust. The conflict resolution led to the establishment of the European Union and the creation of Israel.

Israel's creation upset the neighboring Islamic populations. The intrusion associated the USA and Israel as the alliance threatening Islamic sovereignty. It evoked the Islamic antagonistic dominance spearheading the attack of 9/11. The Islamic youth attacked America in the name of Allah, the one God. America responded by attacking an Islamic dictator. The Iraqi War encouraged questioning Arab authoritarianism and inspired the wave of revolutions, the Arab Spring, rekindling Islamic orthodoxy as Isis aspiring for a caliphate and Taliban espousing orthodoxy, while the sects, Sunnis and Shiites, destroyed Syria and inflicted the Islamic exodus. The Islamic immigrants brought their cultural values into Europe which resisted them by becoming nationalistic with a prevalence of autocratic political rulers. In America, the conflict with Islam in part led to the election of Donald Trump as president. He responded to Jihad's hostilities setting boundaries to the Islamic nationals entering the States. In a parallel manner he canceled America's treaties and alliances, economic, climate, and defense partnerships, while befriending America's political enemies, dictators, North Korea's and Russia's dominant antagonistic leaders. America's president emerged as an aggressive nationalistic leader.

Psychologists diagnosed Trump along DSM illness diagnoses as malignant narcissism, psychopathology defined as a medical diagnosis that may not be disclosed as politicians' privacy is protected by the Goldwater decision. The current "state of the art" psychology neither understands Trump's personality nor that of the Islamic religion. It does not recognize wellness personality types as conflict resolution syndromes, therefore traditional psychology cannot help Trump and Islam.

The Moral Science reverses the medicalization of psychology and reduces the dogma foundation of morality by establishing it as a totally abstract wellness-focused psychodynamic science introducing patterns of conflict resolution as relational modalities applying them both to a person, Trump and a religion, Islam.
Science diagnoses Trump's psychological condition and of the Islamic value system as that of the dominant antagonistic relational modality. This formal analysis clarifies the current political conflicts as evoked by the personal and cultural dominant antagonistic relational modalities.

The Formal Theory offers the wellness relational diagnosis to both Trump and Islam, founded on relational criteria obvious to the public. Everybody agrees that Trump's and Islam's conduct is dominance, antagonism and alienation toward partners. This modality is a syndrome clarified with the attributes of the Wizard of Oz character of the Cowardly Lion, connecting dominance with paranoia, aggression with fears of aggression, eliciting defensiveness, setbacks, and lack of compromise. The scientific psychology identifies the wellness diagnosis as a relational conflict resolving typology applicable to both an individual and a culture. The relational diagnosis explains the individual and the cultural behaviors and also offers corrective information. In a blog 'Educating Trump', I offered advice to Trump upon his election in 2016.

After 20 years at war America failed in thwarting the Taliban oppressive value system. The orthodox Islamics inspired by their faith defended their supremacist oppressive values. Many leaders emerge espousing dominant antagonistic behaviors, such as Putin's invasion of Ukraine. The only solution to psychological, nationalist and religious power postures is insights in psychological and sociological analysis of personalities and moral philosophies as religions' moral thinking. The only path to peace is a meaningful analysis of personalities and religions by recognizing the pathology and obstinacy of relational patterns.

The foremost insight from this analysis is in recognizing that both Trump and Islam suffer of the paranoid distortion of reality based on the dominant antagonistic relational diagnosis. Islam means submit. This moral paradigm has led to the autocratic rule of many Arab nations. It is manifested in the inequity in gender relations, religious zealousness, and sensitivities leading to the jihad spirit manifested in the quest for a caliphate culture and intolerance of criticism. It is difficult to question values as faithful people pray, submit, to the cultural values five times a day.

America uncomfortable with dominant antagonism has sought to correct Trump's insulting behaviors seeking but failing in impeaching him twice. his resistance to transition of power and his assault of the Capitol on January 6, 2021, demonstrates the psychological malignancy of this personality type both distorting reality and escalating conflicts. We experienced Trump's dominant antagonism, in many forms, but it was particularly unacceptable manifested on the January 6 insurrection.

The political and military conduct of several contemporary strongmen exemplifies how difficult it is to address dominant antagonism as leadership options during times of crises. The remedy for this pathology is insights into the psychology of conflict resolution. Trump's conduct has been a momentous opportunity for the public to recognize psychology and religions in terms of the formal analysis of conflict in the psychological and political domains.

Formal Theory's conceptual relevance

The escalation of conflicts between an individual as a president in serious national political conflict and a religion in a problematic word wide disposition, inspiring millions, is a diagnostic problem that needs to be addressed conceptually. It is a conflict that can be explained by applying scientific analysis as advocated by the Formal Theory of Behavior. The challenge is double: to upset the agnostic medicalized psychology and the theistic dated moral values of all religions. This is the moment for a conceptual revolution, the change of paradigms. The public needs to identify the scientific nature of moral order, reconciling psychology, morality, and science, unifying the people of the world divided by the limitations of their psychologically handicapped leaders and the self-righteousness of their moral paradigms. The Moral Science can address the current domestic and international problems by understanding the psychopathology of relational patterns.

The scientific interpretation of metaphors leads to a better understanding of psychology and religion. The analysis of this personal versus cultural conflict represents the opportunity for the conceptual understanding of both psychological and religious relational issues. We can use insights in the psyche of the president and in the nature of a great religion.

Science by attributing moral order to the unconscious, instead of the divine, and attributing it to natural laws characteristic of the mental process, questions psychology as founded on the brain, and morality as determined by revelation. The condition for reconciling psychology and religions is for both domains to espouse the science based moral values in rethinking the unconscious, diagnoses as a wellness typology, and religions' as having a rational foundation. This is indeed a tall order but it is the condition for the world to reign in political leaders and feuding moral paradigms in order to find peace as freedom from extreme conflicts.

Science has the right to overrule agnostic medicalized psychology and theistic religions as they are both misleading the public promoting themselves as representing respectively the total truth. In their obstinacy to prevail along their prejudicial moral normative determinations they are generating conflicts handicapping the social adjustment of the mortals. The new science is Prometheus' fire, the moral authority, stolen from the psychological authorities as well as from traditional belief systems and given to the public. The question is in the receptivity of the scientists and the faithful.

Deprived of proper scientific analysis, and legitimized politically by the Constitution religions have monopolized the concept of morality at the expense of reason and societal normative progress. But science as the new 'deus ex machina' defining morality as independent of the brain and of religions, spiritualizes psychology, while demystifying religions depriving them of their self-righteousness, their entitlement as absolute moral authorities on the basis of dogma.

Science unmasks religions manipulating public opinion but in contrast to Toto's unmasking of the Wizard's machinations and manipulations of the public, science identifies formulas of energy and attitude transformation, moral order as a natural science psychological sociological mechanism. Science questions normative systems making them accountable to natural and civil rights laws. The significance of this development is that science empowers rational people to prevail over both agnostic psychology and also theistic righteousness. Unlike prior criticisms of faiths the Moral Science clarifies morality rather than cancelling it. It places morality on the foundation of science. It informs the public about the means to find inner harmony and societal peace by abiding by universal laws.

We may expect this awareness to moderate religions' self-righteousness and psychology's agnosticism and thus that we can reach a worldwide consensus on moral values as the laws guiding the unconscious to conflict resolution. That should not be difficult as there is overlap between traditional moral laws and science laws. The concept of the divine coincides with the creative process. Genesis coincides with the six-role psychic process. The Ten Commandments injunctions averting conflict coincide with the three laws restoring balance in a system as the traditional moral injunctions coincide with the scientific principles of mastery, cooperation and mutual respect. Traditional psychology impervious of the human need for moral order misunderstands the essence of the unconscious; it has ascribed to it conflict generation. Ignoring the moral makeup of the unconscious is unscientific. Theistic religions relying on dogma based imperatives are misleading the public imposing inequitable gender norms. Such discriminations and their organizational authoritarianism monopolizing normative standards is untenable in our times of the globalization of norms.

The Formal Theory integrates psychology and morality as founded on science instead of on neurology and revelation. Wellness and pathologies are emotional conditions, not medical ones. Morality is not determined by external authorities but by the justice seeking human unconscious. Humans need to be aware of the nature of the psyche, the unconscious as a scientific conflict resolution innate entity to free themselves from illness-based psychiatry and dogma-based morality as the condition to find peace of mind and social justice. Psychology and religions as divisive politicized self-righteous institutions expropriating the notion of wellness and moral authority should be made accountable to reason. Wellness and morality are founded on a psychological sociological scientific phenomenon independent of metaphysics. It is based on rules of emotional processes determined by the unconscious need to reduce psychic and social conflicts. Civil rights laws determine the contemporary norms as what is acceptable. The public needs to be respectful to the norms established by contemporary society's unbiased legislators.

CHAPTER FOUR: THE SCIENTIFIC MORAL PARADIGM

Moral Science's role as the moral authority

The integration of psychology, morality and science is a topic of tremendous clinical, educational and political relevance in our times experiencing an extreme polarization between individuals and cultures. On the one side the field of psychology is dominated by an agnostic, non-psychodynamic, medicalized view of behavior, on the other side a wide public across several religions is inspired by morality as theistic moral paradigms. The science of the process reconciles these fragmented perceptions of the mind and of the divine by understanding the psyche as rational and moral and the divine as the projection of personality determined alternatives.

The Moral Science addresses solving societal conflicts by shifting the normative authority of religions to the civil authority of science-aware legislators. From this perspective morality is the science of the unconscious conflict resolution process while contemporary psychology and religions are misleading partial scientific knowledge. Science demystifies religions as normative institutions representing partial resolutions of conflict that are now accountable to natural laws. Science identifies their normative limitations as partial understanding of the process and requires resolutions to end upon establishing mutual respect between the parties in conflict.

The problem of religions is that they deify particular conflict resolutions as perfect resolutions espousing normative determinations, which eventually are outgrown as society restructures relations and the companion norms. Gods and norms have evolved from matriarchy to patriarchy, from polytheism to monotheism, from the Judaic father son covenant to the Messianic mother child alliances, from theistic absolutes to philosophical belief systems and social justice inspired ideologies. Accordingly gods have evolved as alternative deifications of the newest role models of conflict resolution. Moral authorities are ascribed with the increasingly abstract attributes of the unconscious. This evolution of concepts of the divine as alternative norms explains the current conflicts between reason and faith.

The volume *Science Stealing the Fire of the Gods and Healing the World* and the game of Moral Monopoly retrace the history of religions. They evolved in succession to each other in the course of the history of civilization restructuring family relations improving the family institution as society's ongoing normative evolution. *'The sculptural trail in the history of love'* illustrates paradigm shifts along sociological conflict resolutions generated to rectify social conflicts or injustices. It highlights the accomplishments and limitations of the Abrahamic family. It shows how the Messianic religions, the *Mother-child alliances*, were an adjustment response to *Judaism's Father-Son Covenant.*

The Moral Science's concepts integrate psychology, sociology, diagnosis, assessment, morality with science by placing them on the formal analysis of the creative process. The theory provides a meaningful language that translates all private moral languages into formulas of science that can educate the public and heal cultural conflicts as well as individual ones. The formal six-role process is shown to be the unifying order integrating psychology and morality by placing them on the scientific foundation of the creative process. The emotional transformative effectiveness of the training experience validates the formal theoretical assumption. Test takers recognize the conceptual and technological advantages of the Moral Science utilizing the Conflict Analysis Battery. They recognize that the four new concepts rethink psychology, revamp therapy and education, and reconcile religions among themselves as partial and complementary discoveries of the Moral Science.

The case studies of this volume confirm the educational benefit of implementing this conceptual and technological development. Programs of emotional education, like Power Management, should be used for the education of the public. Education can be improved by delivering in the classroom the integration of the humanities and the sciences, self-knowledge, and clarity of moral values as the scientific principles of the unconscious. This knowledge can also be used to expedite therapy, train workers, political leaders, executives, prisoners, couples in conflict and soldiers involved in cross-cultural warfare.

The world must discover the psychology of wellness and abandon psychology as illness. We no longer need the Oedipal complex neither theistic revelations. We can interpret stories along their natural science alternative conflict resolving dimensions. We must abandon today's psychology treating emotions as symptoms of illness. The science requires therapists to become educators, helping the individual understand patterns, identifying them and becoming responsible in interrupting them by managing attitude and power.

Religions inspire but divide. We do not need to abandon religions. We must examine them critically. We can respect religions as discoveries of the alternative types of conflict resolution, but we must put them in a historical evolutional perspective and explore their integration along the redefinitions for the role of men and women.

Knowledge about morality and psychology as unified into a single science must be introduced into the public's awareness as emotional literacy, as mandatory emotional education; clergy should preach integration of religions as discoveries of the importance of morality as a universal innate order. Their business is still moral education but with less emphasis on one divinity and more on analyzing all cultural patterns. It is important to inform how relational modalities distort reality and that they can mislead. Psychologists must become spiritual, and clergy must become rational, educational. Both psychology and religion must become scientific in their explanations and aspirations.

Science challenges our sanctified paradigms

Formal Theory's unconscious is both a natural science and a conflict resolution physiological homeostatic phenomenon. As both a scientific and moral order entity, it reconciles the rigorous sciences with the humanities, psychology with religions, and transforms behavior into a unified science. By introducing science and morality in the study of the unconscious as a unit order, the Formal Theory departs with a conflict: it questions the norm of the prevailing concepts of agnostic psychology and dogma-abiding religions. It challenges the psychoanalytic conflict evoking, non-rational definition of the unconscious, DSM 5's illness, and non-morality driven diagnoses by introducing psychodynamic thinking guided by formal directional principles into four wellness diagnostic categories. It questions assessments' arbitrary, non-formal distinctions of the unconscious process challenging their credibility. The psychological origin of morality challenges the dogma or divine revelation-based moral values systems. Formal Theory's conflict leads to a resolution; the happy ending is in the fact that the new concepts integrate the social science disciplines into the totally rational relational Moral Science.

The conclusion is that in detecting the formal relationship between the constellation of the six emotions in the plot of stories as a conserved energetic continuum guided by the three formal operations into upgrading order, we avail of the scientific definition of the unconscious. This represents a paradigm shift from stories we believe in at face value, which divide believers, to identifying the structure or plot of stories as a psychological entity with a sociological adaptive function that integrates all stories to the abstractions of scientific laws leading all thinkers to moral consensus.

The unconscious reconciles religions as complementary discoveries of science and completes their unfinished business. Conflict resolution is the driving force manifested in all samples of creativity. The conflict resolving process is an exact natural science phenomenon, the universal harmonic, the common denominator of the social sciences; it is the unit order of the Moral Science. The unconscious redefined as seeking conflict resolution as reduction of psychic tension upon a normative conciliation coincides personal growth with sociological change. Motivation is driven by the need to reduce psychic and social tension as a physiological, psychological, and sociological scientific phenomenon.

The Formal Theory thus recognizes the need for conflict resolution as the key human motivation, identified with the reduction of personal discomfort as the quest for social justice. Morality stems from this unconscious pursuit of conflict resolution coinciding with normative compliance and normative change. The unconscious as a conflict resolution or moral order entity as compliance to norms is the dynamic of faiths, which has been attributed by religions to revelation as stemming from the moral authority of gods. Formal Theory's assumption refutes metaphysical claims showing that religions are of psychological origin and that they represent normative institutions originating in the justice-seeking unconscious: they have evolved toward abstraction and universality. Moral Monopoly shows how religions have evolved as complementary discoveries of the relational modality alternatives as generated by the need to improve the family institution by reducing psychological and sociological conflicts along the four alternative relational paths.

Thus, science reclaims the attributes of the divine as pertaining to the unconscious process. Divinities have evolved, being redefined as projections to external authorities of the qualities of the unconscious. Religions' moral values as in the Ten Commandments, promoting moderation, cooperation, and mutual respect, coincide with the three formal operations as the equilibrial principles of conflict resolution.

Moral Science does not specify norms but recognizes the moral justice principles as constructs and formulas optimizing conflict resolution. Religions evolved succeeding each other as operational improvements following the principles of the unconscious. The study of cultural stories validates Formal Theory's assumption on the scientific and moral nature of the unconscious. Interpreting cultural stories as metaphors, we identify the underlying moral paradigms as discoveries of the set of relational modalities. One of the required formal operations for resolution of conflicts is the operation of correlation, transforming alienation to mutual respect. This is a scientific requirement for conflict resolution that leads to morality as inclusive of all members of an interpersonal realm. This operation is missing in the norm pertaining to the man/woman relationship in all three Abrahamic religions.

The conclusion of this study is that psychology is no longer amoral or agnostic, and one deprived of scientific integrity. Psychology is radically revamped into an exact science. It is established that it is a science that can understand both psychology and morality. Psychology becomes the exact Science of Conflict Resolution. It is totally revamped into an abstract science whose constructs are bound by formulas that are measurable and that are graphically portrayable. A psychological assessment allows the individual to understand one's unconscious as a syndrome with a relational modality diagnosis. The self-study is didactic, diagnostic, and therapeutic.

Religions, theistic metaphysical systems can be understood as measurable scientific normative institutions. They become accountable to science. Science has the moral authority to analyze religions as partial and complementary discoveries of the Science of Conflict Resolution. From the Formal Theoretical perspective, religions are normative institutions that have evolved, restructuring family role relations improving domestic relationships. Religions have followed the path in identifying the unconscious moral operations transforming passivity to activity, from matriarchy to patriarchy in Greece, from antagonism to cooperation in India, and from alienation to mutual respect in Judea's father-son covenant. As norms become, conflictual or dated religions have outgrown earlier variations of resolutions. Religions become immoral from the perspective of the next moral order system. New spiritual leaders seek more inclusive concepts of justice. Moralities have been redefined by the exponents' particular types of conflict resolution. Accordingly, religions have evolved empirically as normative institutions progressing toward reduction of personal and domestic conflicts providing alternative types of moral order abiding by the modality of the prophets. The twentieth century abandoned religions as ideologies promised to resolve the conflicts of the individual with psychoanalysis and the problems of classes with communism.

The Formal Theory claims the moral authority by defining morality as an abstract psychological process determined by the unconscious need of reducing psychic tension. Psychology reclaims the attributes of the divine as projections of the qualities of the unconscious innate pursuit of emotional balance through social justice for all. The science respects religions as sanctifying and deifying the range of relational modalities, but these have evolved as moral monopolies. The new psychology as the Moral Science may intervene by identifying the inequities of the gender relations prevalent in most religions by completing their unfinished business, by reducing their conflicts, and thus attaining their mission for peace in the world.

The world needs the scientific moral paradigm.
The world in the 21st century is torn by psychological and religious conflicts. Psychology is atheoretical, agnostic, non-scientific, and medicalized; it lacks the capacity to both understand wellness and morality; it is unable to assist the public with addressing conflicts by understanding and correcting individual behavior and that of religious institutions.

Education is failing because psychology does not deliver its three objectives: the integration of the humanities and sciences, self-knowledge, and the clarity of values. Society is affected by problematic individuals in high office: decision-making leaders, whom psychology cannot diagnose and assist as it does not avail a psychodynamic understanding of wellness diagnoses. Gun control cannot be managed on the basis of mental illness as the diagnoses do not screen intensity of emotional dispositions. Religious conflicts lead to devastating cross-cultural conflicts.

Critical analysis of personal psychopathology is compromised by the Goldwater ruling forbidding analysis without personally examining individuals; analysis of religions is handicapped by the principle of political correctness. Consequently, societal conflicts are addressed with military containment and personality conflicts with court decisions and therapeutically with medications.

The world needs the scientific psychology to deal effectively with individual behavior and with autocratic moral dogmatism. The formal hypothesis on the conflict resolving nature of the unconscious sheds light on both domains with concepts based on science that are testable.

Timely, upon the conclusion of the Twentieth Century, the Formal Theory completes the task of rational humanists from Aristotle, Freud, and Marx, who aspired to clarify both intrapsychic and interpersonal, intergender, and interclass struggles through scientific principles. Finally, we can show that it is possible to pursue a rational understanding of psychological and sociological phenomena doing justice both to reason and to the inherent need for moral order based on the totally abstract redefinition of the unconscious as an order-striving equilibrial mechanism.

Could the Formal Theory be the final phase in the evolution of abstraction on matters of behavior and morality? The answer is in examining samples of creativity as the object of scientific analysis. Formal Theory's initiative has succeeded in shifting paradigms from advancing stories, theories and religions, to recognizing the structure of all stories as the object of study leading to the psychological and sociological correction of conflicts. The process is now a fathomable entity, a measurable conflict resolution process, the unconscious as a universal order underlying all thinking, hence of all behavior.

Psychology has become an exact science based on the analysis of the creative process as a conflict resolving mechanism reflecting on the nature of the unconscious. The Moral Science is the new psychology. It radically changes the way we conceptualize the unconscious, diagnosis, assessment, therapy, and morality.

1. Instead of an unconscious that is generating conflicts and is non-logical we identify the creative process as a scientific conflict resolving measurable entity. The unconscious resolves conflict in every story as an energy transformation mechanism as a six-role emotional dialectic guided by formal operations to transforming passivity to activity, antagonism to cooperation, and alienation to mutual respect.
2. Instead of illness based diagnoses we identify wellness relational modality syndromes. We recognize four personality types according to how we resolve conflicts corresponding to the three formal operations principles: dominant versus submissive, antagonistic versus cooperative, and alienation as illness versus mutual respect as wellness according to the intensity of conflict experienced.
4. Instead of multiple atheoretical diagnostic assessments the Conflict Analysis Battery identifies the unconscious as a measurable formal relational modality with the help of a personality inventory and as a six role state syndrome by tapping creativity for self-discovery.
5. Instead of multiple divisive moral paradigms we identify morality as the Science of Conflict Resolution where moral values are the three formal operations that guide the process to resolutions. These are: mastery, cooperation and mutual respect.

Religions are psychological phenomena that have evolved, resolving the conflicts of the family institution as discoveries of the alternative paradigms. The Bible is the prototype of a program of emotional education. Dogma consists of very insightful metaphors that may be interpreted as corresponding to science. The Moral Science demystifies religions and interrelates them proceeding to complete their mission for peace in the world as the science of morality.

The world finds in the scientific analysis of the creative process formulas as the new moral paradigm, an explanation integrating meaningfully the diversity of moral paradigms, as these have evolved historically from metaphors, something familiar, to formulas, something meaningful, and measurable. The quest for abstraction and universality has led us to understand the nature of symbolic universes with the abstract concepts of phenomena of science rather than dogma-based approximations. Reconciling morality and science, we attain humanity's long-term quest for meaning. We can proceed from metaphorical thinking with certainty to formulas as definitive abstractions.

Abstract thinking along formulas accounts for psychology and morality, poetry, and religions. Moral Science compels, commands, inspires. It does not cancel God; it rediscovers it simply defining morality as the abstractions of conflict resolution manifested in the physical organization of the creative process unconscious.

Moral Science claims the conditions to achieve emotional growth. They are founded on the clarity of the unconscious as syndromal relational modality diagnoses, the four alternative relational modalities and on our ability to measure it utilizing the battery assessment. The clarity of concepts reduces personal and interpersonal strife by educating students in the classroom, providing couples with premarital counselling, patients with effective psychotherapy, executives_with organizational training, faithful people with clarity of their moral messages. The world needs to find moral consensus by understanding how the modalities differ in their perceptions of reality and how distortions elicit very different responses to the identical stressors. The theory helps individuals by examining their perceptions and distortions in the context of the alternative ways of relating and resolving along their need for power and attitude.

Political and psychological self-awareness is needed

Psychology is medicalized unable to comprehend emotional conflict. Religion-based morality, and their sets of norms, cultural values, generate conflicts in their interface. Psychology and religions must deal with the evolution of conflicts in the world. They must recognize the scientific principles defining psychology and morality as determined by alternative approaches to conflict resolution. We do not need leaders that mislead and moral paradigms that polarize. The world needs to improve our understanding of psychology and morality. We need science integrating psychology and religion into a unified domain of knowledge. All faiths and all individuals need to examine themselves analytically, scientifically, for the individuals and the religions to function optimally in their interactions within the family and within the globe. Current explanations, psychological and religious, are divisive in the pursuit of peace. Unifying the world is only possible by reducing conflict at the conceptual level affecting insights in the personal and interpersonal domains.

Psychology must identify the innateness of the principles of conflict resolution. The new concepts identify the psychological origin of morality and its natural science measurable dimensions. Religions evolved as partial and complementary discoveries of science, improving the family role-relations; they need to continue and complete their mission for peace in the world by recognizing that it is the mind which resolves conflicts. The United Nations need to promote accountability of leaders as well as of religions to laws of science as the means of promoting civil conduct between leaders, religions, and nations. Science-based moral consensus can unify the world.

We need to pay attention to the scientific analysis of metaphors. We need to stop killing each other and destroying the planet in the name of metaphors. We need to change our moral paradigms. Let us explore the dynamics underlying crises and examine the attitude changes as transformative science. Wars can be averted if the world can grow in wisdom by applying the scientific analysis to psychology and religions. Understanding science can diffuse this crisis and be transformative by leading to the global awareness of the scientific nature of psychology and morality. The drama of the world today is summed up as the evolution of the Easter Island, the island of Gods, who doomed its survival. Humanities desperate need for God is threatening the survival of our globe.

CHAPTER FIVE:
EDUCATION INTEGRATING PSYCHOLOGY AND MORALITY INTO THE MORAL SCIENCE

Emotional Education as the application of the science

Suddenly we have formulas accounting for the scientific nature of the unconscious; we can all agree on the nature of the divine as reflecting the unconscious. Morality is the science of the unconscious and religions are solutions of the formulas. They are now accountable to the scientifically defined moral order; they represent partial truths; they are moral monopolies that consider themselves as revelations. They have not finished their business to conflict resolution. They have furthered meaning and civilizations, but they are divisive philosophies that hold people hostage away from the truth by imposing norms that are frozen in time and which are not ethical or moral in our times.

Religions have the attributes of the relational modalities of the individuals who created them as philosophies of life. They represent alternative value systems that have been deified and worshiped as giving meaning and structure to the societies they have inspired. Religions evolved in the last 10,000 years but they are still in the state of evolution. Morality evolved beyond religions as the ideologies of the 20th century, as economic socialism and as psychoanalytic theories, freeing people from repressive norms of economy and sexuality. These twentieth century ideologies eventually failed; the world resumed reliance on faiths and again entered wars based on religious paradigms. Without a sense of inspiration the world is again at the mercy of divisive religiosity and narrow nationalisms.

The Moral Science is of utmost relevance in our times. It clarifies morality as the science of psychology, generating new diagnoses and therapeutic interventions, deliverable as an emotional education. Contemporary agnostic and medicalized psychology misdiagnoses the ailing person. Psychiatry does not understand wellness and relational dysfunctions and does not understand religions and their divisiveness.

The world needs the new psychology and the new moral paradigm. It needs to understand the unconscious, to identify wellness diagnoses for individuals and also for religions. It needs a scientific foundation for psychological services. The Moral Science offers the scientific analysis of the creative process as the scientific moral paradigm. It clarifies the unconscious, wellness diagnostic categories as an insightful personality typology; it offers the effectiveness of an assessment identifying the structure of the thought process, it offers clarity on moral values as the scientific principles of conflict resolution: mastery, cooperation and mutual respect.

The Moral Science examines reality with objectivity. Therapy changes from focus on symptoms and the therapeutic relationship to an emotional education facilitated through the use of the self-assessment, which is made available to the public free of charge. The therapist becomes an educator encouraging understanding the science through self-discovery. The educator becomes a therapist, who can prioritize emotional education as the condition for the effective delivery of the other literacies.

Psychology then and morality as based on science belong to the public as an educational imperative. Emotional Education must deliver this information as moral literacy as a civil right. The public needs guidance; we must educate children and help people in therapy with conflicts away from the medical model as well as the dogma inspired moralities. Civil rights evolved to emancipate oppressed partners, slaves, women or castes, minorities, but also it must serve all faithful hostages of religions. Believers are society's victims. The public needs one more civil right: it needs emotional and moral literacy.

Mission Statement as the implementation of wisdom

The Riddle of the Sphinx has been solved and we are now masters of the passage to the promised land of moral consensus founded on the scientific understanding of the unconscious. The next challenge is technological distribution of information. The objective is to benefit the public, and to avert deterioration of the global moral crisis based on the limitations of current psychology and of religions.

The new moral paradigm promotes inner need for conflict resolution, that is of good will. The world needs to learn about revamping psychology and morality into a science of moral order based on the creative process, defining the unconscious as a scientific phenomenon that is graphically portrayable and that is readily measurable. The public must find out about the scientific breakthrough bridging psychology and religions into the Moral Science demystifying religions, spiritualizing psychology, reconciling religions as partial and complementary discoveries of science integrating wisdoms into the Moral Science, the moral psychology.

The claim for a scientific moral paradigm may and must be scrutinized by responsible experts across all its claims and applications; technologies of the assessment could be improved in all its aspects: constructs, formulas, technological implementation. Among the topics of rethinking psychology as a science we need to clarify the diagnostic categories of wellness and illness, we need to develop an assessment that is more accurate, reliable and valid. We need to clarify the curriculum for emotional education, and we must expect religions to become less dogmatic and more rational. They should be accountable to science.

Knowledge of this science must be shared worldwide with the objective of reducing personal, cultural and cross-cultural conflicts. The program can be delivered as part of public education, in therapeutic settings needs to be repeated yearly. In therapeutic settings, addiction rehabilitation centers as well as institutionalized populations. We need to reduce the ineffectiveness of moral and psychological nonscientific paradigms by understanding that we have a unifying, science-based moral paradigm, and two technologies that can heal the person. The concepts and assessment technologies can achieve a role for global transformation. These concepts and technologies can inspire the world to be responsible, rather than staying conflicted divided and self-destructive.

This transformation, i.e. the successful implementation of the new moral paradigm, will encounter difficulties and challenges. The new psychology and morality as a science will have an impact in many settings, whether personal, organizational or political. These normative changes are strongly resisted.

Let us be partners in recognizing that the world needs a global moral revolution by informing the public about the Moral Science and its educational programs; providing unity to the divided religions and ideologies providing a unifying moral message that integrates psychology, religions and the sciences, that provides a concise emotional education to all individuals and that gives the world clarity on moral values as principles of science.

There are technical problems that we need to address, such as privacy, uniform distribution in many languages, standardizing the programs seeking professional expertise. I am offering the technologies, the assessment instrument of the Moral Monopoly game are available for universal distribution and development. What is important is that the world is educated to avert the destruction of the planet. Big technology is needed to introduce the new technologies that transform education, psychology and religion. There are technical issues to explore such as managing data, distributing information, translating assessment into different languages, delivering the program and storing information. These problems require collaboration with leaders, companies to reduce costs, managing information clearing minimum profit providing a service that puts the entire world on same page. There are always issues that need to be resolved; checks and balances have to be built into the system.

Science is the moral authority, but how do we agree on normative determinations on issues of different perspectives? Issues such as population management, sexual identity, monogamy versus polygamy, age of marriage, number of children, prevention of multiple births in cases of parental disabilities, and physical limitations, ethical normative issues determinations about termination of life, issues like death penalty. So, there are challenges for the successful implementation of the new paradigm.

I am therefore addressing leaders to collaborate as they have the power of communication and technologies to deliver the message that can heal the world from its divisiveness, and from its lack of moral and psychological self-awareness. Research must continue. I would like experts to address Moral Science's merits and deficiencies. I would also like to invite scientists to collaborate in exploring the assumptions, the technology, the delivery. The message can heal the world from its divisiveness, its lack of moral and psychological self-awareness.

Finally, authorities must collaborate as guardians of the public interest to deal with the challenges of the scientific paradigm. Science is the new moral authority, but we need to develop consensus on the power of this authority. Religions and science must be accountable to the public at large.

Accountability of all humanities to the Moral Science

The Moral Science establishes accountability of all humanities to the principles of science. Psychology needs a radical overhaul and so do religions. The Moral Science identifies the unifying order, the unconscious as a natural science phenomenon with the homeostatic function of reducing psychic discomfort by achieving spontaneously attitude modification leading to social adjustment as an energetic transformation.

This concept as the common denominator unifies the disciplines into a pure science, but discovering a scientific premise has consequences. Being a holocaust survivor my quest has been focused on seeking to avert holocausts. I have achieved healing myself from my childhood conflicts: the tragic end of the Jewish communities of Europe, and the deaths of my father and grandfather upon the end of the WWII and during the communist uprising in Athens.

My sense of accomplishment has been introducing the scientific analysis of metaphors, clarifying the unconscious as a scientific mechanism and as the origin of moral thought as the innate human motivation for peace and harmony. This insight spells my activism. Religions reflect the need for improving meaningfulness; gods evolved as the metaphor of the creative process but they have not finished their evolution to moral consensus. It is my duty to share my knowledge with the public and to suggest the overhaul of all moral paradigms.

This educational message must be delivered as a concise program of emotional education, as a new educational standard, in the classroom as well as in therapy. A model version of this program is Creativity and Power Management. It combines first, the scientific study of the creative process viewing the art exhibit at the museum. Second, it uses creativity for self-discovery as a didactic, diagnostic and therapeutic intervention, which does not require professional services. Third, this education delivers clarity on moral paradigms by integrating religions as moral monopolies into the Moral Science by playing the educational game identified as Moral Monopoly retracing the evolution of religions.

The Moral Science disrupts psychology and psychiatry as practiced today; it disrupts religions as self-righteous moral monopolies. It requires that the United Nations charter provide the human right for truth beyond indiscriminate tolerance of religion-based distortions of reality. Religions need to evolve self-awareness and reduce conflicts generated in the minds of the faithful. They need accountability in front of the global moral and climate realities. Religions and psychological theories need to re-examine their differences and revise their concepts to enhance consensus in the delivery of diagnostic and therapeutic services. All religions suffer from the pathologies of the relational modalities they espouse.

The world needs the scientific moral paradigm to heal the person and to reconcile the religions and heal the world. Science provides clarity on the nature of moral order. The world believes stories; the antidote is recognizing what is universal in all stories as a scientific conflict resolution mechanism leading to formally related alternative resolutions.

Science providing clarity in our disciplines is putting all professions on notice. It is the duty of all people to rethink our diverse conceptual systems. The time of enlightenment is here. The science commands accountability from the professional establishment. The world is incurably conflicted by psychology as a medical specialty, education as encyclopedic information, religions as dated moral paradigms, museums lacking understanding of the creative process. The alternative is the Moral Science offering clarity in understanding the unconscious, wellness diagnoses, utilizing an assessment that is didactic, diagnostic and therapeutic, an emotional education for personal growth and for the integration of religions from divisive moral monopolies to the universality of moral psychology as a science. Science commands accountability from all the institutions misleading the public.

Emotional education is a civil right, the right for moral and emotional literacy. Everybody should study relational patterns and clarify values as the scientific principles guiding the process. We must become conscious of the human unconscious and be deliberate in pursuing its wisdom. Using creativity for self-assessment gives a person the opportunity to understand the unconscious pattern and to manage our relational tendencies as our self-driving car. Emotional education is the alternative to therapy and to seeking in religions the total truth.

The educational model is presented in 'Creativity and Power Management' a concise program of emotional education that combines viewing art exhibits to learn about the unconscious as a scientific phenomenon, completing the self-assessment, free online, to find about oneself, and playing the Moral Monopoly game to integrate religions of the world as partial and complementary discoveries of science.

The scientific paradigm puts museums on notice.
Art is displayed as aesthetic statements unrelated to the underlying emotional dialectic and without identifying the alternative ways of resolving personal conflicts. The challenge of art exhibits is to present the artist's perfect symbolic universe as a conflict resolution.

The scientific paradigm puts psychology on notice.
Psychiatry and psychology have become vocational guilds. The guilds' consensus seeks answers in the medical model cancelling out the unconscious, relational wellness diagnoses, and meaningful assessments. The guild ignores religions, morality and creativity as a healing mechanism. Psychology has made itself irrelevant in dealing with political and sociological conflicts as outside its domain of expertise; it is not prepared to understand wellness and deliver emotional education in the classroom.

The scientific paradigm puts religions on notice.
They represent moral monopolies that are now accountable to science. The faithful are not allowed to use critical thinking. Religions have evolved as discoveries of the alternative modes of conflict resolution through metaphors on the nature of God, creation and Commandments. They are normative systems with very different values, very different norms on the roles of men and women. They are inspiring the world along very different versions of how to resolve conflicts. The faithful need to understand that religions are metaphors, stories that inspire but that also mislead. Religions hold the public hostage into partial truths generating pathology that leads people to kill and to self-sacrifice. We have seen their misleading power in the holocaust and in 9/11 responsible for political divisiveness destroying peace, creating global disruptions, unsustainable population explosion and biases in civil rights.

The scientific paradigm puts education on notice.
The current educational curriculum lacks capacity to deliver the three objectives of education: the integration of the humanities and science, self-knowledge and clarity of values. The science changes the focus of education and therapy from encyclopedic information and technologies of psychotherapy to identifying through using one's creativity, one's sample metaphors, how a person can become self-aware and how one needs to optimize one's responses. People need to recognize their own make up having dimensions: syndromal structure leading to the alternative types of resolution.

The alternative to wars
All wars are moral conflicts seeking a resolution. They lead to social transformations. I regard 9/11 as the war of religions, as the Third World War, based on the unresolved conflicts of the Abrahamic religions. Wars seek resolution of conflicts and in this case, the resolution is in a paradigm shift, from art to science, from metaphors to their analysis. Peace in the world to be established needs science to complete the discoveries of religions. Leaders can bring about moral consensus by understanding moral values as principles of science. For peace in the world humans need to understand our unconscious as the scientific moral paradigm. Goodness is inside all of us.

The scientific paradigm puts politicians on notice
Politicians decision making ignores how personal psychological factors distort reality, as well as how religions mislead the use of power in managing conflicts between nations.

Psychology as science belongs in the domain of education
The Moral Science has roots in the history of analytical philosophical thought. Its insights and technologies advance knowledge beyond the traditional schools of thought: the Aristotelian analysis of drama, the Hegelian dialectical thinking, the insights of the Frankfurt school, the psychoanalytic explorations of the unconscious, and Piaget's formal analysis of cognitive concepts. The Moral Science introduces formulas into the analysis of the creative process clarifying the unconscious as both a scientific and moral mechanism unifying psychology and morality. It recognizes the unconscious as a fathomable, universal entity providing a sound scientific foundation accounting for physiological, psychological, and sociological order. The mental process introduces reason in the different domains of traditional social sciences. The Moral Science puts an end to speculations, confusing and ineffectual models of the psyche and of the divine. The orderly and moral unconscious redefines psychology's concepts and reconciles religions.

The new unconscious is of great clinical, educational and political significance, reconciling psychology with morality and with the sciences. The technologies of the assessment, analyzing personal creativity, and the technology of the Moral Monopoly card game, analyzing cultural stories, validate the premises of the Formal Theory and popularize its applications, offering the civil right of emotional literacy, the liberation from personal conflict-generating patterns and blind adherence to partial moral truths. The Formal Theory provides the new moral paradigm apt to inspire the public, educate students and unify the social sciences, guiding us to moral consensus, reconciling knowledge, and self-knowledge into a science-based spirituality centered oncreativity. Psychologists may become spokes-people of healing the person and the world instead of remaining as medical technologists.

Mission statement: Healing the person, healing the world
The process as a measurable harmonic has extraordinary importance in bridging the humanities and the sciences, in reconciling religions among themselves, in defining morality, and clarifying psychology as the Moral Science. Integration of knowledge is a politically relevant scientific discovery in our world divided by its uninterpreted metaphors.

The Formal Theory offers a completely new view of reality. This view integrates morality and psychology with science into a new domain of knowledge. The three components are intrinsically connected by the homeostatic function of the human physiology. The new concept is formulas, and all stories are solutions for alternative values of their variables. Uncertainties about God's wisdom are resolved in the reliability and predictability of science. God is the unit order/formulas that herald peace; the unit is not only science but moral and mental order with a wide range of applications. The unit process clarifies elusive concepts like morality, the unconscious, diagnostic categories, and assessment of associations; it has political relevance and great pertinence to our times of cultural conflicts blocking the smooth evolution of progress.

The case studies show how internal psychological dispositions bring about just as much devastation as cross-cultural conflicts. The cause of our difficulty in making progress is the world's difficulty in interpreting metaphors while the public is holding on to them as beliefs that are sacred. The challenge of the Formal Theory is to reform our imperfect ways of thinking by introducing the abstract language of science as the analytical method; can moral reason prevail over divisive faiths, concrete psychological explanations and medical diagnoses?

We need science to deal with the problem of divisive psychological and belief systems and to effectively respond to the contemporary crises of perceptions that have led us to political and religious conflicts. The War on Terror has been a true clash of civilizations that will not go away because beliefs are entrenched convictions worth dying for. The only path to peace is introducing the scientific paradigm, which will make our many languages compatible and thus lead to moral consensus improving communications. The scientific, moral paradigm is formulas that are testable. Science has multiple rewarding applications enhancing therapy and education, psychology and religions paving the road to peace.

This information is about a simple but pivotal scientific discovery, the anatomy and physiology of the unconscious mental process as the innate adaptive or homeostatic response to stress. It is of true strategic importance for our times. The process has been validated by practice, research, statistics, and multiple experimental studies and art exhibits. The images of the Museum of the Creative Process demonstrate art as evidence of science. The creative process is literally, not metaphorically, the software of the mind. Here we are not talking of another moral paradigm, but of the unit of the social sciences interfacing and bridging the humanities with the rigorous sciences.

The scientific paradigm defines morality. It does not cancel it; it unifies the old paradigms but exposes their limitations. It transforms the playing field by leveling the old paradigms as partial understandings of the universal order. The new paradigm does not eliminate the old paradigms; it reconciles them as steps to science as the total truth, the abstraction of formulas. Religions constitute partial truths. So, the new paradigm is not alienating the world of religions. It simply offers a more elegant and universal abstraction on what religions poetically and intuitively have been trying to grasp and deliver. The new paradigm gives credit to religions but lifts the world to the intelligence of understanding the human unconscious as the origin of all moralities. The remedy to our cultural diversity is the introduction of an integrative paradigm that provides meaningfulness by evolving unifying concepts. Science represents a quantum leap. It introduces the software which interface our diverse cultures flattening our cultural differences. Instead of them dividing us, we may feel secure by interpreting them and uniting them with science.

We need enlightenment that transcends religions and psychological theories by speaking the universal language of science uniting diversity. The means to achieve reconciliation is to go beyond metaphors that inspire but divide. We need to evolve from the era of metaphors to the era of Moral Reason, of the Moral Science, of science understanding the mind, belief systems, and ideologies, by offering a wider and more abstract understanding of the moral, emotional reality inspiring all people.

The Formal Theory of Behavior has identified the nature of the creative process as the unit of the social sciences, the key to interfacing our many languages. Science now understands both psychology and morality. It offers the software needed to integrate the metaphorical languages of the world. This is the importance of my communication: introducing the study of the creative process as the key to understanding metaphors, religions, and ideologies, grasping the universal unit moral order as the common denominator.

Science becomes the believable and meaningful language for all. The unit order, the software of the mind, interfaces all metaphors. The world is ruled and defined by alternative moral values. We must question old values and dated norms to identify the scientific and universal set of values to achieve effectiveness in our global culture. We have the responsibility to promote awareness of this set of new values, as scientific operations to heal the person and the world from their conceptual conflicts.

The challenge for educators and leaders of the world is to discover the wisdom of the unconscious mind in order to unite our divisive paradigms into a reality that is meaningful to all. Military victory will not alter people's belief systems. People need insight and enlightenment to exit one value system and enter the next. The secret for peace in the Global era is in Moral Science's capacity to bridge art and science, psychology, and morality, making behavior into the venerable wisdom of science credible for all. The challenge is in identifying the nature of the psyche and the divine as simple formulas that all of us can understand and agree upon as the unifying paradigm.

My mission has been to advance the integrative paradigm of the Formal Theory, its concepts, and technologies. I have been working reminding myself that I have the responsibility and obligation to promote awareness of my research findings as valuable information that can inspire the general public to heal the person and the world. It has been my odd fortune to discover the conceptual and moral paradigm. It is the fire stolen from the gods, but it is my duty and responsibility to deliver it to the mortals. It has been painful to harbor a useful alternative to the many competing and mutually exclusive approaches to wisdom and to witness the suffering inflicted by the confused individuals considering themselves patriotic, and the faith-inspired warriors considering themselves as defenders of God.

The world lives in an era of illness diagnoses and spiritual metaphors that we believe in as the ultimate truth. They are the many concrete versions of diagnoses and the many theistic moral paradigms. For the world to find peace, for the improvement of mental health, for the public to find political consensus, for peace in the world we need the scientific interpretation of metaphors along the innate process. We need to unify psychology and religions as pertaining to the same scientific unconscious resolving conflict as the unit of the social science disciplines. Understanding the unconscious is the foundation of wellness personality diagnoses, it is useful for personal self-discovery, and in understanding religions as united by scientific principles.

The world needs enlightenment that transcends psychological theories religions by adopting the universal language of science. The means to achieve this is to go beyond metaphors that inspire but also divide, to science, which reconciles and inspires. The religion-based progression of moral paradigms finds its completion with the scientific interpretation of cultural stories as metaphors of conflict resolution. Morality obeys the laws of nature. Moral reason reconciles the diversity of paradigms into the simplicity of science, the language of total abstraction.

The Formal Theory, with its constructs and formulas, its diagnostic categories, and assessment instrument, its clarity of moral values is the unifying rational moral order clarifying abstractly how the unconscious creative process organizes information meaningfully integrating religions among themselves and religion with psychology and science. It is the path to wisdom.

The unit order explains mental health and mental illness, God and the Psyche, Genesis and the Ten Commandments, the messages of the Abrahamic prophets and Buddha, of Aristotle, Maimonides, and Spinoza. The new concepts anchored on the rigorous principles of science redefine psychology, religions, and revamp education. They understand emotions and actions as formally intertwined in a system predicted by the formulas of the Formal Analysis Profile. Moral Science is not dry knowledge. It is the long-sought for spiritual concept; it identifies the nature of the universal moral order. The quest for meaning ends with science understanding the unconscious proceeding spontaneously, predictably from emotions to insights, from art to science, from the particular to the universal. The abstraction, as the automatic programming of the mind to the pursuit of conflict resolution, has a synonym, mindfulness or kindness.

The key to the effectiveness of the Formal Theory is in the value of the interpretation of metaphors generating insights and therapeutic benefits. Deciphering art into science is very important in simplifying communications, understanding order, in intervening to correct problematic situations or patterns, in detecting emotional blocks, and facilitating progress. The examination of metaphors is very important in delivering insights to the test-takers, therapists, educators, in utilizing creativity for self-discovery, in establishing continuity in the personal symbolic system, in deciphering metaphors in terms of understanding art, literature, and religions.

Moral order, present in all stories, all creativity, all art, and music, is based on the unconscious as a scientific phenomenon. This entity allows us to understand psychology, literature, religions, cultures, personal patterns, and attitudes, to explore our makeup, and to grasp moral values as abstract and universal principles. With this publication exposing science, my mission of identifying and presenting the unconscious as a moral process is finding its completion.

BIBLIOGRAPHY

BOOK 1: EPISTEMOLOGY References

American Psychiatric Association. (2013). Diagnostic and statistical manual of mental disorders (DSM-5®). Washington, DC: American Psychiatric Publications.

Bocheński, J. M. (1961). A History of Formal Logic. (Ivo Thomas, Trans.). Notre Dame: University of Notre Dame Press.

Butcher, S. H., & Gassner, J. (1951). Aristotle's theory of poetry and fine art: with a critical text and translation of the Poetics. With a prefatory essay, Aristotelian literary criticism (Vol. 42). Mineola, NY: Dover Publications.

Cohen, M. R., & Nagel, E. (1935). An introduction to logic and scientific method. London: Routledge.
Crouch, J. B. (2004). Reflections on Josiah Royce's logic: Royce on Russell's paradox. Transactions of the Charles S. Peirce Society, 40(4), 607-626.

Flavell, J. H. (1963). The developmental psychology of Jean Piaget. Princeton, NJ: D. Van Nostrand Company.

Freud, A. (2018). The ego and the mechanisms of defense. London: Routledge.

Freud, S. (1955). Psychological Works of Sigmund Freud. Standard edition. London: Hogarth Press.

Gensler, H. J. (2017). Introduction to logic. London: Routledge Press.

Giancoli, D. C. (2016). Physics: principles with applications. Boston: Pearson.

Halliwell, S. (1998). Aristotle's Poetics. Chicago: University of Chicago Press.

Kirk, G. S., Raven, J. E., & Schofield, M. (1983). The presocratic philosophers: a critical history with a selection of texts. Cambridge, UK: Cambridge University Press.

Klein, F. (1945). Elementary Mathematics from an Advanced Standpoint: Arithmetic, Algebra, Analysis. (Hedrick E.R., & Noble, C.A., Trans.). Mineola, NY: Dover Publications.

Levis, A.J., (1988a). Conflict Analysis: The Formal Theory of Behavior. A Theory and its Experimental Validation, Manchester, VT: Normative Publications.

Levis, A.J., (1988b). Conflict Analysis Training, a Program of Emotional Education. Manchester, VT: Normative Publications.

Levis, A.J., & Levis. M., (2011). Science Stealing the Fire of the Gods and Healing the World. Manchester, VT: Normative Publications.

Levis, A.J., & Levis, M., (2016a). Creativity and Power Management, clinical delivery. Manchester, VT: Normative Publications.

Levis, A.J., & Levis, M., (2016b). Creativity and Power Management, psycho-educational and online delivery.

Manchester, VT: Normative Publications, 2016.

Piaget, J. (2015). Structuralism (Psychology Revivals). London: Psychology Press.

Royce, J. (1982). The Philosophy of Josiah Royce. Indianapolis: Hackett Publishing.

Sabelli, H. C. (1984). Mathematical dialectics, scientific logic and the psychoanalysis of thinking. In Hegel and the Sciences (pp. 349-359). New York: Springer.

Vaillant, G. E. (1992). Ego mechanisms of defense: a guide for clinicians and researchers. Washington, DC: American Psychiatric Publications.

Aristotle. (1961). Aristotle's poetics. New York: Hill and Wang,

Costa, P.T. and McCrae R.R., (1988) Personality in Adulthood: A Six Longitudinal Study of Self-reports of Spouse Ratings on the NEO Personality Inventory. *Journal of Personality and Social Psychology*, 54, 853-863.

Householder, A. S. (1939). Lewin, Kurt. Principles of Topological Psychology. Translated by Fritz and Grace Heider. New York: McGraw-Hill, 1936. Pp. 231. *The Pedagogical Seminary and Journal of Genetic Psychology, 54*(1), 249-259.

Leary, T. (1957) Interpersonal Diagnosis of Personality: A Functional Theory and Methodology for Personality Evaluation. New York: Ronald Press

Levis, Albert J., M.D. (1996) The Art to Science Exhibits at The Wilburton Inn. Manchester, Vermont.

Levis, Albert J., M.D. (1996). The Clinical Effectiveness of Creativity and Power Management - A Time-limited, Well-structured, *Comprehensive Integrated Psychotherapy*. Articles.

Levis, Albert J., M.D. (1988). Conflict Analysis the Formal Theory of Behavior: A Theory and its Experimental Validation.

Levis, Albert J., M.D. (1988) Conflict Analysis Training and Metaphoria Studies. Normative Publications.

Levis, Albert J., M.D. (1988). Conflict Analysis Training: A Program of Emotional Education. Normative Publications.

Levis, Albert J., M.D. (1996) The Panels of The Metaphoria Gazebo at The Art to Science Exhibits at The Wilburton Inn. Manchester, Vermont.

Levis, Albert J., M.D. (1996). Three Art as Evidence of Science Exhibits. Articles

Millon, T., Everly, G., & Davis, R. D. (1993). How can knowledge of psychopathology facilitate psychotherapy integration? A view from the personality disorders. *Journal of Psychotherapy Integration*, *3*(4), 331.

Spitzer, R. L., Sheehy, M., & Endicott, J. (1977). DSM-III: guiding principles. In *Psychiatric diagnosis* (pp. 1-24). Palgrave Macmillan, London.

Weissman, Myra M., PhD. and John C. Markowitz, M.D. (1994) Vol. 51, August, *Interpersonal Psychotherapy. Archives of General Psychiatry*

Alden, L. E., Wiggins, J. S., & Pincus, A. L. (1990). Construction of circumplex scales for the Inventory of Interpersonal Problems. Journal of Personality Assessment, 55(3–4), 521–536. https://doi.org/10.1207/s15327752jpa5503&4_10

Barber, J. P., Foltz, C., & Weinryb, R. M. (1998). The Central Relationship Questionnaire: Initial report. Journal of Counseling Psychology, 45(2), 131–142. https://doi.org/10.1037/0022-0167.45.2.131

Barford, K. A., Zhao, K., & Smillie, L. D. (2015). Mapping the interpersonal domain: Translating between the Big Five, HEXACO, and Interpersonal Circumplex. Personality and Individual Differences, 86, 232–237. https://doi.org/10.1016/j.paid.2015.05.038

Bliton, C. F., & Pincus, A. L. (2020). Construction and Validation of the Interpersonal Influence Tactics Circumplex (IIT-C) Scales. Assessment, 27(4), 688–705. https://doi.org/10.1177/1073191119864661

Brenner, C. (2002). Conflict, Compromise Formation, and Structural Theory. The Psychoanalytic Quarterly, 71(3), 397–417. https://doi.org/10.1002/j.2167-4086.2002.tb00519.x

Curtis, J., Silberschatz, G., Sampson, H., & Weiss, J. (1994). The Plan Formulation Method. Psychotherapy Research, 4(3–4), 197–207. https://doi.org/10.1080/10503309412331334032

Ghaed, S. G., & Gallo, L. C. (2006). Distinctions among agency, communion, and unmitigated agency and communion according to the interpersonal circumplex, five-factor model, and social-emotional correlates. Journal of Personality Assessment, 86(1), 77–88. https://doi.org/10.1207/s15327752jpa8601_09

Hopwood, C. J., Pincus, A. L., DeMoor, R. M., & Koonce, E. A. (2008). Psychometric characteristics of the Inventory of Interpersonal Problems–Short Circumplex (IIP–SC) with college students. Journal of Personality Assessment, 90(6), 615–618. https://doi.org/10.1080/00223890802388665

Horowitz, L., & Rosenberg, S. (1994). The Consensual Response Psychodynamic Formulation: Part 1. Method and Research Results. Psychotherapy Research, 4(3–4), 222–233. https://doi.org/10.1080/10503309412331334052

Keltner, D., Gruenfeld, D. H., & Anderson, C. (2003). Power, approach, and inhibition. Psychological Review, 110(2), 265–284. https://doi.org/10.1037/0033-295X.110.2.265

Leary, M. R., Cottrell, C. A., & Phillips, M. (2001). Deconfounding the effects of dominance and social acceptance on self-esteem. Journal of Personality and Social Psychology, 81(5), 898–909. https://doi.org/10.1037/0022-3514.81.5.898

Locke, K. D. (2000). Circumplex scales of interpersonal values: Reliability, validity, and applicability to interpersonal problems and personality disorders. Journal of Personality Assessment, 75(2), 249–267. https://doi.org/10.1207/S15327752JPA7502_6

Luborsky, L. (2000). An introduction to central relationship pattern measures: The Central Relationship Questionnaire. Journal of Psychotherapy Practice & Research, 9(4), 200–200.

Luborsky, L., & Crits-Christoph, P. (1998). Understanding transference: The Core Conflictual Relationship Theme method (2nd ed.). American Psychological Association.
https://doi.org/10.1037/10250-000

McCrae, R. R., & Costa, P. T. (1989). The structure of interpersonal traits: Wiggins's circumplex and the five-factor model. Journal of Personality and Social Psychology, 56(4), 586–595.
https://doi.org/10.1037/0022-3514.56.4.586

Moskowitz, D. S. (1994). Cross-situational generality and the interpersonal circumplex. Journal of Personality and Social Psychology, 66(5), 921.
https://doi.org/10.1037/0022-3514.66.5.921

Perry, J. (1994). Assessing Psychodynamic Patterns Using the Idiographic Conflict Formulation Method. Psychotherapy Research, 4(3–4), 239–252.
https://doi.org/10.1080/10503309412331334072

Russell, J. J., Moskowitz, D. S., Zuroff, D. C., Sookman, D., & Paris, J. (2007). Stability and variability of affective experience and interpersonal behavior in borderline personality disorder. Journal of Abnormal Psychology, 116(3), 578–588.
https://doi.org/10.1037/0021-843X.116.3.578

Smith, J. D., Handler, L., & Nash, M. R. (2010). Therapeutic assessment for preadolescent boys with oppositional defiant disorder: A replicated single-case time-series design. Psychological Assessment, 22(3), 593–602.
https://doi.org/10.1037/a0019697

Wiggins, J. S. (1995). IAS, Interpersonal Adjective Scales: Professional Manual. Psychological Assessment Resources.

CPSIA information can be obtained
at www.ICGtesting.com
Printed in the USA
JSHW070838240123
36574JS00006B/27